Here's what the critics say about

RETIREMENT PLACES R·A·T·E·D

"... immensely helpful ... don't leave home without it."

Richard Nelson Bolles, *What Color is Your Parachute?* (1987)

"... a comprehensive guide to the nation's top retirement areas."

Los Angeles Daily News, November 1990

"A valuable guidebook for anyone looking for domestic retirement spots ..."

Houston Chronicle, December 1991

" ... the lowdown on terrific, affordable places to spend your retirement."

Jordan Goodman, *Everyone's Money Book on Retirement Planning* (2002)

"... the unofficial handbook for mobile senior citizens ..."

Raleigh (NC) *News & Observer*, August 1992

"We assume you want to live in one of the places where you can play golf every day. To find them, you need additional help. There are several books on the market; the best is Retirement Places Rated ..."

Golf Digest, October 1993

"... arguably the most comprehensive book yet published on [where to live in retirement]."

Spokane (WA) *Spokesman Review,* August 1996

"The great resource not only explains the most important retirement location considerations, but it rates big and small towns on key components. Savageau's new book is the best in its field."

Robert J. Bruss, Tribune Media Services, August 1999

"When I came across Savageau's book, I was awed by the extraordinary amount of research that went into its creation. As a reporter who has spent his life gathering information, I could appreciate the effort involved."

Stan Hinden, *How to Retire Happy* (2001 and 2006)

RETIREMENT PLACES R·A·T·E·D®

What You Need to Know to Plan the Retirement You Deserve

7th Edition

David Savageau

Wiley Publishing, Inc.

About the Author

David Savageau lives on Capitol Hill in Washington, D.C. Visit him at www.placesrated.com.

Acknowledgments

This seventh, thoroughly revised, and expanded edition of *Retirement Places Rated* couldn't have gotten off the ground without the criticisms of hundreds of readers. Nor would the book have been finished minus the generous advice from experts. Their affiliations and data are cited throughout.

Thanks to the people at **Wiley Publishing, Inc.,** especially to editors **Michael Kelly, William Travis, Cheri Clark, and M. Faunette Johnston.** Thanks to **Don Larson,** Mapping Specialists, Ltd., and **Brian Davis,** Bombastic Graphics.

Finally, special thanks to **Woods & Poole Economics, Inc.,** for population, income, and job forecasts. The use of this information and conclusions drawn from it are solely the author's responsibility.

Publisher's Note

Published by:

Wiley Publishing, Inc.

111 River St.

Hoboken, NJ 07030-5774

Maps copyright © 2007 by Places Rated Partnership.

ISBN 978-0-470-08959-0

Interior design by Madhouse Studios and contributed to by Marie Kristine Parial-Leonardo
Icons designed by Rashell Smith

Editors: Michael Kelly and William Travis
Production Editor: M. Faunette Johnston
Cartographer: Guy Ruggiero
Photo Editor: Richard Fox
Anniversary Logo Design: Richard Pacifico
Production by Wiley Indianapolis Composition Services

For information on our other products and services or to obtain technical support, please contact our Customer Care Department within the U.S. at 800/762-2974, outside the U.S. at 317/572-3993 or fax 317/572-4002.

Wiley also publishes its books in a variety of electronic formats. Some content that appears in print may not be available in electronic formats.

Manufactured in the United States of America

5 4 3 2 1

CONTENTS

PREFACE

Readers will see differences in the final rankings for places profiled in both the sixth edition of *Retirement Places Rated* and this one. There are five reasons for this:

New Geography. This edition introduces 22 new places, while 25 locations profiled previously have been dropped.

A New, Seventh Chapter. This edition introduces a chapter on *Housing,* covering different shelter choices, utilities, taxes, and costs.

The Interval Effect. Changes in geography necessarily change the ranks of the 178 retirement places common to both editions. Asheville, for example, has its Personal Safety score fall from 43.1 to 36.7. The spot in North Carolina's western mountains isn't getting more dangerous; quite the contrary, criminal activity is down there. The explanation is that a number of newly profiled places with better Personal Safety figures have moved it to a lower ranking.

New Scoring Methods. All the chapters show changes—some slight, others major—in scoring methods. Scores continue to be expressed in percentiles where 50 is average, 100 best, and 0 worst.

Time Series Data. Local population figures (for deriving the number of physicians per capita or access to public golf courses, for example), prices (for gauging living costs), and personal incomes (for measuring how far Social Security benefits will stretch in a given place) have increased at varying rates since the previous edition was published.

As a result of these changes, the rankings more currently reflect what each retirement place has to offer older adults.

AMERICA'S TOP 30 RETIREMENT PLACES

RANK	RETIREMENT PLACE	MEAN SCORE	RANK	RETIREMENT PLACE	MEAN SCORE
1.	Georgetown, TX	72.9	16.	Hanover, NH	66.2
2.	St. George–Zion, UT	72.1	17.	Savannah, GA	66.2
3.	Fort Collins–Loveland, CO	71.9	18.	Las Cruces, NM	66.1
4.	Charleston, SC	71.9	19.	Charlottesville, VA	65.4
4.	Henderson, NV	71.9	20.	Naples, FL	65.3
6.	Kalispell–Flathead Valley, MT	70.3	20.	Tucson, AZ	65.3
7.	Fairhope–Gulf Shores, AL	68.8	22.	Wimberley, TX	65.2
8.	Scottsdale, AZ	68.7	23.	Madison, WI	65.1
9.	Laguna Beach–Dana Point, CA	67.9	24.	Bay St. Louis–Pass Christian, MS	64.4
10.	Sarasota, FL	67.7	25.	Myrtle Beach, SC	64.1
11.	Wickenburg, AZ	67.4	26.	Placer County, CA	63.8
12.	Traverse City, MI	67.3	27.	Medford–Ashland, OR	63.7
13.	Fayetteville, AR	67.2	28.	Asheville, NC	63.5
14.	Fort Myers–Cape Coral, FL	67.2	29.	Bend, OR	63.5
15.	Morro Bay–Cambria, CA	66.3	30.	Iowa City, IA	63.4

Because of rounding, the list above appears to indicate several ties, but there are actually only two ties.

INTRODUCTION

A h, to wear shorts throughout the year in laid-back Key West or to sit on a bench in the evening and watch the locals stroll around the plaza in historic Santa Fe. Oh, for winter quiet and the smell of piñon pine on the western slope of the Colorado Rockies. How about the ambience of a New England college town, painted white Cape and Saltbox houses behind drifting red and gold leaves on a Homecoming Weekend? If you could snap your fingers and find yourself living somewhere else, would you?

Let's put the question another way: What if there were someplace else in America that suited you better for retirement than where you're living now, and you knew nothing about it?

WHY BUDGE AT ALL?

"The best place to retire," advises Dr. Robert Butler, former head of the National Institute on Aging, "is the neighborhood where you spent your life." True enough. Most of us have more power, independence, and plain practical knowledge in the place where we're living than we may ever have in a distant, unfamiliar location.

Certainly the statistics bear this out. For all the hype about moving away, the number of older adults who actually settle each year in another state for retirement wouldn't crowd the route for the Cotton Bowl Parade. Most of us choose to stay where we are.

There's more to this decision than convenience. The emotional connection that comes from raising children, working at a job, and paying off a mortgage in one place may be missed in a new one. When you move, you can take the philodendron, the oak blanket chest, the canoe, and the satellite dish, but you can't pack a deep sense of place.

Perhaps for you, relocation is unthinkable. You've known your neighbors for years; your doctor knows you and your medical history; you don't need to look up the bank's phone number, ask for directions to a discount hardware store, or scratch your head for the name of the one person in City Hall who can get the sewer fixed. What you may ultimately want is R & R in familiar territory, not an agenda that takes high energy and risk to put down new roots.

If all this is true, stay right where you are and travel whenever and wherever you want instead. But possibly—just possibly—there is some other place in this country where you may prosper more than where you now live. And possibly, too, it is a lack of information that keeps you from taking a look.

Over a period of nearly 25 years and six previous editions, *Retirement Places Rated* has profiled hundreds

EIGHTEEN REGIONS

When retirement places are grouped into regions, throw out your notion of political boundaries. Although two regions—the California Coast and the Florida Interior—are found within single states, most regions referred to in this book take in parts of more than one state, and some states are apportioned among more than one region. Places within each region share a distinctive look and feel, geography, outlook, and manners. The Mid-Atlantic Metro Belt has 23 places and the Rocky Mountains 21. The Heartland, North Woods, and California Coast cover large areas but fewer places. There are two in Hawaii.

CALIFORNIA COAST

Carmel–Pebble Beach, CA
Laguna Beach–Dana Point, CA
Mendocino–Fort Bragg, CA
Morro Bay–Cambria, CA
Santa Barbara, CA

DESERT SOUTHWEST

Bisbee, AZ
Cottonwood–Verde Valley, AZ
Henderson, NV
Kingman, AZ
Lake Havasu City, AZ
Pahrump Valley, NV
Palm Springs–Coachella Valley, CA
Payson, AZ
Prescott–Prescott Valley, AZ
St. George–Zion, UT
Scottsdale, AZ
Sedona, AZ
Silver City, NM
Tucson, AZ
Victorville–Apple Valley, CA
Wickenburg, AZ
Yuma, AZ

FLORIDA INTERIOR

Gainesville, FL
Kissimmee–St. Cloud, FL
Lakeland–Winter Haven, FL
Leesburg–Mount Dora, FL
Ocala, FL
Sebring–Avon Park, FL

GULF COAST

Apalachicola, FL
Bay St. Louis–Pass Christian, MS

Bradenton, FL
Fairhope–Gulf Shores, AL
Fort Myers–Cape Coral, FL
Largo, FL
Naples, FL
Panama City, FL
Pensacola, FL
Port Charlotte, FL
Rockport–Aransas Pass, TX
Sarasota, FL
Western St. Tammany Parish, LA

HAWAII

The Big Island, HI
Maui, HI

HEARTLAND

Brown County, IN
Columbia, MO
Iowa City, IA
Madison, WI
Murray–Kentucky Lake, KY

INNER SOUTH

Athens, GA
Chapel Hill–Carrboro, NC
Hattiesburg, MS
Madison, MS
Natchitoches, LA
Oxford, MS
Southern Pines–Pinehurst, NC
Thomasville, GA

MID-ATLANTIC METRO BELT

Annapolis, MD
Berkeley Springs, WV
Charles Town–Shepherdstown, WV

Charlottesville, VA
Chestertown, MD
East End Long Island, NY
Easton–St. Michaels, MD
East Stroudsburg, PA
Fredericksburg–Spotsylvania, VA
Front Royal, VA
Hampshire County, WV
Lake Placid, NY
Loudoun County, VA
Lower Cape May, NJ
Nelson County, VA
Northern Neck, VA
Ocean City, MD
Pike County, PA
Rehoboth Bay–Indian River Bay, DE
State College, PA
Sullivan County, NY
Toms River–Barnegat Bay, NJ
Williamsburg, VA

NEW ENGLAND

Bar Harbor, ME
Brunswick, ME
Burlington, VT
Camden, ME
Hanover, NH
Litchfield Hills, CT
Martha's Vineyard, MA
Middle Cape Cod, MA
Monadnock Region, NH
Northampton–Amherst, MA
St. Jay–Northeast Kingdom, VT
Southern Berkshire County, MA
Woodstock, VT
York Beaches, ME

of retirement spots throughout the country. This new, seventh edition takes the same approach as all of its predecessors and has been thoroughly updated, revised, and expanded.

Retirement Places Rated is meant for those who are planning for retirement and are weighing the pros and cons of moving or staying where they are. This guide offers facts about 200 carefully chosen places

NORTH WOODS
Door Peninsula, WI
Eagle River–Woodruff, WI
Leelanau Peninsula, MI
Petoskey–Harbor Springs, MI
Traverse City, MI

OZARKS & OUACHITAS
Branson, MO
Conway, AR
Eureka Springs, AR
Fayetteville, AR
Hot Springs, AR
Lake of the Cherokees, OK
Lake of the Ozarks, MO
Norfork Lake, AR

PACIFIC NORTHWEST
Anacortes, WA
Bellingham, WA
Bend, OR
Chewelah, WA
Eugene, OR
Grants Pass, OR
Long Beach Peninsula, WA
Medford–Ashland, OR
Newport–Lincoln City, OR
Palmer–Wasilla, AK
Port Angeles–Sequim, WA
Port Townsend, WA
San Juan Islands, WA
Wenatchee, WA
Whidbey Island, WA

RIO GRANDE COUNTRY
Alamogordo, NM
Alpine–Big Bend, TX
Brownsville, TX
Las Cruces, NM
Las Vegas, NM
McAllen–Alamo, TX
Rio Rancho, NM

Roswell, NM
Ruidoso, NM
Santa Fe, NM
Taos, NM

ROCKY MOUNTAINS
Bozeman, MT
Cedar City, UT
Coeur d'Alene, ID
Cortez, CO
Delta County, CO
Driggs, ID
Durango, CO
Fairplay, CO
Flagstaff, AZ
Fort Collins–Loveland, CO
Grand Junction, CO
Hamilton–Bitterroot Valley, MT
Jackson Hole, WY
Kalispell–Flathead Valley, MT
Ketchum–Sun Valley, ID
McCall, ID
Montrose, CO
Pagosa Springs, CO
Park City, UT
Sandpoint–Lake Pend Oreille, ID
Silverthorne–Breckenridge, CO

SOUTH ATLANTIC
Beaufort, SC
Beaufort–Atlantic Beach, NC
Charleston, SC
Dare Outer Banks, NC
Edenton, NC
Hilton Head Island, SC
Key West, FL
Melbourne–Palm Bay, FL
Myrtle Beach, SC
New Bern, NC
Port St. Lucie, FL
St. Augustine, FL

St. Marys, GA
St. Simons–Jekyll Islands, GA
Savannah, GA
Southport–Brunswick Islands, NC
Summerville, SC
Vero Beach, FL

SOUTHERN HIGHLANDS
Asheville, NC
Boone–Blowing Rock, NC
Brevard, NC
Crossville, TN
Dahlonega, GA
Hendersonville–East Flat Rock, NC
Maryville, TN
Pendleton District, SC
Rabun County, GA
Smith Mountain Lake, VA
Tryon, NC
Waynesville, NC

TAHOE BASIN & SIERRAS
Amador County, CA
Carson City–Carson Valley, NV
Grass Valley–Nevada City, CA
Mariposa, CA
Oakhurst–Coarsegold, CA
Paradise–Magalia, CA
Placer County, CA
Sonora–Twain Harte, CA

TEXAS INTERIOR
Boerne, TX
Cedar Creek Lake, TX
Fredericksburg, TX
Georgetown, TX
Kerrville, TX
Lake Conroe, TX
Marble Falls–Lake LBJ, TX
New Braunfels, TX
Wimberley, TX

that have attracted most of the retired persons who move between states.

This guide is more than a collection of interesting and useful information about places, however. It also rates these places on the basis of seven factors influencing the quality of retirement life: climate, the economy, available services, ambience, costs of living, housing, and personal safety.

Retirement Places Rated doesn't treat later life as a kind of autumn or a second career, turning point, third age, journey, or transformation. It does give you the facts you need to start appraising other geographic locations where you may choose to settle.

After using this book, your hunch that you'll never find a better place than your own hometown may well be confirmed. On the other hand, given this country's geographic variety, what are the odds that the place where you happen to live is the right one for you?

WHERE ARE THESE PLACES?

If you were asked, in a kind of geographic word-association test, to name the states that spring to mind when you hear the word retirement, you may well tick off the big ones in the Sun Belt: Arizona, California, Florida, Georgia, Nevada, New Mexico, North Carolina, South Carolina, and Texas.

You'd be right, of course. In the generations since the end of World War II, these states have attracted most of the older adults who packed up and moved to a distant location. Several of their large cities—Scottsdale, San Diego, Fort Myers, Albuquerque, Las Vegas, Asheville, Charleston, and San Antonio—are as synonymous with retirement as any in the country.

But What about Your Own Backyard?

States well above the Sun Belt deserve a place in retirement geography, too. Oregon and Washington continue to attract thousands of equity-rich Californians. The 160-mile stretch of New Jersey's sandy Atlantic coastline from Cape May up to Monmouth owes a good part of its economic health to older newcomers moving in from New York and Philadelphia.

Today, catalogs mailed out by coastal Maine real estate brokers to baby boomers planning their retirement are thick and slick, while requests for relocation packets from Floridians amaze Chambers of Commerce as far away as the Rocky Mountains and even the Puget Sound area in Washington State.

It's no secret that places in every part of the country benefit from older adults moving into them. Roughly every seventh person over 60 is a newcomer in 444 of the country's 3,142 counties, according to recent federal number crunching (see the nearby map, "444 Retirement Magnets"). If these locations were to be daubed in red on a blank map of the United States, the nation would look as if it had measles.

These spots are found along country roads within commuting distance of big cities. They are in the midst of forested federal lands. They are positioned along rocky ocean coastlines, in river valleys, around lakes, on mountain slopes, and in desert crossroads with striking distant vistas.

THE LAST MOVE?

An odd statistic from AT&T market researchers says that we change our address 11 times in a lifetime. The common reasons are job changes or job transfers, shifts out of rental housing into home ownership, moves up to bigger homes, and divorce.

Is retirement still another reason to move? Not at all. Each year, fewer than half a million persons between the ages of 55 and 65 pack up and relocate to another state. Another million and a half simply trade the big family house for a smaller place within the same city. Consider your own options. You may:

- Stay at your current address—49 out of 50 persons over age 65 do.
- Stay close to town but sell or rent your home and move into an apartment, condominium, or smaller home—1 in 60 older adults take this route.
- Move to another state—among 93 older adults, only 1 will take this course.
- Move out of town to another part of the state to occupy a vacation home year-round, perhaps—just 1 in 116 older adults does this.
- Move abroad—the longest shot of all, just 1 of 1,006 retired persons does this and most that do are returning to their native country.

Clearly, hometown turf beats the distant happy valley. A basic rule for successful relocation says that the day-to-day attractions of a destination must be much, much stronger than the day-to-day attractions of home.

Even if you're not thrilled with your current location, you still have to decide whether moving is the key to a more satisfying later life. The anecdotes of people who moved, became disillusioned, and later moved again or returned home are getting more common.

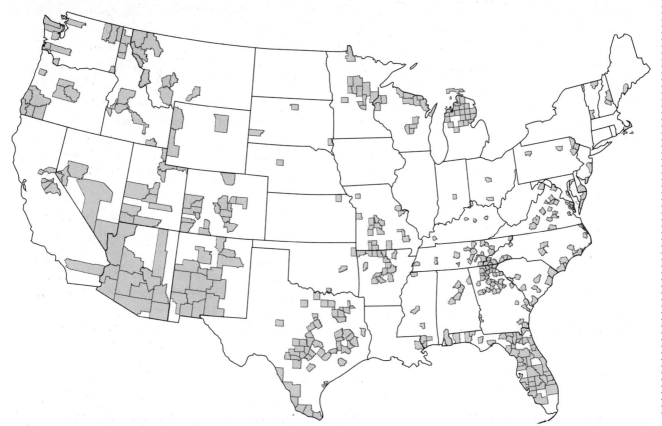

One out of seven persons over the age of 60 in the 444 counties shown here moved in from outside the area over the most recent 10-year period. Source: Economic Research Service, U.S. Department of Agriculture

Why These 200?

To identify likely places from among the hundreds of possibilities, *Retirement Places Rated* uses several criteria:

- **The place should have a 2008 area population greater than 10,000.** A smaller population may signal a lower level of human services. Moreover, the place should be growing. In the years between 2008 and 2015, the U.S. population is projected to grow by 7 percent. Over the same time period, the retirement places profiled here will together grow 13 percent.

- **The place should be attractive to older adults.** In almost all of the retirement places in this book, the number of persons 60 to 65 years of age in residence today is greater than the number of persons 50 to 55 years of age 10 years ago. This simple demographic exercise means that older newcomers have moved into the area over the previous decade.

- **The place should be relatively safe.** The U.S. annual average crime rate, for example, is 3,899 per 100,000 people. In 8 out of 10 of the places profiled here, the crime rate is less than the national average.

- **The place should be affordable.** The money it takes to live in 9 out of 10 of the places included in this book is much less than U.S. average estimated costs for a retired household.

- **The place should have natural endowments.** Most of the locations included here have at least one of the following: large areas of federal recreation land, state recreation land, large areas of inland water, or an ocean coastline. Several places are blessed with all four.

Based on repeated visits and recommendations from hundreds of older adults, *Retirement Places Rated* profiles 200 places. Of these, 98 are in the 9 Sun Belt states noted above. Retirement relocation is still a march to low-cost living and milder winters, that much is certain. Because there is a growing counter-movement to attractive places outside the Sun Belt, 102 of these are profiled. In all, locations in 42 states—from the Florida Keys to the Big Island of Hawaii and from the Down East Maine Coast to Southern California—are represented.

Although this selection of places does not by any means include every desirable destination, it does include many of the country's best, and it does represent the variety of choices many persons have for retirement living.

SOME WORDS ABOUT PLACE NAMES

None of the 200 places profiled here coincides with the corporate limits of towns or cities. For good reason, most of them are counties. Thanks to the car, the space you can cover on a typical day has expanded since the nostalgic era when Main Street truly was the noisy, exciting center of things. Now people likely live in one town, work in another, visit friends in still another, shop at a mall miles away, and escape to open country—all within an easy drive.

It is no different in retirement places. Metropolitan Tucson, with a population just short of a million, not only takes in the country's 33rd largest city but also includes Casas Adobes, Drexel Heights, Flowing Wells, Green Valley, Oro Valley, and other suburban places in surrounding Pima County. (For a complete list of cities, towns, and unincorporated places within each retirement place, see the "Retirement Contacts & Place Finder" in this book's Appendix.)

County names ring a bell with travelers. Hawaii's Maui, Wisconsin's Door County, and New Jersey's Cape May are three such places. Other counties—Mississippi's Madison, Santa Fe in New Mexico, and Yuma in Arizona—have the same name as their well-known seats of government. In these instances, it's natural to call the retirement place by its county name.

But county names aren't usually tossed around in your basic where-to-retire scuttlebutt. Washington County, Arkansas, is one of 31 counties honoring the first president of the United States. The name draws a blank to Texans, Louisianans, Missourians, and Oklahomans (neighboring states that have their *own* Washington County). But more recognizable is Fayetteville, the seat of Washington County and home of the University of Arkansas.

Another case is Barnstable County, Massachusetts, which includes all of Cape Cod from Buzzards Bay out old U.S. 6 on the famous sandy spit of land to Provincetown. Centuries ago, Cape Cod elbowed Barnstable County aside in popular New England usage.

Sometimes the name given a retirement place is that of the one or two biggest population centers. Thus North Carolina's Orange County becomes Chapel Hill–Carrboro, Florida's Charlotte County changes into Port Charlotte, and California's Nevada County turns into Grass Valley–Nevada City.

In other instances, the name of a town may be paired with a well-known natural feature. Alpine–Big Bend identifies the county seat and one of our finest national parks, all in sparsely peopled Brewster County, Texas. Murray–Kentucky Lake names the college town and one of the world's largest man-made lakes, both in Calloway County, Kentucky.

The following chart identifies the 200 places as they are used throughout *Retirement Places Rated* and details the geography—usually a county—that defines the place. Included in the chart are population figures for today and an economist's forecast of what they will be by the year 2015.

200 Retirement Places

RETIREMENT PLACE & COUNTY	POPULATION 2008	POPULATION 2015	GROWTH 2008–2015
Alamogordo, New Mexico Otero County	66,164	72,043	9%
Alpine–Big Bend, Texas Brewster County	9,421	10,189	8%
Amador County, California Amador County	41,014	46,769	14%
Anacortes, Washington Skagit County	118,676	131,064	10%
Annapolis, Maryland Anne Arundel County	539,310	603,598	12%
Apalachicola, Florida Franklin County	10,705	11,897	11%

RETIREMENT PLACE & COUNTY	POPULATION 2008	POPULATION 2015	GROWTH 2008–2015
Asheville, North Carolina Buncombe County	228,406	249,792	9%
Athens, Georgia Clarke County	108,604	117,920	9%
Bar Harbor, Maine Hancock County	55,053	58,119	6%
Bay St. Louis–Pass Christian, Mississippi Hancock and Harrison counties	236,397	260,261	10%
Beaufort, South Carolina Beaufort County	150,457	179,339	19%
Beaufort–Atlantic Beach, North Carolina Carteret County	65,669	72,702	11%
Bellingham, Washington Whatcom County	193,634	216,569	12%
Bend, Oregon Deschutes County	153,961	182,573	19%
Berkeley Springs, West Virginia Morgan County	16,439	17,353	6%
The Big Island, Hawaii Hawaii County	177,744	201,459	13%
Bisbee, Arizona Cochise County	132,294	146,229	11%
Boerne, Texas Kendall County	30,492	34,760	14%
Boone–Blowing Rock, North Carolina Watauga County	44,491	49,033	10%
Bozeman, Montana Gallatin County	85,072	100,736	18%
Bradenton, Florida Manatee County	328,737	378,566	15%
Branson, Missouri Taney County	48,061	59,665	24%
Brevard, North Carolina Transylvania County	30,561	32,638	7%
Brown County, Indiana Brown County	15,816	17,298	9%
Brownsville, Texas Cameron County	398,275	443,184	11%
Brunswick, Maine Cumberland County	281,548	296,006	5%
Burlington, Vermont Chittenden County	154,837	166,503	8%
Camden, Maine Knox County	42,810	46,368	8%
Carmel–Pebble Beach, California Monterey County	430,489	471,731	10%
Carson City–Carson Valley, Nevada Carson City and Douglas County	109,607	124,383	14%
Cedar City, Utah Iron County	41,766	49,626	19%
Cedar Creek Lake, Texas Henderson County	86,085	99,868	16%
Chapel Hill–Carrboro, North Carolina Orange County	126,286	144,206	14%
Charleston, South Carolina Charleston County	347,387	385,752	11%
Charles Town–Shepherdstown, West Virginia Jefferson County	50,948	54,826	8%

continued

200 Retirement Places (cont.)

RETIREMENT PLACE & COUNTY	POPULATION 2008	POPULATION 2015	GROWTH 2008–2015
Charlottesville, Virginia Charlottesville City and Albemarle County	137,546	151,931	10%
Chestertown, Maryland Kent County	20,312	21,203	4%
Chewelah, Washington Stevens County	43,910	48,172	10%
Coeur d'Alene, Idaho Kootenai County	138,572	163,425	18%
Columbia, Missouri Boone County	149,845	164,450	10%
Conway, Arkansas Faulkner County	104,253	120,374	15%
Cortez, Colorado Montezuma County	25,948	28,577	10%
Cottonwood–Verde Valley, Arizona Yavapai County	217,134	259,126	19%
Crossville, Tennessee Cumberland County	54,035	60,084	11%
Dahlonega, Georgia Lumpkin County	26,024	29,884	15%
Dare Outer Banks, North Carolina Dare County	36,824	43,405	18%
Delta County, Colorado Delta County	31,362	34,549	10%
Door Peninsula, Wisconsin Door County	29,288	31,381	7%
Driggs, Idaho Teton County	8,082	9,483	17%
Durango, Colorado La Plata County	51,773	61,624	19%
Eagle River–Woodruff, Wisconsin Vilas County	23,276	25,391	9%
East End Long Island, New York Suffolk County	1,505,473	1,571,843	4%
Easton–St. Michaels, Maryland Talbot County	36,797	39,262	7%
East Stroudsburg, Pennsylvania Monroe County	173,727	197,487	14%
Edenton, North Carolina Chowan County	14,894	15,691	5%
Eugene, Oregon Lane County	347,308	374,364	8%
Eureka Springs, Arkansas Carroll County	28,359	31,420	11%
Fairhope–Gulf Shores, Alabama Baldwin County	180,331	214,058	19%
Fairplay, Colorado Park County	18,941	23,473	24%
Fayetteville, Arkansas Washington County	190,004	211,673	11%
Flagstaff, Arizona Coconino County	131,072	147,360	12%
Fort Collins–Loveland, Colorado Larimer County	288,826	327,033	13%
Fort Myers–Cape Coral, Florida Lee County	585,799	678,995	16%
Fredericksburg, Texas Gillespie County	24,142	26,512	10%

RETIREMENT PLACE & COUNTY	POPULATION 2008	POPULATION 2015	GROWTH 2008–2015
Fredericksburg–Spotsylvania, Virginia Spotsylvania County	147,247	169,924	15%
Front Royal, Virginia Warren County	37,061	40,433	9%
Gainesville, Florida Alachua County	232,146	250,689	8%
Georgetown, Texas Williamson County	374,970	469,243	25%
Grand Junction, Colorado Mesa County	135,760	149,006	10%
Grants Pass, Oregon Josephine County	85,377	95,807	12%
Grass Valley–Nevada City, California Nevada County	106,091	123,531	16%
Hamilton–Bitterroot Valley, Montana Ravalli County	42,730	49,025	15%
Hampshire County, West Virginia Hampshire County	22,857	24,715	8%
Hanover, New Hampshire Grafton County	87,990	95,330	8%
Hattiesburg, Mississippi Forrest County	80,337	81,059	1%
Henderson, Nevada Clark County	1,890,570	2,300,121	22%
Hendersonville–East Flat Rock, North Carolina Henderson County	101,160	109,988	9%
Hilton Head Island, South Carolina Beaufort County	150,457	179,339	19%
Hot Springs, Arkansas Garland County	97,850	106,442	9%
Iowa City, Iowa Johnson County	124,487	141,295	14%
Jackson Hole, Wyoming Teton County	20,945	25,314	21%
Kalispell–Flathead Valley, Montana Flathead County	89,888	105,059	17%
Kerrville, Texas Kerr County	48,225	52,088	8%
Ketchum–Sun Valley, Idaho Blaine County	24,054	30,706	28%
Key West, Florida Monroe County	80,527	89,998	12%
Kingman, Arizona Mohave County	204,205	242,892	19%
Kissimmee–St. Cloud, Florida Osceola County	252,454	300,173	19%
Laguna Beach–Dana Point, California Orange County	3,106,174	3,370,410	9%
Lake Conroe, Texas Montgomery County	413,847	485,316	17%
Lake Havasu City, Arizona Mohave County	204,205	242,892	19%
Lakeland–Winter Haven, Florida Polk County	559,720	596,655	7%
Lake of the Cherokees, Oklahoma Delaware County	41,716	47,530	14%
Lake of the Ozarks, Missouri Camden County	42,768	50,361	18%

continued

200 Retirement Places (cont.)

RETIREMENT PLACE & COUNTY	POPULATION 2008	POPULATION 2015	GROWTH 2008–2015
Lake Placid, New York Essex County	39,198	40,284	3%
Largo, Florida Pinellas County	951,019	1,001,530	5%
Las Cruces, New Mexico Dona Ana County	198,653	219,380	10%
Las Vegas, New Mexico San Miguel County	30,946	34,125	10%
Leelanau Peninsula, Michigan Leelanau County	23,276	25,797	11%
Leesburg–Mount Dora, Florida Lake County	290,364	320,294	10%
Litchfield Hills, Connecticut Litchfield County	195,525	207,582	6%
Long Beach Peninsula, Washington Pacific County	22,037	23,035	5%
Loudoun County, Virginia Loudoun County	283,691	348,250	23%
Lower Cape May, New Jersey Cape May County	102,693	110,292	7%
Madison, Mississippi Madison County	93,634	108,754	16%
Madison, Wisconsin Dane County	479,489	527,449	10%
Marble Falls–Lake LBJ, Texas Burnet County	45,380	53,823	19%
Mariposa, California Mariposa County	18,682	20,047	7%
Martha's Vineyard, Massachusetts Dukes County	16,458	18,415	12%
Maryville, Tennessee Blount County	123,615	142,039	15%
Maui, Hawaii Maui County	149,640	171,575	15%
McAllen–Alamo, Texas Hidalgo County	733,807	860,192	17%
McCall, Idaho Valley County	8,746	9,680	11%
Medford–Ashland, Oregon Jackson County	210,054	243,517	16%
Melbourne–Palm Bay, Florida Brevard County	550,018	591,573	8%
Mendocino–Fort Bragg, California Mendocino County	90,565	95,872	6%
Middle Cape Cod, Massachusetts Barnstable County	237,664	262,772	11%
Monadnock Region, New Hampshire Cheshire County	79,053	82,914	5%
Montrose, Colorado Montrose County	39,089	42,702	9%
Morro Bay–Cambria, California San Luis Obispo County	269,181	300,095	11%
Murray–Kentucky Lake, Kentucky Calloway County	35,935	37,707	5%
Myrtle Beach, South Carolina Horry County	246,184	289,938	18%
Naples, Florida Collier County	332,330	389,405	17%

RETIREMENT PLACE & COUNTY	POPULATION 2008	POPULATION 2015	GROWTH 2008–2015
Natchitoches, Louisiana Natchitoches Parish	39,717	40,513	2%
Nelson County, Virginia Nelson County	15,345	15,867	3%
New Bern, North Carolina Craven County	93,636	99,925	7%
New Braunfels, Texas Comal County	101,981	115,472	13%
Newport–Lincoln City, Oregon Lincoln County	47,499	50,846	7%
Norfork Lake, Arkansas Baxter County	42,230	46,501	10%
Northampton–Amherst, Massachusetts Hampshire County	158,390	169,619	7%
Northern Neck, Virginia Lancaster and Northumberland counties	24,994	26,132	4%
Oakhurst–Coarsegold, California Madera County	151,979	172,762	14%
Ocala, Florida Marion County	319,070	354,252	11%
Ocean City, Maryland Worcester County	50,878	55,652	9%
Oxford, Mississippi Lafayette County	43,126	48,257	12%
Pagosa Springs, Colorado Archuleta County	13,565	17,414	28%
Pahrump Valley, Nevada Nye County	42,646	47,503	11%
Palmer–Wasilla, Alaska Matanuska–Susitna County	81,240	93,111	15%
Palm Springs–Coachella Valley, California Riverside County	2,081,878	2,389,079	15%
Panama City, Florida Bay County	169,989	186,878	10%
Paradise–Magalia, California Butte County	222,595	241,515	8%
Park City, Utah Summit and Wasatch counties	62,043	80,453	30%
Payson, Arizona Gila County	54,964	62,440	14%
Pendleton District, South Carolina Oconee County	71,014	74,137	4%
Pensacola, Florida Escambia County	311,493	340,670	9%
Petoskey–Harbor Springs, Michigan Emmet County	35,540	39,982	12%
Pike County, Pennsylvania Pike County	59,985	68,246	14%
Placer County, California Placer County	344,339	406,261	18%
Port Angeles–Sequim, Washington Clallam County	72,209	77,832	8%
Port Charlotte, Florida Charlotte County	176,711	220,512	25%
Port St. Lucie, Florida St. Lucie County	251,509	274,325	9%
Port Townsend, Washington Jefferson County	30,794	35,623	16%

continued

RETIREMENT PLACE & COUNTY	POPULATION 2008	POPULATION 2015	GROWTH 2008–2015
Prescott–Prescott Valley, Arizona Yavapai County	217,134	259,126	19%
Rabun County, Georgia Rabun County	16,757	18,259	9%
Rehoboth Bay–Indian River Bay, Delaware Sussex County	184,703	203,027	10%
Rio Rancho, New Mexico Sandoval County	117,097	139,060	19%
Rockport–Aransas Pass, Texas Aransas County	25,730	28,179	10%
Roswell, New Mexico Eddy County	52,715	55,523	5%
Ruidoso, New Mexico Lincoln County	22,345	25,377	14%
St. Augustine, Florida St. Johns County	170,195	189,709	11%
St. George–Zion, Utah Washington County	137,509	180,274	31%
St. Jay–Northeast Kingdom, Vermont Caledonia County	31,303	33,212	6%
St. Marys, Georgia Camden County	47,409	51,097	8%
St. Simons–Jekyll Islands, Georgia Glynn County	73,763	77,949	6%
Sandpoint–Lake Pend Oreille, Idaho Bonner County	44,080	51,299	16%
San Juan Islands, Washington San Juan County	16,033	17,741	11%
Santa Barbara, California Santa Barbara County	409,355	428,069	5%
Santa Fe, New Mexico Santa Fe County	151,711	176,397	16%
Sarasota, Florida Sarasota County	384,400	425,278	11%
Savannah, Georgia Chatham County	243,527	254,498	5%
Scottsdale, Arizona Maricopa County	3,892,546	4,474,285	15%
Sebring–Avon Park, Florida Highlands County	101,646	115,589	14%
Sedona, Arizona Coconino County	131,072	147,360	12%
Silver City, New Mexico Grant County	30,287	31,442	4%
Silverthorne–Breckenridge, Colorado Summit County	27,063	31,990	18%
Smith Mountain Lake, Virginia Bedford and Franklin counties	129,751	147,727	14%

Introduction

RETIREMENT PLACE & COUNTY	POPULATION 2008	POPULATION 2015	GROWTH 2008–2015
Sonora–Twain Harte, California Tuolumne County	62,030	67,975	10%
Southern Berkshire County, Massachusetts Berkshire County	132,715	134,301	1%
Southern Pines–Pinehurst, North Carolina Moore County	85,298	93,396	9%
Southport–Brunswick Islands, North Carolina Brunswick County	96,585	113,503	18%
State College, Pennsylvania Centre County	145,946	158,042	8%
Sullivan County, New York Sullivan County	77,656	80,019	3%
Summerville, South Carolina Dorchester County	117,495	127,861	9%
Taos, New Mexico Taos County	34,058	39,364	16%
Thomasville, Georgia Thomas County	46,273	49,792	8%
Toms River–Barnegat Bay, New Jersey Ocean County	586,549	650,086	11%
Traverse City, Michigan Grand Traverse County	88,809	99,743	12%
Tryon, North Carolina Polk County	20,296	22,923	13%
Tucson, Arizona Pima County	976,294	1,092,601	12%
Vero Beach, Florida Indian River County	137,091	156,359	14%
Victorville–Apple Valley, California San Bernardino County	2,071,156	2,314,060	12%
Waynesville, North Carolina Haywood County	58,770	63,894	9%
Wenatchee, Washington Chelan County	72,286	77,856	8%
Western St. Tammany Parish, Louisiana St. Tammany Parish	285,142	301,330	6%
Whidbey Island, Washington Island County	82,921	91,165	10%
Wickenburg, Arizona Parts of Maricopa County	3,892,546	4,474,285	15%
Williamsburg, Virginia Williamsburg city and James City County	73,544	83,263	13%
Wimberley, Texas Hays County	135,899	162,064	19%
Woodstock, Vermont Windsor County	59,762	63,604	6%
York Beaches, Maine York County	208,764	223,087	7%
Yuma, Arizona Yuma County	214,805	244,915	14%

Source: Woods & Poole Economics, Inc., population forecasts.

San Juan Islands
Bellingham
Port Angeles-Sequim
Anacortes
Port Townsend
Whidbey Island
WA
Long Beach Peninsula
Wenatchee
Sandpoint-Lake Pend Oreille
Chewelah
KALISPELL—FLATHEAD VALLEY
Coeur d' Alene
MT
ND
OR
Newport-Lincoln City
Hamilton-Bitterroot Valley
Eugene
BEND
McCall
Bozeman
SD
Grants Pass
Ketchum-Sun Valley
WY
MEDFORD-ASHLAND
CA
Driggs
Jackson Hole
ID
Mendocino-Fort Bragg
NV
UT
NE
Paradise-Magalia
Park City
Grass Valley-Nevada City
PLACER COUNTY
CO
FORT COLLINS-LOVELAND
Carson City-Carson Valley
Amador County
Grand Junction
Silverthorne—Breckenridge
KS
Sonora-Twain Harte
Delta County
Fairplay
Mariposa
Montrose
Oakhurst-Coarsegold
Cedar City
Cortez
Carmel-Pebble Beach
ST. GEORGE-ZION
Durango
Pagosa Springs
MORRO BAY—CAMBRIA
HENDERSON
AZ
NM
Pahrump Valley
Taos
OK
Lake of the Cherokees
Santa Barbara
Victorville-Apple Valley
Flagstaff
Santa Fe
Kingman
Sedona
Las Vegas
TX
Lake Havasu City
Cottonwood-Verde Valley
Rio Rancho
LAGUNA BEACH-DANA POINT
Prescott-Prescott Valley
Palm Springs-Coachella Valley
WICKENBURG
Payson
SCOTTSDALE
Yuma
Ruidoso
Roswell
Silver City
Alamogordo
Cedar Creek Lake
TUCSON
LAS CRUCES
Bisbee
Alpine-Big Bend
Marble Falls-Lake LBJ
GEORGETOWN
Lake Conroe
Fredericksburg
WIMBERLY
Kerrville
New Braunfels
Boerne
Maui
AK
The Big Island
Palmer-Wasilla
Rockport-Aransas Pass
McAllen-Alamo
Brownsville

Population

● 250,000 and over

◉ 100,000 to 249,000

⊙ 30,000 to 99,000

○ less than 29,999

ASHEVILLE = One of the
top 30 retirement places

MAKING
RETIREMENT
PLACES RATED
WORK FOR YOU

W hen it comes to rating places for livability, there are three points of view. The first says that defining what's good for all people all the time isn't just unfair, it's impossible and shouldn't be attempted at all. "Livable for whom?" the argument goes. The artist who wants mountain vistas? The businessman who wants low taxes and no red tape? The new college graduate starting a career? The retired person looking for a healthful climate? The parents searching for good public schools?

The second view says that you *can* rate places but shouldn't, because measuring a prickly thing like livability makes places unwilling rivals of one another. When you claim that your own turf is the most livable, you're implying that others aren't. Look at the old jokes and occasional ill will between neighbors such as Dallas and Ft. Worth, Minneapolis and St. Paul, or San Francisco and Oakland. According to this view, rating places from best to worst is an unbecoming exercise. Every place is habitable, which is why people live in them.

The third point of view says nonsense to the first two. Of course you can measure livability. As long as you know who your audience is and make clear what your statistical yardsticks are and use them consistently, you'll be doing what's done all the time by Chambers of Commerce from Key West, Florida, to communities around Bremerton, Washington, and from West Quoddy Head, Maine, to San Diego, California.

Although one can argue with confidence for viewpoints one and two, *Retirement Places Rated* takes sides with the third.

RATING PLACES: AN AMERICAN TRADITION

It may seem the height of effrontery, this business of judging places from best to worst with numbers. After all, how can intangible things such as friendliness and optimism be measured with statistics? Yet *numeracy* is almost as strong a national character trait as *literacy*. When it comes to choosing a new place to live, we've been digesting numbers for a long, long time.

To sell colonists on settling in Maryland rather than in Virginia, 17th-century boosters assembled figures showing heavier livestock, more plentiful game, and lower mortality from summer diseases and Indian attacks.

California for Health, Wealth, and Residence, just one volume in a library of post–Civil War guides touting the West's superior quality of life, gathered data to show the climate along the southern Pacific Coast to be the world's best. Not so, countered the Union Pacific Railroad's land office in 1871; settlers will find the most "genial and healthy seasons" in western Kansas.

In our own century, the statistical nets were flung even wider. "There are plenty of Americans who regard Kansas as almost barbaric," noted H.L. Mencken back in 1931, "just as there are other Americans who shudder whenever they think of Arkansas, Ohio, Indiana, Oklahoma, Texas, or California." Mencken wrote these words in his *American Mercury* magazine to introduce his formula for measuring the progress of civilization in each of the states. He mixed the number of Boy Scouts and *Atlantic Monthly* subscribers with lynchings and pellagra cases, added a dash of *Who's Who* listings along with rates for divorce and murder, threw in figures for rainfall and gasoline consumption, and found that, hands down, Mississippi was the worst American state. Mencken hated the South. Massachusetts, a state he liked, came out best.

Decades later, in 1978, the Bay State was demoted when Chase Econometrics, an economic consulting firm, rated it the worst state for retirement. And the best state according to the Chase forecasters? Utah.

Fast forwarding to 2003, *Kiplinger's* magazine elevated tiny Delaware to the "most retirement-friendly" of all the states, at least in the favorable

tax treatment of retirement income and a lack of sales tax. And the worst state according to the Kiplinger analysts? Pennsylvania, right next door.

RATING RETIREMENT PLACES: ONE WAY

Retirement Places Rated is more useful than any system that just looks at states. When it comes to finding your own spot for retirement, you would do well to ignore the shopworn truisms about states and their track records in attracting older adults.

Thinking of Florida as a destination still means having to make a choice from among thousands of cities, towns, and unincorporated places that stretch from the Gulf beaches and farming backcountry in Escambia County in the western panhandle all the way some 900 miles down the peninsula to the causeway to subtropical Key West. People don't retire to states; they retire to specific places.

Moreover, statewide averages hide local realities. For some persons, there may be a world of difference between Laguna Beach and Palm Springs in California, and these differences may be more important in retirement than the differences between California and Florida.

Certainly, this book is more objective than the hearsay that travelers share at an interstate highway rest stop or at an airport gate. Each of the 200 locations is rated by seven factors that most persons planning for retirement consider highly important.

- **Climate** reviews winter discomfort factors such as wind chill and summer discomfort factors such as humidity. Psychological factors such as cloudiness, rain, darkness, and fog, plus hazards such as snow, thunderstorms, and high wind also receive scrutiny.

- **The Economy** compares the prospects for jobs in four basic industries most promising to older adults: government; finance, insurance, and real estate; retail trade; and services. The chapter also scans how vulnerable a spot is to recessions and how competitive the part-time job market is.

- **Services** looks at physician specialists, the supply of hospital services, air travel, public library, and continuing-education assets in each place.

- **Ambience** looks at historic preservation, water recreation, protected scenic and recreation areas, good restaurants, bookstores, and the fine arts scene.

- **Costs of Living** measures typical expenses such as housing, food, transportation, and healthcare. The chapter also looks at the bite that various state personal income and sales taxes take from retirement income.

- **Housing** considers home prices for a "starter" home, a "move up" home, and an "elite" home, as well as alternative housing choices such as condos, mobile homes, and apartments.

- **Personal Safety** measures the annual rate of violent and property crime in each place and looks also at the latest 5-year trends: up, down, or unchanged.

Go ahead and fault *Retirement Places Rated*'s criteria. Admittedly, this book's measurements for healthcare, services, and ambience favor big places over small ones. On the other hand, the ratings for crime and costs of living favor small places over big ones. The standards for climate mildness certainly aren't everyone's. But they have nothing to do with population size.

RATING RETIREMENT PLACES: YOUR WAY

At the end of this book, in the chapter titled "Putting It All Together," climate, the local economy, community services, ambience, costs of living, housing, and personal safety get equal weight to identify retirement places with across-the-board strengths.

A MAP FOR THE CHAPTERS

Each of *Retirement Places Rated*'s seven core chapters has four parts:

- The **Introduction** gives basic information on the chapter's topic, peppered with facts and figures to help you evaluate places.

- The **Judging** and **Rankings** sections explain how the places are rated. Sample comparisons of retirement places are often included.

- The **Place Profiles** are capsule comparisons, arranged alphabetically by place, covering all the elements used in the ratings. Here you can see differences among places at a glance.

- The **Et Cetera** section expands on topics mentioned in the introduction and also has essays on related subjects. These range all the way from state-by-state tax treatment of retirement income to tactics for avoiding property crime.

The last chapter, "Putting It All Together," factors the scores to identify America's best all-around retirement places and describes the strengths and weaknesses of each place.

You may not agree with this system. You may prefer year-round sunshine to an abundance of medical specialists. You may give more weight to personal safety than to good fishing spots. For you, a place where retirement income goes further might be more important than historic homes and good restaurants. To identify which factors are more important and which are less, you may want to take stock of your own preferences, using the following Preference Inventory.

YOUR PREFERENCE INVENTORY

Retirement Places Rated's Preference Inventory has 63 pairs of statements. For each pair, decide which statement is more important to you when judging a retirement place. Even if both statements are equally important or neither is important, select one anyway. If you can't decide quickly, pass up the item but return to it after you complete the rest of the inventory.

Don't worry about being consistent. The paired statements aren't repeated. You won't find right or wrong answers, only answers that are best for you. Although the inventory takes about 10 minutes to finish, there is no time limit. You may want to ask your spouse or a friend to use one of the extra preference profiles on the last page of this chapter. Comparing your own Preference Inventory with another person's is an interesting exercise.

PREFERENCE INVENTORY DIRECTIONS

For each numbered item, decide which of the two statements is *more important* to you when choosing a place to retire. Mark the box next to that statement. Be sure to make a choice for all of the items.

1. A. ❏ The duration of the winter.
   B. ❏ Opportunities for part-time work.
2. C. ❏ Opportunities for taking college courses.
   A. ❏ A mild, four-season climate.
3. E. ❏ Where the living is inexpensive.
   D. ❏ Beaches and boating.
4. F. ❏ The variety of rental housing.
   G. ❏ The odds of being a crime victim.
5. D. ❏ Local performing arts calendar.
   C. ❏ Specialized medical care.
6. C. ❏ Public library collections.
   G. ❏ Whether crime is a major problem.
7. C. ❏ Accredited short-term hospitals.
   B. ❏ Competition for part-time work.
8. E. ❏ The bite state and local taxes take.
   G. ❏ Where criminal activity is least.
9. B. ❏ Launching a part-time business.
   D. ❏ Nearby national parks and forests.
10. A. ❏ Elevation, humidity, and temperatures.
    F. ❏ Typical apartment rents.
11. D. ❏ National parks and wildlife refuges.
    F. ❏ Typical apartment rents.
12. C. ❏ Medical specialists and hospitals.
    F. ❏ Residential property taxes.
13. A. ❏ A mild, four-season climate.
    G. ❏ Crime-free neighborhoods.
14. E. ❏ State and local tax bites.
    B. ❏ Seasonal jobs in the tourist season.
15. E. ❏ An area's typical household income.
    F. ❏ Recent home price appreciation.

16. B. ❏ Jobs in the service sector.
    G. ❏ Crime-free neighborhoods.
17. B. ❏ Outlook for part-time employment.
    F. ❏ Choices for home heating fuels.
18. D. ❏ Nearby national parks and forests.
    G. ❏ Crime-free neighborhoods.
19. A. ❏ Annual temperature highs and lows.
    E. ❏ Where physician fees are low.
20. D. ❏ Historic neighborhoods and bookstores.
    A. ❏ The number of thunderstorms in a year.
21. C. ❏ Medical specialists and good hospitals.
    E. ❏ State income and sales taxes.
22. A. ❏ Annual temperature extremes.
    C. ❏ Public library branches and collections.
23. D. ❏ Historic houses and good bookstores.
    B. ❏ Forecasted employment growth.
24. F. ❏ Residential property taxes.
    G. ❏ The burglary and auto theft rate.
25. C. ❏ The supply of medical specialists.
    D. ❏ Boating and fishing.
26. E. ❏ The cost of food.
    B. ❏ Jobs in the service sector.
27. A. ❏ The potential for cloudy days.
    F. ❏ The price of a move-up home.
28. D. ❏ The local performing arts calendar.
    F. ❏ Recent house price appreciation.
29. B. ❏ A recession-proof local economy.
    C. ❏ The area's public transportation.
30. C. ❏ Public libraries and bus routes.
    F. ❏ Recent house price appreciation.

31. E. ❏ Making retirement income stretch.

D. ❏ Historic homes and buildings.

32. G. ❏ An area's crime rate.

C. ❏ Academic programs at local colleges.

33. E. ❏ Tax breaks for older adults.

G. ❏ The odds of being a crime victim.

34. A. ❏ Annual amounts of rain and snow.

G. ❏ The local crime rate.

35. F. ❏ Variety of rental housing.

B. ❏ Variety of seasonal job prospects.

36. E. ❏ The costs for physician services.

A. ❏ Humidity, elevation, and wind speed.

37. A. ❏ The area's foggy and rainy days.

B. ❏ Local threat of unemployment.

38. D. ❏ Local performing arts.

G. ❏ The robbery and burglary rate.

39. A. ❏ Elevation, windiness, and cloudiness.

D. ❏ Performing arts and concert halls.

40. C. ❏ The variety of local college courses.

E. ❏ An area's typical household income.

41. B. ❏ Jobs in retail trade or real estate.

G. ❏ The area's criminal activity.

42. E. ❏ Where the living is inexpensive.

F. ❏ The variety of rental housing.

43. A. ❏ The duration of the summer.

B. ❏ The part-time job market.

44. C. ❏ Local community college courses.

A. ❏ A rigorous four-season climate.

45. E. ❏ Where the taxes are bearable.

D. ❏ National parks, fishing, and boating.

46. F. ❏ Rental apartment options.

G. ❏ The odds of being a crime victim.

47. D. ❏ Good restaurants and performing arts.

C. ❏ Specialized medical care.

48. C. ❏ Public library collections.

G. ❏ Whether auto theft is a problem.

49. C. ❏ Accredited hospital services.

B. ❏ Competition for part-time work.

50. E. ❏ The bite state and local taxes take.

G. ❏ Where the crime rate is low.

51. B. ❏ Finding a good part-time job.

D. ❏ Nearby national parks and forests.

52. A. ❏ Elevation, humidity, and temperatures.

F. ❏ Median home prices.

53. D. ❏ Wildlife refuges and scenic areas.

F. ❏ Local rental housing market.

54. C. ❏ Medical specialists and hospitals.

F. ❏ Residential property taxes.

55. A. ❏ Annual precipitation or cloudiness.

G. ❏ Crime-free neighborhoods.

56. E. ❏ Tax breaks for older adults.

B. ❏ Seasonal jobs in tourist season.

57. E. ❏ Typical household incomes.

F. ❏ Recent home price appreciation.

58. B. ❏ Jobs in the retail sector.

G. ❏ Low-crime neighborhoods.

59. B. ❏ Competition for part-time work.

F. ❏ Home heating fuel choices.

60. D. ❏ Nearby lakes and rivers.

G. ❏ Low auto-theft and burglary rates.

61. A. ❏ Annual temperature highs and lows.

E. ❏ Where medical specialists practice.

62. D. ❏ Historic neighborhoods.

A. ❏ The number of storms in a year.

63. C. ❏ Air travel connections.

E. ❏ State income and sales taxes.

Source: Adapted from "The Prospering Test," courtesy Thomas F. Bowman, Ph.D.; George Giuliani, Ph.D.; and M. Ronald Minge, Ph.D.

PLOTTING YOUR PREFERENCE PROFILE

It is important that you make a choice for each of the 63 items. Have you left any unchecked? If not, you're ready to draw your Preference Profile.

1. Count all the marks you've made in the boxes next to the letter A. Then enter the number of "A" statements on the line next to the word "Climate" on your Preference Profile. In the same way, count the number of statements for each of the other letters. Enter their totals in their respective places on your Preference Profile.

2. Now plot your totals on the blank chart. Place a dot on the appropriate line for each of the numbers and connect the dots to form a line graph of your results (see the Sample Preference Profile).

ANALYZING YOUR PREFERENCE PROFILE

Each of the seven factors in your Preference Profile—climate, the economy, community services, ambience, costs of living, housing, and personal safety—is not only a major concern when finding a likely place to retire, but also has a complete chapter in this book. The purpose of the Preference Inventory is to help you decide the relative importance of each of the chapters to you personally.

If your scores are high for one or two of these factors, you may want to give extra attention to the chapters covering them. Likewise, if your scores are low for any of the six, you may not need to give as much consideration to them as you would the ones with high scores. Bear in mind that the inventory orders your preferences in a hierarchy, that each of the factors has some importance to you, and that none should be entirely ignored.

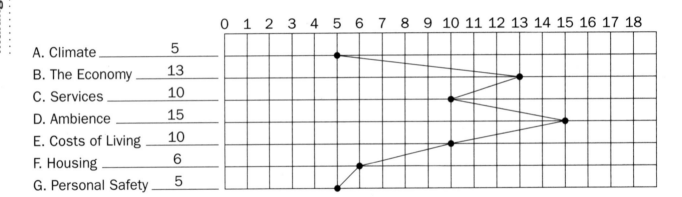

A. Climate _____ 5
B. The Economy _____ 13
C. Services _____ 10
D. Ambience _____ 15
E. Costs of Living _____ 10
F. Housing _____ 6
G. Personal Safety _____ 5

0 1 2 3 4 5 6 7 8 9 10 11 12 13 14 15 16 17 18

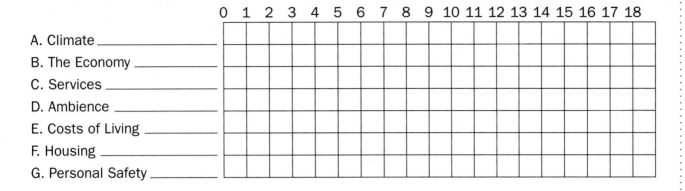

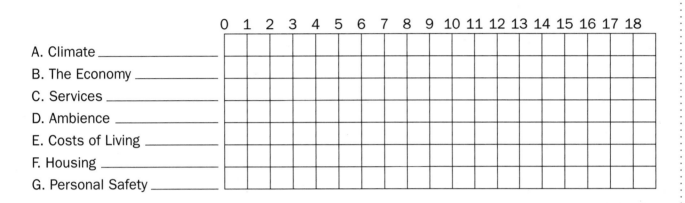

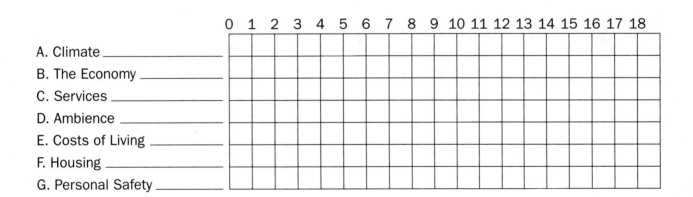

Climate

Canadian-born economist John Kenneth Galbraith once wrote, "The fortunate people of the planet are those who live by the seasons. There is far more difference between a Vermont farm in the summer and that farm in the winter than there is between San Diego and São Paulo. This means that people who live where the seasons are good and strong have no need to travel; they can stay at home and let change come to them. This simple truth will one day be recognized and then we will see a great reverse migration from Florida to Maine and on into Quebec."

That extraordinary prediction might cause many a lacquered Sun Belt real estate saleswoman to put down her cellphone and say, "Huh?" She can relax. Demographers forecast that the march to the sun will continue well into the 21st century.

What else is new? Most of us say we prefer a mild, sunny climate. When asked where in the country these climates are, we point to the lower half of the Pacific Coast, the Desert Southwest, Florida, and anywhere along the South Atlantic and Gulf coasts. Sure enough, this area between 25 and 35 degrees latitude has been drawing older adults for decades.

But other places above the Sun Belt and hundreds of miles from beaches are drawing older adults. Many of these locations see mild climates, too. The names of some may surprise you.

What always surprises is the variety of global climates found right here at home. Northern maritime, mild Mediterranean, southerly mountain, desert, tropical "paradise," desert highland, rugged northern continental, windward slope, leeward slope, and humid subtropical climates—name it and you'll meet up with it somewhere in the United States.

Climate can't be bought, built, remodeled, or relocated. A place's climate is there for keeps, and the weather events that make up its climate—rain, snow, heat, cold, drought, wind—will have a profound effect on the rest of your life.

KEEP THESE SIMPLE FACTORS IN MIND

If you can live anywhere you wish and are open to all the variety this country offers, recognize that a combination of water, latitude and longitude, elevation, prevailing winds, mountains, and urban development lies behind any area's climate.

1

If You Can, Choose Water

A waterfront location—even one with just a water view—doesn't come cheap. As Will Rogers once said, "They aren't making any more of it." Water, particularly an ocean, takes the edge off temperature. It warms up slowly, holds the heat, and cools more slowly. Places on the water tend to be cooler in summer and warmer in winter than other places inland. The hottest it gets in July on the Santa Monica Pier in Los Angeles is 75°F; meanwhile, 15 miles north in the San Fernando Valley, it's 95°F. Golfers in Boston's western suburbs must store their clubs during the cold-weather months from Thanksgiving to the onset of spring. Golfers 45 miles southeast on Cape Cod, with the Gulf Stream flowing by the beaches, can play almost all year-round.

Don't Move Centrally & Northerly

Over the past 200 years, America's center of population has shifted westward some 1,000 miles from Chestertown, Maryland, to near the college town of Rolla, Missouri. Alas, places located in the heartland see wide swings of temperature. Continental climates tend to be even harsher the higher the latitude. The closer to the North Pole you get, the more exaggerated are the seasonal shifts because polar and very northerly locations undergo the greatest seasonal variation in the amount and intensity of sunlight.

In Alaska's Palmer–Wasilla area, for example, *Retirement Places Rated*'s northernmost spot, a December day is only 5 hours long, overcast with occasional snow. In late June the day has lengthened to 18 hours, the sun's heat is intense, 50-pound cabbages show up in roadside markets, and golfers can play until midnight.

Far to the southwest, at this book's southernmost location, the solar energy pouring over the island of Hawaii (20.52 N) in June is double what it is in December, but in Palmer–Wasilla (61.36 N) it is 20 times as great. Places in the north and far north, then, experience Siberian winters and short, sunlit summers as well.

High Is Cooler

Though some medical studies show reduced odds of heart disease and cancer the higher one lives above sea level, a higher elevation can have the same negative effect on comfort as higher latitude. Each 1,000 feet above sea level lowers a thermometer reading by 3.3 degrees. In New Mexico, there are just 3 degrees difference in annual average temperature between Clayton and Lordsburg, two places with similar elevations. But Clayton is on the edge of the plains while Lordsburg is 440 miles southwest in high desert. However, at two weather stations just 15 miles apart but differing in elevation by 4,700 feet, the average annual temperatures vary by 16 degrees.

Something in the Wind

To understand how prevailing winds influence climate, consider a pair of places 3,200 miles apart: Bellingham, Washington, and Bar Harbor, Maine. On their respective coasts, both sit high in northern latitudes and both peek through some of the foggiest mornings in the United States. You'd naturally suppose the two have similar climates. But Bellingham is milder because it is

CLIMATE IN BRIEF

Chambers of commerce and retirement guidebooks that quote annual average temperatures are misleading. By this measure, San Diego, California, and Oxford, Mississippi, are identical at 60°F.

Beware of promoters highlighting winter temperatures but excluding summer temperatures *adjusted upward by humidity*. One out of three places profiled in this book has a July humidex (air temperature heightened by relative humidity) topping 100°F. And the dry Desert Southwest isn't immune: The humidex in Lake Havasu City, Arizona, is 123°F; in Palm Springs, California, it's 118°F; and in Scottsdale, Arizona, it's 115°F.

Consider the psychological impact, or *seasonal affect,* of differing climates. Locations in the Pacific Northwest and North Woods regions see cloudy skies 3 out of 4 days in the year. Wet days are strongly associated with cloudiness. High latitudes mean much earlier winter darkness. And don't discount periodic hazards such as Rocky Mountain snows, Florida afternoon thunderstorms, Ozark ice storms, California coastal sea fogs, and low strati. They're nearly everywhere.

If a mild climate is most important to you, think about living in two places—June to October in State College, Pennsylvania, for example, and November to May in Natchitoches, Louisiana. Or rotate Yuma, Arizona, winters with Montrose, Colorado, summers. The costs of living in two inexpensive places are still less than the costs in year-round paradise climates of coastal Southern California and Hawaii. But there's a less obvious benefit: You have alternating senses of place and sets of friendships.

a landfall for air that has moved thousands of miles over the Pacific. Far inland in Washington State, even Wenatchee and Spokane feel the beneficial effects of the Pacific winds. Interior cities in the East, however, experience few consequences of the Atlantic save on rare occasions when the prevailing wind direction turns. Alas, this reversal often means a storm.

Choose the Right Slope

The only barriers big enough to deflect and channel winds, rain, and snow are mountains. Mountain people aren't relating folk tales when they tell visitors that the weather on one side of a mountain range is radically different from that on the other. In winter, the Great Divide shields Divide–Cripple Creek, Colorado, from much of the Arctic air that moves down the continent. In summer, the windward side of the location's mountain setting is a lush, evergreen parkland at lower elevations; some 30 miles east, a semiarid steppe descends to dry, shortgrass prairie.

Downtown Is Hot

Finally, urban development makes heat islands within the surrounding countryside. Downtown Scottsdale, Arizona, has night temperatures 8 degrees warmer than they were 60 years ago when the area was a 1-square-mile farming cluster with 2,000 people. Population here has increased 100-fold, concrete and asphalt store the sun's radiant energy better than desert sand ever did, and automobile pollution is trapped overhead in a high-pressure cell. Wind speed, visibility, sunshine, and heating needs are less in the center of cities than in nearby country, but temperature, cloudiness, thunderstorm frequency, and air pollution levels are higher.

CLIMATE REGIONS

Mountains indeed mark the climate regions of the United States. The Pacific Coast is mild and the northern portion of the Great Plains is rigorous. The Great Basin between the Cascade and Sierra Nevada ranges to the west and the Rocky Mountains to the east is dry.

CLIMATE REGIONS OF THE UNITED STATES

Some of the best climates for variety and mildness are found in the southern part of this area. The southern part of the Appalachian Mountains, too, offers mild and variable climates.

Millions of Americans live in the Great Plains and Central Lowlands, ironically the least comfortable region. If you live in the northern part, you're hit by severe winters and hot, humid summers with springs and autumns that are all too short. If you live in the southern part, winters are milder, springs and autumns are longer, but the summer air hits you in the face like a warm, wet towel.

The climate of the East Coast is like the Central Lowlands, but milder and somewhat damper. On the coast, winters are milder and summers are noticeably cooler. Retirement places with excellent climates are here, especially New Jersey's Cape May and Ocean counties, Ocean City in Maryland, and Rehoboth Bay–Indian River Bay in southern Delaware.

The high country that includes the Rockies, the Cascades, the Sierra Nevadas, and the northern half of the Appalachians is home to resort areas, thanks to the cool, crisp, sunny summers with cold nights and winters that produce snow for outdoor sports. Several places in the valleys are popular with older adults who prefer a stimulating yet not too mild climate.

Hawaii is the only state situated in the tropical zone, officially defined as any area where temperatures don't drop below 64°F. These islands experience small temperature changes, with summer averaging only 4 to 8 degrees higher than winter. Moisture-bearing trade winds from over the Pacific provide a system of natural ventilation for the heat associated with these tropical climates.

SO, WHAT'S COMFORTABLE?

Mop the sweat from pulling a balky lawnmower's starter cord a dozen times on a July afternoon, hack away at the ice on the car's windshield one morning in January, or look out the window on a sodden and gray day and you're forgiven for fantasizing about a place where it's never hot or cold and always bright.

It is a fantasy, indeed. Not only would you likely get bored with an endless sequence of identically dry sunny days with tepid temperatures, but you'd also find that none of the places profiled in *Retirement Places Rated* have climates that match this pattern 365 days a year.

SNOWY PLACES

Most locations profiled in these pages see less than 6 inches of snow, and 40 places experience less than a trace. But other places get a bit more than that. Below are 15 places that receive more than 6 feet in a normal year:

PLACE	ANNUAL SNOWFALL
Palmer–Wasilla, AK	130 inches
Pagosa Springs, CO	116
Flagstaff, AZ	100
Leelanau Peninsula, MI	98
Woodstock, VT	89
Sandpoint–Lake Pend Oreille, ID	89
Traverse City, MI	88
Petoskey–Harbor Springs, MI	88
Jackson Hole, WY	87
McCall, ID	86
St. Jay–Northeast Kingdom, VT	86
Lake Placid, NY	86
Driggs, ID	80
Burlington, VT	77
Hanover, NH	77
Retirement Places Average	**22**

Source: NOAA, Climatography of the United States

Temperature

Beware of chamber of commerce blandishments about a place's annual average temperature. San Francisco's is 57°F. So is St. Louis's. But San Francisco enjoys both a diurnal (24-hour) temperature range of 12 degrees and an annual range (the difference between January's and July's average temperatures) of 12 degrees. St. Louis has a diurnal range of 17 degrees and an annual range of 47 degrees. The temperature swings in these two cities highlight the difference between a marine climate and a continental climate. San Francisco's climate is somewhat cool and remarkably stable year-round. St. Louis's is neither.

Among retirement regions, the greatest annual temperature ranges (up to 77 degrees) are found in the North Woods, the Rocky Mountains, and northern parts of New England. The greatest diurnal temperature swings (up to 40 degrees) are in high desert parts of the Rio Grande and Desert Southwest regions. The smallest diurnal and annual temperature swings are in Hawaii and along the Pacific Coast.

CLOUDY PLACES

A day is *clear* if clouds form less than 30 percent of the daytime sky, *partly cloudy* if they form 40 to 70 percent of it, and *cloudy* if they form more than 80 percent. Some popular spots see cloudiness 2 of every 3 of their days.

PLACE	ANNUAL CLOUDY DAYS
Palmer–Wasilla, AK	240
Newport–Lincoln City, OR	238
Anacortes, WA	231
Bellingham, WA	231
San Juan Islands, WA	231
Port Townsend, WA	230
Port Angeles–Sequim, WA	229
Whidbey Island, WA	228
Long Beach Peninsula, WA	223
Kalispell–Flathead Valley, MT	213
Petoskey–Harbor Springs, MI	210
Traverse City, MI	210
Hamilton–Bitterroot Valley, MT	208
Burlington, VT	206
Leelanau Peninsula, MI	206
Retirement Places Average	**141**

Source: NOAA, Local Climatological Data. Some of the above figures come from the nearest "first order" station.

DRY PLACES

In some locations with low humidity, it's cheaper and more efficient to cool interiors with roof-mounted evaporative air conditioners, locally called "swamp coolers," rather than the more expensive refrigerated air conditioners.

PLACE	RELATIVE HUMIDITY
Henderson, NV	24%
Pahrump Valley, NV	24%
St. George–Zion, UT	24%
Tucson, AZ	30%
Wickenburg, AZ	31%
Kingman, AZ	32%
Lake Havasu City, AZ	32%
Palm Springs–Coachella Valley, CA	32%
Scottsdale, AZ	32%
Victorville–Apple Valley, CA	32%
Yuma, AZ	32%
Alamogordo, NM	33%
Alpine–Big Bend, TX	33%
Cottonwood–Verde Valley, AZ	33%
Las Cruces, NM	33%
Retirement Places Average	**56%**

Source: NOAA, Local Climatological Data. Some of the above figures come from the nearest "first order" station.

Humidity

After air temperature, humidity is the major factor in climatic comfort. Anyone who has sweated out a hot, humid summer knows humidity heightens heat. In hot, humid climates, heat is retained in the damp air even after the sunset, resulting in nights that are almost as hot as the days. (See the "Heat Index" chart below.)

Wind Chill

Wind chill (air temperature reduced by wind, derived according to newly revised National Oceanic and Atmospheric Administration standards—see the "Wind Chill" chart below) is the same thing as heat loss. Anyone who has turned their face away from a stiff winter blow swears to this. When the wind rises over 5 miles per hour and the thermometer reads 45°F or less, you'll start to feel temperatures on exposed skin colder than still air.

Approaching a Climatic Ideal

Is searching for the ideal year-round retirement climate an illusion, like the quest for perfect health, an honest man, or the Holy Grail?

Perhaps it is. More than 100 years ago, the Santa Fe Railroad's *Healthseeker* guidebook advised newcomers to Arizona to winter in Phoenix but head north to Flagstaff's 7,000-foot elevation for the summer. Thousands still take that advice, and many bypass Flagstaff for a place farther north in the Idaho panhandle, or in the Rocky Mountain regions of Utah or Colorado.

In Florida, thousands of retired persons vacate the Sunshine State's buggy summers for a cottage on the Jersey Shore, the New England coast, or a cabin in the southern Appalachians. Still others, absolutely bored by the unvarying paradise-like climate in the Virgin Islands or Hawaii, head back to the mainland for a fix of four-season weather.

Heat Index

AIR TEMPERATURE (°F)	APPARENT TEMPERATURE (°F)																		
110	99	102	105	108	112	117	123	130	137	143	150								
105	95	97	100	102	105	109	113	118	123	129	135	142	149						
100	91	93	95	97	99	101	104	107	110	115	120	126	132	138	144				
95	87	88	90	91	93	94	96	98	101	104	107	110	114	119	124	130	136		
90	83	84	85	86	87	88	90	91	93	95	96	98	100	102	106	109	113	117	122
85	78	79	80	81	82	83	84	85	86	87	88	89	90	91	93	95	97	99	102
80	73	74	75	76	77	77	78	79	79	80	81	81	82	83	85	86	86	87	88
75	69	69	70	71	72	72	73	73	74	74	75	75	76	76	77	77	78	78	79
70	64	64	65	65	66	66	67	67	68	68	69	69	70	70	70	70	71	71	71
	0%	5%	10%	15%	20%	25%	30%	35%	40%	45%	50%	55%	60%	65%	70%	75%	80%	85%	90%

RELATIVE HUMIDITY (%)

Wind Chill

WIND SPEED (MPH)	APPARENT TEMPERATURE (°F)																
60	25	17	10	3	-4	-11	-19	-26	-33	-40	-48	-55	-62	-69	-76	-84	-91
55	25	18	11	4	-3	-11	-18	-25	-32	-39	-46	-54	-61	-68	-75	-82	-89
50	26	19	12	4	-3	-10	-17	-24	-31	-38	-45	-52	-60	-67	-74	-81	-88
45	26	19	12	5	-2	-9	-16	-23	-30	-37	-44	-51	-58	-65	-72	-79	-86
40	27	20	13	6	-1	-8	-15	-22	-29	-36	-43	-50	-57	-64	-71	-78	-84
35	28	21	14	7	0	-7	-14	-21	-27	-34	-41	-48	-55	-62	-69	-76	-82
30	28	22	15	8	1	-5	-12	-19	-26	-33	-39	-46	-53	-60	-67	-73	-80
25	29	23	16	9	3	-4	-11	-17	-24	-31	-37	-44	-51	-58	-64	-71	-78
20	30	24	17	11	4	-2	-9	-15	-22	-29	-35	-42	-48	-55	-61	-68	-74
15	32	25	19	13	6	0	-7	-13	-19	-26	-32	-39	-45	-51	-58	-64	-71
10	34	27	21	15	9	3	-4	-10	-16	-22	-28	-35	-41	-47	-53	-59	-66
5	36	31	25	19	13	7	1	-5	-11	-16	-22	-28	-34	-40	-46	-52	-57
	40	35	30	25	20	15	10	5	0	-5	-10	-15	-20	-25	-30	-35	-40

AIR TEMPERATURE (°F)

This migration isn't exclusively American. Older adults from northern Europe who live in Spain, southern Italy, Greece, or North Africa routinely pack up and return to their native country for a summer climate that's milder than the one on the Mediterranean coast.

Having acknowledged all this, it is still possible to rate places that approach a climatic ideal by pointing to conditions that detract from maximum comfort.

JUDGING: CLIMATE

Mild doesn't mean a winterless, perpetually Mediterranean climate. It is simply the absence of great variations or extremes of temperature. As we get older, we tend to be better off in comfortable, stable weather conditions than we are in climates that make large physiological demands and where radical weather changes come on quickly.

WINTER MILDNESS

To measure how mild the winters are, *Retirement Places Rated* takes into account the wind chill, the number of days the temperature falls to 32°F or lower, and the average 24-hour temperature for the coldest month. Santa Barbara, California, has the highest figure for these months, resulting in a winter mildness score of 100. Nelson County, Virginia, and Pahrump Valley, Nevada, each hit the middle with a 50 score, meaning they see a milder winter than half of the places profiled here. Alas, locations high in the snowy Rocky Mountains (particularly Jackson Hole, Wyoming, with a score of 0), with their perfect weather for skiing, score at the bottom for winter mildness.

SUMMER MILDNESS

To measure how mild the summers are, *Retirement Places Rated* considers humidity, the average 24-hour temperature of the hottest month, and the number of days the thermometer tops 90°F. Fairplay, Colorado, has a summer mildness score of 100. Two regions in North Carolina—Chapel Hill–Carrboro and Southern Pines–Pinehurst—each get a score of 50, meaning they see a milder summer than half of the other retirement areas. Madison, Mississippi, hot and humid during the summer months, gets a 0. These retirement places are respectively the best, average, and worst for summer mildness.

HAZARD FREE

Bad weather isn't just inconvenient—it is downright dangerous. Aside from delaying and canceling social and business events, it contributes to injury and even death. The general hazardousness of an area is measured by normal winter snowfall and the frequencies of two other elements: strong winds and thunderstorms.

To score for relative freedom from these hazards, *Retirement Places Rated* counts snow three times as heavily as thunderstorms, and thunderstorms three times as heavily as strong winds. The higher the score, the freer the metro area is from these weather hazards.

Santa Barbara, Morro Bay–Cambria, and Laguna Beach–Dana Point on the Southern California coast do best here. Chapel Hill–Carrboro, North Carolina, and Oxford, Mississippi, are average, at 50. The Leelanau Peninsula in northern Michigan earns a hazard-ridden score of 0.

SEASONAL AFFECT

If you need something to blame for tiredness, depression, irritability, lack of sleep, lack of focus, lack of ambition, lack of interest in sex or food, headaches, chest and joint pains, hallucinations, and any other ailments, stick it to the weather.

To measure the local weather's seasonal affect, or psychological impact, the number of cloudy days (more than 80 percent cloud cover) and wet days (precipitation greater than 0.1 in.) are weighted twice as heavily as the number of fog (visibility less than ½ mile) days, and fog days are weighted twice as heavily as latitude, an indicator of potential sunlight. Yuma, Arizona, earns a perfect 100 score. Port St. Lucie, Florida, and St. Marys, Georgia, get 50. Palmer–Wasilla, Alaska, scores at the bottom. These metro areas are respectively the best, average, and worst for bright seasons and seasonal affect.

RANKINGS: CLIMATE

To rank places for mild climate, four factors get equal weight: (1) **summer mildness;** (2) **winter mildness;** (3) **seasonal affect,** or the psychological impact of cloudiness, darkness, fog, and rain; and (4) **hazard free,** or the relative absence of snow, thunderstorms, and high wind. A place's score is its percentile on a scale of 0 to 100, corresponding to its rank. Locations with tie scores get the same rank and are listed alphabetically.

Retirement Places from First to Last

RANK	PLACE	SCORE		RANK	PLACE	SCORE
1.	Santa Barbara, CA	100.0		11.	Wickenburg, AZ	94.9
2.	Carmel–Pebble Beach, CA	99.4		12.	The Big Island, HI	94.4
3.	Laguna Beach–Dana Point, CA	98.9		13.	Maui, HI	93.9
4.	Morro Bay–Cambria, CA	98.4		14.	Paradise–Magalia, CA	93.4
5.	Scottsdale, AZ	97.9		15.	Kingman, AZ	92.9
6.	Palm Springs–Coachella Valley, CA	97.4		16.	Sonora–Twain Harte, CA	92.4
7.	Yuma, AZ	96.9		17.	Placer County, CA	91.9
8.	Lake Havasu City, AZ	96.4		18.	Henderson, NV	91.4
9.	Victorville–Apple Valley, CA	95.9		19.	Sarasota, FL	90.9
10.	Mendocino–Fort Bragg, CA	95.4		20.	Fort Myers–Cape Coral, FL	90.4

continued

Retirement Places from First to Last (cont.)

RANK	PLACE	SCORE
21.	Alpine–Big Bend, TX	89.9
22.	Carson City–Carson Valley, NV	89.4
23.	Bisbee, AZ	88.9
24.	Bradenton, FL	88.4
25.	Prescott–Prescott Valley, AZ	87.9
26.	Cottonwood–Verde Valley, AZ	87.4
27.	Melbourne–Palm Bay, FL	86.9
28.	Port Angeles–Sequim, WA	86.4
29.	Port Townsend, WA	85.9
30.	Naples, FL	85.4
31.	Largo, FL	84.4
31.	Pahrump Valley, NV	84.4
33.	Amador County, CA	83.9
34.	St. Simons–Jekyll Islands, GA	83.4
35.	Grants Pass, OR	82.9
36.	St. Augustine, FL	82.4
37.	Tucson, AZ	81.9
38.	Mariposa, CA	81.4
39.	Oakhurst–Coarsegold, CA	80.9
40.	Payson, AZ	80.4
41.	Leesburg–Mount Dora, FL	79.8
42.	Medford–Ashland, OR	79.3
43.	Port Charlotte, FL	78.8
44.	Ruidoso, NM	78.3
45.	Kissimmee–St. Cloud, FL	77.8
46.	Lakeland–Winter Haven, FL	77.3
47.	McAllen–Alamo, TX	76.8
48.	Gainesville, FL	76.3
49.	Sedona, AZ	75.8
50.	Vero Beach, FL	75.3
51.	Grass Valley–Nevada City, CA	74.8
52.	Alamogordo, NM	74.3
53.	Ocala, FL	73.8
54.	Sebring–Avon Park, FL	73.3
55.	Brownsville, TX	72.8
56.	Apalachicola, FL	72.3
57.	St. Marys, GA	71.8
58.	Las Cruces, NM	71.3
59.	Kerrville, TX	70.3
59.	Thomasville, GA	70.3
61.	San Juan Islands, WA	69.8
62.	Port St. Lucie, FL	69.3
63.	Silver City, NM	68.8
64.	Boerne, TX	68.3
65.	St. George–Zion, UT	67.8
66.	Fredericksburg, TX	67.3
67.	Panama City, FL	66.8
68.	New Braunfels, TX	66.3
69.	Savannah, GA	65.8
70.	Newport–Lincoln City, OR	65.3
71.	Whidbey Island, WA	64.8
72.	Anacortes, WA	64.3
73.	Bellingham, WA	63.8
74.	Georgetown, TX	63.3
75.	Bend, OR	62.8
76.	Rockport–Aransas Pass, TX	62.3
77.	Lake Conroe, TX	61.8
78.	Marble Falls–Lake LBJ, TX	61.3
79.	Athens, GA	60.8
80.	Charleston, SC	59.7
80.	Flagstaff, AZ	59.7
82.	Delta County, CO	59.2
83.	Key West, FL	58.7
84.	Hilton Head Island, SC	58.2
85.	Montrose, CO	57.7

RANK	PLACE	SCORE
86.	Beaufort, SC	56.7
86.	Santa Fe, NM	56.7
88.	Pendleton District, SC	56.2
89.	Las Vegas, NM	55.7
90.	Rio Rancho, NM	55.2
91.	Hot Springs, AR	54.7
92.	Southport–Brunswick Islands, NC	54.2
93.	Myrtle Beach, SC	53.7
94.	Grand Junction, CO	53.2
95.	Tryon, NC	52.7
96.	Durango, CO	52.2
97.	Hamilton–Bitterroot Valley, MT	51.2
97.	Taos, NM	51.2
99.	Cedar Creek Lake, TX	50.2
99.	Eugene, OR	50.2
101.	Roswell, NM	49.7
102.	Chapel Hill–Carrboro, NC	49.2
103.	Western St. Tammany Parish, LA	48.7
104.	Bay St. Louis–Pass Christian, MS	48.2
105.	Wimberley, TX	47.7
106.	Pagosa Springs, CO	46.7
106.	Southern Pines–Pinehurst, NC	46.7
108.	Smith Mountain Lake, VA	46.2
109.	Dahlonega, GA	45.7
110.	Fairhope–Gulf Shores, AL	45.2
111.	Beaufort–Atlantic Beach, NC	44.7
112.	Kalispell–Flathead Valley, MT	44.2
113.	Cortez, CO	43.7
114.	Rabun County, GA	43.2
115.	Fort Collins–Loveland, CO	42.7
116.	Oxford, MS	42.2
117.	Madison, MS	41.7
118.	Pensacola, FL	41.2
119.	Natchitoches, LA	40.7
120.	Asheville, NC	40.2
121.	Waynesville, NC	39.6
122.	Hattiesburg, MS	39.1
123.	Lower Cape May, NJ	38.6
124.	Brevard, NC	38.1
125.	Charlottesville, VA	37.6
126.	Edenton, NC	37.1
127.	Easton–St. Michaels, MD	36.6
128.	Hendersonville–East Flat Rock, NC	36.1
129.	Summerville, SC	35.1
129.	Wenatchee, WA	35.1
131.	Long Beach Peninsula, WA	34.6
132.	Murray–Kentucky Lake, KY	33.6
132.	Ocean City, MD	33.6
134.	Ketchum–Sun Valley, ID	33.1
135.	Conway, AR	32.6
136.	Annapolis, MD	32.1
137.	Lake of the Cherokees, OK	31.6
138.	Fredericksburg–Spotsylvania, VA	31.1
139.	Rehoboth Bay–Indian River Bay, DE	30.6
140.	Charles Town–Shepherdstown, WV	30.1
141.	Park City, UT	29.6
142.	State College, PA	29.1
143.	Norfork Lake, AR	28.6
144.	Crossville, TN	28.1
145.	Eureka Springs, AR	27.6
146.	Silverthorne–Breckenridge, CO	27.1
147.	New Bern, NC	26.6
148.	East End Long Island, NY	25.1
148.	Maryville, TN	25.1
148.	Williamsburg, VA	25.1

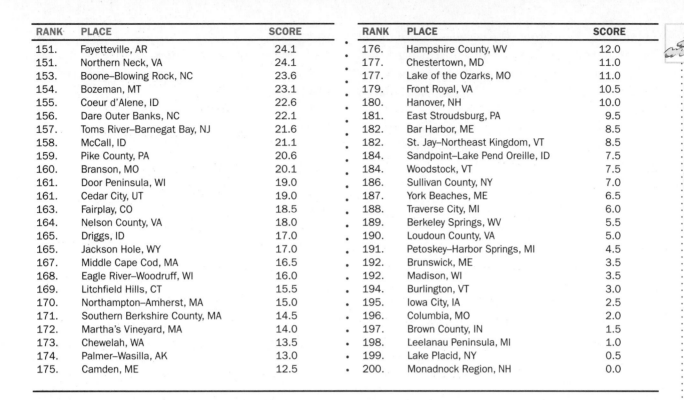

RANK	PLACE	SCORE
151.	Fayetteville, AR	24.1
151.	Northern Neck, VA	24.1
153.	Boone–Blowing Rock, NC	23.6
154.	Bozeman, MT	23.1
155.	Coeur d'Alene, ID	22.6
156.	Dare Outer Banks, NC	22.1
157.	Toms River–Barnegat Bay, NJ	21.6
158.	McCall, ID	21.1
159.	Pike County, PA	20.6
160.	Branson, MO	20.1
161.	Door Peninsula, WI	19.0
161.	Cedar City, UT	19.0
163.	Fairplay, CO	18.5
164.	Nelson County, VA	18.0
165.	Driggs, ID	17.0
165.	Jackson Hole, WY	17.0
167.	Middle Cape Cod, MA	16.5
168.	Eagle River–Woodruff, WI	16.0
169.	Litchfield Hills, CT	15.5
170.	Northampton–Amherst, MA	15.0
171.	Southern Berkshire County, MA	14.5
172.	Martha's Vineyard, MA	14.0
173.	Chewelah, WA	13.5
174.	Palmer–Wasilla, AK	13.0
175.	Camden, ME	12.5

RANK	PLACE	SCORE
176.	Hampshire County, WV	12.0
177.	Chestertown, MD	11.0
177.	Lake of the Ozarks, MO	11.0
179.	Front Royal, VA	10.5
180.	Hanover, NH	10.0
181.	East Stroudsburg, PA	9.5
182.	Bar Harbor, ME	8.5
182.	St. Jay–Northeast Kingdom, VT	8.5
184.	Sandpoint–Lake Pend Oreille, ID	7.5
184.	Woodstock, VT	7.5
186.	Sullivan County, NY	7.0
187.	York Beaches, ME	6.5
188.	Traverse City, MI	6.0
189.	Berkeley Springs, WV	5.5
190.	Loudoun County, VA	5.0
191.	Petoskey–Harbor Springs, MI	4.5
192.	Brunswick, ME	3.5
192.	Madison, WI	3.5
194.	Burlington, VT	3.0
195.	Iowa City, IA	2.5
196.	Columbia, MO	2.0
197.	Brown County, IN	1.5
198.	Leelanau Peninsula, MI	1.0
199.	Lake Placid, NY	0.5
200.	Monadnock Region, NH	0.0

PLACE PROFILES: CLIMATE

The following are the primary sources for the data referred to in this section:

• Temperature and precipitation data come from the National Oceanic and Atmospheric Administration (NOAA) *Series 20* publications.

The temperature and precipitation data are NOAA's "30-Year Normals" or averages collected over 3 decades. Every 10 years, the data for the new decade are added into the normal, and the data for the earliest 10 years are dropped to flatten out anomalies and weather extremes. Events such as a freak blizzard in Albuquerque or a heat wave that might occur once every 50 years in Coeur d'Alene have little effect on each place's 30-year normals.

• Data for humidity, wind speed, and days with fog and thunderstorms, as well as the clear, partly cloudy, and cloudy days, are derived from the closest station reporting in NOAA's *Local Climatological Data*.

The text summaries describe each place's location and its distinctive climate and landscape features.

Location details the place's elevation and its latitude north of the equator and longitude west of Greenwich, England. With these coordinates, you can roughly determine whether one place is farther north, south, east, or west than another.

When **Landscape** is described, it is usually how the terrain influences a place's climate and what varieties of vegetation grow there naturally. Few people would deny that landscape is an important element on its own; for many, it is as important as climate. Some prefer mountains or seacoasts, others rolling hills or flatwoods forests, while still others favor stark desert vistas. Landscapes are not rated; rather, they are described briefly here and the decision is left up to you.

The descriptions for **Climate** are capsule summaries of each location's type and general features.

The tables to the right of each description include monthly high and low temperatures, relative humidity observed nearest to noon, wind speed, precipitation, and snowfall. Each profile also includes a visual legend for the number of days per year that a place sees such conditions as a partly cloudy sky, temperatures below zero, and thunderstorms (see sample legend to the right).

A star (★) preceding a place's name highlights it as one of the top 30 places for climate mildness.

(sun)	125	Annual number of clear days (days with less than 30% cloud cover)
(partly cloudy)	175	Annual number of partly-cloudy days (days with less than 70% but more than 30% cover)
(cloudy)	65	Annual number of cloudy days (days with more than 70% cover)
90°	67	Annual number of days temperature tops 90°F
32°	60	Annual number of days temperature hits freezing
0°	0	Annual number of days temperature hits 0°F
(fog)	50	Annual number of days fog limits visibility
(precip)	72	Annual number of days precipitation exceeds one-tenth of an inch
(thunderstorm)	43	Annual number of days with one or more thunderstorm cells

Alamogordo, NM — Rank: 52

Location: 32.54 N and 105.57 W at 4,303 feet, some 200 miles south of Albuquerque and 55 miles north of El Paso, Texas.

Landscape: Low mountains. The city is near the western base of the Sacramento Mountains that peak around 4,500 feet and form the eastern rim of the Tularosa Basin. The area has the typical high desert look with native thorny shrubs of mesquite and creosote bush. White gypsum dunes of the White Sands National Monument stretch across the west toward the San Andreas Mountains. Juniper and piñon pine forests stand in higher elevations and in the Lincoln National Forest.

Climate: Desert character with long, hot, bright, and usually dry summers. Temperature changes from daytime highs to nighttime lows can be dramatic at all seasons. Rains are widespread and usually gentle except for July and August, when they typically come in heavy thunderstorms. Winters are moderate but subject to occasional frosts from November to March. Infrequent snowfalls melt within days.

Summer mildness: 41   **Seasonal affect:** 93
Winter mildness: 47   **Hazard free:** 60

(sun)	193
(partly cloudy)	100
(cloudy)	72
90°	103
32°	84
0°	0
(fog)	2
(precip)	27
(thunderstorm)	36

	High °F	Low °F	Hum %	Wind mph	Precip inches	Snow inches
JAN	57	28	42	8.4	0.7	1.7
FEB	62	32	34	9.2	0.5	1.0
MAR	69	38	27	11.0	0.5	0.5
APR	78	45	21	11.1	0.3	0
MAY	87	54	21	10.3	0.5	0
JUN	95	62	23	9.3	0.9	0
JUL	95	66	35	8.3	2.2	0
AUG	92	64	39	7.8	2.4	0
SEP	86	58	41	7.6	2.0	0
OCT	78	47	36	7.5	1.3	0
NOV	66	36	37	8.0	0.7	0
DEC	58	29	42	7.9	0.8	1.1

★ Alpine–Big Bend, TX — Rank: 21

Location: 30.21 N and 103.39 W at 4,480 feet in west Texas, 190 miles southeast of El Paso and 75 miles north of the Rio Grande and Mexico.

Landscape: Plains with low mountains. Located in a high desert valley flanked by the Davis Mountains to the north and the Glass Mountains to the east. Dry canyons and extensive, sparse rangeland contrast with the forests of the mountain elevations. In the valleys and on the lower slopes are many varieties of cactus, and a soaking rain makes wildflowers abundant.

Climate: Chihuahuan Desert moderated by altitude. Summers are long and sunny. Winters are brief and mild, though subject to occasional morning frosts, the first of which occurs in early November and the last in early April. Most of the area's 17 inches of rain falls from July to September as spectacular afternoon thunderheads build over the mountains and move across the countryside.

Summer mildness: 59   **Seasonal affect:** 94
Winter mildness: 54   **Hazard free:** 62

(sun)	193
(partly cloudy)	100
(cloudy)	72
90°	67
32°	60
0°	0
(fog)	2
(precip)	28
(thunderstorm)	36

	High °F	Low °F	Hum %	Wind mph	Precip inches	Snow inches
JAN	61	30	42	8.4	0.5	1.1
FEB	65	33	34	9.2	0.5	1.1
MAR	72	39	27	11.0	0.4	0
APR	80	46	21	11.1	0.5	0
MAY	86	54	21	10.3	1.2	0
JUN	90	61	23	9.3	2.2	0
JUL	89	63	35	8.3	2.7	0
AUG	88	61	39	7.8	3.0	0
SEP	83	57	41	7.6	3.3	0
OCT	78	47	36	7.5	1.5	0
NOV	69	38	37	8.0	0.6	0
DEC	62	32	42	7.9	0.5	0.3

★ = in the top 30 places for climate mildness

Amador County, CA — Rank: 33

Location: The weather station is the county seat at Jackson, 38.21 N and 120.46 W at 1,975 feet, 45 miles southeast of Sacramento and 100 miles southwest of Reno, Nevada.

Landscape: Low mountains. In the higher grassy foothills of the western slope of the Sierra Nevadas, with steep gradients from mountain to valley. Canyons cut the forested slope, giving dramatic relief. Snow-fed rivers, lakes, and reservoirs promote wildflowers and low-growing shrubs. Digger pine and blue oak are found at higher elevations.

Climate: Sierran Forest, in the transition zone between the dry western desert and the wetter Pacific Coast. Mountain temperature changes can vary greatly both daily and seasonally. Prevailing west winds together with elevation influence local conditions. The summers are long, hot, and generally dry. About half of the annual precipitation falls as snow. Frost appears in early November and departs by late April.

Summer mildness: 54	Seasonal affect: 74
Winter mildness: 73	Hazard free: 57

Icon column values: 189, 75, 100, 90° 59, 32° 77, 0° 0, 34, 49, 14

	High °F	Low °F	Hum %	Wind mph	Precip inches	Snow inches
JAN	57	34	80	7.3	5.2	5.3
FEB	62	37	75	7.4	4.4	3.1
MAR	65	39	65	7.9	5.0	3.0
APR	72	42	55	8.3	2.7	0
MAY	81	47	48	8.3	0.7	0
JUN	90	52	44	8.5	0.3	0
JUL	97	56	44	9.5	0.2	0
AUG	96	55	45	8.9	0.2	0
SEP	90	52	45	7.3	0.6	0
OCT	80	46	53	6.6	1.8	0
NOV	65	40	65	6.9	4.5	0
DEC	57	35	77	7.2	4.5	2.7

Anacortes, WA — Rank: 72

Location: 48.30 N and 122.36 W at 75 feet on Fidalgo Island in upper Puget Sound. Via a bridge eastward to the mainland, Seattle is 80 miles south and Vancouver, British Columbia, is 90 miles north.

Landscape: High mountains. Fidalgo Island is relatively big with many low-rise hills. The original coniferous forest of Sitka spruce and western hemlock has largely given way to fruit farms. The shoreline has many small harbors and embayments. Distantly visible on the mainland to the east are Mount Baker and the North Cascade Mountains.

Climate: Marine, characterized by moderate temperatures, a pronounced rainy season, and constant cloud cover during the winter. Anacortes is modified by its position within the rain shadow of the Olympic Mountain range to the south, resulting in more sun and less rain than other Pacific Coast places. Summers are pleasantly cool with low precipitation. Winter days are mild with prevailing temperatures in the 40s; nights are chilly. The first frost arrives November 12 and the last frost departs March 22.

Summer mildness: 88	Seasonal affect: 1
Winter mildness: 74	Hazard free: 63

Icon column values: 50, 84, 231, 90° 0, 32° 68, 0° 0, 90, 95, 5

	High °F	Low °F	Hum %	Wind mph	Precip inches	Snow inches
JAN	45	34	77	7.1	3.6	5.2
FEB	49	36	74	7.2	2.5	1.3
MAR	52	38	70	7.4	2.1	2.4
APR	56	41	67	7.4	1.8	0
MAY	62	46	64	6.9	1.6	0
JUN	67	50	62	6.7	1.3	0
JUL	71	52	62	6.2	1.0	0
AUG	72	52	63	6.0	1.0	0
SEP	67	49	68	5.7	1.5	0
OCT	59	44	75	5.9	2.3	0
NOV	50	39	78	6.9	3.6	0
DEC	46	35	80	7.3	3.8	4.4

Annapolis, MD — Rank: 136

Location: 38.58 N and 76.29 W at 41 feet on the Severn River near its mouth on the western shore of the Chesapeake Bay. Baltimore is 27 miles northwest, and Washington, D.C., 35 miles southwest.

Landscape: Irregular plains. The wide Severn River drains low, long rolling hills into the upper Bay. The surrounding area is extensively developed suburban and agricultural land. Whatever native vegetation remains flourishes in the mild winters and hot summers of the coastal plains and are typically southern trees, such as the loblolly pine and the magnolia.

Climate: Subtropical with a definite marine influence. Summer days are hot and humid, though a Bay breeze often lifts in the afternoons. Winters are overcast, chilly, and rainy. Frost comes as soon as November 1 and departs in early April. Snowfalls are brief and melt within hours. Spring arrives early for this latitude.

Summer mildness: 56	Seasonal affect: 43
Winter mildness: 30	Hazard free: 42

Icon column values: 107, 108, 150, 90° 28, 32° 93, 0° 0, 26, 72, 28

	High °F	Low °F	Hum %	Wind mph	Precip inches	Snow inches
JAN	42	25	57	9.7	3.3	4.5
FEB	45	27	54	10.3	3.2	5.3
MAR	55	35	50	10.9	3.6	2.6
APR	66	44	49	10.6	3.4	0
MAY	76	54	53	9.2	4.1	0
JUN	84	63	52	8.5	3.4	0
JUL	88	68	53	8.0	3.6	0
AUG	86	67	56	7.8	3.9	0
SEP	80	60	55	8.0	3.3	0
OCT	69	48	54	8.7	3.3	0
NOV	58	39	55	9.3	3.5	0
DEC	47	30	57	9.3	3.4	2.0

★ = in the top 30 places for climate mildness

Apalachicola, FL — Rank: 56

Location: 29.43 N and 84.59 W at 30 feet at the mouth of the Apalachicola River on Apalachicola Bay and the Gulf of Mexico 65 miles southwest of the state capital at Tallahassee.

Landscape: Flat plains. Much of the area is gently sloping, but nowhere is there relief greater than 100 feet. Marshes, swamps, and lakes are common. The trees include ever-green oaks, short palm, and members of the magnolia and laurel families.

Climate: Subtropical, with warm summers with sporadic heavy thunderstorms and humidity slightly tempered by sea breezes. Winters fare extremely mild though somewhat cool, with unpredictable, brief cold spells.

Summer mildness: 6   **Seasonal affect:** 58
Winter mildness: 83   **Hazard free:** 90

	106
	123
	136
90°	67
32°	12
0°	0
	178
	66
	68

	High °F	Low °F	Hum %	Wind mph	Precip inches	Snow inches
JAN	61	39	72	9.0	3.9	0
FEB	63	41	70	9.4	3.8	0
MAR	69	48	71	9.7	4.3	0
APR	76	55	71	9.5	2.7	0
MAY	82	62	73	8.6	2.7	0
JUN	87	69	73	7.6	4.6	0
JUL	88	72	76	7.0	7.4	0
AUG	88	71	78	6.7	7.5	0
SEP	86	68	75	7.6	7.5	0
OCT	79	56	70	7.9	3.4	0
NOV	71	48	72	8.4	3.2	0
DEC	64	41	74	8.9	4.1	0

Asheville, NC — Rank: 120

Location: 35.36 N and 82.33 W at 2,134 feet, in western North Carolina. Charlotte is 120 miles east and Knoxville, Tennessee, is 120 miles west.

Landscape: Low mountains. Two miles upstream from the city, the Swannanoa and French Broad rivers join to form the Asheville Plateau valley, flanked on the east and west by mountain ranges. Thirty miles south, the Blue Ridge Mountains form an escarpment with 2,700 feet average elevation. Nearby peaks include Mount Mitchell (6,684 ft.) and Big Pisgah (5,721 ft.). Tall oak, hickory, walnut, maple, and basswood trees produce a dense canopy in summer. There are lower layers of small trees, dogwood, blueberry, and haw.

Climate: Temperate but invigorating. Considerable variation in temperature occurs from day to day throughout the year. The valley has a pronounced effect on wind direction, which is mostly from the northwest. Destructive weather events are rare. The first frost arrives October 24 and the last frost departs in early April.

Summer mildness: 58   **Seasonal affect:** 29
Winter mildness: 60   **Hazard free:** 37

	103
	113
	149
90°	10
32°	86
0°	0
	78
	75
	45

	High °F	Low °F	Hum %	Wind mph	Precip inches	Snow inches
JAN	45	26	59	9.7	2.5	5.0
FEB	49	29	56	9.6	3.3	4.8
MAR	58	37	53	9.4	3.9	2.6
APR	67	45	50	8.9	3.1	0
MAY	74	52	57	7.1	3.6	0
JUN	81	60	59	6.1	3.3	0
JUL	84	64	63	5.8	2.9	0
AUG	83	63	63	5.4	3.8	0
SEP	77	57	64	5.6	3.2	0
OCT	67	45	57	6.8	2.8	0
NOV	58	37	57	8.1	2.9	0
DEC	49	30	59	8.9	2.8	1.9

Athens, GA — Rank: 79

Location: 33.57 N and 83.22 W at 662 feet, in Georgia's Piedmont Plateau. Atlanta is 60 miles west.

Landscape: Irregular plains. Local elevations range between 600 and 800 feet in rolling terrain. Streams drain eastward to the Savannah River. The countryside is agricultural, with occasional stands of trees dominated by southern yellow pine, with some mixed hardwood.

Climate: The city's climate is influenced by the Atlantic Ocean 200 miles southeast, the Gulf of Mexico 275 miles south, and the southern Appalachian Mountains to the north and northwest. Summers are warm and humid, but without prolonged periods of extreme heat. Precipitation is evenly distributed throughout the year. The mountains to the north partially block extremely cold air, softening the city's winters. Cold spells are short-lived, broken up by periods of warm southerly airflow. Frost arrives just after Halloween, and the last frost departs before April Fools' Day.

Summer mildness: 29   **Seasonal affect:** 57
Winter mildness: 73   **Hazard free:** 61

	114
	106
	146
90°	70
32°	70
0°	0
	39
	70
	51

	High °F	Low °F	Hum %	Wind mph	Precip inches	Snow inches
JAN	52	32	58	8.5	4.6	0.9
FEB	56	35	55	8.9	4.4	0.7
MAR	65	42	53	8.8	5.5	0.4
APR	73	50	50	8.3	4.0	0
MAY	81	58	54	7.1	4.4	0
JUN	87	66	55	6.6	3.9	0
JUL	90	70	59	6.3	4.9	0
AUG	88	69	59	5.8	3.7	0
SEP	83	63	60	6.4	3.4	0
OCT	74	51	54	6.8	3.3	0
NOV	64	42	54	7.4	3.7	0
DEC	55	35	57	8.0	4.1	0.2

★ = *in the top 30 places for climate mildness*

Bar Harbor, ME — Rank: 182

Location: 44.23 N and 68.12 W at 20 feet on the northeast shore of Mount Desert Island off Maine's Atlantic Coast. Augusta, the capital, is 35 miles west. Boston, Massachusetts, is 165 miles south.

Landscape: Plains with high hills. Glacial features are characteristic in many lakes, islands, and the rocky coastline. Elevations range from sea level to 1,530-foot Mount Cadillac, producing a dramatic combination of mountains, sheer cliff, and ocean. Tortuous trails crisscross Mount Desert. Native vegetation includes a mix of northern hardwoods and spruce.

Climate: Warm continental, with winters that are moderately long and occasionally severe if the predominant weather is coming from the Carolina coast. The first frost hits October 4. The Atlantic Ocean moderates the cold winds from the Canadian Arctic. Spring arrives late, with the last freeze occurring May 9. Summer weather is mild, changeable, and influenced by tropical storms that sweep up the Atlantic Coast. Autumn is bright and mild.

Summer mildness: 84 **Seasonal affect:** 10
Winter mildness: 12 **Hazard free:** 13

	102
	99
	164
90°	4
32°	158
0°	13
	49
	76
	18

	High °F	Low °F	Hum %	Wind mph	Precip inches	Snow inches
JAN	30	11	61	9.2	3.6	20.3
FEB	33	12	58	9.4	3.4	18.2
MAR	41	23	58	10.0	3.7	13.3
APR	52	32	55	10.0	4.1	3.0
MAY	63	42	58	9.2	3.9	0
JUN	73	51	60	8.2	3.2	0
JUL	78	57	59	7.6	3.3	0
AUG	77	56	59	7.5	3.1	0
SEP	69	48	59	7.8	3.7	0
OCT	58	39	50	8.4	3.9	0
NOV	46	31	62	8.8	5.2	4.0
DEC	34	17	62	9.0	4.7	15.9

Bay St. Louis–Pass Christian, MS — Rank: 104

Location: 30.18 N and 89.19 W at 28 feet, on the state's thickly settled Gulf Coast. New Orleans, Louisiana, is 60 miles west, and Mobile, Alabama, is 70 miles east.

Landscape: Flat, consisting of low-lying delta flood plains sloping to sand beaches and shallow harbors and bays. Native trees are a temperate rainforest of evergreen, oak, laurel, and magnolia, with large stands of loblolly and slash pine in the sandy upland areas.

Climate: Subtropical. The Gulf waters modify local climate. Summers are hot and humid, though temperatures of 90°F or higher occur only half as often here as they do in Hattiesburg, 60 miles north. However, there's no such reverse effect on cold air moving down from the north in winter. November 30 marks the first frost; the last frost occurs in mid-February. Rainfall is plentiful and heaviest in July. Damage from hurricanes and tropical storms can occur six to seven times a year.

Summer mildness: 10 **Seasonal affect:** 56
Winter mildness: 71 **Hazard free:** 60

	103
	116
	146
90°	55
32°	15
0°	0
	28
	73
	74

	High °F	Low °F	Hum %	Wind mph	Precip inches	Snow inches
JAN	60	42	66	10.4	5.4	0.3
FEB	63	45	63	10.7	5.9	0.1
MAR	69	52	60	10.9	5.3	0.1
APR	76	60	60	10.2	4.4	0
MAY	83	67	60	8.9	4.8	0
JUN	88	73	63	7.7	5.0	0
JUL	90	75	66	7.0	6.5	0
AUG	90	74	66	6.8	6.6	0
SEP	87	70	65	7.9	5.3	0
OCT	80	60	60	8.2	3.3	0
NOV	71	52	62	9.3	4.1	0
DEC	63	46	66	10.1	5.4	0.2

Beaufort, SC — Rank: 86

Location: 32.26 N and 80.40 W at 11 feet on Port Royal, one of the Sea Islands, 45 miles south of Charleston and 35 miles north of Savannah, Georgia.

Landscape: Flat plains. The land is low with elevations averaging less than 25 feet. Port Royal is one of dozens of islands of various shapes and sizes with fresh and saltwater streams, inlets, rivers, and sounds. Most have many swampy areas. Coastal Plain forests of beech, sweet gum, magnolia, pine, and oak are common.

Climate: Subtropical. The island group is on the edge of the balmy climate enjoyed by Florida. The surrounding water produces a maritime climate with mild winters, hot summers with regular thunderstorms, and seasonal temperatures that shift slowly. The inland Appalachian Mountains block cold air from the northern interior, and the Gulf Stream moderates the climate considerably. November 20 heralds the arrival of first frost, and the last frost departs March 9.

Summer mildness: 16 **Seasonal affect:** 48
Winter mildness: 75 **Hazard free:** 74

	104
	109
	152
90°	56
32°	28
0°	0
	28
	71
	56

	High °F	Low °F	Hum %	Wind mph	Precip inches	Snow inches
JAN	59	39	57	9.1	3.7	0.1
FEB	62	41	55	9.9	3.3	0.2
MAR	70	48	53	10.0	4.1	0
APR	77	55	50	9.7	2.9	0
MAY	83	63	55	8.7	4.0	0
JUN	88	69	60	8.4	6.1	0
JUL	90	73	66	7.9	6.4	0
AUG	89	72	70	7.4	7.9	0
SEP	85	68	67	7.8	5.0	0
OCT	78	58	70	8.1	2.6	0
NOV	70	49	60	8.1	2.4	0
DEC	62	42	60	8.5	3.2	0

★ = in the top 30 places for climate mildness

Beaufort–Atlantic Beach, NC   Rank: 111

Location: 34.43 N and 76.40 W at 15 feet at the north end of Onslow Bay on the Atlantic Coast. Wilmington is 100 miles southwest.

Landscape: Flat plains. The Bogue Banks, a series of offshore island reefs, separate Bogue Sound, part of the Intracoastal Waterway, from the Atlantic. Typical of the Carolina coast, the Banks are composed of dunes, marshes, and maritime forest. Sea oats grow on the dunes. Salt marsh cordgrass, saltmeadow hay, sea ox-eye, and black needlebrush predominate in the marsh. The forest includes oak, pine, cedar, youpon, and wax myrtle.

Climate: Subtropical, moderated by the ocean. Summers are warm and humid, with frequent thunderstorms. Winters are mild with little or no snow. Spring and fall are long lasting and pleasant. Frost first appears November 19 and departs 4 months later in mid-March. Rain falls consistently throughout the year, and tropical storms are a threat from late summer to early fall.

Summer mildness: 29   **Seasonal affect:** 42
Winter mildness: 65   **Hazard free:** 54

	111
	104
	150
90°	14
32°	37
0°	0
	174
	65
	47

	High °F	Low °F	Hum %	Wind mph	Precip inches	Snow inches
JAN	55	35	68	9.0	4.6	0.7
FEB	57	36	65	9.7	4.2	1.0
MAR	63	43	67	10.1	4.0	1.1
APR	71	51	64	10.2	2.9	0
MAY	78	60	71	9.1	4.6	0
JUN	84	68	72	8.5	4.4	0
JUL	87	72	75	7.9	6.8	0
AUG	87	72	78	7.4	6.2	0
SEP	83	67	76	7.8	5.3	0
OCT	76	56	72	8.0	3.9	0
NOV	68	47	70	8.1	3.7	0
DEC	59	39	69	8.4	4.2	0.3

Bellingham, WA   Rank: 73

Location: 48.45 N and 122.29 W at 60 feet, on Bellingham Bay in the northwest corner of Washington State. Seattle is 90 miles south, and Vancouver, British Columbia, is 50 miles north.

Landscape: High mountains. Dominated by the broad, glacier-carved Skagit River Valley with fjords and deep undersea troughs. East of Bellingham are the North Cascade Mountains and Mount Baker at 10,775 feet. The San Juan Islands are offshore in Puget Sound. The natural vegetation is a predominantly needleleaf forest of Douglas fir, red cedar, and spruce.

Climate: Marine. Winter days are mild, but the nights are chilly. Six months lie between the first frost in November and the last frost in mid- to late April. Summers are cool with low precipitation. The cooler air temperatures reduce evaporation and produce a very damp, humid climate with heavy cloud cover.

Summer mildness: 87   **Seasonal affect:** 1
Winter mildness: 71   **Hazard free:** 63

	50
	84
	231
90°	0
32°	68
0°	0
	90
	91
	5

	High °F	Low °F	Hum %	Wind mph	Precip inches	Snow inches
JAN	43	32	77	7.1	4.7	5.2
FEB	48	35	74	7.2	3.6	1.3
MAR	51	36	70	7.4	3.0	2.4
APR	56	40	67	7.4	2.7	0
MAY	62	45	64	6.9	2.3	0
JUN	67	51	62	6.7	1.8	0
JUL	71	53	62	6.2	1.3	0
AUG	71	54	63	6.0	1.4	0
SEP	67	48	68	5.7	1.9	0
OCT	58	42	75	5.9	3.4	0
NOV	50	37	78	6.9	5.0	0
DEC	44	33	80	7.3	5.0	4.4

Bend, OR   Rank: 75

Location: 44.03 N and 121.19 W at 3,629 feet near the center of the state along the western border of the Harney Basin and Great Sandy Desert. Portland is 130 miles northwest.

Landscape: Open high mountains. The Cascades terrace upward to crests of 10,000 feet about 10 miles west. A rolling plateau extends south and east into California, Nevada, and Idaho. To the north, canyons and streams that feed into the Columbia River cut the plateau. The lower elevation is a shortgrass prairie of grama, needlegrass, and wheatgrass. Mountain forests are Douglas fir, red cedar, and spruce.

Climate: Continental. The Cascades restrain extreme summer temperatures and also block moisture-laden Pacific winds. Rains are generally light with only a rare rainfall of an inch or more. The average growing season is about 82 days, with frost coming as early as late August and departing as late as July. Moderate days and cool nights characterize temperatures here.

Summer mildness: 94   **Seasonal affect:** 45
Winter mildness: 43   **Hazard free:** 41

	117
	79
	169
90°	13
32°	196
0°	4
	50
	31
	8

	High °F	Low °F	Hum %	Wind mph	Precip inches	Snow inches
JAN	42	22	81	4.1	1.8	12.3
FEB	46	25	77	4.5	1.0	4.7
MAR	51	26	66	5.3	0.9	5.6
APR	58	29	57	5.7	0.6	2.0
MAY	65	35	50	5.7	0.8	0
JUN	74	41	44	5.9	0.9	0
JUL	81	45	40	5.8	0.5	0
AUG	81	45	40	5.3	0.6	0
SEP	73	38	42	4.5	0.5	0
OCT	63	32	57	3.7	0.7	0
NOV	48	27	80	3.6	1.6	5.0
DEC	42	22	85	3.6	2.0	9.4

★ = in the top 30 places for climate mildness

Berkeley Springs, WV
Rank: 189

Location: 39.33 N and 78.15 W at 730 feet at the extreme northern edge of West Virginia's Eastern Panhandle, some 85 air miles northwest of Washington, D.C.

Landscape: Open low mountains. Most of the area is rolling. On the east, the Appalachian Mountains produce high relief. The naturally occurring vegetation is a typical deciduous forest of oak, beech, hickory, and ash. Second growth is rapidly growing pine. In spring, a luxuriant low layer of herbs quickly develops.

Climate: Hot continental, with cold and somewhat snowy winters, but mild summers thanks to elevation. Precipitation is adequate in all months but greater in summer when moisture demands are high. The first frost arrives October 18 and the last frost departs April 25. This is one of the cloudier locations for retirement, mainly in winter and spring.

Summer mildness: 58 **Seasonal affect:** 11
Winter mildness: 18 **Hazard free:** 17

☀	58
🌤	103
☁	204
90°	7
32°	124
0°	5
🌧	178
💧	71
⚡	35

	High °F	Low °F	Hum %	Wind mph	Precip inches	Snow inches
JAN	34	19	69	10.6	2.4	11.3
FEB	37	20	68	10.5	2.5	9.3
MAR	49	30	65	10.7	3.1	8.7
APR	60	39	65	10.3	3.2	1.7
MAY	71	48	71	8.9	4.1	0.1
JUN	79	57	70	8.0	3.4	0
JUL	83	62	65	7.3	3.5	0
AUG	81	60	65	6.9	3.3	0
SEP	74	54	70	7.4	2.8	0
OCT	63	42	66	8.4	3.4	0.4
NOV	50	34	68	9.8	3.1	3.3
DEC	39	24	68	10.4	2.7	8.3

★ The Big Island, HI
Rank: 12

Location: The weather station is at Hilo, 19.43 N and 115.05 W at 38 feet on the island's east coast some 200 air miles from Honolulu.

Landscape: Plains with high mountains. All the islands are volcanoes in various stages of erosion. Hawaii, the largest and most easterly of the islands, has peaks higher than 13,000 feet and some active volcanoes. Coastlines are mostly rocky and rough. Native flora are unique, and forests vary by availability of moisture.

Climate: Mild marine tropical. Daily and seasonal temperature changes are small, secondary to the surrounding ocean and persistent northeast trade winds. Summer days can be hot, owing to high humidity, but temperature and precipitation vary greatly with altitude and exposure. There's marked variation in rainfall depending on the season and place. Severe storms are rare.

Summer mildness: 39 **Seasonal affect:** 87
Winter mildness: 77 **Hazard free:** 95

☀	90
🌤	180
☁	95
90°	21
32°	0
0°	0
🌧	0
💧	54
⚡	13

	High °F	Low °F	Hum %	Wind mph	Precip inches	Snow inches
JAN	80	64	74	9.5	9.9	0
FEB	80	64	73	10.1	10.3	0
MAR	80	64	72	11.4	13.9	0
APR	80	66	72	11.8	15.3	0
MAY	81	67	72	11.8	9.9	0
JUN	83	68	70	12.7	6.2	0
JUL	83	69	70	13.2	9.7	0
AUG	84	69	71	12.8	9.3	0
SEP	84	69	71	11.2	8.5	0
OCT	83	68	75	10.5	9.6	0
NOV	81	67	74	10.7	14.5	0
DEC	80	65	74	10.4	12.0	0

★ Bisbee, AZ
Rank: 23

Location: 31.23 N and 109.55 W at 5,490 feet in southeast Arizona just 7 miles above the Mexico border. Phoenix is 180 miles northwest.

Landscape: Plains with high mountains. The city was built in two steep-sided canyons, Mule Pass Gulch and Brewery Gulch. The surrounding topography is Sonoran desert. The vegetation is very sparse, with bare ground between individual plants. On the rocky slopes of the mountains, paloverde, ocotillo, and saguaro are common.

Climate: Desert, with a long summer that starts in late March and ends in October, and produces high temperatures modified by the low humidity. Winters are ideal with warm days and cool nights. Like other locations in the Desert Southwest, nearly every day is clear.

Summer mildness: 18 **Seasonal affect:** 96
Winter mildness: 84 **Hazard free:** 70

☀	194
🌤	90
☁	81
90°	140
32°	18
0°	0
🌧	3
💧	12
⚡	42

	High °F	Low °F	Hum %	Wind mph	Precip inches	Snow inches
JAN	64	39	48	8.0	0.9	0.2
FEB	68	41	43	8.1	0.7	0.2
MAR	73	45	39	8.5	0.7	0.1
APR	81	50	29	8.9	0.3	0.1
MAY	90	58	24	8.8	0.2	0
JUN	100	68	23	8.7	0.2	0
JUL	99	74	43	8.4	2.4	0
AUG	97	72	49	7.9	2.2	0
SEP	93	68	41	8.3	1.7	0
OCT	84	57	39	8.2	1.1	0
NOV	73	46	41	8.1	0.7	0.1
DEC	64	40	49	7.8	1.1	0.2

★ = in the top 30 places for climate mildness

Boerne, TX — Rank: 64

Location: 29.47 N and 98.44 W at 1,405 feet in the south-central Texas Blacklands, 30 miles NW of San Antonio.

Landscape: High hills. Between the southern rim of the Edwards Plateau and the Gulf Coastal Plain, the area is characterized by rolling hills and open prairie. Limestone caverns, bluffs, and creeks that run to the Guadalupe River are common. Vegetation includes prairie grasses, mesquite, cacti, Texas live oak, cypress, and sycamore.

Climate: Subtropical. Winters are mild, but the rest of the year amounts to one long, hot summer. Moist Gulf air adds humidity to the heat. Rainfall is fairly steady, but is heaviest from May to September. Thunderstorms occur throughout the year. Frost arrives in early November and departs before April.

Summer mildness: 38   **Seasonal affect:** 73
Winter mildness: 49   **Hazard free:** 75

108
118
139
90° 90
32° 45
0° 0
22
46
37

	High °F	Low °F	Hum %	Wind mph	Precip inches	Snow inches
JAN	59	33	59	9.0	1.7	0
FEB	63	37	57	9.7	2.1	0.5
MAR	71	44	54	10.4	2.1	0
APR	79	53	56	10.3	3.1	0
MAY	84	61	59	10.0	4.1	0
JUN	89	67	56	9.9	3.8	0
JUL	93	69	51	9.2	2.2	0
AUG	93	68	51	8.5	2.9	0
SEP	88	64	55	8.5	4.2	0
OCT	80	54	54	8.4	3.6	0
NOV	70	44	55	8.8	2.7	0.1
DEC	62	36	57	8.5	1.8	0

Boone–Blowing Rock, NC — Rank: 153

Location: 36.13 N and 81.40 W at 3,266 feet atop the Blue Ridge Mountains in North Carolina's northwestern corner. Asheville is 50 miles southwest.

Landscape: Low mountains. Rough highland with the deep gorges, mountain trails, and rising elevations of the southern Appalachians. Many streams cut through the forests. A typical heavy Appalachian oak forest covers the mountains with a mix of pine, oak, maple, beech, hickory, and birch.

Climate: Hot continental moderated by the altitude. Winters are long and cold with the first frost showing up by October 2 and the last frost not leaving until May 12. The rest of the year is mild and invigorating. Considerable variation in temperature occurs from day to night throughout the year. Precipitation is constant and plentiful, with long, snowy winters and rainy seasons in spring and summer. Destructive weather events are rare.

Summer mildness: 83   **Seasonal affect:** 16
Winter mildness: 45   **Hazard free:** 11

103
113
149
90° 0
32° 133
0° 4
78
96
45

	High °F	Low °F	Hum %	Wind mph	Precip inches	Snow inches
JAN	41	20	59	9.7	3.8	11.3
FEB	44	22	56	9.6	3.9	11.4
MAR	53	30	53	9.4	4.8	9.3
APR	60	37	50	8.9	4.2	1.0
MAY	68	45	57	7.1	4.8	0
JUN	74	52	59	6.1	4.5	0
JUL	77	56	63	5.8	4.7	0
AUG	76	55	63	5.4	4.7	0
SEP	71	50	64	5.6	4.1	0
OCT	63	39	57	6.8	4.0	0
NOV	54	31	57	8.1	3.9	4.0
DEC	45	24	59	8.9	3.2	7.9

Bozeman, MT — Rank: 154

Location: 45.41 N and 111.02 W at 5,950 feet in southwest Montana, 112 miles west of Billings and 72 miles east southeast of Butte.

Landscape: High mountains. The Continental Divide, with elevations well over 10,000 feet, provides a scenic backdrop to the city. The Gallatin National Forest is near here and Yellowstone National Park is 45 miles south. The naturally occurring woods are mainly Douglas fir with secondary growth of ponderosa pine, aspen, and lodgepole pine.

Climate: Rigorous mountain, with extremely bright, mild summer days and cool nights and with severe, cloudy winter days and cold nights. Mountains shield the area somewhat from moisture from the Pacific and from bitterly cold arctic air. The first frost arrives August 18 and the last frost departs July 12.

Summer mildness: 84   **Seasonal affect:** 8
Winter mildness: 37   **Hazard free:** 26

115
92
153
90° 21
32° 137
0° 15
67
115
23

	High °F	Low °F	Hum %	Wind mph	Precip inches	Snow inches
JAN	32	14	81	8.0	2.8	12.5
FEB	36	20	77	6.0	2.0	7.7
MAR	40	25	69	7.0	2.7	5.9
APR	48	32	61	8.0	3.2	2.1
MAY	58	39	61	8.0	4.6	0.8
JUN	67	46	61	8.0	4.2	0
JUL	76	50	52	8.0	2.1	0
AUG	75	49	51	8.0	2.5	0
SEP	64	40	60	7.0	3.2	0
OCT	54	31	70	7.0	2.7	0.9
NOV	40	24	80	6.0	2.6	5.8
DEC	33	17	83	7.0	2.5	10.6

★ = in the top 30 places for climate mildness

★ Bradenton, FL — Rank: 24

Location: 27.30 N and 82.34 W at 19 feet, on the south bank of the Manatee River near its mouth at Tampa Bay. Tampa is 50 miles north.

Landscape: The southern Gulf Coastal Plains are flat and irregular with less than 300 feet variation in altitude over the gently rolling area. Most of the streams are sluggish. Marshes, swamps, and lakes are numerous. Evergreen oaks, laurel, and magnolia are common, but the trees aren't tall and the leaf canopy isn't dense. There is an understory of various shrubs, with ferns and herbaceous plants as ground cover.

Climate: Subtropical. Summer and winter extremes are checked by the influence of the Gulf. Winter days are bright and warm. Nights are moderately cool. Rainfall averages more than 50 inches annually, with two-thirds coming daily between June and September. Most rain falls in late-afternoon or early-evening thunderstorms, bringing relief from the heat.

Summer mildness: 20   **Seasonal affect:** 72
Winter mildness: 92   **Hazard free:** 83

| | 102 | 142 | 121 | 90° 78 | 32° 0 | 0° 0 | 22 | 69 | 93 |

	High °F	Low °F	Hum %	Wind mph	Precip inches	Snow inches
JAN	71	49	56	8.6	2.5	0
FEB	73	51	56	9.2	3.0	0
MAR	77	55	53	9.5	3.2	0
APR	82	59	47	9.3	1.2	0
MAY	87	65	49	8.7	2.8	0
JUN	90	70	56	8.0	7.8	0
JUL	91	72	60	7.2	8.9	0
AUG	91	72	60	7.0	9.5	0
SEP	89	71	60	7.8	8.0	0
OCT	85	65	56	8.5	2.6	0
NOV	79	57	56	8.4	2.1	0
DEC	73	51	56	8.5	2.3	0

Branson, MO — Rank: 160

Location: 36.38 N and 93.13 W at 722 feet, 50 miles south of Springfield near the Arkansas state line.

Landscape: High hills. There are several important lakes and rivers in this area of the Ozark Plateau. The rounded mountains rise somewhat steeply from river valleys and impounded lakes. Oak-hickory forests are tall, providing a dense, high, and leafy cover in summer and colorful foliage in fall, but are completely bare in winter. Pines are evidence of second-growth forest. Lower understory layers of shrub and flowering trees are common throughout.

Climate: Hot continental with hot summers and cool winters. Precipitation is adequate throughout the year and usually falls as rain. Winters may be cold enough for snow, but the typical precipitation is icy rain during brief, intense cold snaps that begin with the first frost around October 16. Spring arrives early and is pleasant.

Summer mildness: 46   **Seasonal affect:** 60
Winter mildness: 21   **Hazard free:** 22

| | 116 | 97 | 153 | 90° 57 | 32° 101 | 0° 1 | 20 | 61 | 56 |

	High °F	Low °F	Hum %	Wind mph	Precip inches	Snow inches
JAN	45	19	60	11.7	1.9	4.4
FEB	50	23	60	11.9	2.4	4.3
MAR	60	32	56	12.9	3.9	3.4
APR	71	42	55	12.2	3.9	0
MAY	79	50	59	10.4	4.5	0
JUN	86	59	59	9.6	4.3	0
JUL	92	63	56	8.5	3.4	0
AUG	90	61	54	8.6	3.4	0
SEP	83	55	58	9.3	3.9	0
OCT	73	42	54	10.1	3.3	0
NOV	60	33	59	11.3	3.9	1.0
DEC	49	24	63	11.6	3.3	3.0

Brevard, NC — Rank: 124

Location: 35.14 N and 82.44 W at 2,230 feet in the mountains close to the South Carolina border, near the French Broad River, and 40 miles southwest of Asheville.

Landscape: Low mountains. High rounded slopes of the southern Appalachians, with steep gorges, precipitous cliffs, and numerous waterfalls. Nearby are the Appalachian Trail and the Blue Ridge Parkway. Also near are the Pisgah and Nantahala national forests, with oak, beech, walnut, ash, sweet chestnut, and hornbeam. Native laurel blooms in spring along with other common understory trees like dogwood and redbud.

Climate: Hot continental moderated by the altitude. This is especially notable in summer, with markedly less humidity and cooler nights than cities of similar latitude. Winters are typically cold and cloudy, heralded by the first frost around October 8. Early May sees the last frost. Precipitation, mainly mountain rain, is plentiful and well distributed throughout the year.

Summer mildness: 61   **Seasonal affect:** 19
Winter mildness: 52   **Hazard free:** 47

| | 103 | 113 | 149 | 90° 9 | 32° 111 | 0° 1 | 78 | 91 | 45 |

	High °F	Low °F	Hum %	Wind mph	Precip inches	Snow inches
JAN	50	25	59	9.7	4.9	3.4
FEB	54	27	56	9.6	5.4	3.5
MAR	62	34	53	9.4	6.4	2.5
APR	70	41	50	8.9	4.7	0
MAY	77	49	57	7.1	5.9	0
JUN	82	57	59	6.1	5.6	0
JUL	85	61	63	5.8	5.9	0
AUG	84	61	63	5.4	6.5	0
SEP	79	55	64	5.6	5.1	0
OCT	71	42	57	6.8	5.3	0
NOV	62	34	57	8.1	5.4	0
DEC	53	28	59	8.9	5.9	1.5

★ = in the top 30 places for climate mildness

Brown County, IN — Rank: 197

Location: 39.12 N and 86.15 W at 629 feet 12 miles east of Bloomington and 60 miles south of Indianapolis.

Landscape: Open hills. The terrain is rolling with tumbled hills and narrow valleys in contrast to the flat, glacier-scoured land of northern Indiana. Ridges, knolls, bluffs, caves, and waterfalls are all found in this area. The surrounding forests have been regrowing for decades, and a wide variety of trees, including oak, maple, beech, sycamore, hickory, walnut, and elm cover the hills.

Climate: Continental. Warm summers and cold winters are the norm. Temperatures may vary widely in winter. The first frost arrives before mid-October and it will be the end of April before frost departs. Snowfall is moderate with accumulation in the hills. Summers vary from humid to dry. Spring and fall are long and pleasant. Rainfall is moderate, with occasional thunderstorms in summer.

Summer mildness: 36	Seasonal affect: 6
Winter mildness: 13	Hazard free: 23

	88
	99
	179
90°	29
32°	121
0°	6
	163
	78
	43

	High °F	Low °F	Hum %	Wind mph	Precip inches	Snow inches
JAN	37	17	76	10.9	2.6	7.6
FEB	41	20	74	10.8	2.6	4.9
MAR	53	30	71	11.7	4.4	4.8
APR	65	40	68	11.2	4.0	0.2
MAY	74	50	69	9.5	4.8	0
JUN	83	59	69	8.5	4.0	0
JUL	86	63	74	7.5	4.5	0
AUG	85	61	76	7.2	3.9	0
SEP	79	54	74	8.0	2.8	0
OCT	67	41	72	8.8	3.3	0
NOV	54	33	76	10.4	3.7	1.7
DEC	41	22	78	10.5	3.5	3.5

Brownsville, TX — Rank: 55

Location: 26.00 N and 97.00 W at 30 feet at the extreme southern tip of Texas on the north bank of the Rio Grande. Across the river is Mexico.

Landscape: Flat plains. Tidal marshlands make up more than half the land toward the coast. Winding through the city, the Rio Grande River makes Brownsville a port with a deepwater channel to the Gulf of Mexico. The fertile valley between the coastal prairie and the western desert flourishes with palm trees and bougainvillea as well as citrus groves.

Climate: Humid subtropical. Citrus fruits, cotton, and warm-weather vegetables thrive. Man-made irrigation adds to the humidity. Summer temperatures are in the lower 90s in the day and middle 70s at night. Gulf breezes help temper the summer heat. Snowbirds—persons fleeing cold northerly weather—flock here to the comparative warmth of normal January minimum temperatures.

Summer mildness: 10	Seasonal affect: 67
Winter mildness: 70	Hazard free: 93

	96
	133
	138
90°	116
32°	2
0°	0
	112
	40
	22

	High °F	Low °F	Hum %	Wind mph	Precip inches	Snow inches
JAN	69	69	67	11.2	1.6	0
FEB	72	72	63	12.0	1.1	0
MAR	78	78	59	13.3	0.5	0
APR	84	84	59	13.7	1.6	0
MAY	88	88	60	13.0	2.9	0
JUN	91	91	59	11.9	2.7	0
JUL	93	93	55	11.3	1.9	0
AUG	94	94	56	10.3	2.8	0
SEP	90	90	60	9.4	6.0	0
OCT	85	85	59	9.5	2.8	0
NOV	78	78	60	10.6	1.5	0
DEC	72	72	65	10.7	1.3	0

Brunswick, ME — Rank: 192

Location: 44.00 N and 70.23 W at 70 feet on a harbored section of southern Maine's Atlantic Coast some 20 miles northeast of Portland.

Landscape: Plains with high hills. Terrain is rolling, coastal lowland, penetrated extensively by ocean inlets. The forest is primarily evergreen with oak, maple, and other hardwoods throughout.

Climate: Continental, ensuring a strong annual temperature cycle. As a rule, the area sees pleasant summers and falls, cold winters with frequent thaws, and disagreeable muddy springs. Autumn has the greatest number of sunny days. Winters are seldom severe, but they extend deep into what is normally considered springtime, and temperatures well below zero are recorded frequently. The first frost arrives October 15 and the last frost departs April 27.

Summer mildness: 47	Seasonal affect: 5
Winter mildness: 22	Hazard free: 15

	101
	99
	165
90°	5
32°	156
0°	15
	170
	81
	15

	High °F	Low °F	Hum %	Wind mph	Precip inches	Snow inches
JAN	30	30	68	9.2	3.5	19.0
FEB	33	33	67	9.4	3.3	17.4
MAR	41	41	66	10.0	3.7	13.0
APR	52	52	64	10.0	4.1	3.1
MAY	63	63	67	9.2	3.6	0.2
JUN	73	73	69	8.3	3.4	0
JUL	79	79	70	7.6	3.1	0
AUG	77	77	71	7.5	2.9	0
SEP	69	69	73	7.9	3.1	0
OCT	59	59	72	8.4	3.9	0.2
NOV	47	47	72	8.7	5.2	3.0
DEC	35	35	70	9.0	4.6	14.6

★ = in the top 30 places for climate mildness

Burlington, VT — Rank: 194

Location: 44.29 N and 73.13 W on the eastern shore of Lake Champlain, some 75 miles south of Montreal, Quebec.
Landscape: Open low mountains. The highest peaks of the Adirondacks are visible 35 miles across the lake, and the Green Mountain foothills begin 10 miles to the east. Northern white pine, eastern hemlock, maple, oak, and beech are common trees in the surrounding forest.
Climate: The last freeze here occurs in late May, followed by a short, extremely pleasant summer. Fall is cool; the first freeze hits in late September. Winters are cold, with brief intense cold snaps formed by high-pressure systems moving down from central Canada and Hudson Bay. Lake Champlain moderates the cold somewhat. Burlington is one of the cloudiest cities in the country.

Summer mildness: 62   **Seasonal affect:** 7
Winter mildness: 7   **Hazard free:** 8

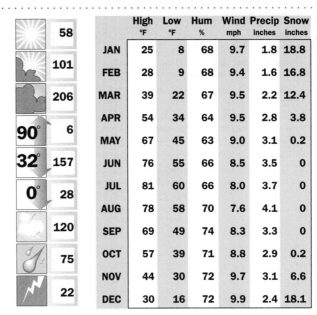

	58
	101
	206
90°	6
32°	157
0°	28
	120
	75
	22

	High °F	Low °F	Hum %	Wind mph	Precip inches	Snow inches
JAN	25	8	68	9.7	1.8	18.8
FEB	28	9	68	9.4	1.6	16.8
MAR	39	22	67	9.5	2.2	12.4
APR	54	34	64	9.5	2.8	3.8
MAY	67	45	63	9.0	3.1	0.2
JUN	76	55	66	8.5	3.5	0
JUL	81	60	66	8.0	3.7	0
AUG	78	58	70	7.6	4.1	0
SEP	69	49	74	8.3	3.3	0
OCT	57	39	71	8.8	2.9	0.2
NOV	44	30	72	9.7	3.1	6.6
DEC	30	16	72	9.9	2.4	18.1

Camden, ME — Rank: 175

Location: 44.12 N and 69.04 W at 33 feet, on Penobscot Bay in the center of Maine's seacoast. Portland is 70 air miles southwest.
Climate: The Atlantic Ocean has a considerable modifying effect on the local climate, resulting in cool summers and winters that are mild for so northerly a location. Winter snows can be heavy, however. Though fall is generally mild, spring comes late and the weather isn't really warm until late June. Early October will bring in the first frost, and the last frost comes May 9.

Summer mildness: 79   **Seasonal affect:** 10
Winter mildness: 16   **Hazard free:** 20

	102
	99
	164
90°	5
32°	155
0°	16
	49
	76
	18

	High °F	Low °F	Hum %	Wind mph	Precip inches	Snow inches
JAN	32	11	61	9.2	3.5	14.4
FEB	35	12	58	9.4	3.3	17.9
MAR	43	23	58	10.0	3.9	10.2
APR	54	32	55	10.0	4.4	2.0
MAY	65	42	58	9.2	4.2	0
JUN	75	51	60	8.2	3.5	0
JUL	80	57	59	7.6	3.1	0
AUG	79	56	59	7.5	3.2	0
SEP	71	48	60	7.8	3.6	0
OCT	60	39	59	8.4	4.3	0
NOV	47	31	62	8.8	5.4	2.0
DEC	36	17	61	9.0	4.9	13.7

★ Carmel–Pebble Beach, CA — Rank: 2

Location: 36.33 N and 121.55 W at 237 feet, on the Carmel River at the southern point of Monterey Bay, 80 miles south of San Francisco.
Landscape: High mountains. Monterey Bay is a great sweeping coastal indentation on the Pacific Coast. Sandy and rocky beaches verge on tidepools along the shore. Local relief comes mainly from the Diablo and Santa Lucia mountains that rise to the east in high, grassy bluffs. Cypress and pine groves predominate in the mixed evergreen forest.
Climate: Marine, with year-round mild temperatures moving through gradual transitions. Nighttime cooling produces low-stratus clouds, known as California stratus, and early-morning fog. Most afternoons are clear and sunny. Cool temperatures and sea breezes keep the weather mild all year long. There may be a frost around December 8. Precipitation falls only from October to March. Summers are dry and thunderstorms rare.

Summer mildness: 76   **Seasonal affect:** 83
Winter mildness: 99   **Hazard free:** 94

	147
	116
	103
90°	2
32°	1
0°	0
	19
	35
	4

	High °F	Low °F	Hum %	Wind mph	Precip inches	Snow inches
JAN	60	43	57	4.8	3.5	0.1
FEB	62	45	58	6.3	2.7	0
MAR	62	45	60	6.7	3.2	0
APR	63	46	61	7.6	1.7	0
MAY	64	48	63	7.1	0.4	0
JUN	67	50	66	6.8	0.2	0
JUL	68	52	67	6.5	0.1	0
AUG	69	53	68	6.1	0.1	0
SEP	72	53	67	5.8	0.3	0
OCT	70	51	64	5.5	0.9	0
NOV	65	47	57	5.3	2.8	0
DEC	60	44	55	5.0	2.8	0

★ = in the top 30 places for climate mildness

★ **Carson City–Carson Valley, NV** **Rank: 22**

Location: 39.10 N and 119.46 W at 4,665 feet, 14 miles east of Lake Tahoe. Reno is 30 miles north.

Landscape: Plains with high mountains. Near the eastern foothills and the wind shadow of the Sierra Nevada Range and on the edge of the Great Basin, a major drainage sink for the Rockies. The rivers here flow into landlocked lakes or simply evaporate in the desert. Sagebrush and saltbrush are common in this high country desert. The Sierran forest is mountain hemlock, red fir, lodgepole pine, and western white pine.

Climate: Mediterranean highland characterized by a long, unbroken, dry summer. Winters are cold but short. The first frost arrives by September 21, and the last frost won't depart until May 29. West winds prevail and influence the temperature and humidity. The mountains block much of the moisture from the Pacific that would otherwise fall as rain. At higher elevations, winter precipitation will fall as snow.

Summer mildness: 87 **Seasonal affect:** 85
Winter mildness: 43 **Hazard free:** 53

	159
	93
	112
90°	32
32°	170
0°	4
	7
	23
	0

	High °F	Low °F	Hum %	Wind mph	Precip inches	Snow inches
JAN	47	21	60	5.6	1.9	6.8
FEB	52	24	52	6.2	1.6	4.4
MAR	57	28	44	7.8	1.0	4.7
APR	63	32	36	8.2	0.5	1.0
MAY	72	39	32	8.0	0.6	0
JUN	82	46	29	7.6	0.4	0
JUL	90	50	25	7.0	0.3	0
AUG	88	48	24	6.5	0.3	0
SEP	80	41	30	5.8	0.5	0
OCT	70	32	36	5.4	0.7	0
NOV	55	26	49	5.5	1.4	1.0
DEC	47	21	58	5.2	1.7	6.0

Cedar City, UT **Rank: 161**

Location: 37.41 N and 113.04 W at 5,834 feet, located 45 miles northeast of St. George and 220 miles southwest of Salt Lake City.

Landscape: High mountains. On a tableland with Zion National Park to the south and Cedar Breaks National Monument to the east. The terrain is moderately to extremely rugged; elevations vary from 3,000 to over 8,000 feet. Lodgepole pine and aspen are dominant trees.

Climate: Rigorous mountain with cool, pleasant summers and long, cold, snowy winters. The first frost arrives September 20 and the last frost departs May 29. Fall and spring are short transitional seasons here. Thanks to elevation, the climate here contrasts sharply with St. George.

Summer mildness: 49 **Seasonal affect:** 39
Winter mildness: 32 **Hazard free:** 28

	137
	107
	122
90°	62
32°	134
0°	5
	26
	107
	36

	High °F	Low °F	Hum %	Wind mph	Precip inches	Snow inches
JAN	36	15	81	5.7	0.7	7.3
FEB	45	24	77	6.7	0.9	4.2
MAR	56	31	69	8.3	1.4	3.8
APR	66	39	61	9.4	1.1	1.1
MAY	76	48	61	9.6	0.8	0.1
JUN	88	57	61	9.7	0.4	0
JUL	94	64	52	9.3	1.1	0
AUG	91	62	51	9.1	1.5	0
SEP	81	53	60	9.0	1.0	0.1
OCT	68	42	70	7.9	1.0	0.5
NOV	51	29	80	6.8	1.0	2.7
DEC	39	19	83	5.9	0.7	5.3

Cedar Creek Lake, TX **Rank: 99**

Location: 32.10 N and 96.04 W at 460 feet, in East Texas, about 70 air miles southeast of Dallas.

Landscape: Plains with hills. The surrounding rolling-to-hilly terrain drains to the Neches River on the east and the Trinity River on the west. The grass is bluestem prairie. The trees are pine, post oak, blackjack oak, and Texas hickory.

Climate: Prairie, with hot summers. Rainfall is about 39 inches annually, evenly distributed, though July and August are somewhat dry. Winters are mild, with temperatures almost always rising above freezing in the daytime, with no zero temperatures on record. Spring and fall are the best seasons. November 20 sees the first frost; the last frost departs March 15. This provides a long growing season, but there are sufficient changes to make the weather interesting. Flowers bloom as late as December and as early as March.

Summer mildness: 23 **Seasonal affect:** 78
Winter mildness: 45 **Hazard free:** 53

	138
	98
	130
90°	102
32°	44
0°	0
	11
	50
	45

	High °F	Low °F	Hum %	Wind mph	Precip inches	Snow inches
JAN	55	33	59	11.2	2.2	1.3
FEB	60	37	59	11.9	2.8	1.0
MAR	68	45	57	12.9	3.1	0.2
APR	77	54	56	12.6	3.6	0
MAY	83	62	60	11.2	5.8	0
JUN	90	69	55	10.6	3.1	0
JUL	94	72	48	9.6	2.1	0
AUG	95	72	49	9.0	1.9	0
SEP	88	66	55	9.4	3.4	0
OCT	79	55	54	9.8	4.2	0
NOV	68	44	57	10.8	2.9	0
DEC	58	36	59	11.0	2.9	0.3

★ = in the top 30 places for climate mildness

Chapel Hill–Carrboro, NC — Rank: 102

Location: 35.54 N and 79.03 W at 503 feet, in central North Carolina, 35 miles west of Raleigh.

Landscape: Irregular plains. The topography of the Piedmont is rolling, with elevations from 200 to 500 feet within a 10-mile radius. Broadleaf deciduous and needle-leaf evergreen trees make up the medium-tall forests. Loblolly and other southern yellow pine mix with hickory, sweet gum, red maple, and winged elm. Low shrubs of dogwood, viburnum, and blueberry are common.

Climate: Subtropical. Because the Blue Ridge is a partial barrier to cold air masses moving eastward from the nation's interior, there are very few days in winter when the temperature falls below 20°F. Tropical air is present during much of summer, bringing warm temperatures and high humidity. Rainfall is well distributed throughout the year. Frost arrives by late October and departs on April 15.

Summer mildness: 50 **Seasonal affect:** 40
Winter mildness: 57 **Hazard free:** 50

	112								
	106		High °F	Low °F	Hum %	Wind mph	Precip inches	Snow inches	
	147	JAN	49	26	55	8.5	3.7	2.7	
90°	39	FEB	52	28	52	8.9	3.9	2.4	
32°	91	MAR	62	36	49	9.3	4.2	1.9	
0°	0	APR	71	44	45	9.0	3.2	0	
	34	MAY	78	53	54	7.7	4.5	0	
	74	JUN	85	61	56	7.0	4.4	0	
	44	JUL	89	65	58	6.7	4.1	0	
		AUG	87	64	60	6.4	4.4	0	
		SEP	82	57	59	6.8	3.2	0	
		OCT	72	45	53	7.1	3.5	0	
		NOV	63	37	52	7.6	3.5	0	
		DEC	53	29	55	8.0	3.5	0.9	

Charleston, SC — Rank: 80

Location: 32.46 N and 79.56 W at 118 feet, between the Ashley and Cooper rivers on South Carolina's central coast.

Landscape: Flat plains. Generally level with sandy to sandy-loam soil. Because of the low elevation, a portion of the city and nearby coastal islands are vulnerable to tidal flooding. The coastal marshes and interior swamps are dominated by moss-draped oak, sweet and black gums, and bald cypress. Grasses and cattails grow in the more open marsh areas.

Climate: Temperate subtropical modified considerably by the ocean. Summer is warm and humid, but temperatures over 100°F are infrequent; nearly half the year's rain falls during this time. From late September to early November the weather is cool and sunny. Winters are mild; temperatures of 32°F or less are unusual. The first frost appears on November 30; the last frost departs in late February, leading to a warm, windy, and stormy spring.

Summer mildness: 21 **Seasonal affect:** 55
Winter mildness: 76 **Hazard free:** 65

	104								
	109		High °F	Low °F	Hum %	Wind mph	Precip inches	Snow inches	
	152	JAN	57	39	57	9.1	3.7	0.1	
90°	35	FEB	60	41	55	9.9	3.5	0.2	
32°	19	MAR	67	48	53	10.0	4.4	0.1	
0°	0	APR	74	56	50	9.7	2.7	0	
	28	MAY	81	64	55	8.7	3.5	0	
	66	JUN	86	71	60	8.4	5.4	0	
	56	JUL	89	74	66	7.9	5.1	0	
		AUG	88	73	70	7.4	7.1	0	
		SEP	84	69	67	7.8	4.5	0	
		OCT	78	59	60	8.1	3.5	0	
		NOV	70	50	60	8.1	2.9	0	
		DEC	62	43	59	8.5	3.4	0.3	

Charles Town–Shepherdstown, WV — Rank: 140

Location: 39.17 N and 77.51 W at 513 feet, near the meeting point of Virginia, Maryland, and West Virginia. Washington, D.C., is 53 miles southeast.

Landscape: Irregular plains. In the midst of rolling farmland and Allegheny Mountain foothills west of the Blue Ridge Parkway. Steep hills and mountains rise up in long ridges, curving north to south. The Shenandoah and Potomac rivers offer both white-water rapids and lazy stretches of calm fishing waters. Continuous dense covering is provided in summer by the Appalachian oak forest dominated by tall, broadleaf trees. Other common trees are beech, birch, hickory, maple, and shrub undergrowth. Pines are a secondary growth.

Climate: Hot continental with warm, humid summers, cool falls, and somewhat cold and snowy winters. Mid-October brings the first frost, while the last frost is late April. Precipitation is evenly distributed throughout the year, snow or rain in season.

Summer mildness: 55 **Seasonal affect:** 47
Winter mildness: 38 **Hazard free:** 27

	102								
	113		High °F	Low °F	Hum %	Wind mph	Precip inches	Snow inches	
	150	JAN	39	21	55	9.5	2.4	6.8	
90°	31	FEB	42	23	53	9.7	2.5	7.7	
32°	119	MAR	53	32	51	10.1	3.1	6.1	
0°	1	APR	64	41	50	9.8	3.2	0	
	23	MAY	74	50	55	7.9	4.1	0	
	71	JUN	83	59	56	6.9	3.4	0	
	36	JUL	87	64	58	6.5	3.5	0	
		AUG	85	62	59	6.1	3.3	0	
		SEP	78	55	60	6.1	2.8	0	
		OCT	66	42	56	6.9	3.4	0	
		NOV	55	34	55	8.3	3.1	1.0	
		DEC	43	26	55	8.8	2.7	5.6	

★ = in the top 30 places for climate mildness

Charlottesville, VA   Rank: 125

Location: 38.01 N and 78.32 W at 480 feet, in the center of Virginia's Piedmont Plateau. Washington, D.C., is 110 miles northeast.

Landscape: Open low mountains. The Blue Ridge Mountains rise to the west. These and smaller ranges produce a rolling to steep relief. The land is agricultural, with occasional stands of oak, hickory, sweet gum, red maple, loblolly, and shortleaf pine. There is undergrowth of dogwood, viburnum, blueberry, youpon, and numerous woody vines.

Climate: Modified continental, with mild winters and warm, humid summers. The first frost arrives November 4, and the last frost leaves April 7. The mountains produce various steering and blocking effects on storms and air masses. Chesapeake Bay modifies the climate, making it warmer in winter, cooler in summer. Precipitation is well distributed throughout the year, with the maximum in July and August and the minimum in January. Tornadoes and violent storms are rare, but severe thunderstorms occur in July.

Summer mildness: 51   **Seasonal affect:** 44
Winter mildness: 53   **Hazard free:** 29

	113
	107
	145
90°	31
32°	87
0°	0
	39
	72
	40

	High °F	Low °F	Hum %	Wind mph	Precip inches	Snow inches
JAN	43	26	55	8.6	3.2	6.7
FEB	47	28	52	8.6	3.3	6.9
MAR	57	36	50	9.1	3.8	5.1
APR	68	45	47	9.0	3.3	0
MAY	76	54	54	7.9	4.9	0
JUN	83	62	56	6.9	3.7	0
JUL	87	66	59	6.5	4.8	0
AUG	85	65	60	6.3	4.7	0
SEP	79	59	60	6.9	4.1	0
OCT	68	48	55	7.3	4.6	0
NOV	59	39	53	7.9	3.7	1.0
DEC	47	29	56	7.9	3.3	3.6

Chestertown, MD   Rank: 177

Location: 39.13 N and 76.04 W at 35 feet on the eastern shore of Chesapeake Bay, 30 miles east of Baltimore and 60 miles northeast of Washington, D.C.

Landscape: The topography is generally flat with unvarying relief. Inland from the Bay the land is suburban and developed agricultural. The remaining naturally occurring vegetation is a typical southeastern mixed forest with broadleaf deciduous and needleleaf evergreen.

Climate: Subtropical with a definite marine influence from the Bay. Summer days are hot and humid and a Bay breeze is welcome. Winters are cloudy, dripping, and chilly. Snowfalls are brief and melt quickly. The first frost arrives November 1 and the last frost departs April 7.

Summer mildness: 28   **Seasonal affect:** 29
Winter mildness: 31   **Hazard free:** 36

	105
	109
	151
90°	31
32°	97
0°	0
	146
	70
	27

	High °F	Low °F	Hum %	Wind mph	Precip inches	Snow inches
JAN	40	28	65	9.7	3.2	5.9
FEB	43	30	63	10.3	3.1	6.5
MAR	53	38	62	10.8	3.7	3.8
APR	64	48	61	10.5	3.2	0.1
MAY	74	58	65	9.1	4.0	0
JUN	83	67	66	8.5	4.4	0
JUL	87	72	67	8.0	3.7	0
AUG	86	71	70	7.8	4.0	0
SEP	79	63	70	8.0	3.6	0
OCT	68	51	69	8.6	3.1	0
NOV	57	42	67	9.2	3.4	1.0
DEC	45	33	66	9.3	3.8	3.5

Chewelah, WA   Rank: 173

Location: 48.17 N and 117.44 W at 1,671 feet in northeast Washington, 50 miles midway between Spokane and the Canadian border.

Landscape: Low mountains. Situated in meadowlands on the floor of the Colville River Valley, the town is surrounded by mountainous benchland. The nearby Selkirk and Huckleberry mountains are forested by a variety of evergreens including cedar, larch, fir, and pine.

Climate: Warm continental. The seasonal temperature shifts are moderated because of mountain protection from wind and severe storms. Summer days are warm with little humidity. The seasons are well defined and include a winter with much snow. The first frost arrives September 6 and the last frost departs June 3.

Summer mildness: 80   **Seasonal affect:** 5
Winter mildness: 19   **Hazard free:** 25

	86
	87
	192
90°	21
32°	141
0°	5
	101
	78
	11

	High °F	Low °F	Hum %	Wind mph	Precip inches	Snow inches
JAN	33	21	82	8.8	2.4	16.2
FEB	41	26	77	9.2	1.9	7.7
MAR	48	30	68	9.6	1.9	4.1
APR	57	35	61	10.0	1.5	0.6
MAY	66	42	59	9.3	2.0	0.1
JUN	75	49	55	9.2	1.5	0
JUL	83	54	47	8.6	0.9	0
AUG	83	54	46	8.2	1.1	0
SEP	72	46	53	8.3	1.1	0
OCT	59	36	64	8.1	1.3	0.4
NOV	41	29	82	8.6	2.7	6.2
DEC	34	22	86	8.6	3.1	15.1

★ = in the top 30 places for climate mildness

Coeur d'Alene, ID — Rank: 155

Location: 47.40 N and 116.46 W at 2,152 feet, on Lake Coeur d'Alene in Idaho's panhandle. Boise is 400 miles south and Spokane, Washington, 30 miles west.

Landscape: High mountains. The Coeur d'Alene Mountains are a division of the Bitterroot Range of the northern Rockies. They shelter the city with a triangle of forested hills or low mountains for 60 miles along the Montana border from Lake Pend Oreille to the St. Joe River. The Coeur d'Alene National Forest spreads across most of the range. To the north and northwest lies Rathdrum Prairie. Within a 10-mile radius, several mountain peaks rise over 4,000 feet.

Climate: Can be described as temperate, with clear, dry summers and rainy, snowy winters. The first frost shows up by the beginning of October and the last frost leaves by May 11. Though seasonal variation is large, it's less so than most other locations this far north. Precipitation is heaviest from autumn to early spring.

Summer mildness: 82 **Seasonal affect:** 23
Winter mildness: 24 **Hazard free:** 24

Icon values: 86, 87, 192, 90° 27, 32° 139, 0° 3, 47, 66, 11

	High °F	Low °F	Hum %	Wind mph	Precip inches	Snow inches
JAN	36	23	80	8.8	3.5	24.0
FEB	43	26	78	9.3	2.5	9.9
MAR	50	30	65	9.7	2.3	5.1
APR	60	35	55	10.0	1.7	0
MAY	69	42	51	9.2	2.1	0
JUN	77	49	47	9.2	2.0	0
JUL	85	53	37	8.6	0.9	0
AUG	86	53	40	8.2	1.3	0
SEP	76	45	45	8.3	1.2	0
OCT	62	38	59	8.2	1.6	0
NOV	46	32	75	8.7	3.3	5.0
DEC	37	26	83	8.6	3.7	15.9

Columbia, MO — Rank: 196

Location: 38.57 N and 92.20 W at 758 feet, in north-central Missouri. Kansas City is 120 miles west and St. Louis is 100 miles east.

Landscape: Open hills. Here are the gently rolling plains of the broad Missouri River Valley meeting just at the point where prairie and eastern forest ecologies come together. The natural vegetation is a transitional intermingling of prairie, groves, and woodlands. Efforts are underway to increase the diversity of native species.

Climate: Hot continental. Winters are moderately cold but often interrupted by days that are almost balmy, with temperatures as high as the 50s and 60s. First frost rolls in by October 30 and rolls out by April 10. Summers are warm, with days topping 100°F, and it often is very humid. Late spring and early summer are the rainiest.

Summer mildness: 25 **Seasonal affect:** 25
Winter mildness: 16 **Hazard free:** 14

Icon values: 104, 91, 170, 90° 40, 32° 114, 0° 6, 123, 65, 52

	High °F	Low °F	Hum %	Wind mph	Precip inches	Snow inches
JAN	37	19	73	10.8	1.5	5.6
FEB	41	23	72	11.0	1.8	6.5
MAR	53	33	69	12.0	3.2	4.3
APR	66	44	67	11.5	3.8	0.7
MAY	74	53	73	9.1	5.0	0
JUN	83	61	73	8.6	4.3	0
JUL	89	66	72	8.3	3.7	0
AUG	87	64	73	7.9	3.3	0
SEP	79	57	73	8.6	3.9	0
OCT	68	46	71	9.5	3.2	0
NOV	54	35	73	10.6	2.9	1.8
DEC	40	23	75	10.8	2.5	4.2

Conway, AR — Rank: 135

Location: 35.00 N and 92.00 W at 330 feet near Ozark foothills some 30 miles north of Little Rock.

Landscape: Flat plains. The Ouachita Mountains are visible to the west. The flat lowlands of the Mississippi River Valley lie to the east. This is prime land for farming and raising cattle or poultry.

Climate: Modified four-season continental climate. The area is exposed to all North American air-mass types, but the Gulf of Mexico gives the summer season prolonged periods of warmer and more humid weather. There is a long frost-free growing season of 233 days, during which nearly two-thirds of the normal annual precipitation occurs. Winters are mild, but polar and Arctic outbreaks are not uncommon. Glaze and ice storms, though infrequent, can be severe.

Summer mildness: 2 **Seasonal affect:** 37
Winter mildness: 81 **Hazard free:** 51

Icon values: 119, 100, 147, 90° 73, 32° 57, 0° 0, 142, 72, 53

	High °F	Low °F	Hum %	Wind mph	Precip inches	Snow inches
JAN	49	49	71	8.5	3.4	2.3
FEB	54	54	70	8.9	3.6	1.4
MAR	64	64	68	9.6	4.9	0.5
APR	73	73	70	9.0	5.5	0
MAY	81	81	73	7.7	5.2	0
JUN	89	89	71	7.2	3.6	0
JUL	92	92	72	6.7	3.6	0
AUG	91	91	73	6.3	3.3	0
SEP	85	85	74	6.7	4.1	0
OCT	75	75	70	6.8	3.8	0
NOV	63	63	71	8.0	5.2	0.2
DEC	53	53	71	8.2	4.8	0.7

★ = in the top 30 places for climate mildness

Cortez, CO — Rank: 113

Location: 37.21 N and 108.35 W at 6,201 feet in extreme southwestern Colorado. The Four Corners area, where Utah, New Mexico, Colorado, and Arizona meet, is the archaeological center of America.

Landscape: High mountains. McPhee Lake is Colorado's second-largest lake. The Dolores River rises in the San Juan Mountains and cuts through red-rock canyons to the west. Ponderosa pine fills the San Juan National Forest; while at lower elevations there are mixed grasses, chaparral brush, oak-juniper, or piñon-juniper woodland.

Climate: Mountain steppe, with considerable seasonal variety that goes with altitude. Average annual temperature is about 55°F in the lower foothills and 40°F on the upper mountain slopes. During late spring, there is a moisture deficit until the arrival of summer rains, which appear as thunderstorms. Rains also come in early autumn and winter. In the mountains, most precipitation is snow. The first frost arrives October 1 and the last frost departs May 22.

Summer mildness: 86   **Seasonal affect:** 87
Winter mildness: 10   **Hazard free:** 7

Icon values: 168, 110, 87, 90° 30, 32° 177, 0° 10, 5, 33, 34

	High °F	Low °F	Hum %	Wind mph	Precip inches	Snow inches
JAN	39	11	63	8.0	0.9	12.2
FEB	45	17	55	8.8	0.9	8.2
MAR	51	24	41	10.0	1.4	9.8
APR	61	30	32	10.8	0.9	3.0
MAY	71	38	31	10.5	0.9	0.5
JUN	82	46	25	9.9	0.5	0
JUL	88	54	27	9.0	1.3	0
AUG	85	53	30	8.2	1.5	0
SEP	77	44	33	8.5	1.3	0.1
OCT	66	33	37	8.2	1.5	0.3
NOV	52	23	48	7.9	1.2	4.8
DEC	41	14	60	7.7	1.2	11.8

★ Cottonwood–Verde Valley, AZ — Rank: 26

Location: 34.44 N and 112.00 W at 3,314 feet, 100 miles north of Phoenix and 10 miles east of Prescott.

Landscape: Open high mountains. The Verde River runs through this high valley near the western edge of the Mongollon Rim. Near are many high peaks, canyons, and mesas. Cottonwood trees line the river. Ponderosa pine and other conifers are in the high country, and sagebrush and native grasses cover the valley floor. The shrubs must tolerate alkaline conditions, as soils are poorly drained.

Climate: Mountain steppe, with strong daily and seasonal temperature changes. The usual winter flow of air is from the Pacific Ocean, bringing snows. Cold air masses from Canada sometimes force temperatures well below 0°F higher up in the mountains. Frost arrives October 9 and departs as late as May 17. Moisture-bearing winds from the southeast Gulf bring brief summer rains from July to September.

Summer mildness: 67   **Seasonal affect:** 88
Winter mildness: 62   **Hazard free:** 45

Icon values: 212, 84, 69, 90° 32, 32° 150, 0° 0, 11, 39, 24

	High °F	Low °F	Hum %	Wind mph	Precip inches	Snow inches
JAN	59	25	45	5.3	1.6	4.5
FEB	63	28	40	5.9	1.5	3.5
MAR	66	31	36	6.7	1.8	6.8
APR	74	35	25	7.0	0.7	2.0
MAY	84	42	20	7.1	0.4	0
JUN	94	49	18	6.8	0.2	0
JUL	98	61	28	7.2	1.6	0
AUG	95	61	33	6.7	2.4	0
SEP	90	52	34	6.3	1.5	0
OCT	80	40	34	5.8	1.0	0
NOV	68	30	37	5.4	1.6	1.0
DEC	60	26	46	5.1	1.5	5.1

Crossville, TN — Rank: 144

Location: 35.57 N and 85.50 W at 1,863 feet, on the Cumberland Plateau near the center of the state. Knoxville is 62 miles east and Nashville is 110 miles west.

Landscape: Open low mountains. High, rolling foothills of the Appalachians are on the eastern horizon. This is a timberland plateau of the eastern deciduous forest. Common trees are hickory, oak, beech, birch, walnut, and maple. These tall broadleaf trees provide dense foliage during summer and are bare in winter. Low shrubs develop in spring.

Climate: Hot continental climate characterized by long, mild summers and cool winters. Daily and seasonal temperature changes aren't dramatic. The first frost will come by October 15, and the last frost is April 26. Precipitation is well distributed throughout the year.

Summer mildness: 62   **Seasonal affect:** 14
Winter mildness: 56   **Hazard free:** 33

Icon values: 112, 96, 157, 90° 10, 32° 110, 0° 4, 34, 90, 51

	High °F	Low °F	Hum %	Wind mph	Precip inches	Snow inches
JAN	42	21	63	4.8	5.2	5.2
FEB	46	24	62	5.0	4.8	5.2
MAR	56	34	59	5.3	6.2	2.7
APR	65	43	55	5.7	5.0	0
MAY	73	50	60	4.5	5.6	0
JUN	80	58	61	4.2	4.4	0
JUL	83	62	63	3.9	5.5	0
AUG	83	60	63	3.7	3.9	0
SEP	77	55	63	3.8	4.2	0
OCT	67	42	63	3.6	3.7	0
NOV	56	35	64	4.1	5.1	1.0
DEC	46	26	67	4.5	5.7	2.3

★ = in the top 30 places for climate mildness

Dahlonega, GA — Rank: 109

Location: 34.00 N and 84.00 W at 1,390 feet in the northern Georgia foothills at the edge of the Chattahoochee National Forest. Atlanta is 100 miles southwest.

Landscape: Low mountains. To the north, there are mountains above 3,000 feet. Chattahoochee National Forest is a mixed deciduous forest, with oak, beech, birch, walnut, maple, ash, and hornbeam. Pines readily develop as second growth where there has been logging or fire.

Climate: Mountains have marked influences on summer heat, producing warm days and cool nights. Winters are cold but not severe. The contrast of valley and hill exposures results in wide variations in winter low temperatures. Frost appears by the end of October and departs by the end of April. Midway on mountain slopes, temperatures remain warmer during winter nights than the valley floor. Spring is changeable and sometimes stormy. Fall is clear and sunny, with chilly nights.

Summer mildness: 63 **Seasonal affect:** 21
Winter mildness: 46 **Hazard free:** 62

	105
	114
	147
90°	5
32°	90
0°	0
	80
	92
	41

	High °F	Low °F	Hum %	Wind mph	Precip inches	Snow inches
JAN	48	28	65	9.7	6.4	0.4
FEB	52	30	61	9.6	6.1	0.6
MAR	61	37	56	9.4	7.4	0.4
APR	70	44	53	8.9	5.4	0
MAY	77	52	60	7.1	6.8	0
JUN	83	60	61	6.1	5.4	0
JUL	86	64	63	5.8	5.8	0
AUG	85	64	63	5.4	6.1	0
SEP	79	58	62	5.6	5.7	0
OCT	70	46	57	6.8	5.1	0
NOV	61	38	60	8.1	5.9	0
DEC	52	31	66	8.9	6.7	0.2

Dare Outer Banks, NC — Rank: 156

Location: 35.54 N and 75.40 W at 5 feet, on North Carolina's northeast coast, 60 miles south of Virginia Beach.

Landscape: Flat plains. Principally barrier islands with white-sand beaches, dunes, wetland habitats, and a hardwood forest of Atlantic white cedar and bald cypress, with many types of wildflowers and shrubs. Nags Head Woods is a biologically diverse maritime forest, one of the best remaining examples of mid-Atlantic maritime forest. Cape Hatteras National Seashore, extending 75 miles along the coast, protects more than 30,000 acres.

Climate: Subtropical, with humid, hot summers and mild winters. Frost arrives as late as November 4 and departs as early as April 6. January and February nights can be freezing due to the wind chill. Rain falls throughout the year. Summer brings heavy thunderstorms. Occasional tropical storms from the Atlantic may strike this coastal location.

Summer mildness: 26 **Seasonal affect:** 33
Winter mildness: 39 **Hazard free:** 55

	108
	101
	156
90°	32
32°	67
0°	0
	15
	76
	42

	High °F	Low °F	Hum %	Wind mph	Precip inches	Snow inches
JAN	52	34	68	12.1	4.3	0.4
FEB	54	36	65	12.3	3.8	0.6
MAR	61	42	63	12.0	4.2	0.5
APR	70	50	59	11.8	3.4	0
MAY	77	59	65	10.9	4.4	0
JUN	84	67	68	10.7	4.6	0
JUL	87	71	70	10.0	5.5	0
AUG	87	71	69	9.5	5.8	0
SEP	82	66	67	10.5	5.0	0
OCT	72	56	65	11.1	3.9	0
NOV	64	47	64	11.0	3.6	0
DEC	56	39	66	11.5	3.6	0.6

Delta County, CO — Rank: 82

Location: The weather station is Delta, the county seat, 38.44 N and 108.04 W at 4,953 feet on Colorado's western slope. Grand Junction is 45 miles northwest.

Landscape: High mountains. Within the sage desert and shortgrass prairie of the Colorado Plateau. Ranchland and orchards mark the gently rolling lowland. Lakes and streams are fed from mountain snows. The Gunnison and Uncompahgre rivers flow through steep canyons, where sagebrush and cactus are found. Pine, spruce, and aspen forests cover the subalpine areas.

Climate: Desert-steppe brings varied seasonal and daily temperature changes. Summers are dry and comfortable due to the high altitude. Winters are cold with moderate snow cover in the elevations through May. First frost is October 5; last frost is May 17. Humidity is low, and precipitation is scant except for brief mountain thunderstorms.

Summer mildness: 85 **Seasonal affect:** 81
Winter mildness: 29 **Hazard free:** 21

	137
	107
	121
90°	23
32°	165
0°	4
	8
	34
	35

	High °F	Low °F	Hum %	Wind mph	Precip inches	Snow inches
JAN	38	15	64	5.6	0.9	10.5
FEB	44	20	52	6.7	0.8	7.9
MAR	52	27	43	8.4	1.2	7.0
APR	62	33	33	9.5	0.9	2.4
MAY	72	41	32	9.6	1.1	0.6
JUN	83	50	34	9.7	0.8	0
JUL	88	56	28	9.3	1.0	0
AUG	85	54	30	9.0	1.2	0
SEP	77	46	33	8.9	1.3	0
OCT	65	36	38	7.9	1.5	0.9
NOV	50	26	51	6.7	1.1	4.9
DEC	40	17	62	5.9	1.1	9.2

★ = in the top 30 places for climate mildness

Door Peninsula, WI — Rank: 161

Location: The weather station is Sturgeon Bay, 44.51 N and 87.23 W at 660 feet on Wisconsin's Door Peninsula between Green Bay and Lake Michigan. The site is 180 miles northeast of Madison.

Landscape: Irregular plains. Characterized by rolling woodlands, limestone bluffs, and 250 miles of rocky shoreline and sandy beaches. Glacier effects predominate. The woods contain northern hardwoods of maple, oak, beech, and birch mixed with pine, eastern hemlock, and eastern red cedar.

Climate: Continental, and largely influenced by Lake Michigan and Lake Superior. This is certainly a four-season climate that is relatively temperate and extends the growing season. Winters are moderately long and can be severe. First frost snaps in by October 8; the last frost departs May 17. Snow falls early and lasts late. Summers are mild, with cool evenings and nights. Springs and autumns are all too short.

Summer mildness: 91   **Seasonal affect:** 35
Winter mildness: 5   **Hazard free:** 18

87 / 102 / 176 / 3 / 159 / 19 / 24 / 63 / 33

	High °F	Low °F	Hum %	Wind mph	Precip inches	Snow inches
JAN	25	9	72	11.0	1.5	10.4
FEB	28	11	69	10.6	1.1	7.2
MAR	38	22	64	10.9	2.1	8.0
APR	52	33	55	11.3	2.7	2.0
MAY	65	42	50	10.2	3.1	0
JUN	74	51	55	9.2	3.3	0
JUL	80	58	54	8.2	3.4	0
AUG	77	57	60	8.0	3.4	0
SEP	69	50	63	9.0	3.9	0
OCT	57	40	65	9.9	2.7	0
NOV	43	30	73	11.0	2.5	2.0
DEC	30	17	77	10.7	1.9	9.5

Driggs, ID — Rank: 165

Location: 43.43 N and 111.06 W at 6,116 feet in eastern Idaho. Wyoming and the Teton Mountains are immediately east.

Landscape: High mountains. Teton Valley is located on the west side of the famous Tetons and is characterized by rolling plains and tablelands of moderate relief in a broad belt that slopes gradually eastward.

Climate: Temperate semiarid steppe regime with average annual temperatures ranging from 35°F to 45°F in most of the region, but reaching 50°F in the lower valleys. The prevailing west winds and the general north–south orientation of the mountain ranges influence weather events. Summer and early fall are ideal; winter is long, cold, and snowy. Frost occurs nearly year-round.

Summer mildness: 97   **Seasonal affect:** 41
Winter mildness: 1   **Hazard free:** 5

125 / 87 / 153 / 5 / 255 / 40 / 50 / 49 / 25

	High °F	Low °F	Hum %	Wind mph	Precip inches	Snow inches
JAN	29	7	60	13.0	1.5	20.8
FEB	35	10	59	12.2	1.0	16.2
MAR	41	17	57	11.4	1.1	10.0
APR	52	26	55	11.5	1.3	4.3
MAY	63	33	56	10.7	2.2	0.6
JUN	72	41	55	10.1	1.9	0
JUL	81	47	48	9.5	1.3	0
AUG	80	45	46	9.5	1.2	0
SEP	70	36	51	10.2	1.5	0
OCT	59	27	52	11.0	1.2	0.7
NOV	41	19	59	12.1	1.3	8.3
DEC	31	8	60	13.1	1.4	19.3

Durango, CO — Rank: 96

Location: 37.16 N and 107.52 W at 6,523 feet, in Colorado's Four Corners area, 250 air miles southwest of Denver.

Landscape: High mountains. High in the Animas River Valley surrounded by red bluffs. The sharply uplifted San Juan Mountains provide dramatic relief. Much of the area is within the San Juan National Forest, a pine and aspen woods with a subalpine growth of scrub oak and grasses.

Climate: Semiarid continental, which causes definite seasonal temperature variations. Daily temperature changes are notable throughout the year as mountain nights chill considerably. Warm, dry summers blend into short, cool, dry falls. Mid-September, the first frost jacks into the area; June 4, the last frost bites. Winters are long and extremely snowy. Due to deep snow in the mountains, rivers and reservoirs stay relatively full in summer, though city water is frequently rationed.

Summer mildness: 93   **Seasonal affect:** 80
Winter mildness: 20   **Hazard free:** 8

137 / 107 / 121 / 18 / 211 / 11 / 8 / 44 / 35

	High °F	Low °F	Hum %	Wind mph	Precip inches	Snow inches
JAN	40	10	63	5.6	1.6	20.4
FEB	46	16	55	6.7	1.4	12.6
MAR	53	22	41	8.4	1.7	12.1
APR	62	29	32	9.5	1.2	4.0
MAY	71	36	31	9.6	1.1	0
JUN	82	42	25	9.7	0.7	0
JUL	87	51	27	9.3	1.8	0
AUG	84	49	30	9.0	2.4	0
SEP	76	41	33	8.9	1.9	0
OCT	66	31	37	7.9	2.0	0
NOV	52	22	48	6.7	1.7	6.0
DEC	41	13	60	5.9	1.8	17.4

★ = in the top 30 places for climate mildness

Eagle River–Woodruff, WI Rank: 168

Location: 45.55 N and 89.14 W at 1,647 feet, near where Michigan's Upper Peninsula meets northern Wisconsin. Green Bay is 140 miles southeast.

Landscape: Irregular plains. Generally level. The entire area was once part of a great, dense white pine forest but is now covered with second growth. Within a 20-mile radius of the town are more than 200 lakes, some with identical names.

Climate: Continental, and largely determined by the movement and interaction of large air masses. Weather changes can be expected every few days in winter and spring. Winters are long and cold with an average of 39 days when the temperature drops below 0°F. Summer days are warm and pleasant, with comfortably cool nights. Spring and fall are short, with rapid transition from winter to summer and vice versa. First frost is in by September 23; last frost out May 19.

Summer mildness: 92 **Seasonal affect:** 34
Winter mildness: 2 **Hazard free:** 12

	87
	102
	176
90°	3
32°	181
0°	44
	24
	63
	33

	High °F	Low °F	Hum %	Wind mph	Precip inches	Snow inches
JAN	21	-1	72	11.0	1.1	10.6
FEB	26	2	69	10.6	0.8	8.3
MAR	38	15	64	10.9	1.5	9.0
APR	53	29	55	11.3	2.4	2.0
MAY	67	41	50	10.2	3.2	0
JUN	75	50	55	9.2	3.8	0
JUL	80	56	54	8.2	3.4	0
AUG	77	53	60	8.0	4.3	0
SEP	67	45	63	9.0	4.3	0
OCT	55	35	65	9.9	2.6	0
NOV	39	22	73	11.0	1.9	4.0
DEC	25	6	77	10.7	1.4	11.1

East End Long Island, NY Rank: 148

Location: 40.58 N and 72.11 W at 55 feet, at the extreme tip of Long Island. New York City is 120 miles west.

Landscape: Irregular plains. The eastern end of Long Island, where the Atlantic Ocean meets Long Island Sound, is divided into two narrow peninsulas by four bays. The surrounding land is suburban and agricultural. Small understory trees and shrubs make up the lower growth of the woodlands. Common specimen trees are oak, beech, birch, hickory, tulip tree, and sweet chestnut.

Climate: Hot continental, with fewer seasonal and daily temperature fluctuations where tempered by the effects of the surrounding salt water. Precipitation is distributed throughout the year. Summers have hot and humid stretches but are generally warm and dry. Winters can be cold with icy rain. Snowfall is light and lasts but a little while. Frost extends from October 21 to April 27, leaving a modest growing season.

Summer mildness: 64 **Seasonal affect:** 33
Winter mildness: 25 **Hazard free:** 35

	100
	118
	148
90°	7
32°	121
0°	2
	39
	74
	28

	High °F	Low °F	Hum %	Wind mph	Precip inches	Snow inches
JAN	39	21	62	9.7	3.9	7.2
FEB	40	22	61	10.1	3.7	4.4
MAR	49	30	56	10.5	4.2	3.4
APR	59	38	56	10.0	4.3	0
MAY	69	47	58	9.0	4.0	0
JUN	78	57	58	8.5	4.0	0
JUL	83	63	62	7.5	3.5	0
AUG	82	62	61	7.4	4.3	0
SEP	76	55	61	7.5	3.4	0
OCT	65	44	59	8.3	3.6	0
NOV	55	36	60	9.9	4.4	1.0
DEC	43	26	58	9.4	4.3	3.9

Easton–St. Michaels, MD Rank: 127

Location: 38.46 N and 76.04 W at 38 feet in the tidewater region along the eastern shore of Chesapeake Bay near the head of the Tred Avon River. Baltimore is 55 miles northwest by bridge.

Landscape: Flat plains. There's precious little relief in the long, low hills cut by streams and inlets from the Bay. Inland, the land is developed agricultural fields. The native vegetation is a typical southeastern mixed forest with broadleaf deciduous and needleleaf evergreen trees. In the towns are holly and magnolias.

Climate: Subtropical with a definite marine influence. Summers are hot and humid though often lifted somewhat by a bay breeze. Some winters can be freezing and snowy but normally are chilly and rainy. The first frost rolls in at the end of October, and the last one appears 3 weeks into spring. Snow is minimal and is quickly gone.

Summer mildness: 59 **Seasonal affect:** 40
Winter mildness: 35 **Hazard free:** 42

	107
	108
	150
90°	27
32°	85
0°	0
	26
	73
	28

	High °F	Low °F	Hum %	Wind mph	Precip inches	Snow inches
JAN	43	26	57	9.7	3.6	4.5
FEB	46	28	54	10.3	3.2	5.3
MAR	56	36	50	10.9	3.9	2.6
APR	66	44	49	10.6	3.3	0
MAY	76	54	53	9.2	4.1	0
JUN	84	63	52	8.5	3.5	0
JUL	88	67	52	8.0	4.4	0
AUG	86	66	56	7.8	4.5	0
SEP	81	60	55	8.0	3.4	0
OCT	70	48	55	8.7	3.0	0
NOV	60	40	55	9.3	3.4	0
DEC	49	31	57	9.3	3.6	2.0

★ = in the top 30 places for climate mildness

East Stroudsburg, PA — Rank: 181

Location: 41.05 N and 75.10 W at 520 feet at the foot of Pennsylvania's Pocono Mountains. The Delaware River is just east and on the opposite bank is New Jersey.

Landscape: Low mountains. There is a winter deciduous forest dominated by tall broadleaf trees that provide a dense, continuous canopy in summer and shed their leaves completely in winter. Lower layers of small trees and shrubs develop weakly. In spring, a luxuriant ground cover of herbs quickly develops.

Climate: The continental climatic regime here ensures a strong annual temperature cycle, with cold winters and warm summers. Average annual temperatures range from 40°F to 60°F. There is year-round precipitation, averaging from 35 to 60 inches per year. The first frost arrives September 30 and the last frost departs May 13.

Summer mildness: 47	Seasonal affect: 22
Winter mildness: 27	Hazard free: 25

	93
	111
	161
90°	15
32°	123
0°	1
	187
	70
	28

	High °F	Low °F	Hum %	Wind mph	Precip inches	Snow inches
JAN	34	34	58	10.7	3.2	8.4
FEB	38	38	57	10.8	3.0	8.9
MAR	49	49	53	11.0	3.3	5.8
APR	60	60	49	10.5	3.5	0.7
MAY	71	71	49	8.8	4.2	0
JUN	80	80	55	8.1	3.8	0
JUL	85	85	55	7.6	4.1	0
AUG	82	82	57	7.6	4.3	0
SEP	75	75	59	8.1	3.9	0
OCT	64	64	59	8.9	2.9	0.1
NOV	52	52	60	9.9	3.9	1.3
DEC	39	39	62	10.4	3.5	6.1

Edenton, NC — Rank: 126

Location: 36.03 N and 76.36 W at 5 feet, on Albemarle Sound in North Carolina's northeast coastal area. Raleigh is 120 miles west and Virginia Beach, Virginia, is 65 miles north.

Landscape: Flat plains. At the mouth of the Chowan River on Albemarle Sound west of Kitty Hawk and the Barrier Islands. The woods are evergreens, oak, bald cypress, laurel, and magnolia mixed with loblolly and slash pine. The native undergrowth consists of typical coastal plain plants of fern, and other herbaceous plants, small palms, and shrubs.

Climate: Subtropical, with humid, hot, coastal plain summers. Winters are mild but with some freezing nights. Frost rolls in late around November 10 and leaves early by March 24. Snow is negligible, but rain falls throughout the year. Spring and summer can bring heavy thunderstorms, and occasional tropical storms from the Atlantic may reach this location.

Summer mildness: 43	Seasonal affect: 46
Winter mildness: 40	Hazard free: 48

	106
	107
	152
90°	31
32°	52
0°	0
	20
	73
	42

	High °F	Low °F	Hum %	Wind mph	Precip inches	Snow inches
JAN	52	32	60	12.1	4.2	1.7
FEB	55	34	58	12.3	3.8	2.2
MAR	63	41	56	12.0	4.0	1.1
APR	72	49	52	11.8	3.3	0
MAY	79	58	58	10.9	4.5	0
JUN	85	66	58	10.7	4.5	0
JUL	88	70	61	10.0	5.4	0
AUG	87	70	62	9.5	5.4	0
SEP	82	64	62	10.5	4.3	0
OCT	73	53	61	11.1	3.2	0
NOV	65	44	58	11.0	2.8	0
DEC	56	36	60	11.5	3.2	0.5

Eugene, OR — Rank: 99

Location: 44.00 N and 123.00 W at 370 feet at the southern end of the fertile Willamette Valley and bounded by mountain ranges. The Cascades lie to the east and the Coastal Ranges to the west. Portland is 110 miles north.

Landscape: High mountains. The valley widens and levels out to the north, while hills of the rolling, wooded Coastal Ranges begin about 5 miles west of the airport and rise to between 1,500 feet and 2,000 feet midway between the city and Pacific Ocean, 60 miles to the west. The Cascades, 75 miles east, reach heights of 10,000 feet.

Climate: Mild maritime climate. The sheltering ranges and the proximity of the ocean contribute to the extremely mild climate. Temperatures below 20°F occur only five times a year. The temperature rarely reaches the mid-90s. Seasonal change is gradual. The first frost arrives October 16 and the last frost departs May 17.

Summer mildness: 37	Seasonal affect: 3
Winter mildness: 82	Hazard free: 77

	75
	82
	209
90°	15
32°	54
0°	0
	137
	90
	2

	High °F	Low °F	Hum %	Wind mph	Precip inches	Snow inches
JAN	46	46	86	7.9	7.9	3.7
FEB	51	51	82	7.8	5.6	0.8
MAR	56	56	78	8.3	5.5	0.5
APR	61	61	75	7.8	3.1	0
MAY	67	67	73	7.4	2.2	0
JUN	74	74	70	7.5	1.4	0
JUL	82	82	63	8.0	0.5	0
AUG	82	82	64	7.6	1.1	0
SEP	76	76	66	7.4	1.7	0
OCT	65	65	78	6.7	3.4	0
NOV	52	52	86	7.4	8.3	0.3
DEC	46	46	89	7.6	8.6	1.3

★ = in the top 30 places for climate mildness

Eureka Springs, AR   Rank: 145

Location: 36.23 N and 93.44 W at 1,420 feet in the Ozark Mountains near the Arkansas and Missouri border, 33 miles northeast of Fayetteville.

Landscape: High hills. Encircled by two great lakes and two scenic rivers. The country is rugged and wooded, with farms small and scattered. A dense deciduous forest of oak and hickory surrounds the area. In spring, a luxurious low layer of herbs develops, but this is arrested when the trees leaf out and shade the ground.

Climate: Hot continental, with warm summers due to the elevation and mild winters thanks to the latitude. Summer can vary from warm and humid maritime to dry continental. Winter occasionally produces dangerous ice storms. The first frost arrives October 25 and the last frost departs April 12.

Summer mildness: 42   **Seasonal affect:** 59
Winter mildness: 27   **Hazard free:** 33

	127
	103
	136
90°	56
32°	105
0°	1
	92
	62
	50

	High °F	Low °F	Hum %	Wind mph	Precip inches	Snow inches
JAN	46	23	60	10.3	2.0	3.0
FEB	51	27	60	10.8	2.8	3.9
MAR	61	37	56	12.1	4.1	2.4
APR	72	47	55	11.9	4.2	0
MAY	78	55	59	10.6	4.9	0
JUN	85	63	59	10.0	4.4	0
JUL	91	68	56	9.4	3.3	0
AUG	90	66	54	8.9	3.8	0
SEP	82	59	58	9.1	4.1	0
OCT	72	47	54	9.7	3.7	0
NOV	60	37	59	10.3	3.8	1.0
DEC	49	28	63	10.2	3.4	1.0

Fairhope–Gulf Shores, AL   Rank: 110

Location: 30.31 N and 87.54 W at 122 feet, 35 miles south of Mobile on the Gulf of Mexico near the entrance to Mobile Bay.

Landscape: Irregular plains. Gulf coastal plain where ecologies appear to be flat plains, but contain coastal lagoons, sandy beaches, swampy lowlands, and salt marshes to typical southern forests of loblolly, shortleaf, and pond pines, with some sweet gum and oaks. Local relief ranges from sea level to less than 250 feet inland.

Climate: Subtropical. Although destructive hurricanes from the West Indies and the Gulf of Mexico are extremely infrequent, this seems due more to chance than to location. The normal annual rainfall amount is one of the highest in the continental United States. It's evenly distributed throughout the year, with a slight maximum at the height of the summer thunderstorm season. First frost arrives by Thanksgiving; last frost departs February 25. This means a long growing season, enough for citrus.

Summer mildness: 23   **Seasonal affect:** 34
Winter mildness: 67   **Hazard free:** 67

	103
	116
	146
90°	74
32°	21
0°	0
	41
	80
	74

	High °F	Low °F	Hum %	Wind mph	Precip inches	Snow inches
JAN	59	39	61	10.4	5.0	0.1
FEB	63	41	56	10.7	6.1	0.2
MAR	70	49	55	10.9	6.1	0
APR	77	56	52	10.2	4.1	0
MAY	83	63	54	8.9	5.4	0
JUN	89	70	55	7.7	6.6	0
JUL	90	72	60	7.0	7.3	0
AUG	89	72	61	6.8	6.7	0
SEP	87	68	59	7.9	5.7	0
OCT	79	56	52	8.2	3.2	0
NOV	70	49	57	9.3	4.2	0
DEC	62	42	61	10.1	4.9	0

Fairplay, CO   Rank: 163

Location: 39.00 N and 106.00 W at 10,010 feet. This is one of the highest incorporated places in the United States. It sits at the northern end of Colorado's South Park, a huge grassland basin.

Landscape: High mountains. Directly below town is the subalpine zone dominated by Engelmann spruce and sub-alpine fir. Farther below, tall ponderosa pine predominates on lower, drier, more exposed slopes, and taller Douglas fir predominates in higher, moister, more sheltered areas.

Climate: Temperate semiarid steppe regime with average annual temperatures ranging from 35°F to 45°F in most of the region, but reaching 50°F in the lower valleys. Spring and fall are short transitions. Summer is ideal. Winter is long, snowy, and cold, and is influenced by prevailing west winds and the general north–south orientation of the mountain ranges. The first frost arrives September 18 and the last frost departs June 1.

Summer mildness: 100   **Seasonal affect:** 45
Winter mildness: 2   **Hazard free:** 1

	113
	113
	139
90°	0
32°	212
0°	30
	10
	81
	31

	High °F	Low °F	Hum %	Wind mph	Precip inches	Snow inches
JAN	27	-1	71	11.5	1.4	23.0
FEB	31	1	61	10.7	1.2	14.0
MAR	34	8	50	11.1	1.6	11.0
APR	44	17	43	11.0	1.5	4.0
MAY	55	25	40	9.7	1.6	1.0
JUN	65	33	32	8.9	1.6	0
JUL	73	37	35	8.2	2.7	0
AUG	71	37	38	7.9	2.5	0
SEP	63	30	39	8.3	1.5	1.0
OCT	52	21	46	9.4	1.2	2.0
NOV	38	10	59	10.5	1.3	8.0
DEC	30	3	69	10.7	1.5	16.0

★ = *in the top 30 places for climate mildness*

Fayetteville, AR — Rank: 151

Location: 36.03 N and 94.09 W at 1,334 feet, in northwest Arkansas, 30 miles from the Oklahoma line and 40 miles south of Missouri. Little Rock is 170 miles southeast.

Landscape: High hills. On the White River in the Boston Mountains. Elevations near here reach over 2,000 feet in the highest parts of the Ozark Plateau. This is rugged, wooded mountain country. Broadleaf deciduous oak and hickory predominate, with lower layers of scattered small trees and shrubs, especially redbud and dogwood.

Climate: Modified continental, with hot, humid summers and briefer winters than other locations at this latitude. Winter to winter can vary from warm and humid maritime to cold and dry continental but are relatively free from climatic extremes. Mid-October sees the first frost, and late April marks the last frost. Snowfalls are minimal, but precipitation in January and February can be dangerous icy rain.

Summer mildness: 49 **Seasonal affect:** 56
Winter mildness: 23 **Hazard free:** 29

| | 116 |
| 97 |
| 153 |
90°	44
32°	103
0°	1
	20
	66
	56

	High °F	Low °F	Hum %	Wind mph	Precip inches	Snow inches
JAN	45	23	60	11.7	1.8	3.0
FEB	50	27	60	11.9	2.5	3.9
MAR	59	37	56	12.9	3.9	2.4
APR	69	47	55	12.2	4.3	0
MAY	76	55	59	10.4	5.0	0
JUN	84	63	59	9.6	5.0	0
JUL	89	68	56	8.5	2.9	0
AUG	88	66	54	8.6	3.6	0
SEP	81	59	58	9.3	4.5	0
OCT	71	47	54	10.1	3.8	0
NOV	59	37	59	11.3	3.7	1.0
DEC	49	28	63	11.6	3.1	1.4

Flagstaff, AZ — Rank: 80

Location: 35.08 N and 111.40 W, at 7,000 feet in north-central Arizona, 80 miles south of the Grand Canyon and 120 miles north-northeast of Phoenix.

Landscape: Tablelands, with very high relief. Part the Colorado Plateau, a series of generally level plateaus mostly separated by steep-sided chasms. There is little arable land. Near here is Arizona's highest point, 12,633-foot Humphreys Peak in the San Francisco Mountains. The city sits on the northern border of the Prescott National Forest.

Climate: Vigorous, with cool to cold winters and with warm summers. Frost arrives by October 21 and departs May 14. Flagstaff gets about 23 inches of precipitation yearly, and the surrounding mountains and plateaus receive somewhat more moisture, 20 to 40 inches, with up to 5 feet of snow falling in peak areas.

Summer mildness: 96 **Seasonal affect:** 84
Winter mildness: 35 **Hazard free:** 2

| | 162 |
| 102 |
| 101 |
90°	1
32°	210
0°	8
	12
	39
	38

	High °F	Low °F	Hum %	Wind mph	Precip inches	Snow inches
JAN	42	15	63	6.8	2.0	20.7
FEB	45	18	60	6.7	2.1	18.3
MAR	49	21	57	7.2	2.6	22.3
APR	58	27	49	7.6	1.5	9.5
MAY	67	33	46	7.3	0.7	1.8
JUN	78	41	38	6.9	0.4	0
JUL	82	51	53	5.5	2.8	0
AUG	79	49	60	5.1	2.8	0
SEP	73	41	55	5.7	2.0	0.1
OCT	63	31	54	5.8	1.6	2.0
NOV	51	22	57	6.8	2.0	10.2
DEC	43	16	62	6.7	2.4	15.9

Fort Collins–Loveland, CO — Rank: 115

Location: 40.35 N and 105.05 W at 5,003 feet, on the Cache la Poudre River in the eastern foothills of the Rockies' Front Range, 55 miles north of Denver.

Landscape: High mountains. Lies near some of the most spectacular mountain terrain in the country. Steep cliffs, high waterfalls, and forested mountain slopes cut by swift rivers are found to the west. Thirty miles east, the landscape settles into grassland prairies of the Great Plains.

Climate: Near the center of the continent, Fort Collins and Loveland are removed from any major source of airborne moisture and are further shielded from rainfall by the high Rockies to the west. In winter, cold air from Canada may bring snow and subfreezing temperatures at night. Frost arrives October 1 and departs by early May. In summer, hot air from the desert southwest brings daytime temperatures of 90°F. However, felt heat is low because of dryness.

Summer mildness: 81 **Seasonal affect:** 82
Winter mildness: 18 **Hazard free:** 6

| | 115 |
| 130 |
| 120 |
90°	22
32°	167
0°	11
	10
	33
	42

	High °F	Low °F	Hum %	Wind mph	Precip inches	Snow inches
JAN	41	14	46	8.7	0.4	7.3
FEB	46	19	44	8.9	0.4	6.3
MAR	52	25	41	9.7	1.4	12.0
APR	61	34	38	10.1	1.8	6.0
MAY	70	43	38	9.4	2.7	1.0
JUN	80	52	37	8.9	1.9	0
JUL	86	57	35	8.3	1.8	0
AUG	83	55	35	8.0	1.3	0
SEP	75	46	35	8.0	1.3	0
OCT	64	35	37	7.9	1.0	2.0
NOV	51	24	45	8.3	0.7	6.0
DEC	42	16	46	8.5	0.5	6.7

★ = in the top 30 places for climate mildness

★ **Fort Myers–Cape Coral, FL** Rank: 20

Location: 26.38 N and 81.52 W at 10 feet, on the broad Caloosahatchee River in southwestern Florida, 120 miles south of Tampa.

Landscape: Flat plains. This area is the western terminus of the Okeechobee Waterway, linking the Atlantic Ocean and the Gulf of Mexico, about 15 miles away. The land is level and low. The climax growth of the coastal plain in this area north of the Everglades is evergreen-oak and magnolia. Spanish moss trails from Evangeline oak and bald cypress. Tree ferns, small palms, and shrubs make up the lower layer.

Climate: Subtropical. Summer and winter temperature extremes are checked by the influence of the Gulf. Mild winters have many bright, warm days. Nights are moderately cool. Rainfall averages more than 50 inches annually, two-thirds of this coming daily between June and September. Most rain falls as late-afternoon or early-evening thunderstorms, bringing relief from the heat.

Summer mildness: 11	**Seasonal affect:** 73	
Winter mildness: 97	**Hazard free:** 88	

	100
	168
	98
90°	101
32°	0
0°	0
	21
	72
	93

	High °F	Low °F	Hum %	Wind mph	Precip inches	Snow inches
JAN	74	53	57	8.4	1.8	0
FEB	75	54	55	9.0	2.2	0
MAR	80	59	52	9.4	3.1	0
APR	84	62	47	8.9	1.1	0
MAY	89	68	50	8.1	3.9	0
JUN	90	73	58	7.3	9.5	0
JUL	91	75	59	6.7	8.3	0
AUG	91	75	60	6.8	9.7	0
SEP	90	74	61	7.6	7.8	0
OCT	86	69	56	8.5	2.9	0
NOV	81	61	56	8.2	1.6	0
DEC	76	55	56	8.0	1.5	0

Fredericksburg, TX Rank: 66

Location: 30.16 N and 98.52 W at 1,702 feet, on the Pedernales River in central Texas. Austin is 80 miles east and San Antonio is 80 miles southeast.

Landscape: Plains with high hills. In a high, green valley where a transition from rich Blacklands to Edwards Plateau foothills occurs. Encircled by hills with outcroppings of a large, dissected plateau, formed of thick layers of limestone and other sedimentary rocks lifted about 2,000 feet along the Balcones Escarpment. Erosion carved the uplifted areas into hilly, rocky terrain. Among the peach orchards and many wineries are native vegetation stands of cedar, juniper, oak, and prairie grasses.

Climate: Prairie. Summer days are hot but nights pleasantly cool. Winters are mild with few, brief cold spells. Fall arrives around mid-October though the first frost waits until November 11. The last frost leaves March 24. Snow is negligible. Rainfall is distributed evenly throughout the year. Humidity is generally comfortable.

Summer mildness: 34	**Seasonal affect:** 77	
Winter mildness: 56	**Hazard free:** 64	

	117
	115
	134
90°	97
32°	39
0°	0
	23
	43
	41

	High °F	Low °F	Hum %	Wind mph	Precip inches	Snow inches
JAN	60	35	60	9.7	1.3	0.2
FEB	64	39	59	10.2	1.8	0.7
MAR	72	47	56	10.8	1.4	0.1
APR	79	55	57	10.5	2.5	0
MAY	84	62	60	9.6	4.2	0
JUN	89	67	56	9.1	3.6	0
JUL	93	69	51	8.3	2.2	0
AUG	93	68	50	7.9	2.7	0
SEP	87	64	55	7.9	3.6	0
OCT	79	55	55	8.1	3.6	0
NOV	69	46	58	9.0	1.9	0
DEC	62	38	59	9.2	1.3	0.1

Fredericksburg–Spotsylvania, VA Rank: 138

Location: 38.18 N and 77.27 W at 60 feet, 42 miles south of Washington, D.C., and 40 miles north of Richmond.

Landscape: Irregular plains. Rolling hill country at the head of navigation of the Rappahannock River in northeastern Virginia. The woods are a southeastern mixed forest of medium-tall to tall broadleaf deciduous oak, hickory, sweet gum, red maple, and winged elm, together with loblolly and shortleaf pine. The undergrowth is dogwood, viburnum, blueberry, youpon, and numerous woody vines.

Climate: Modified continental, with cool winters and warm, humid summers. The Blue Ridge Mountains west of here produce steering and blocking effects on storms and air masses. Chesapeake Bay further modifies the climate, making it warmer in winter and cooler in summer. The first frost rolls in on October 15, and the last frost departs April 21. Precipitation is well distributed throughout the year.

Summer mildness: 39	**Seasonal affect:** 54	
Winter mildness: 42	**Hazard free:** 34	

	113
	107
	145
90°	49
32°	112
0°	1
	23
	72
	40

	High °F	Low °F	Hum %	Wind mph	Precip inches	Snow inches
JAN	44	22	60	9.5	3.1	6.2
FEB	47	23	58	9.7	2.9	4.9
MAR	58	33	56	10.1	3.6	3.7
APR	68	41	52	9.8	3.1	0
MAY	77	51	58	7.9	3.9	0
JUN	85	60	58	6.9	3.4	0
JUL	89	65	61	6.5	3.7	0
AUG	87	63	62	6.1	3.6	0
SEP	81	56	62	6.1	3.5	0
OCT	70	43	61	6.9	3.4	0
NOV	59	34	58	8.3	3.4	0
DEC	48	26	60	8.8	3.3	2.1

★ = in the top 30 places for climate mildness

Front Royal, VA — Rank: 179

Location: 38.55 N and 78.10 W at 680 feet in northern Virginia at the north end of Skyline Drive, an extension of the Blue Ridge Parkway through Shenandoah National Park. Washington, D.C., is 60 miles east.

Landscape: Open low mountains. Terrain varies from rolling hills to rugged in the mountains visible to the west. Tall, broadleaf trees that provide a continuous dense canopy in summer dominate the surrounding forest.

Climate: Warm continental, with mild winters and warm, humid summers. The mountains provide steering, blocking, and modifying effects on storms and air masses. All seasons are pleasant for this latitude. Summer, especially July, can be hot. The first frost arrives October 17 and the last frost departs April 19.

Summer mildness: 70   **Seasonal affect:** 12
Winter mildness: 18   **Hazard free:** 23

	58
	103
	204
90°	8
32°	134
0°	9
	178
	71
	35

	High °F	Low °F	Hum %	Wind mph	Precip inches	Snow inches
JAN	34	23	55	10.6	2.4	10.1
FEB	37	26	53	10.5	2.4	8.7
MAR	49	35	51	10.7	3.4	5.1
APR	60	43	50	10.3	3.8	0.9
MAY	71	52	55	8.9	4.1	0
JUN	79	60	56	8.0	4.1	0
JUL	83	64	58	7.3	4.3	0
AUG	81	63	59	6.9	3.9	0
SEP	74	57	59	7.4	3.3	0
OCT	63	44	55	8.4	2.8	0.2
NOV	50	36	55	9.8	3.5	2.2
DEC	39	28	57	10.4	3.0	5.1

Gainesville, FL — Rank: 48

Location: 29.39 N and 82.19 W at 147 feet, in north-central Florida. Jacksonville is 65 miles northeast.

Landscape: Flat plains and some rolling ranch and farm country, with some geological relief in limestone sinkholes and caverns. Native trees are longleaf and slash pines. Gallberry, saw palmetto, and fetterbush make up the undergrowth. Plants normally found in ravines of the Appalachian Mountains are at home here. There are lakes and wetlands in the county.

Climate: Subtropical, with a small annual range of temperature change. Humid, hot summer afternoons are cooled by frequent heavy thunderstorms or cool breezes from the Gulf. Winters tend to be dry and mild, with warm days and cool nights. First frost comes as late as November 27, with the last frost as early as March 3 yielding a long growing season. Measurable snowfalls are rare.

Summer mildness: 14   **Seasonal affect:** 57
Winter mildness: 97   **Hazard free:** 78

	92
	148
	125
90°	99
32°	18
0°	0
	42
	75
	81

	High °F	Low °F	Hum %	Wind mph	Precip inches	Snow inches
JAN	66	43	61	6.9	3.4	0.1
FEB	68	44	57	7.3	4.2	0
MAR	75	51	55	7.4	3.7	0
APR	81	56	50	7.0	2.6	0
MAY	86	63	50	6.7	3.8	0
JUN	90	68	59	5.9	6.8	0
JUL	91	71	63	5.6	6.8	0
AUG	90	71	65	5.3	8.0	0
SEP	87	69	65	5.9	5.3	0
OCT	81	60	62	6.6	1.8	0
NOV	74	51	63	6.2	2.3	0
DEC	68	45	62	5.9	3.3	0

Georgetown, TX — Rank: 74

Location: 30.16 N and 97.44 W at 501 feet, on the Balcones Escarpment separating the Texas hill country from the blackland prairies of East Texas. Austin is 20 miles south.

Landscape: Tablelands, moderate relief. Low hills and wide terraces intermingle, supporting a variety of native vegetation, including oak, cedar, walnut, pecan, and mesquite. It varies with some stretches of grasslands, others of cliffs and bluffs. Located on the San Gabriel River, with nearby Lake Georgetown, impounded in 1980, providing a typical highland reservoir.

Climate: Prairie. Summers are hot and humid, though evenings can be cool. Winters are mild, only occasionally reaching below-freezing temperatures. November 25 brings the first frost, while the last frost leaves March 7. Late spring and early fall bring peak precipitation and thunderstorm activity. Winds are predominantly southerly, with occasional strong and cool northerlies. Snowfall is virtually nonexistent.

Summer mildness: 21   **Seasonal affect:** 75
Winter mildness: 58   **Hazard free:** 69

	117
	115
	134
90°	106
32°	30
0°	0
	23
	46
	41

	High °F	Low °F	Hum %	Wind mph	Precip inches	Snow inches
JAN	56	35	60	9.7	1.9	0.5
FEB	61	38	59	10.2	2.7	0.3
MAR	70	46	56	10.8	2.5	0
APR	78	55	57	10.5	2.9	0
MAY	84	63	60	9.6	4.6	0
JUN	91	70	56	9.1	3.6	0
JUL	95	73	51	8.3	2.0	0
AUG	96	73	50	7.9	2.3	0
SEP	89	67	55	7.9	3.8	0
OCT	80	57	55	8.1	3.3	0
NOV	69	46	58	9.0	2.9	0
DEC	60	38	59	9.2	2.3	0

★ = in the top 30 places for climate mildness

Grand Junction, CO — Rank: 94

Location: 39.04 N and 108.33 W at 4,597 feet, in the Grand Valley of western Colorado. Denver is 250 miles east and the Utah border 20 miles west.

Landscape: Open high mountains. Near to lake-studded Grand Mesa, the Colorado National Monument, and Uncompahgre National Forest. Sagebrush and prickly pear cactus are found in the canyons. Pine, spruce, and aspen forests cover the subalpine areas.

Climate: The interior location, coupled with the ring of high mountains, results in low rainfall. Winter snows are frequent and light and don't remain long. First frost arrives in late September and the last frost is gone by mid-May. Low summer humidity makes the region as dry as parts of Arizona. Sunny days predominate in all seasons. The city's climate is marked by wide seasonal temperature changes. The surrounding mountains protect from sudden and severe weather changes.

Summer mildness: 65 **Seasonal affect:** 84
Winter mildness: 21 **Hazard free:** 32

	137
	107
	121
90°	67
32°	174
0°	9
	8
	24
	35

	High °F	Low °F	Hum %	Wind mph	Precip inches	Snow inches
JAN	36	10	64	5.6	0.6	7.4
FEB	46	18	53	6.7	0.5	4.2
MAR	55	26	43	8.4	0.9	4.0
APR	65	33	34	9.5	0.7	1.0
MAY	76	43	31	9.6	0.9	0
JUN	87	50	25	9.7	0.5	0
JUL	92	57	29	9.3	0.8	0
AUG	90	55	31	9.0	0.9	0
SEP	81	45	33	8.9	0.8	0
OCT	69	34	39	7.9	0.9	0
NOV	52	23	50	6.7	0.7	2.0
DEC	40	14	61	5.9	0.7	5.3

Grants Pass, OR — Rank: 35

Location: 42.26 N and 123.19 W at 948 feet, on the Rogue River in southwestern Oregon. Eugene is 120 miles north and Medford 20 miles east. California is 60 miles south.

Landscape: High mountains. This is the rugged terrain of the foothills of the Siskiyous. The Rogue River is swift white water here. Southwest is the "Redwood Highway" and the Illinois Valley. The common trees in the dense Pacific conifer forest are Douglas fir, western red cedar, western hemlock, silver fir, and Sitka spruce.

Climate: Generally mild highland. The moderate temperatures of the Pacific are altered somewhat by the Coast Range bringing a reputation of "Sun Belt" of southern Oregon. Nights are always cool, as are the days but for a brief period between July and August. Winter is the rainy season. Summers are dry. The first frost delays until October 20; last frost bides until April 30.

Summer mildness: 69 **Seasonal affect:** 30
Winter mildness: 78 **Hazard free:** 80

	117
	79
	169
90°	53
32°	68
0°	0
	50
	62
	8

	High °F	Low °F	Hum %	Wind mph	Precip inches	Snow inches
JAN	48	33	83	4.1	5.2	2.4
FEB	55	34	77	4.5	3.8	0.7
MAR	61	36	66	5.3	3.5	0.7
APR	67	38	57	5.7	1.8	0
MAY	75	44	50	5.7	1.2	0
JUN	83	50	42	5.9	0.5	0
JUL	90	53	38	5.8	0.2	0
AUG	90	53	39	5.3	0.5	0
SEP	83	47	42	4.5	0.9	0
OCT	70	41	58	3.7	2.4	0
NOV	54	38	80	3.6	5.3	0
DEC	46	34	85	3.6	5.7	1.5

Grass Valley–Nevada City, CA — Rank: 51

Location: 39.15 N and 121.01 W at 2,519 feet, on the western slope of the Sierra Nevadas, 60 miles northeast of Sacramento.

Landscape: High mountains. In a long, steeply sloping mountainous region. The Sacramento Valley to the west softens the terrain somewhat. The transition zone between grassland and Sierran forest is found here. Conifers and shrubs cover the slopes, and at higher elevations, digger pine and blue oak form open stands. At 4,000 to 6,000 feet, the most important trees are western yellow pine, Douglas fir, sugar pine, white fir, and incense cedar.

Climate: Mediterranean, characterized by winter rainfall and dry summers. The higher elevation of the Sierra foothills tempers the summer heat. Winters are milder than at other locations on the eastern slope of the Sierras. There are frequent freezing temperatures at night as well as an occasional blizzard. Mid-October heralds the first frost and the last frost departs May 17.

Summer mildness: 73 **Seasonal affect:** 70
Winter mildness: 48 **Hazard free:** 51

	189
	75
	100
90°	39
32°	117
0°	0
	34
	59
	14

	High °F	Low °F	Hum %	Wind mph	Precip inches	Snow inches
JAN	50	30	80	7.2	10.3	6.5
FEB	53	31	75	7.6	8.8	3.5
MAR	56	33	65	8.6	8.4	4.0
APR	62	37	55	8.7	4.2	0
MAY	71	42	48	9.2	1.5	0
JUN	80	49	44	9.7	0.5	0
JUL	88	53	44	9.0	0.2	0
AUG	87	52	45	8.6	0.3	0
SEP	80	47	45	7.5	1.1	0
OCT	70	41	53	6.4	3.3	0
NOV	56	35	65	6.0	8.7	0
DEC	50	30	77	6.6	8.8	2.7

★ = in the top 30 places for climate mildness

Hamilton–Bitterroot Valley, MT   Rank: 97

Location: 46.14 N and 114.09 W at 3,572 feet on the Bitterroot River in extreme western Montana. Missoula is at the head of the valley, 45 miles north.

Landscape: High mountains. The valley of rolling subalpine woodland is 25 miles wide and 96 miles long. Surrounding is the open parkland of the high valley, and the lakes and high, glaciated peaks of the Bitterroot Mountains. Conditions are good for prairie shortgrasses. Scattered shrubs and low trees give way to forests of ponderosa pine, piñon juniper, and Douglas fir.

Climate: Semiarid steppe, with most precipitation falling as snow in winter from October to May. With the variety of elevation and bodies of water, there are many microclimates in the Valley. Snow is especially heavy in the higher altitudes. Winters are cold and long with the first frost arriving September 20 and the last frost not leaving until May 24. Summers are hot, dry, clear, and all too brief.

Summer mildness: 90	**Seasonal affect:** 43
Winter mildness: 37	**Hazard free:** 30

Icon values: 75, 82, 208, 90° 17, 32° 170, 0° 10, 27, 37, 24

	High °F	Low °F	Hum %	Wind mph	Precip inches	Snow inches
JAN	34	16	79	5.2	1.3	12.5
FEB	41	21	76	5.7	0.8	6.2
MAR	48	25	65	6.7	0.8	8.1
APR	57	31	52	7.6	1.0	3.0
MAY	66	38	51	7.3	1.7	0
JUN	74	45	52	7.1	1.6	0
JUL	83	49	42	6.9	0.9	0
AUG	81	47	46	6.6	1.2	0
SEP	70	39	54	6.0	1.2	0
OCT	59	31	65	5.0	0.8	0
NOV	43	23	77	5.1	1.0	4.0
DEC	34	17	81	4.8	1.1	9.5

Hampshire County, WV   Rank: 176

Location: The weather station is Romney, the county seat. The town sits at 39.20 N and 78.45 W, at 830 feet in the eastern Panhandle section of West Virginia in the midst of 2,500-foot mountains.

Landscape: Open low mountains. The slopes are covered by a deciduous forest dominated by tall broadleaf trees that provide a dense, continuous canopy in summer but are completely bare in winter. Lower layers of small trees and shrubs develop weakly. In spring, a luxuriant ground cover of herbs quickly develops.

Climate: The continental climatic regime here ensures a strong annual temperature cycle, with cold winters and warm summers. Average annual temperatures range from 40°F to 60°F. There is year-round precipitation, averaging from 35 to 60 inches per year. The first frost arrives October 10 and the last frost departs May 5.

Summer mildness: 44	**Seasonal affect:** 4
Winter mildness: 46	**Hazard free:** 31

Icon values: 63, 99, 203, 90° 15, 32° 108, 0° 2, 178, 91, 39

	High °F	Low °F	Hum %	Wind mph	Precip inches	Snow inches
JAN	39	18	71	8.6	2.2	8.7
FEB	43	20	69	8.6	2.1	4.9
MAR	54	29	66	9.1	2.9	3.0
APR	64	38	63	9.0	2.9	0.3
MAY	75	47	70	7.5	3.4	0
JUN	83	56	73	6.9	3.3	0
JUL	86	61	75	6.5	3.7	0
AUG	85	59	76	6.3	3.2	0
SEP	78	52	76	6.9	3.0	0
OCT	67	40	71	7.3	2.8	0
NOV	55	32	70	7.9	2.7	1.8
DEC	43	24	72	7.9	2.3	3.6

Hanover, NH   Rank: 180

Location: 43.42 N and 72.17 W at 531 feet, on the Connecticut River in western New Hampshire. Boston, Massachusetts, is 135 miles southeast.

Landscape: Low mountains. The Green Mountains of Vermont lie west and the White Mountains lie northeast of this upper Connecticut River Valley location. Low hills flank the river. The surrounding forest is mixed conifer and deciduous, with northern white pine, eastern hemlock, maple, oak, and beech.

Climate: Northerly latitude assures the variety and vigor of a true New England climate. The summer, while not long, is pleasant. Fall is cool and clear and runs through October. First frost comes September 30 and the last frost delays until May 17. Winters are cold, with brief, intense cold snaps formed by high-pressure systems moving down from central Canada and Hudson Bay. Snows are deep and long lasting. Spring is called breakup, or mud season.

Summer mildness: 82	**Seasonal affect:** 12
Winter mildness: 14	**Hazard free:** 12

Icon values: 91, 110, 164, 90° 7, 32° 167, 0° 23, 50, 75, 20

	High °F	Low °F	Hum %	Wind mph	Precip inches	Snow inches
JAN	28	7	58	9.0	2.5	18.7
FEB	33	10	57	9.4	2.4	17.9
MAR	43	21	53	9.9	2.7	13.7
APR	56	32	49	10.0	2.9	3.0
MAY	70	43	49	8.9	3.6	0
JUN	78	52	55	8.1	3.3	0
JUL	83	57	55	7.5	3.3	0
AUG	80	56	57	7.2	3.6	0
SEP	71	48	59	7.3	3.3	0
OCT	59	37	59	7.8	3.3	0
NOV	45	28	60	8.5	3.5	5.0
DEC	32	15	62	8.7	3.1	18.5

★ = *in the top 30 places for climate mildness*

Hattiesburg, MS   Rank: 122

Location: 31.1937 N and 89.1725 W at 161 feet in southern Mississippi, 70 miles north of Biloxi and the Gulf of Mexico. Jackson is 90 miles northwest.

Landscape: Irregular plains. This is the Piney Woods section of the Gulf Coastal Plain—a wide belt of longleaf yellow pine that covers southern Mississippi to within a few miles of the coastal-plain grasslands. The DeSoto National Forest lies to the south, southeast, and northeast. Slash and loblolly pine mix with dogwoods along the sloping plains. Marshes, lakes, and swamps are common. The soil is sandstone and clay.

Climate: Subtropical. Hattiesburg averages 60 to 70 inches of rain a year. Thunderstorms are frequent in summer, and hurricanes are a threat from late summer to early autumn. Summers are hot and humid, while winters are mild with negligible amounts of snow and sleet. November 8 will bring the first frost, and March 17 will usher out the last frost.

Summer mildness: 3	**Seasonal affect:** 26
Winter mildness: 84	**Hazard free:** 68

	111
	104
	150
90°	95
32°	44
0°	0
	195
	75
	68

	High °F	Low °F	Hum %	Wind mph	Precip inches	Snow inches
JAN	58	34	76	8.4	5.8	0.4
FEB	62	37	74	8.6	5.7	0.3
MAR	70	45	72	9.1	6.3	0
APR	78	54	73	8.5	4.8	0
MAY	84	61	74	7.3	5.2	0
JUN	90	68	74	6.4	4.2	0
JUL	92	71	77	5.9	5.5	0
AUG	92	70	77	5.6	5.2	0
SEP	88	65	76	6.4	3.6	0
OCT	79	52	73	6.5	3.2	0
NOV	70	44	74	7.6	4.8	0
DEC	62	38	76	8.3	6.3	0

★ Henderson, NV   Rank: 18

Location: 36.10 N and 115.08 W at 2,028 feet, just west of the Colorado River Valley. Las Vegas is 15 miles northwest.

Landscape: Plains with high mountains. Near the center of a broad desert valley surrounded by mountains from 2,000 to 10,000 feet higher than the valley floor. These mountains act as effective barriers to moisture-laden storms moving in from the Pacific Ocean. The thick-branched Joshua tree grows among creosote bushes and jumbled boulders in the Mohave Desert region.

Climate: Typical desert. Humidity is low with maximum temperatures at the 100°F level. Nearby mountains and Lake Mead contribute to relatively cool nights. Spring and fall are ideal, rarely interrupted by adverse weather conditions. Winters, too, are mild, with daytime averages of 60°F, clear skies, and warm sunshine. First frost is delayed until mid-December; last frost is seen February 17. There are very few overcast or rainy days.

Summer mildness: 28	**Seasonal affect:** 93
Winter mildness: 54	**Hazard free:** 96

	221
	79
	65
90°	123
32°	14
0°	0
	1
	13
	14

	High °F	Low °F	Hum %	Wind mph	Precip inches	Snow inches
JAN	55	39	35	7.5	0.6	1.0
FEB	62	43	30	8.6	0.6	0.1
MAR	68	46	25	10.3	0.7	0
APR	77	53	20	11.0	0.3	0
MAY	87	61	17	11.1	0.2	0
JUN	97	70	14	11.1	0.1	0
JUL	102	76	15	10.3	0.5	0
AUG	100	74	19	9.6	0.9	0
SEP	92	68	20	9.0	0.6	0
OCT	80	58	22	8.1	0.3	0
NOV	65	46	30	7.7	0.5	0
DEC	56	39	36	7.3	0.5	0.1

Hendersonville–East Flat Rock, NC   Rank: 128

Location: 35.19 N and 82.27 W at 2,146 feet, just above the South Carolina border in the western part of the state, 20 miles south of Asheville.

Landscape: Low mountains. The relief is mostly broken, mountainous, and rugged, with some very steep slopes and high waterfalls. The city lies in the midst of a large intermountain valley, with rolling to strongly rolling mountain meadows. The Appalachian oak forest includes the variety of deciduous trees common throughout, including birch, hickory, maple, ash, and sweet chestnut, with an understory of small trees and shrubs.

Climate: Warm continental, with considerable temperature differences between winter and summer. It is mild and pleasant from late spring to late fall, and summer nights are always cool even following hot afternoons. Winters are short, with light snowfalls. October 12 will bring in the first frost; April 26 will usher out the last.

Summer mildness: 56	**Seasonal affect:** 22
Winter mildness: 52	**Hazard free:** 46

	103
	113
	149
90°	11
32°	109
0°	0
	78
	82
	45

	High °F	Low °F	Hum %	Wind mph	Precip inches	Snow inches
JAN	48	25	59	9.7	3.9	3.2
FEB	51	28	56	9.6	4.5	3.6
MAR	60	35	53	9.4	5.7	2.8
APR	69	42	50	8.9	3.9	0
MAY	76	51	57	7.1	5.0	0
JUN	82	58	59	6.1	4.8	0
JUL	85	62	63	5.8	4.7	0
AUG	83	61	63	5.4	6.0	0
SEP	78	55	64	5.6	4.4	0
OCT	69	43	57	6.8	4.5	0
NOV	59	35	57	8.1	4.3	0
DEC	51	29	59	8.9	4.4	1.4

★ = in the top 30 places for climate mildness

Hilton Head Island, SC — Rank: 84

Location: 32.13 N and 80.45 W at 8 feet, in the Sea Islands, 45 miles south of Charleston.

Landscape: Flat plains. The land is low and flat, with elevations mostly under 25 feet. There are dozens of islands of various shapes and sizes, and on them are fresh and saltwater streams, inlets, rivers, and sounds. Hilton Head, with excellent beaches, is an exception to the usual swampy conditions of the islands. The interior forests are medium to tall stands of mixed loblolly and shortleaf pines, plus deciduous oak, hickory, red maple, and winged elm.

Climate: Subtropical. The island group is just on the edge of the subtropical climate enjoyed by Florida and the Caribbean. The surrounding water produces a maritime climate, with mild winters, hot and humid summers, and temperatures that shift slowly. The inland mountains block much cold air from the interior. First frost after November 20; last frost leaves March 9.

Summer mildness: 16 **Seasonal affect:** 49
Winter mildness: 75 **Hazard free:** 76

	104
	109
	152
90°	56
32°	28
0°	0
	28
	71
	47

	High °F	Low °F	Hum %	Wind mph	Precip inches	Snow inches
JAN	59	39	57	9.1	3.7	0.1
FEB	62	41	55	9.9	3.3	0.2
MAR	70	48	53	10.0	4.1	0
APR	77	55	50	9.7	2.9	0
MAY	83	63	55	8.7	4.0	0
JUN	88	69	60	8.4	6.1	0
JUL	90	73	66	7.9	6.4	0
AUG	89	72	70	7.4	7.9	0
SEP	85	68	67	7.8	5.0	0
OCT	78	58	60	8.1	2.6	0
NOV	70	49	60	8.1	2.4	0
DEC	62	42	59	8.5	3.2	0

Hot Springs, AR — Rank: 91

Location: 34.30 N and 93.03 W at 579 feet, 36 miles southwest of Little Rock.

Landscape: Open low mountains. On the eastern edge of the Ouachita Mountains and the Ouachita National Forest. There are 47 thermal springs here. In the protected forests, mixed broadleaf deciduous trees such as oak, maple, sweet gum, and hickory thrive. Needleleaf evergreens and lower layers of redbud and dogwood are common.

Climate: The irregular topography, with elevations varying from 400 to 1,000 feet, has considerable effect on the area's microclimate, particularly on temperature extremes, ground fog, and precipitation. The climate is generally mild, not seeing frost until November 9, and bidding farewell to it by late March. However, the area is subject to storms, flash floods, and extreme heat and cold. Winter is short and wet, with temperatures falling below freezing half the nights. Summers are hot, humid, and long. Spring and fall are changeable and usually pleasant.

Summer mildness: 26 **Seasonal affect:** 62
Winter mildness: 67 **Hazard free:** 52

	119
	100
	146
90°	78
32°	56
0°	0
	16
	72
	57

	High °F	Low °F	Hum %	Wind mph	Precip inches	Snow inches
JAN	50	29	61	8.6	3.3	2.3
FEB	55	32	59	9.0	3.9	1.4
MAR	65	41	56	9.7	5.4	0.4
APR	74	50	56	9.1	5.5	0
MAY	81	58	58	7.7	6.4	0
JUN	89	66	55	7.2	4.7	0
JUL	93	70	56	6.7	5.0	0
AUG	92	68	56	6.4	3.5	0
SEP	86	62	58	6.7	4.0	0
OCT	76	51	53	6.8	4.3	0
NOV	63	41	59	8.0	5.6	0
DEC	53	32	62	8.2	5.0	0.6

Iowa City, IA — Rank: 195

Location: 41.394 N and 91.3148 W at 654 feet, along both banks of the Iowa River in eastern Iowa. Cedar Rapids is 25 miles northeast and Des Moines 110 miles west.

Landscape: Irregular plains. In the midst of rolling to steep hills and highly developed farmland. The soil is prairie, high in organic content. The Iowa River provides an extensive drainage basin. Prehistoric coral formations were revealed in the 1993 floods, providing further evidence that the area was part of a huge sea many millions of years ago.

Climate: Continental, with extremes in temperature and precipitation. Summer highs can hit 100°F accompanied by high humidity. Winter temperatures average 15°F to 25°F but can get much colder. Frost appears by October 11 and disappears after April 22. Precipitation can be highly variable, with large amounts falling all at once and then long dry periods. The potential for violent storms is high.

Summer mildness: 33 **Seasonal affect:** 27
Winter mildness: 6 **Hazard free:** 16

	90
	100
	175
90°	26
32°	139
0°	15
	130
	59
	41

	High °F	Low °F	Hum %	Wind mph	Precip inches	Snow inches
JAN	30	12	74	11.5	1.0	6.7
FEB	35	17	74	11.4	1.0	6.0
MAR	48	28	74	12.4	2.4	5.6
APR	63	40	69	12.7	3.7	1.5
MAY	75	51	68	11.1	4.0	0
JUN	84	60	69	10.0	4.5	0
JUL	88	65	73	8.6	4.9	0
AUG	85	62	75	8.4	4.4	0
SEP	78	54	74	9.2	3.9	0
OCT	66	43	70	10.2	2.8	0.3
NOV	50	31	75	11.2	2.1	1.7
DEC	34	18	77	11.2	1.6	6.8

★ = in the top 30 places for climate mildness

Jackson Hole, WY — Rank: 165

Location: 43.2848 N and 110.4542 W at 6,234 feet, in western Wyoming south of Yellowstone National Park. Billings, Montana, is 110 miles north.

Landscape: High mountains. In a valley encompassing Bridger-Teton National Forest, Grand Teton National Park, and the National Elk Refuge. Jackson Hole is surrounded by the Rocky Mountains, of which the Teton Range is the youngest. The Snake River cuts through the valley and passes through Jackson Lake. The alpine geography supports a variety of vegetation, including sagebrush, lodgepole pine, fir, spruce, and aspen. Cottonwood, elder, and willow grow in the valley itself.

Climate: The mountains shield the valley from moist air, making for crisp, clear, dry summers. Winters are long with heavy snowfall, but are not too severe. First frost comes early by August 12, and there will be frost potential until July 13. Rainfall amounts are small; most precipitation comes in the form of light, powdery snow from October to April.

Summer mildness: 98 **Seasonal affect:** 44
Winter mildness: 0 **Hazard free:** 2

	120
	90
	155
90°	2
32°	252
0°	42
	48
	45
	27

	High °F	Low °F	Hum %	Wind mph	Precip inches	Snow inches
JAN	26	4	60	13.0	1.5	23.3
FEB	32	7	59	12.2	1.0	12.2
MAR	41	16	57	11.4	1.1	12.5
APR	51	24	55	11.5	1.2	6.8
MAY	62	30	56	10.7	2.0	1.3
JUN	72	37	55	10.1	1.7	0.2
JUL	82	41	48	9.5	1.1	0
AUG	80	38	46	9.5	1.3	0
SEP	70	31	51	10.2	1.4	0.3
OCT	58	23	52	11.0	1.2	2.2
NOV	39	16	59	12.1	1.5	9.2
DEC	27	5	60	13.1	1.6	18.6

Kalispell–Flathead Valley, MT — Rank: 112

Location: 48.11 N and 114.18 W at 2,946 feet, in the Flathead Valley at the western gateway to Glacier National Park, about 70 air miles north of Missoula.

Landscape: High mountains. The Continental Divide is 50 miles east. In addition to Flathead, the largest natural lake west of the Mississippi, the valley contains four smaller lakes and numerous streams and sloughs. Scattered prairie grasses, shrubs, and low trees give way to evergreen forests. Ponderosa pine, piñon juniper, and Douglas fir are frequent associates.

Climate: In winter, the mountains to the east block cold air from Alberta and assure beneficial seasonal rains by cooling the ocean air arriving from the west. There's more precipitation on the eastern side of the valley than the western. It's windy, with intense winds often reaching 30 to 40 mph. Winter is cold and snowy. First frost arrives September 20; last frost departs finally by May 20. Summers are pleasant and dry.

Summer mildness: 95 **Seasonal affect:** 31
Winter mildness: 33 **Hazard free:** 32

	71
	81
	213
90°	12
32°	171
0°	12
	33
	44
	22

	High °F	Low °F	Hum %	Wind mph	Precip inches	Snow inches
JAN	28	13	79	6.0	1.5	12.5
FEB	35	18	76	6.2	1.1	6.2
MAR	43	24	65	7.2	1.0	8.1
APR	55	31	52	8.2	1.1	3.0
MAY	64	38	51	7.6	1.9	0
JUN	71	44	52	7.2	2.2	0
JUL	80	47	42	6.7	1.1	0
AUG	79	46	46	6.6	1.4	0
SEP	68	39	54	6.4	1.3	0
OCT	54	29	65	5.3	0.9	0
NOV	38	24	77	5.7	1.3	4.0
DEC	30	16	81	5.6	1.7	9.5

Kerrville, TX — Rank: 59

Location: 30.03 N and 99.08 W at 1,645 feet, at the edge of the Edwards Plateau. Austin is 80 miles east.

Landscape: High hills. Kerr County lies across the hills, valleys, and uplands of the rolling hill country of central Texas. There are breaks into the deep valleys of the Guadalupe River and its tributaries. The area is covered with cedars and live oaks.

Climate: Prairie continental in character, with wide swings of temperature both daily and seasonally, especially in winter. First frost arrives by November 11 and the last frost leaves March 24. Winter precipitation is mostly slow, steady, light rain. Summers are drier and hot. Falls are pleasant but can be stormy due to northers and Gulf storms moving north.

Summer mildness: 34 **Seasonal affect:** 78
Winter mildness: 56 **Hazard free:** 69

	117
	115
	134
90°	97
32°	39
0°	0
	23
	43
	41

	High °F	Low °F	Hum %	Wind mph	Precip inches	Snow inches
JAN	60	35	60	9.7	1.3	0.1
FEB	64	39	59	10.2	1.8	0.6
MAR	72	47	56	10.8	1.4	0.1
APR	79	55	57	10.5	2.5	0
MAY	84	62	60	9.6	4.2	0
JUN	89	67	56	9.1	3.6	0
JUL	93	69	51	8.3	2.2	0
AUG	93	68	50	7.9	2.7	0
SEP	87	64	55	7.9	3.6	0
OCT	79	55	55	8.1	3.6	0
NOV	69	46	58	9.0	1.9	0
DEC	62	38	59	9.2	1.3	0

★ = in the top 30 places for climate mildness

Ketchum–Sun Valley, ID   Rank: 134

Location: 43.41 N and 114.21 W at 5,821 feet, at the edge of Idaho's Sawtooth National Recreation Area, 100 miles east of Boise.

Landscape: High mountains. Sits high among even higher, rugged mountains. There are several flat or nearly flat glaciated valleys, some of which are several miles wide. The native vegetation is a mixed coniferous forest composed of Douglas fir, Engelmann spruce, and cedar-hemlock.

Climate: Semiarid steppe. Summers are crisp, clear, and dry. Winters are long and cold. First frost heralds by September 10 and the frost will last until June 14. Annual precipitation comes almost entirely as light and dry snow and accumulates to some depth. The prevailing winds are westerlies. Seasonal and daily temperature changes are extreme but would be even more so if not moderated by the mountains.

Summer mildness: 93   **Seasonal affect:** 51
Winter mildness: 6   **Hazard free:** 22

	121
	90
	154
90°	15
32°	205
0°	20
	47
	36
	15

	High °F	Low °F	Hum %	Wind mph	Precip inches	Snow inches
JAN	29	6	80	8.0	2.4	21.6
FEB	35	9	78	9.0	1.7	9.7
MAR	43	17	65	10.0	1.3	6.7
APR	55	27	55	10.0	1.1	0.7
MAY	67	34	51	9.5	1.2	0.1
JUN	76	41	47	9.0	1.1	0
JUL	86	46	37	8.4	0.7	0
AUG	84	44	40	8.2	0.6	0
SEP	74	35	45	8.2	0.8	0
OCT	63	27	59	8.3	0.8	0.3
NOV	44	19	75	8.4	2.0	6.1
DEC	31	7	83	8.1	2.3	15.0

Key West, FL   Rank: 83

Location: 24.33 N and 81.47 W, at 7 feet, at the end of the long island chain swinging in a southwesterly arc from the tip of the Florida peninsula, 160 miles south of Miami.

Landscape: Flat plains. Key West sits on a sand-and-coral island 3½ miles long and 1 mile wide. The average elevation along the entire island chain is just 8 feet. The waters surrounding these islands are shallow, and there is little wave action because outlying reefs break the surf. Much of the shoreline is filled mangrove swamp.

Climate: Because of the Gulf Stream, the Florida Keys have a notably mild, tropical-maritime climate in which the average winter temperatures are only about 14 degrees lower than in summer. Summers are hot, humid, and stormy, although prevailing easterly trade winds and sea breezes make the heat tolerable. There is no known record of frost, ice, sleet, or snow.

Summer mildness: 1   **Seasonal affect:** 51
Winter mildness: 82   **Hazard free:** 82

	75
	175
	115
90°	139
32°	0
0°	0
	39
	84
	74

	High °F	Low °F	Hum %	Wind mph	Precip inches	Snow inches
JAN	75	59	69	9.5	2.0	0
FEB	75	60	67	10.2	1.8	0
MAR	79	64	66	10.6	1.7	0
APR	82	68	63	10.5	1.8	0
MAY	85	72	65	9.7	3.5	0
JUN	88	75	68	8.4	5.1	0
JUL	89	76	66	8.0	3.6	0
AUG	89	77	67	7.9	5.0	0
SEP	88	76	69	8.2	5.9	0
OCT	84	72	69	9.3	4.4	0
NOV	80	67	69	9.7	2.8	0
DEC	76	62	69	9.2	2.0	0

★ Kingman, AZ   Rank: 15

Location: 35.11 N and 114.03 W at 3,334 feet, in the dry Peacock Mountains of northwestern Arizona. Las Vegas is 90 miles northwest.

Landscape: Plains with high mountains. Sits some 2,000 feet above the Colorado River Valley in high plateau country. Lakes Mead, Mohave, and Havasu are principal sources of water and recreation. Ground cover is primarily sagebrush and native grasses. In the upper elevations are sparse conifer stands.

Climate: Arid steppe, with strong daily and seasonal temperature changes. Winters are clear, long, and extremely mild, with some flow of air from as far as the Pacific Ocean. The first frost delays until November 14 and the last frost departs around April 8. There's a short, hot, sun-baked stretch from July to September. Except for brief periods in spring and summer, there's no measurable precipitation.

Summer mildness: 35   **Seasonal affect:** 96
Winter mildness: 72   **Hazard free:** 81

	242
	75
	48
90°	101
32°	61
0°	0
	2
	23
	7

	High °F	Low °F	Hum %	Wind mph	Precip inches	Snow inches
JAN	54	31	40	7.3	0.9	0.5
FEB	59	34	35	7.4	0.9	0.3
MAR	63	38	30	7.9	1.1	1.0
APR	71	44	25	8.3	0.6	0
MAY	81	53	23	8.3	0.2	0
JUN	91	62	22	8.5	0.2	0
JUL	96	69	32	9.5	1.1	0
AUG	94	68	35	8.9	1.5	0
SEP	88	60	35	7.3	0.8	0
OCT	78	50	32	6.6	0.7	0
NOV	64	39	34	6.9	0.8	0
DEC	55	32	41	7.2	1.0	0.6

★ = *in the top 30 places for climate mildness*

Kissimmee–St. Cloud, FL — Rank: 45

Location: 28.17 N and 81.24 W at 19 feet at the head of Lake Tohopekaliga in central Florida, 30 miles southwest of Orlando.

Landscape: Flat plains. Situated amid clear lakes in gently rolling hill country. Flood-plain grasses and pine flatwoods mix with live oak hammocks. Forests are a typical southern coastal mix of hardwood, longleaf, and slash pine. Aromatic and evergreen bayberry and sweet bay are scattered throughout.

Climate: Subtropical, with a small annual range of temperature change. First frost comes as late as December 27 and the last frost is gone by February 6. Warmed by both the Gulf of Mexico and the Atlantic, winters are sunny, mild, and dry. Summers are hot, humid, and beset by frequent thunderstorms that provide half the area's annual precipitation.

Summer mildness: 12 **Seasonal affect:** 63
Winter mildness: 87 **Hazard free:** 86

Icon values: 92, 148, 125, 108, 6, 0, 27, 74, 82

	High °F	Low °F	Hum %	Wind mph	Precip inches	Snow inches
JAN	73	49	56	8.9	2.2	0
FEB	75	50	52	9.6	3.1	0
MAR	79	55	50	9.9	2.9	0
APR	84	59	46	9.4	1.5	0
MAY	88	65	49	8.8	3.7	0
JUN	91	70	56	8.0	6.1	0
JUL	91	72	59	7.4	7.0	0
AUG	91	72	60	7.1	6.7	0
SEP	90	71	60	7.7	5.7	0
OCT	85	65	56	8.6	2.8	0
NOV	80	57	55	8.6	2.2	0
DEC	75	51	57	8.6	2.2	0

★ Laguna Beach–Dana Point, CA — Rank: 3

Location: 33.32 N and 117.47 W at 44 feet, on the Pacific Ocean 40 miles south of Los Angeles. San Diego is another 60 miles south.

Landscape: Open low mountains. The shore is somewhat rocky, and steep hills rise from two lagoons at the head of Laguna canyon. Trees and shrubs must withstand severe summer drought and evaporation. Following a wet winter, hard-leaved evergreens such as piñon and cypress are more abundant.

Climate: Ocean breezes keep the weather mild throughout the year. Days when the temperature tops 90°F or falls to 32°F are rare. It is a long growing season, with the first frost coming in January 5 and the last frost departing by January 25. Morning fog and low clouds are common in cooler seasons. There isn't much precipitation, and what rain there is falls mostly in winter.

Summer mildness: 71 **Seasonal affect:** 82
Winter mildness: 98 **Hazard free:** 99

Icon values: 147, 116, 103, 2, 3, 0, 38, 21, 4

	High °F	Low °F	Hum %	Wind mph	Precip inches	Snow inches
JAN	66	42	55	6.7	2.3	0
FEB	67	43	58	7.4	2.3	0
MAR	66	44	61	8.2	2.2	0
APR	69	46	60	8.5	0.9	0
MAY	70	52	65	8.4	0.3	0
JUN	72	55	68	8.0	0.1	0
JUL	76	59	68	7.8	0.0	0
AUG	77	59	68	7.7	0.1	0
SEP	78	58	65	7.3	0.4	0
OCT	75	53	59	6.9	0.3	0
NOV	70	46	55	6.7	1.7	0
DEC	66	42	53	6.5	1.7	0

Lake Conroe, TX — Rank: 77

Location: 30.21 N and 95.33 W at 201 feet, in the Texas Gulf coastal plain, 40 miles north of downtown Houston.

Landscape: Irregular plains. Rolling hills on a flood plain at the southern edge of the Big Thicket area. The Sam Houston National Forest abuts the northern shore of this 22,000-acre artificial lake. The area is rapidly becoming suburbanized, with some loss to the piney woods and dense deciduous forests.

Climate: Subtropical. Summer days are long, hot, and humid, but the nights are pleasantly cool. Winters are mild with few, brief cold spells. Thanksgiving brings in the first frost, and the last frost is out before St. Patrick's Day. Rainfall is distributed evenly throughout the year but arrives in brief, heavy, and sometimes violent thunderstorms.

Summer mildness: 9 **Seasonal affect:** 53
Winter mildness: 85 **Hazard free:** 75

Icon values: 94, 115, 157, 108, 28, 0, 31, 64, 61

	High °F	Low °F	Hum %	Wind mph	Precip inches	Snow inches
JAN	60	38	63	8.3	3.6	0.1
FEB	64	41	61	8.8	3.2	0.2
MAR	72	48	59	9.4	2.9	0
APR	79	57	57	9.2	3.8	0
MAY	85	63	59	8.2	5.4	0
JUN	91	70	59	7.7	4.5	0
JUL	94	72	58	7.0	3.5	0
AUG	95	72	58	6.3	3.6	0
SEP	89	67	60	6.9	5.0	0
OCT	81	56	56	7.0	3.7	0
NOV	72	48	57	7.9	4.2	0
DEC	63	40	61	8.0	4.0	0

★ = in the top 30 places for climate mildness

★ Lake Havasu City, AZ — Rank: 8

Location: 34.29 N and 114.19 W at 602 feet, in extreme western Arizona above Parker Dam on the Colorado River. Las Vegas, Nevada, is 100 miles northwest.

Landscape: Plains with high mountains. On the Colorado River, west of the Mojave Mountains. The center is the 45-mile-long Lake Havasu, with red wall limestone canyons, steep slopes, and gorges. This is the edge of the Sonoran Desert, where growth is low shrub and saguaro. Creosote bush, geraniums, and sedums are common, especially after a wet winter.

Climate: Desert, with strong daily and seasonal temperature changes. Winters are clear, long, and extremely mild, with some flow of air from as far away as the Pacific Ocean. First frost comes December 9; last frost is gone by February 7. From May to October is a long, hot, sunbaked stretch. Except for a handful of days in spring and summer, there is no measurable precipitation.

Summer mildness: 19	Seasonal affect: 99
Winter mildness: 91	Hazard free: 97

Icon values: 242, 75, 48, 90° 178, 32° 14, 0° 0, 2, 11, 7

	High °F	Low °F	Hum %	Wind mph	Precip inches	Snow inches
JAN	67	39	40	7.3	0.6	0
FEB	73	44	35	7.4	0.4	0
MAR	79	48	30	7.9	0.5	0
APR	87	54	25	8.3	0.2	0
MAY	96	63	23	8.3	0.1	0
JUN	105	72	22	8.5	0.0	0
JUL	109	79	32	9.5	0.3	0
AUG	107	79	35	8.9	0.5	0
SEP	101	71	35	7.3	0.5	0
OCT	91	59	32	6.6	0.4	0
NOV	77	47	34	6.9	0.5	0
DEC	67	39	41	7.2	0.6	0

Lakeland–Winter Haven, FL — Rank: 46

Location: 28.02 N and 81.57 W at 211 feet, in central Florida, 42 miles east of Tampa.

Landscape: Flat plains. In the rolling lake-ridge section, 50 miles from the Gulf of Mexico and 70 miles from the Atlantic Ocean. Here one can find the highest elevation in the Florida peninsula. Flood-plain prairies and pine flatwoods mix with live oak hammocks. Forests are a typical mix of hardwood, longleaf, and slash pine. Aromatic and evergreen bayberry and sweet bay are scattered throughout.

Climate: Subtropical. The proximity of the Gulf of Mexico and the Atlantic Ocean bring pleasant winters. Days are bright and warm, nights are cool, and rainfall is light to moderate. The high temperature and humidity during the long summers are moderated by afternoon thundershowers. Occasional major cold waves overspread the area, bringing temperatures down below freezing. The first frost comes late on December 27, and the last frost leaves a short time later on February 6.

Summer mildness: 8	Seasonal affect: 64
Winter mildness: 88	Hazard free: 86

Icon values: 92, 148, 125, 90° 108, 32° 6, 0° 0, 27, 74, 82

	High °F	Low °F	Hum %	Wind mph	Precip inches	Snow inches
JAN	72	50	56	8.9	2.3	0
FEB	74	52	52	9.6	3.0	0
MAR	80	57	50	9.9	3.4	0
APR	84	61	46	9.4	1.4	0
MAY	89	67	49	8.8	4.2	0
JUN	91	71	56	8.0	6.8	0
JUL	92	73	59	7.4	7.0	0
AUG	92	73	60	7.1	7.6	0
SEP	90	72	60	7.7	5.7	0
OCT	85	66	56	8.6	2.0	0
NOV	78	58	55	8.6	2.1	0
DEC	73	53	57	8.6	2.2	0

Lake of the Cherokees, OK — Rank: 137

Location: 36.33 N and 94.45 W at 739 feet, near the western slope of the Ozark Mountains. Tulsa is 75 miles southwest.

Landscape: Tablelands with moderate relief. The forested hills drop to the 1,300-mile shore of Grand Lake, a major impoundment on the Neosho River. Foothills give way to a low-relief plain and rivers. Forest and prairie grow side by side: Deciduous oak-hickory forests with elm, sycamore, bur oak, redbud, and buckeye stand next to vast stretches of bluestem grasses.

Climate: Prairie, with hot summers and winters that are moderate, with occasional hard freezes. October 22 brings in the first frost; last frost departs by April 15. Spring arrives in mid-March and autumn ends in late October. Annual precipitation is moderate and, except for snow in January, usually falls as rain. Humidity is mild.

Summer mildness: 39	Seasonal affect: 70
Winter mildness: 25	Hazard free: 37

Icon values: 128, 103, 135, 90° 72, 32° 96, 0° 1, 10, 61, 51

	High °F	Low °F	Hum %	Wind mph	Precip inches	Snow inches
JAN	45	23	59	10.5	1.8	3.3
FEB	51	27	57	10.9	2.0	2.4
MAR	61	37	53	12.1	4.0	1.5
APR	72	47	51	12.0	3.8	0
MAY	78	56	58	10.7	5.1	0
JUN	86	64	58	10.0	4.7	0
JUL	92	68	53	9.3	3.0	0
AUG	92	66	53	9.0	3.8	0
SEP	84	60	56	9.2	5.1	0
OCT	73	48	53	9.7	3.8	0
NOV	60	37	57	10.4	3.8	0
DEC	48	27	60	10.3	2.5	1.6

★ = in the top 30 places for climate mildness

Lake of the Ozarks, MO — Rank: 177

Location: 38.00 N and 92.44 W at 1,043 feet, on the Osage River at Bagnell Dam. Kansas City is 170 miles northwest and St. Louis 180 miles northeast.

Landscape: Open hills. There are 1,150 miles of irregular shoreline on the lake, formed when the Osage River was dammed in the rolling, open country of south-central Missouri. The slopes are wooded with oak, maple, sweet gum, and hickory, mixed with second-growth spruce and pine.

Climate: Hot continental with hot, humid summers and cold winters. Apparent temperatures, especially those caused by cold and wind, are pronounced throughout the year. First frost arrives by October 20 and the last frost departs mid-April. Snow is neither deep nor long lasting.

Summer mildness: 33
Winter mildness: 20
Seasonal affect: 53
Hazard free: 17

	116
	97
	153
90°	58
32°	104
0°	3
	20
	66
	56

	High °F	Low °F	Hum %	Wind mph	Precip inches	Snow inches
JAN	43	21	59	11.7	1.6	5.2
FEB	48	26	61	11.9	2.2	4.5
MAR	60	35	57	12.9	3.8	4.3
APR	71	46	57	12.2	4.0	0
MAY	78	55	60	10.4	5.1	0
JUN	85	63	61	9.6	4.2	0
JUL	90	68	60	8.5	3.6	0
AUG	89	66	56	8.6	3.9	0
SEP	82	58	58	9.3	4.5	0
OCT	73	47	57	10.1	4.4	0
NOV	59	37	60	11.3	3.4	1.0
DEC	47	26	64	11.6	2.9	3.4

Lake Placid, NY — Rank: 199

Location: 44.16 N and 73.59 W at 1,800 feet in northeast New York, in the Adirondack Mountains, surrounding Mirror Lake. Plattsburgh is 40 miles northeast.

Landscape: Open low mountains. Lake Placid Trail connects the Adirondack foothills and High Peaks region to the northeast. The land is sharply rolling with relatively deep valleys. Natural lakes abound and a dense mixed conifer and deciduous forest covers the area.

Climate: Rigorous continental, with severe, snowy winters impacted by air and moisture from the Canadian Arctic. The first frost arrives September 14 and the last frost departs May 31. Summer days are bright and approach the ideal: a long period of mild, dry days with cool nights. Springs and falls are all too short.

Summer mildness: 56
Winter mildness: 3
Seasonal affect: 13
Hazard free: 4

	63
	98
	205
90°	14
32°	189
0°	19
	129
	70
	27

	High °F	Low °F	Hum %	Wind mph	Precip inches	Snow inches
JAN	26	6	72	10.8	2.2	14.0
FEB	29	9	69	10.7	2.0	13.0
MAR	39	22	66	10.8	2.4	10.0
APR	50	33	62	10.5	2.7	9.0
MAY	64	44	66	9.0	3.3	5.0
JUN	72	53	69	8.3	3.8	0
JUL	77	58	70	8.0	3.9	0
AUG	74	56	74	7.7	4.5	0
SEP	67	48	76	8.2	3.8	1.0
OCT	55	37	73	8.8	3.2	9.0
NOV	42	29	73	10.2	3.4	12.0
DEC	30	15	74	10.4	2.8	13.0

Largo, FL — Rank: 31

Location: 27.54 N and 82.48 W at 50 feet, on the Gulf Coast 15 miles west of Tampa and 20 miles north of St. Petersburg.

Landscape: Flat plains. Largo occupies a high coastal area on the west coast of a peninsula separating the Gulf of Mexico from Tampa Bay. Sand-reef islands line the coast. Coastal vegetation consists of southern yellow pine and laurel, with cultivated citrus groves farther inland.

Climate: Subtropical. The Gulf of Mexico heavily influences the weather. Summers are long, hot, and humid, interrupted by frequent afternoon thunderstorms. Winters are very mild and cool at night, with snow and below-freezing temperatures extremely rare.

Summer mildness: 7
Winter mildness: 94
Seasonal affect: 71
Hazard free: 85

	102
	142
	121
90°	78
32°	0
0°	0
	22
	69
	86

	High °F	Low °F	Hum %	Wind mph	Precip inches	Snow inches
JAN	68	53	59	8.6	2.2	0
FEB	70	54	56	9.2	3.1	0
MAR	75	60	55	9.5	3.6	0
APR	80	65	51	9.3	1.3	0
MAY	86	70	52	8.7	3.1	0
JUN	89	75	60	8.0	6.2	0
JUL	90	76	63	7.2	6.8	0
AUG	90	76	64	7.0	8.6	0
SEP	88	75	62	7.8	7.1	0
OCT	83	69	57	8.5	2.3	0
NOV	76	62	57	8.4	2.1	0
DEC	71	55	59	8.5	2.4	0

★ = in the top 30 places for climate mildness

Las Cruces, NM — Rank: 58

Location: 32.18 N and 106.46 W at 3,883 feet, 40 miles northwest of El Paso, Texas.

Landscape: Plains with high mountains. The wide, level Rio Grande Valley runs northwest to southeast through here. Rolling desert borders the southwest and west. About 12 miles east, the Organ Mountains, with peaks above 8,500 feet, form a rugged backdrop. The northwest portion of the valley narrows to low hills and buttes. The vegetation is dry-desert with negligible ground cover. Only plants adapted to the highly alkaline conditions survive. These include thorn scrub, savanna or steppe grass, prickly pear, and saguaro cactus. In this higher altitude are belts of oak and juniper woodland.

Climate: Desert continental, characterized by low rainfall, hot summers with cool nights, and mild, sunny winters. There are freezes, with the first frost coming October 23 and the last frost leaving April 18. The rainfall is light, almost all falling in occasional, brief summer showers. Drizzles are unknown.

Summer mildness: 48	Seasonal affect: 95
Winter mildness: 38	Hazard free: 56

Sidebar icon values: 193, 100, 72, 90° 105, 32° 120, 0° 0, 2, 22, 36

	High °F	Low °F	Hum %	Wind mph	Precip inches	Snow inches
JAN	58	23	42	8.4	0.5	1.3
FEB	63	26	34	9.2	0.4	0.9
MAR	69	33	27	11.0	0.2	0.4
APR	77	40	21	11.1	0.2	0
MAY	86	48	21	10.3	0.3	0
JUN	94	56	23	9.3	0.6	0
JUL	95	63	35	8.3	1.9	0
AUG	92	61	39	7.8	2.2	0
SEP	87	54	41	7.6	1.6	0
OCT	79	41	36	7.5	1.0	0
NOV	67	30	37	8.0	0.6	1.0
DEC	59	23	42	7.9	0.8	1.7

Las Vegas, NM — Rank: 89

Location: 35.37 N and 105.13 W at 6,600 feet in northeast New Mexico, some 50 miles east from Santa Fe.

Landscape: Tablelands with considerable relief. Mountains of the Mesa Montosa surround this San Miguel County seat. Engelmann spruce and subalpine fir cover the higher elevations; ponderosa pine is on the lower, drier, more exposed slopes; grasses cover the parks and valleys.

Climate: Highland steppe, with crisp and clear, but cold, winter days. The first frost arrives October 6 and the last frost departs May 15. Summers and falls are the best seasons: pleasant, warm, dry, and invigorating. Long periods of cloudiness are unknown.

Summer mildness: 91	Seasonal affect: 85
Winter mildness: 17	Hazard free: 16

Sidebar icon values: 168, 110, 87, 90° 23, 32° 157, 0° 2, 14, 38, 38

	High °F	Low °F	Hum %	Wind mph	Precip inches	Snow inches
JAN	40	18	50	8.0	0.9	5.4
FEB	44	21	42	8.8	0.8	5.4
MAR	50	26	32	10.0	1.2	6.9
APR	59	33	25	10.8	1.0	4.0
MAY	68	42	23	10.5	1.2	0
JUN	78	51	22	9.9	1.4	0
JUL	81	55	30	9.0	3.3	0
AUG	78	53	34	8.2	3.5	0
SEP	71	47	35	8.5	2.1	0
OCT	62	38	35	8.2	1.3	1.0
NOV	49	27	38	7.9	1.0	4.0
DEC	41	19	46	7.7	1.1	7.0

Leelanau Peninsula, MI — Rank: 198

Location: 45.01 N and 85.45 W at 656 feet in the northwest mainland on the eastern shore of Lake Michigan. Southeast, Traverse City is 20 miles and Detroit 270 miles.

Landscape: Plains with hills. The peninsula is hilly, ranging from rolling to steep. Dunes predominate in the coastal areas, with lakes and bogs inland. Maples and cherry trees are common, as are pine, hemlock, and birch. Trilliums and other wildflowers grow in the hills. Swamp marigolds can be found in the boglands.

Climate: Winters are severe, with frequent cold snaps and heavy snow. It is a long season, too, with the first frost on October 17 and the last frost on May 10. Summers, however, are mild and pleasant, thanks to the tempering effect of the Great Lakes. Autumns are cool and long. Cloudy to partly cloudy days are the norm throughout the year, but rainfall is light.

Summer mildness: 61	Seasonal affect: 9
Winter mildness: 7	Hazard free: 0

Sidebar icon values: 64, 95, 206, 90° 4, 32° 155, 0° 8, 137, 71, 34

	High °F	Low °F	Hum %	Wind mph	Precip inches	Snow inches
JAN	30	17	77	11.5	2.2	29.1
FEB	33	17	75	10.7	1.5	16.0
MAR	42	24	72	11.1	2.0	11.0
APR	56	35	68	11.0	2.7	3.0
MAY	68	44	66	9.7	2.5	0.3
JUN	76	53	68	8.9	3.3	0
JUL	81	59	70	8.2	2.7	0
AUG	79	58	74	7.9	3.6	0
SEP	72	52	75	8.3	4.0	0
OCT	61	43	74	9.4	3.2	0.6
NOV	47	33	77	10.5	2.9	12.1
DEC	34	22	79	10.7	2.5	26.0

★ = in the top 30 places for climate mildness

Leesburg–Mount Dora, FL — Rank: 41

Location: 28.48 N and 81.52 W at 80 feet, in Florida's central lakes region, 40 miles northwest of Orlando.

Landscape: Flat plains. Composed of lakes, rivers, forests, and sand hills, there is interesting variety. Withlacoochee State Forest is a typical mix of hardwood, longleaf, and slash pine. Aromatic and evergreen bayberry and sweet bay are scattered throughout.

Climate: Subtropical, with a small range of annual temperature change. Humid, hot summers are cooled by frequent afternoon thunderstorms. Winters are extremely mild, with warm days and cool nights. Frost season is quite short, lasting but a few weeks from the first frost on January 2 to the last frost by that month's end.

Summer mildness: 15	Seasonal affect: 65
Winter mildness: 87	Hazard free: 86

Icon values: 92, 148, 125, 90° 106, 32° 4, 0° 0, 27, 73, 82

	High °F	Low °F	Hum %	Wind mph	Precip inches	Snow inches
JAN	70	47	56	8.9	2.7	0
FEB	71	48	52	9.6	3.3	0
MAR	76	53	50	9.9	3.5	0
APR	82	58	46	9.4	2.2	0
MAY	87	64	49	8.8	3.4	0
JUN	90	69	56	8.0	6.5	0
JUL	92	71	59	7.4	6.2	0
AUG	91	72	60	7.1	7.2	0
SEP	89	71	60	7.7	5.9	0
OCT	83	64	56	8.6	3.1	0
NOV	77	56	55	8.6	2.5	0
DEC	72	50	57	8.6	2.4	0

Litchfield Hills, CT — Rank: 169

Location: 41.48 N and 73.07 W at 593 feet, in the state's northwest corner, some 35 miles northwest of Hartford.

Landscape: Open low mountains. The low Berkshire Mountain foothills surround the area, with many forest-rimmed lakes next to open fields and meadows. The woods are an eastern hardwood forest dominated by tall, broadleaf trees that provide dense cover in summer and brilliant color in fall and are bare in winter. Common varieties are maple, oak, beech, birch, walnut, ash, and sweet chestnut.

Climate: Hot continental, with large temperature variations from season to season. Winters receive Canadian air that sweeps down the Hudson Valley to the west. First frost descends on October 2 and deepens until the last frost on May 14. December to February is cold with long-lasting snow. Spring is short. Summers are clear, warm, and ideal. Falls extend to mid-November. Precipitation is moderate and evenly distributed throughout the year.

Summer mildness: 96	Seasonal affect: 9
Winter mildness: 17	Hazard free: 19

Icon values: 81, 109, 175, 90° 0, 32° 165, 0° 14, 29, 90, 21

	High °F	Low °F	Hum %	Wind mph	Precip inches	Snow inches
JAN	27	11	58	9.0	4.0	16.3
FEB	30	12	57	9.4	3.9	14.1
MAR	40	22	53	9.9	4.2	10.7
APR	52	32	49	10.0	4.5	2.0
MAY	65	43	49	8.9	4.6	0
JUN	73	52	55	8.1	4.6	0
JUL	78	58	55	7.5	4.2	0
AUG	75	56	57	7.2	4.6	0
SEP	68	48	59	7.3	4.1	0
OCT	56	38	59	7.8	3.9	0
NOV	44	29	60	8.5	4.6	4.0
DEC	32	17	62	8.7	4.4	15.1

Long Beach Peninsula, WA — Rank: 131

Location: 46.39 N and 123.48 W at 110 feet on the Pacific Ocean at a point where explorers Lewis and Clark ended their expedition west. At 28 continuous miles, Long Beach is the country's longest stretch of sand and surf. The Columbia River is immediately south.

Landscape: Low mountains to the east. At the lowest elevations, there is a dense conifer forest of Douglas fir, western red cedar, western hemlock, grand fir, silver fir, Sitka spruce, and Alaska cedar. Numerous species of shrubs grow exceptionally well in this forest and around its margins.

Climate: Because this location is directly on the Pacific Ocean, its climate is characterized by generally mild average temperatures ranging from 35°F to 70°F throughout the year. Rainfall is heavy, 30 to 150 inches per year, with a maximum in winter. Humidity is always high. The southern part of this area is winter-wet with no snow; fog partially compensates for the summer drought. The first frost arrives November 12 and the last frost departs April 10.

Summer mildness: 72	Seasonal affect: 2
Winter mildness: 51	Hazard free: 47

Icon values: 68, 74, 223, 90° 10, 32° 44, 0° 0, 56, 103, 6

	High °F	Low °F	Hum %	Wind mph	Precip inches	Snow inches
JAN	47	32	81	11.2	5.4	1.0
FEB	51	34	77	10.7	3.9	0.5
MAR	54	35	73	11.2	3.6	0.5
APR	57	37	71	11.0	2.4	0
MAY	63	42	69	9.7	2.1	0
JUN	68	46	67	8.9	1.5	0
JUL	73	49	64	8.2	0.6	0
AUG	74	49	65	7.9	1.1	0
SEP	71	46	68	8.3	1.8	0
OCT	62	40	76	9.4	2.7	0
NOV	52	37	81	10.5	5.3	0
DEC	47	33	83	10.7	6.1	1.0

★ = in the top 30 places for climate mildness

Loudoun County, VA — Rank: 190

Location: The weather station is Leesburg, the county seat, sitting at 39.00 N and 77.00 W at 320 feet in extreme northeast Virginia. Maryland is east across the Potomac River. Washington, D.C., is 35 miles southeast.

Landscape: Open low mountains. The surrounding naturally occurring trees are remnants of a northeastern hardwood forest composed of birch, beech, maple, elm, red oak, and basswood, with an admixture of hemlock and white pine.

Climate: Temperate mid-latitude climate. Summers are warm and humid, winters mild. Typically, the best weather is in the spring and autumn. The coldest weather occurs in late January and early February; the warmest month is July. There are no pronounced wet and dry seasons. Thunderstorms during the summer often bring sudden heavy rains and damaging winds, hail, or lightning. In winter, snow accumulations of more than 10 inches are rare. The first frost arrives October 28 and the last frost departs April 14.

Summer mildness: 13   **Seasonal affect:** 8
Winter mildness: 41   **Hazard free:** 36

Icons: 97, 105, 163, 34 (90°), 71 (32°), 0 (0°), 127, 87, 28

	High °F	Low °F	Hum %	Wind mph	Precip inches	Snow inches
JAN	42	42	63	10.0	2.7	5.3
FEB	46	46	61	10.4	2.7	5.3
MAR	57	57	60	10.9	3.2	2.1
APR	67	67	60	10.5	2.7	0
MAY	76	76	63	9.3	3.7	0
JUN	85	85	64	8.9	3.4	0
JUL	89	89	65	8.3	3.8	0
AUG	87	87	68	8.1	3.9	0
SEP	80	80	69	8.4	3.3	0
OCT	69	69	67	8.7	3.0	0
NOV	58	58	65	9.3	3.1	0.8
DEC	47	47	65	9.6	3.1	3.1

Lower Cape May, NJ — Rank: 123

Location: 38.56 N and 74.54 W at 10 feet, where the Intracoastal Waterway swings into Delaware Bay. Atlantic City is 50 miles north, Philadelphia 85 miles northwest.

Landscape: Flat plains. Surrounding flat terrain is composed of tidal marshes and beach sand. The Wildwood resorts are on a barrier island to the northeast. The interior woods are evergreen and laurel.

Climate: Continental, but the moderating influence of the Atlantic is apparent throughout the year. Summers are cooler, winters warmer than those of other places at the same latitude. During the warm season, sea breezes in the late morning and afternoon prevent excessive heat. On occasion, these may lower the temperature between 15 and 20 degrees within a half-hour. Fall is long, lasting to mid-November. Warming is somewhat delayed in spring. The first frost arrives November 12 and the last frost departs March 30. Precipitation is moderate and well distributed throughout the year.

Summer mildness: 70   **Seasonal affect:** 38
Winter mildness: 30   **Hazard free:** 43

Icons: 95, 110, 160, 8 (90°), 72 (32°), 0 (0°), 44, 64, 21

	High °F	Low °F	Hum %	Wind mph	Precip inches	Snow inches
JAN	40	26	62	11.0	3.5	4.8
FEB	42	28	59	11.4	3.2	5.4
MAR	50	35	56	11.9	3.9	2.8
APR	59	43	54	11.8	3.4	0
MAY	68	52	55	10.2	3.5	0
JUN	78	61	56	9.2	3.2	0
JUL	83	67	57	8.5	3.3	0
AUG	82	67	58	8.1	3.7	0
SEP	77	60	58	8.4	3.0	0
OCT	66	50	57	9.0	3.1	0
NOV	56	41	57	10.5	3.2	0
DEC	46	31	62	10.6	3.5	2.1

Madison, MS — Rank: 117

Location: 32.00 N and 90.00 W at 340 feet on the historic Natchez Trace Trail some 15 miles north of Jackson.

Landscape: Irregular, alluvial plains. Rolling hills of the central coastal plain are predominant but there are bluffs along the river. Forests are mixed broadleaf deciduous and southern yellow pine.

Climate: Humid maritime climate. One short cold season and one long warm one, and humid year-round. The frost-free period totals 235 days. In summer, the southerly winds and accompanying warm Gulf air masses predominate, resulting in significant humidity. Summer days are hot and the nights aren't much different. In winter, colder northern air occasionally invades the region, causing rapid and sometimes dramatic temperature shifts. The first frost arrives November 1 and the last frost departs March 29.

Summer mildness: 0   **Seasonal affect:** 32
Winter mildness: 89   **Hazard free:** 63

Icons: 111, 104, 150, 84 (90°), 50 (32°), 0 (0°), 195, 72, 63

	High °F	Low °F	Hum %	Wind mph	Precip inches	Snow inches
JAN	56	56	76	8.4	5.2	0.5
FEB	60	60	74	8.6	4.7	0.2
MAR	69	69	72	9.1	5.8	0.2
APR	77	77	73	8.5	5.6	0
MAY	84	84	74	7.3	5.1	0
JUN	91	91	74	6.4	3.2	0
JUL	92	92	77	5.9	4.5	0
AUG	92	92	77	5.6	3.8	0
SEP	88	88	76	6.4	3.6	0
OCT	79	79	73	6.5	3.3	0
NOV	69	69	74	7.6	4.8	0
DEC	60	60	76	8.3	5.9	0

★ = in the top 30 places for climate mildness

Madison, WI — Rank: 192

Location: 43.0423 N and 89.2404 W at 860 feet in southern Wisconsin on an 8-block-wide stretch of land between Lakes Mendota and Monona. Milwaukee is 75 miles east.

Landscape: Open hills. The metro area includes 18,000 acres of lake surface, which is frozen over from December to April. Outside the urban area, dairy farms predominate, with field crops of corn, oats, alfalfa, apples, strawberries, and raspberries.

Climate: Continental. Like much of the interior of North America, summer high and winter low temperatures are extreme, with much variation within seasons. Winters are long and cold due to frequent blasts of arctic air. Even so, the first frost doesn't arrive until October 3, though the last frost will delay leaving until May 6. Snowfall is moderate, however. Summers are warm and often humid.

Summer mildness: 53 **Seasonal affect:** 21
Winter mildness: 4 **Hazard free:** 11

	90
	96
	179
90°	7
32°	159
0°	22
	140
	64
	40

	High °F	Low °F	Hum %	Wind mph	Precip inches	Snow inches
JAN	24	6	74	10.5	1.2	8.2
FEB	29	10	73	10.4	1.2	7.3
MAR	41	23	72	11.2	2.6	9.6
APR	57	35	68	11.4	3.2	2.1
MAY	68	46	67	10.0	3.4	0.2
JUN	78	55	69	9.2	3.8	0
JUL	82	60	72	8.1	4.1	0
AUG	79	58	75	8.0	4.4	0
SEP	71	49	76	8.7	3.7	0
OCT	59	39	73	9.6	2.4	0.2
NOV	43	26	76	10.8	2.2	3.3
DEC	29	12	78	10.3	1.8	9.2

Marble Falls–Lake LBJ, TX — Rank: 78

Location: 30.45 N and 98.25 W at 1,270 feet, on the Colorado River at the northern end of the Highland Lakes region, 50 miles northwest of Austin.

Landscape: Open high hills in central Texas. Granite cliffs, limestone bluffs, and caverns are prominent geologic features. Cedar and oak are prevalent; cypress trees grow on the banks of rivers; and Texas bluebonnet and other wildflowers bloom profusely with sufficient spring rainfall.

Climate: Prairie. Summer days are hot but nights pleasantly cool. Winters are mild with few cold spells that also tend to be brief. The first frost arrives November 8; the season's last frost departs March 23. Rainfall is distributed evenly throughout the year. Humidity is generally comfortable.

Summer mildness: 25 **Seasonal affect:** 79
Winter mildness: 48 **Hazard free:** 69

	117
	115
	134
90°	118
32°	55
0°	0
	23
	40
	41

	High °F	Low °F	Hum %	Wind mph	Precip inches	Snow inches
JAN	58	32	60	9.7	1.7	0.5
FEB	62	36	59	10.2	2.0	0.3
MAR	69	44	56	10.8	2.1	0
APR	77	54	57	10.5	2.7	0
MAY	83	61	60	9.6	4.8	0
JUN	89	68	56	9.1	3.5	0
JUL	93	70	51	8.3	1.9	0
AUG	93	70	50	7.9	2.0	0
SEP	87	64	55	7.9	3.5	0
OCT	79	53	55	8.1	3.5	0
NOV	68	44	58	9.0	2.1	0
DEC	60	35	59	9.2	1.5	0

Mariposa, CA — Rank: 38

Location: 37.29 N and 119.57 W at 1,962 feet, 15 miles southwest of Yosemite National Park. Merced and California's central valley lie another 20 miles southwest. San Francisco is 150 miles west.

Landscape: High mountains. Lying in a canyon valley in the foothills of the Sierra Nevadas, the area is surrounded by ranchland, and the hills are covered with a mixed forest of oak and pine. Part of Yosemite National Park and Stanislaus National Forest fall within Mariposa County.

Climate: Continental. The area is protected from the humid air of the Pacific, so warm summers and dry, cool winters are the norm. A rain shadow effect is cast, so winter snow and summer thunderstorms are rare. It does freeze, with the first frost around November 12; the last frost leaves with the tax return, April 15.

Summer mildness: 51 **Seasonal affect:** 77
Winter mildness: 68 **Hazard free:** 58

	189
	75
	100
90°	83
32°	64
0°	0
	34
	43
	14

	High °F	Low °F	Hum %	Wind mph	Precip inches	Snow inches
JAN	55	32	80	7.3	5.6	4.3
FEB	59	34	75	7.6	5.0	3.1
MAR	61	36	65	8.7	5.3	3.0
APR	67	40	55	8.7	2.7	0
MAY	77	45	48	9.4	0.8	0
JUN	87	51	44	9.7	0.2	0
JUL	95	57	44	9.1	0.1	0
AUG	94	56	45	8.6	0.2	0
SEP	87	51	45	7.5	0.6	0
OCT	77	43	53	6.4	1.8	0
NOV	62	36	65	6.0	4.8	0
DEC	54	32	77	6.6	4.6	2.7

★ = in the top 30 places for climate mildness

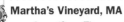

Martha's Vineyard, MA Rank: 172

Location: The weather station is Edgartown, 41.23 N and 70.32 W at 20 feet on southeast Martha's Vineyard, and 27 miles southeast of New Bedford in the Atlantic and 70 miles south of Boston.

Landscape: Irregular plains. On a 100-square-mile island reachable by ferry off the southeast Massachusetts coast, separated from the Elizabeth Islands and Cape Cod by Vineyard and Nantucket sounds. As a result of glaciation, the island has morainal hills composed of boulders and clay deposits in the north, and low, sandy plains in the south. The island once was thickly covered by typical deciduous trees of the northeast forest, but now is relatively bare.

Climate: Mild, cool, and maritime with a distinct four-season climate of warm, damp, foggy summers; cold, wet winters; brief springs; and a long, bright, and pleasant fall. The first frost arrives October 22 and the last frost departs April 28.

Summer mildness: 66 **Seasonal affect:** 26
Winter mildness: 11 **Hazard free:** 28

| 98 | 104 | 163 | 90° 3 | 32° 118 | 0° 1 | 24 | 75 | 19 |

	High °F	Low °F	Hum %	Wind mph	Precip inches	Snow inches
JAN	38	24	64	13.8	3.8	9.1
FEB	38	25	62	13.8	3.6	9.8
MAR	45	31	62	13.7	3.9	6.1
APR	54	38	60	13.2	4.1	0
MAY	63	46	63	12.2	4.0	0
JUN	72	55	66	11.5	3.4	0
JUL	78	61	67	11.0	2.9	0
AUG	78	61	68	10.8	3.6	0
SEP	71	56	69	11.3	3.5	0
OCT	62	48	67	12.0	3.8	0
NOV	53	39	67	12.9	4.4	0
DEC	43	29	66	13.6	4.3	5.0

Maryville, TN Rank: 148

Location: 35.45 N and 83.58 W at 945 feet, in the foothills of the Great Smoky Mountains of eastern Tennessee. Knoxville is 16 miles north.

Landscape: Low mountains. To the east are the highest peaks in eastern North America. In the nearby Great Smoky Mountains National Park is a large stand of virgin red spruce. Common trees are hickory, oak, beech, birch, walnut, and maple. These tall broadleaf trees provide dense foliage in summer and completely shed their leaves in winter. Low shrubs develop in spring.

Climate: Hot continental, characterized by hot, humid summers and cool, cloudy, and wet winters. Daily and seasonal temperature changes aren't abrupt. The first frost will come by October 27; the last frost leaves by April 13. On summer nights, there's a pleasant moderating effect where a steady wind, a draw caused by the many streams and waterfalls, pulls the cool air down from the mountains to the lowlands.

Summer mildness: 40 **Seasonal affect:** 15
Winter mildness: 59 **Hazard free:** 44

| 97 | 107 | 161 | 90° 39 | 32° 95 | 0° 0 | 31 | 86 | 47 |

	High °F	Low °F	Hum %	Wind mph	Precip inches	Snow inches
JAN	46	26	65	7.9	4.2	4.1
FEB	51	29	61	8.3	4.1	3.7
MAR	61	37	56	8.7	5.1	1.5
APR	70	45	53	8.6	3.7	0
MAY	78	53	60	7.0	4.1	0
JUN	85	62	61	6.5	4.0	0
JUL	87	66	63	6.1	4.7	0
AUG	87	65	63	5.6	3.1	0
SEP	81	59	62	5.8	3.1	0
OCT	71	46	57	5.8	2.8	0
NOV	60	38	60	6.9	3.8	0
DEC	50	30	66	7.3	4.5	1.6

★ Maui, HI Rank: 13

Location: The weather station is Lahaina, 20.52 N and 156.41 W at 20 feet, on the island's west coast, 125 air miles from Honolulu.

Landscape: Plains with high mountains. At 728 square miles, Maui is the second-largest island of the Hawaiian chain. Created by two volcanoes, which make up east and west peninsulas connected by a valley-like isthmus 7 miles wide, hence the nickname of Valley Isle. The peaks of west Maui rise to almost 6,000 feet, and those to the southeast to over 10,000 feet. Native plants include varieties of fern and palm, shrub, forest, bog, and moss lichen.

Climate: Mild marine tropical. Daily and seasonal temperature changes are small. Summer days can be hot, owing to high humidity. There's marked variation in rainfall depending on the season and place. Leeward coastal areas are drier than the lower mountains of western Maui. Winds are persistently from the northeast. Severe storms are rare.

Summer mildness: 37 **Seasonal affect:** 90
Winter mildness: 74 **Hazard free:** 95

| 54 | 182 | 129 | 90° 17 | 32° 0 | 0° 0 | 0 | 19 | 8 |

	High °F	Low °F	Hum %	Wind mph	Precip inches	Snow inches
JAN	82	64	74	10.9	3.5	0
FEB	82	63	73	11.4	2.4	0
MAR	83	64	72	12.4	1.8	0
APR	84	65	72	13.2	1.1	0
MAY	85	67	72	12.5	0.6	0
JUN	87	68	70	12.9	0.1	0
JUL	88	69	70	13.5	0.2	0
AUG	88	70	71	12.8	0.2	0
SEP	89	70	71	11.5	0.3	0
OCT	88	69	75	11.3	1.1	0
NOV	86	67	74	12.0	2.2	0
DEC	83	65	74	11.5	3.2	0

★ = in the top 30 places for climate mildness

McAllen–Alamo, TX — Rank: 47

Location: 26.12 N and 98.13 W at 124 feet, on the border with Mexico in the lower Rio Grande Valley of southernmost Texas. The Rio Grande empties into the Gulf of Mexico 75 miles east of here.

Landscape: Smooth plains. Flat topography with little relief. Date palms, bougainvillea, and winter poinsettias color the valley towns, but the native upland sage and chaparral have lost out to intensive development, both agricultural and urban.

Climate: Subtropical, influenced by the Gulf of Mexico. The valley is usually windy. Winters are clear, with warm days and cool nights. The frost arrives late in December and departs by the end of January. Summers are long, hot, and humid. The Sierra Madre Oriental Mountains in Mexico block dry air from the Chihuahuan Desert, but both affect the climate of this river plain.

Summer mildness: 9
Winter mildness: 65
Seasonal affect: 79
Hazard free: 93

	98
	132
	135
90°	157
32°	4
0°	0
	27
	34
	26

	High °F	Low °F	Hum %	Wind mph	Precip inches	Snow inches
JAN	68	47	67	11.3	1.4	0
FEB	72	50	63	12.1	1.3	0
MAR	80	57	59	13.4	0.6	0
APR	86	64	59	13.9	1.3	0
MAY	89	70	60	13.1	2.8	0
JUN	93	73	59	12.0	2.7	0
JUL	95	74	55	11.3	1.7	0
AUG	96	74	56	10.3	2.4	0
SEP	92	72	60	9.4	4.4	0
OCT	87	64	59	9.5	2.6	0
NOV	79	56	60	10.7	1.0	0
DEC	71	49	65	10.8	1.1	0

McCall, ID — Rank: 158

Location: 44.54 N and 116.06 W at 5,031 feet in the Payette River Valley 100 miles north of Boise.

Landscape: High mountains. Slopes vary from the flat river and lake bottomlands to rolling foothills and steep mountain slopes. Though all aspects are found, most face east and west. Elevations range from about 4,800 to 7,500 feet. Mixed coniferous-deciduous forest predominates. The area's major parent material is granite from the Idaho Batholith. A small area in the northwestern part of the county is underlaid by basalt of the Columbia River formation.

Climate: Highland continental characterized by wide daily and seasonal temperature changes. Winters are severe, with among the heaviest snowfall amounts of any retirement places profiled here. First frost comes early, by August 26; last frost occurs June 23. Summer days are warm to hot and usually dry because westerly air masses draw the dry climate of the Pacific Coast.

Summer mildness: 95
Winter mildness: 10
Seasonal affect: 37
Hazard free: 10

	120
	90
	155
90°	4
32°	224
0°	18
	51
	54
	15

	High °F	Low °F	Hum %	Wind mph	Precip inches	Snow inches
JAN	31	22	76	8.0	3.8	14.0
FEB	37	28	70	8.9	2.8	13.0
MAR	42	32	60	9.9	2.6	10.0
APR	51	37	53	9.9	2.0	9.0
MAY	62	44	52	9.5	2.1	5.0
JUN	71	52	49	9.0	2.1	0
JUL	81	58	38	8.4	0.8	0
AUG	80	57	38	8.2	1.2	0
SEP	70	48	44	8.2	1.7	1.0
OCT	58	39	53	8.3	1.9	9.0
NOV	41	31	69	8.4	3.2	12.0
DEC	32	23	76	8.1	3.5	13.0

Medford–Ashland, OR — Rank: 42

Location: 42.19 N and 122.52 W at 1,374 feet, in southwest Oregon, 25 miles north of the California border.

Landscape: High mountains. Located in a mountain valley formed by the Rogue River and Bear Creek. The valley's outlet to the ocean 80 miles west is the narrow Canyon of the Rogue. Principal trees of the dense coniferous Pacific forest are Douglas fir, western red cedar, western hemlock, silver fir, and Sitka spruce.

Climate: Moderate continental. Late fall, winter, and early spring are cloudy, damp, and cool. The remainder of the year is warm, dry, and sunny. The shadow afforded by the Siskiyous and the Coast Range results in lighter rainfall. Snowfalls are light and usually melt within 24 hours. Winters are mild, with temperatures just dipping below freezing during December and January nights. Summer days can reach 90°F, but nights are cool. Frost arrives by October 20 and leaves by April 30.

Summer mildness: 69
Winter mildness: 78
Seasonal affect: 30
Hazard free: 73

	117
	79
	169
90°	53
32°	68
0°	0
	50
	62
	8

	High °F	Low °F	Hum %	Wind mph	Precip inches	Snow inches
JAN	48	33	83	4.1	5.2	3.7
FEB	55	34	77	4.5	3.8	1.6
MAR	61	36	66	5.3	3.5	1.3
APR	67	38	57	5.7	1.8	0
MAY	75	44	50	5.7	1.2	0
JUN	83	50	42	5.9	0.5	0
JUL	90	53	38	5.8	0.2	0
AUG	90	53	39	5.3	0.5	0
SEP	83	47	42	4.5	0.9	0
OCT	70	41	58	3.7	2.4	0
NOV	54	38	80	3.6	5.3	0
DEC	46	34	85	3.6	5.7	2.3

★ = in the top 30 places for climate mildness

★ Melbourne–Palm Bay, FL — Rank: 27

Location: 28.04 N and 80.36 W at 21 feet, on the Intracoastal Waterway in the center of Florida's Atlantic Coast, 58 miles southeast of Orlando.

Landscape: Flat plains. Florida coastal topography, with miles of hard, sandy beach. Inland, the land rises slightly to 30 feet. Native vegetation includes sea-oat grass, sea-grape, and cabbage palm.

Climate: Subtropical. Nearness to the Atlantic results in a climate tempered by land and sea breezes. Temperatures in summer may top 90°F during the late morning or early afternoon, but they're cut short by midday sea breezes, and afternoon convective thundershowers lower temperatures to comfortable levels. Winters can have cold airflows from the north, but they're usually mild because of the city's ocean setting and southerly latitude. There is hardly a freezing season, with frost arriving January 16 and departing a few days later, on January 19.

Summer mildness: 15	Seasonal affect: 68
Winter mildness: 90	Hazard free: 89

	99
	134
	133
90°	65
32°	2
0°	0
	28
	65
	77

	High °F	Low °F	Hum %	Wind mph	Precip inches	Snow inches
JAN	71	51	58	8.7	2.2	0
FEB	72	51	56	9.2	2.8	0
MAR	77	56	56	9.9	2.7	0
APR	81	61	54	9.2	1.6	0
MAY	85	67	59	9.1	4.0	0
JUN	88	71	65	7.9	6.1	0
JUL	90	72	64	7.1	5.2	0
AUG	89	73	64	6.5	5.2	0
SEP	88	72	66	7.6	6.6	0
OCT	83	67	62	8.9	4.1	0
NOV	77	59	61	8.9	3.0	0
DEC	73	53	59	8.1	2.1	0

★ Mendocino–Fort Bragg, CA — Rank: 10

Location: 39.25 N and 123.21 W at 120 feet in a valley in the Coast Ranges of northwest California, 130 miles north of San Francisco.

Landscape: Low mountains are visible to the east. The location lies at the mouth of Big River. Redwood and pine timber are found in Mendocino National Forest off to the east and at Jackson State Forest to the west.

Climate: Mendocino experiences a short growing season, with late frosts in spring, early rains and frosts in fall, and higher average rainfall than Napa and Sonoma counties and the central coast. Summer daytime temperatures are warm, while cold nights often dip into the 30s. This dramatic fluctuation softens the tannins of locally produced cabernet sauvignon and zinfandel.

Summer mildness: 75	Seasonal affect: 67
Winter mildness: 64	Hazard free: 97

	160
	101
	104
90°	0
32°	11
0°	0
	100
	42
	0

	High °F	Low °F	Hum %	Wind mph	Precip inches	Snow inches
JAN	57	46	76	7.2	6.5	0
FEB	57	49	75	8.7	5.5	0
MAR	58	49	73	10.5	6.0	0
APR	61	50	71	12.2	2.8	0
MAY	62	51	71	13.4	1.2	0
JUN	64	53	71	13.9	0.3	0
JUL	65	54	73	13.6	0.1	0
AUG	66	55	74	12.8	0.4	0
SEP	67	56	72	11.1	0.8	0
OCT	64	55	71	9.4	2.9	0
NOV	60	52	73	7.5	6.2	0
DEC	56	47	76	7.1	6.4	0

Middle Cape Cod, MA — Rank: 167

Location: The weather station is Harwich at 41.40 N and 70.04 W, at 19 feet and 60 miles southeast of Boston on a hooked peninsula jutting out 65 miles into the Atlantic Ocean.

Landscape: Irregular plains. The area falls between the hilly western end of the Cape and the flat and treeless eastern or "outer cape." The soil is sandy and arranged in hills and dunes. There are also marshes and lakes. Tree cover is mostly pinewood.

Climate: Cape Cod extends into the Gulf Stream, making for a markedly milder climate than that of the rest of southern New England. Summers are warm, but temperatures rarely exceed 90°F. Winters are mild, with light to moderate snowfall mixed with periods of thaw and rain. First frost arrives on October 22, last frost on April 28.

Summer mildness: 85	Seasonal affect: 20
Winter mildness: 9	Hazard free: 27

	99
	104
	162
90°	1
32°	122
0°	1
	24
	77
	19

	High °F	Low °F	Hum %	Wind mph	Precip inches	Snow inches
JAN	38	21	57	13.9	3.8	9.1
FEB	38	22	56	13.8	3.6	9.8
MAR	45	29	56	13.7	3.9	6.1
APR	54	37	55	13.2	4.1	0.3
MAY	63	46	60	12.2	4.0	0
JUN	72	56	59	11.5	3.4	0
JUL	78	62	57	11.0	2.9	0
AUG	78	62	59	10.8	3.6	0
SEP	71	55	60	11.3	3.5	0
OCT	62	45	58	12.0	3.8	0
NOV	53	37	59	13.0	4.4	0.2
DEC	43	27	59	13.6	4.3	5.2

★ = in the top 30 places for climate mildness

Retirement Places Rated

Monadnock Region, NH — Rank: 200

Location: 42.561 N and 72.1643 W at 487 feet, in southwestern New Hampshire, 15 miles from the Vermont and Massachusetts borders.

Landscape: Open low mountains. The terrain is hilly to mountainous forestland. Nearby, Mount Monadnock rises to 3,165 feet, with Boston visible 85 miles southeast. The Connecticut River lies to the west and forms the border with Vermont. Vegetation is mixed forest, with pine and maple predominating. Mountain laurel and flowering dogwood are also common in this part of the state.

Climate: The typical New England climate makes for warm summers, long and pleasant autumns, cold winters, and short, wet springs. Heat waves are infrequent in summer, but cold snaps are common in winter. Frost comes in by September 25 and will not leave until May 19. Snowfall amounts can vary greatly from year to year, with limited thaws.

Summer mildness: 52 **Seasonal affect:** 7
Winter mildness: 3 **Hazard free:** 9

	98
	104
	163
90°	13
32°	166
0°	18
	185
	81
	19

	High °F	Low °F	Hum %	Wind mph	Precip inches	Snow inches
JAN	32	10	67	13.8	2.9	16.9
FEB	36	13	66	13.8	2.7	16.1
MAR	45	23	65	13.7	2.9	13.2
APR	59	33	62	13.2	3.2	2.8
MAY	71	44	62	12.2	3.8	0.1
JUN	79	53	67	11.5	3.6	0
JUL	84	57	68	11.0	3.6	0
AUG	82	56	71	10.8	3.9	0
SEP	73	48	73	11.3	3.0	0
OCT	62	37	71	12.0	3.2	0.1
NOV	49	30	72	12.9	3.5	3.9
DEC	36	17	71	13.6	3.3	16.1

Montrose, CO — Rank: 85

Location: 38.28 N and 107.52 W at 5,801 feet, in the Uncompahgre River Valley, 50 miles southeast of Grand Junction.

Landscape: Open low mountains. The sage desert and shortgrass prairie of the Colorado Plateau. The western vista is the Uncompahgre Plateau, rising over 9,000 feet. Ranchland and orchards mark the gently rolling lowland. Lakes and streams here are fed from mountain snows. The Uncompahgre River flows through steep canyons. Mixed forests of pine, spruce, and aspen cover the subalpine areas; sagebrush and cactus are found in the canyons.

Climate: Desert-steppe brings varied seasonal and daily temperature changes. Summers are dry and comfortable due to the high altitude. Winters are cold with moderate snow cover in the elevations through May. Winters are long, with the first frost arriving October 8 and the last frost not leaving until May 12. Humidity is low, and summer precipitation is scant but for brief mountain thunderstorms.

Summer mildness: 78 **Seasonal affect:** 83
Winter mildness: 26 **Hazard free:** 26

	137
	107
	121
90°	34
32°	168
0°	7
	8
	27
	35

	High °F	Low °F	Hum %	Wind mph	Precip inches	Snow inches
JAN	37	12	63	5.6	0.5	7.3
FEB	44	19	54	6.7	0.4	5.7
MAR	53	26	43	8.4	0.7	3.7
APR	62	34	33	9.5	0.8	2.0
MAY	72	42	32	9.6	0.9	0
JUN	83	51	26	9.7	0.6	0
JUL	88	57	28	9.3	1.0	0
AUG	86	54	31	9.0	1.1	0
SEP	77	46	33	8.9	1.2	0
OCT	66	35	38	7.9	1.1	0
NOV	50	25	49	6.7	0.8	4.0
DEC	40	16	60	5.9	0.7	7.5

★ Morro Bay–Cambria, CA — Rank: 4

Location: 35.21 N and 120.50 W at 89 feet, on the Pacific Ocean roughly 230 miles midway between San Francisco and Los Angeles.

Landscape: Open low mountains. The Santa Lucia Mountains end in cliffs that slice into the ocean to the north, with sandy beaches elsewhere on the coast. Forests are mixed evergreen, with pine and cypress in abundance. Cultivated groves of almond, walnut, and apple trees are common, as are vineyards.

Climate: Weather is stable, ranging from mild and warm in summer to mild and cool in winter. Fog and cloudy mornings usually give way to bright sunshine with cool ocean breezes. The high elevation and coastal location are responsible for the consistently mild climate. There is a long growing season between the last frost of January 25 and the first frost of December 30.

Summer mildness: 63 **Seasonal affect:** 86
Winter mildness: 99 **Hazard free:** 99

	147
	116
	103
90°	12
32°	3
0°	0
	19
	28
	4

	High °F	Low °F	Hum %	Wind mph	Precip inches	Snow inches
JAN	63	42	57	4.8	5.0	0
FEB	65	43	58	6.3	4.6	0
MAR	65	43	60	6.7	3.8	0
APR	68	45	61	7.6	1.6	0
MAY	70	47	63	7.1	0.3	0
JUN	74	50	66	6.8	0.0	0
JUL	78	52	67	6.5	0.0	0
AUG	79	53	68	6.1	0.1	0
SEP	79	53	67	5.8	0.4	0
OCT	76	50	64	5.5	1.1	0
NOV	69	46	57	5.3	2.8	0
DEC	64	42	55	5.0	3.8	0

★ = in the top 30 places for climate mildness

Murray–Kentucky Lake, KY — Rank: 132

Location: 36.36 N and 88.19 W at 480 feet, just above the Tennessee state line in the extreme western part of Kentucky. Nashville, Tennessee, is 100 miles southeast.

Landscape: Irregular plains. Kentucky Lake is one of the world's largest artificial lakes, formed more than 50 years ago by damming the Tennessee River. Relief is minimal. The surrounding country is gently rolling and heavily forested with oak, hickory, walnut, maple, elm, ash, and sweet chestnut, with lower layers of small trees and shrubs.

Climate: Hot continental, with moderately cold winters and warm, humid summers. Precipitation is ample and well distributed throughout the year. October 26 ushers in the first frost; April 5 sees the last frost out. Most days, even those in winter, are suitable for outdoor activity. Spring and fall are the most comfortable seasons. Fall, the sunniest season, is remarkably free from storms or cold.

Summer mildness: 44   **Seasonal affect:** 36
Winter mildness: 53   **Hazard free:** 40

	109
	99
	157
90°	51
32°	84
0°	1
	20
	74
	60

	High °F	Low °F	Hum %	Wind mph	Precip inches	Snow inches
JAN	43	25	62	9.3	3.8	4.3
FEB	49	29	65	9.2	4.4	3.1
MAR	60	39	57	9.6	5.1	2.4
APR	71	48	50	8.6	5.1	0
MAY	79	57	56	7.5	4.9	0
JUN	87	65	55	6.5	4.1	0
JUL	90	68	58	6.1	4.7	0
AUG	88	67	59	5.6	3.6	0
SEP	82	60	56	6.2	3.9	0
OCT	71	48	56	6.9	3.6	0
NOV	59	40	61	8.9	5.2	0
DEC	48	30	63	8.9	5.3	1.0

Myrtle Beach, SC — Rank: 93

Location: 33.41 N and 78.53 W at 30 feet, 100 miles northeast of Charleston.

Landscape: Flat plains. The area known as the Grand Strand is flat, has a populated area only a few blocks wide, and extends 60 miles up and down the shore. Elevations are no greater than 50 feet above sea level. There are many more wooded areas than are usually found in a beach area. The beaches themselves are white sand. Inland is low and swampy, with stands of southern yellow pine mixed with hickory, sweet gum, and other deciduous trees. The grasses are bluestem, panicums, and longleaf uniola in the coastal marshes.

Climate: Subtropical. Mild winters and warm summers are the rule. The ocean has a pronounced modifying effect on temperatures, and the Blue Ridge Mountains block cold air from the interior. Some tropical storms reach the area every few years. First frost comes by November 20; the last frost leaves by March 11.

Summer mildness: 27   **Seasonal affect:** 52
Winter mildness: 66   **Hazard free:** 59

	112
	104
	150
90°	45
32°	35
0°	0
	24
	72
	47

	High °F	Low °F	Hum %	Wind mph	Precip inches	Snow inches
JAN	58	36	56	9.1	3.9	0.5
FEB	62	38	52	9.8	3.7	0.6
MAR	69	45	52	10.2	4.2	0.3
APR	76	52	48	10.3	2.7	0
MAY	83	61	55	9.2	4.4	0
JUN	87	68	59	8.5	5.6	0
JUL	90	71	63	8.0	6.5	0
AUG	89	71	64	7.4	6.5	0
SEP	85	66	62	7.9	5.2	0
OCT	78	55	56	8.1	4.0	0
NOV	70	47	53	8.1	3.1	0
DEC	62	39	55	8.5	3.5	0.3

★ Naples, FL — Rank: 30

Location: 26.08 N and 81.47 W at 9 feet, on Florida's Gulf of Mexico coast, 25 miles south of Ft. Myers.

Landscape: Flat plains. The area lies on a 7-mile mainland beach. Nearby are mangrove islands. To the east is the Big Cypress Swamp, and beyond, the Everglades. Native vegetation includes cypress, evergreen oaks, laurel, small palms, and tropical shrubs.

Climate: Subtropical. Summer and winter temperature extremes are checked by the influence of the Gulf. Summer heat is exacerbated by humidity. Winters have many bright, warm days and moderately cool nights. Rainfall averages more than 50 inches annually, with two-thirds coming daily between June and September. Most rain falls as late-afternoon or early-evening thunderstorms, bringing welcome relief from the heat.

Summer mildness: 11   **Seasonal affect:** 68
Winter mildness: 96   **Hazard free:** 83

	102
	142
	121
90°	101
32°	0
0°	0
	21
	72
	93

	High °F	Low °F	Hum %	Wind mph	Precip inches	Snow inches
JAN	76	53	56	8.6	1.7	0
FEB	77	54	56	9.2	2.2	0
MAR	81	58	53	9.5	2.3	0
APR	85	61	47	9.3	1.5	0
MAY	88	66	49	8.7	4.1	0
JUN	90	71	56	8.0	8.6	0
JUL	91	72	60	7.2	7.8	0
AUG	92	73	60	7.0	8.2	0
SEP	91	72	60	7.8	8.4	0
OCT	87	67	56	8.5	3.1	0
NOV	82	61	56	8.4	1.8	0
DEC	78	55	56	8.5	1.4	0

Natchitoches, LA — Rank: 119

Location: 31.46 N and 93.06 W at 130 feet in northwest Louisiana, 65 miles southeast from Shreveport and 225 miles east of Dallas, Texas.

Landscape: Irregular plains. The topography is gently sloping, with relief varying between 100 and 250 feet. Most of the numerous streams are sluggish; marshes, swamps, and lakes are numerous. The naturally occurring forest is laurel, magnolia, and evergreen oak.

Climate: Moderately uniform throughout the year: Mild winters and hot summers are the rule. Precipitation exceeds evaporation, but summer droughts occur. The growing season is long, but frost occurs every winter. The first frost arrives November 11 and the last frost departs March 10. Snow falls rarely but melts almost immediately.

Summer mildness: 2   **Seasonal affect:** 48
Winter mildness: 77   **Hazard free:** 57

	114
	100
	151
90°	90
32°	36
0°	0
	107
	64
	57

	High °F	Low °F	Hum %	Wind mph	Precip inches	Snow inches
JAN	57	35	74	9.2	4.9	0.8
FEB	62	38	71	9.6	4.6	0.5
MAR	70	46	70	10.1	4.7	0.2
APR	78	54	72	9.7	4.3	0
MAY	85	62	75	8.3	6.0	0
JUN	91	69	75	7.5	4.3	0
JUL	94	72	74	7.1	3.5	0
AUG	93	71	73	6.7	3.2	0
SEP	88	66	74	7.2	3.4	0
OCT	79	54	72	7.4	3.8	0
NOV	69	45	73	8.5	4.2	0
DEC	60	37	74	8.9	6.1	0.2

Nelson County, VA — Rank: 164

Location: The weather station is Lovingston, the county seat, sitting at 37.45 N and 78.52 W at 760 feet. Visible to the northwest are the Blue Ridge Mountains. Charlottesville is 30 miles north.

Landscape: Open low mountains. The country is agricultural and forested by a remnant of the northeastern hardwood forest. Birch, beech, maple, elm, red oak, and basswood, with some hemlock and white pine, predominate.

Climate: Temperate mid-latitude climate. Summers are warm and humid, winters mild. Typically, the best weather is in the spring and autumn. The coldest weather occurs in late January and early February; the warmest month is July. There are no pronounced wet and dry seasons. Thunderstorms during the summer often bring sudden heavy rains and damaging winds, hail, or lightning. In winter, snow accumulations of more than 10 inches are rare. The first frost arrives November 4 and the last frost departs April 7.

Summer mildness: 36   **Seasonal affect:** 27
Winter mildness: 50   **Hazard free:** 31

	112
	107
	147
90°	31
32°	92
0°	0
	122
	75
	32

	High °F	Low °F	Hum %	Wind mph	Precip inches	Snow inches
JAN	45	23	63	8.6	3.2	7.2
FEB	48	25	61	8.6	3.2	7.6
MAR	59	33	61	9.1	3.9	6.3
APR	69	41	59	9.0	3.3	0.5
MAY	76	50	67	7.5	4.6	0
JUN	84	59	69	6.9	3.2	0
JUL	87	64	72	6.5	4.6	0
AUG	86	63	74	6.3	3.6	0
SEP	80	56	73	6.9	3.7	0
OCT	70	44	69	7.3	4.4	0
NOV	61	36	66	7.9	3.4	1.5
DEC	49	27	65	7.9	3.2	4.5

New Bern, NC — Rank: 147

Location: 35.06 N and 77.02 W at 15 feet, on a triangle of land where the Neuse and Trent rivers meet and empty into Pamlico Sound. Raleigh is 100 miles northwest. The Atlantic Ocean is 35 miles east.

Landscape: Flat plains. In this central tidewater savanna are bluffs, marshes, lakes, and rivers. Narrow-leafed grasses are found in the salt marshes; cattails, ricegrass, and parrotfeathers are found in the freshwater marshes. The trees are oak-hickory, not as tall, with smaller and more leathery leaves, and a sparse canopy. In town are live oak, laurel, holly, and magnolia, with underbrush of shrubs and herbaceous plants.

Climate: Subtropical, with humid, hot summers and mild winters. Rain falls throughout the year. Spring and summer can bring heavy thunderstorms. Occasional tropical storms from the Atlantic may strike this coastal location. Since first frost comes November 9 and the last frost leaves March 23, the growing season is relatively long.

Summer mildness: 34   **Seasonal affect:** 36
Winter mildness: 42   **Hazard free:** 49

	106
	107
	152
90°	39
32°	53
0°	0
	20
	77
	49

	High °F	Low °F	Hum %	Wind mph	Precip inches	Snow inches
JAN	54	33	56	12.1	4.3	1.1
FEB	57	35	52	12.3	4.2	1.0
MAR	65	42	52	12.0	3.9	0.8
APR	73	50	48	11.8	3.2	0
MAY	80	59	55	10.9	4.6	0
JUN	86	66	59	10.7	5.4	0
JUL	88	71	63	10.0	7.0	0
AUG	87	70	64	9.5	6.6	0
SEP	83	64	62	10.5	5.1	0
OCT	75	53	56	11.1	3.0	0
NOV	67	44	53	11.0	3.2	0
DEC	58	36	55	11.5	3.7	0.3

★ = in the top 30 places for climate mildness

Climate

51

New Braunfels, TX

Rank: 68

Location: 29.42 N and 98.07 W at 623 feet, on the Balcones Escarpment in south-central Texas. San Antonio is 30 miles southwest.

Landscape: Open high hills amid arid grassland with shrubs and low trees and low hills. The deep, winding Comal River flows into the Guadalupe River. While the spring-fed Comal is predictably smooth and safe, conditions on the white-water Guadalupe frequently change. Nearby Landa Park, Natural Bridge Caverns, and Canyon Lake mark the region. Caladium grows along the riverbanks. As the land rises to the Edwards Plateau, oak, hickory, and juniper mix with mesquite and buffalo grass. Open grassland and savanna are less common because ranching is predominant.

Climate: Prairie, with warm days and cool nights in winter and a long, hot summer. Though miles from the Gulf, the area is influenced by moist, marine air. Most of the annual precipitation falls as rain in May and September. The first frost comes at Thanksgiving, around November 26, and the last frost is out early, by March 9.

Summer mildness: 19	Seasonal affect: 74
Winter mildness: 59	Hazard free: 76

Weather icon scale: 108 / 118 / 139 / 90° 122 / 32° 28 / 0° 0 / 22 / 46 / 37

	High °F	Low °F	Hum %	Wind mph	Precip inches	Snow inches
JAN	60	37	59	9.0	1.9	0.1
FEB	65	40	57	9.7	2.2	0.4
MAR	73	48	54	10.4	1.8	0
APR	81	56	56	10.3	2.6	0
MAY	86	64	59	10.0	5.0	0
JUN	92	70	56	9.9	4.1	0
JUL	95	72	51	9.2	2.0	0
AUG	96	72	51	8.5	2.5	0
SEP	90	68	55	8.5	4.1	0
OCT	82	57	54	8.4	3.5	0
NOV	72	48	55	8.8	2.8	0
DEC	63	39	57	8.5	2.0	0

Newport–Lincoln City, OR

Rank: 70

Location: 44.38 N and 124.03 W at 177 feet, on Oregon's Pacific Coast, 55 miles west of Salem.

Landscape: Low mountains. Parts of the cities sit at the water's edge, and more are built on level bench land about 150 feet above sea level. Just to the east, the foothills of the Coast Range begin a steep ascent to ridges 2,000 to 3,000 feet high. The principal trees of the dense Pacific conifer forests nearby are Douglas fir, western red cedar, western hemlock, silver fir, and Sitka spruce.

Climate: Marine climate typical of Oregon's coastal area. Temperature extremes are almost nonexistent. Warm, moist air from the Pacific makes summers mild and pleasant. In winter, the air releases moisture over the cold landmass, resulting in a constant cloud cover and rain from November to March. Most of the annual precipitation falls during these months. The first frost arrives November 18; the last frost leaves April 16.

Summer mildness: 75	Seasonal affect: 3
Winter mildness: 68	Hazard free: 81

Weather icon scale: 49 / 78 / 238 / 90° 0 / 32° 30 / 0° 0 / 41 / 126 / 7

	High °F	Low °F	Hum %	Wind mph	Precip inches	Snow inches
JAN	50	38	80	9.1	11.1	0.8
FEB	53	39	79	9.1	8.1	0.2
MAR	54	39	77	9.0	8.2	0.4
APR	55	40	72	8.7	4.8	0
MAY	59	43	71	8.5	3.5	0
JUN	62	48	71	8.6	2.7	0
JUL	65	50	73	8.7	1.0	0
AUG	65	50	73	8.1	1.3	0
SEP	65	48	72	7.6	2.6	0
OCT	61	45	77	7.6	5.4	0
NOV	55	42	78	8.8	10.9	0
DEC	51	38	80	9.1	12.3	0.6

Norfork Lake, AR

Rank: 143

Location: 36.20 N and 92.23 W at 756 feet, near the center of the Arkansas–Missouri border, 100 air miles north of Little Rock.

Landscape: High hills. Though in the center of the Ozark Mountains, gently rolling hills surround Lake Norfork, formed decades ago by damming the White River. The thick woods are broadleaf deciduous forests of oak, hickory, maple, sweet gum, and walnut.

Climate: Hot continental, with warm summers and winters of mild days and freezing nights. In a given year, the climate can vary from warm and humid maritime to cold and dry continental, but it's relatively free from climatic extremes. Winters may be cold enough for snow, but an icy rain is more typical during brief, intense cold snaps. First frost has hit by October 26; last frost strikes April 6, bringing an early spring that is pleasant.

Summer mildness: 45	Seasonal affect: 59
Winter mildness: 28	Hazard free: 34

Weather icon scale: 116 / 97 / 153 / 90° 56 / 32° 90 / 0° 1 / 20 / 63 / 56

	High °F	Low °F	Hum %	Wind mph	Precip inches	Snow inches
JAN	45	23	60	11.7	2.5	3.1
FEB	50	27	60	11.9	3.0	3.2
MAR	60	37	56	12.9	4.4	2.0
APR	71	47	55	12.2	4.1	0
MAY	78	55	59	10.4	4.9	0
JUN	85	63	59	9.6	4.1	0
JUL	91	67	56	8.5	2.6	0
AUG	90	66	54	8.6	2.9	0
SEP	82	59	58	9.3	4.1	0
OCT	73	47	54	10.1	3.3	0
NOV	59	37	59	11.3	4.4	1.0
DEC	48	27	63	11.6	3.8	1.6

★ = in the top 30 places for climate mildness

Northampton–Amherst, MA — Rank: 170

Location: 42.22 N and 72.31 W at 320 feet, in the western part of the state, 70 miles west of Boston and 20 miles north of Springfield.

Landscape: Open low mountains. Situated in the center of the long Connecticut Valley, with the Berkshire Hills of the Appalachians visible to the west. This is the Berkshire Taconic forest plateau with curved ridges covered by diverse and transitional forests of red oak, beech, birch, walnut, sugar maple, elm, and sweet chestnut. Cottonwood, basswood, or silver maple found in poorly drained coves. There are areas of isolated wetlands. Quabbin Reservoir lies to the east.

Climate: Hot continental, with typical New England seasonal temperature extremes. Summers are generally mild and free of thunderstorms, but with occasional hot, muggy days. September 29 heralds the first frost; May 9 bids the last frost adieu. Winters are long with a snow cover that's deep and lasting.

Summer mildness: 77 **Seasonal affect:** 16
Winter mildness: 25 **Hazard free:** 20

Weather icon counts: 81, 109, 175, 90° 10, 32° 151, 0° 11, 29, 75, 33

	High °F	Low °F	Hum %	Wind mph	Precip inches	Snow inches
JAN	35	12	58	9.0	3.2	11.6
FEB	38	15	57	9.4	2.9	11.4
MAR	48	25	53	9.9	3.2	8.8
APR	60	34	49	10.0	3.6	1.0
MAY	72	44	49	8.9	3.9	0
JUN	80	54	55	8.1	3.8	0
JUL	85	59	55	7.5	3.8	0
AUG	83	57	57	7.2	3.7	0
SEP	76	49	59	7.3	3.4	0
OCT	65	39	59	7.8	3.4	0
NOV	52	31	60	8.5	3.8	2.0
DEC	39	19	62	8.7	3.7	10.0

Northern Neck, VA — Rank: 151

Location: 37.46 N and 76.28 W at 98 feet, on a peninsula between Virginia's Rappahannock and Potomac rivers extending into Chesapeake Bay. Richmond is 40 miles southeast.

Landscape: Irregular plains. Tidewater country of low hills, streams, and marsh of the Chesapeake Bay watershed. The woods inland are a typical southeastern mixed forest, with tall oak, hickory, sweet gum, red maple, and winged elm. At least half of the stands are filled with second-growth loblolly and shortleaf pine. Coastal marshes and interior wetlands are dominated by gums and cypress trees, cattails, and rush. An understory of dogwood, viburnum, blueberry, youpon, and numerous woody vines is prevalent.

Climate: Subtropical, with mild winters and hot, humid summers. Spring and autumn are especially pleasant. First frost of October 22 will set the woods in color; last frost of April 15 will signal spring greening. Precipitation is evenly distributed throughout the year, mostly as rain. Thunderstorms are likely in mid-summer.

Summer mildness: 43 **Seasonal affect:** 55
Winter mildness: 29 **Hazard free:** 30

Weather icon counts: 106, 107, 152, 90° 39, 32° 88, 0° 0, 20, 70, 37

	High °F	Low °F	Hum %	Wind mph	Precip inches	Snow inches
JAN	45	26	60	11.5	3.2	5.4
FEB	49	29	58	12.0	2.8	5.4
MAR	59	36	56	12.5	3.5	3.4
APR	69	44	52	11.8	2.9	0
MAY	77	54	58	10.5	4.6	0
JUN	85	62	58	9.8	3.7	0
JUL	88	67	61	9.0	4.2	0
AUG	87	65	62	8.9	4.2	0
SEP	81	59	62	9.6	4.2	0
OCT	70	47	61	10.4	3.4	0
NOV	61	39	58	10.7	3.2	0
DEC	50	31	60	11.2	3.1	2.5

Oakhurst–Coarsegold, CA — Rank: 39

Location: 37.19 N and 119.39 W at 2,289 feet, in California's Southern Mines country in the Sierra foothills. San Francisco is 150 miles west.

Landscape: High mountains. In these high foothills are ravines, buttes, and wooded peaks, watered by streams from the Sierra Nevada Mountains. Yosemite National Park is immediately north with waterfalls, acres of forest, and glacier-carved valleys. Rivers drain into the broad San Joaquin Valley to the west. The lower hills are covered by close-growing cypress and piñon. In the higher elevations is a combination of digger pine and blue oak.

Climate: Sierran forest climate in the transition zone between the dry west coast desert and the wet west coast farther north. Prevailing west winds influence conditions jointly with elevation. Therefore the summers are long and generally dry, with most of the precipitation falling as rain rather than snow. First frost comes October 22 while the last frost leaves April 15.

Summer mildness: 57 **Seasonal affect:** 75
Winter mildness: 66 **Hazard free:** 56

Weather icon counts: 189, 75, 100, 90° 59, 32° 77, 0° 0, 34, 49, 14

	High °F	Low °F	Hum %	Wind mph	Precip inches	Snow inches
JAN	56	31	80	7.2	6.0	5.3
FEB	58	33	75	7.6	5.6	3.1
MAR	60	35	65	8.6	5.5	3.0
APR	66	38	55	8.7	3.0	0
MAY	75	44	48	9.2	1.0	0
JUN	85	51	44	9.7	0.3	0
JUL	93	57	44	9.0	0.1	0
AUG	93	57	45	8.6	0.1	0
SEP	86	52	45	7.5	0.7	0
OCT	76	44	53	6.4	1.4	0
NOV	64	36	65	6.0	4.3	0
DEC	57	31	77	6.6	4.9	2.7

★ = in the top 30 places for climate mildness

Climate

Ocala, FL Rank: 53

Location: 29.11 N and 82.08 W at 99 feet, in north-central Florida, 25 miles south of Gainesville and 90 miles west of Daytona Beach and the Atlantic Ocean.

Landscape: Flat plains. This is low ridge country with deposits of pure limestone, just west of Ocala National Forest. Artesian springs and outlets form the Silver River. Stands of sand pine, longleaf, slash, and other yellow southern pine mix with a variety of hardwoods of the Eastern deciduous forest, evergreen oaks, laurel, and a lower stratum of tree ferns, small palms, and shrubs.

Climate: Subtropical, with a small annual range of temperature changes. Precipitation is light, except from May to September. Summers are hotter and more humid than those of coastal locations but are cooled by afternoon thunderstorms. Winters are mild, with warm days and cool nights. First frost comes early December; the last frost leaves mid-February.

Summer mildness: 12 **Seasonal affect:** 58
Winter mildness: 85 **Hazard free:** 86

	92
	148
	125
90°	120
32°	12
0°	0
	27
	77
	82

	High °F	Low °F	Hum %	Wind mph	Precip inches	Snow inches
JAN	70	45	56	8.9	3.2	0
FEB	72	46	52	9.6	3.8	0
MAR	79	53	50	9.9	3.5	0
APR	84	57	46	9.4	2.8	0
MAY	89	63	49	8.8	4.1	0
JUN	92	69	56	8.0	7.2	0
JUL	92	71	59	7.4	7.8	0
AUG	92	71	60	7.1	6.7	0
SEP	90	69	60	7.7	5.5	0
OCT	84	61	56	8.6	2.1	0
NOV	77	53	55	8.6	2.3	0
DEC	72	47	57	8.6	2.7	0

Ocean City, MD Rank: 132

Location: 38.20 N and 75.05 W at 8 feet, on the Atlantic Coast of southeastern Maryland, 100 miles southeast of Washington, D.C.

Landscape: Flat plains. A 10-mile barrier beach forming a chain of bays along the Atlantic shore. Assateague Island National Seashore is a narrow barrier island and a southern extension of Ocean City's barrier beach. The coastal marshes and interior swamps of the region are dominated by gums and cypress. There is an understory of grasses and sedges. Undrained shallow depressions in these savannas form upland bogs where evergreen shrubs predominate.

Climate: Subtropical, characterized by milder winters than those in locations farther north, thanks to the Atlantic. Summers are somewhat hot and humid. Precipitation is evenly distributed throughout the year as rain, though there may be summer drought. Snow is infrequent though frost occurs nearly every winter, with the first frost on October 19 and the last frost on April 22.

Summer mildness: 60 **Seasonal affect:** 32
Winter mildness: 33 **Hazard free:** 48

	97
	104
	164
90°	26
32°	93
0°	0
	34
	70
	28

	High °F	Low °F	Hum %	Wind mph	Precip inches	Snow inches
JAN	43	26	61	9.8	3.6	4.2
FEB	46	28	59	10.4	3.5	3.5
MAR	55	35	53	11.2	4.2	2.4
APR	65	43	52	10.6	3.2	0
MAY	74	53	55	9.1	3.6	0
JUN	82	62	55	8.5	3.6	0
JUL	86	67	55	7.8	4.3	0
AUG	85	66	58	7.5	5.3	0
SEP	79	58	58	7.8	3.7	0
OCT	68	47	58	8.2	3.4	0
NOV	59	38	58	9.2	3.2	0
DEC	48	30	61	9.4	3.7	1.8

Oxford, MS Rank: 116

Location: 34.22 N and 89.31 W at 416 feet, in north-central Mississippi, 75 miles southeast of Memphis, Tennessee.

Landscape: Irregular plains. Rolling hill country near the Sardis Reservoir and two other lakes. The surrounding Holly Springs National Forest protects a typical southeastern mixed forest. Before the Holly Springs National Forest was formed, much of the land was abandoned farmland with rapidly eroding soils. These rolling hills are now covered with loblolly and shortleaf pines, and upland hardwoods of oak-hickory woodlands.

Climate: Hot continental to subtropical. Though not in the path of storms coming up from the Gulf or down from Canada, the area is influenced by both. Winter is wet with frequent drizzle and infrequent light snowfall. Usually there are mild days and cold nights. October 27 greets the first frost; April 4 bids adieu to the last frost. Summer is hot and humid. Spring and autumn are pleasant and long lasting.

Summer mildness: 32 **Seasonal affect:** 61
Winter mildness: 44 **Hazard free:** 50

	120
	96
	149
90°	77
32°	76
0°	0
	10
	72
	53

	High °F	Low °F	Hum %	Wind mph	Precip inches	Snow inches
JAN	49	28	63	10.1	4.6	1.7
FEB	54	31	60	10.2	4.8	1.0
MAR	64	40	56	10.8	6.0	0.2
APR	74	49	53	10.3	5.3	0
MAY	81	57	55	8.8	5.9	0
JUN	88	65	56	8.0	4.1	0
JUL	91	68	57	7.5	4.4	0
AUG	91	66	56	7.0	3.1	0
SEP	85	60	56	7.5	3.7	0
OCT	76	46	51	7.7	3.5	0
NOV	65	39	56	9.1	5.8	0
DEC	54	31	61	9.8	6.1	0.4

★ = in the top 30 places for climate mildness

Pagosa Springs, CO
Rank: 106

Location: 37.16 N and 107.00 W at 7,105 feet, on the San Juan River in southwestern Colorado, 230 air miles from Denver.

Landscape: On a high mountain plateau with peaks of the San Juan Mountains a distant vista to the north and east. The geothermal springs, canyons, mesas, and mountains provide dramatic relief. Mostly forested and dominated by Engelmann spruce and fir forest, scattered aspen groves cover the subalpine areas. The upper reaches grade into alpine tundra.

Climate: Semiarid steppe. High altitude brings just two seasons: an 8-month winter and a 4-month summer. Still, there are, on average, 300 sunny days a year. Temperature variations are great both daily and annually. Snowfall in this region is legendary. First frost arrives early, by September 3; last frost is late departing, not leaving until June 25.

Summer mildness: 99 **Seasonal affect:** 80
Winter mildness: 14 **Hazard free:** 1

	115
	130
	120
90°	2
32°	243
0°	36
	8
	47
	35

	High °F	Low °F	Hum %	Wind mph	Precip inches	Snow inches
JAN	37	1	63	5.6	1.7	31.0
FEB	42	7	55	6.7	1.3	19.9
MAR	48	16	41	8.4	1.6	18.0
APR	57	22	32	9.5	1.2	6.0
MAY	67	30	31	9.6	1.1	1.0
JUN	77	37	25	9.7	0.8	0
JUL	82	46	27	9.3	1.9	0
AUG	80	45	30	9.0	2.5	0
SEP	72	36	33	8.9	2.2	0
OCT	63	26	37	7.9	2.1	3.0
NOV	49	16	48	6.7	1.7	11.0
DEC	39	5	60	5.9	1.8	26.5

Pahrump Valley, NV
Rank: 31

Location: 36.10 N and 115.08 W at 2,028 feet, just west of the Colorado River Valley. Las Vegas is 40 miles east.

Landscape: Plains with high mountains. A desert valley with mountains from 2,000 to 10,000 feet on the horizon. These mountains act as effective barriers to moisture-laden storms moving in from the Pacific Ocean. In the environs, thick-branched Joshua trees grow among creosote bushes and jumbled boulders.

Climate: Summers are typical of a desert climate. Humidity is low, with maximum temperatures topping 100°F. Desert temperatures fall and nearby mountains contribute to relatively cool nights. Spring and fall are ideal, rarely interrupted by adverse weather conditions. Winters, too, are mild, with daytime averages of 60°F, clear skies, and warm sunshine. First frost comes December 11; last frost leaves February 17. There are very few overcast or rainy days.

Summer mildness: 31 **Seasonal affect:** 97
Winter mildness: 50 **Hazard free:** 80

	221
	79
	65
90°	123
32°	14
0°	0
	1
	13
	14

	High °F	Low °F	Hum %	Wind mph	Precip inches	Snow inches
JAN	57	26	35	7.5	0.6	1.0
FEB	62	31	30	8.6	0.6	0.1
MAR	67	36	25	10.3	0.6	0
APR	74	42	20	11.0	0.4	0
MAY	84	51	17	11.1	0.2	0
JUN	95	60	14	11.1	0.1	0
JUL	101	67	15	10.3	0.4	0
AUG	99	65	19	9.6	0.5	0
SEP	91	56	20	9.0	0.3	0
OCT	81	45	22	8.1	0.2	0
NOV	67	33	30	7.7	0.5	0
DEC	57	25	36	7.3	0.4	0.1

Palmer–Wasilla, AK
Rank: 174

Location: 61.36 N and 149.063 W at 239 feet in the Matanuska-Susitna Valley in south-central Alaska, 42 miles northeast of Anchorage. Seattle, Washington, is 1,450 air miles southeast.

Landscape: Plains with low mountains. Level to gently rolling farmland, surrounded by the Chugach and Talkeetna mountain ranges. Pioneer Peak, Knik Glacier, Matanuska Peak, and Lazy Mountain are prominent features in view. The nearby forests are dense conifer stands of Douglas fir, western red cedar, western hemlock, Sitka spruce, and Alaska cedar.

Climate: Four well-marked seasons, though summers are brief. Fifty miles northwest, the Alaska Range blocks much of the cold air from the vast interior. Consequently, winter temperatures are warmer by 30 degrees. The first frost, coming by mid-September, signals the onset of autumn; the last frost, April 1, shouts spring is coming. By mid-April to the beginning of May, the rivers and lakes have thawed.

Summer mildness: 79 **Seasonal affect:** 0
Winter mildness: 31 **Hazard free:** 18

	61
	64
	240
90°	0
32°	178
0°	21
	73
	148
	0

	High °F	Low °F	Hum %	Wind mph	Precip inches	Snow inches
JAN	31	16	73	6.4	6.7	20.4
FEB	35	19	70	6.8	6.8	23.6
MAR	38	22	64	6.9	6.3	27.3
APR	44	29	60	7.2	5.7	16.0
MAY	52	36	56	8.4	6.3	1.5
JUN	58	43	62	8.3	6.0	0
JUL	62	47	68	7.3	5.6	0
AUG	62	46	71	6.9	9.2	0
SEP	56	40	71	6.7	13.8	0
OCT	46	33	72	6.7	13.0	3.7
NOV	37	23	75	6.5	7.7	10.8
DEC	32	18	77	6.2	9.1	26.8

★ = in the top 30 places for climate mildness

★ Palm Springs–Coachella Valley, CA — Rank: 6

Location: 33.49 N and 116.32 W at 466 feet, in California's desert country, 100 miles east of Los Angeles.

Landscape: High mountains. In the Coachella Valley at the foot of Mt. San Jacinto, where the San Gorgonio Pass funnels warmed air from the Pacific that sometimes includes Los Angeles smog. This is the edge of the Sonoran Desert, known sometimes as the Upper Colorado Desert. Joshua Tree National Monument is immediately northeast. Desert cactus, palm, and broadleaf evergreen scrub pine are typical.

Climate: Arid desert surrounding rapid urbanization. Summers are dry and hot with afternoon temperatures topping 100°F. Nights are cooler, as is typical of deserts. Most of the annual precipitation, such as it is, falls in winter as brief rain. The first frost is late arriving in mid-December; the last frost is out by late January.

Summer mildness: 22		Seasonal affect: 99
Winter mildness: 96		Hazard free: 94

	242
	75
	48
90°	180
32°	7
0°	0
	2
	9
	7

	High °F	Low °F	Hum %	Wind mph	Precip inches	Snow inches
JAN	70	43	40	7.3	1.0	0.1
FEB	76	46	35	7.4	0.8	0
MAR	80	49	30	7.9	0.5	0
APR	87	54	25	8.3	0.1	0
MAY	95	61	23	8.3	0.1	0
JUN	104	68	22	8.5	0.1	0
JUL	109	75	32	9.5	0.2	0
AUG	107	75	35	8.9	0.4	0
SEP	101	69	35	7.3	0.4	0
OCT	92	60	32	6.6	0.2	0
NOV	79	49	34	6.9	0.7	0
DEC	70	42	41	7.2	0.8	0

Panama City, FL — Rank: 67

Location: 30.09 N and 85.39 W at 33 feet, on the Gulf of Mexico in Florida's northwestern panhandle. Tallahassee is 120 miles east.

Landscape: Flat plains. Sandy coastal region of shallow bays, white beaches, and dunes. Elevations range from a few feet above sea level to more than 100 feet, providing relief from usual flat topography. The interior swamp includes evergreen oaks and members of the laurel and magnolia families. The longleaf, loblolly, and slash pines represent second-growth forest.

Climate: Subtropical. The Florida panhandle is cooler in summer than the central part of the state and still pleasant in winter. The Yucatan Current runs near here, bringing its moderating influence. This is basically a two-season climate with little temperature swing.

Summer mildness: 14		Seasonal affect: 65
Winter mildness: 78		Hazard free: 73

	108
	122
	135
90°	75
32°	39
0°	0
	35
	66
	69

	High °F	Low °F	Hum %	Wind mph	Precip inches	Snow inches
JAN	60	37	62	9.0	5.0	0.1
FEB	64	39	59	9.4	5.8	0.1
MAR	70	46	59	9.7	5.8	0
APR	78	53	56	9.5	3.7	0
MAY	85	61	58	8.6	4.0	0
JUN	90	68	60	7.6	6.1	0
JUL	91	71	64	7.0	8.5	0
AUG	91	71	65	6.7	7.2	0
SEP	88	66	61	7.6	5.8	0
OCT	80	54	55	7.9	4.3	0
NOV	71	46	60	8.4	4.1	0
DEC	64	40	64	9.0	4.8	0

★ Paradise–Magalia, CA — Rank: 14

Location: 39.44 N and 121.38 W at 1,708 feet, on Paradise Ridge in the Sierra Nevada foothills, 92 miles north of Sacramento.

Landscape: Low mountains. Known locally as "the Ridge" where steep slopes climb to high mountains. Stream-cut canyons drain to the Sacramento River. Tall digger pine, ponderosa and sugar pine, and blue oak dominate the mixed conifer forest. Lower rounded hills are grass and chaparral scrub covered. Open meadows and woodlands alternate.

Climate: Distinctly four seasons. The altitude moderates temperature. Winter is the rainy season, and summer is long and dry. First frost is in mid-October; last frost is in mid-May.

Summer mildness: 60		Seasonal affect: 76
Winter mildness: 62		Hazard free: 92

	178
	78
	110
90°	39
32°	117
0°	0
	13
	59
	5

	High °F	Low °F	Hum %	Wind mph	Precip inches	Snow inches
JAN	54	37	80	7.3	10.0	0.2
FEB	57	40	75	7.4	7.6	0
MAR	59	41	65	7.9	7.9	0
APR	66	45	55	8.3	3.8	0
MAY	75	51	48	8.3	1.2	0
JUN	84	58	44	8.5	0.5	0
JUL	91	64	44	9.5	0.1	0
AUG	90	63	45	8.9	0.3	0
SEP	84	59	45	7.3	1.1	0
OCT	74	52	53	6.6	3.2	0
NOV	60	43	65	6.9	8.5	0
DEC	53	37	77	7.2	8.5	0.2

★ = *in the top 30 places for climate mildness*

Park City, UT — Rank: 141

Location: 40.3846 N and 111.295 W at 6,970 feet, 30 miles east of Salt Lake City.

Landscape: High mountains. This alpine area is located in a high valley of the Wasatch Range with many limestone terraces, lakes, and high mountain streams. Near the junction with the Uinta Mountains where the Wasatch National Forest is mixed conifer, with spruce, fir, and aspen. The many mine tailings are covered and planted with salt grass for erosion control. Open rangeland is nearby. Cottonwood predominates in the valley streams. Alpine wildflowers are abundant in spring and summer.

Climate: This is a four-season area. Summers are warm and dry, winters long and cold. Autumn is short but pleasant, while spring is longer but often stormy. First frost hits early, by September 10; last frost leaves late, June 8. Almost all precipitation falls in the form of snow, some 70 inches in a typical year.

Summer mildness: 88 **Seasonal affect:** 66
Winter mildness: 8 **Hazard free:** 5

	125
	101
	139
90°	20
32°	210
0°	21
	42
	43
	38

	High °F	Low °F	Hum %	Wind mph	Precip inches	Snow inches
JAN	34	8	75	7.5	1.8	19.3
FEB	40	13	69	8.1	1.6	13.1
MAR	48	22	59	9.3	1.4	7.9
APR	60	29	53	9.6	1.4	3.2
MAY	70	36	49	9.5	1.2	1.0
JUN	79	42	43	9.4	0.9	0
JUL	87	48	37	9.5	0.9	0
AUG	86	47	39	9.7	1.0	0
SEP	77	39	45	9.1	1.3	0.1
OCT	65	30	55	8.5	1.5	1.9
NOV	48	22	67	7.9	1.7	8.1
DEC	36	12	75	7.5	1.6	13.6

Payson, AZ — Rank: 40

Location: 34.14 N and 111.19 W at 4,887 feet, in the Tonto Basin near Arizona's Mogollon Rim. Phoenix is 65 miles southeast.

Landscape: Open high mountains. Surrounded by the Tonto National Forest. The Mazatzal Mountains of central Arizona and higher peaks of the White Mountains are nearby, though this is gentle rolling hill country. In the higher ridges the cover is ponderosa, juniper, and piñon pine. Lower, sagebrush and native grasses grow in the dry alkaline soil.

Climate: Semiarid mountain steppe. There are strong daily and seasonal temperature changes. The usual winter flow of air is from the Pacific Ocean, bringing snow. Cold air masses from Canada sometimes drive temperatures well below freezing in the high plateau and mountainous regions. First frost arrives by October 21; last frost leaves May 14. Moisture-bearing winds from the southeast Gulf region bring rain from July to September.

Summer mildness: 67 **Seasonal affect:** 91
Winter mildness: 55 **Hazard free:** 40

	212
	84
	69
90°	64
32°	144
0°	0
	2
	40
	24

	High °F	Low °F	Hum %	Wind mph	Precip inches	Snow inches
JAN	54	24	45	5.3	2.0	5.3
FEB	58	26	40	5.9	1.9	4.1
MAR	62	29	36	6.7	2.4	5.6
APR	70	34	25	7.0	1.1	1.0
MAY	79	41	20	7.1	0.6	0
JUN	90	49	18	6.8	0.4	0
JUL	93	58	28	7.2	2.6	0
AUG	90	57	33	6.7	3.2	0
SEP	84	50	34	6.3	2.1	0
OCT	74	40	34	5.8	1.7	0
NOV	62	30	37	5.4	1.9	2.0
DEC	54	24	46	5.1	2.3	6.4

Pendleton District, SC — Rank: 88

Location: 34.41 N and 82.57 W at 950 feet in the extreme northwestern part of the state, 25 miles southwest of Greenville.

Landscape: Low mountains. The high parts of the Blue Ridge foothills yield a broken outline. Here's a curving valley with typical Up Country broadleaf forests of beech, sweet gum, magnolia, and oak forests with scattered pine. Rhododendrons, azaleas, and kalmias are the understory bloom in spring.

Climate: Transition between hot continental and subtropical. Winters are brief, with negligible snowfalls. First frost arrives fairly late on November 1; last frost leaves a little early by April 3. Summers are longer than those in more northerly locations and less humid and stormy than those in the Lowcountry, 150 miles southeast. Precipitation is distributed throughout the year, with the most falling as early spring rain.

Summer mildness: 46 **Seasonal affect:** 35
Winter mildness: 70 **Hazard free:** 59

	122
	100
	143
90°	49
32°	70
0°	0
	34
	81
	43

	High °F	Low °F	Hum %	Wind mph	Precip inches	Snow inches
JAN	51	28	56	7.4	5.2	1.2
FEB	55	31	53	8.0	4.9	1.5
MAR	63	38	52	8.1	6.0	1.1
APR	72	47	49	7.9	4.2	0
MAY	79	55	55	6.9	4.3	0
JUN	86	63	56	6.4	4.2	0
JUL	89	67	58	5.9	4.6	0
AUG	88	67	61	5.7	4.4	0
SEP	82	60	61	6.1	3.7	0
OCT	73	48	53	6.5	4.1	0
NOV	64	39	55	6.8	4.1	0
DEC	54	31	58	7.3	4.8	0.6

★ = in the top 30 places for climate mildness

Pensacola, FL   Rank: 118

Location: 30.25 N and 87.13 W at 39 feet, in the Florida Panhandle on Pensacola Bay, 195 miles west of Tallahassee. Mobile, Alabama, is 50 miles west.

Landscape: Irregular plains. On a somewhat hilly, sandy slope separated from the Gulf of Mexico by a long, narrow island forming a natural breakwater for the harbor. Salt marshes and white-sand beaches are common. The forested area is southern mixed with various deciduous hardwoods, conifers of loblollies, and shortleaf pine. Elevations don't reach much more than 100 feet above sea level, but most of the city is safely above storm tides.

Climate: Warm, humid summers and cool winters are the expected norm. Rainfall is likely throughout the year, becoming heavy with summer thunderstorms. Sea breezes off the Gulf of Mexico temper the humidity in summer. More than a trace amount of snow per winter is rare.

Summer mildness: 4   **Seasonal affect:** 28
Winter mildness: 81   **Hazard free:** 72

	106
	123
	136
90°	84
32°	30
0°	0
	178
	82
	68

	High °F	Low °F	Hum %	Wind mph	Precip inches	Snow inches
JAN	60	41	66	9.0	4.7	0.3
FEB	63	44	63	9.4	5.4	0
MAR	69	51	64	9.7	5.6	0
APR	77	59	63	9.5	3.8	0
MAY	83	66	69	8.6	4.2	0
JUN	89	72	70	7.6	6.4	0
JUL	90	74	72	7.0	7.4	0
AUG	89	74	75	6.7	7.4	0
SEP	86	70	74	7.6	5.3	0
OCT	79	59	69	7.9	4.2	0
NOV	70	51	68	8.4	3.5	0
DEC	63	44	67	8.9	4.3	0

Petoskey–Harbor Springs, MI   Rank: 191

Location: 45.22 N and 84.57 W at 786 feet, on the south shore of Little Traverse Bay on Lake Michigan, some 30 miles south of the Mackinac Straits separating Michigan's upper and lower peninsulas.

Landscape: Plains with hills. Generally level or gently undulating, with sandy and gravelly soils. The region abounds with lakes. Local beaches and gravel pits yield colorful fossilized stones. Elevations in the area provide access to both downhill and cross-country skiing. The forest is pine and hemlock.

Climate: Though rigorous because of its interior and northerly location, the climate is modified by the presence of two Great Lakes. As a consequence, summer temperatures average at least 5 degrees cooler than locations in the southern part of the state. However, winters are severe, with cold spells that may last for a week and snowfall that averages almost 75 inches. First frost arrives early, by September 22; the last frost won't leave until May 31.

Summer mildness: 74   **Seasonal affect:** 17
Winter mildness: 4   **Hazard free:** 3

	67
	89
	210
90°	5
32°	169
0°	18
	23
	73
	24

	High °F	Low °F	Hum %	Wind mph	Precip inches	Snow inches
JAN	28	12	77	12.6	2.0	23.1
FEB	31	9	72	11.6	1.2	15.4
MAR	41	19	66	11.9	1.5	10.4
APR	55	31	60	11.8	2.4	2.0
MAY	69	40	58	10.1	2.6	0
JUN	77	49	61	9.5	2.8	0
JUL	81	55	63	8.7	2.8	0
AUG	79	53	64	8.5	3.2	0
SEP	71	47	66	9.4	4.3	0
OCT	60	38	68	10.8	3.4	0
NOV	45	30	72	11.9	3.0	12.0
DEC	33	19	78	12.1	2.4	25.5

Pike County, PA   Rank: 159

Location: 41.19 N and 74.48 W at 1,185 feet, across the Delaware River from New York State. New York City is 80 miles southeast.

Landscape: Low mountains. The Delaware River drains this highland region between the Catskills and the Pocono Mountains. These are long flat-topped or rounded ridges rising to 4,000 feet. Many streams and glacial lakes lie among the wooded hills. White pine, eastern hemlock, and red spruce mix with deciduous trees like red maple, sassafras, oak, beech, and birch. Mountain laurel, dogwood, dwarf sumac, and fern fill out the lower growth layers.

Climate: Hot continental, with summers moderated by altitude. Winter is cold and cloudy. Precipitation is evenly distributed throughout the year, with snow likely to fall in December and last until spring. The first frost will arrive by October 7; the last frost will leave May 9. Severe weather disturbances are unlikely.

Summer mildness: 73   **Seasonal affect:** 20
Winter mildness: 36   **Hazard free:** 24

	69
	113
	183
90°	16
32°	145
0°	6
	19
	76
	32

	High °F	Low °F	Hum %	Wind mph	Precip inches	Snow inches
JAN	34	16	58	8.3	3.1	11.3
FEB	38	18	57	9.0	3.0	10.7
MAR	49	26	53	9.5	3.5	10.4
APR	62	36	49	9.2	3.7	1.0
MAY	73	46	49	7.6	4.5	0
JUN	80	55	55	6.8	3.7	0
JUL	85	60	55	6.2	4.2	0
AUG	82	59	57	5.8	3.6	0
SEP	73	52	59	6.1	3.7	0
OCT	62	40	59	6.6	3.0	0
NOV	51	32	60	7.8	3.9	2.0
DEC	38	22	62	8.0	3.4	9.7

★ = in the top 30 places for climate mildness

★ Placer County, CA — Rank: 17

Location: The weather station is Auburn, the county seat, sitting at 39.00 N and 121.00 W at 1,290 feet in California's Sierra Nevadas. Sacramento is 30 miles southwest.

Landscape: High mountains. On steep hill and mountain slopes too dry to support oak woodland or oak forest, much of the vegetation is scrub or "dwarf forest" known as chaparral, which varies in composition with elevation and exposure. It consists of chamise and various manzanitas that are adapted to periodic occurrences of fire.

Climate: Mediterranean highland. Hot, dry summers and rainy, mild winters characterize this climate. Annual precipitation ranges from 10 to 50 inches, with a pronounced summer drought. This coastal area has a more moderate climate than the interior and receives some moisture from fog in summer. Fire is common, usually set by lightning during the summer dry season. The first frost arrives October 17 and the last frost departs May 23.

Summer mildness: 17	Seasonal affect: 69
Winter mildness: 89	Hazard free: 98

				189
				76
				101
	90°			93
	32°			17
	0°			0
				95
				37
				2

	High °F	Low °F	Hum %	Wind mph	Precip inches	Snow inches
JAN	54	54	83	7.2	4.1	0
FEB	62	62	76	7.5	3.2	0
MAR	67	67	71	8.6	3.0	0
APR	74	74	65	8.7	1.5	0
MAY	83	83	60	9.2	0.4	0
JUN	90	90	55	9.7	0.2	0
JUL	96	96	54	9.0	0.1	0
AUG	94	94	56	8.6	0.1	0
SEP	89	89	57	7.5	0.4	0
OCT	79	79	62	6.4	1.4	0
NOV	64	64	74	6.0	3.3	0
DEC	54	54	83	6.7	3.4	0

★ Port Angeles–Sequim, WA — Rank: 28

Location: 48.07 N and 123.25 W at 32 feet, on Washington's Olympic Peninsula. Victoria, British Columbia, is 20 miles by ferry across the Strait of Juan de Fuca.

Landscape: High mountains. A variety of terrain, from the rocky coastline to peaks rising nearly 8,000 feet in the Olympic Mountains immediately to the south. Rivers and lakes drain the forested peninsula. Pacific needleleaf forests grow densely and have some of the world's largest trees. Douglas fir, western red cedar, and Sitka spruce are dominant. There is shrub undergrowth present in the forests.

Climate: Generally mild throughout the year because of the modifying influence of the Pacific Ocean. Annual rainfall is moderate-heavy, with maximum precipitation in winter due to the maritime polar air masses. There are traces of snow. A late first frost arrives November 10; the last frost leaves early, April 7. Summer tends to be foggy.

Summer mildness: 89	Seasonal affect: 15
Winter mildness: 79	Hazard free: 79

				52
				84
				229
	90°			0
	32°			41
	0°			0
				90
				64
				5

	High °F	Low °F	Hum %	Wind mph	Precip inches	Snow inches
JAN	45	34	86	7.1	4.0	2.7
FEB	48	35	83	7.2	2.6	0.8
MAR	51	37	77	7.4	2.0	1.1
APR	55	39	68	7.4	1.3	0
MAY	60	44	64	6.9	1.0	0
JUN	65	48	64	6.7	0.8	0
JUL	69	51	63	6.2	0.5	0
AUG	69	51	64	6.0	0.8	0
SEP	66	48	70	5.7	1.2	0
OCT	58	43	78	5.9	2.3	0
NOV	50	38	82	6.9	4.0	0
DEC	46	34	87	7.3	4.4	1.5

Port Charlotte, FL — Rank: 43

Location: 26.58 N and 82.05 W at 11 feet, at the northern end of Charlotte Harbor on the Gulf of Mexico, 44 miles south of Sarasota.

Landscape: Flat plains crossed by rivers and streams. The woods are temperate broadleaf evergreen of laurel, and magnolia. The lower level of growth includes tree ferns, small palms, and shrubs.

Climate: Subtropical. Summer and winter temperature extremes are checked by the influence of the Gulf. Mild winters have many bright, warm days. Nights are moderately cool. Rainfall averages more than 50 inches annually, with two-thirds of this total coming daily between June and September. Most rain falls as late-afternoon or early-evening thunderstorms, bringing welcome relief from the heat. With a first frost coming late, December 11, and the last frost leaving early, February 16, there is a long growing season.

Summer mildness: 5	Seasonal affect: 69
Winter mildness: 92	Hazard free: 83

				102
				142
				121
	90°			120
	32°			1
	0°			0
				21
				71
				93

	High °F	Low °F	Hum %	Wind mph	Precip inches	Snow inches
JAN	74	51	56	8.6	2.0	0
FEB	76	52	56	9.2	2.5	0
MAR	80	57	53	9.5	2.6	0
APR	85	60	47	9.3	1.3	0
MAY	89	66	49	8.7	3.6	0
JUN	91	71	56	8.0	8.1	0
JUL	92	73	60	7.2	7.3	0
AUG	92	73	60	7.0	7.9	0
SEP	90	72	61	7.8	6.5	0
OCT	86	66	57	8.5	2.8	0
NOV	80	59	57	8.4	1.8	0
DEC	76	53	56	8.5	1.8	0

★ = in the top 30 places for climate mildness

Port St. Lucie, FL — Rank: 62

Location: 27.26 N and 80.19 W at 16 feet off Florida Atlantic Coast, some 120 miles north of Miami.

Landscape: Flat plains, with local relief less than 300 feet, although some areas are gently rolling. Common trees include evergreen oaks and members of the laurel and magnolia families. Sandy uplands have forests of loblolly and slash pine. Bald Cypress is a dominant tree in swamps. Sometimes the trees are festooned with Spanish moss.

Climate: Subtropical, with high year-round relative humidity near 90 percent at night and dipping to 50 percent in the afternoon. The rainy season extends from June to September; afternoon thundershowers occur daily. Rain is light during the winter, and snow and sleet are rare. Winter temperatures may drop to freezing at night, but days are clear and dry, with brilliant sunshine. The first frost arrives December 12 and the last frost departs January 22.

Summer mildness: 4   **Seasonal affect:** 50
Winter mildness: 92   **Hazard free:** 90

	98
	133
	135
90°	55
32°	1
0°	0
	39
	76
	67

	High °F	Low °F	Hum %	Wind mph	Precip inches	Snow inches
JAN	73	52	74	8.6	2.1	0
FEB	74	53	72	9.1	2.8	0
MAR	78	58	71	9.7	3.1	0
APR	82	62	68	9.4	1.9	0
MAY	86	67	70	9.2	4.8	0
JUN	89	71	75	7.9	5.7	0
JUL	90	73	76	7.0	5.8	0
AUG	90	73	78	6.5	5.6	0
SEP	89	72	77	7.5	7.5	0
OCT	85	68	75	8.7	5.7	0
NOV	79	60	75	9.2	2.9	0
DEC	75	54	73	8.0	2.3	0

★ Port Townsend, WA — Rank: 29

Location: 48.07 N and 122.45 W at 16 feet, on Washington's Olympic Peninsula, at the eastern end of the Strait of Juan de Fuca, where Admiralty Inlet leads into Puget Sound. Seattle is 45 air miles south.

Landscape: High mountains. In the midst of a variety of terrain, from the rocky, glaciated coastline to peaks rising nearly 8,000 feet in the Olympic Mountains to the west. Rivers and lakes drain the forested peninsula. Nearby Pacific needleleaf forests are thick and contain some of the world's largest trees. Douglas fir, western red cedar, and Sitka spruce are dominant. Shrub undergrowth is present in the forests.

Climate: Predominantly marine, with cool summers, mild winters, moist air, and small daily temperature variation. Summers are cool and dry. Like most other places in this region, the area is often foggy and cloudy. First frost comes by November 10; the last frost is gone by April 7.

Summer mildness: 89   **Seasonal affect:** 14
Winter mildness: 79   **Hazard free:** 79

	53
	83
	230
90°	0
32°	41
0°	0
	90
	64
	5

	High °F	Low °F	Hum %	Wind mph	Precip inches	Snow inches
JAN	45	34	86	7.1	4.0	2.7
FEB	48	35	83	7.2	2.6	0.8
MAR	51	37	77	7.4	2.0	1.1
APR	55	39	68	7.4	1.3	0
MAY	60	44	64	6.9	1.0	0
JUN	65	48	64	6.7	0.8	0
JUL	69	51	63	6.2	0.5	0
AUG	69	51	64	6.0	0.8	0
SEP	66	48	70	5.7	1.2	0
OCT	58	43	78	5.9	2.3	0
NOV	50	38	82	6.9	4.0	0
DEC	46	34	87	7.3	4.4	1.5

★ Prescott–Prescott Valley, AZ — Rank: 25

Location: 34.32 N and 112.28 W at 5,368 feet, in Arizona's mountainous west-central section. Phoenix is 96 miles southeast; Flagstaff 90 miles northeast.

Landscape: Open high mountains. Found in a mile-high basin among pine-dotted mountains rich in minerals. The higher ridges of the Prescott National Forest hold the world's largest stand of ponderosa. Sagebrush and native grasses dominate the dry alkaline soil at lower elevations.

Climate: Semiarid mountain steppe, with strong daily and seasonal temperature changes. Prescott is Arizona's mile-high city, and its high elevation and mountain breezes keep temperatures from reaching the grueling levels of low-lying Phoenix. The usual winter flow of air is from the Pacific Ocean, bringing frequent snow. Cold air masses from Canada sometimes drive temperatures below freezing in the high plateau and mountainous regions. First frost is in by October 9; last frost leaves by May 17. Moisture-bearing winds from the southeast Gulf region bring rain from July to September.

Summer mildness: 78   **Seasonal affect:** 89
Winter mildness: 51   **Hazard free:** 45

	212
	84
	69
90°	32
32°	150
0°	0
	11
	39
	24

	High °F	Low °F	Hum %	Wind mph	Precip inches	Snow inches
JAN	50	22	45	5.3	1.5	4.5
FEB	54	24	40	5.9	1.5	3.5
MAR	57	28	36	6.7	1.8	6.8
APR	65	34	25	7.0	0.8	2.0
MAY	74	41	20	7.1	0.6	0
JUN	85	50	18	6.8	0.5	0
JUL	88	58	28	7.2	3.2	0
AUG	85	56	33	6.7	3.4	0
SEP	80	49	34	6.3	2.0	0
OCT	71	38	34	5.8	1.1	0
NOV	60	29	37	5.4	1.5	1.0
DEC	51	22	46	5.1	1.6	5.1

Rabun County, GA — Rank: 114

Location: The weather station is at Clayton, 34.52 N and 83.24 W at 1,925 feet in Georgia's northeast mountains. Atlanta is 90 miles southwest.

Landscape: Low mountains. In the southern Appalachians, terrain is hilly to mountainous, with elevations averaging 1,500 feet. To the north, some mountains rise above 3,000 feet. Chattahoochee National Forest is a mixed deciduous forest, with oak, beech, birch, walnut, maple, ash, and hornbeam. Pines readily develop as second growth where there has been logging or fire.

Climate: Nearby mountains have marked influences on summer heat, producing warm days and cool nights. Winters are cold but not severe. The contrast of valley and hill exposures results in wide variations in winter low temperatures. First frost makes its appearance by October 21; last frost departs by April 24. Generally, places halfway up the mountain slopes remain warmer during winter nights than do places on the valley floor. Spring is changeable and sometimes stormy. Fall is clear and sunny, with chilly nights.

Summer mildness: 55 **Seasonal affect:** 18
Winter mildness: 61 **Hazard free:** 54

	103
	113
	149
90°	14
32°	93
0°	0
	78
	95
	45

	High °F	Low °F	Hum %	Wind mph	Precip inches	Snow inches
JAN	51	27	65	9.7	6.4	1.6
FEB	55	29	61	9.6	6.1	1.9
MAR	63	35	56	9.4	7.4	1.7
APR	71	42	53	8.9	5.4	0
MAY	77	50	60	7.1	6.8	0
JUN	83	57	61	6.1	5.4	0
JUL	85	62	63	5.8	5.8	0
AUG	84	61	63	5.4	6.1	0
SEP	79	55	62	5.6	5.7	0
OCT	72	43	57	6.8	5.1	0
NOV	63	36	60	8.1	5.9	0
DEC	54	29	66	8.9	6.7	0.8

Rehoboth Bay–Indian River Bay, DE — Rank: 139

Location: 38.43 N and 75.04 W at 16 feet, on Delaware Bay and the Atlantic Coast, 100 miles east of Washington, D.C.

Landscape: Flat plains. Very nearly a flat topography. A long barrier beach separates the Bays from the Atlantic Ocean. Coastal sand dunes and beaches are a sharp contrast, with stands of pine. Streams flow from inland lakes to coastal marshlands before emptying into the bays.

Climate: Experiences the northern edge of the subtropical zone. Seasonal and daily temperature variations are moderate. Winters can be cold, with snow that's scant and usually doesn't last long. First frost is October 27; last frost is April 13. Summers can be hot and humid but are tempered by onshore breezes.

Summer mildness: 66 **Seasonal affect:** 28
Winter mildness: 34 **Hazard free:** 41

	97
	104
	164
90°	18
32°	91
0°	0
	34
	71
	30

	High °F	Low °F	Hum %	Wind mph	Precip inches	Snow inches
JAN	43	26	62	9.8	3.8	5.1
FEB	45	28	59	10.4	3.3	5.2
MAR	54	35	55	11.2	4.1	2.7
APR	64	43	52	10.6	3.6	0
MAY	73	53	51	9.1	3.8	0
JUN	81	62	51	8.5	3.4	0
JUL	85	67	53	7.8	4.0	0
AUG	84	66	54	7.5	5.2	0
SEP	78	60	54	7.8	3.1	0
OCT	68	49	54	8.2	3.2	0
NOV	59	40	54	9.2	3.3	0
DEC	48	31	57	9.4	3.7	1.9

Rio Rancho, NM — Rank: 90

Location: 35.14 N and 106.39 W at 5,290 feet, 10 miles northwest of Albuquerque. Santa Fe is 60 miles northeast.

Landscape: Plains with high mountains. Perched on a mesa overlooking the upper Rio Grande River and bounded by parts of the Cibola National Forest. The Sandia and Manzano mountains are to the east. The land is a typical steppe or shortgrass prairie, with scattered shrubs and low trees. Common vegetation includes sagebrush or shadscale and a mixture of shortgrasses. There may be willows and sedges along streams.

Climate: Arid continental. The dry air lessens the effect of the heat, which frequently tops 100°F in summer. Summer nights are cool. Winters are cool also, with light snow in higher elevations. First frost is in by October 11; last frost is out by May 5. In mid- to late summer there are frequent and intense thunderstorms, accounting for half the area's annual precipitation.

Summer mildness: 54 **Seasonal affect:** 91
Winter mildness: 24 **Hazard free:** 39

	169
	111
	85
90°	75
32°	151
0°	1
	6
	24
	41

	High °F	Low °F	Hum %	Wind mph	Precip inches	Snow inches
JAN	47	22	50	8.1	0.4	2.5
FEB	54	26	42	8.9	0.5	2.2
MAR	61	32	32	10.1	0.5	1.8
APR	71	40	25	11.0	0.5	0.6
MAY	80	49	23	10.6	0.5	0
JUN	90	58	22	10.0	0.6	0
JUL	93	64	30	9.1	1.4	0
AUG	89	63	34	8.3	1.6	0
SEP	82	55	35	8.6	1.0	0
OCT	71	43	35	8.3	0.9	0.1
NOV	57	31	38	7.9	0.4	1.3
DEC	48	23	46	7.7	0.5	2.6

★ = in the top 30 places for climate mildness

Rockport–Aransas Pass, TX   Rank: 76

Location: 28.01 N and 97.03 W at 6 feet, on the Gulf of Mexico, 30 miles northeast of Corpus Christi.

Landscape: Flat plains. Aransas County is a flat coastal plain, with many bays and inlets. Elevations range from sea level to a mere 50 feet. The sandy loam and coastal clay soils are dotted with mesquite and live oak.

Climate: Humid subtropical. The heat is moderated by the prevailing southeasterly winds off the Gulf, producing a climate that's predominantly maritime. Summers are warm and humid. Winters are pleasantly mild, with freezing temperatures occurring only at night, and only about 10 times per year. First frost is late arriving on December 9; last frost departs early, by February 16. Spring and fall are the most pleasant, with moderate temperatures and changeable weather.

Summer mildness: 6	Seasonal affect: 71
Winter mildness: 63	Hazard free: 82

	103
	121
	140
90°	135
32°	9
0°	0
	29
	38
	29

	High °F	Low °F	Hum %	Wind mph	Precip inches	Snow inches
JAN	68	45	68	12.1	1.5	0.1
FEB	72	48	65	13.0	1.8	0
MAR	79	55	61	14.1	0.9	0
APR	85	63	62	14.3	1.6	0
MAY	89	68	66	12.8	3.4	0
JUN	92	72	63	11.8	4.0	0
JUL	95	74	57	11.5	2.2	0
AUG	96	73	58	11.0	2.9	0
SEP	92	70	62	10.4	4.3	0
OCT	86	62	59	10.3	2.7	0
NOV	78	55	62	11.6	1.4	0
DEC	71	47	64	11.5	1.0	0

Roswell, NM   Rank: 101

Location: 33.2342 N and 104.3136 W at 3,557 feet, roughly 175 miles midway between El Paso, Texas, and Lubbock, Texas. Albuquerque is 180 miles northwest.

Landscape: Open high hills. The area is situated in the high desert plains of the Pecos Valley, with mountains to the west and south. The dry land forms into cliffs, terraces, buttes, mesas, and canyons. Carlsbad Caverns National Park lies to the south and Lincoln National Forest to the west. Mesquite, creosote, yucca, and cacti mix with desert willows, Rio Grande cottonwood, and native grasses.

Climate: Typical desert, with long, hot, and dry summers. Winters range from daytime warm to cold nights. The first frost arrives in late October; the last frost leaves by April 13. Most precipitation falls in the form of summer thunderstorms, with trace snowfall in winter.

Summer mildness: 32	Seasonal affect: 81
Winter mildness: 44	Hazard free: 42

	157
	104
	104
90°	105
32°	107
0°	1
	57
	21
	47

	High °F	Low °F	Hum %	Wind mph	Precip inches	Snow inches
JAN	54	25	57	7.7	0.4	2.4
FEB	60	29	50	8.5	0.5	2.9
MAR	68	36	40	10.1	0.3	1.5
APR	77	45	37	10.1	0.5	0.2
MAY	85	55	42	9.8	1.0	0
JUN	94	62	45	9.5	1.6	0
JUL	95	67	51	8.7	1.7	0
AUG	92	65	55	7.8	2.6	0
SEP	86	59	57	8.0	2.0	0
OCT	77	47	53	7.8	1.1	0.2
NOV	66	35	53	7.8	0.5	1.2
DEC	56	26	55	7.5	0.5	1.9

Ruidoso, NM   Rank: 44

Location: 33.20 N and 105.41 W at 6,641 feet, in south-central New Mexico. El Paso, Texas, is 155 miles south.

Landscape: Low mountains. On the eastern slope of the Sacramento Mountains with the Tularosa Valley to the west. Thorny desert shrubs of mesquite and creosote bush thrive in lower elevations; juniper and piñon are found in higher elevations to the east.

Climate: Highland, with cold winters, and short hot summers. Daily and seasonal temperature changes are pronounced. Because of the mountain location, the first frost arrives early, by September 19, and the last frost does not leave until June 11. There are traces of snow, but most precipitation falls as light rain and is evenly distributed throughout the year. The higher elevations of the Lincoln National Forest, which includes the ski area, usually remain snow-covered all winter.

Summer mildness: 99	Seasonal affect: 86
Winter mildness: 15	Hazard free: 49

	193
	100
	72
90°	5
32°	200
0°	4
	6
	49
	36

	High °F	Low °F	Hum %	Wind mph	Precip inches	Snow inches
JAN	42	20	42	8.4	1.6	2.7
FEB	43	21	34	9.2	1.4	1.7
MAR	49	25	27	11.0	1.5	1.1
APR	57	32	21	11.1	0.5	0
MAY	65	38	21	10.3	1.0	0
JUN	73	46	23	9.3	2.0	0
JUL	72	49	35	8.3	4.4	0
AUG	70	47	39	7.8	5.0	0
SEP	66	43	41	7.6	3.3	0
OCT	59	35	36	7.5	1.8	0
NOV	49	26	37	8.0	1.3	1.0
DEC	43	22	42	7.9	2.0	2.6

Rockport–Aransas Pass, TX   Rank: 76

★ = in the top 30 places for climate mildness

St. Augustine, FL Rank: 36

Location: 29.51 N and 81.16 W at 5 feet, on the Atlantic Coast in northeastern Florida, 40 miles south of Jacksonville.

Landscape: Flat plains. Located on a peninsula with the Matanzas and North rivers on the east and south and the San Sebastian on the west. These rivers and saltwater lagoons lie between the city and Anastasia Island and the Atlantic Ocean beyond, serving as a port of entry on the Atlantic Intracoastal Waterway. There are Coquina quarries. The surrounding terrain is level. The pines begin to yield to palms. Broadleaf deciduous trees are a rarity in the coastal pine forest.

Climate: Subtropical. The atmosphere is heavily humid. Average daily sunshine ranges from 5½ hours in December to 9 hours in May. The greatest amount of rain, mostly in the form of daily afternoon thundershowers, falls during late summer. There is a short frost season with first frost delayed until mid-December; last frost exits mid-February.

Summer mildness: 22	Seasonal affect: 52
Winter mildness: 90	Hazard free: 91

	97
	127
	141
90°	104
32°	8
0°	0
	38
	73
	66

	High °F	Low °F	Hum %	Wind mph	Precip inches	Snow inches
JAN	66	46	57	8.2	3.1	0
FEB	68	47	53	9.0	3.8	0
MAR	74	53	50	9.0	3.6	0
APR	79	58	48	8.6	2.4	0
MAY	84	64	50	8.0	3.6	0
JUN	88	70	57	7.8	5.5	0
JUL	90	72	58	7.1	5.5	0
AUG	89	72	60	6.8	6.3	0
SEP	86	71	62	7.6	6.1	0
OCT	81	64	58	8.1	3.7	0
NOV	74	55	56	7.7	2.3	0
DEC	69	48	58	7.8	3.0	0

St. George–Zion, UT Rank: 65

Location: 37.06 N and 113.34 W at 2,880 feet, in extreme southwestern Utah. Las Vegas, Nevada, is 130 miles southwest.

Landscape: Plains with high mountains. Fifteen miles north, the Pine Valley Mountains rise to over 10,000 feet. The same distance west are the Beaver Dam Mountains, rising to 7,000 feet. Canyon walls of red, gray, yellow, and brown sandstone and volcanic cinder-cone rock formations provide relief. As it's on the northern edge of the Mohave Desert, vegetation is sparse. Cacti, thorny shrubs, creosote bush, and chamisa are most prevalent.

Climate: Semiarid desert steppe. The most striking features are bright sunshine, small annual precipitation, dryness and purity of air, and large daily variations in temperature. Summers are characterized by hot, dry weather and low humidity. Winters are short and mild, with the Rocky Mountains blocking cold air masses from the north and east. First frost comes in November 4; last frost leaves on March 31.

Summer mildness: 29	Seasonal affect: 95
Winter mildness: 36	Hazard free: 74

	221
	79
	65
90°	125
32°	89
0°	0
	1
	20
	14

	High °F	Low °F	Hum %	Wind mph	Precip inches	Snow inches
JAN	54	27	35	7.5	1.1	1.6
FEB	61	32	30	8.6	0.9	0.7
MAR	68	38	25	10.3	1.1	0
APR	77	44	20	11.0	0.5	0
MAY	86	53	17	11.1	0.4	0
JUN	97	62	14	11.1	0.2	0
JUL	102	69	15	10.3	0.6	0
AUG	100	67	19	9.6	0.8	0
SEP	93	58	20	9.0	0.5	0
OCT	81	46	22	8.1	0.5	0
NOV	65	35	30	7.7	0.9	0
DEC	54	28	36	7.3	0.7	0.7

St. Jay–Northeast Kingdom, VT Rank: 182

Location: 44.25 N and 72.01 W at 588 feet, in Vermont's Upper Connecticut River Valley, 33 miles east of Montpelier and 75 miles east of Burlington.

Landscape: Open low mountains. The Green Mountains form the western boundary, the Connecticut River the eastern. This area is composed of low rugged hills, lowlands dotted with glacial lakes, ponds, bogs, and swamps. The Passumpsic, Moose, and Sleeper river valleys create interesting relief. The woods are a transitional forest of mixed conifer and deciduous trees. Northern white pine, eastern hemlock, maple, oak, and beech are common.

Climate: Northerly latitude ensures the variety and vigor of a true New England climate. Summers, though not long, are pleasant. Falls are cool, extending through October. Winters are cold and snowy, with brief, intense cold snaps formed by high-pressure systems moving down from central Canada and Hudson Bay. The first frost arrives September 25; the last frost departs May 22.

Summer mildness: 80	Seasonal affect: 18
Winter mildness: 11	Hazard free: 10

	91
	110
	164
90°	9
32°	173
0°	28
	15
	81
	20

	High °F	Low °F	Hum %	Wind mph	Precip inches	Snow inches
JAN	27	6	58	9.0	2.3	21.3
FEB	31	7	57	9.4	2.1	19.5
MAR	42	19	53	9.9	2.5	14.3
APR	55	31	49	10	2.7	3.0
MAY	70	42	49	8.9	3.3	0
JUN	78	52	55	8.1	3.8	0
JUL	82	56	55	7.5	3.7	0
AUG	80	55	57	7.2	4.0	0
SEP	71	47	59	7.3	3.1	0
OCT	59	36	59	7.8	3.1	0
NOV	44	28	60	8.5	3.5	6.0
DEC	31	13	62	8.7	3.2	21.9

★ = in the top 30 places for climate mildness

St. Marys, GA — Rank: 57

Location: 30.00 N and 81.00 W at 10 feet in extreme southeast Georgia on the Atlantic Coast. It is the state's oldest city. Immediately south is Florida and greater Jacksonville.

Landscape: Flat plains. Like Florida to the south, relief is less than 300 feet, although some areas are gently rolling. There are typical southern mixed forests of loblolly and slash pine, and bald cypress is a dominant tree in swamps.

Climate: Subtropical. Average temperatures compare with those of southern portions of California, Brazil, China, and Australia. In contrast to places farther south, there is a more definite march of the four seasons here. There is considerable winter rain and less sunshine. Summer is the least pleasant time of year, with humidity and high temperatures bringing discomfort. The freeze-free growing season is from early March to mid-November.

Summer mildness: 1   **Seasonal affect:** 50
Winter mildness: 95   **Hazard free:** 91

95
127
143
90° 82
32° 12
0° 0
175
70
58

	High °F	Low °F	Hum %	Wind mph	Precip inches	Snow inches
JAN	64	64	73	8.2	3.3	0
FEB	67	67	70	9.0	3.9	0
MAR	73	73	68	9.0	3.7	0
APR	79	79	67	8.6	2.8	0
MAY	85	85	68	8.0	3.6	0
JUN	89	89	72	7.7	5.7	0
JUL	91	91	73	7.1	5.6	0
AUG	91	91	76	6.7	7.9	0
SEP	87	87	77	7.5	7.1	0
OCT	80	80	75	8.0	2.9	0
NOV	74	74	73	7.8	2.2	0
DEC	67	67	73	7.8	2.7	0

St. Simons–Jekyll Islands, GA — Rank: 34

Location: 31.13 N and 81.21 W at 10 feet, on the Intracoastal Waterway, 65 miles south of Savannah, and 54 miles north of Jacksonville, Florida.

Landscape: Flat plains, with no elevation higher than 20 feet. Shell beaches blend into the surrounding marshlands. The low terrain and low-latitude location make the area vulnerable to occasional tropical storms, though their full force is felt infrequently. The outer coastal plain, reached by a causeway, is a temperate rainforest with Evangeline oak, long-leaf pine, laurel, Bayonet palmettos, holly, and magnolia. Flowers bloom through the winter, and climbing vines are prevalent.

Climate: The area enjoys mild and relatively short winters due to the moderating effect of coastal waters. Summers are warm and humid, but very high temperatures are rare. Heat waves are usually interrupted by thundershowers. Even in summer the nights are usually pleasant. With first frost on December 3 and last frost on February 24, there is a long growing season.

Summer mildness: 31   **Seasonal affect:** 62
Winter mildness: 86   **Hazard free:** 78

97
127
141
90° 42
32° 16
0° 0
38
68
66

	High °F	Low °F	Hum %	Wind mph	Precip inches	Snow inches
JAN	60	42	54	8.2	3.3	0
FEB	62	44	50	9.0	3.9	0.1
MAR	69	51	48	9.0	3.9	0
APR	76	58	45	8.6	2.5	0
MAY	82	66	50	8.0	3.3	0
JUN	87	72	54	7.8	5.0	0
JUL	90	74	57	7.1	5.6	0
AUG	88	74	61	6.8	7.0	0
SEP	85	71	60	7.6	6.5	0
OCT	77	61	53	8.1	2.9	0
NOV	70	52	52	7.7	2.6	0
DEC	63	45	55	7.8	3.1	0

Sandpoint–Lake Pend Oreille, ID — Rank: 184

Location: 48.16 N and 116.33 W at 2,086 feet, in the Idaho panhandle, 50 miles south of the Canadian border. Spokane, Washington, is 75 miles southwest.

Landscape: High mountains. Lake Pend Oreille, near the outflow of the Pend Oreille River, is 43 miles long and 6 miles at its widest. The surface of the lake reflects the surrounding Selkirk, Cabinet, and Coeur d'Alene mountain ranges, with peaks rising over 6,000 feet. The Kaniksu National Forest is mixed coniferous and deciduous. Douglas fir, hemlock, and cedar predominate in this high valley surrounded by mountain ranges.

Climate: Continental and generally described as rigorous. Summers are dry and bright. Falls are pleasant but all too short. Winters are long, cold, and snowy. First frost by September 11; last frost by early June. Though seasonal temperature variation is large, it's less so than in most other locations this far north.

Summer mildness: 94   **Seasonal affect:** 6
Winter mildness: 8   **Hazard free:** 9

86
87
192
90° 15
32° 187
0° 7
47
80
11

	High °F	Low °F	Hum %	Wind mph	Precip inches	Snow inches
JAN	30	19	80	8.8	4.0	31.0
FEB	37	22	78	9.3	3.1	14.1
MAR	45	26	65	9.7	2.8	8.3
APR	56	31	55	10.0	2.1	0
MAY	66	38	51	9.2	2.4	0
JUN	74	45	47	9.2	2.1	0
JUL	82	47	37	8.6	1.2	0
AUG	82	47	40	8.2	1.5	0
SEP	71	40	45	8.3	1.5	0
OCT	56	33	59	8.2	2.0	0
NOV	38	28	75	8.7	4.3	10.0
DEC	30	22	83	8.6	4.5	25.9

★ = in the top 30 places for climate mildness

San Juan Islands, WA — Rank: 61

Location: The weather station is Friday Harbor, 48.32 N and 123.00 W at 91 feet, in the midst of an archipelago of 172 islands that make up San Juan County in northwestern Washington. Bellingham is 20 miles east by ferry.

Landscape: Plains with low mountains. The islands are a submerged mountain chain in upper Puget Sound, where the straits of Juan de Fuca and Georgia meet at the Canadian border. Mt. Constitution, at 2,409 feet, is the highest point on the islands. Many are low flat or flat-topped hills, with wooded forests of Sitka spruce and western hemlock. Madrona, with a red-skinned trunk, is scattered throughout the coniferous forests at these low levels.

Climate: Marine, with mild summers and cool winters, moist air, and small daily temperature variation. First frost comes October 20; last frost leaves April 21. Summers are dry. Like most other places in this region, the area is often foggy and cloudy.

Summer mildness: 86   **Seasonal affect:** 2
Winter mildness: 71   **Hazard free:** 77

	High °F	Low °F	Hum %	Wind mph	Precip inches	Snow inches
JAN	43	32	77	7.1	4.7	2.7
FEB	48	35	74	7.2	3.6	0.6
MAR	51	36	71	7.4	3.0	1.1
APR	56	40	68	7.4	2.7	0
MAY	62	45	65	6.9	2.3	0
JUN	67	51	64	6.7	1.8	0
JUL	71	53	63	6.2	1.3	0
AUG	71	54	63	6.0	1.4	0
SEP	67	48	67	5.7	1.9	0
OCT	58	42	74	5.9	3.4	0
NOV	50	37	77	6.9	5.0	0
DEC	44	33	79	7.3	5.0	1.8

Weather icon values: 50, 84, 231, 90° 0, 32° 68, 0° 0, 90, 91, 5

★ Santa Barbara, CA — Rank: 1

Location: 34.25 N and 119.42 W at 100 feet, in the Santa Maria Valley, 150 miles northwest of Los Angeles.

Landscape: High mountains. The valley is flat and fertile, opening onto the Pacific Ocean at the base of the Santa Ynez Mountains. The foothills of the San Rafael Mountains, the Solomon Hills, and the Casmalia Hills bound it. Cypress and pine groves predominate in the mixed evergreen forest.

Climate: Mediterranean, including a rainy season typical of the California coast in winter. Particularly from June to October, there's little or no precipitation. Clear, sunny afternoons prevail on most days. At night and in the morning, however, the California stratus and fog appear.

Summer mildness: 74   **Seasonal affect:** 89
Winter mildness: 100   **Hazard free:** 100

	High °F	Low °F	Hum %	Wind mph	Precip inches	Snow inches
JAN	64	40	56	4.8	3.2	0
FEB	65	43	57	6.3	3.6	0
MAR	65	45	59	6.7	2.8	0
APR	67	47	60	7.6	1.1	0
MAY	69	50	62	7.1	0.2	0
JUN	71	54	66	6.8	0.0	0
JUL	74	57	66	6.5	0.0	0
AUG	75	58	67	6.1	0.1	0
SEP	75	57	65	5.8	0.5	0
OCT	73	52	62	5.5	0.5	0
NOV	69	45	56	5.3	2.0	0
DEC	64	40	54	5.0	2.2	0

Weather icon values: 147, 116, 103, 90° 3, 32° 0, 0° 0, 19, 17, 3

Santa Fe, NM — Rank: 86

Location: 35.40 N and 105.56 W at 6,947 feet, in the north-central part of the state, 60 miles from Albuquerque.

Landscape: Plains with high mountains. The city lies in the northern Rio Grande Valley on the Santa Fe River amid rolling foothills of the rugged Sangre de Cristo Mountains. Westward, the terrain slopes to the Rio Grande River some 20 miles away. The high mountains protect the city from much of the winter cold. Engelmann spruce and subalpine fir cover the higher slopes; ponderosa pine is on the lower, drier, and more exposed slopes.

Climate: Highland steppe. Winters are crisp, clear, and sunny, with considerable daytime warming. First frost makes appearance by October 6; last frost lingers until May 15. Summers are warm, pleasant, dry, and invigorating. Long cloudy periods are unknown.

Summer mildness: 98   **Seasonal affect:** 90
Winter mildness: 12   **Hazard free:** 13

	High °F	Low °F	Hum %	Wind mph	Precip inches	Snow inches
JAN	40	18	50	8.1	0.9	5.4
FEB	44	21	42	8.9	0.8	5.4
MAR	50	26	32	10.1	1.2	6.9
APR	59	33	25	11.0	1.0	4.0
MAY	68	42	23	10.6	1.2	0
JUN	78	51	22	10.0	1.4	0
JUL	81	55	30	9.1	3.3	0
AUG	78	53	34	8.3	3.5	0
SEP	71	47	35	8.6	2.1	0
OCT	62	38	35	8.3	1.3	1.0
NOV	49	27	38	7.9	1.0	4.0
DEC	41	19	46	7.7	1.1	7.0

Weather icon values: 169, 111, 85, 90° 8, 32° 169, 0° 4, 6, 33, 41

★ = in the top 30 places for climate mildness

★ Sarasota, FL   Rank: 19

Location: 27.20 N and 82.32 W at 27 feet, sheltered from the Gulf of Mexico behind Longboat Key on Sarasota Bay. Tampa is 50 miles north; Fort Myers 75 miles south.

Landscape: Flat plains. The southern Gulf Coastal Plains are flat and irregular. There's less than 200 feet variation in altitude over the gently rolling areas. Most of the streams are sluggish; marshes, swamps, and lakes are numerous. Evergreen oaks, laurel, and magnolia are common. Trees aren't tall, and the leaf canopy is less dense. There is a well-developed underbrush of ferns, shrubs, and herbaceous plants.

Climate: Subtropical. The waters of the Gulf of Mexico and surrounding bays modify temperature throughout the year. Thunderstorms are frequent during late-summer afternoons, rapidly cooling the hot, humid days. Winters are mild. Snow and freezing temperatures are rare.

Summer mildness: 18	Seasonal affect: 72
Winter mildness: 95	Hazard free: 85

			High °F	**Low** °F	**Hum** %	**Wind** mph	**Precip** inches	**Snow** inches

	102
	142
	121
90°	78
32°	0
0°	0
	22
	69
	86

	High °F	Low °F	Hum %	Wind mph	Precip inches	Snow inches
JAN	72	52	56	8.6	2.2	0
FEB	72	53	56	9.2	2.7	0
MAR	77	58	53	9.5	3.2	0
APR	81	61	47	9.3	1.6	0
MAY	86	67	49	8.7	2.6	0
JUN	89	72	56	8.0	6.5	0
JUL	90	73	60	7.2	6.5	0
AUG	91	73	60	7.0	7.9	0
SEP	89	73	60	7.8	7.2	0
OCT	85	66	56	8.5	2.6	0
NOV	79	59	56	8.4	2.1	0
DEC	74	54	56	8.5	2.1	0

Savannah, GA   Rank: 69

Location: 32.05 N and 81.06 W at 42 feet, at the mouth of the Savannah River and Atlantic Ocean. Jacksonville, Florida, is 140 miles down the coast, and Charleston, South Carolina, is 100 miles up the coast.

Landscape: Flat plains, low and marshy to the north and east, rising to several feet above sea level to the west and south. About half the land to the west and south is clear of trees and the other half is woods, much of which lies in swamp. The outer coastal plain is a temperate rainforest that includes live oak, loblolly pine, laurel, and magnolia.

Climate: Subtropical. Summer temperatures are moderated by thundershowers almost every afternoon. Sunshine is adequate in all seasons; seldom are there more than 2 or 3 days in succession without it. First frost makes an appearance by November 14; last frost is gone by March 11. There's abundant rain during the long growing season.

Summer mildness: 24	Seasonal affect: 49
Winter mildness: 83	Hazard free: 71

	104
	111
	150
90°	76
32°	33
0°	0
	39
	70
	61

	High °F	Low °F	Hum %	Wind mph	Precip inches	Snow inches
JAN	60	38	54	8.5	3.6	0.1
FEB	62	41	50	9.2	3.2	0.2
MAR	70	48	48	9.2	3.8	0
APR	78	55	45	8.7	3.0	0
MAY	84	63	50	7.7	4.1	0
JUN	89	69	54	7.5	5.7	0
JUL	91	72	57	7.1	6.4	0
AUG	90	72	61	6.6	7.5	0
SEP	85	68	60	7.2	4.5	0
OCT	78	57	53	7.4	2.4	0
NOV	70	48	52	7.5	2.2	0
DEC	62	41	54	7.9	3.0	0.1

★ Scottsdale, AZ   Rank: 5

Location: 33.30 N and 111.53 W at 1,259 feet, 10 miles immediately east of Phoenix.

Landscape: Open high mountains. The area lies in the center of the oval-shaped flat Salt River Valley. Mountain ranges surround the valley on all sides, with the famous Superstition Mountain to the east. Although this is a desert, cotton and citrus are cultivated. Native vegetation includes creosote bush, saguaro, cholla, and cereus. An underground water table contributes to the local water supply, along with the Salt and Verde rivers.

Climate: Arid desert climate, with little rainfall and low humidity. Summers are hot with temperatures frequently above 100°F. Winters are cool and can drop below freezing at night. The growing season is long, with the first frost coming late, on December 4, and the last frost coming early, February 14. Cloudy days are rare.

Summer mildness: 24	Seasonal affect: 98
Winter mildness: 98	Hazard free: 96

	212
	84
	69
90°	163
32°	20
0°	0
	2
	19
	24

	High °F	Low °F	Hum %	Wind mph	Precip inches	Snow inches
JAN	66	41	45	5.3	0.7	0
FEB	71	45	39	5.9	0.7	0
MAR	76	49	34	6.7	0.9	0
APR	85	55	23	7.0	0.2	0
MAY	94	64	18	7.1	0.1	0
JUN	104	73	16	6.8	0.1	0
JUL	106	81	28	7.2	0.8	0
AUG	104	79	33	6.7	1.0	0
SEP	98	73	31	6.3	0.9	0
OCT	88	61	31	5.8	0.7	0
NOV	75	49	37	5.4	0.7	0
DEC	66	42	46	5.1	1.0	0

Sebring–Avon Park, FL   Rank: 54

Location: 27.29 N and 81.26 W at 131 feet, circling Lake Jackson in south-central Florida. Orlando is 90 miles north. Sarasota, on the Gulf Coast, is 60 miles west. Ft. Pierce, on the Atlantic Coast, is 60 miles east.

Landscape: Flat plains. Highland lakes region, with sandy ridges giving relief to low-level muckland and flatland. Most of the surrounding acreage is citrus groves and ranches. Hardwood hammock and cabbage palms are dense in the rainforest of Highlands Hammock State Park.

Climate: Subtropical, with a surplus of moisture. As in other Florida locations, the humid, hot summer is cooled by afternoon thunderstorms. Winters are mild and the first frost comes late, December 31; the last frost leaves early, January 23. Annual range of temperature changes is small.

Summer mildness: 7   **Seasonal affect:** 60
Winter mildness: 87   **Hazard free:** 86

	92
	148
	125
90°	137
32°	4
0°	0
	27
	76
	82

	High °F	Low °F	Hum %	Wind mph	Precip inches	Snow inches
JAN	73	48	56	8.9	2.2	0
FEB	75	49	52	9.6	2.8	0
MAR	79	54	50	9.9	3.0	0
APR	85	59	46	9.4	1.7	0
MAY	89	65	49	8.8	4.0	0
JUN	91	70	56	8.0	8.4	0
JUL	92	71	59	7.4	7.7	0
AUG	92	72	60	7.1	7.2	0
SEP	90	71	60	7.7	6.1	0
OCT	85	64	56	8.6	2.8	0
NOV	80	57	55	8.6	1.9	0
DEC	74	51	57	8.6	1.9	0

Sedona, AZ   Rank: 49

Location: 34.52 N and 111.45 W at 4,280 feet, in Oak Creek Canyon. Phoenix is 90 miles south; Flagstaff 20 miles north.

Landscape: Tablelands with very high relief, overlooking red-hued rocks and buttes of the canyon, whose steep walls rise 1,200 feet. The forest is ponderosa pine, Douglas fir, and (at higher elevations) subalpine fir and Engelmann spruce.

Climate: Semiarid mountain steppe. There are strong daily and seasonal temperature changes. The usual winter flow of air is from the Pacific Ocean, bringing frequent snows. Cold air from Canada sometimes drives temperatures below freezing. First frost is October 13; last frost is May 17. Moisture-bearing winds from the southeast Gulf region bring brief rains from July to September.

Summer mildness: 53   **Seasonal affect:** 92
Winter mildness: 55   **Hazard free:** 44

	212
	84
	69
90°	66
32°	155
0°	0
	11
	29
	24

	High °F	Low °F	Hum %	Wind mph	Precip inches	Snow inches
JAN	56	29	45	7.0	1.7	4.5
FEB	60	32	40	6.9	1.8	3.5
MAR	64	35	36	7.5	2.2	6.8
APR	73	41	25	7.9	1.2	2.0
MAY	82	48	20	7.5	0.6	0
JUN	93	56	18	7.1	0.4	0
JUL	97	64	28	5.7	1.8	0
AUG	94	62	33	5.3	2.1	0
SEP	88	56	34	6.0	2.0	0
OCT	78	47	34	6.1	1.5	0
NOV	65	36	37	7.1	1.6	1.0
DEC	56	30	46	7.0	1.8	5.1

Silver City, NM   Rank: 63

Location: 32.46 N and 108.16 W at 5,851 feet, in southwestern New Mexico. Tucson, Arizona, is 170 miles west and El Paso, Texas, 140 miles east.

Landscape: High mountains. East of the Continental Divide in the foothills of the Pinos Altos Range at the edge of the Gila National Forest. There are wild ranges, high cliffs, and remote canyons. The Chihuahuan Desert vegetation includes creosote, ceniza, and ocotillo shrubs. Juniper and piñons are common on rocky outcrops. Ponderosa pine, Douglas fir, white fir, and spruce occur in the high forests.

Climate: Desert continental. The rainfall, at 8 inches per year, is light and falls in brief showers through late summer and fall. Drizzles are unknown. Summers are hot, but the nights are cool. Winters tend to be mild and sunny, with freezing nights. The arrival of the first frost on October 30 and the departure of the last frost on April 22 make for a short growing season.

Summer mildness: 38   **Seasonal affect:** 94
Winter mildness: 41   **Hazard free:** 61

	193
	100
	72
90°	112
32°	110
0°	0
	2
	23
	24

	High °F	Low °F	Hum %	Wind mph	Precip inches	Snow inches
JAN	58	25	42	8.4	0.9	2.1
FEB	63	27	34	9.2	0.6	1.8
MAR	70	33	27	11.0	0.7	1.9
APR	78	39	21	11.1	0.2	0
MAY	87	47	21	10.3	0.3	0
JUN	96	57	23	9.3	0.5	0
JUL	96	65	35	8.3	2.0	0
AUG	93	62	39	7.8	2.1	0
SEP	88	56	41	7.6	1.5	0
OCT	79	43	36	7.5	1.2	0
NOV	67	31	37	8.0	0.7	0
DEC	58	25	42	7.9	1.2	0.8

★ = in the top 30 places for climate mildness

Silverthorne–Breckenridge, CO — Rank: 146

Location: The weather station is Breckenridge, 39.29 N and 106.02 W at 9,602 feet near the Continental Divide. Denver is 60 miles east.

Landscape: High mountains. The two most visible elevations are Buffalo (12,777 ft.) and Ptarmigan (13,739 ft.) mountains. Visible below their summits around 11,000 feet is the tree line. Above it is the short-growing, sparse vegetation of the tundra. On the slopes below are thick stands of Engelmann spruce and tall Douglas fir.

Climate: The climate is a temperate semiarid steppe regime that is influenced by the prevailing west winds and the general north–south orientation of the mountain ranges. Winters are cold, snowy, and windy. The first frost arrives September 25 and the last frost departs May 22. Summers are ideal.

Summer mildness: 92 **Seasonal affect:** 64
Winter mildness: 1 **Hazard free:** 4

	113
	113
	139
90°	32
32°	188
0°	10
	32
	61
	31

	High °F	Low °F	Hum %	Wind mph	Precip inches	Snow inches
JAN	29	-1	71	10.1	1.4	19.1
FEB	32	1	61	10.2	1.2	11.2
MAR	36	9	50	10.8	1.6	8.0
APR	45	18	43	10.3	1.5	2.8
MAY	55	26	40	8.8	1.6	0.3
JUN	66	33	32	8.0	1.6	0
JUL	73	39	35	7.5	2.7	0
AUG	71	37	38	7.0	2.5	0
SEP	63	30	39	7.5	1.5	0
OCT	53	22	46	7.7	1.2	0.8
NOV	39	11	59	9.1	1.3	6.3
DEC	30	3	69	9.8	1.5	14.4

Smith Mountain Lake, VA — Rank: 108

Location: 37.02 N and 79.32 W at 795 feet, in foothills on the eastern slope of the Blue Ridge Mountains in southwest Virginia. Roanoke is 30 miles northwest and Greensboro, North Carolina, 100 miles south.

Landscape: Low mountains. This 22,000-acre artificial lake is located in a natural notch in a 7-mile-long ridge, Smith Mountain, just below the confluence of the Blackwater and Roanoke rivers. The woods on the slopes are a typical southeastern mixed forest of medium-tall to tall oak, hickory, sweet gum, and red maple, together with loblolly and shortleaf pine. The undergrowth is dogwood, viburnum, blueberry, youpon, and numerous woody vines.

Climate: Hot continental, with four distinct seasons. First frost arrives by October 14; last frost departs on April 26. Winters are short, summers somewhat hot and humid. Spring and autumn are ideal. Precipitation is evenly distributed throughout the year, mostly as rain. In mid-summer, mountain thunderstorms are likely.

Summer mildness: 64 **Seasonal affect:** 54
Winter mildness: 39 **Hazard free:** 38

	102
	113
	150
90°	17
32°	123
0°	2
	23
	69
	36

	High °F	Low °F	Hum %	Wind mph	Precip inches	Snow inches
JAN	42	20	55	9.5	2.3	5.8
FEB	45	22	52	9.7	2.3	4.7
MAR	55	30	50	10.1	2.9	3.5
APR	65	38	47	9.8	2.8	0
MAY	73	48	54	7.9	3.6	0
JUN	81	56	56	6.9	2.8	0
JUL	85	61	59	6.5	3.5	0
AUG	84	59	60	6.1	3.7	0
SEP	77	52	60	6.1	3.5	0
OCT	67	39	55	6.9	3.6	0
NOV	57	32	53	8.3	3.0	0
DEC	46	24	56	8.8	2.4	2.0

★ Sonora–Twain Harte, CA — Rank: 16

Location: The weather station is Sonora, 37.59 N and 120.23 W at 1,854 feet. Sacramento is 90 miles northwest. Modesto, in the central valley, is 40 miles southwest.

Landscape: Situated in the foothills of the Sierra Nevada Mountains at the edge of the Stanislaus National Forest. There are five rivers that drain the region. Chaparral in the low elevations gives way to digger pine and several oak species in the higher mountains.

Climate: Sierran forest climate in the transition zone between the dry west coast desert and the wet west coast farther north. Prevailing west winds influence conditions jointly with elevation. Therefore, the summers are long and generally dry. Most of the annual precipitation falls as rain rather than snow. The first frost arrives on November 12 and the last frost leaves April 14.

Summer mildness: 51 **Seasonal affect:** 76
Winter mildness: 69 **Hazard free:** 83

	189
	75
	100
90°	83
32°	64
0°	0
	34
	43
	14

	High °F	Low °F	Hum %	Wind mph	Precip inches	Snow inches
JAN	55	32	80	7.2	5.6	0.4
FEB	59	34	75	7.6	5.0	0
MAR	61	36	65	8.6	5.3	0.4
APR	67	40	55	8.7	2.7	0
MAY	77	45	48	9.2	0.8	0
JUN	87	51	44	9.7	0.2	0
JUL	95	57	44	9.0	0.1	0
AUG	94	56	45	8.6	0.2	0
SEP	87	51	45	7.5	0.6	0
OCT	77	43	53	6.4	1.8	0
NOV	62	36	65	6.0	4.8	0
DEC	54	32	77	6.6	4.6	0.1

★ = in the top 30 places for climate mildness

Southern Berkshire County, MA   Rank: 171

Location: The weather station is Great Barrington, 42.11 N and 73.21 W at 721 feet, in the rural corner where Massachusetts, New York, and Connecticut meet.

Landscape: Open low mountains. The Berkshire Plateau in the east and the Taconic Mountains in the west enclose the Berkshire Valley. Rolling, open meadows are watered by the headwaters of the Housatonic River. A typical northern deciduous forest covers the uplands with maple, birch, beech, oak, and a scattering of pine. The low growth is shrub, herb, and fern.

Climate: Hot continental, with large temperature variations from season to season. Winters receive Canadian air sweeping down the Hudson Valley to the west and bring the first frost by October 15; the last frost departs a little late, April 27. December to February is cold, with long-lasting snow. Springs are short. Summers are clear, warm, and ideal. Falls are bright and extend through mid-November.

Summer mildness: 77   **Seasonal affect:** 17
Winter mildness: 23   **Hazard free:** 19

	81
	109
	175
90°	19
32°	135
0°	6
	29
	75
	21

	High °F	Low °F	Hum %	Wind mph	Precip inches	Snow inches
JAN	31	9	58	9.0	3.0	16.3
FEB	33	12	57	9.4	2.9	14.1
MAR	43	22	53	9.9	3.2	10.7
APR	56	32	49	10.0	3.8	2.0
MAY	68	42	49	8.9	4.5	0
JUN	76	51	55	8.1	4.1	0
JUL	80	56	55	7.5	4.0	0
AUG	78	54	57	7.2	4.6	0
SEP	71	46	59	7.3	3.7	0
OCT	60	35	59	7.8	3.5	0
NOV	48	28	60	8.5	3.9	4.0
DEC	35	17	62	8.7	3.6	15.1

Southern Pines–Pinehurst, NC   Rank: 106

Location: 35.10 N and 79.23 W at 512 feet, 75 miles south of Chapel Hill in the southern heartland of the state.

Landscape: Irregular plains. This area is in gently rolling sand-hill country between the foothills of the Uwharrie Mountains and the coastal plains. The woods are a hardwood swamp forest, with broadleaf deciduous and needleleaf evergreens.

Climate: Subtropical, with mild winters and hot, humid summers. Precipitation is evenly distributed throughout the year, but peaks slightly in midsummer or early spring thunderstorms. Occasionally there will be summer droughts. Unprotected by the mountains, the first frost will come by September 29 and the last frost departs on May 9. Snow is rare.

Summer mildness: 50   **Seasonal affect:** 42
Winter mildness: 48   **Hazard free:** 55

	112
	106
	147
90°	43
32°	111
0°	0
	34
	74
	44

	High °F	Low °F	Hum %	Wind mph	Precip inches	Snow inches
JAN	49	24	55	8.5	4.0	2.1
FEB	53	27	52	8.9	4.0	1.8
MAR	62	35	49	9.3	4.4	1.3
APR	71	43	45	9.0	3.2	0
MAY	78	52	54	7.7	4.5	0
JUN	85	60	56	7.0	4.0	0
JUL	88	64	58	6.7	4.9	0
AUG	87	63	60	6.4	4.8	0
SEP	82	56	60	6.8	3.5	0
OCT	72	43	54	7.1	3.7	0
NOV	63	35	55	7.6	3.2	0
DEC	53	28	55	8.0	3.5	0.5

Southport–Brunswick Islands, NC   Rank: 92

Location: 33.55 N and 78.01 W at 34 feet, on the Atlantic Ocean in North Carolina's extreme southeastern corner. Wilmington is 30 miles north.

Landscape: Flat plains. The surrounding low-lying terrain is typical of the state's coastal plain. The average elevation is less than 40 feet and level. Many rivers, creeks, and lakes are nearby, with considerable swampy growth surrounding them. Large tracts of southern mixed forest alternate with cultivated fields.

Climate: A strong maritime influence. Summers are warm and humid, but excessive heat is rare. During the colder part of the year, polar air reaches the coastal areas, causing sharp temperature drops. Rainfall is ample and well distributed, with most occurring in summer thundershowers. In winter, rain may fall steadily for several days. Snowfall is slight. Some tropical storms reach the Cape Fear area every few years. November 11 will see the first frost and March 21 will see the last frost.

Summer mildness: 41   **Seasonal affect:** 47
Winter mildness: 60   **Hazard free:** 58

	112
	104
	150
90°	20
32°	42
0°	0
	24
	74
	48

	High °F	Low °F	Hum %	Wind mph	Precip inches	Snow inches
JAN	55	32	56	9.1	4.7	0.5
FEB	57	34	52	9.8	4.4	0.6
MAR	64	42	52	10.2	4.4	0.3
APR	72	50	48	10.3	3.0	0
MAY	79	59	55	9.2	4.0	0
JUN	85	67	59	8.5	4.9	0
JUL	88	71	63	8.0	6.9	0
AUG	88	70	64	7.4	7.1	0
SEP	83	64	62	7.9	6.8	0
OCT	75	52	56	8.1	3.3	0
NOV	68	43	53	8.1	3.3	0
DEC	59	35	55	8.5	4.1	0.3

★ = in the top 30 places for climate mildness

State College, PA   Rank: 142

Location: 40.47 N and 77.51 W at 1,157 feet. Philadelphia is 190 miles east; Pittsburgh 140 miles west.

Landscape: Open low mountains. The ridges and valleys of the Appalachians run northeast to southwest, with elevations varying from 977 to 2,400 feet. In the Nittany Valley rolling meadows and where the foothills of the Allegheny Plateau rise to the west, forests of pine, hemlock, and hardwoods of beech, maple, oak, ash, and cherry were once more common before the clear-cut harvests. The surrounding higher elevations are now covered with second-growth forests.

Climate: Hot continental, with temperatures moderated by the surrounding mountain elevations. The city is protected by its eastern slope location, producing drier, somewhat less humid seasons. Winters are cold and relatively dry, with thick cloud cover. The first frost comes on October 15; the last frost leaves April 27. Summer and fall are the most pleasant seasons.

Summer mildness: 81   **Seasonal affect:** 24
Winter mildness: 40   **Hazard free:** 21

	87
	109
	169
90°	8
32°	131
0°	5
	19
	76
	32

	High °F	Low °F	Hum %	Wind mph	Precip inches	Snow inches
JAN	33	17	58	8.3	2.4	11.7
FEB	36	18	55	9.0	2.6	11.7
MAR	46	27	52	9.5	3.2	11.1
APR	58	37	49	9.2	2.9	1.0
MAY	70	48	52	7.6	3.6	0
JUN	78	56	53	6.8	4.0	0
JUL	82	61	52	6.2	3.6	0
AUG	80	59	55	5.8	3.2	0
SEP	73	52	56	6.1	3.2	0
OCT	62	41	54	6.6	2.8	0
NOV	49	33	57	7.8	3.2	3.0
DEC	37	23	58	8.0	2.7	9.5

Sullivan County, NY   Rank: 186

Location: 41.00 N and 74.00 W at 1,580 feet in the southern part of New York State in the midst of the Catskill Mountains. New York City is 75 miles southeast.

Landscape: Low mountains. Rolling hills occur in many places; there are lakes, poorly drained depressions, morainic hills, drumlins, eskers, outwash plains, and other glacial features that are typical of the area. A transitional forest includes mixed stands of a few coniferous species and a few deciduous species, principally yellow birch, sugar maple, and the American beech. Where the soil is good, a more pure deciduous forest exists.

Climate: Continental with moderately long winters that are somewhat severe, but with more than 120 days that have temperatures above 50°F. Snow usually stays on the ground all winter. The area is north of the main cyclonic belt during winter; but during summer it lies within this belt, and the weather is changeable.

Summer mildness: 65   **Seasonal affect:** 4
Winter mildness: 34   **Hazard free:** 14

	55
	101
	209
90°	4
32°	150
0°	10
	175
	89
	18

	High °F	Low °F	Hum %	Wind mph	Precip inches	Snow inches
JAN	30	11	75	11.5	3.0	17.2
FEB	33	12	73	11.6	2.9	19.5
MAR	42	22	71	11.7	3.2	16.1
APR	55	33	66	11.4	3.8	4.7
MAY	66	43	67	10.0	4.5	0.2
JUN	74	51	70	9.3	4.1	0
JUL	79	56	71	8.4	4.0	0
AUG	78	54	75	8.2	4.6	0
SEP	70	47	77	8.8	3.7	0
OCT	59	36	74	9.8	3.5	0.6
NOV	47	29	76	10.9	3.9	6.4
DEC	34	17	76	11.2	3.6	16.6

Summerville, SC   Rank: 129

Location: 33.0106 N and 80.1033 W at 75 feet, 25 miles northwest of Charleston.

Landscape: Flat plains. The local terrain is mostly swampland and forest. Southeast is the Atlantic Ocean, and east is the Francis Marion National Forest. Tree cover includes oak, sweet and black gums, and bald cypress.

Climate: Subtropical, with moderation from the ocean. Summer is a period of heat and humidity, with frequent thunderstorms. Fall and winter are cool but rarely cold. With the first frost arriving fairly late, on November 6, and the last frost leaving rather early, on March 27, the growing season is extended. Spring is warm, windy, and sunny.

Summer mildness: 8   **Seasonal affect:** 38
Winter mildness: 64   **Hazard free:** 65

	104
	109
	152
90°	59
32°	50
0°	0
	28
	74
	56

	High °F	Low °F	Hum %	Wind mph	Precip inches	Snow inches
JAN	57	33	70	9.1	4.0	0
FEB	61	35	67	9.9	3.6	0.6
MAR	69	43	67	10.0	4.5	0
APR	76	49	67	9.7	3.1	0
MAY	83	58	69	8.7	4.3	0
JUN	88	66	72	8.4	6.1	0
JUL	90	70	75	7.9	6.1	0
AUG	89	69	77	7.4	6.9	0
SEP	85	64	76	7.8	4.8	0
OCT	77	52	72	8.1	3.1	0
NOV	70	43	70	8.1	2.5	0
DEC	61	36	69	8.5	3.3	0.1

★ = in the top 30 places for climate mildness

Taos, NM   Rank: 97

Location: 36.24 N and 105.34 W at 6,983 feet, 40 miles south of the Colorado border. Santa Fe is 70 miles south and Albuquerque 130 miles southwest.

Landscape: High mountains. In an area where the western flank of the Sangre de Cristo range meets the semiarid high desert of the upper Rio Grande Valley. Wheeler Peak (13,161 ft.), the highest point in New Mexico, is nearby. The relief includes deep gorges, mountainous skylines, and wide valleys. Typical steppe vegetation consists of numerous shortgrasses, scattered shrubs, and low trees. Engelmann spruce and subalpine fir cover the intermediate slopes, and ponderosa pine is on the lower, drier, more exposed areas.

Climate: Steppe and semiarid continental. Precipitation is evenly distributed throughout the year, falling as rain in summer storms and snow in the cold winters. Summers are clear, mild, and ideal. First frost comes by October 4; last frost departs May 12.

Summer mildness: 97   **Seasonal affect:** 88
Winter mildness: 9   **Hazard free:** 6

| | 169 | | 111 | | 85 | | 9 | | 163 | | 5 | | 6 | | 34 | | 41 |

	High °F	Low °F	Hum %	Wind mph	Precip inches	Snow inches
JAN	39	7	50	8.1	0.6	8.2
FEB	44	14	42	8.9	0.5	7.5
MAR	52	21	32	10.1	0.8	6.8
APR	61	28	25	11.0	0.8	5.0
MAY	71	37	23	10.6	0.9	1.0
JUN	81	45	22	10.0	1.1	0
JUL	85	51	30	9.1	1.6	0
AUG	82	49	34	8.3	2.0	0
SEP	75	42	35	8.6	1.5	0
OCT	65	31	35	8.3	1.1	2.0
NOV	51	20	38	7.9	0.8	7.0
DEC	41	10	46	7.7	0.8	8.2

Thomasville, GA   Rank: 59

Location: 30.50 N and 83.58 W at 250 feet, in the extreme southern part of the state. Tallahassee, Florida, is 35 miles southwest.

Landscape: Irregular plains. At the western edge of the coastal plain in low, gently sloping pinelands near the Ochlockonee River. Stands of temperate rainforest of evergreen and laurel occur. The city is noted for a profusion of moss-covered live oaks, and roses, azaleas, camellias, and other ornamental shrubs.

Climate: Subtropical, with no freezing winters. Summers are hot and humid. The annual temperature range is small to moderate. Rainfall is abundant and well distributed throughout the year. The first frost comes November 11 and the last frost goes March 12.

Summer mildness: 13   **Seasonal affect:** 60
Winter mildness: 93   **Hazard free:** 71

| | 102 | | 130 | | 133 | | 94 | | 34 | | 0 | | 50 | | 71 | | 83 |

	High °F	Low °F	Hum %	Wind mph	Precip inches	Snow inches
JAN	63	39	58	6.8	4.5	0.1
FEB	67	41	54	7.4	5.0	0.3
MAR	74	48	52	7.5	5.1	0
APR	81	54	47	6.9	3.6	0
MAY	87	61	50	6.3	4.2	0
JUN	91	68	55	5.8	5.4	0
JUL	92	71	61	5.2	6.2	0
AUG	92	70	62	5.0	5.1	0
SEP	89	66	59	5.9	3.6	0
OCT	82	55	52	6.3	2.2	0
NOV	74	47	55	6.1	3.1	0
DEC	66	41	52	6.4	4.3	0

Toms River–Barnegat Bay, NJ   Rank: 157

Location: 39.57 N and 74.12 W at 40 feet, in the center of New Jersey's Atlantic Coast. New York City is 95 miles north; Atlantic City 50 miles south.

Landscape: Smooth plains composed of tidal marshes and beach sand. The dunes provide vantages for observing bird migrations along the Atlantic flyway. Inland is a forest of mixed evergreens.

Climate: Hot continental, with the moderating influence of the Atlantic apparent throughout the year. Summers are relatively cooler and winters warmer than those of other places at the same latitude. During the warm season, sea breezes in the late morning and afternoon prevent excessive heat and may lower the temperature 15 degrees within half an hour. Fall is long, lasting until mid-November. On the other hand, warming is delayed in spring. Precipitation is moderate and well distributed throughout the year. First frost may come as early as October 30; last frost leaves by mid-April.

Summer mildness: 68   **Seasonal affect:** 24
Winter mildness: 22   **Hazard free:** 39

| | 95 | | 110 | | 160 | | 12 | | 98 | | 0 | | 44 | | 73 | | 27 |

	High °F	Low °F	Hum %	Wind mph	Precip inches	Snow inches
JAN	39	22	58	11.0	3.6	5.3
FEB	41	24	56	11.4	3.4	5.5
MAR	49	32	54	11.9	4.1	2.6
APR	58	40	52	11.8	4.1	0
MAY	68	50	56	10.2	4.3	0
JUN	77	59	56	9.2	3.5	0
JUL	82	65	57	8.5	4.4	0
AUG	81	64	58	8.1	4.4	0
SEP	75	58	60	8.4	3.6	0
OCT	65	47	60	9.0	3.5	0
NOV	55	38	64	10.5	4.2	0
DEC	44	28	67	10.6	4.0	2.3

★ = in the top 30 places for climate mildness

Climate

Traverse City, MI — Rank: 188

Location: 44.45 N and 85.37 W at 599 feet, on Grand Traverse Bay. Detroit is 245 miles southeast.

Landscape: Plains with hills. The tip of the 20-mile Old Mission Peninsula, jutting into the bay from the city, is exactly midway between the Equator and the North Pole. The terrain is generally level or gently undulating, with sandy and gravelly soils. The region abounds with lakes. The forest is second-growth pine and hemlock. Maple, oak, and birch are occasional deciduous trees.

Climate: Though rigorous because of its interior and northerly location, the climate is modified by the Great Lakes on either side of the Michigan peninsula. Consequently, summer temperatures average at least 5 degrees cooler than in locations in the southern part of the state. However, winters are severe, with cold spells that may last for a week and snowfall that averages almost 75 inches. First frost comes by October 17; last frost by May 10.

Summer mildness: 72   **Seasonal affect:** 25
Winter mildness: 5   **Hazard free:** 3

	67
	89
	210
90°	5
32°	143
0°	5
	23
	71
	23

	High °F	Low °F	Hum %	Wind mph	Precip inches	Snow inches
JAN	30	17	77	12.6	2.2	23.1
FEB	33	17	72	11.6	1.5	15.4
MAR	42	24	66	11.9	2.0	10.4
APR	56	35	60	11.8	2.7	2.0
MAY	68	44	58	10.1	2.5	0
JUN	76	53	61	9.5	3.3	0
JUL	81	59	63	8.7	2.7	0
AUG	79	58	64	8.5	3.6	0
SEP	72	52	66	9.4	4.0	0
OCT	61	43	68	10.8	3.2	0
NOV	47	33	72	11.9	2.9	12.0
DEC	34	22	78	12.1	2.5	25.5

Tryon, NC — Rank: 95

Location: 35.12 N and 82.14 W at 1,085 feet, just above the South Carolina border. Asheville is 30 miles north.

Landscape: Low mountains. Central mountain region of North Carolina, with the Blue Ridge to the north. Nearby are waterfalls, and valleys of rolling farmland, together with lakes and ski areas. The surrounding Appalachian oak forest also includes tulip trees, sweet chestnut, birch, hickory, walnut, and maple. In spring, a low layer of herbaceous plants quickly develops but is reduced after the trees reach full foliage.

Climate: Hot continental, with a strong annual cycle of cool winters and warm summers. The surrounding mountains and valleys produce a variety of microclimates, and the presence of thermal winds provides a pleasingly mild climate in lower elevations. Precipitation, usually rain, is adequate in all months. Spring comes earlier in this "thermal belt" than just a few miles north or south. First frost won't arrive until late October; last frost leaves in early April.

Summer mildness: 44   **Seasonal affect:** 31
Winter mildness: 75   **Hazard free:** 52

	122
	100
	143
90°	41
32°	70
0°	0
	34
	83
	43

	High °F	Low °F	Hum %	Wind mph	Precip inches	Snow inches
JAN	52	30	55	7.4	5.2	2.7
FEB	56	32	53	8.0	5.4	2.8
MAR	66	39	52	8.1	6.5	1.7
APR	74	46	48	7.9	4.7	0
MAY	81	55	54	6.9	5.9	0
JUN	86	62	54	6.4	5.7	0
JUL	88	66	60	5.9	5.3	0
AUG	87	65	62	5.7	5.9	0
SEP	82	59	62	6.1	5.4	0
OCT	73	48	55	6.5	5.4	0
NOV	64	40	54	6.8	4.8	0
DEC	55	33	55	7.3	5.1	1.0

Tucson, AZ — Rank: 37

Location: 32.13 N and 110.55 W at 2,437 feet, on the Santa Cruz River, 120 miles southeast of Phoenix and 60 miles above the Mexican border.

Landscape: At the foot of the Catalina Mountains in a broad, flat to gently rolling valley floor rimmed by mountains. Northeast, the Coronado National Forest is typical of pine, spruce, and fir forests of the higher elevations.

Climate: Desert, with a sunny, dry climate and a unique desert-mountain location. There's a long, hot season beginning in April and ending in October. High temperatures are modified by low humidity. Tucson lies in the zone receiving more sunshine than any other in the United States. Clear skies or very thin, high clouds permit intense surface heating during the day and active radiation cooling at night. Summer is the rainy season with robust, active thunderstorms. The first frost arrives November 2 and the last frost departs April 15.

Summer mildness: 30   **Seasonal affect:** 92
Winter mildness: 63   **Hazard free:** 68

	195
	90
	80
90°	93
32°	112
0°	0
	2
	33
	42

	High °F	Low °F	Hum %	Wind mph	Precip inches	Snow inches
JAN	64	39	40	7.9	0.9	0.3
FEB	68	41	35	8.1	0.7	0.2
MAR	73	45	29	8.5	0.7	0.3
APR	81	50	21	8.9	0.3	0
MAY	90	58	17	8.7	0.2	0
JUN	100	68	17	8.6	0.2	0
JUL	99	74	33	8.4	2.4	0
AUG	97	72	38	7.8	2.2	0
SEP	93	68	32	8.3	1.7	0
OCT	84	57	30	8.1	1.1	0
NOV	73	46	32	8.1	0.7	0
DEC	64	40	39	7.8	1.1	0.3

★ = in the top 30 places for climate mildness

Vero Beach, FL — Rank: 50

Location: 27.38 N and 80.24 W at 17 feet, near the center of Florida's Atlantic Coast. Palm Beach is 50 miles south.

Landscape: Flat plains, with miles of dunes and barrier beach on the coastal plain northeast of Lake Okeechobee. Native vegetation includes sea-oat grass, seagrape, and cabbage palm. Live oaks shade many of the residential streets while oleander, hibiscus, and bougainvillea lend a tropical atmosphere.

Climate: Subtropical, on the northern border of Florida's warmest thermal belt. Nearness to the Atlantic results in a climate tempered by land and sea breezes. Apparent temperatures in summer may top 90°F during the late morning or early afternoon but are cut short by midday sea breezes and afternoon convective thundershowers. Winters can have cold airflows from the north but usually are mild because of the area's ocean setting and southerly latitude.

Summer mildness: 17 **Seasonal affect:** 63
Winter mildness: 91 **Hazard free:** 72

Weather icons: 99, 134, 133, 90° 58, 32° 1, 0° 0, 15, 77, 70

	High °F	Low °F	Hum %	Wind mph	Precip inches	Snow inches
JAN	73	50	59	8.7	2.2	0
FEB	74	51	56	9.2	2.9	0
MAR	78	56	56	9.9	3.1	0
APR	82	60	52	9.2	2.0	0
MAY	86	65	57	9.1	4.6	0
JUN	88	70	64	7.9	6.7	0
JUL	90	72	65	7.1	6.4	0
AUG	90	72	64	6.5	6.5	0
SEP	89	72	64	7.6	7.4	0
OCT	84	66	61	8.9	5.8	0
NOV	79	59	62	8.9	3.3	0
DEC	74	53	59	8.1	2.1	0.2

★ Victorville–Apple Valley, CA — Rank: 9

Location: 34.32 N and 117.17 W at 2,715 feet, in the high desert of the Victor Valley, 78 miles northeast of Los Angeles.

Landscape: Plains with low mountains. On the southwestern edge of the Mohave Desert and north of the San Bernardino Mountains and National Forest. This is dramatic country where mountain peaks thousands of feet high look down on valleys lying below sea level.

Climate: Desert. Nights are invariably much cooler than the days. Springs and summers in the Victor Valley are warm to hot, often topping 100°F. Humidity remains low during those months. In contrast, fall and winter temperatures occasionally drop to freezing or below. The first frost is late on November 5; last frost, a little early on April 13. Most of the annual precipitation falls in the winter as rain on the lower slopes and in great amounts of snow in the higher mountains and just a trace on the valley floor.

Summer mildness: 48 **Seasonal affect:** 98
Winter mildness: 69 **Hazard free:** 89

Weather icons: 242, 75, 48, 90° 104, 32° 79, 0° 0, 2, 12, 7

	High °F	Low °F	Hum %	Wind mph	Precip inches	Snow inches
JAN	58	30	40	7.3	0.8	0.8
FEB	63	34	35	7.4	0.9	0.1
MAR	66	37	30	7.9	0.9	0.1
APR	73	41	25	8.3	0.4	0
MAY	81	48	23	8.3	0.2	0
JUN	91	55	22	8.5	0.1	0
JUL	97	61	32	9.5	0.2	0
AUG	96	61	35	8.9	0.3	0
SEP	90	55	35	7.3	0.4	0
OCT	80	45	32	6.6	0.3	0
NOV	67	36	34	6.9	0.6	0
DEC	59	30	41	7.2	0.7	0.2

Waynesville, NC — Rank: 121

Location: 35.00 N and 83.00 W at 2,660 feet in a valley amid 6,000-foot mountains—including the famed Cold Mountain—in the southern Appalachians. Asheville is 30 miles northeast.

Landscape: Low mountains. The surrounding forest is hardwood, composed of birch, beech, maple, elm, red oak, and basswood, with an admixture of hemlock and white pine.

Climate: Temperate, with distinct summer and winter, and all areas are subject to frost. Average annual temperatures range from below 50°F in the north to about 64°F at the south end of the highlands. The average length of the frost-free period is about 100 days in the northern mountains, and about 220 days in the low southern parts of the Appalachian Highlands.

Summer mildness: 68 **Seasonal affect:** 19
Winter mildness: 58 **Hazard free:** 37

Weather icons: 100, 113, 152, 90° 7, 32° 92, 0° 0, 78, 78, 42

	High °F	Low °F	Hum %	Wind mph	Precip inches	Snow inches
JAN	47	23	59	9.2	2.6	3.8
FEB	51	26	56	9.3	3.5	4.4
MAR	60	33	53	9.4	3.9	3.2
APR	68	40	50	8.8	3.2	0.1
MAY	75	47	57	7.3	3.6	0
JUN	80	55	59	6.3	3.3	0
JUL	83	59	63	6.1	2.9	0
AUG	82	58	63	5.4	3.8	0
SEP	76	52	64	5.7	3.2	0
OCT	68	40	57	6.7	2.5	0
NOV	59	33	57	8.2	2.9	0.7
DEC	51	27	59	8.9	2.5	2.1

★ = in the top 30 places for climate mildness

Wenatchee, WA   Rank: 129

Location: 47.25 N and 120.18 W at 645 feet, in central Washington, roughly 150 miles midway between Seattle to the west and Spokane to the east.

Landscape: High mountains. Here is the juncture of the Wenatchee and Columbia rivers. The rounded, shrubbed Wenatchee Mountains are off to the southwest, and the Columbia Plain stretches east in juniper grasslands. The uplands are moderately dissected, hilly, and steep. The tablelands are fertile and covered with loess.

Climate: Steppe grassland, generally shielded from the wet Pacific-driven weather by the Cascade Range. Summers are warm and nearly rainless. Winters are cool, foggy, and rainy. Snow is plentiful in the higher mountains. The first frost arrives October 20; last frost leaves April 17.

Summer mildness: 71   **Seasonal affect:** 41
Winter mildness: 28   **Hazard free:** 35

86
87
192
90° 33
32° 118
0° 1
48
26
11

	High °F	Low °F	Hum %	Wind mph	Precip inches	Snow inches
JAN	35	22	80	8.8	1.3	11.7
FEB	43	27	77	9.3	0.9	4.1
MAR	55	33	67	9.7	0.6	1.8
APR	64	40	53	10.0	0.6	0
MAY	73	48	49	9.2	0.5	0
JUN	81	55	45	9.2	0.6	0
JUL	88	60	37	8.6	0.2	0
AUG	87	59	38	8.2	0.5	0
SEP	78	50	40	8.3	0.4	0
OCT	64	40	56	8.2	0.5	0
NOV	47	32	79	8.7	1.3	3.0
DEC	36	25	84	8.6	1.5	10.1

Western St. Tammany Parish, LA   Rank: 103

Location: 30.28 N and 90.06 W at 30 feet, on the north shore of Lake Pontchartrain. A 24-mile causeway across the lake connects the parish with New Orleans.

Landscape: Flat plains. On a low-level area of alluvial plain in the Lower Mississippi Valley. Swamp and marshlands support cypress, small palms, tree ferns, shrubs, and herbaceous plants. Evergreen-oak and magnolia forests are the natural climax vegetation.

Climate: Subtropical and best described as humid. Lake Pontchartrain and the nearby Gulf of Mexico modify the temperature and decrease its range. Heavy and frequent rains are typical, with daily afternoon thunderstorms from mid-June to September. From December to March, precipitation is likely to be steady rain of 2 or 3 days' duration. During winter and spring, cold rain forms fogs. The first frost comes in November 11 and the last frost goes March 14. Hurricanes are a threat from July to October.

Summer mildness: 5   **Seasonal affect:** 46
Winter mildness: 80   **Hazard free:** 66

103
119
144
90° 91
32° 32
0° 0
28
76
69

	High °F	Low °F	Hum %	Wind mph	Precip inches	Snow inches
JAN	61	39	66	9.4	5.0	0.2
FEB	65	41	63	9.9	6.1	0.2
MAR	72	48	60	9.9	5.9	0
APR	79	55	59	9.4	4.7	0
MAY	85	62	60	8.1	5.0	0
JUN	90	68	63	6.9	4.9	0
JUL	92	70	66	6.1	6.5	0
AUG	91	70	66	6.0	5.8	0
SEP	88	66	65	7.3	5.1	0
OCT	80	55	59	7.5	3.2	0
NOV	71	48	62	8.7	4.5	0
DEC	64	42	66	9.1	6.0	0.1

Whidbey Island, WA   Rank: 71

Location: The weather station is Coupeville, 48.08 N and 122.35 W at 50 feet, on the Saratoga Passage in Puget Sound, 40 miles above Seattle.

Landscape: Tablelands with moderate relief. At 40 miles long, Whidbey is one of the largest offshore islands in the continental United States. The coast has rocky banks indented by coves and inlets. Inland there are gently rolling hills with patches of Garry Oak, fir, red cedar, and spruce. Penn Cove and Crockett's Lake are important feeding grounds for shorebirds and waterfowl.

Climate: Marine, characterized by moderate temperatures, a pronounced though not sharply defined rainy season, and considerable cloudiness, particularly during winter. Occasionally, severe winter storms come in from the north. Summers are warm and pleasant and winters mild and rainy. The first frost glazes foliage on October 28, and deepens until the last frost departs April 15.

Summer mildness: 89   **Seasonal affect:** 23
Winter mildness: 47   **Hazard free:** 67

57
81
228
90° 0
32° 52
0° 0
43
62
7

	High °F	Low °F	Hum %	Wind mph	Precip inches	Snow inches
JAN	45	34	77	9.8	2.5	2.9
FEB	49	35	74	9.6	1.8	1.1
MAR	53	37	70	9.8	1.8	1.1
APR	57	40	67	9.6	1.8	0
MAY	63	44	64	8.9	1.7	0
JUN	68	48	62	8.7	1.3	0
JUL	72	50	62	8.3	0.8	0
AUG	73	50	63	7.9	1.0	0
SEP	68	46	68	8.1	1.4	0
OCT	59	42	75	8.5	1.7	0
NOV	50	38	78	9.3	2.6	0
DEC	45	35	80	9.6	2.9	1.5

★ = in the top 30 places for climate mildness

★ Wickenburg, AZ   Rank: 11

Location: 33.58 N and 112.43 W at 2,903 feet, in west-central Arizona. Phoenix is 30 miles southeast.

Landscape: In the Harcuvar Mountains on the Hassayampa River at the northern edge of the Sonoran Desert. A typical desert river, the Hassayampa moves underground for much of the 100-mile length. Where it appears, there is an oasis with cottonwood and willows and supporting a diverse riparian culture. Native vegetation includes mixed grasses, chaparral brush, and oak-juniper woodlands. These uplands of high desert also include the Joshua tree, saguaro, cholla, and ironwood.

Climate: Semiarid mountain steppe, with strong daily and seasonal temperature changes. The usual winter flow of air is from the Pacific, though cold air from Canada sometimes drives temperatures below freezing in the high plateau and mountainous regions. Mid-November ushers in the first frost, late March sees the last frost exit. Summer is dry with daytime temperatures topping 100°F.

Summer mildness: 27   **Seasonal affect:** 97
Winter mildness: 86   **Hazard free:** 92

	212
	84
	69
90°	152
32°	63
0°	0
	2
	20
	24

	High °F	Low °F	Hum %	Wind mph	Precip inches	Snow inches
JAN	65	32	44	5.3	1.2	0
FEB	69	35	37	5.9	1.1	0
MAR	74	39	32	6.7	1.6	0
APR	82	43	22	7.0	0.5	0
MAY	91	51	27	7.1	0.2	0
JUN	101	59	15	6.8	0.1	0
JUL	105	69	27	7.2	1.4	0
AUG	102	68	32	6.7	1.9	0
SEP	96	60	30	6.3	1.4	0
OCT	87	48	30	5.8	0.7	0
NOV	74	38	35	5.4	1.0	0
DEC	66	32	44	5.1	1.3	0.2

Williamsburg, VA   Rank: 148

Location: 37.16 N and 76.42 W at 86 feet, on a tidewater peninsula between the James and York rivers 40 miles midway between Richmond and Norfolk.

Landscape: Irregular plains. Elevated slightly on a ridge, the country is low and level to gently rolling field. Salt flats along brackish rivers are predominantly marsh grass. The southeastern mixed forest has medium-tall to tall oak, hickory, sweet gum, red maple, and winged elm. At least half the stands are filled with loblolly and shortleaf pine. Gums and cypress dominate the coastal marshes and interior swamps. Live oak and wax myrtle grow only in Tidewater.

Climate: Hot continental. Winter is mild, while spring and fall are ideal. First frost arrives by October 28; last frost leaves by April 14. Summers are warm, humid, and long. Precipitation is evenly distributed as rain, though there's occasional snow. The area lies north of the hurricane and tropical storm track and south of high-latitude storm systems.

Summer mildness: 41   **Seasonal affect:** 39
Winter mildness: 31   **Hazard free:** 46

	106
	107
	152
90°	37
32°	85
0°	0
	20
	75
	37

	High °F	Low °F	Hum %	Wind mph	Precip inches	Snow inches
JAN	48	27	60	11.5	3.8	4.2
FEB	51	29	58	12.0	3.5	2.5
MAR	61	36	56	12.5	4.2	1.8
APR	70	44	52	11.8	3.0	0
MAY	78	54	58	10.5	4.5	0
JUN	85	62	58	9.8	4.0	0
JUL	88	67	61	9.0	5.0	0
AUG	87	66	62	8.9	4.7	0
SEP	81	60	62	9.6	4.3	0
OCT	71	48	61	10.4	3.2	0
NOV	63	39	58	10.7	3.5	0
DEC	52	31	60	11.2	3.4	1.2

Wimberley, TX   Rank: 105

Location: 29.59 N and 98.03 W at 840 feet, in the central Texas hill country, 35 miles midway between Austin and San Antonio.

Landscape: Open high hills. The San Marcos River rises from springs here. Caves and lakes dot the nearby green meadows and low-rise hill country. Along the watercourses are cypress and juniper-oak stands.

Climate: Prairie. Though summers are hot, night temperatures usually drop into the 70s. Winters are mild. November 17 sees the first frost arrive; March 17 bids the last frost farewell. Prevailing winds are southerly, though strong northers may bring cold spells that rarely last more than a few days. Precipitation is well distributed but heaviest in late spring, with a secondary rainfall peak in September. Summer brings some heavy thunderstorms. Winter rains are slow and steady.

Summer mildness: 3   **Seasonal affect:** 66
Winter mildness: 61   **Hazard free:** 66

	116
	114
	135
90°	107
32°	21
0°	0
	115
	47
	41

	High °F	Low °F	Hum %	Wind mph	Precip inches	Snow inches
JAN	59	32	69	9.6	1.7	0.5
FEB	63	35	67	10.1	2.2	0.3
MAR	72	42	64	10.8	1.9	0
APR	79	49	67	10.4	2.6	0
MAY	85	58	72	9.5	4.8	0
JUN	91	66	70	9.1	3.7	0
JUL	95	70	65	8.3	2.0	0
AUG	96	69	64	7.9	2.1	0
SEP	91	63	68	7.9	3.3	0
OCT	82	50	67	8.1	3.4	0
NOV	72	42	68	9.0	2.4	0.1
DEC	62	35	68	9.1	1.9	0

★ = in the top 30 places for climate mildness

Woodstock, VT — Rank: 184

Location: 43.37 N and 72.31 W at 705 feet, just west of the Connecticut River and New Hampshire line and 60 miles south of Montpelier.

Landscape: Low mountains. In the upper Connecticut River Valley with the Green Mountains rising to the west. Rivers cut through steep gorges, giving high relief to the winding valleys. The forests are transitional stands of mixed conifer and deciduous trees. Northern white pine, eastern hemlock, maple, oak, and beech are common.

Climate: Northerly latitude assures the variety and vigor of a true New England climate. The summer, while not long, is clear and warm. Fall is cool, extending through October. Winters are cold, with brief, intense cold snaps formed by high-pressure systems moving down from central Canada and Hudson Bay. Snows are deep and long lasting. First frost comes in late September; last frost delays leaving until mid-May. Spring is called breakup or mud season.

Summer mildness: 82 **Seasonal affect:** 13
Winter mildness: 14 **Hazard free:** 7

Icon values: 91, 110, 164, 90° 7, 32° 167, 0° 23, 50, 75, 20

	High °F	Low °F	Hum %	Wind mph	Precip inches	Snow inches
JAN	28	7	58	9.0	2.5	20.9
FEB	33	10	57	9.4	2.4	20.6
MAR	43	21	53	9.9	2.7	16.9
APR	56	32	49	10.0	2.9	5.0
MAY	70	43	49	8.9	3.6	0
JUN	78	52	55	8.1	3.3	0
JUL	83	57	55	7.5	3.3	0
AUG	80	56	57	7.2	3.6	0
SEP	71	48	59	7.3	3.3	0
OCT	59	37	59	7.8	3.3	0
NOV	45	28	60	8.5	3.5	5.0
DEC	32	15	62	8.7	3.1	20.9

York Beaches, ME — Rank: 187

Location: 43.23 N and 70.32 W at 51 feet, on Maine's southern Atlantic Coast. Portland is 35 miles north, Boston, Massachusetts, is 60 miles south.

Landscape: Plains with high hills. Low hills drained by marsh and stream rise at the mouth of the York River on the Atlantic Ocean. Coastal watersheds include upstream areas, wetlands, estuaries, beaches, near-shore waters, and offshore habitats. Natural harbors, inlets, and sandy beaches mark the shore. Native vegetation is mixed evergreen of pine and spruce, with some maple and oak. The low-lying areas support typical marsh grasses and cattails.

Climate: Hot continental. Moderated somewhat by the ocean, winters can be cold, damp, and snowy. The first frost arrives October 15 and the last frost departs April 22. Spring arrives late. Summer days are clear and warm, the nights pleasantly cool. Fall is bright, mild, and long lasting.

Summer mildness: 76 **Seasonal affect:** 11
Winter mildness: 13 **Hazard free:** 15

Icon values: 102, 99, 164, 90° 6, 32° 157, 0° 14, 49, 76, 19

	High °F	Low °F	Hum %	Wind mph	Precip inches	Snow inches
JAN	30	11	62	9.2	3.5	19.3
FEB	33	14	59	9.4	3.3	17.2
MAR	41	25	59	10.0	3.7	12.3
APR	52	34	57	10.0	4.1	2.0
MAY	63	43	57	9.2	3.6	0
JUN	73	52	60	8.2	3.4	0
JUL	79	58	60	7.6	3.1	0
AUG	77	57	60	7.5	2.9	0
SEP	69	49	60	7.8	3.1	0
OCT	59	38	60	8.4	3.9	0
NOV	47	30	62	8.8	5.2	3.0
DEC	35	18	62	9.0	4.6	14.9

★ Yuma, AZ — Rank: 7

Location: 32.43 N and 114.37 W at 137 feet, in the extreme southwestern corner of Arizona, 21 miles north of the Mexican border. The city is 150 miles midway between Phoenix to the east and San Diego to the west.

Landscape: Plains with low mountains. The land is typical desert steppe, with dry, sandy, and dusty soil. There's scant vegetation. Craggy buttes and mountains take their characteristic texture from wind erosion. The surrounding Trigo, Chocolate, Castle Dome, Mohawk, and Gila ranges are the dominant geologic feature.

Climate: Desert, with many places in the world receiving more rain in a year than has fallen here in the past century. There is a first frost by December 9 and a last frost by February 7. Home heating is necessary during the nights from late October to mid-April. Of all of America's First Order weather stations, the one here records the most sunny days.

Summer mildness: 20 **Seasonal affect:** 100
Winter mildness: 93 **Hazard free:** 97

Icon values: 242, 75, 48, 90° 178, 32° 14, 0° 0, 2, 11, 7

	High °F	Low °F	Hum %	Wind mph	Precip inches	Snow inches
JAN	69	44	40	7.3	0.4	0
FEB	74	47	35	7.4	0.2	0
MAR	79	51	30	7.9	0.2	0
APR	86	57	25	8.3	0.1	0
MAY	94	64	23	8.3	0.0	0
JUN	103	72	22	8.5	0.0	0
JUL	107	81	32	9.5	0.3	0
AUG	105	80	35	8.9	0.6	0
SEP	101	73	35	7.3	0.3	0
OCT	90	62	32	6.6	0.3	0
NOV	77	51	34	6.9	0.2	0
DEC	69	44	41	7.2	0.5	0

★ = in the top 30 places for climate mildness

ET CETERA: CLIMATE

CLIMATE & HEALTH

A bogus fact sometimes getting into print has it that men get an extra 12 months of life and women an extra 18 simply by moving to Florida.

There is no proven link between longevity and climate. True, the three places with the highest portion of centenarians—the Caucasus Mountains, the mountains of Bolivia, and northwestern India—are in southern latitudes at high elevations. But in America, the longest average life spans are recorded in three states with northern latitudes, flat terrain, and severe winters—Minnesota, North Dakota, and Iowa.

People with specific chronic diseases are much more comfortable in some climates than in others. Asthmatics do best in warm, dry places that have a minimum of airborne allergens and no molds. People with rheumatism or arthritis find comfort in warm, moist southerly climates where the weather is constant and the atmospheric pressure swings least. Those suffering from tuberculosis or emphysema seem to do best in the lower elevations of mountains with lots of clear air and sunshine.

A small classic in bioclimatology is H.E. Landsberg's *Weather and Health,* which details the relationships between climate and the aggravation of physical afflictions. Drawing on this and other sources, *Retirement Places Rated* describes some basic weather phenomena and suggests how they can affect the way you feel.

Weather Stages: Beware of 3 & 4

The weather changes that cause the body to react have been studied by meteorologists and classified into six basic stages that make up the clear-stormy-clear cycle repeated all over the planet. The stages in the cycle are linked to some of the joys and tragedies of existence.

- **Stage 1.** Cool, high-pressure air, with few clouds and moderate winds, followed by . . .

- **Stage 2.** Perfectly clear, dry air, high pressure, and little wind, leading to . . .

- **Stage 3.** Considerable warming, steady or slightly falling pressure, and some high clouds, until . . .

- **Stage 4.** The warm, moist air gets into the lower layers; pressure falls, clouds thicken, precipitation is common, and the wind picks up speed; then . . .

- **Stage 5.** An abrupt change takes place; showery precipitation is accompanied by cold, gusty winds, rapidly rising pressure, and falling humidity as the moisture in the air is released.

- **Stage 6.** Gradually, the pressure rises still further and the clouds diminish; temperatures reach low levels and the humidity continues to drop, leading back to . . .

- **Stage 1.** Cool, high-pressure air . . .

Of course, these phases aren't equally long, either in any given sequence or in the course of a year. During winter, all six stages may follow one another within 3 days, whereas in the summer 2 weeks may pass before the cycle is completed.

The beautiful-weather stages 1 and 2 stimulate the body very little. They make no demands that can't be met by adequate clothing and shelter. In contrast, weather stages 4 and 5 are often violent. They stir us up mentally and physically.

There is no question weather stages affect the body. Hospital birth and death records prove it. In pregnancy, in far more cases than statistical accident permits, labor begins on days that are in weather stage 3. Heart attacks peak in weather stages 3 and 4 and drop in stages 1 and 6. Bleeding ulcers and migraines peak in stage 4.

Weather influences mood and conduct. There is a strong link between weather stage 3 and suicide, behavior problems in schoolchildren, and street riots. A study in Poland showed that accident rates in factory workers doubled during cyclonic weather conditions (stages 3 and 4: periods of falling pressure and rising temperatures and humidity signaling the onset of stormy weather) and returned to normal low levels in fair weather. Animals are affected, too. Dogcatchers are busiest during stages 3, 4, and 5 because dogs become restless, stray from their homes, and wander through the streets.

More about Comfort

As the six weather stages suggest, everyday comfort is influenced by three basic climatic factors: humidity, temperature, and barometric pressure.

Humidity. The amount of moisture in the air is closely related to air temperature in determining the comfort level of the atmosphere. Much of the discomfort and nervous tension experienced at the approach of stormy weather (weather stage 4) is the product of rising temperatures and humidity.

High levels of atmospheric moisture, such as those felt most of the time in the Pacific Northwest and along the Gulf Coast and South Atlantic Coast, aren't usually the cause of direct discomfort except in persons suffering from certain types of arthritis or rheumatism. But even in these cases, the mild temperatures found in these locations do much to offset discomfort. In fact, the stability of the barometric pressure in these areas makes them ideal for people with muscle and joint pain.

But damp air combined with low temperatures can be uncomfortable. Most people who live through damp winters, especially in places with high winds, complain that the cold, wet wind goes right through them. Moreover, the harmful effect of cold, damp air on pulmonary diseases has long been known. With this in mind, it's smart to think carefully about moving to New England coastal locations—Cape Cod and the Maine coast, for example—where these conditions are winter trademarks.

Perhaps the most noticeable drawback to very moist air is the variety of organisms it supports. Bacteria and the spores of fungi and molds thrive in moist air but are almost absent in dry air. If the air is moist and also warm, the problem is multiplied. People susceptible to bacterial skin infections, fungal infections such as athlete's foot, or mold allergies should consider places with high humidities carefully.

On the other end of the spectrum, very dry air produces perceptible effects immediately and can cause discomfort within a day. When the relative humidity falls below 50 percent, most persons experience dry nasal passages and perhaps a dry, tickling throat. In the Desert Southwest, where the humidity can drop to 20 percent or less in some locations, many people experience nosebleeds, flaking skin, and constant sore throats.

Temperature. Some bioclimatologists maintain that the body is most comfortable and productive at "65-65," meaning an air temperature of 65°F with 65 percent humidity. High relative humidity intensifies the felt effect of high temperatures because it impairs the evaporative cooling effect of sweating.

APPARENT TEMPERATURES (JULY)

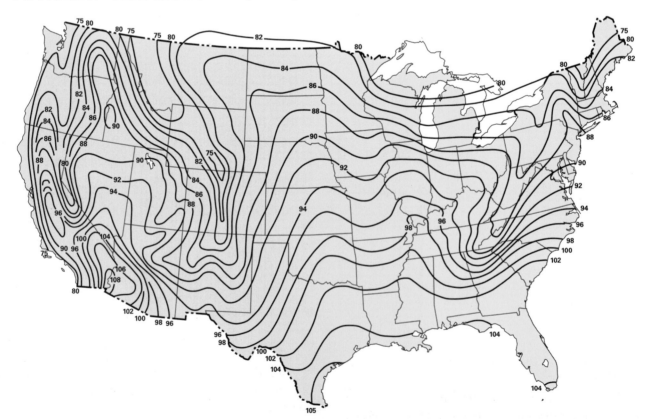

At apparent temperatures as low as 80°F to 90°F, a person may begin to suffer symptoms of heat stress. The degree of heat stress experienced will vary depending on age, health, and body characteristics. Infants, young children, and older adults are most likely to be affected by high temperature/humidity combinations.

The map "Apparent Temperatures (July)" shows how felt temperatures vary across the country. The places with the highest temperatures are in the southern half of the plateau between the Sierra Nevada to the west and the Rocky Mountains to the east, the Great Interior Valley of California, and parts of the high plains regions of New Mexico, Oklahoma, and Texas. These areas are generally dry, so the effects of the high temperatures on the body are not particularly noticeable or damaging. This is especially true of locations west of eastern New Mexico.

States along the Gulf Coast and the South Atlantic Coast have temperatures that are less spectacularly high but humidity that can be oppressive. Most people would find a 90°F day in Savannah, Georgia, Daytona Beach, Florida, or Rockport–Aransas Pass, Texas, far more uncomfortable than they would a day of the same temperature in Silver City, New Mexico, or Yuma, Arizona.

What about cold temperatures? Throughout the 1960s and 1970s, older adults shunned cold weather in favor of the hot and sunny beach climates of the Sun Belt. Now, many are discovering the benefits of seasonal change and some cold weather, particularly around the holiday season.

But cold weather can have an adverse effect on persons with heart or circulatory ailments. These diseases follow a seasonal pattern, with a peak of deaths occurring in January and February. The cooling of the extremities places greater stress on the heart as it tries to maintain a safe body temperature. Breathing very cold air can tax the heart-lung system, and some persons who have hardening of the coronary arteries may get chest pains when outdoors in a cold wind.

Cold weather can also increase blood pressure with adverse consequences for those with circulatory problems. Although polar weather inhibits the survival of respiratory germs, these microbes thrive in a damp, cloudy, cool climate and contribute to a high incidence of influenza, bronchitis, and colds.

As the body gets older, its circulatory system gets less effective. Add to this another natural consequence of aging—the decreased rate of metabolism that keeps the body warm—and you have explained older adults' needs for higher household temperatures. The expense of heating costs in a cool climate, therefore, may offset the appeal of seasonal changes and winter weather.

But despite the dangers of heat or cold extremes, sudden wide shifts of temperature in either direction constitute a threat to health. When the weather—and especially the temperature—changes suddenly and dramatically, the rates of cardiac arrest, respiratory distress, stroke, and other medical emergencies skyrocket.

Sudden atmospheric cooling can bring on attacks of asthma, bronchitis, and stroke. Heart attacks and associated symptoms are more frequent following these periods. Often in autumn, changing air masses produce these attacks, particularly by the passage of a cold frontal system following a dropping barometer.

A sudden rise in the temperature may precipitate its own assortment of medical emergencies, among them heat stroke, heart attack, and stroke. Because the body recuperates during the night, the nighttime maximum air temperature is far more significant than the daytime maximum during a heat wave. A hot night prevents the body from reestablishing its thermal equilibrium and tends to lessen the amount of sleep a person gets, increasing fatigue. Hospital employees call these sudden temperature shifts, which cause so much discomfort and harm, "ambulance weather."

Barometric pressure. Though most people may be unaware of the source of their discomfort, barometric pressure and its wide and rapid fluctuations are powerful influences on performance, comfort, and health. Pressure changes are felt more keenly by older adults, whose bodies are generally more sensitive to change.

Recalling weather stage 4, the rapid fall of pressure that signals the arrival of storms and advancing cold fronts can trigger episodes of asthma, heart disease, stroke, and pain in the joints. People with rheumatism or arthritis may suffer unduly if they live in places where pressure changes are continual and rapid. The map "Pressure Changes from Day to Day (February)" shows the regions with greatest and least pressure changes during an average day in February, when joint pain and other discomforts reach their peak.

As the map shows, the northern and eastern sections of the country experience the biggest swings, averaging a barometric change of .20 inch to .25 inch from one day to the next. In summer, when pressure changes are relatively small, the average change in

Retirement Places Rated

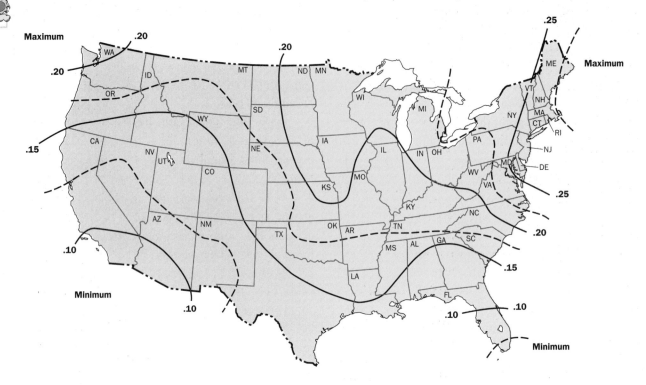

these regions is approximately .10 inch. States in the southern latitudes, particularly Florida and Southern California, show the least change, only about .10 inch in February and less than .05 inch in summer. Of course, these figures are averages, and along the Gulf and Atlantic coasts, large and rapid pressure changes are occasionally caused by hurricanes.

The map offers another reason why so many older adults choose Florida and the Gulf Coast. Additionally, due to the stabilizing and modifying effects that large bodies of water have on temperature and pressure, weather conditions by seacoasts are steadier than those of most inland, desert, or mountain locations.

Although the year-round climates found in Florida and the other Gulf states aren't as pleasant as they are hyped, subtropical climates—hot, humid, monotonous, and even wearying as they are to some— are just about perfect for people with severe rheumatoid joint pain or those who cannot tolerate sudden changes in the weather.

Questing for Relief

People with heart conditions should definitely avoid extreme heat and cold, rapid temperature variations, and wide and sudden pressure swings. This can rule out most interior regions as well as northerly ones, even those on coastal locations.

Recommended are places that have warm, mild, and steady weather. Mountains and high altitudes should be avoided on two counts: less oxygen and strain caused by steep grades. Best bets are southerly coastal locations where sea level, oxygen-rich air, and stable pressures and temperatures predominate most of the year.

Look along the coast of the Mid-Atlantic Metro Belt southward all the way around the Florida peninsula and westward along the Gulf. Also look along the southern third of the Pacific coastline.

Emphysema brings a completely different set of problems and solutions. In general, excessive dampness combined with cool or cold weather is harmful. This eliminates the Pacific Northwest, New England, and the North Woods. Southerly coastal locations are better, but the air is perhaps still too damp. Seek out warm, sunny, and dry climates such as those found in Arizona, New Mexico, Utah, Nevada, and the interior valleys of California. Remember to avoid high elevations.

Asthma is a complex disorder not completely understood. While it is believed to be an autoimmune disorder similar to allergies, it may be precipitated or worsened by different things in different individuals.

Your wisest course is to consult medical specialists first to determine the specific cause of your attacks. Asthmatics seem to do best in the pollen-free, dry, warm air found in the Desert Southwest. Because the air on the desert floor can be dusty, seeking a moderate altitude there may be beneficial.

Tuberculosis, recently considered a waning disease, is on the rise. It generally strikes people who have weakened resistance to infection, making older adults more susceptible than the rest of the population. Treatment is multifaceted, but an area that is mild, dry, sunny, and has clear air helps a great deal.

Mountain locations have always been popular and can provide relief if the altitude isn't excessive. Because dampness isn't recommended, the dry, sunny places in the southern Rockies are preferable to locations in the Southern Highlands. Ocean breezes are thought to be beneficial, too, and may be better for people who cannot tolerate the more rugged climate of the interior mountains. Hawaii or the Southern California coast are ideal.

For people with rheumatic pains and discomfort in amputated limbs or in old scar tissue, the warm and steady climates of the subtropics are perfect. Here the surrounding water keeps temperatures and pressures from shifting quickly, and the prevailing warmth is soothing. It would be hard to miss with any seafront location from Myrtle Beach, South Carolina, south to the Florida Keys, around and up the west coast of the Florida peninsula, westward along the Gulf and down all the way to the mouth of the Rio Grande.

Life at the Top

Mountain resorts usually got their start as 19th-century health retreats when "night air" and "bad air" were seen as causes for chronic respiratory diseases. The antidote prescribed was "pine air" and a high altitude.

While mountain air tends to be clear and relatively free from pollutants, it also contains less oxygen. A rapid change to a high altitude is risky for people with heart diseases and arteriosclerosis. If you suffer from asthma, emphysema, or anemia, you should consult local physicians before moving to any place more than 2,000 feet above sea level. Even if all indications point to a positive reaction, it would be wise to take up residence for at least several months before making a permanent move.

Since altitude puts a certain amount of stress on the body's circulatory system and lungs, becoming acclimated to high places leads to good health. A higher altitude accelerates respiration and increases the lung capacity, strengthens the heart, increases the metabolic rate, and boosts the number and proportion of red blood cells.

In the United States, the highest town with a post office is Climax, Colorado. At 11,350 feet, Climax is beyond the comfort range of many older adults. Up here, a 3-minute egg takes 7 minutes to boil, corn on the cob needs to be on the fire 45 minutes, and home-brewed beer matures in half the expected time. Yet many of the 4,000 residents love it. The incidence of infection is amazingly low, and insects are practically unknown. In the East, the highest town of any size is Highlands, North Carolina, in the Great Smoky Mountains. Though less than half as high as Climax, Highlands and the neighboring towns offer the cool, clear air and invigorating climate that have long drawn people to the mountains.

NATURAL HAZARDS

Risk management firms whose clients include the insurance industry now rate areas as small as a zip code for the damage from future hurricanes, tornadoes, and earthquakes. These natural hazards follow definite geographic patterns, and some places are at greater risk than others.

The Sun Belt Is Also a Storm Belt

Most severe storms occur in the southern half of the nation. For this reason, you might say the Sun Belt is also a storm belt.

Thunderstorms & Lightning. Thunderstorms are common and don't usually cause death. But lightning, the most common natural danger, kills 200 Americans a year. At any given moment there are about 2,000 thunderstorms in progress around the globe. In the time it takes you to read this paragraph, lightning will have struck 700 times.

Florida, the Sunshine State, is actually the country's stormiest state, with three times as much thunder and lightning as any other. California, Oregon, and Washington are the three most storm-free states. In a typical year, coastal California locations average between 2 and 5 thunderstorm episodes. Most American locations average between 35 and 50. Florida's Gulf Coast averages 90.

Tables in the "Place Profiles: Climate" section earlier in this chapter tell how many thunderstorm days on average each place can expect in a year. The southeastern quadrant of our country generally receives more rain and thunderstorms than the rest, although the thunderstorms of the Great Plains are awesome spectacles.

Tornadoes. While they aren't nearly as large or long-lived as hurricanes and release much less force, tornadoes have more killing power concentrated in a small area than any other storm. For absolute ferocity and wind speed, a tornado hasn't a rival.

The hallmark of this vicious inland storm is the huge funnel cloud that sweeps and bounces along the ground, destroying buildings, sweeping up cars, trains, livestock, and trees, and sucking them up hundreds of feet into the whirling vortex. Wind speeds close to 300 miles per hour have been recorded.

FLORIDA'S STORMY COAST

The minimum requirement for the recording of a thunderstorm is the presence of a single storm cell. On a bad day in summer, locations on Florida's west coast can record three or four in a single afternoon.

PLACE	STORMS PER YEAR
Bradenton, FL	93
Fort Myers–Cape Coral, FL	93
Naples, FL	93
Port Charlotte, FL	93
Largo, FL	86
Sarasota, FL	86
Thomasville, GA	83
Kissimmee–St. Cloud, FL	82
Lakeland–Winter Haven, FL	82
Leesburg–Mount Dora, FL	82
Ocala, FL	82
Sebring–Avon Park, FL	82
Gainesville, FL	81
Melbourne–Palm Bay, FL	77
Port St. Lucie, FL	75
200 Retirement Places Average	**36**

Source: NOAA, local climatological data. Some of the above figures come from the nearest "First Order" station.

Although no one can tell for certain just where particular tornadoes might touch down, their season, origin, and direction of travel are predictable using decades of records. Tornado season reaches its peak in late spring and early summer. After forming in the intense heat and rising air of the plains, these storms proceed toward the northeast at speeds averaging 25 to 40 miles per hour. Most tornadoes do not last long or travel far. Half of all tornadoes reported travel less than 5 miles on the ground; a rare few have been tracked for more than 200 miles.

Nearly one-third of all twisters ever reported in the United States touched down somewhere in Kansas, Oklahoma, and Texas. Indeed, Tornado Alley is an area 150 miles on either side of a line drawn from Abilene, Texas, to Omaha, Nebraska. Among retirement spots, the lake locations in Oklahoma and Missouri, any location in Texas or Arkansas, and even spots in Kentucky and Tennessee have a high potential for tornado damage and danger.

Hurricanes. Along Louisiana's and Mississippi's Gulf coasts, the plain is so low that a serious storm surge in front of a hurricane will flood escape routes 80 miles inland. In the months following Katrina's devastation, safety officials recommended at least a 3-day evacuation window even if forecasters couldn't accurately plot a hurricane's track and strength.

Giant tropical cyclonic storms that start at sea, hurricanes are unmatched for sheer power over a very large area. They last for days, measure hundreds of miles across, and release tremendous energy in the form of high winds, torrential rains, lightning, and tidal surges. They usually occur in late summer and fall, and strike the Gulf States and southern segments of the Atlantic Coast. Like thunderstorms, hurricanes are much less frequent and less severe on the Pacific Coast.

Hurricanes usually originate in the tropical waters of the Atlantic Ocean. They occur toward summer's end because it takes that long for the water temperature and evaporation rate to rise sufficiently to begin the cyclonic, counterclockwise rotation of a wind system around a low-pressure system. When the winds are less than 39 miles per hour, the cyclone becomes a tropical depression. When winds speed up to between 39 and 74 miles per hour, the depression becomes a tropical storm. When the winds top 74 miles per hour, the storm becomes a hurricane.

Often the greatest danger and destruction from hurricanes aren't winds but tidal surges that sweep ashore with seas 15 feet or more higher than normal high tides. Although Florida and the southern coasts are most vulnerable to hurricanes, low-lying locations as far north as Cape Cod and the Maine coast aren't invulnerable. The map "Tornado & Hurricane Risk Areas" shows the nation's danger areas for these natural hazards.

Earthquake Risks

California and the Pacific Northwest may be relatively free of the thunderstorms, tornadoes, and hurricanes that buffet other parts of the country. But these states are in the area most prone to earthquake damage. A glance at the map "Earthquake Hazard Zones," which predicts not only the probability of earthquakes but also their severity, confirms this.

TORNADO & HURRICANE RISK AREAS

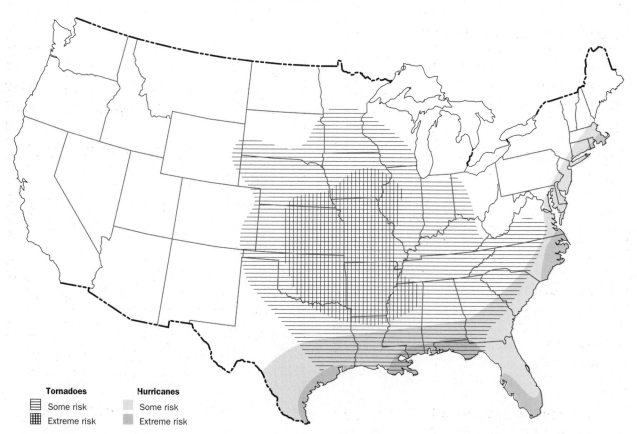

Tornadoes	Hurricanes
Some risk	Some risk
Extreme risk	Extreme risk

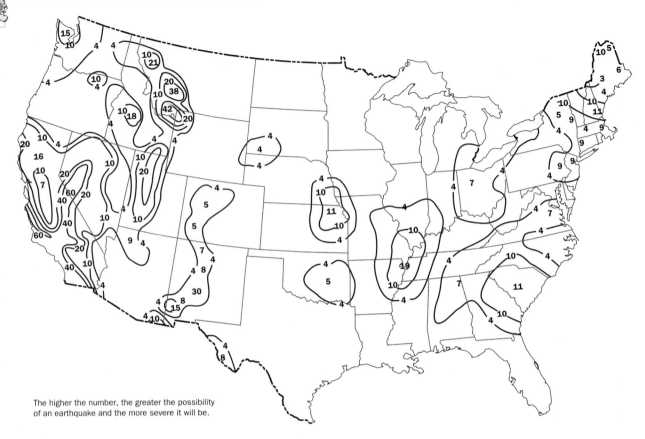

The higher the number, the greater the possibility
of an earthquake and the more severe it will be.

All retirement places in California, Nevada, and Utah have the potential for substantial earthquake damage. Locations in Oregon are relatively safe, but the Puget Sound area of Washington has experienced three major shocks in the past 35 years. Portions of Montana and Idaho also are vulnerable.

Other pockets of earthquake risk may surprise you. In New Mexico, Albuquerque is situated in a danger area, and so is Silver City. The resorts on the South Carolina and Georgia coasts sit in the middle of a quake-sensitive zone that was the site of the 1886 Charleston quake, the strongest ever measured east of the Mississippi. The entire New England region shares a danger roughly comparable to this area. Boston has suffered a severe quake and remains prone today. A series of quakes occurred in southeastern Missouri in 1811 and 1812, changing the course of the Mississippi River and creating a major lake. There is still some risk in this area, which includes retirement places in western Kentucky and Tennessee and part of the Ozarks.

Can Anyone Win?

After studying the maps, you may come to the dismal conclusion that you cannot win: Where one natural disaster area stops, another begins. Some areas, like the coasts of South Carolina and Georgia, appear to possess a triple-whammy combination of earthquake, tornado, and hurricane hazards.

Studying the map more closely, you might begin to detect retirement areas that seem safer than others. One such area is the Pacific Northwest, with the exception of the significant earthquake risk around Puget Sound. Parts of Arizona, Utah, and New Mexico, too, are relatively free from disaster risk. The southern Appalachians, despite a moderate earthquake risk, do not experience many storms due to the protection of the mountains. But some parts of that region are flood-prone. And moderate earthquake risk seems almost unavoidable anywhere but the frigid north-central plains or the steamy, tornado-ridden flatlands of Texas and the Gulf states.

So, as with most things in life, when it comes to avoiding natural disasters, you can only pay your money and take your chances.

HAY FEVER SUFFERERS, TAKE NOTE

It does not come from hay nor does it cause a fever, but that's little consolation to the 18 million Americans afflicted. Hay fever is an allergic reaction of the eyes, nose, or throat to certain airborne particles. These particles may be pollen from seed-bearing trees, grasses, and weeds, or spores from certain molds. The term originated in Britain when people assumed its fever-like symptoms had something to do with the fall haying.

Most persons might think that once they're into adulthood, they already know whether they have hay fever. But if you move, would you suddenly develop a baffling runny nose and minor sore throat? Allergy problems aren't always alleviated by relocation, and sometimes a new allergen, absent where you used to live, can turn up to cause you problems.

In the Arctic, because of low temperature, poor soil, and small and primitive vegetation, nobody suffers from it. In the tropics and subtropics, because the plants are generally flowered and produce pollen so heavy it cannot become airborne, few complain of it.

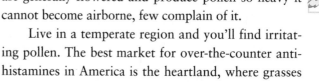

Live in a temperate region and you'll find irritating pollen. The best market for over-the-counter antihistamines in America is the heartland, where grasses and trees without flowers predominate. Farming disrupts the soil here, encouraging the growth of weeds (especially the most devilish of them all, ragweed). It extends from the Rockies to the Appalachian chain, and from the Canadian border down to the mid-South.

Alas, nowhere in this country except Alaska and the southern half of Florida will you entirely escape. It's simply a question of degree. Some places that were once havens for asthmatics and hay fever sufferers aren't any longer. Examples include many of the fast-growing areas of the Desert Southwest. In the 1950s, Tucson was virtually free of ragweed pollen. Its desert location prevented the growth of weeds, grasses, and trees that cause hay fever. As more and more people moved into the area, more trees were planted and lawns seeded. The result? A pollen index that's still good but not nearly as good as it used to be.

The Economy

For years, politicians and economic boosters in attractive locations around the country considered an interesting possibility: Enticing affluent persons to move in would be a much cleaner and easier strategy than chasing after smokestack employers. The impact of just one couple moving in and spending their retirement income locally, so the argument went, could be the same as three new jobs in light industry.

Several states have taken up the idea and started "retiree attraction" programs. Mississippi stresses its authentic, welcoming small towns and low living costs. Arkansas pushes its natural environment. Wyoming emphasizes hiking and skiing in the state's rugged outdoors. Louisiana bases its appeal on great food. Florida, aware that the Carolinas and other nearby states were poaching its older residents, began its own program.

For all that, diesel logging trucks—their exhaust stacks roaring—are still a common sight on coastal U.S. 17 from Virginia Beach, Virginia, to Savannah, Georgia; on route 12 in Vermont; and on U.S. 93 in western Montana. On Colorado's western slope, Montrose still has a Russell Stover candy factory, a composites plastics plant, and several boutique fishing-gear manufacturers. In Silver City, New Mexico, the Phelps Dodge copper mine is still king. In the Arkansas Ozarks, FM stations still broadcast help-wanted ads for workers at chicken processor Tyson Foods. On the Chesapeake Bay, fishing boats still lightly bob and bump at wooden docks.

If places had to rely on free-spending older newcomers for their economic futures, they'd starve. Paychecks everywhere are still earned the old-fashioned way—in agriculture, mining, manufacturing, construction, and a lot of retail trade and services. If you're thinking of starting a second career or finding an interesting part-time or seasonal job, consider places that aren't prone to recession and that can expect to gain good new jobs over the next 8 years.

OLDER PERSONS DO WORK

Near Fayetteville, Arkansas, a man and wife, both retired from the U.S. Army Corps of Engineers, breed AKC Schipperke dogs and take in stray animals for later adoption. They advertise their Skips in *Dog World,* and buyers come from all over the Mississippi and Ohio valleys. For them, it's a matter of being your own boss and doing something you love rather than working a temporary job at Tyson's

Foods, in nearby Springdale, when that employer is especially busy.

In a Chapel Hill, North Carolina, haberdashery, a woman stands near the Kenneth Cole and Pendleton shelves in the shirt alcove. The boys from Duke, UNC, and State are her customers, especially during the job-interviewing season. They haven't a clue about what goes into a good shirt or even how best to wash it. She likes this retail job much better than the one she had selling linens and bedding at a department store in a mall near Raleigh.

In Eagle River, Wisconsin, a World War II veteran tells how his teenage friend is mystified that the man doesn't quit his penny-ante Commander's job at American Legion Post #431 and get behind the counter at McDonald's out on Highway 17. The teenager promises to pull strings with the day manager to start the older friend at $8. For some odd reason, says the man, he can't drum into the kid's head that the Commander's job requires organizational and human relations skills, and is far more fun and interesting than fast food, even if it were done for free.

A thousand miles south, a charming woman runs the visitor's drop-in center on Central Avenue in downtown Hot Springs, Arkansas. Amid racks full of brochures, booklets, maps, pamphlets, and broadsides, she talks with American and foreign tourists all day long. "Ask me a question and I'll be happy to answer it. And if I don't know the answer," she adds, "I'll be happy to make one up." Her work is voluntary; so are other options such as working at St. Joseph's Health Center's hospital auxiliary, or helping high-school kids with reading problems.

Many retired persons work in their own way—as a volunteer, through self-employment, or at a part-time job. Though having a job after retirement is by no means a concern of every older adult, it may be to you. In the years immediately after retirement, nearly one in four people takes a short-schedule, seasonal, or temporary job. Another one in four would do the same thing according to surveys, but several things stand in the way.

Social Security Rules

If you're going back to work, "Social Security giveth, and Social Security taketh away," notes retirement expert Bob Menchin. The amount of money you can earn on the job and still collect the benefits coming to you is limited. If you're under FRA, or *full retirement age* (in 2007, FRA is 65 years 8 months), and your

THE ECONOMY IN BRIEF

Talk about a generational shift! When your parents retired, it meant the end of work. Now, a third of persons receiving pension income have a full- or part-time job.

Coming up: Boomers, 8 out of 10 of whom say they'll find another job after retiring. "Forget leisure. Retirement is . . . a transition to another work life, although at a more relaxed pace," says the opening line in a recent *Business Week* article on the "working late" trend.

It makes a difference in *which* industry you look. The best ones offer the most part-time and seasonal jobs: services, retail trade, government, and financial. Somewhere in those sectors is interesting, fun, stimulating, and rewarding work.

It also makes some difference *where* you look. For all the attractions of smaller towns, they offer little variety in local employment. You may need to commute to better opportunity. Some larger places, where you'd expect more variety and quality, might be dominated by single industries such as mining or the military.

Large summer resorts are excellent because you can start earlier in the season and finish up later than college students, the group that traditionally shows up for hospitality jobs. But college students increase the competition for good work in college towns that are attractive for retirement.

There must be many reasons to work besides putting today's food on the table. Two of the best ones you'll ever need: A mental and physical workout, and a sure way of increasing your assets by regularly saving even modest amounts that can compound over the long haul.

income exceeds $12,960 ($1,080 monthly), your benefits will be reduced by $1 for every $2 you're earning over that amount. In the year you reach FRA, $1 in benefits will be deducted from every $3 you earn above a new limit of $34,440 ($2,870 monthly). *Starting with the month you hit FRA*, however, you get your benefits with no limit on your earnings.

Keeping your earnings under the exempt amount is understandable. Not only would half or more of your excess earnings be lost through Social Security reductions, but also they would be subject to income taxes as well as Social Security withholding. Unfortunately, explaining this to an employer makes it seem as if you're limited in motivation.

The Market for Part-Time Jobs

In spite of the rapid growth in the number of part-time jobs, most of these positions are dead-end, low-skill, mind-numbing, low-paid ones with few benefits.

The big reason that there aren't more better-paying and challenging part-time jobs is the high cost to employers. Training and administrative costs, for instance, are the same for full- and part-time workers. A short workweek boosts the hourly costs to employers for these expenses. In contrast, jobs that require little training—such as hamburger flipping, counter help, aisle sweeping, or cashiering—won't significantly raise the costs to employers, particularly if the job has no benefit package.

Age Discrimination

In spite of the law protecting anyone between the ages of 40 and 70 from being passed over in hiring or being involuntarily retired solely on the basis of age, this kind of discrimination still happens everywhere in the job market.

It is also one of the most difficult job-market issues to identify. Few, if any, employers support discriminatory business practices; they are open to lawsuits if they do. Yet a large number of older workers have experienced discrimination. About the only advice career counselors can offer is that fair treatment usually comes from working for a supervisor older than you.

MILITARY ECONOMIES

Hilton Head and Beaufort share Beaufort County, South Carolina, with the Marine Corps Recruiting Depot Parris Island, the area's largest employer. Near New Bern, North Carolina, is Cherry Point, the world's largest Marine Corps Air Station. At least 1 in every 30 workers in the following 12 locations gets a paycheck from the Department of Defense. Not for nothing are several of their congressmen sitting on Armed Services Committees.

Alamogordo, NM
Annapolis, MD
Bay St. Louis–Pass Christian, MS
Beaufort, SC
Charleston, SC
Hilton Head Island, SC
New Bern, NC
Panama City, FL
Pensacola, FL
St. Marys, GA
Savannah, GA
Whidbey Island, WA

Source: Woods & Poole Economics, Inc., employment forecasts.

JOB FORECASTS IN RETIREMENT PLACES

Economists who follow job trends have an old joke: If you take each local planner's numbers for job growth in his or her area and add them all together, the total jobs forecasted would require that every man, woman, and child hold down one day-job and moonlight two others.

Fortunately, economists with a national view have a better perspective. Although no one sees the future with certainty, forecasting where jobs will be plentiful over the next few years isn't a matter of gazing into a crystal ball.

Start by asking this question: Do people move to where the jobs are, or do jobs come to where the people are? While this is a good topic to argue about over beers at an academic convention, most economists think jobs come to where the people are. In other words, any growing place that has a concentration of people with a variety of worker skills is a jobs mecca.

But there's more to it than that. Some spots are saddled with sunset industries—shipbuilding, textiles, sawmills, and mining, for example—while others have sunrise industries—healthcare, higher education, software, and, yes, government. Most locations have varying mixes of the dying and the growing.

Forecasting which spots will gain jobs is as much a matter of determining the prospects for certain industries as it is predicting population shifts. The great American job machine has churned out record numbers of jobs for decades and, depending on which expert is talking, the machine either is showing wear and tear or has shifted into a new and different gear. Still, millions of new jobs will be added to the U.S. economy by 2010. Although employment increases will occur at half the pace of the 1990s, the prospects for certain occupations look quite rosy.

The hot industries—retail trade; services; and finance, insurance, and real estate (known as FIRE in employment shorthand)—will stay hot. With variation between places, this is where the real action is expected to occur. And with variation among employers, these hot industries are precisely the ones where *good* part-time jobs are found.

UNEMPLOYMENT RISK

If you see a good number of light-manufacturing plants with full parking lots and notice lots of hard-hat construction workers aboard growling earth-moving machines at new residential and commercial developments, you'll know that in flush times jobs are easy to find here and the pay is just great. You can also assume that, should a recession roll in, this place may be hard hit by unemployment.

One of the few things you'll find economists agreeing on is that places with large numbers of workers in manufacturing and construction are harshly affected during business slumps.

In contrast to boom-and-bust places, there are others where the pace isn't quite as fast, and where large numbers of white-collar workers commute to downtown or suburban jobs with financial, real estate, and insurance firms. Others find their work at colleges and universities, at big medical centers in the area, or at local resorts. The employment mix in these areas is more balanced, with most of the weight going to the white-collar sector.

Finally, there are places at the opposite extreme from industrial places, not because they are thriving, but because manufacturing plays no part in their existence. These have nearly pure white-collar economies characterized by people working almost exclusively in retail trade, services, finance, insurance, and real estate.

Even though in retirement you may have little to worry about if you don't have a full-time job, local unemployment may still affect you in unforeseen ways. By boosting the competition for available work, high unemployment limits your chances of finding a part-time job should you ever want one.

Just as places can be rated for mild climates and their supply of public golf links, so also can they be rated for how vulnerable they are to joblessness during a bad business cycle. The two yardsticks are the local portion of workers in manufacturing, construction, and the military, plus the place's most recent 120-month unemployment record versus national averages. For each of *Retirement Places Rated*'s 200 locations, the unemployment threat is very high (↑↑), higher (↑), average (↔), low (↓), and very low (↓↓).

THE PART-TIME JOB MARKET

If relocation is a definite option in your retirement and if finding work in your destination isn't a hallucination, are there any immutable laws for finding a comfortable, well-paying, flexible, interesting, challenging part-time job with a sympathetic employer?

FARMS, FORESTS, & MINES

Just outside the residential fringe of many retirement places is a kind of muscular outback. Equipment-sales yards along the commercial strips leading into town offer the clue: John Deere tractors, Ingersoll-Rand pumps, Dresser rock drills, and Homelite chain saws. At least 1 in 10 workers in the following areas has a job in slow-growing or no-growing farming, forestry, and mining industries.

Carmel–Pebble Beach, CA
Cedar Creek Lake, TX
Chewelah, WA
Delta County, CO
Driggs, ID
Eureka Springs, AR
Fredericksburg, TX
Hampshire County, WV
Lake of the Cherokees, OK
Leelanau Peninsula, MI
Nelson County, VA
Oakhurst–Coarsegold, CA
Roswell, NM
Silver City, NM
Wenatchee, WA

Source: Woods & Poole Economics, Inc., employment forecasts.

Gee no, there aren't. But there are common sense rules for judging whether one place is more promising than another. Consider the variety of jobs, their quality, and the competition to land one of them.

Tinker, Tailor . . . Parachute Packer

The U.S. Department of Labor's *Dictionary of Occupational Titles* should be recommended bedtime reading for job seekers. You'll either quickly nod off or sit right up when you read how many jobs there are somewhere that you've never heard of—some 20,000 job titles between "abalone diver" and "zoo veterinarian."

All of which leads into something important: If you spent your career as an actuary, a geographer, a real-estate appraiser, or a webmaster, are there any part-time or seasonal opportunities in retirement places besides the local Wal-Mart, the county hospital, or the paddle-boat concession at the local state park?

Answer: Of course, but almost always in bigger places. When it comes to the *variety* of interesting jobs, size does matter. By looking at how many new jobs in hot industries are projected by 2015, it's possible to break our retirement places into five groups: Where the variety of jobs is very high (↑↑), where it's high (↑), where it's just average (↔), where the variety is low (↓), and where it's very low (↓↓).

Job Quality: Show Me the Money

Sure, somewhere over the rainbow is a job waiting where colleagues are like family, fringes are fabulous, the cafeteria is gourmet, and the parking is close in—and where there's no pecking order, no performance reviews, and no prohibition on catnaps.

A quality job? For some, perhaps. But in the view of economists, there is just one benchmark that counts: the worker's paycheck. The big difference between earnings in Loudoun County, Virginia, and Fairplay, high in the Colorado Rockies, is somewhat due to cost-of-living differences. But it's mainly due to differences in skills and the employer productivity.

To broadly describe job quality, we adopt this simple view: A quality job pays more. Based on earnings figures for people in FIRE (finance, insurance, and real estate industries), services, and retail trade in each retirement place, it's possible to break the places into five groups: Where the quality of jobs is very high (↑↑), where it's high (↑), where it's just average (↔), where the variety is low (↓), and where it's very low (↓↓).

What Are the Odds?

Think of how much competition you'll meet in tracking down a good seasonal or short-schedule job. Are there crowds of voluntary part-time workers pounding the pavement everywhere, or are the odds more favorable in Tucson, Arizona, and Chapel Hill, North Carolina, than in Las Cruces, New Mexico, or Port Angeles, Washington?

"Voluntary" part-timers are persons who want only part-time jobs rather than persons who resignedly take a temporary, seasonal, or short-schedule job because nothing else is available. There are 20 million voluntary part-timers in this country. Most are older adults, 19- to 24-year-old college students, and women age 38 to 54 easing back into the workplace.

To measure competition, *Retirement Places Rated* compares the population of the latter two groups to persons in their early 60s. In each place, the part-time job competition is:

- Very high (↑↑) if the number of college-age persons and women re-entering the job market is more than 6½ times the number of persons in their early 60s.

- High (↑) if the number of college-age persons and women re-entering the job market is between 5½ and 6½ times the number of persons in their early 60s.

- Average (↔) if the number of college-age persons and women re-entering the job market is between 4½ and 5½ times the number of persons in their early 60s.

- Low (↓) if the number of college-age persons and women re-entering the job market is between 3½ and 4½ times the number of persons in their early 60s.

- Very low (↓↓) if the number of college-age persons and women re-entering the job market is less than 3½ times the number of persons in their early 60s.

JUDGING: THE ECONOMY

If you've taken early retirement from your lifelong career and want to launch a new one or simply land an interesting part-time job, are the prospects rosier in Rehoboth Bay, Reno, or Ruidoso (Delaware, Nevada, and New Mexico, respectively)?

To help you answer the question, *Retirement Places Rated* compares three factors in each place: (1) the rate of job growth to the year 2015; (2) the total number of new full-time equivalent jobs forecasted in government, retail trade, services, and the FIRE industries (finance, insurance, and real estate); and (3) job quality, determined by how much local workers in these industries see on their paychecks in each place. *Note:* One worker typically holds a full-time equivalent job; occasionally, two workers share it. Two full-time equivalent jobs roughly translate into three part-time jobs of 25 hours per week.

Which of these factors is more important? A rosy growth forecast, such as the 16.1 percent for Fairplay, Colorado, always looks good at first view, and it does

SKI TOWNS & COLLEGE TOWNS: TOUGH COMPETITION

For all the liveliness of college towns or ski areas, they aren't the best places for older adults to find part-time or seasonal work. The competition is especially stiff in these places where the number of younger persons who look for part-time work is more than two-and-a-half times the number of persons in their early 60s searching for the same thing.

translate into some 700 new jobs in services, retail trade, and FIRE each year. In contrast, the more modest 7.8 percent forecast for Pensacola, Florida, results in almost 13,000 new jobs in these industries during the same period.

And what about job quality in these two locations? Not only do full- and part-time workers in Pensacola make more money than similar workers up high on the Continental Divide in Fairplay, but also they make more money than the national average. True, the difference points to different costs of living, but it also points to the quality of the work.

To produce a score, the three factors—number of new jobs, job quality, and rate of growth—get equal weight. The result is then scaled against a standard from 0 to 100 in which 50 is average. Suburban Henderson, Nevada, has a score of 100. Grand Junction, in Colorado's Western Slope region midway between Denver and Salt Lake City, scores a 50. Nelson County, Virginia, has a score of 0. These three areas are respectively the best, average, and worst retirement places for job growth between now and 2015.

RANKINGS: THE ECONOMY

To rank 200 places for part-time and seasonal job prospects, *Retirement Places Rated* weights three criteria equally: (1) the number of new jobs forecasted by 2015 in government, services, retail trade, and the FIRE industries (finance, insurance, and real estate); (2) the rate of growth; and (3) the quality of new jobs.

Forecasts are for the entire county in which the place is located. Scores are rounded to one decimal place. Locations with tie scores get the same rank and are listed alphabetically.

Retirement Places from First to Last

RANK	PLACE	SCORE
1.	Henderson, NV	100.0
2.	Georgetown, TX	99.4
3.	Loudoun County, VA	98.9
4.	Scottsdale, AZ	97.9
4.	Wickenburg, AZ	97.9
6.	Naples, FL	97.4
7.	Placer County, CA	96.9
8.	Bradenton, FL	96.4
9.	Fort Myers–Cape Coral, FL	95.9
10.	Beaufort, SC	94.9
10.	Hilton Head Island, SC	94.9
12.	Annapolis, MD	93.9
12.	Lake Conroe, TX	93.9
14.	Palm Springs–Coachella Valley, CA	93.4
15.	Laguna Beach–Dana Point, CA	92.9
16.	Sarasota, FL	92.4
17.	Fort Collins–Loveland, CO	91.9
18.	Tucson, AZ	91.4
19.	Victorville–Apple Valley, CA	90.9
20.	Madison, WI	89.9
20.	Rio Rancho, NM	89.9
22.	Carmel–Pebble Beach, CA	89.4
23.	Charleston, SC	88.9
24.	Myrtle Beach, SC	88.4
25.	Bay St. Louis–Pass Christian, MS	87.9
26.	Kissimmee–St. Cloud, FL	87.4
27.	Chapel Hill–Carrboro, NC	86.9
28.	Charlottesville, VA	86.4
29.	Pensacola, FL	85.9
30.	Santa Fe, NM	85.4
31.	Maui, HI	84.9
32.	Bend, OR	84.4
33.	Iowa City, IA	83.9
34.	Medford–Ashland, OR	83.4
35.	Kingman, AZ	82.4
35.	Lake Havasu City, AZ	82.4
37.	Jackson Hole, WY	81.9
38.	McAllen–Alamo, TX	81.4
39.	Morro Bay–Cambria, CA	80.9
40.	Conway, AR	80.4
41.	Fayetteville, AR	79.8
42.	St. George–Zion, UT	79.3
43.	Coeur d'Alene, ID	78.8
44.	Fredericksburg–Spotsylvania, VA	78.3
45.	Madison, MS	77.8
46.	Maryville, TN	77.3
47.	Panama City, FL	76.8
48.	Park City, UT	76.3
49.	Largo, FL	75.8
50.	Santa Barbara, CA	75.3
51.	Flagstaff, AZ	74.3
51.	Sedona, AZ	74.3
53.	Brunswick, ME	73.3
53.	East End Long Island, NY	73.3
55.	Ketchum–Sun Valley, ID	72.8
56.	Port Charlotte, FL	72.3
57.	Cottonwood–Verde Valley, AZ	71.3
57.	Prescott–Prescott Valley, AZ	71.3
59.	Southport–Brunswick Islands, NC	70.8
60.	Wimberley, TX	70.3
61.	Fairhope–Gulf Shores, AL	69.8
62.	Grass Valley–Nevada City, CA	69.3
63.	Anacortes, WA	68.3
63.	Kalispell–Flathead Valley, MT	68.3
65.	Melbourne–Palm Bay, FL	67.8
66.	Asheville, NC	67.3

RANK	PLACE	SCORE
67.	Oakhurst–Coarsegold, CA	66.8
68.	Bellingham, WA	66.3
69.	Durango, CO	65.8
70.	Pahrump Valley, NV	65.3
71.	Burlington, VT	64.8
72.	Traverse City, MI	64.3
73.	Bozeman, MT	63.3
73.	Williamsburg, VA	63.3
75.	Toms River–Barnegat Bay, NJ	62.8
76.	Columbia, MO	62.3
77.	Vero Beach, FL	61.8
78.	Lakeland–Winter Haven, FL	61.3
79.	East Stroudsburg, PA	60.8
80.	Carson City–Carson Valley, NV	60.3
81.	St. Augustine, FL	59.7
82.	Eugene, OR	59.2
83.	Branson, MO	58.7
84.	State College, PA	58.2
85.	New Braunfels, TX	57.7
86.	Ocala, FL	57.2
87.	Savannah, GA	56.7
88.	Silverthorne–Breckenridge, CO	56.2
89.	Gainesville, FL	55.7
90.	Middle Cape Cod, MA	55.2
91.	New Bern, NC	54.7
92.	Hanover, NH	54.2
93.	Payson, AZ	53.7
94.	Bisbee, AZ	53.2
95.	Brownsville, TX	52.7
96.	Thomasville, GA	52.2
97.	Yuma, AZ	51.7
98.	St. Simons–Jekyll Islands, GA	51.2
99.	Amador County, CA	50.7
100.	Grand Junction, CO	50.2
101.	Summerville, SC	49.2
101.	York Beaches, ME	49.2
103.	Key West, FL	48.7
104.	Las Cruces, NM	48.2
105.	Cedar City, UT	47.7
106.	Athens, GA	47.2
107.	Western St. Tammany Parish, LA	46.7
108.	Leesburg–Mount Dora, FL	46.2
109.	Litchfield Hills, CT	45.7
110.	Rehoboth Bay–Indian River Bay, DE	45.2
111.	Southern Pines–Pinehurst, NC	44.7
112.	Northampton–Amherst, MA	44.2
113.	Wenatchee, WA	43.7
114.	Dare Outer Banks, NC	43.2
115.	Lake of the Ozarks, MO	42.7
116.	Paradise–Magalia, CA	42.2
117.	Hendersonville–East Flat Rock, NC	41.2
117.	Oxford, MS	41.2
119.	Whidbey Island, WA	40.7
120.	St. Marys, GA	40.2
121.	Marble Falls–Lake LBJ, TX	39.6
122.	Crossville, TN	39.1
123.	Southern Berkshire County, MA	38.6
124.	Palmer–Wasilla, AK	38.1
125.	Port Townsend, WA	37.6
126.	Port St. Lucie, FL	37.1
127.	Petoskey–Harbor Springs, MI	36.6
128.	The Big Island, HI	36.1
129.	Cedar Creek Lake, TX	35.6
130.	Dahlonega, GA	35.1
131.	Sandpoint–Lake Pend Oreille, ID	34.6
132.	Taos, NM	34.1

continued

The Economy

Retirement Places from First to Last (cont.)

RANK	PLACE	SCORE
133.	Boone–Blowing Rock, NC	33.6
134.	Pagosa Springs, CO	33.1
135.	Pendleton District, SC	32.6
136.	Beaufort–Atlantic Beach, NC	32.1
137.	Roswell, NM	31.6
138.	Hamilton–Bitterroot Valley, MT	31.1
139.	Fairplay, CO	30.6
140.	Camden, ME	30.1
141.	San Juan Islands, WA	29.6
142.	Hot Springs, AR	29.1
143.	Port Angeles–Sequim, WA	28.6
144.	Montrose, CO	28.1
145.	Monadnock Region, NH	27.6
146.	Eagle River–Woodruff, WI	27.1
147.	Grants Pass, OR	26.6
148.	Sonora–Twain Harte, CA	26.1
149.	Hattiesburg, MS	25.6
150.	Boerne, TX	25.1
151.	Pike County, PA	24.6
152.	Easton–St. Michaels, MD	23.6
152.	Lower Cape May, NJ	23.6
154.	Sullivan County, NY	23.1
155.	Alamogordo, NM	22.6
156.	Murray–Kentucky Lake, KY	22.1
157.	Smith Mountain Lake, VA	21.1
157.	Waynesville, NC	21.1
159.	Norfork Lake, AR	20.6
160.	Martha's Vineyard, MA	20.1
161.	Ocean City, MD	19.5
162.	Sebring–Avon Park, FL	19.0
163.	Tryon, NC	18.5
164.	Woodstock, VT	18.0
165.	Lake of the Cherokees, OK	17.5
166.	Kerrville, TX	17.0

RANK	PLACE	SCORE
167.	Bar Harbor, ME	16.5
168.	Cortez, CO	16.0
169.	Door Peninsula, WI	15.5
170.	Brown County, IN	15.0
171.	Silver City, NM	14.5
172.	Brevard, NC	14.0
173.	Newport–Lincoln City, OR	13.5
174.	Front Royal, VA	13.0
175.	Fredericksburg, TX	12.5
176.	Leelanau Peninsula, MI	12.0
177.	Las Vegas, NM	11.5
178.	McCall, ID	11.0
179.	Lake Placid, NY	10.5
180.	Delta County, CO	10.0
181.	Mendocino–Fort Bragg, CA	9.5
182.	St. Jay–Northeast Kingdom, VT	9.0
183.	Chewelah, WA	8.5
184.	Driggs, ID	8.0
185.	Mariposa, CA	7.5
186.	Ruidoso, NM	7.0
187.	Charles Town–Shepherdstown, WV	6.5
188.	Alpine–Big Bend, TX	6.0
189.	Eureka Springs, AR	5.5
190.	Chestertown, MD	4.5
190.	Natchitoches, LA	4.5
192.	Apalachicola, FL	4.0
193.	Rockport–Aransas Pass, TX	3.5
194.	Edenton, NC	3.0
195.	Northern Neck, VA	2.5
196.	Berkeley Springs, WV	2.0
197.	Long Beach Peninsula, WA	1.5
198.	Rabun County, GA	1.0
199.	Hampshire County, WV	0.5
200.	Nelson County, VA	0.0

PLACE PROFILES: THE ECONOMY

The following table shows job features for each place. The percent figure under *Forecast* is the rate of growth forecasted from 2007 to 2015 in all industries. Detailed under *New Jobs in . . .* are the number of new positions forecasted in government, FIRE (finance, insurance, and real estate industries), retail trade, and services—industries where older adults find opportunity and also where most part-time, seasonal, and short-schedule jobs are found.

The next column, *Typical Hourly Pay,* offers average dollar amounts that local employers pay to workers in each of the four listed job categories (government, FIRE, retail trade, and services). The figures are derived from earning and employment forecasts for each local industry.

The arrows seen throughout stand for five intervals: very high (↑↑), high (↑), average (↔), low (↓), and very low (↓↓). Under *Part-time Job Market, Competition*

compares the number of persons in their early 20s and women in their late 40s reentering the job market with the number of persons in their early 60s; *Job Quality* describes typical earnings for workers in government, FIRE, retail trade, and services compared with the average figure for all of the retirement places; and *Job Variety* describes the absolute number of new jobs in those industries. *Unemployment Risk* is based on each area's portion of blue-collar and military jobs and its most recent 120-month unemployment rate compared with the national average.

All forecasts are county totals and are derived from current Complete Economic and Demographic Data Source (CEDDS) data from July 1, 2007, to July 1, 2015, by forecaster Woods & Poole Economics, Inc., of Washington, D.C., and are used here with permission. Forecasts are uncertain and future data may differ substantially from Woods & Poole projections. The use of these data and the conclusions drawn from them are solely the responsibility of the author.

A star (★) in front of a place's name highlights it as one of the top 30 places for part-time job opportunities between 2007 and 2015.

PLACE	FORE-CAST	New Jobs In . . .				Typical Hourly Pay				Part-time Job Market			UNEMPLOY-MENT RISK	RANK
		GOVERN-MENT	FIRE	RETAIL	SERV-ICES	GOVERN-MENT	FIRE	RETAIL	SERV-ICES	COMPETI-TION	JOB QUALITY	JOB VARIETY		
Alamogordo, NM	5.4%	369	134	107	739	$13.28	$13.57	$6.99	$9.75	↑	↔	↓	↑	155
Alpine–Big Bend, TX	6.1%	38	9	92	233	$14.10	$19.99	$6.94	$9.51	↔	↓	↓↓	↓↓	188
Amador County, CA	9.5%	492	85	186	972	$19.87	$15.41	$8.98	$10.86	↓	↔	↓	↑	99
Anacortes, WA	7.5%	703	197	358	2,469	$18.48	$24.52	$11.07	$14.72	↑	↑↑	↔	↑↑	63
★ Annapolis, MD	8.3%	1,229	2,660	2,018	17,289	$22.60	$24.98	$11.63	$17.83	↑	↑↑	↑↑	↓	12
Apalachicola, FL	6.8%	15	97	38	261	$16.01	$17.17	$7.40	$8.06	↓↓	↓↓	↓↓	↔	192
Asheville, NC	7.1%	855	627	2,053	5,291	$17.07	$28.79	$8.40	$14.00	↔	↑	↑↑	↓	66
Athens, GA	5.3%	1,031	217	352	1,849	$20.45	$21.87	$8.32	$14.48	↑↑	↑↑	↔	↓↓	106
Bar Harbor, ME	5.4%	172	145	346	842	$15.98	$21.87	$8.99	$12.19	↓	↓	↓	↑	167
★ Bay St. Louis–Pass Christian, MS	8.8%	1,541	553	1,746	7,223	$15.46	$21.71	$7.92	$14.21	↑	↑	↑↑	↔	25
★ Beaufort, SC	12.5%	1,355	996	3,216	4,643	$18.40	$37.48	$10.05	$14.57	↔	↑↑	↑↑	↓↓	10
Beaufort-Atlantic Beach, NC	8.0%	261	236	541	1,175	$16.80	$20.12	$7.26	$10.38	↓↓	↓↓	↔	↔	136
Bellingham, WA	7.3%	1,332	345	976	3,456	$17.63	$26.08	$8.85	$12.39	↑	↑	↑	↑	68
Bend, OR	10.8%	445	550	1,662	4,994	$20.66	$36.01	$9.29	$12.64	↔	↔	↑	↑↑	32
Berkeley Springs, WV	3.9%	38	17	42	69	$16.15	$15.04	$7.90	$8.61	↓	↓	↓↓	↔	196
The Big Island, HI	5.2%	645	330	537	2,229	$21.22	$32.21	$9.58	$12.96	↔	↔	↔	↑	128
Bisbee, AZ	6.8%	321	324	727	2,109	$16.47	$12.26	$6.98	$11.91	↔	↑	↔	↑↑	94
Boerne, TX	9.3%	85	131	250	509	$16.49	$19.31	$8.80	$8.49	↔	↓↓	↓↓	↓↓	150
Boone–Blowing Rock, NC	7.6%	380	76	551	1,119	$18.04	$27.83	$7.55	$11.10	↑↑	↓	↓	↓↓	133
Bozeman, MT	10.9%	580	444	1,252	2,539	$17.03	$22.06	$9.28	$12.38	↑↑	↔	↑	↓↓	73
★ Bradenton, FL	16.5%	1,052	733	1,547	24,899	$19.63	$25.29	$9.99	$13.83	↓	↑	↑↑	↓	8
Branson, MO	14.7%	363	371	1,317	2,167	$15.96	$31.07	$7.91	$12.33	↓	↓	↔	↑↑	83
Brevard, NC	6.4%	105	82	215	474	$16.50	$18.98	$6.42	$9.48	↓↓	↓	↓↓	↔	172
Brown County, IN	8.8%	85	34	97	338	$14.95	$17.23	$5.17	$6.22	↓↓	↓↓	↓↓	↓↓	170
Brownsville, TX	7.5%	3,443	350	1,497	5,310	$16.59	$22.50	$8.09	$9.91	↑↑	↓	↑↑	↑↑	95
Brunswick, ME	5.6%	1,434	940	1,732	7,380	$19.36	$47.78	$11.17	$16.38	↑	↑↑	↑↑	↓↓	53
Burlington, VT	5.7%	831	454	555	4,347	$21.20	$48.32	$10.09	$16.22	↑↑	↑↑	↑	↓↓	71
Camden, ME	7.2%	174	430	197	824	$18.41	$24.84	$8.31	$12.98	↓	↓	↓	↓	140
★ Carmel–Pebble Beach, CA	7.7%	5,073	912	1,617	5,941	$23.24	$30.38	$13.89	$16.24	↑↑	↑↑	↑↑	↑↑	22
Carson City–Carson Valley, NV	7.0%	672	892	687	1,780	$22.23	$22.04	$10.84	$14.11	↓	↑↑	↔	↑	80
Cedar City, UT	13.6%	894	410	309	914	$14.63	$14.67	$6.87	$7.69	↑↑	↓↓	↔	↓	105
Cedar Creek Lake, TX	9.6%	295	239	619	1,245	$15.25	$18.58	$7.83	$9.63	↓	↓↓	↔	↔	129
★ Chapel Hill-Carrboro, NC	8.5%	2,660	320	842	2,302	$22.25	$34.87	$10.27	$16.36	↑↑	↑↑	↑	↓↓	27
★ Charleston, SC	7.9%	1,785	1,316	2,238	13,512	$18.04	$42.38	$9.29	$15.17	↑	↑↑	↑↑	↔	23
Charles Town–Shepherdstown, WV	5.1%	174	46	112	628	$16.97	$19.44	$7.55	$9.97	↔	↓	↓↓	↓↓	187
★ Charlottesville, VA	7.9%	2,651	170	949	3,888	$21.11	$33.15	$9.64	$12.38	↑↑	↑↑	↑	↓↓	28
Chestertown, MD	4.8%	-2	36	97	357	$18.80	$15.71	$7.39	$11.98	↓	↓	↓↓	↑	190
Chewelah, WA	6.0%	174	68	205	437	$16.53	$11.81	$7.98	$9.98	↓	↓	↓↓	↑↑	183
Coeur d'Alene, ID	12.6%	876	972	1,711	3,521	$16.89	$24.97	$9.34	$11.30	↔	↔	↑	↑↑	43
Columbia, MO	7.2%	2,593	292	1,386	2,563	$16.82	$39.41	$7.63	$11.96	↑↑	↑	↑	↓↓	76
Conway, AR	11.6%	403	419	1,191	2,840	$17.15	$18.89	$7.78	$15.89	↑↑	↑	↑	↔	40
Cortez, CO	7.5%	318	68	79	474	$14.19	$17.97	$7.52	$9.61	↔	↓↓	↓↓	↑	168
Cottonwood–Verde Valley, AZ	11.6%	906	790	1,109	5,234	$16.72	$13.93	$8.21	$10.93	↓↓	↓	↑	↓	57
Crossville, TN	8.5%	119	114	600	1,268	$15.95	$26.98	$8.04	$12.61	↓↓	↓	↓	↑	122
Dahlonega, GA	8.7%	102	55	193	272	$17.67	$19.30	$7.82	$9.00	↑↑	↔	↓↓	↓↓	130
Dare Outer Banks, NC	10.7%	171	407	931	1,275	$17.63	$22.21	$9.48	$10.20	↔	↓↓	↔	↑	114
Delta County, CO	7.5%	165	81	204	356	$15.36	$14.16	$5.57	$8.65	↓	↓↓	↓↓	↑	180
Door Peninsula, WI	7.0%	149	286	302	552	$16.78	$14.70	$7.02	$10.27	↓↓	↓↓	↓	↑	169
Driggs, ID	7.7%	38	4	41	146	$12.37	$15.64	$6.80	$6.74	↑↑	↓↓	↓↓	↓↓	184

continued

★ = in the top 30 places for part-time job opportunities

Retirement Places Rated

PLACE	FORE-CAST	New Jobs In... GOVERN-MENT	FIRE	RETAIL	SERV-ICES	Typical Hourly Pay GOVERN-MENT	FIRE	RETAIL	SERV-ICES	Part-time Job Market COMPETI-TION	JOB QUALITY	JOB VARIETY	UNEMPLOY-MENT RISK	RANK
Durango, CO	11.2%	519	324	415	1,842	$17.05	$21.41	$9.30	$14.75	↑	↔	↔	↓	69
Eagle River-Woodruff, WI	9.6%	329	9	179	358	$15.83	$14.72	$7.20	$9.25	↓↓	↓↓	↓↓	↑	146
East End Long Island, NY	3.9%	3,964	834	4,490	13,416	$26.64	$55.13	$11.22	$16.84	↑	↑↑	↑↑	↓	53
Easton-St. Michaels, MD	5.1%	47	194	266	848	$19.29	$21.38	$10.30	$14.89	↓↓	↔	↓	↓↓	152
East Stroudsburg, PA	7.6%	889	297	1,540	2,367	$18.74	$17.27	$8.18	$12.55	↑	↑	↑	↑	79
Edenton, NC	4.1%	74	8	24	206	$16.52	$19.78	$6.74	$11.64	↔	↓	↓↓	↔	194
Eugene, OR	6.0%	1,209	610	2,153	6,030	$19.36	$28.55	$9.61	$11.81	↔	↑	↑↑	↑	82
Eureka Springs, AR	6.3%	79	41	224	403	$14.11	$16.82	$7.01	$8.57	↓	↓↓	↓↓	↔	189
Fairhope-Gulf Shores, AL	11.9%	598	1,213	3,128	3,017	$16.92	$23.05	$8.76	$10.69	↔	↓	↑	↓	61
Fairplay, CO	16.1%	94	157	70	400	$14.79	$11.21	$4.77	$6.97	↑	↓↓	↓↓	↓	139
Fayetteville, AR	8.3%	555	371	1,360	4,839	$17.96	$25.95	$8.22	$14.77	↑↑	↑	↑	↓↓	41
Flagstaff, AZ	10.7%	1,123	921	1,840	4,048	$17.59	$15.33	$7.72	$11.79	↑↑	↔	↑	↑↑	51
★Fort Collins-Loveland, CO	9.2%	1,811	1,163	3,047	6,855	$18.71	$19.90	$8.99	$14.50	↑↑	↑↑	↑↑	↓	17
★Fort Myers-Cape Coral, FL	11.8%	4,310	1,528	6,547	16,276	$20.76	$35.89	$11.26	$14.05	↓↓	↑	↑↑	↓	9
Fredericksburg, TX	7.8%	61	103	163	485	$15.76	$15.95	$7.54	$9.50	↓↓	↓↓	↓↓	↓↓	175
Fredericksburg-Spotsylvania, VA	9.3%	1,188	480	1,575	2,313	$18.54	$23.23	$10.31	$15.53	↑↑	↑	↑	↓	44
Front Royal, VA	6.7%	105	30	233	534	$16.49	$14.27	$7.54	$10.61	↑	↓	↓↓	↓↓	174
Gainesville, FL	5.7%	747	405	765	6,165	$16.56	$36.75	$7.35	$13.65	↑↑	↑	↑↑	↓↓	89
★Georgetown, TX	15.5%	2,581	1,991	1,919	7,391	$17.20	$26.54	$8.46	$11.71	↑↑	↑↑	↑↑	↓↓	2
Grand Junction, CO	7.5%	578	416	1,111	2,495	$18.65	$23.33	$8.24	$12.39	↑	↔	↔	↔	100
Grants Pass, OR	7.1%	222	153	508	1,298	$19.31	$17.62	$9.86	$10.67	↓↓	↓	↓	↑↑	147
Grass Valley-Nevada City, CA	10.3%	584	615	768	3,279	$20.39	$21.63	$9.18	$12.24	↓↓	↔	↑	↑	62
Hamilton-Bitterroot Valley, MT	9.2%	151	62	215	948	$15.65	$18.55	$8.05	$10.31	↓↓	↓↓	↓	↑	138
Hampshire County, WV	4.3%	11	64	31	165	$16.70	$16.62	$6.68	$9.02	↓	↓↓	↓↓	↔	199
Hanover, NH	5.6%	337	68	650	2,379	$16.25	$28.10	$10.78	$18.58	↑	↑↑	↔	↓↓	92
Hattiesburg, MS	3.7%	824	36	26	1,179	$15.87	$22.54	$8.93	$14.00	↑↑	↑	↓	↔	149
★Henderson, NV	15.1%	15,928	22,958	24,013	64,467	$24.71	$35.99	$11.90	$18.69	↑	↑↑	↑↑	↔	1
Hendersonville-East Flat Rock, NC	6.2%	479	165	553	977	$17.25	$23.83	$8.96	$11.39	↓	↑	↓	↓↓	117
★Hilton Head Island, SC	12.5%	1,355	996	3,216	4,643	$18.40	$37.48	$10.05	$14.57	↔	↑↑	↑↑	↓↓	10
Hot Springs, AR	6.5%	194	226	519	1,808	$17.07	$16.37	$7.84	$12.18	↓	↓	↔	↔	142
Iowa City, IA	8.1%	2,267	344	1,401	3,305	$20.57	$31.85	$7.36	$13.04	↑↑	↑	↑	↓↓	33
Jackson Hole, WY	11.9%	221	491	694	1,148	$19.06	$25.64	$10.13	$17.26	↑	↔	↔	↓↓	37
Kalispell-Flathead Valley, MT	11.5%	284	244	607	4,641	$17.66	$21.95	$9.83	$11.74	↔	↓	↑	↑	63
Kerrville, TX	6.4%	131	244	410	521	$16.98	$16.82	$8.32	$12.96	↓	↓	↓	↓↓	166
Ketchum-Sun Valley, ID	14.2%	61	482	386	1,259	$18.66	$35.35	$9.32	$12.38	↔	↔	↓	↓	55
Key West, FL	7.2%	427	256	739	2,177	$21.69	$30.66	$10.04	$12.66	↓↓	↔	↔	↓↓	103
Kingman, AZ	12.8%	1,572	888	2,004	2,918	$17.02	$18.40	$9.40	$13.13	↓↓	↔	↑	↑	35
★Kissimmee-St. Cloud, FL	12.1%	1,984	1,024	2,166	3,159	$18.61	$38.78	$9.10	$12.87	↑	↔	↑↑	↓	26
★Laguna Beach-Dana Point, CA	7.7%	10,069	23,637	16,692	68,206	$24.16	$54.18	$12.63	$19.50	↑↑	↑↑	↑↑	↓	15
★Lake Conroe, TX	12.0%	1,226	985	2,982	8,204	$17.39	$21.23	$9.33	$16.35	↑	↑	↑↑	↓	12
Lake Havasu City, AZ	12.8%	1,572	888	2,004	2,918	$17.02	$18.40	$9.40	$13.13	↓↓	↔	↑	↑	35
Lakeland-Winter Haven, FL	5.6%	1,941	250	1,980	7,697	$18.48	$33.38	$11.45	$11.97	↔	↑	↑↑	↑	78
Lake of the Cherokees, OK	8.5%	70	53	636	219	$15.80	$15.87	$6.21	$9.96	↓↓	↓↓	↓↓	↔	165
Lake of the Ozarks, MO	11.1%	128	554	1,017	1,058	$15.32	$22.55	$7.25	$11.28	↓↓	↓↓	↔	↑	115
Lake Placid, NY	5.1%	326	102	59	555	$18.78	$18.76	$7.94	$9.06	↔	↓	↓↓	↑↑	179
Largo, FL	5.9%	3,273	812	5,101	19,813	$20.34	$39.65	$9.85	$13.74	↓	↑↑	↑↑	↓	49
Las Cruces, NM	7.0%	1,260	189	617	2,820	$15.79	$20.03	$8.58	$11.94	↑↑	↔	↑	↑↑	104
Las Vegas, NM	7.2%	289	29	120	517	$15.17	$14.97	$7.72	$8.23	↔	↓↓	↓↓	↑↑	177
Leelanau Peninsula, MI	7.2%	242	53	61	289	$17.10	$16.80	$7.62	$8.29	↓	↓↓	↓↓	↓	176
Leesburg-Mount Dora, FL	6.7%	1,125	364	1,265	3,037	$17.99	$24.65	$8.81	$13.93	↓	↔	↑	↓	108
Litchfield Hills, CT	4.3%	289	154	864	2,329	$21.84	$31.36	$10.34	$13.22	↔	↑↑	↔	↓	109
Long Beach Peninsula, WA	4.5%	130	31	33	230	$18.48	$14.71	$7.22	$8.22	↓↓	↓↓	↓↓	↑↑	197

★ = in the top 30 places for part-time job opportunities

PLACE	FORE-CAST	New Jobs In . . .				Typical Hourly Pay				Part-time Job Market			UNEMPLOY-MENT RISK	RANK
		GOVERN-MENT	FIRE	RETAIL	SERV-ICES	GOVERN-MENT	FIRE	RETAIL	SERV-ICES	COMPETI-TION	JOB QUALITY	JOB VARIETY		
★Loudoun County, VA	12.7%	2,138	657	3,751	5,970	$21.78	$28.51	$11.58	$32.15	↑↑	↑↑	↑↑	↓↓	3
Lower Cape May, NJ	3.7%	537	227	497	915	$21.07	$24.77	$9.17	$11.91	↓	↔	↓	↑↑	152
Madison, MS	9.7%	415	716	989	2,450	$15.84	$31.49	$10.34	$15.48	↑↑	↑	↔	↓	45
★Madison, WI	7.6%	3,865	1,900	3,864	15,543	$21.47	$38.95	$9.93	$16.18	↑↑	↑↑	↑↑	↓↓	20
Marble Falls–Lake LBJ, TX	11.8%	185	673	338	1,090	$16.48	$14.72	$7.87	$8.01	↔	↓↓	↔	↓	121
Mariposa, CA	6.5%	122	25	106	219	$17.70	$10.18	$6.13	$10.67	↓	↓	↓↓	↑↑	185
Martha's Vineyard, MA	7.1%	105	148	134	391	$19.69	$21.87	$12.70	$10.20	↔	↓	↓↓	↓	160
Maryville, TN	8.5%	545	288	800	1,767	$16.49	$23.58	$14.59	$12.28	↔	↑↑	↔	↓	46
Maui, HI	10.0%	633	655	2,139	4,111	$21.65	$32.45	$11.44	$13.13	↔	↑	↑	↑	31
McAllen–Alamo, TX	10.2%	6,775	1,081	3,814	10,210	$16.50	$26.93	$10.46	$10.17	↑↑	↓	↑↑	↑↑	38
McCall, ID	7.8%	64	63	144	101	$15.53	$15.57	$6.03	$7.79	↓	↑	↑↑	↑↑	178
Medford–Ashland, OR	8.5%	471	555	2,262	5,019	$19.55	$27.54	$10.06	$13.51	↓	↑	↑↑	↑	34
Melbourne–Palm Bay, FL	5.1%	1,526	941	2,377	6,304	$19.63	$29.39	$8.24	$16.62	↔	↑↑	↑↑	↔	65
Mendocino–Fort Bragg, CA	3.7%	302	122	323	778	$18.58	$16.48	$9.33	$10.87	↓	↓	↓	↑↑	181
Middle Cape Cod, MA	6.1%	836	921	1,457	4,288	$21.93	$22.31	$11.59	$14.85	↓	↑	↑	↔	90
Monadnock Region, NH	4.4%	108	129	501	1,005	$15.48	$33.80	$8.90	$10.82	↑	↑	↓	↓↓	145
Montrose, CO	7.8%	249	122	266	736	$17.10	$15.62	$9.65	$10.12	↔	↓	↓	↑	144
Morro Bay–Cambria, CA	7.6%	1,169	596	1,726	5,627	$21.55	$20.56	$9.52	$13.28	↑	↑	↑↑	↔	39
Murray–Kentucky Lake, KY	6.7%	473	17	281	199	$15.10	$23.16	$8.19	$10.92	↔	↔	↓↓	↑	156
★Myrtle Beach, SC	12.9%	1,521	2,276	4,920	6,490	$19.05	$31.53	$9.18	$12.86	↓	↔	↑↑	↔	24
★Naples, FL	12.3%	1,814	1,502	3,800	11,373	$21.12	$43.05	$11.27	$16.14	↓↓	↑↑	↑↑	↔	6
Natchitoches, LA	3.5%	207	5	20	239	$13.94	$14.94	$7.70	$11.40	↑	↓	↓↓	↑	190
Nelson County, VA	3.8%	33	12	37	71	$16.35	$18.53	$6.34	$8.23	↓	↓↓	↓↓	↓↓	200
New Bern, NC	6.0%	776	137	354	1,884	$16.53	$22.47	$7.61	$13.22	↑	↑↑	↔	↑	91
New Braunfels, TX	10.1%	453	468	1,098	1,448	$16.86	$14.74	$11.15	$12.15	↑	↔	↔	↓	85
Newport–Lincoln City, OR	5.5%	229	8	141	968	$19.34	$15.64	$9.50	$10.23	↓↓	↓	↓	↑↑	173
Norfork Lake, AR	7.2%	79	88	179	1,066	$14.49	$14.88	$7.19	$12.60	↓↓	↓↓	↓	↔	159
Northampton–Amherst, MA	6.1%	496	59	231	4,145	$20.17	$20.99	$8.66	$12.36	↑↑	↔	↑	↓↓	112
Northern Neck, VA	5.3%	67	31	101	293	$15.01	$20.78	$8.27	$9.73	↓↓	↓↓	↓↓	↑↑	195
Oakhurst–Coarsegold, CA	9.5%	885	250	467	2,564	$19.08	$12.05	$11.19	$16.42	↑↑	↔	↔	↑↑	67
Ocala, FL	7.3%	1,769	382	1,443	4,023	$17.26	$25.78	$9.15	$12.97	↓	↔	↑	↔	86
Ocean City, MD	6.5%	247	195	602	1,075	$19.54	$19.37	$8.92	$10.94	↓	↓	↓	↑↑	161
Oxford, MS	7.7%	344	151	297	738	$16.59	$18.73	$7.47	$14.99	↑↑	↔	↓	↓	117
Pagosa Springs, CO	14.5%	112	180	144	505	$15.14	$17.76	$7.04	$5.56	↔	↓↓	↓↓	↔	134
Pahrump Valley, NV	9.8%	235	326	261	295	$20.60	$18.31	$7.67	$18.59	↓↓	↑↑	↑	↑	70
Palmer–Wasilla, AK	7.3%	139	113	392	916	$21.12	$14.60	$12.26	$11.83	↑↑	↔	↓	↑↑	124
★Palm Springs–Coachella Valley, CA	9.5%	10,723	3,590	13,482	26,430	$21.31	$19.98	$11.01	$13.88	↑↑	↑↑	↑↑	↑↑	14
Panama City, FL	8.2%	206	413	927	5,391	$18.27	$25.50	$8.32	$13.53	↔	↑	↑	↑	47
Paradise–Magalia, CA	5.7%	1,071	496	833	3,057	$19.18	$23.59	$9.16	$13.10	↑	↔	↑	↑↑	116
Park City, UT	17.4%	423	1,066	1,141	3,533	$18.04	$20.85	$8.18	$13.66	↑↑	↓	↑	↔	48
Payson, AZ	11.5%	660	352	470	877	$15.23	$10.17	$6.49	$9.55	↓↓	↓	↔	↑↑	93
Pendleton District, SC	4.4%	231	106	247	506	$17.52	$19.57	$9.27	$13.60	↓	↑↑	↓	↑	135
★Pensacola, FL	7.8%	320	419	999	11,137	$17.53	$28.62	$9.39	$12.33	↑	↑	↑↑	↔	29
Petoskey–Harbor Springs, MI	7.1%	178	64	364	728	$17.89	$15.05	$10.13	$13.95	↔	↑	↓	↑↑	127
Pike County, PA	7.1%	229	86	285	465	$18.82	$16.97	$8.22	$11.99	↑	↓	↓	↔	151
★Placer County, CA	11.0%	2,614	1,667	3,950	7,561	$21.03	$32.36	$11.84	$16.74	↑	↑↑	↑↑	↔	7
Port Angeles–Sequim, WA	6.4%	555	256	158	1,047	$19.27	$15.39	$9.35	$10.20	↓↓	↔	↓	↑↑	143
Port Charlotte, FL	11.9%	866	415	1,419	5,302	$19.80	$20.36	$8.84	$11.86	↓↓	↓	↑	↔	56
Port St. Lucie, FL	6.3%	782	260	977	1,946	$19.55	$24.28	$8.44	$13.25	↔	↔	↔	↑↑	126
Port Townsend, WA	11.6%	75	80	157	1,255	$18.39	$11.73	$7.14	$8.95	↓↓	↓↓	↓	↑	125
Prescott–Prescott Valley, AZ	11.6%	906	790	1,109	5,234	$16.72	$13.93	$8.21	$10.93	↓↓	↓	↑	↓	57
Rabun County, GA	5.1%	80	26	50	193	$15.07	$17.30	$8.13	$9.75	↓↓	↓↓	↓↓	↓↓	198
Rehoboth Bay–Indian River Bay, DE	6.6%	246	895	1,697	2,379	$18.99	$23.96	$10.73	$11.53	↓	↔	↑	↓	110

continued

★ = *in the top 30 places for part-time job opportunities*

		New Jobs In . . .				Typical Hourly Pay				Part-time Job Market				
PLACE	FORE-CAST	GOVERN-MENT	FIRE	RETAIL	SERV-ICES	GOVERN-MENT	FIRE	RETAIL	SERV-ICES	COMPETI-TION	JOB QUALITY	JOB VARIETY	UNEMPLOY-MENT RISK	RANK
★Rio Rancho, NM	14.4%	1,937	271	659	868	$16.39	$16.11	$7.38	$9.33	↑	↑↑	↔	↔	20
Rockport-Aransas Pass, TX	6.3%	91	187	50	264	$15.88	$12.18	$7.00	$7.91	↓↓	↓↓	↓↓	↑	193
Roswell, NM	5.1%	130	52	289	583	$18.17	$18.91	$8.39	$11.42	↔	↑↑	↓	↑	137
Ruidoso, NM	7.2%	87	53	130	435	$16.93	$14.52	$7.25	$9.58	↓↓	↓↓	↓↓	↑	186
St. Augustine, FL	7.7%	252	559	745	2,732	$18.28	$33.07	$8.21	$13.85	↓	↑	↔	↓↓	81
St. George-Zion, UT	19.1%	907	1,475	2,028	4,842	$15.76	$15.26	$9.23	$11.48	↑↑	↓	↑↑	↓	42
St. Jay-Northeast Kingdom, VT	5.5%	156	32	69	576	$16.25	$20.91	$8.57	$11.06	↔	↓	↓↓	↔	182
St. Marys, GA	5.7%	154	4	167	947	$13.66	$15.07	$7.06	$10.92	↑↑	↑↑	↓	↔	120
St. Simons-Jekyll Islands, GA	7.3%	150	98	571	2,159	$18.30	$25.82	$7.99	$12.36	↔	↑	↔	↓	98
Sandpoint-Lake Pend Oreille, ID	9.8%	143	313	569	799	$15.67	$16.18	$8.11	$9.12	↓	↓↓	↓	↑↑	131
San Juan Islands, WA	10.9%	62	91	55	804	$17.04	$12.83	$8.14	$8.33	↓↓	↓↓	↓↓	↔	141
Santa Barbara, CA	5.6%	2,360	1,186	1,787	6,964	$21.23	$33.79	$10.21	$17.34	↑	↑↑	↑↑	↔	50
★Santa Fe, NM	9.0%	1,128	822	1,305	3,724	$18.94	$31.37	$13.65	$14.65	↓	↑↑	↑	↓	30
★Sarasota, FL	9.8%	914	1,073	1,779	16,181	$21.08	$39.63	$11.43	$14.41	↓↓	↑	↑↑	↓↓	16
Savannah, GA	4.6%	554	-102	2,102	4,700	$19.07	$20.86	$9.06	$15.58	↑	↑↑	↑	↔	87
★Scottsdale, AZ	11.1%	23,429	26,766	34,556	109,089	$20.66	$42.30	$10.91	$18.02	↑	↑↑	↑↑	↓	4
Sebring-Avon Park, FL	7.1%	500	6	-33	1,433	$17.25	$20.95	$8.55	$10.86	↓↓	↓↓	↓	↑↑	162
Sedona, AZ	10.7%	1,123	921	1,840	4,048	$17.59	$15.33	$7.72	$11.79	↑↑	↔	↑	↑↑	51
Silver City, NM	6.7%	277	82	181	206	$14.91	$13.08	$5.68	$7.17	↓↓	↓	↓↓	↑↑	171
Silverthorne-Breckenridge, CO	11.5%	268	366	548	1,393	$18.02	$23.22	$9.00	$12.58	↑↑	↓	↔	↓↓	88
Smith Mountain Lake, VA	6.2%	502	40	514	1,831	$16.57	$15.46	$7.86	$9.65	↓	↓↓	↔	↓	157
Sonora-Twain Harte, CA	5.9%	721	153	60	662	$19.20	$13.62	$7.94	$12.93	↓	↔	↓	↑↑	148
Southern Berkshire County, MA	3.8%	294	125	174	2,491	$18.60	$34.85	$10.79	$13.33	↔	↑	↔	↔	123
Southern Pines-Pinehurst, NC	6.7%	287	165	256	1,736	$15.54	$25.14	$8.57	$16.73	↓	↑	↔	↔	111
Southport-Brunswick Islands, NC	13.1%	391	990	874	2,051	$16.46	$16.54	$9.24	$10.45	↓↓	↓	↔	↑	59
State College, PA	7.4%	3,495	403	943	2,450	$14.81	$22.09	$7.43	$13.09	↑↑	↔	↑	↓↓	84
Sullivan County, NY	3.6%	238	99	133	591	$25.09	$23.70	$7.67	$12.21	↔	↑	↓	↑	154
Summerville, SC	8.5%	302	110	537	1,508	$15.94	$17.81	$8.28	$11.05	↑	↔	↔	↓	101
Taos, NM	9.8%	295	259	271	755	$15.81	$17.25	$8.53	$9.16	↓	↓↓	↓	↑↑	132
Thomasville, GA	7.9%	122	55	175	1,669	$15.54	$21.97	$8.46	$14.94	↑	↑	↓	↔	96
Toms River-Barnegat Bay, NJ	5.5%	1,069	619	2,669	6,097	$22.41	$25.61	$10.89	$13.74	↔	↑↑	↑↑	↑	75
Traverse City, MI	7.3%	229	355	1,077	2,087	$18.03	$23.02	$10.36	$14.39	↑	↑↑	↔	↔	72
Tryon, NC	8.6%	54	62	90	306	$16.24	$16.10	$6.44	$10.30	↓↓	↓↓	↓↓	↓↓	163
★Tucson, AZ	8.8%	6,749	2,201	5,453	22,096	$18.37	$21.76	$9.07	$13.17	↑	↑	↑↑	↓	18
Vero Beach, FL	7.9%	582	355	615	2,553	$20.63	$35.08	$9.07	$14.63	↓↓	↑	↔	↑↑	77
★Victorville-Apple Valley, CA	7.7%	8,426	2,966	10,766	24,009	$22.52	$34.20	$11.10	$14.43	↑↑	↑↑	↑↑	↑	19
Waynesville, NC	6.7%	280	171	401	638	$16.29	$17.68	$8.67	$9.63	↓↓	↓	↓	↔	157
Wenatchee, WA	7.1%	384	113	634	1,833	$20.87	$21.65	$8.93	$14.05	↑	↔	↔	↑↑	113
Western St. Tammany Parish, LA	6.8%	923	594	1,986	4,276	$17.10	$19.49	$8.29	$12.87	↑	↓	↑	↔	107
Whidbey Island, WA	6.3%	161	292	374	1,057	$18.84	$13.64	$9.09	$9.34	↔	↑	↓	↑	119
★Wickenburg, AZ	11.1%	23,429	26,766	34,556	109,089	$20.66	$42.30	$10.91	$18.02	↑	↑↑	↑↑	↓	4
Williamsburg, VA	8.7%	647	835	1,065	1,958	$17.86	$30.49	$8.20	$12.54	↑	↔	↔	↑↑	73
Wimberley, TX	14.4%	1,199	1,073	2,235	3,151	$15.50	$15.95	$8.91	$9.47	↑↑	↓↓	↑	↓	60
Woodstock, VT	4.4%	178	109	135	953	$17.66	$21.74	$8.17	$12.25	↓	↔	↓	↓↓	164
York Beaches, ME	5.8%	687	317	799	3,100	$18.31	$20.45	$9.45	$12.01	↔	↑	↑	↓	101
Yuma, AZ	6.7%	1,197	301	1,161	2,261	$16.44	$20.81	$9.31	$11.27	↑	↔	↑	↑↑	97

★ = in the top 30 places for part-time job opportunities

It's dryly said that job searching means having to listen to no, no, no, no, no . . . and no one more time, before finally hearing yes. Landing a good part-time job isn't any different, except when it means *creating* one with an employer who isn't looking, or interviewing with an employer who is looking but hasn't the slightest idea what to do with an older applicant. In these situations, you may be in for a long series of no's.

SOME UNVOICED EMPLOYER OBJECTIONS

Are we getting mixed signals, or what? We hear that our 60s are the new 40s. We read that within a few years, government and business may face an "experience crisis" as one in five seasoned workers heads out the door for retirement.

So what do we make of scuttlebutt that finding a good, interesting, and challenging part-time or seasonal job is tough? Actually, it is tough for anyone. But while job discrimination on the basis of age is against the law, you may still be a victim of what labor economists call "statistical" discrimination when an employer makes the following assumptions about all older persons applying for a job:

- You want a job that isn't available.

- You have old-fashioned, conservative values.

- You haven't the same economic incentive to work that younger workers have.

- You don't have the stamina or the flexibility.

- You want more money because you have more experience.

- You'll call in sick more often than younger workers.

- Your fringe coverage—life insurance, health insurance, and pension benefits—will cost more than fringes for younger applicants.

- Your prospects for staying with a job and justifying the employer's investment in on-the-job training are less than those of a younger worker.

- You're preoccupied with the past, a slate upon which nothing more can be written.

All of these objections somehow work themselves into the "overqualified" catchall; it's the word most frequently used by an employer when turning down older people who've applied for a job.

Anyone who has worked 20, 30, or 40 years is overqualified by standard definition. Why not ask the employer what he or she means by being overqualified? If you'll go to work at the going rate, plus bring experience and maturity to the job, won't that mean that the cost of your productivity will be less than or equal to a younger worker's? If you're already covered by Medicare and Social Security, won't the employer avoid the cost of health insurance and a pension plan if you're hired? If the average tenure of younger workers in certain jobs is less than the shelf life of yogurt, mightn't that make you a better bet for longevity?

JOB SEARCHING

The number of part-time jobs has rocketed since the 1990s, often as a consequence of corporate downsizing. Most of these jobs are found in retail trade; in services; and in finance, insurance, and real estate. Here are some useful strategies for searching out good opportunities.

Focus on Small Businesses & Nonprofit Organizations

Large employers often have policies against part-time employment. Smaller companies are more flexible. Moreover, small businesses compete with larger employers for good workers, not by offering more money, but by offering informal, adaptable working conditions. Finally, older workers cast off from large corporations start small businesses (fewer than 250 employees), and economists expect more job creation in these organizations than in larger firms.

Many of the most interesting jobs are found in the nonprofit sector—libraries, museums, colleges and universities, hospitals, and human service organizations. Like small businesses, they offer flexibility instead of big money.

PART-TIME EMPLOYERS:
A SHORT DIRECTORY

Depending on the product or service they sell, America's millions of businesses are pigeonholed into more than 20,000 slots by the federal government. Here's a selected list, grouped under the three broadest classes—finance, insurance, and real estate; retail trade; and services—that (1) are found nearly everywhere; (2) offer part-time and seasonal flexibility; and (3) are businesses where older adults are finding jobs.

FINANCE, INSURANCE & REAL ESTATE

Depository Institutions
Commercial banks
Savings institutions
Credit unions

Nondepository Institutions
Federally sponsored credit institutions
Personal credit institutions
Business credit institutions
Mortgage bankers and brokers

Insurance Carriers
Life insurance
Medical service and health insurance
Fire, marine, and casualty insurance
Surety insurance
Title insurance
Pension, health, and welfare funds

Real Estate
Real estate operators and lessors
Real estate agents and managers
Title abstract offices
Subdividers and developers

RETAIL TRADE

Building Materials & Garden Supplies
Lumber and other building materials
Paint, glass, and wallpaper stores
Hardware stores
Retail nurseries and garden stores
Mobile home dealers

General Merchandise Stores
Department stores
Variety stores

Food Stores
Grocery stores
Meat and fish markets
Fruit and vegetable markets
Candy, nut, and confectionery stores
Dairy products stores
Retail bakeries

Automotive Dealers & Service Stations
New and used car dealers
Auto and home supply stores
Gasoline service stations
Boat dealers
Recreational vehicle dealers
Motorcycle dealers

Apparel & Accessory Stores
Men's and boys' clothing stores
Women's clothing stores
Women's accessory and specialty stores
Children's and infants' wear stores
Family clothing stores
Shoe stores

Furniture & Home Furnishings Stores
Furniture stores
Household appliance stores
Radio, TV, and electronic stores

Miscellaneous Retail
Drug stores and proprietary stores
Liquor stores
Used merchandise stores
Nonstore retailers (mail-order firms)

SERVICES

Hotels & Other Lodging Places
Hotels and motels
Rooming and boarding houses
Camps and recreational vehicle parks
Membership-basis organization hotels

Personal Services
Laundry, cleaning, and garment services
Photographic studios, portrait
Beauty shops
Barber shops
Shoe repair and shoeshine parlors
Funeral service and crematories

Business Services

Advertising

Credit reporting and collection

Mailing, reproduction, stenographic

Services to buildings

Miscellaneous equipment rental and leasing

Personnel supply services

Computer and data processing services

Auto Repair, Services & Parking

Automotive rentals

Automobile parking

Automotive repair shops

Miscellaneous Repair Services

Electrical repair shops

Watch, clock, and jewelry repair

Reupholstery and furniture repair

Motion Pictures

Motion picture production and services

Motion picture distribution and services

Motion picture theaters

Video tape rental

Amusement & Recreation Services

Dance studios, schools, and halls

Producers, orchestras, entertainers

Bowling centers

Commercial sports

Miscellaneous amusement, recreation services

Health Services

Offices and clinics of medical doctors

Offices and clinics of dentists

Offices of osteopathic physicians

Offices of other health practitioners

Nursing and personal care facilities

Hospitals

Medical and dental laboratories

Home healthcare services

Legal Services

Legal services

Educational Services

Elementary and secondary schools

Colleges and universities

Libraries

Vocational schools

Social Services

Individual and family services

Job training and related services

Child day-care services

Residential care

Museums, Botanical, Zoological Gardens

Museums and art galleries

Botanical and zoological gardens

Membership Organizations

Business associations

Professional organizations

Labor organizations

Civic and social associations

Political organizations

Religious organizations

Engineering & Management Services

Engineering and architectural services

Accounting, auditing, and bookkeeping

Research and testing services

Management and public relations

Respond to Full-Time Job Openings

If you've identified an employer that can use your skills, buttonhole the boss for a full-time job. If he or she hasn't any, suggest a part-time alternative. If the company has no experience with part-timers, suggest a trial period.

Too often part-timers pass by advertised positions that are full-time. Many 8-hour-a-day jobs can be shared.

Don't Forget the Government

Part-time opportunities are expanding within the federal government, partly because of a regulation that requires federal agencies to introduce short-schedule positions and prorate compensation and benefits according to the number of hours worked. The good jobs, however, are reserved for persons who've previously worked for Uncle Sam for at least 3 years.

All state governments have agencies with part-time positions. The key is identifying the agencies and where in the state the positions are (don't assume there are no state government jobs outside of the capital city). A good place to start is the state's aging or adult services office.

Try Temporary Work

One major reason why agencies that supply temporary workers are hiring older persons is that the work is

The Economy

101

usually full-time for a limited period. For job seekers with child-care needs, this isn't the most attractive situation. Agencies specializing in clerical work dominate the Yellow Pages, but firms that engage part-time engineers, accountants, and healthcare professionals are growing.

Volunteer

The "Me Decade" has given way to the "Decency Decade," if you follow pop sociologists on the talk shows. Today, one of every four Americans over the age of 14 is involved in some kind of volunteer work. The value of all their volunteered time adds up to more than $100 billion a year.

Volunteer positions frequently turn into paid positions. If anything, they provide the setting for polishing up existing job skills and acquiring new skills and experience for seeking paid employment.

Services

A generation ago, local planners in attractive rural spots whispered to one another, "Here comes the Gray Peril. They'll bid up real estate, string out the visiting nurses, slow down traffic, tap into Meals on Wheels, and vote down school bond issues, all without contributing a nickel to the economy."

How times change. Today, places are courting retired persons as ardently as they're chasing fickle tourists and light industry. A few years ago, Alamogordo, New Mexico, offered to pay half your moving costs. Hot Springs, Arkansas, calls out the volunteer Blue Coats to show you around and even buy you lunch. Mississippi canceled taxes on Social Security and all public and private pensions and is pondering free license plates.

Not for nothing. A retired household moving in from outside can have the same impact as three new light industrial jobs, some planners figure. Local economies get better when they float on a cushion of Social Security, pensions, and asset income. Talk to a trust officer in a bank in downtown Grand Junction, Colorado, or Eagle River, Wisconsin, and he or she will go on at length about how banks wouldn't be in business if not for the millions they oversee for older depositors.

Some rural spots owe their growth to older adults who moved there *because* the area was short on services—and short on taxes too. To the confusion of municipal officials, after bouncing over dirt roads, smelling landfill effluvia, and looking in vain for the *Wall Street Journal* at the public library, the newcomers soon show up at public meetings demanding better services and offering higher property taxes in return.

In many rural areas, however, the myth persists that footloose older adults want big-city benefits without paying for them. This chapter focuses on five public services: **airports, hospitals, physicians, public libraries,** and **continuing education.** Wouldn't it be better to know that the services you expect are in place, rather than being disappointed that they aren't?

GENERAL HOSPITAL SERVICES

For many of us, healthcare determines whether to stay in familiar territory or move to a distant place. When you're in your 60s, the odds of sitting in a doctor's waiting room triple from when you were in your 30s. Checking into the hospital for a short stay is also likely. With each passing year, the bills for physician fees and prescriptions get bigger and bigger.

Retirement Places Rated doesn't judge the quality of healthcare; it simply looks at the place's supply. While larger places have an edge, this doesn't mean quality healthcare in a small Ozark clinic is a contradiction in terms. Nor does it necessarily mean you're better off in a university medical center in Chapel Hill, North Carolina. The quality of medical care that people get depends on their ability to pay for it, the luck of the draw, professional competence, and human error.

The term *health* can also refer to its opposite: illness. A hospital isn't really a healthcare institution; its business is to take care of sick people. The truly healthy need little medical care except for an occasional shot or checkup; the unhealthy need a lot more.

Just as not all M.D.s see patients, not all hospitals handle typical illnesses and emergencies. Many of the 5,465 facilities certified by Medicare for inpatient treatment are hospitals that exclusively treat chronic diseases or alcohol and drug addiction, or they may be burn centers, psychiatric hospitals, or rehabilitation hospitals. *Retirement Places Rated* counts only general hospitals where most patients stay less than 30 days. In addition to Medicare certification, most are accredited for acute care by the Joint Commission on Accreditation of Health Care Organizations (JCAHO).

Though most operate as nonprofits, general hospitals are actually businesses that can't afford to go deeply into the red. They offer common services such as an emergency department, respiratory therapy, intensive care, ultrasound, a blood bank, a histopathology laboratory, and outpatient surgery. Some stake out market niches with an additional menu—a sports medicine clinic, a women's health center, an open-heart surgery unit, a certified trauma center, or an X-ray radiation therapy unit.

Most hospitals are *nonteaching*. That is, they're staffed almost entirely by "attending physicians" who have an outside practice, are paid by the patient, and have admitting privileges at the hospital.

Teaching hospitals grant admitting privileges to attending physicians, but they also employ full-time "house staff," taking in first-year and advanced residents and a teaching faculty. The attending physician heads a team of house staff members to make important decisions about a patient's care. The patient pays the attending physician; the hospital pays the house staff.

If an area appeals to you but it doesn't have a hospital, don't be discouraged. There are usually good

Of course your health is excellent. For a point in your life that's supposed to be upbeat, *acute care, Medicare,* and *continuing care* are discouraging words indeed. Sure you detest niggling taxes that fund an elaborate menu of municipal services. Fleeing these taxes is one reason you're moving. Education after retirement? You haven't thought about it and probably won't. Your race is run; there's no further need for courses and credentials.

If you agree with all of the above, heed some advice from others who had the same convictions about learning, death, and taxes when they made their own move.

You won't miss the congestion and tension of city life if you settle in the bucolic sticks, but you will miss the services you took for granted before you moved.

Though you'll rarely see sobering pictures of ambulances, gowned surgeons, and wheelchairs in slick literature promoting retirement places, in time the whole household will become a big consumer of medical care. Make sure specialists and hospitals are available *before* you settle in.

Position and possessions ultimately won't matter in later life. What matters are friends, a sense of humor, and a well-furnished mind. It's said that college towns have high percentages of young people *and* retired people because both groups are there for a good time. But college towns also offer a definite advantage: a higher level of human services than places of similar or even larger size. In retirement, these human services truly count.

facilities a short drive away. Residents of Ocean City on Maryland's Eastern Shore may have to drive to Baltimore for specialized care, but Dorchester General Hospital up the shore in Cambridge or Peninsula General Hospital in Salisbury are more than adequate for routine care.

OFFICE-BASED PHYSICIANS

Not every M.D. is listed in the Yellow Pages. Some are hospital administrators, medical school professors, journalists, lawyers, or researchers for pharmaceutical companies. Others work for the federal government's Public Health Service, Veteran's Administration, or Department of Defense. Still others are in residency training or are full-time members of hospital staffs. When it comes to doctors, what really counts is the number of physicians who have offices and see patients.

PAGING DR. FINDER

Learning whether cardiologists, urologists, psychiatrists, or other specialists practice in a distant area needn't be a telephonic drudgery. Call the local hospital's public relations office for a free copy of their Physician Locator or M.D. Directory. Hospitals in competitive markets know they'll more likely have you as a customer when you're ill if they can introduce you early on to an M.D. who uses their facilities.

These "Dr. Finders" aren't mere telephone contact sheets. Often they're photo galleries of physicians with capsule résumés on their education from college through medical school to residency, their specialties, and their board certifications. You can also learn if they take walk-in patients or accept Medicare assignments and whether another doctor will cover for them on their day off. Some of these guides even detail their civic clubs and what they like to do on weekends.

Sentiment, their perceptions of local quality of life, or both determine where doctors end up practicing. But mainly it's economics. The beginning physician has invested 3 to 7 years in graduate medical education and frequently has to start out with an enormous loan to repay. Some begin work on a hospital staff, develop a practice, get loose from the hospital, and open an office. Others are recruited into partnerships or group practices through ads like these from the *Journal of the American Medical Association*:

North Carolina: Expanding group recruiting two experienced Emergency Physicians. Double coverage and flexible schedule. Excellent total compensation package includes paid vacation. CME time and occurrence malpractice. 22,000 census. Waterfront community. Community hospital closest to Outer Banks and ocean. Send C.V. to Box 1945, c/o JAMA.

Cardiologist—BC/BE wanted to join a well-established solo, Board Certified, noninvasive Cardiologist in a nice Oregon coastal community. Facility available for Echo-Doppler, Holter, Stress test, Cardiac Nuclear Studies, Temporary and Permanent Pacemaker, Swan Ganz, HIS bundle. Excellent salary and benefits. Early partnership. Send C.V. to Box 6199, c/o JAMA.

By whatever means they launch themselves professionally, the major concern of new M.D.s who wish to specialize is a place's "covered census" or, to be blunt, the number of potential patients who are insured.

Services

AMA PHYSICIAN CATEGORIES

The American Medical Association (AMA) classifies a physician as a general practitioner, a specialist in family medicine, a medical specialist, a surgeon, or another specialist by 35 specialties in which the physician reports spending the largest number of his or her professional hours.

GENERAL PRACTITIONERS/FAMILY MEDICINE

General practice
Family medicine

MEDICAL SPECIALISTS

Allergy
Cardiovascular diseases
Dermatology
Gastroenterology
Internal medicine
Pediatric allergy
Pediatric cardiology
Pediatrics
Pulmonary diseases

SURGICAL SPECIALISTS

Colon and rectal surgery
General surgery
Neurological surgery
Obstetrics and Gynecology
Ophthalmology
Orthopedic surgery
Otolaryngology
Plastic surgery
Thoracic surgery
Urology

OTHER SPECIALISTS

Aerospace medicine
Anesthesiology

Child psychiatry
Diagnostic radiology
Forensic pathology
General preventive medicine
Neurology
Occupational medicine
Pathology
Physical medicine and rehabilitation
Psychiatry
Public health
Radiology
Therapeutic radiology

The American Hospital Association (AHA) defines 108 hospital services. Here are the 85 major ones.

Adult day-care program

Alcohol/drug abuse or dependency inpatient unit

Alcohol/drug abuse or dependency outpatient services

Alzheimer's diagnostic/assessment services

Angioplasty

Arthritis treatment center

Birthing room/LDRP room

Blood bank

Burn-care unit

Cardiac catheterization laboratory

Cardiac intensive-care unit

Cardiac rehabilitation program

Chaplaincy/Pastoral care services

Chronic obstructive pulmonary disease services

Community health promotion

Comprehensive geriatric assessment

CT scanner

Diagnostic radioisotope facility

Emergency department

Emergency department social work services

Emergency response (geriatric)

Ethics committee

Extracorporeal shock wave lithotripter

Fitness center

General inpatient care for AIDS/ARC

Genetic counseling/screening services

Geriatric acute-care unit

Geriatric clinics

Health sciences library

Hemodialysis

Histopathology laboratory

HIV/AIDS unit

Home health services

Hospice

Magnetic resonance imaging

Mammography diagnostic

Mammography screening

Medical surgical or other intensive-care unit

Megavoltage radiation therapy

Neonatal intensive-care unit

Noninvasive cardiac assessment services

Obstetrics unit

Occupational health services

Occupational therapy services

Oncology services

Open-heart surgery

Organ/tissue transplant

Organized outpatient services

Organized social work services

Orthopedic surgery

Outpatient social work services

Outpatient surgery services

Patient education

Patient representative services

Pediatric acute inpatient unit

Physical therapy services

Psychiatric child/adolescent services

Psychiatric consultation/liaison services

Psychiatric education services

Psychiatric emergency services

Psychiatric geriatric services

Psychiatric inpatient services

Psychiatric outpatient services

Psychiatric partial hospitalization program

Radioactive implants

Recreational therapy services

Rehabilitation inpatient unit

Rehabilitation outpatient services

Reproductive health services

Respiratory therapy services

Respite care

Senior membership program

Single photon emission computed tomography (SPECT)

Skilled nursing or other long-term-care facility

Specialized outpatient program for AIDS/ARC

Speech therapy services

Sports medicine clinic/services

Therapeutic radioisotope facility

Trauma center (certified)

Ultrasound

Volunteer services department

Women's health center/services

Worksite health promotion

X-ray radiation therapy

The American Medical Association (AMA) classifies office-based physicians into four groups, depending on how they spend their professional hours. Unless they specialize in pediatrics, obstetrics, or child psychiatry, physicians are waking up to the reality that their typical patients are now older than 55—in contrast to a generation just past when they were younger than 50.

General practitioners and specialists in family medicine use all accepted methods of medical care. They treat diseases and injuries, provide preventive care, give routine checkups, prescribe drugs, and do some surgery. According to the new AMA physician classifications, M.D.s in family medicine may have subspecialties in geriatric medicine, psychiatry, sports medicine, and internal medicine. They also refer patients to medical specialists.

Medical specialists focus on specific medical disciplines such as cardiology, allergy, gastroenterology, and dermatology. They're the largest of the AMA groups because, frankly, specializing is where the money is.

They're likely to give attention to surgical and non-surgical approaches to treatment. If it's decided that surgery is the method of treatment, they refer patients to surgeons.

Surgical specialists, the best paid of the AMA's groups, operate on a regular basis several times a week. The letters F.A.C.S. (Fellow of the American College of Surgeons) after a surgeon's name indicate that he or she has passed an evaluation of surgical training and skills as well as ethical fitness.

Other specialists concentrate on disciplines as familiar as psychiatry and neurology or as exotic as diagnostic radiology, aerospace medicine, and forensic pathology.

PUBLIC LIBRARIES

Enter the handsome Craven County library on a summer afternoon in the heart of New Bern, North Carolina, plop down in a comfortable wingback chair among the local histories, bestsellers, out-of-town newspapers, and data terminals, and you'll get so comfortable in the air-conditioned quiet you'll want to hang out there all day long.

Until its door is padlocked after a municipal budget cut or a treasured librarian is laid off, one service taken for granted is the local public library. There are more than 9,000 systems in this country. From all that, you may expect libraries to be the most plentiful of public services. They are. Though you'll find current fiction and nonfiction on the shelves everywhere, you won't always locate issues of the *Wall Street Journal, Morningstar, Vanity Fair,* or *Wired.* Nor will you always find a community fax machine or an Internet connection to look up that book mentioned on one of the talk shows.

Libraries and library resources are concentrated in larger places. Tucson's 1.2 million books are shelved in the main building on North Stone Avenue and in 20 neighborhood branches throughout surrounding Pima County. Laguna Beach is part of the huge Orange County Public Library system, with more than 2.5 million books dispersed among 31 branches. But the size of the collection tells only half the story. Measured by the number of books per person, the supply is greater in smaller places, especially college towns and towns in New England, where some endowed public libraries are beginning their third century of operation.

SHOW ME YOUR RECENTLY USED LIBRARY CARD

When a library's annual circulation figure is divided by the number of books in its collection, the result is the collection turnover—a sign of local reading. The average turnover for places in this book is 2.8. In these 15 locations, it's nearly twice that number.

CONTINUING EDUCATION

When we look back over our lives, the autobiographies we wanted to write are different from the ones that finally get written. There's one thread in the stories: the quick passage through school in youth to a long period of raising a family and working throughout the middle years, ending up in a retirement that's all too short. "Is that all there is?" sang the late Peggy Lee.

School, then work, then retirement—the *linear life pattern* some call it—no longer fits people's lengthening lives. Today the post-retirement pattern might be this: retirement, school, work, retirement, school, work, more school, retirement, work. If you will miss the world of work, an idle retirement will certainly be an empty time if there weren't opportunities for learning new things.

Read the smarmy feature articles in newspapers 20 or so years ago about the grandmother who started her masters in social work or the retired U.S. Marine Corps major general who got an A in art history and you'll realize older students were looked on as interlopers in the classroom.

They aren't any longer. Gray-haired students cruise the stadium parking lot at the University of Arkansas looking for an open slot. They push a tray down the cafeteria line at the Viking Union at Western Washington University, and they scold you for smoking on the steps at the University of Vermont's library. Like any student, they buttonhole instructors after class, bang out assigned papers, and cram for final exams.

The average age of students is rising, particularly at public colleges. To fill classrooms, colleges and universities cut tuition fees or waive them for retired people who want to earn a degree, finish one, or just study for no reason other than fulfillment.

Of the 200 places featured in this book, 139 have at least one college. *Two-year colleges* include junior colleges, community colleges, and technical institutes that offer at least 1 year of college-level courses leading to an associate degree or are creditable toward a bachelor's degree. Most 2-year colleges are nonprofit and public. *Four-year colleges* offer undergraduate courses leading to a Bachelor of Arts or Bachelor of Science degree and may also offer graduate courses. Though most students in 4-year colleges are attending publicly controlled ones, most 4-year colleges are nonprofit and private.

JUDGING: SERVICES

Services are in greater supply in bigger places than in smaller ones—that's simple common sense. This doesn't mean your need for a cardiologist or an allergist, a public library that gets *Value Line* and *Architectural Digest,* and a schedule of college courses can be met only in places the size of Tucson or Santa Barbara.

Rating places by their services can't be done to everyone's satisfaction, *Retirement Places Rated* admits. Services constitute a laundry list of everything from trash pickup and street repair to emergency medical teams and firefighters to gypsy moth spraying and sewage treatment.

If you agree that air travel, a broad range of hospital services, a choice of general practice and specialist physicians, public libraries that are well looked after, and the chance to take a college course or finish a degree is as good a set of services as any other, then you won't always be disappointed by smaller places, particularly college towns with a medical school.

In spotlighting these services, *Retirement Places Rated* doesn't judge the quality of local hospitals, the credentials of local physicians, the breadth of local college course offerings, or the staff attentiveness at the local public library. This guide simply indicates the presence of selected services that most persons agree enhance retirement living.

A place's final score is derived from the scores it receives in the following four areas.

GENERAL HOSPITAL SERVICES

Grading here is based on accessibility of hospital services defined by the American Hospital Association (AHA). This figure is then scaled against a standard in which the accessibility of all 108 AHA services gets a 100, the average number of services a 50, and no services a 0.

For example, the menu of services available at Durango, Colorado's hospital—the Mercy Medical Center—is good for a middling score of 56. Consider retirement places with medical schools: Columbia, Missouri; Iowa City, Iowa; and Hanover, New Hampshire. The choice of hospital services in those smaller areas is nearly as good as it is in Maricopa County in Arizona and Orange County in California, where retirement places found in each of those populous areas earn a score of 100 in this category.

OFFICE-BASED PHYSICIANS

From a consumer's viewpoint, the fewer patients per physician the better. The M.D. will more likely accept new patients and Medicare reimbursement, and medical specialties may be more varied. On average there is a specialist in family medicine for every 4,847 persons, a medical specialist for every 1,030 persons, and a surgeon for every 1,379 persons in the places profiled in this book.

Each place's figures for their own three physician groups are set against a standard where the best number gets 100, the average 50, and the worst a 0. No surprise, the three top locations for this factor—Chapel Hill–Carrboro, North Carolina; Charlottesville, Virginia; and Iowa City, Iowa—are university towns with renowned medical schools.

PUBLIC LIBRARIES

The 805 million books in America's public libraries circulated more than 2 billion times, for an average turnover rate of 2.5. Turnover rate is calculated by dividing any library's annual circulation by its number of books, that is, its holdings. The result shows the activity of a library's collection, indicating the number of times each book would have circulated during the year if circulation had been spread evenly throughout the collection. Among our 200 retirement places, the average turnover rate is 3.2.

Libraries stocking bestsellers will have a higher turnover rate than libraries that emphasize subject depth in their collections and have extensive reference collections—frankly, libraries that are open fewer hours and have books that no one likes to read.

Each place's library turnover rate is scaled against a standard where the highest number gets 100, the average a 50, and the lowest a 0. Places that are part of larger library systems are graded by the figures for the library system's entire legal service area. Fredericksburg–Spotsylvania, Virginia; Alamogordo, New Mexico; and Apalachicola in Florida's panhandle are, respectively, the best, average, and worst for library turnover.

CONTINUING EDUCATION

Grading here is based on the percentage of a place's population enrolled in colleges and universities. Because 2-year institutions cost less and are more likely to grant fee waivers to older adults, they're weighted 1½ times more than private 4-year colleges. Because public 4-year colleges have the same cost advantages plus a greater variety of courses listed in their catalogs as 2-year institutions, they're weighted 2½ times more than private 4-year colleges.

The resulting figure is then scaled against a standard where the highest number gets 100, the average a 50, and the lowest a 0. Enrollment figures are the sum of full-time and part-time students. Institutions offering only graduate-level courses aren't counted.

RANKINGS: SERVICES

Four criteria make up the score for a retirement place's supply of selected services: (1) *short-term general hospital services,* (2) *physicians who treat patients,* (3) *public libraries,* and (4) *continuing education.*

Scores are rounded to one decimal place. Locations with tie scores get the same rank and are listed alphabetically.

Retirement Places from First to Last

RANK	PLACE	SCORE	RANK	PLACE	SCORE
1.	Chapel Hill–Carrboro, NC	100.0	68.	Rehoboth Bay–Indian River Bay, DE	66.3
2.	Iowa City, IA	99.4	69.	Kalispell–Flathead Valley, MT	65.8
3.	Columbia, MO	98.9	70.	Conway, AR	65.3
4.	Madison, WI	98.4	71.	Myrtle Beach, SC	64.8
5.	Gainesville, FL	97.9	72.	Panama City, FL	64.3
6.	Charlottesville, VA	97.4	73.	Jackson Hole, WY	63.8
7.	Thomasville, GA	96.9	74.	Hilton Head Island, SC	62.8
8.	Tucson, AZ	96.4	74.	Beaufort, SC	62.8
9.	Fort Collins–Loveland, CO	95.9	76.	Branson, MO	62.3
10.	Santa Barbara, CA	95.4	77.	East End Long Island, NY	61.8
11.	Bellingham, WA	94.4	78.	Chestertown, MD	61.3
11.	Fayetteville, AR	94.4	79.	Palm Springs–Coachella Valley, CA	60.8
13.	Traverse City, MI	93.9	80.	Mendocino–Fort Bragg, CA	60.3
14.	Laguna Beach–Dana Point, CA	93.4	81.	Fort Myers–Cape Coral, FL	59.7
15.	Burlington, VT	92.9	82.	Bradenton, FL	59.2
16.	Charleston, SC	92.4	83.	Toms River–Barnegat Bay, NJ	58.7
17.	Murray–Kentucky Lake, KY	91.9	84.	Middle Cape Cod, MA	57.7
18.	Asheville, NC	91.4	84.	Wimberley, TX	57.7
19.	Williamsburg, VA	90.9	86.	St. Augustine, FL	57.2
20.	Sedona, AZ	89.9	87.	Southern Pines–Pinehurst, NC	56.7
20.	Flagstaff, AZ	89.9	88.	Naples, FL	56.2
22.	Eugene, OR	89.4	89.	Sonora–Twain Harte, CA	55.7
23.	Hot Springs, AR	88.9	90.	Dahlonega, GA	55.2
24.	Wickenburg, AZ	87.9	91.	Crossville, TN	54.7
24.	Scottsdale, AZ	87.9	92.	Leesburg–Mount Dora, FL	54.2
26.	Athens, GA	87.4	93.	Anacortes, WA	52.7
27.	Boone–Blowing Rock, NC	86.9	93.	East Stroudsburg, PA	52.7
28.	Hattiesburg, MS	86.4	93.	The Big Island, HI	52.7
29.	Pensacola, FL	85.9	96.	Southern Berkshire County, MA	52.2
30.	Bend, OR	85.4	97.	Fairhope–Gulf Shores, AL	51.7
31.	Durango, CO	84.9	98.	Silver City, NM	51.2
32.	Cottonwood–Verde Valley, AZ	83.9	99.	Woodstock, VT	50.7
32.	Prescott–Prescott Valley, AZ	83.9	100.	Cedar City, UT	50.2
34.	Brunswick, ME	83.4	101.	McAllen–Alamo, TX	49.7
35.	Hendersonville–East Flat Rock, NC	82.9	102.	Brevard, NC	49.2
36.	Hanover, NH	81.9	103.	Vero Beach, FL	48.7
36.	Largo, FL	81.9	104.	Grass Valley–Nevada City, CA	48.2
38.	Paradise–Magalia, CA	81.4	105.	Monadnock Region, NH	47.7
39.	Morro Bay–Cambria, CA	80.9	106.	New Bern, NC	47.2
40.	Savannah, GA	80.4	107.	Key West, FL	46.7
41.	Northampton–Amherst, MA	79.8	108.	Lakeland–Winter Haven, FL	46.2
42.	Sarasota, FL	79.3	109.	Georgetown, TX	45.7
43.	Annapolis, MD	78.8	110.	Port St. Lucie, FL	45.2
44.	State College, PA	78.3	111.	Waynesville, NC	44.7
45.	Henderson, NV	77.8	112.	Natchitoches, LA	44.2
46.	Bozeman, MT	77.3	113.	Brownsville, TX	43.7
47.	Carmel–Pebble Beach, CA	76.3	114.	York Beaches, ME	43.2
47.	Fredericksburg–Spotsylvania, VA	76.3	115.	Ocala, FL	42.7
49.	Melbourne–Palm Bay, FL	75.8	116.	Kerrville, TX	42.2
50.	Petoskey–Harbor Springs, MI	75.3	117.	Western St. Tammany Parish, LA	41.7
51.	Grand Junction, CO	74.8	118.	Easton–St. Michaels, MD	40.7
52.	Oxford, MS	74.3	118.	Yuma, AZ	40.7
53.	New Braunfels, TX	73.8	120.	Port Townsend, WA	40.2
54.	St. George–Zion, UT	73.3	121.	St. Jay–Northeast Kingdom, VT	39.6
55.	Placer County, CA	72.8	122.	Lake Havasu City, AZ	38.6
56.	Wenatchee, WA	71.8	122.	Kingman, AZ	38.6
56.	Coeur d'Alene, ID	71.8	124.	Sebring–Avon Park, FL	38.1
58.	Port Angeles–Sequim, WA	71.3	125.	Port Charlotte, FL	37.6
59.	Norfork Lake, AR	70.8	126.	Lake Conroe, TX	37.1
60.	Maryville, TN	70.3	127.	Southport–Brunswick Islands, NC	36.6
61.	St. Simons–Jekyll Islands, GA	69.8	128.	Ruidoso, NM	36.1
62.	Medford–Ashland, OR	69.3	129.	Maui, HI	35.6
63.	Las Cruces, NM	68.8	130.	Sandpoint–Lake Pend Oreille, ID	35.1
64.	Santa Fe, NM	68.3	131.	Taos, NM	34.6
65.	Grants Pass, OR	67.8	132.	Montrose, CO	34.1
66.	Victorville–Apple Valley, CA	67.3	133.	Whidbey Island, WA	33.6
67.	Carson City–Carson Valley, NV	66.8	134.	Camden, ME	33.1

RANK	PLACE	SCORE
135.	Bar Harbor, ME	32.6
136.	Bay St. Louis–Pass Christian, MS	32.1
137.	Martha's Vineyard, MA	31.6
138.	Alamogordo, NM	31.1
139.	Boerne, TX	30.6
140.	Alpine–Big Bend, TX	30.1
141.	Litchfield Hills, CT	29.6
142.	Bisbee, AZ	29.1
143.	Madison, MS	28.1
143.	Las Vegas, NM	28.1
145.	Smith Mountain Lake, VA	27.6
146.	Newport–Lincoln City, OR	27.1
147.	Charles Town–Shepherdstown, WV	26.6
148.	Northern Neck, VA	26.1
149.	Loudoun County, VA	25.6
150.	Fredericksburg, TX	25.1
151.	Lake of the Ozarks, MO	24.6
152.	Door Peninsula, WI	24.1
153.	Beaufort–Atlantic Beach, NC	23.6
154.	Cedar Creek Lake, TX	23.1
155.	Park City, UT	22.6
156.	St. Marys, GA	22.1
157.	Chewelah, WA	21.6
158.	Pendleton District, SC	21.1
159.	Front Royal, VA	20.6
160.	Roswell, NM	20.1
161.	Summerville, SC	19.5
162.	Kissimmee–St. Cloud, FL	19.0
163.	Long Beach Peninsula, WA	18.5
164.	Edenton, NC	18.0
165.	Rabun County, GA	17.5
166.	Tryon, NC	17.0
167.	Sullivan County, NY	16.5

RANK	PLACE	SCORE
168.	Hamilton–Bitterroot Valley, MT	16.0
169.	San Juan Islands, WA	15.0
169.	Ketchum–Sun Valley, ID	15.0
171.	Marble Falls–Lake LBJ, TX	14.5
172.	Delta County, CO	14.0
173.	Payson, AZ	13.5
174.	Lake of the Cherokees, OK	13.0
175.	Cortez, CO	12.5
176.	Nelson County, VA	12.0
177.	Leelanau Peninsula, MI	11.5
178.	Lower Cape May, NJ	11.0
179.	Lake Placid, NY	10.5
180.	Driggs, ID	10.0
181.	Dare Outer Banks, NC	9.5
182.	Eureka Springs, AR	9.0
183.	Rio Rancho, NM	8.5
184.	Palmer–Wasilla, AK	8.0
185.	Silverthorne–Breckenridge, CO	7.5
186.	Ocean City, MD	7.0
187.	Pagosa Springs, CO	6.5
188.	Amador County, CA	6.0
189.	Oakhurst–Coarsegold, CA	5.5
190.	Pike County, PA	5.0
191.	Pahrump Valley, NV	4.5
192.	Brown County, IN	4.0
193.	Hampshire County, WV	3.5
194.	Apalachicola, FL	3.0
195.	Rockport–Aransas Pass, TX	2.5
196.	Eagle River–Woodruff, WI	2.0
197.	Mariposa, CA	1.5
198.	Berkeley Springs, WV	1.0
199.	McCall, ID	0.5
200.	Fairplay, CO	0.0

PLACE PROFILES: SERVICES

The following pages detail general hospital services, physicians treating patients and their specialties, local public libraries, and college-level continuing education in each of the 200 places.

Under the heading *Airline Service* is the location of the nearest Federal Aviation Administration (FAA) "primary" airport, that is, an airport from which more than 10,000 passengers fly out on scheduled commercial airlines per year.

Next to the heading *General Hospitals* is the number of short-stay, Medicare-certified general hospitals and their total beds in parentheses. Numbered underneath are hospitals accredited by the Joint Commission on Accreditation of Health Care Organizations (JCAHO) and institutions that are American Medical Association–approved teaching hospitals. The last figure is the total number of American Hospital Association–defined services available from all general hospitals in the retirement place.

Office-Based Physicians details how many patient-treating M.D.s practice, according to the AMA's basic classifications of Family Medicine, Medical Specialties, and Surgery. To the left of the entries are four letter ratings (AA, A, B, and C, where AA is best and C is fair) describing physician supply per capita.

Public Libraries is a listing of the library system serving the retirement place.

Under the heading *Continuing Education* are the number of community or 2-year college campuses and their enrollment figures (in parentheses) and the names and enrollment figures (in parentheses) of local 4-year institutions—defined here as granting at least a bachelor's degree. Public 4-year institutions, which typically charge less for tuition and often waive or reduce tuition for older adults, are italicized.

The sources for the information include the American Hospital Association, *Guide to the Health Care Field* (hospital accreditation and services), 2006;

American Library Association, *Output Measures for Public Libraries* (public library quality standards), 1987; American Medical Association, *Physician Characteristics and Distribution* (office-based physician classifications and number by county), 2006; U.S. Department of Education, National Center for Education Statistics, online Integrated Postsecondary Education Data System IPEDS (college and university types and enrollments), 2007; and online Library Statistics Program LSP (public library collections and budgets), 2007; and U.S. Department of Health and Human Services, Bureau of Health-Care Professions, Area Resource File (hospital services by county), 2005.

A star (★) preceding a place's name highlights it as one of the top 30 for services.

Alamogordo, NM
Airline Service
El Paso International (ELP)
General Hospitals: 1 (110 beds)
1 accredited, 24 services
Office-Based Physicians
B Family Medicine: 17
C Medical Specialists: 14
C Surgeons: 14
Public Libraries
Alamogordo Public Library
Continuing Education
Two-Year
1 campus, 2,952 students
Rank: 138

Alpine–Big Bend, TX
Airline Service
El Paso International (ELP)
General Hospitals: 1 (29 beds)
1 accredited, 31 services
Office-Based Physicians
AA Family Medicine: 4
C Medical Specialists: 2
C Surgeons: 2
Public Libraries
Alpine Public Library
Continuing Education
Four-Year
Sul Ross State (3,951)
Rank: 140

Amador County, CA
Airline Service
Reno/Tahoe International (RNO)
General Hospitals: 1 (66 beds)
1 accredited, 20 services
Office-Based Physicians
A Family Medicine: 13
C Medical Specialists: 13
C Surgeons: 8
Public Libraries
Amador County Library
Rank: 188

Anacortes, WA
Airline Service
Bellingham International (BLI)
General Hospitals: 2 (231 beds)
1 accredited, 39 services

Office-Based Physicians
AA Family Medicine: 63
C Medical Specialists: 47
C Surgeons: 48
Public Libraries
Anacortes Public Library
Continuing Education
Two-Year
1 campus, 9,383 students
Rank: 93

Annapolis, MD
Airline Service
Baltimore/Washington International (BWI)
General Hospitals: 2 (530 beds)
2 accredited, 103 services
Office-Based Physicians
C Family Medicine: 90
AA Medical Specialists: 361
AA Surgeons: 230
Public Libraries
Anne Arundel Public Library
Continuing Education
Two-Year
1 campus, 20,928 students
Four-Year
St. John's College (629)
U.S. Naval Academy (5,587)
Rank: 43

Apalachicola, FL
Airline Service
Panama City-Bay County International (PFN)
General Hospitals: 1 (25 beds)
15 services
Office-Based Physicians
A Family Medicine: 3
C Medical Specialists: 2
C Surgeons: 2
Public Libraries
Apalachicola Municipal Library
Rank: 194

★ Asheville, NC
Airline Service
Asheville Regional (AVL)
General Hospitals: 2 (971 beds)
2 accredited, 2 teaching, 146 services

Office-Based Physicians
AA Family Medicine: 110
A Medical Specialists: 231
A Surgeons: 178
Public Libraries
Asheville-Buncombe Library
Continuing Education
Two-Year
1 campus, 8,797 students
Four-Year
Montreat College (1,466)
University of North Carolina Asheville (4,107)
Warren Wilson College (940)
Rank: 18

★ Athens, GA
Airline Service
Hartsfield-Jackson Atlanta International (ATL)
General Hospitals: 2 (617 beds)
2 accredited, 117 services
Office-Based Physicians
C Family Medicine: 16
AA Medical Specialists: 87
AA Surgeons: 86
Public Libraries
Athens Regional Library
Continuing Education
Two-Year
1 campus, 5,716 students
Four-Year
University of Georgia (38,863)
Rank: 26

Bar Harbor, ME
Airline Service
Hancock County-Bar Harbor (BHB)
General Hospitals: 3 (98 beds)
1 accredited, 121 services
Office-Based Physicians
AA Family Medicine: 30
C Medical Specialists: 22
C Surgeons: 22
Public Libraries
23 independent libraries
Continuing Education
Four-Year
Maine Maritime Academy (773)
Rank: 135

Retirement Places Rated

Bay St. Louis–Pass Christian, MS

Airline Service
  Gulfport-Biloxi International (GPT)
General Hospitals: 5 (1,758 beds)
  5 accredited, 2 teaching,
    175 services
Office-Based Physicians
  C   Family Medicine: 31
  AA Medical Specialists: 147
  AA Surgeons: 129
Public Libraries
  Hancock County Library System
  Harrison County Library System
Rank: 136

Beaufort, SC

Airline Service
  Hilton Head (HXD)
General Hospitals: 2 (301 beds)
  2 accredited, 105 services
Office-Based Physicians
  B   Family Medicine: 31
  A   Medical Specialists: 96
  AA Surgeons: 100
Public Libraries
  Beaufort County Library
Continuing Education
  Two-Year
  1 campus, 2,531 students
  Four-Year
  University of South Carolina
    Beaufort (1,752)
Rank: 74

Beaufort–Atlantic Beach, NC

Airline Service
  Craven Regional (EWN)
General Hospitals: 1 (221 beds)
  1 accredited
Office-Based Physicians
  B   Family Medicine: 11
  A   Medical Specialists: 25
  A   Surgeons: 23
Public Libraries
  Craven-Pamlico-Carteret Library
Continuing Education
  Two-Year
  1 campus, 2,456 students
Rank: 153

★ **Bellingham, WA**

Airline Service
  Bellingham International (BLI)
General Hospitals: 1 (226 beds)
  1 accredited, 71 services
Office-Based Physicians
  AA Family Medicine: 83
  B   Medical Specialists: 106
  B   Surgeons: 82
Public Libraries
  Bellingham Public Library
  Whatcom County Library System

Continuing Education
  Two-Year
  3 campuses, 13,200 students
  Four-Year
  Western Washington University
    (16,389)
Rank: 11

★ **Bend, OR**

Airline Service
  Roberts Field-Redmond Municipal
    (RDM)
General Hospitals: 2 (220 beds)
  2 accredited, 1 teaching,
    92 services
Office-Based Physicians
  A   Family Medicine: 51
  B   Medical Specialists: 79
  A   Surgeons: 91
Public Libraries
  Deschutes Public Library
Continuing Education
  Two-Year
  1 campus, 6,596 students
  Four-Year
  Oregon State University-Cascades
    (610)
Rank: 30

Berkeley Springs, WV

Airline Service
  Washington Dulles International (IAD)
General Hospitals: 1 (41 beds)
  27 services
Office-Based Physicians
  B   Family Medicine: 3
  C   Medical Specialists: 3
Public Libraries
  Morgan County Public Library
Rank: 198

The Big Island, HI

Airline Service
  Hilo International (ITO)
General Hospitals: 6 (495 beds)
  3 accredited, 151 services
Office-Based Physicians
  A   Family Medicine: 41
  B   Medical Specialists: 91
  B   Surgeons: 52
Public Libraries
  Part of Hawaii State Library
Continuing Education
  Two-Year
  1 campus, 2,977 students
  Four-Year
  University of Hawaii Hilo (4,124)
Rank: 93

Bisbee, AZ

Airline Service
  Tucson International (TUS)
General Hospitals: 5 (186 beds)
  2 accredited, 67 services

Office-Based Physicians
  C   Family Medicine: 15
  B   Medical Specialists: 27
  B   Surgeons: 14
Public Libraries
  8 independent libraries
Continuing Education
  Two-Year
  1 campus, 12,890 students
Rank: 142

Boerne, TX

Airline Service
  San Antonio International (SAT)
Office-Based Physicians
  AA Family Medicine: 12
  A   Medical Specialists: 29
  B   Surgeons: 17
Public Libraries
  3 independent libraries
Rank: 139

★ **Boone–Blowing Rock, NC**

Airline Service
  Hickory Regional (HKY)
General Hospitals: 2 (195 beds)
  2 accredited, 46 services
Office-Based Physicians
  A   Family Medicine: 15
  A   Medical Specialists: 29
  A   Surgeons: 31
Public Libraries
  Appalachian Regional Library
Continuing Education
  Four-Year
  Appalachian State University
    (16,713)
Rank: 27

Bozeman, MT

Airline Service
  Gallatin Field (BZN)
General Hospitals: 1 (69 beds)
  43 services
Office-Based Physicians
  AA Family Medicine: 35
  B   Medical Specialists: 36
  B   Surgeons: 33
Public Libraries
  5 independent libraries
Continuing Education
  Four-Year
  Montana State University (13,838)
Rank: 46

Bradenton, FL

Airline Service
  Sarasota Bradenton International
    (SRQ)
General Hospitals: 2 (810 beds)
  2 accredited, 39 services
Office-Based Physicians
  C   Family Medicine: 51
  AA Medical Specialists: 197
  AA Surgeons: 137

continued

★ = *one of the top 30 places for services*

Services

Public Libraries
Manatee County Library System
Continuing Education
Two-Year
2 campuses, 14,900 students
Rank: 82

Branson, MO
Airline Service
Springfield-Branson National (SGF)
General Hospitals: 1 (132 beds)
1 accredited, 63 services
Office-Based Physicians
B   Family Medicine: 9
B   Medical Specialists: 20
B   Surgeons: 10
Public Libraries
Taneyhills Community Library
Continuing Education
Four-Year
College of the Ozarks (1,517)
Rank: 76

Brevard, NC
Airline Service
Asheville Regional (AVL)
General Hospitals: 1 (55 beds)
1 accredited, 33 services
Office-Based Physicians
A   Family Medicine: 10
B   Medical Specialists: 15
A   Surgeons: 15
Public Libraries
Transylvania County Library
Continuing Education
Four-Year
Brevard College (653)
Rank: 102

Brown County, IN
Airline Service
Indianapolis International (IND)
Office-Based Physicians
A   Family Medicine: 5
C   Medical Specialists: 2
Public Libraries
Brown County Public Library
Rank: 192

Brownsville, TX
Airline Service
Brownsville/South Padre Island
International (BRO)
General Hospitals: 6 (1,055 beds)
5 accredited, 1 teaching,
234 services
Office-Based Physicians
C   Family Medicine: 55
A   Medical Specialists: 176
A   Surgeons: 97
Public Libraries
8 independent libraries

Continuing Education
Two-Year
1 campus, 5,997 students
Four-Year
University of Texas Brownsville
(14,365)
Rank: 113

Brunswick, ME
Airline Service
Portland International Jetport (PWM)
General Hospitals: 6 (879 beds)
5 accredited, 1 teaching,
252 services
Office-Based Physicians
AA   Family Medicine: 104
AA   Medical Specialists: 326
A   Surgeons: 204
Public Libraries
33 independent libraries
Continuing Education
Two-Year
2 campuses, 4,970 students
Four-Year
Bowdoin College (1,739)
Saint Joseph's College (5,609)
University of Southern Maine
(15,147)
Rank: 34

★ Burlington, VT
Airline Service
Burlington International (BTV)
General Hospitals: 1 (519 beds)
1 accredited, 1 teaching,
85 services
Office-Based Physicians
AA   Family Medicine: 70
AA   Medical Specialists: 205
A   Surgeons: 123
Public Libraries
16 independent libraries
Continuing Education
Four-Year
Champlain College (2,981)
Saint Michael's College (3,235)
University of Vermont (12,656)
Rank: 15

Camden, ME
Airline Service
Knox County Regional (RKD)
General Hospitals: 1 (171 beds)
1 accredited, 55 services
Office-Based Physicians
A   Family Medicine: 12
A   Medical Specialists: 30
A   Surgeons: 1
Public Libraries
17 independent libraries
Rank: 134

Carmel–Pebble Beach, CA
Airline Service
Monterey Peninsula (MRY)
General Hospitals: 4 (637 beds)
4 accredited, 1 teaching,
125 services
Office-Based Physicians
B   Family Medicine: 102
A   Medical Specialists: 210
A   Surgeons: 156
Public Libraries
5 independent libraries
Continuing Education
Two-Year
4 campuses, 45,565 students
Four-Year
California State University Monterey
Bay (4,239)
Institute of International Studies
(922)
Naval Postgraduate School (2,652)
Rank: 47

Carson City–Carson Valley, NV
Airline Service
Reno/Tahoe International (RNO)
General Hospitals: 1 (131 beds)
1 accredited, 58 services
Office-Based Physicians
A   Family Medicine: 33
B   Medical Specialists: 54
B   Surgeons: 40
Public Libraries
Carson City Library
Douglas County Public Library
Continuing Education
Two-Year
1 campus, 7,192 students
Rank: 67

Cedar City, UT
Airline Service
Cedar City Regional (CDC)
General Hospitals: 1 (46 beds)
1 accredited, 46 services
Office-Based Physicians
C   Family Medicine: 6
B   Medical Specialists: 7
B   Surgeons: 8
Public Libraries
3 independent libraries
Continuing Education
Four-Year
Southern Utah University (11,503)
Rank: 100

Cedar Creek Lake, TX
Airline Service
Dallas Love Field (DAL)
General Hospitals: 1 (117 beds)
1 accredited, 21 services

Office-Based Physicians
B Family Medicine: 22
C Medical Specialists: 10
C Surgeons: 14
Public Libraries
3 independent libraries
Continuing Education
Two-Year
1 campus, 9,720 students
Rank: 154

★ **Chapel Hill–Carrboro, NC**
Airline Service
Raleigh-Durham International (RDU)
General Hospitals: 1 (670 beds)
1 accredited, 1 teaching,
92 services
Office-Based Physicians
AA Family Medicine: 74
AA Medical Specialists: 338
AA Surgeons: 160
Public Libraries
Chapel Hill Public Library
Continuing Education
Four-Year
University of North Carolina
(29,750)
Rank: 1

★ **Charleston, SC**
Airline Service
Charleston International (CHS)
General Hospitals: 7 (1,668 beds)
6 accredited, 4 teaching,
264 services
Office-Based Physicians
A Family Medicine: 113
AA Medical Specialists: 451
AA Surgeons: 338
Public Libraries
Charleston County Library
Continuing Education
Two-Year
1 campus, 16,563 students
Four-Year
Charleston Southern University
(4,139)
Citadel Military College (5,165)
College of Charleston (14,196)
Johnson & Wales University (1,508)
Medical University of South Carolina
(2,762)
Rank: 16

Charles Town–Shepherdstown, WV
Airline Service
Washington Dulles International
(IAD)
General Hospitals: 1 (60 beds)
1 accredited, 1 teaching,
33 services

Office-Based Physicians
B Family Medicine: 10
B Medical Specialists: 11
C Surgeons: 6
Public Libraries
3 independent libraries
Continuing Education
Four-Year
Shepherd University (5,850)
Rank: 147

★ **Charlottesville, VA**
Airline Service
Charlottesville-Albemarle (CHO)
General Hospitals: 2 (687 beds)
2 accredited, 1 teaching,
140 services
Office-Based Physicians
AA Family Medicine: 61
AA Medical Specialists: 374
AA Surgeons: 142
Public Libraries
Jefferson-Madison Regional Library
Continuing Education
Two-Year
1 campus, 6,497 students
Four-Year
University of Virginia (30,307)
Rank: 6

Chestertown, MD
Airline Service
Baltimore/Washington International
(BWI)
General Hospitals: 1 (46 beds)
1 accredited, 41 services
Office-Based Physicians
AA Family Medicine: 10
C Medical Specialists: 9
B Surgeons: 11
Public Libraries
Kent County Public Library
Continuing Education
Four-Year
Washington College (1,549)
Rank: 78

Chewelah, WA
Airline Service
Spokane International (GEG)
General Hospitals: 2 (133 beds)
65 services
Office-Based Physicians
AA Family Medicine: 16
C Medical Specialists: 9
C Surgeons: 3
Public Libraries
Chewelah Public Library
Rank: 157

Coeur d'Alene, ID
Airline Service
Spokane International (GEG)
General Hospitals: 1 (246 beds)
1 accredited, 63 services
Office-Based Physicians
A Family Medicine: 49
C Medical Specialists: 51
B Surgeons: 54
Public Libraries
3 independent libraries
Continuing Education
Two-Year
1 campus, 5,661 students
Rank: 56

★ **Columbia, MO**
Airline Service
Columbia Regional (COU)
General Hospitals: 4 (976 beds)
4 accredited, 4 teaching,
252 services
Office-Based Physicians
AA Family Medicine: 56
AA Medical Specialists: 192
AA Surgeons: 141
Public Libraries
Daniel Boone Regional Library
Continuing Education
Four-Year
Columbia College (18,832)
Stephens College (811)
University of Missouri (30,386)
Rank: 3

Conway, AR
Airline Service
Little Rock National (LIT)
General Hospitals: 1 (149 beds)
1 accredited, 63 services
Office-Based Physicians
B Family Medicine: 24
B Medical Specialists: 31
B Surgeons: 31
Public Libraries
Faulkner-Van Buren Regional Library
System
Continuing Education
Four-Year
Central Baptist College (576)
Hendrix College (1,078)
University of Central Arkansas
(11,117)
Rank: 70

Cortez, CO
Airline Service
Durango-La Plata County (DRO)
General Hospitals: 1 (61 beds)
1 accredited, 27 services
Office-Based Physicians
AA Family Medicine: 13
C Medical Specialists: 6
C Surgeons: 10

continued

★ = *one of the top 30 places for services*

Services

Public Libraries
3 independent libraries
Rank: 175

Cottonwood–Verde Valley, AZ
Airline Service
Flagstaff Pulliam (FLG)
General Hospitals: 2 (463 beds)
2 accredited, 139 services
Office-Based Physicians
B   Family Medicine: 43
B   Medical Specialists: 88
A   Surgeons: 71
Public Libraries
18 independent libraries
Continuing Education
Two-Year
1 campus, 15,024 students
Four-Year
Embry-Riddle Aeronautical University
(1,779)
Prescott College (1,410)
Rank: 32

Crossville, TN
Airline Service
Knoxville-McGhee Tyson (TYS)
General Hospitals: 1 (154 beds)
1 accredited, 41 services
Office-Based Physicians
A   Family Medicine: 13
A   Medical Specialists: 31
A   Surgeons: 21
Public Libraries
Art Circle Public Library
Continuing Education
Two-Year
1 campus, 386 students
Rank: 91

Dahlonega, GA
Airline Service
Hartsfield-Jackson Atlanta
International (ATL)
General Hospitals: 1 (49 beds)
1 accredited, 28 services
Office-Based Physicians
C   Family Medicine: 3
B   Medical Specialists: 5
A   Surgeons: 6
Public Libraries
Part of Chestatee Regional Library
System
Continuing Education
Four-Year
*North Georgia College & State
University* (5,413)
Rank: 90

Dare Outer Banks, NC
Airline Service
Pitt-Greenville (PGV)
General Hospitals: 1 (19 beds)
1 accredited, 26 services

Office-Based Physicians
A   Family Medicine: 11
C   Medical Specialists: 5
C   Surgeons: 7
Public Libraries
Part of East Albemarle Regional
Library System
Rank: 181

Delta County, CO
Airline Service
Grand Junction-Walker Field (GJT)
General Hospitals: 1 (35 beds)
1 accredited, 39 services
Office-Based Physicians
AA Family Medicine: 13
C   Medical Specialists: 5
C   Surgeons: 6
Public Libraries
Delta County Public Library
Rank: 172

Door Peninsula, WI
Airline Service
Green Bay Straubel International
(GRB)
General Hospitals: 1 (73 beds)
1 accredited, 54 services
Office-Based Physicians
A   Family Medicine: 11
B   Medical Specialists: 11
C   Surgeons: 3
Public Libraries
Door County Library
Rank: 152

Driggs, ID
Airline Service
Jackson Hole (WY [JAC])
General Hospitals: 1 (13 beds)
46 services
Office-Based Physicians
B   Family Medicine: 2
C   Medical Specialists: 1
Public Libraries
Valley of The Tetons District
Rank: 180

Durango, CO
Airline Service
Durango-La Plata County (DRO)
General Hospitals: 1 (92 beds)
1 accredited, 56 services
Office-Based Physicians
AA Family Medicine: 24
B   Medical Specialists: 31
A   Surgeons: 39
Public Libraries
3 independent libraries
Continuing Education
Four-Year
Fort Lewis College (4,834)
Rank: 31

Eagle River–Woodruff, WI
Airline Service
Green Bay Straubel International
(GRB)
General Hospitals: 1 (8 beds)
27 services
Office-Based Physicians
AA Family Medicine: 11
C   Surgeons: 1
Public Libraries
9 independent libraries
Rank: 196

East End Long Island, NY
Airline Service
Long Island Islip MacArthur (ISP)
General Hospitals: 12 (3,909 beds)
12 accredited, 3 teaching,
557 services
Office-Based Physicians
C   Family Medicine: 202
AA Medical Specialists: 1,151
AA Surgeons: 664
Public Libraries
56 independent libraries
Continuing Education
Two-Year
1 campus, 28,731 students
Four-Year
Dowling College (8,622)
Farmingdale State University
(8,173)
Long Island University Brentwood
(1,329)
New York IT (911)
St. Joseph's College (4,368)
Southampton College of Long Island
University (1,599)
Stony Brook University (27,278)
Rank: 77

Easton–St. Michaels, MD
Airline Service
Salisbury-Ocean City-Wicomico
Regional (SBY)
General Hospitals: 1 (109 beds)
1 accredited, 48 services
Office-Based Physicians
A   Family Medicine: 11
AA Medical Specialists: 46
AA Surgeons: 41
Public Libraries
Talbot County Free Library
Rank: 118

East Stroudsburg, PA
Airline Service
Wilkes-Barre/Scranton International
(AVP)
General Hospitals: 1 (192 beds)
1 accredited, 54 services

★ = *one of the top 30 places for services*

Office-Based Physicians

C Family Medicine: 23
AA Medical Specialists: 66
A Surgeons: 37

Public Libraries

5 independent libraries

Continuing Education

Two-Year

1 campus, 1,774 students

Four-Year

East Stroudsburg University (8,263)

Rank: 93

Edenton, NC

Airline Service

Pitt-Greenville (PGV)

General Hospitals: 1 (82 beds)

1 accredited, 34 services

Office-Based Physicians

A Family Medicine: 5
C Medical Specialists: 4
A Surgeons: 10

Public Libraries

Pettigrew Regional Library

Rank: 164

★ **Eugene, OR**

Airline Service

Eugene-Mahlon Sweet Field (EUG)

General Hospitals: 4 (604 beds)

3 accredited, 123 services

Office-Based Physicians

A Family Medicine: 113
B Medical Specialists: 211
B Surgeons: 151

Public Libraries

7 independent libraries

Continuing Education

Two-Year

1 campus, 14,923 students

Four-Year

Northwest Christian College (535)
University of Oregon (23,866)

Rank: 22

Eureka Springs, AR

Airline Service

Northwest Arkansas Regional (XNA)

General Hospitals: 2 (60 beds)

1 accredited, 75 services

Office-Based Physicians

A Family Medicine: 10
C Medical Specialists: 1
C Surgeons: 5

Public Libraries

Eureka Springs Carnegie Library

Rank: 182

Fairhope–Gulf Shores, AL

Airline Service

Mobile Regional (MOB)

General Hospitals: 4 (335 beds)

2 accredited, 70 services

Office-Based Physicians

A Family Medicine: 48
B Medical Specialists: 60
B Surgeons: 59

Public Libraries

10 independent libraries

Continuing Education

Two-Year

1 campus, 3,235 students

Four-Year

United States Sports Academy
(938)

Rank: 97

Fairplay, CO

Airline Service

Denver International (DEN)

Office-Based Physicians

C Family Medicine: 2
B Medical Specialists: 2

Public Libraries

Park County Public Library

Rank: 200

★ **Fayetteville, AR**

Airline Service

Northwest Arkansas Regional (XNA)

General Hospitals: 4 (489 beds)

3 accredited, 177 services

Office-Based Physicians

A Family Medicine: 60
B Medical Specialists: 92
A Surgeons: 96

Public Libraries

Fayetteville Library

Continuing Education

Two-Year

1 campus, 68 students

Four-Year

University of Arkansas (18,503)

Rank: 11

★ **Flagstaff, AZ**

Airline Service

Flagstaff Pulliam (FLG)

General Hospitals: 2 (336 beds)

2 accredited, 72 services

Office-Based Physicians

A Family Medicine: 46
B Medical Specialists: 62
B Surgeons: 64

Public Libraries

5 independent libraries

Continuing Education

Two-Year

1 campus, 6,084 students

Four-Year

Northern Arizona University
(23,892)

Rank: 20

★ **Fort Collins–Loveland, CO**

Airline Service

Fort Collins-Loveland Municipal
(FNL)

General Hospitals: 3 (445 beds)

2 accredited, 164 services

Office-Based Physicians

AA Family Medicine: 129
B Medical Specialists: 130
B Surgeons: 121

Public Libraries

6 independent libraries

Continuing Education

Four-Year

Colorado State University (34,049)

Rank: 9

Fort Myers–Cape Coral, FL

Airline Service

Southwest Florida International
(RSW)

General Hospitals: 5 (1,735 beds)

4 accredited, 98 services

Office-Based Physicians

C Family Medicine: 67
AA Medical Specialists: 314
AA Surgeons: 248

Public Libraries

3 independent libraries

Continuing Education

Two-Year

4 campuses, 19,729 students

Four-Year

Florida Gulf Coast University (7,560)

Rank: 81

Fredericksburg, TX

Airline Service

Austin-Bergstrom International (AUS)

General Hospitals: 1 (77 beds)

1 accredited, 37 services

Office-Based Physicians

AA Family Medicine: 13
B Medical Specialists: 15
B Surgeons: 17

Public Libraries

Pioneer Memorial Library

Rank: 150

Fredericksburg–Spotsylvania, VA

Airline Service

Washington Dulles International
(IAD)

General Hospitals: 1 (318 beds)

1 accredited, 61 services

Office-Based Physicians

B Family Medicine: 28
AA Medical Specialists: 85
A Surgeons: 58

Public Libraries

Central Rappahannock Library

continued

Services

Continuing Education
Four-Year
University of Mary Washington
(5,585)
Rank: 47

Front Royal, VA
Airline Service
Washington Dulles International
(IAD)
General Hospitals: 1 (166 beds)
1 accredited, 40 services
Office-Based Physicians
B   Family Medicine: 8
C   Medical Specialists: 7
B   Surgeons: 8
Public Libraries
Samuels Public Library
Rank: 159

★ Gainesville, FL
Airline Service
Gainesville Regional (GNV)
General Hospitals: 4 (1,634 beds)
4 accredited, 3 teaching, 150 serv-
ices
Office-Based Physicians
AA Family Medicine: 92
AA Medical Specialists: 358
AA Surgeons: 198
Public Libraries
Alachua County Library
Continuing Education
Two-Year
1 campus, 19,470 students
Four-Year
City College Branch Campus (606)
University of Florida (56,217)
Rank: 5

Georgetown, TX
Airline Service
Austin-Bergstrom International (AUS)
General Hospitals: 3 (267 beds)
3 accredited, 94 services
Office-Based Physicians
B   Family Medicine: 76
B   Medical Specialists: 84
C   Surgeons: 60
Public Libraries
7 independent libraries
Continuing Education
Four-Year
Southwestern University (1,315)
Rank: 109

Grand Junction, CO
Airline Service
Walker Field (GJT)
General Hospitals: 3 (769 beds)
3 accredited, 86 services

Office-Based Physicians
AA Family Medicine: 60
C   Medical Specialists: 55
B   Surgeons: 64
Public Libraries
Mesa County Public Library
Continuing Education
Four-Year
Mesa State College (6,942)
Rank: 51

Grants Pass, OR
Airline Service
Rogue Valley International-Medford
(MFR)
General Hospitals: 1 (98 beds)
1 accredited, 49 services
Office-Based Physicians
A   Family Medicine: 29
B   Medical Specialists: 32
C   Surgeons: 27
Public Libraries
Josephine County Library
Continuing Education
Two-Year
1 campus, 7,592 students
Rank: 65

Grass Valley–Nevada City, CA
Airline Service
Sacramento International (SMF)
General Hospitals: 2 (148 beds)
1 accredited, 72 services
Office-Based Physicians
AA Family Medicine: 40
B   Medical Specialists: 49
B   Surgeons: 50
Public Libraries
Nevada County Library
Rank: 104

Hamilton–Bitterroot Valley, MT
Airline Service
Missoula International (MSO)
General Hospitals: 1 (48 beds)
34 services
Office-Based Physicians
A   Family Medicine: 12
C   Medical Specialists: 10
B   Surgeons: 12
Public Libraries
3 independent libraries
Rank: 168

Hampshire County, WV
Airline Service
Washington Dulles International
(IAD)
General Hospitals: 1 (47 beds)
1 accredited, 15 services

Office-Based Physicians
C   Family Medicine: 1
B   Medical Specialists: 3
B   Surgeons: 1
Public Libraries
2 independent libraries
Rank: 193

Hanover, NH
Airline Service
Lebanon Municipal (LEB)
General Hospitals: 5 (484 beds)
1 accredited, 1 teaching, 237
services
Office-Based Physicians
AA Family Medicine: 45
AA Medical Specialists: 163
AA Surgeons: 109
Public Libraries
38 independent libraries
Continuing Education
Two-Year
1 campus, 603 students
Four-Year
Dartmouth College (6,562)
Plymouth State University (6,877)
Rank: 36

★ Hattiesburg, MS
Airline Service
Hattiesburg-Laurel Regional (PIB)
General Hospitals: 1 (537 beds)
1 accredited, 45 services
Office-Based Physicians
AA Family Medicine: 43
A   Medical Specialists: 111
AA Surgeons: 93
Public Libraries
Library of Hattiesburg
Continuing Education
Four-Year
University of Southern Mississippi
(19,222)
William Carey College (4,045)
Rank: 28

Henderson, NV
Airline Service
Las Vegas-McCarran International
(LAS)
General Hospitals: 11 (2,897 beds)
10 accredited, 2 teaching, 340
services
Office-Based Physicians
C   Family Medicine: 245
AA Medical Specialists: 920
A   Surgeons: 521
Public Libraries
4 independent libraries

Retirement Places Rated

Continuing Education
Two-Year
1 campus, 41 students
Four-Year
University of Southern Nevada
(53,951)
Nevada State College (806)
University of Nevada Las Vegas
(32,874)
Rank: 45

Hendersonville–East Flat Rock, NC
Airline Service
Asheville Regional (AVL)
General Hospitals: 2 (279 beds)
2 accredited, 109 services
Office-Based Physicians
A Family Medicine: 35
A Medical Specialists: 65
B Surgeons: 52
Public Libraries
Henderson County Library
Continuing Education
Two-Year
1 campus, 3,205 students
Rank: 35

Hilton Head Island, SC
Airline Service
Hilton Head (HXD)
General Hospitals: 2 (301 beds)
2 accredited, 105 services
Office-Based Physicians
B Family Medicine: 31
A Medical Specialists: 96
AA Surgeons: 100
Public Libraries
Beaufort County Library
Continuing Education
Two-Year
1 campus, 2,531 students
Four-Year
University of South Carolina
Beaufort (1,752)
Rank: 74

★ Hot Springs, AR
Airline Service
Little Rock National (LIT)
General Hospitals: 4 (485 beds)
3 accredited, 141 services
Office-Based Physicians
AA Family Medicine: 36
B Medical Specialists: 62
A Surgeons: 55
Public Libraries
Garland County Library
Continuing Education
Two-Year
1 campus, 4,661 students
Rank: 23

★ Iowa City, IA
Airline Service
Cedar Rapids-Eastern Iowa (CID)
General Hospitals: 2 (975 beds)
2 accredited, 2 teaching, 204 services
Office-Based Physicians
AA Family Medicine: 61
AA Medical Specialists: 231
AA Surgeons: 165
Public Libraries
6 independent libraries
Continuing Education
Four-Year
University of Iowa (33,224)
Rank: 2

Jackson Hole, WY
Airline Service
Jackson Hole (JAC)
General Hospitals: 1 (108 beds)
1 accredited, 57 services
Office-Based Physicians
A Family Medicine: 6
A Medical Specialists: 16
AA Surgeons: 26
Public Libraries
Teton County Library
Rank: 73

Kalispell–Flathead Valley, MT
Airline Service
Glacier Park International (GPI)
General Hospitals: 2 (190 beds)
1 accredited, 89 services
Office-Based Physicians
A Family Medicine: 32
B Medical Specialists: 45
A Surgeons: 57
Public Libraries
Flathead County Library
Continuing Education
Two-Year
1 campus, 3,786 students
Rank: 69

Kerrville, TX
Airline Service
San Antonio International (SAT)
General Hospitals: 1 (104 beds)
1 accredited, 43 services
Office-Based Physicians
A Family Medicine: 15
A Medical Specialists: 39
A Surgeons: 29
Public Libraries
Butt-Holdsworth Library
Continuing Education
Four-Year
Schreiner University (848)
Rank: 116

Ketchum–Sun Valley, ID
Airline Service
Twin Falls-Magic Valley Regional
(TWF)
General Hospitals: 1 (32 beds)
1 accredited
Office-Based Physicians
AA Family Medicine: 14
C Medical Specialists: 11
B Surgeons: 21
Public Libraries
3 independent libraries
Rank: 169

Key West, FL
Airline Service
Key West International (EYW)
General Hospitals: 3 (203 beds)
2 accredited, 103 services
Office-Based Physicians
B Family Medicine: 13
A Medical Specialists: 34
AA Surgeons: 40
Public Libraries
Monroe County Library System
Continuing Education
Two-Year
1 campus, 2,594 students
Rank: 107

Kingman, AZ
Airline Service
Laughlin/Bullhead International (IFP)
General Hospitals: 3 (361 beds)
3 accredited, 85 services
Office-Based Physicians
C Family Medicine: 18
A Medical Specialists: 61
A Surgeons: 38
Public Libraries
Mohave County Library District
Continuing Education
Two-Year
1 campus, 11,556 students
Rank: 122

Kissimmee–St. Cloud, FL
Airline Service
Orlando International (MCO)
General Hospitals: 2 (239 beds)
1 accredited, 53 services
Office-Based Physicians
C Family Medicine: 30
A Medical Specialists: 72
A Surgeons: 48
Public Libraries
Osceola County Library
Rank: 162

continued

Services

★ Laguna Beach–Dana Point, CA
Airline Service
John Wayne-Orange County (SNA)
General Hospitals: 29 (4,962 beds)
26 accredited, 3 teaching,
710 services
Office-Based Physicians
B   Family Medicine: 729
A   Medical Specialists: 2,374
A   Surgeons: 1,471
Public Libraries
11 independent libraries
Continuing Education
Two-Year
9 campuses, 220,305 students
Four-Year
California State University Fullerton
(38,055)
Chapman University (11,310)
Concordia University (2,192)
Hope International University
(1,770)
South Baylo University (878)
University of California Irvine
(26,042)
Vanguard University (2,573)
Rank: 14

Lake Conroe, TX
Airline Service
Houston-George Bush
Intercontinental (IAH)
General Hospitals: 2 (272 beds)
1 accredited, 51 services
Office-Based Physicians
B   Family Medicine: 92
A   Medical Specialists: 159
B   Surgeons: 109
Public Libraries
Montgomery County Library
Rank: 126

Lake Havasu City, AZ
Airline Service
Laughlin/Bullhead International (IFP)
General Hospitals: 3 (361 beds)
3 accredited, 85 services
Office-Based Physicians
C   Family Medicine: 18
A   Medical Specialists: 61
A   Surgeons: 38
Public Libraries
Mohave County Library
Continuing Education
Two-Year
1 campus, 11,556 students
Rank: 122

Lakeland–Winter Haven, FL
Airline Service
Tampa International (TPA)
General Hospitals: 4 (1,190 beds)
4 accredited, 205 services

Office-Based Physicians
C   Family Medicine: 61
AA Medical Specialists: 285
AA Surgeons: 195
Public Libraries
Polk County Library Coop
Continuing Education
Two-Year
3 campuses, 12,861 students
Four-Year
Florida Southern College (3,123)
Southeastern University (1,968)
Warner Southern College (1,359)
Webber International University (716)
Rank: 108

Lake of the Cherokees, OK
Airline Service
Tulsa International (TUL)
General Hospitals: 1 (72 beds)
1 accredited, 39 services
Office-Based Physicians
A   Family Medicine: 14
C   Medical Specialists: 4
C   Surgeons: 4
Public Libraries
Eastern Oklahoma Library
Rank: 174

Lake of the Ozarks, MO
Airline Service
Columbia Regional (COU)
General Hospitals: 1 (140 beds)
1 accredited, 54 services
Office-Based Physicians
B   Family Medicine: 7
B   Medical Specialists: 13
A   Surgeons: 11
Public Libraries
Camden County Library
Rank: 151

Lake Placid, NY
Airline Service
Burlington (VT) International (BTV)
General Hospitals: 2 (15 beds)
Office-Based Physicians
B   Family Medicine: 9
C   Medical Specialists: 6
C   Surgeons: 5
Public Libraries
16 independent libraries
Continuing Education
Two-Year
1 campus, 1,741 students
Rank: 179

Largo, FL
Airline Service
St. Petersburg-Clearwater
International (PIE)
General Hospitals: 14 (3,673 beds)
12 accredited, 3 teaching,
337 services

Office-Based Physicians
B   Family Medicine: 191
AA Medical Specialists: 776
AA Surgeons: 469
Public Libraries
Pinellas Public Library Coop
Continuing Education
Two-Year
2 campuses, 4,027 students
Four-Year
Clearwater Christian College (686)
Eckerd College (1,781)
St. Petersburg College (35,021)
Rank: 36

Las Cruces, NM
Airline Service
El Paso (TX) International (ELP)
General Hospitals: 2 (314 beds)
2 accredited, 1 teaching,
88 services
Office-Based Physicians
B   Family Medicine: 37
B   Medical Specialists: 64
B   Surgeons: 46
Public Libraries
4 independent libraries
Continuing Education
Two-Year
1 campus, 8,280 students
Four-Year
New Mexico State University
(19,206)
Rank: 63

Las Vegas, NM
Airline Service
Santa Fe Municipal (SAF)
General Hospitals: 1 (54 beds)
1 accredited, 23 services
Office-Based Physicians
B   Family Medicine: 7
B   Medical Specialists: 13
C   Surgeons: 4
Public Libraries
Carnegie Public Library
Continuing Education
Two-Year
1 campus, 3,572 students
Four-Year
New Mexico Highlands University
(5,117)
Rank: 143

Leelanau Peninsula, MI
Airline Service
Traverse City-Cherry Capital (TVC)
General Hospitals: 1 (95 beds)
0 accredited, 32 services
Office-Based Physicians
C   Family Medicine: 3
C   Medical Specialists: 2
C   Surgeons: 1

Public Libraries
4 independent libraries
Rank: 177

Leesburg–Mount Dora, FL
Airline Service
Orlando International (MCO)
General Hospitals: 3 (664 beds)
3 accredited, 92 services
Office-Based Physicians
C   Family Medicine: 50
A   Medical Specialists: 137
A   Surgeons: 87
Public Libraries
3 independent libraries
Continuing Education
Two-Year
1 campus, 4,648 students
Rank: 92

Litchfield Hills, CT
Airline Service
Windsor Locks-Bradley International
(BDL)
General Hospitals: 3 (244 beds)
3 accredited, 144 services
Office-Based Physicians
C   Family Medicine: 21
AA Medical Specialists: 136
AA Surgeons: 74
Public Libraries
28 independent libraries
Continuing Education
Two-Year
1 campus, 1,949 students
Rank: 141

Long Beach Peninsula, WA
Airline Service
Portland (OR) International (PDX)
General Hospitals: 2 (32 beds)
27 services
Office-Based Physicians
C   Family Medicine: 2
C   Surgeons: 1
Public Libraries
Part of Timberland Regional Library
Rank: 163

Loudoun County, VA
Airline Service
Washington Dulles International
(IAD)
General Hospitals: 1 (92 beds)
1 accredited
Office-Based Physicians
C   Family Medicine: 41
A   Medical Specialists: 114
A   Surgeons: 71
Public Libraries
Loudoun County Library
Rank: 149

Lower Cape May, NJ
Airline Service
Atlantic City International (ACY)
General Hospitals: 1 (208 beds)
1 accredited, 45 services
Office-Based Physicians
C   Family Medicine: 11
A   Medical Specialists: 27
A   Surgeons: 20
Public Libraries
2 independent libraries
Rank: 178

Madison, MS
Airline Service
Jackson-Evers International (JAN)
General Hospitals: 1 (34 beds)
16 services
Office-Based Physicians
AA Family Medicine: 34
A   Medical Specialists: 93
B   Surgeons: 32
Public Libraries
Madison County Library
Continuing Education
Four-Year
Tougaloo College (1,042)
Rank: 143

★ Madison, WI
Airline Service
Dane County Municipal-Truax Field
(MSN)
General Hospitals: 4 (1,264 beds)
4 accredited, 4 teaching,
315 services
Office-Based Physicians
AA Family Medicine: 207
A   Medical Specialists: 495
B   Surgeons: 289
Public Libraries
18 independent libraries
Continuing Education
Two-Year
2 campuses, 36,953 students
Four-Year
Edgewood College (2,787)
University of Wisconsin (46,153)
Rank: 4

Marble Falls–Lake LBJ, TX
Airline Service
Austin-Bergstrom International (AUS)
General Hospitals: 1 (26 beds)
1 accredited, 34 services
Office-Based Physicians
A   Family Medicine: 14
C   Medical Specialists: 9
C   Surgeons: 7
Public Libraries
Burnet County Library
Rank: 171

Mariposa, CA
Airline Service
Modesto City-County/Sham Field
(MOD)
General Hospitals: 1 (34 beds)
Office-Based Physicians
C   Family Medicine: 3
C   Medical Specialists: 1
Public Libraries
Mariposa County Library
Rank: 197

Martha's Vineyard, MA
Airline Service
Martha's Vineyard (MVY)
General Hospitals: 1 (96 beds)
39 services
Office-Based Physicians
B   Family Medicine: 3
A   Medical Specialists: 9
A   Surgeons: 6
Public Libraries
7 independent libraries
Rank: 137

Maryville, TN
Airline Service
Knoxville-McGhee Tyson (TYS)
General Hospitals: 1 (250 beds)
1 accredited, 70 services
Office-Based Physicians
B   Family Medicine: 23
A   Medical Specialists: 63
B   Surgeons: 33
Public Libraries
2 independent libraries
Continuing Education
Four-Year
Maryville College (1,105)
Rank: 60

Maui, HI
Airline Service
Kahului (OGG)
General Hospitals: 3 (240 beds)
1 accredited, 1 teaching,
29 services
Office-Based Physicians
B   Family Medicine: 36
A   Medical Specialists: 92
B   Surgeons: 51
Public Libraries
Part of Hawaii State Library
Continuing Education
Four-Year
Maui Community College (4,247)
Rank: 129

McAllen–Alamo, TX
Airline Service
McAllen-Miller International (MFE)
General Hospitals: 8 (1,405 beds)
7 accredited, 1 teaching,
280 services

continued

Office-Based Physicians
C Family Medicine: 122
A Medical Specialists: 247
B Surgeons: 133
Public Libraries
12 independent libraries
Continuing Education
Four-Year
South Texas College (21,927)
University of Texas-Pan American
(20,414)
Rank: 101

McCall, ID
Airline Service
Boise (BOI)
General Hospitals: 2 (25 beds)
25 services
Office-Based Physicians
AA Family Medicine: 8
C Medical Specialists: 2
Public Libraries
2 independent libraries
Rank: 199

Medford–Ashland, OR
Airline Service
Rogue Valley International-Medford
(MFR)
General Hospitals: 3 (539 beds)
3 accredited, 128 services
Office-Based Physicians
A Family Medicine: 63
A Medical Specialists: 144
A Surgeons: 98
Public Libraries
Jackson County Library
Continuing Education
Four-Year
Southern Oregon University (7,781)
Rank: 62

Melbourne–Palm Bay, FL
Airline Service
Melbourne International (MLB)
General Hospitals: 5 (1,108 beds)
4 accredited, 128 services
Office-Based Physicians
B Family Medicine: 109
A Medical Specialists: 344
A Surgeons: 217
Public Libraries
Brevard County Library
Continuing Education
Two-Year
1 campus, 21,448 students
Four-Year
Florida Institute of Technology
(5,468)
Rank: 49

Mendocino–Fort Bragg, CA
Airline Service
San Francisco International (SFO)
General Hospitals: 3 (155 beds)
3 accredited, 75 services
Office-Based Physicians
AA Family Medicine: 41
B Medical Specialists: 46
B Surgeons: 45
Public Libraries
Mendocino County Library
Continuing Education
Two-Year
1 campus, 8,220 students
Rank: 80

Middle Cape Cod, MA
Airline Service
Barnstable Municipal/Boardman-
Polando Field (HYA)
General Hospitals: 2 (306 beds)
2 accredited, 107 services
Office-Based Physicians
B Family Medicine: 42
AA Medical Specialists: 200
AA Surgeons: 123
Public Libraries
30 independent libraries
Continuing Education
Two-Year
1 campus, 5,459 students
Four-Year
Massachusetts Maritime Academy
(959)
Rank: 84

Monadnock Region, NH
Airline Service
Manchester-Boston Regional (MHT)
General Hospitals: 1 (146 beds)
1 accredited, 62 services
Office-Based Physicians
AA Family Medicine: 29
B Medical Specialists: 31
C Surgeons: 20
Public Libraries
24 independent libraries
Continuing Education
Four-Year
Antioch New England Graduate
School (1,120)
Franklin Pierce College (3,743)
Keene State College (6,698)
Rank: 105

Montrose, CO
Airline Service
Montrose Regional (MTJ)
General Hospitals: 1 (47 beds)
1 accredited, 54 services

Office-Based Physicians
A Family Medicine: 13
C Medical Specialists: 12
B Surgeons: 19
Public Libraries
2 independent libraries
Rank: 132

Morro Bay–Cambria, CA
Airline Service
San Luis Obispo County Regional
(SBP)
General Hospitals: 4 (366 beds)
4 accredited, 67 services
Office-Based Physicians
A Family Medicine: 80
A Medical Specialists: 162
A Surgeons: 122
Public Libraries
2 independent libraries
Continuing Education
Two-Year
1 campus, 14,623 students
Four-Year
Cal Poly State University (19,448)
Rank: 39

★ Murray–Kentucky Lake, KY
Airline Service
Paducah-Barkley Regional (PAH)
General Hospitals: 1 (332 beds)
1 accredited, 59 services
Office-Based Physicians
B Family Medicine: 8
A Medical Specialists: 17
AA Surgeons: 20
Public Libraries
Calloway County Public Library
Continuing Education
Four-Year
Murray State University (12,387)
Rank: 17

Myrtle Beach, SC
Airline Service
Myrtle Beach International (MYR)
General Hospitals: 3 (571 beds)
3 accredited, 156 services
Office-Based Physicians
C Family Medicine: 32
AA Medical Specialists: 116
AA Surgeons: 91
Public Libraries
2 independent libraries
Continuing Education
Two-Year
1 campus, 7,020 students
Four-Year
Coastal Carolina University (8,501)
Rank: 71

Naples, FL
Airline Service
Naples Municipal (APF)
General Hospitals: 1 (539 beds)
1 accredited, 60 services
Office-Based Physicians
C   Family Medicine: 34
AA Medical Specialists: 232
AA Surgeons: 164
Public Libraries
Collier County Public Library
Continuing Education
Four-Year
International College (2,220)
Rank: 88

Natchitoches, LA
Airline Service
Alexandria International (AEX)
General Hospitals: 1 (211 beds)
1 accredited, 38 services
Office-Based Physicians
B   Family Medicine: 6
B   Medical Specialists: 12
B   Surgeons: 9
Public Libraries
Natchitoches Parish Library
Continuing Education
Two-Year
1 campus, 840 students
Four-Year
Northwestern State University
(13,336)
Rank: 112

Nelson County, VA
Airline Service
Charlottesville-Albemarle (CHO)
Office-Based Physicians
AA Family Medicine: 6
C   Medical Specialists: 5
C   Surgeons: 1
Public Libraries
Jefferson-Madison Library
Rank: 176

New Bern, NC
Airline Service
Craven Regional (EWN)
General Hospitals: 1 (307 beds)
1 accredited, 67 services
Office-Based Physicians
C   Family Medicine: 14
AA Medical Specialists: 77
AA Surgeons: 57
Public Libraries
Craven-Pamlico-Carteret Library
Continuing Education
Two-Year
1 campus, 4,607 students
Rank: 106

New Braunfels, TX
Airline Service
San Antonio International (SAT)
General Hospitals: 1 (132 beds)
1 accredited, 50 services
Office-Based Physicians
A   Family Medicine: 33
C   Medical Specialists: 30
C   Surgeons: 30
Public Libraries
3 independent libraries
Continuing Education
Two-Year
1 campus, 11,685 students
Rank: 53

Newport–Lincoln City, OR
Airline Service
Eugene-Mahlon Sweet Field (EUG)
General Hospitals: 2 (73 beds)
2 accredited, 50 services
Office-Based Physicians
B   Family Medicine: 7
B   Medical Specialists: 12
A   Surgeons: 13
Public Libraries
5 independent libraries
Continuing Education
Two-Year
1 campus, 1,066 students
Rank: 146

Norfork Lake, AR
Airline Service
Springfield-Branson National (SGF)
General Hospitals: 1 (264 beds)
46 services
Office-Based Physicians
AA Family Medicine: 16
B   Medical Specialists: 24
B   Surgeons: 22
Public Libraries
Baxter County Library
Continuing Education
Two-Year
1 campus, 1,857 students
Rank: 59

Northampton–Amherst, MA
Airline Service
Windsor Locks-Bradley International
(BDL)
General Hospitals: 2 (156 beds)
2 accredited, 98 services
Office-Based Physicians
AA Family Medicine: 58
AA Medical Specialists: 174
B   Surgeons: 56
Public Libraries
22 independent libraries

Continuing Education
Four-Year
Amherst College (2,458)
Hampshire College (1,407)
Mount Holyoke College (2,489)
Smith College (3,294)
University of Massachusetts
(29,044)
Rank: 41

Northern Neck, VA
Airline Service
Newport News/Williamsburg
International (PHF)
General Hospitals: 1 (67 beds)
1 accredited, 44 services
Office-Based Physicians
AA Family Medicine: 13
C   Medical Specialists: 14
C   Surgeons: 9
Public Libraries
2 independent libraries
Rank: 148

Oakhurst–Coarsegold, CA
Airline Service
Modesto City-County/Sham Field
(MOD)
General Hospitals: 2 (106 beds)
1 accredited, 35 services
Office-Based Physicians
C   Family Medicine: 10
AA Medical Specialists: 62
AA Surgeons: 22
Public Libraries
Madera County Library
Rank: 189

Ocala, FL
Airline Service
Gainesville Regional (GNV)
General Hospitals: 2 (610 beds)
2 accredited, 87 services
Office-Based Physicians
C   Family Medicine: 36
AA Medical Specialists: 164
AA Surgeons: 103
Public Libraries
Marion County Library
Continuing Education
Two-Year
2 campuses, 9,712 students
Rank: 115

Ocean City, MD
Airline Service
Salisbury-Ocean City-Wicomico
Regional (SBY)
General Hospitals: 1 (62 beds)
1 accredited, 38 services

continued

Services

Office-Based Physicians
B   Family Medicine: 11
B   Medical Specialists: 16
C   Surgeons: 6
Public Libraries
Worcester County Library
Rank: 186

Oxford, MS
Airline Service
Memphis (TN) International (MEM)
General Hospitals: 1 (217 beds)
1 accredited, 39 services
Office-Based Physicians
B   Family Medicine: 8
AA Medical Specialists: 30
AA Surgeons: 26
Public Libraries
First Regional Library
Continuing Education
Four-Year
University of Mississippi (15,898)
Rank: 52

Pagosa Springs, CO
Airline Service
Durango-La Plata County (DRO)
Office-Based Physicians
AA Family Medicine: 6
C   Medical Specialists: 4
C   Surgeons: 1
Public Libraries
Upper San Juan Library
Rank: 187

Pahrump Valley, NV
Airline Service
Las Vegas-McCarran International
(LAS)
General Hospitals: 1 (44 beds)
12 services
Office-Based Physicians
C   Family Medicine: 5
B   Medical Specialists: 6
C   Surgeons: 1
Public Libraries
5 independent libraries
Rank: 191

Palmer–Wasilla, AK
Airline Service
Ted Stevens Anchorage International
(ANC)
General Hospitals: 1 (36 beds)
1 accredited
Office-Based Physicians
B   Family Medicine: 20
C   Medical Specialists: 8
C   Surgeons: 15
Public Libraries
7 independent libraries
Rank: 184

Palm Springs–Coachella Valley, CA
Airline Service
Palm Springs International (PSP)
General Hospitals: 15 (2,889 beds)
14 accredited, 2 teaching,
373 services
Office-Based Physicians
C   Family Medicine: 242
A   Medical Specialists: 621
A   Surgeons: 458
Public Libraries
Palm Springs Public Library
Continuing Education
Two-Year
4 campuses, 77,268 students
Four-Year
California Baptist University (3,141)
La Sierra University (2,659)
University of California Riverside
(18,646)
Rank: 79

Panama City, FL
Airline Service
Panama City-Bay County
International (PFN)
General Hospitals: 2 (547 beds)
2 accredited, 113 services
Office-Based Physicians
C   Family Medicine: 28
A   Medical Specialists: 85
AA Surgeons: 80
Public Libraries
Northwest Regional Library
Continuing Education
Two-Year
2 campuses, 11,059 students
Rank: 72

Paradise–Magalia, CA
Airline Service
Chico Municipal (CIC)
General Hospitals: 4 (450 beds)
2 accredited, 174 services
Office-Based Physicians
A   Family Medicine: 56
A   Medical Specialists: 109
A   Surgeons: 91
Public Libraries
Butte County Library
Continuing Education
Two-Year
1 campus, 18,399 students
Four-Year
California State University Chico
(17,398)
Rank: 38

Park City, UT
Airline Service
Salt Lake City International (SLC)
General Hospitals: 1 (19 beds)

Office-Based Physicians
A   Family Medicine: 22
B   Medical Specialists: 32
C   Surgeons: 17
Public Libraries
3 independent libraries
Rank: 155

Payson, AZ
Airline Service
Phoenix Sky Harbor International
(PHX)
General Hospitals: 2 (96 beds)
2 accredited, 67 services
Office-Based Physicians
A   Family Medicine: 18
C   Medical Specialists: 16
C   Surgeons: 14
Public Libraries
8 independent libraries
Rank: 173

Pendleton District, SC
Airline Service
Greenville-Spartanburg International
(GSP)
General Hospitals: 1 (201 beds)
1 accredited, 48 services
Office-Based Physicians
A   Family Medicine: 23
C   Medical Specialists: 21
B   Surgeons: 23
Public Libraries
Oconee County Library
Rank: 158

★ **Pensacola, FL**
Airline Service
Pensacola Regional (PNS)
General Hospitals: 3 (1,325 beds)
3 accredited, 2 teaching,
210 services
Office-Based Physicians
A   Family Medicine: 90
A   Medical Specialists: 197
A   Surgeons: 146
Public Libraries
West Florida Regional Library
Continuing Education
Two-Year
2 campuses, 17,347 students
Four-Year
University of West Florida (12,177)
Rank: 29

Petoskey–Harbor Springs, MI
Airline Service
Charlevoix Municipal (CVX)
General Hospitals: 1 (213 beds)
1 accredited, 63 services
Office-Based Physicians
A   Family Medicine: 10
AA Medical Specialists: 44
AA Surgeons: 40

Public Libraries
3 independent libraries
Continuing Education
Two-Year
1 campus, 3,941 students
Rank: 50

Pike County, PA
Airline Service
Wilkes-Barre/Scranton International (AVP)
Office-Based Physicians
C Family Medicine: 4
A Medical Specialists: 14
A Surgeons: 9
Public Libraries
Pike County Public Library
Rank: 190

Placer County, CA
Airline Service
Sacramento International (SMF)
General Hospitals: 2 (230 beds)
2 accredited, 41 services
Office-Based Physicians
A Family Medicine: 109
A Medical Specialists: 226
B Surgeons: 148
Public Libraries
3 independent libraries
Continuing Education
Two-Year
1 campus, 27,707 students
Rank: 55

Port Angeles–Sequim, WA
Airline Service
Fairchild International (CLM)
General Hospitals: 2 (256 beds)
1 accredited, 79 services
Office-Based Physicians
AA Family Medicine: 38
C Medical Specialists: 29
C Surgeons: 27
Public Libraries
North Olympic Library
Continuing Education
Two-Year
1 campus, 8,062 students
Rank: 58

Port Charlotte, FL
Airline Service
Southwest Florida International (RSW)
General Hospitals: 3 (722 beds)
3 accredited, 97 services
Office-Based Physicians
C Family Medicine: 19
AA Medical Specialists: 114
AA Surgeons: 73
Public Libraries
Charlotte-Glades Library

Continuing Education
Two-Year
1 campus, 1,025 students
Rank: 125

Port St. Lucie, FL
Airline Service
Palm Beach International (PBI)
General Hospitals: 2 (539 beds)
2 accredited, 90 services
Office-Based Physicians
C Family Medicine: 26
A Medical Specialists: 85
AA Surgeons: 59
Public Libraries
St. Lucie County Library
Continuing Education
Two-Year
1 campus, 24,588 students
Rank: 110

Port Townsend, WA
Airline Service
Seattle-Tacoma International (SEA)
General Hospitals: 1 (25 beds)
43 services
Office-Based Physicians
AA Family Medicine: 16
C Medical Specialists: 12
C Surgeons: 10
Public Libraries
Port Townsend Public Library
Rank: 120

Prescott–Prescott Valley, AZ
Airline Service
Phoenix Sky Harbor International (PHX)
General Hospitals: 2 (463 beds)
2 accredited, 139 services
Office-Based Physicians
B Family Medicine: 43
B Medical Specialists: 88
A Surgeons: 71
Public Libraries
18 independent libraries
Continuing Education
Two-Year
1 campus, 15,024 students
Four-Year
Embry-Riddle Aeronautical University (1,779)
Prescott College (1,410)
Rank: 32

Rabun County, GA
Airline Service
Asheville (NC) Regional (AVL)
General Hospitals: 1 (21 beds)
25 services
Office-Based Physicians
B Family Medicine: 4
B Medical Specialists: 4
C Surgeons: 3

Public Libraries
Northeast Georgia System
Rank: 165

Rehoboth Bay–Indian River Bay, DE
Airline Service
Salisbury-Ocean City-Wicomico (MD [SBY])
General Hospitals: 2 (437 beds)
2 accredited, 111 services
Office-Based Physicians
B Family Medicine: 36
A Medical Specialists: 106
A Surgeons: 66
Public Libraries
12 independent libraries
Continuing Education
Two-Year
2 campuses, 5,184 students
Rank: 68

Rio Rancho, NM
Airline Service
Albuquerque International Sunport (ABQ)
Office-Based Physicians
A Family Medicine: 35
C Medical Specialists: 33
C Surgeons: 10
Public Libraries
14 independent libraries
Rank: 183

Rockport–Aransas Pass, TX
Airline Service
Corpus Christi International (CRP)
Office-Based Physicians
B Family Medicine: 5
B Medical Specialists: 6
C Surgeons: 3
Public Libraries
Aransas County Public Library
Rank: 195

Roswell, NM
Airline Service
Roswell International Air Center (ROW)
General Hospitals: 2 (147 beds)
1 accredited, 53 services
Office-Based Physicians
C Family Medicine: 6
A Medical Specialists: 14
A Surgeons: 12
Public Libraries
2 independent libraries
Continuing Education
Two-Year
1 campus, 1,936 students
Rank: 160

continued

★ = one of the top 30 places for services

Ruidoso, NM
  Airline Service
    El Paso (TX) International (ELP)
  General Hospitals: 1 (39 beds)
    1 accredited, 27 services
  Office-Based Physicians
    A Family Medicine: 5
    C Medical Specialists: 3
    A Surgeons: 9
  Public Libraries
    2 independent libraries
  Continuing Education
    Two-Year
    1 campus, 1,419 students
  Rank: 128

St. Augustine, FL
  Airline Service
    Jacksonville International (JAX)
  General Hospitals: 1 (274 beds)
    1 accredited, 40 services
  Office-Based Physicians
    B Family Medicine: 42
    AA Medical Specialists: 139
    A Surgeons: 63
  Public Libraries
    St. Johns County Library
  Continuing Education
    Two-Year
    1 campus, 2,283 students
    Four-Year
    Flagler College (2,321)
  Rank: 86

St. George–Zion, UT
  Airline Service
    St. George Municipal (SGU)
  General Hospitals: 1 (196 beds)
    1 accredited, 52 services
  Office-Based Physicians
    B Family Medicine: 25
    B Medical Specialists: 40
    A Surgeons: 43
  Public Libraries
    Washington County Library
  Continuing Education
    Four-Year
    Dixie State College (9,536)
  Rank: 54

St. Jay–Northeast Kingdom, VT
  Airline Service
    Lebanon (NH) Municipal (LEB)
  General Hospitals: 1 (49 beds)
    1 accredited, 49 services
  Office-Based Physicians
    AA Family Medicine: 11
    C Medical Specialists: 10
    B Surgeons: 11
  Public Libraries
    14 independent libraries

  Continuing Education
    Four-Year
    Lyndon State College (1,983)
  Rank: 121

St. Marys, GA
  Airline Service
    Jacksonville (FL) International (JAX)
  General Hospitals: 1 (40 beds)
    1 accredited, 37 services
  Office-Based Physicians
    C Family Medicine: 8
    A Medical Specialists: 13
    B Surgeons: 10
  Public Libraries
    Part of Three Rivers Regional Library
      System
  Rank: 156

St. Simons–Jekyll Islands, GA
  Airline Service
    Brunswick Golden Isles (BQK)
  General Hospitals: 1 (278 beds)
    1 accredited, 61 services
  Office-Based Physicians
    B Family Medicine: 14
    AA Medical Specialists: 48
    AA Surgeons: 52
  Public Libraries
    Part of Three Rivers Regional Library
      System
  Continuing Education
    Two-Year
    1 campus, 4,030 students
  Rank: 61

Sandpoint–Lake Pend Oreille, ID
  Airline Service
    Spokane (WA) International (GEG)
  General Hospitals: 1 (41 beds)
    1 accredited, 31 services
  Office-Based Physicians
    A Family Medicine: 11
    C Medical Specialists: 11
    B Surgeons: 15
  Public Libraries
    East Bonner County Libraries
  Rank: 130

San Juan Islands, WA
  Airline Service
    Friday Harbor (FHR)
  Office-Based Physicians
    AA Family Medicine: 8
    C Medical Specialists: 6
    C Surgeons: 4
  Public Libraries
    San Juan Island Libraries
  Rank: 169

★ Santa Barbara, CA
  Airline Service
    Santa Barbara Municipal (SBA)
  General Hospitals: 6 (874 beds)
    5 accredited, 1 teaching,
      136 services
  Office-Based Physicians
    A Family Medicine: 109
    A Medical Specialists: 302
    A Surgeons: 203
  Public Libraries
    Santa Barbara Public Library
  Continuing Education
    Two-Year
    2 campuses, 46,605 students
    Four-Year
    Fielding Graduate University (1,626)
    University of California Santa
      Barbara (22,982)
    Westmont College (1,393)
  Rank: 10

Santa Fe, NM
  Airline Service
    Santa Fe Municipal (SAF)
  General Hospitals: 1 (285 beds)
    1 accredited, 1 teaching,
      86 services
  Office-Based Physicians
    AA Family Medicine: 66
    A Medical Specialists: 112
    B Surgeons: 64
  Public Libraries
    5 independent libraries
  Continuing Education
    Two-Year
    1 campus, 9,747 students
    Four-Year
    College of Santa Fe (2,582)
    St. John's College (600)
  Rank: 64

Sarasota, FL
  Airline Service
    Sarasota Bradenton International
      (SRQ)
  General Hospitals: 5 (1,013 beds)
    4 accredited, 172 services
  Office-Based Physicians
    B Family Medicine: 85
    AA Medical Specialists: 343
    AA Surgeons: 249
  Public Libraries
    Sarasota County Libraries
  Continuing Education
    Two-Year
    1 campus, 125 students
    Four-Year
    New College of Florida (715)
    Ringling School of Art and Design
      (1,004)
  Rank: 42

    ★ = one of the top 30 places for services

Savannah, GA
Airline Service
Savannah/Hilton Head International (SAV)
General Hospitals: 3 (990 beds)
3 accredited, 1 teaching, 200 services
Office-Based Physicians
B Family Medicine: 52
AA Medical Specialists: 214
AA Surgeons: 186
Public Libraries
Live Oak Public Library
Continuing Education
Two-Year
1 campus, 6,483 students
Four-Year
Armstrong Atlantic State University (8,845)
Savannah College of Art and Design (6,714)
Savannah State University (3,262)
Rank: 40

★ Scottsdale, AZ
Airline Service
Phoenix Sky Harbor International (PHX)
General Hospitals: 28 (6,577 beds)
25 accredited, 7 teaching, 1,160 services
Office-Based Physicians
C Family Medicine: 636
AA Medical Specialists: 1,989
AA Surgeons: 1,353
Public Libraries
Scottsdale Public Library
Continuing Education
Two-Year
10 campuses, 219,268 students
Four-Year
Arizona State University (74,452)
Midwestern University (1,288)
Ottawa University (3,776)
Thunderbird School of Management (1,852)
Rank: 24

Sebring–Avon Park, FL
Airline Service
Tampa International (TPA)
General Hospitals: 2 (230 beds)
2 accredited, 73 services
Office-Based Physicians
C Family Medicine: 16
AA Medical Specialists: 59
A Surgeons: 34
Public Libraries
Heartland Library Coop
Continuing Education
Two-Year
1 campus, 4,179 students
Rank: 124

★ Sedona, AZ
Airline Service
Flagstaff Pulliam (FLG)
General Hospitals: 2 (336 beds)
2 accredited, 72 services
Office-Based Physicians
A Family Medicine: 46
B Medical Specialists: 62
B Surgeons: 64
Public Libraries
5 independent libraries
Continuing Education
Two-Year
1 campus, 6,084 students
Four-Year
Northern Arizona University (23,892)
Rank: 20

Silver City, NM
Airline Service
El Paso (TX) International (ELP)
General Hospitals: 1 (68 beds)
1 accredited, 37 services
Office-Based Physicians
AA Family Medicine: 11
B Medical Specialists: 15
B Surgeons: 14
Public Libraries
Public Library of Silver City
Continuing Education
Four-Year
Western New Mexico University (3,762)
Rank: 98

Silverthorne–Breckenridge, CO
Airline Service
Denver International (DEN)
Office-Based Physicians
AA Family Medicine: 17
C Medical Specialists: 11
C Surgeons: 13
Public Libraries
Summit County Library
Rank: 185

Smith Mountain Lake, VA
Airline Service
Roanoke Regional (ROA)
General Hospitals: 1 (37 beds)
1 accredited, 30 services
Office-Based Physicians
A Family Medicine: 44
C Medical Specialists: 16
C Surgeons: 19
Public Libraries
Bedford Public Library
Continuing Education
Two-Year
1 campus, 2,377 students
Four-Year
Ferrum College (982)
Rank: 145

Sonora–Twain Harte, CA
Airline Service
Modesto City-County/Sham Field (MOD)
General Hospitals: 2 (206 beds)
2 accredited, 78 services
Office-Based Physicians
B Family Medicine: 11
A Medical Specialists: 32
B Surgeons: 15
Public Libraries
Tuolumne County Library
Continuing Education
Two-Year
1 campus, 5,599 students
Rank: 89

Southern Berkshire County, MA
Airline Service
Windsor Locks-Bradley International (BDL)
General Hospitals: 3 (435 beds)
3 accredited, 1 teaching, 128 services
Office-Based Physicians
C Family Medicine: 20
AA Medical Specialists: 141
AA Surgeons: 63
Public Libraries
30 independent libraries
Continuing Education
Two-Year
1 campus, 3,139 students
Four-Year
Massachusetts College of Liberal Arts (3,003)
Williams College (2,208)
Rank: 96

Southern Pines–Pinehurst, NC
Airline Service
Fayetteville Regional-Grannis Field (FAY)
General Hospitals: 1 (362 beds)
1 accredited, 72 services
Office-Based Physicians
C Family Medicine: 11
AA Medical Specialists: 73
AA Surgeons: 71
Public Libraries
Southern Pines Public Library
Continuing Education
Two-Year
1 campus, 4,939 students
Rank: 87

Southport–Brunswick Islands, NC
Airline Service
Wilmington International (ILM)
General Hospitals: 2 (160 beds)
2 accredited, 37 services

continued

★ = *one of the top 30 places for services*

Office-Based Physicians
C   Family Medicine: 12
B   Medical Specialists: 15
B   Surgeons: 16
Public Libraries
Brunswick County Library
Continuing Education
Two-Year
1 campus, 1,626 students
Rank: 127

State College, PA
Airline Service
University Park Airport (UNV)
General Hospitals: 2 (168 beds)
1 accredited, 54 services
Office-Based Physicians
B   Family Medicine: 31
A   Medical Specialists: 81
A   Surgeons: 48
Public Libraries
Schlow Memorial Library
Continuing Education
Four-Year
Pennsylvania State University
(46,281)
Rank: 44

Sullivan County, NY
Airline Service
Newburgh-Stewart International
(SWF)
General Hospitals: 1 (238 beds)
1 accredited
Office-Based Physicians
C   Family Medicine: 11
AA Medical Specialists: 33
B   Surgeons: 14
Public Libraries
9 independent libraries
Continuing Education
Two-Year
1 campus, 2,574 students
Rank: 167

Summerville, SC
Airline Service
Charleston International (CHS)
General Hospitals: 1 (94 beds)
Office-Based Physicians
B   Family Medicine: 25
C   Medical Specialists: 14
C   Surgeons: 21
Public Libraries
Dorchester County Library
Rank: 161

Taos, NM
Airline Service
Santa Fe Municipal (SAF)
General Hospitals: 1 (49 beds)
38 services

Office-Based Physicians
AA Family Medicine: 14
C   Medical Specialists: 11
C   Surgeons: 13
Public Libraries
Taos Public Library
Continuing Education
Two-Year
1 campus, 1,829 students
Rank: 131

★ Thomasville, GA
Airline Service
Tallahassee (FL) Regional (TLH)
General Hospitals: 1 (328 beds)
1 accredited, 76 services
Office-Based Physicians
A   Family Medicine: 11
A   Medical Specialists: 38
AA Surgeons: 36
Public Libraries
Thomas County Libraries
Continuing Education
Two-Year
1 campus, 2,676 students
Four-Year
Thomas University (1,037)
Rank: 7

Toms River–Barnegat Bay, NJ
Airline Service
Newark Liberty International (EWR)
General Hospitals: 5 (1,161 beds)
4 accredited, 186 services
Office-Based Physicians
C   Family Medicine: 29
AA Medical Specialists: 322
AA Surgeons: 173
Public Libraries
Ocean County Library
Continuing Education
Two-Year
1 campus, 11,673 students
Four-Year
Beth Medrash Govoha (4,506)
Georgian Court University (3,680)
Rank: 83

★ Traverse City, MI
Airline Service
Traverse City-Cherry Capital (TVC)
General Hospitals: 1 (368 beds)
1 accredited, 1 teaching, 82 services
Office-Based Physicians
A   Family Medicine: 30
AA Medical Specialists: 92
AA Surgeons: 66
Public Libraries
Traverse Area Library
Continuing Education
Two-Year
1 campus, 5,916 students
Rank: 13

Tryon, NC
Airline Service
Greenville-Spartanburg International
(GSP)
General Hospitals: 1 (55 beds)
1 accredited, 28 services
Office-Based Physicians
B   Family Medicine: 4
A   Medical Specialists: 7
AA Surgeons: 10
Public Libraries
Polk County Public Library
Rank: 166

★ Tucson, AZ
Airline Service
Tucson International (TUS)
General Hospitals: 8 (2,276 beds)
8 accredited, 4 teaching,
278 services
Office-Based Physicians
B   Family Medicine: 193
AA Medical Specialists: 666
AA Surgeons: 433
Public Libraries
Tucson-Pima Library
Continuing Education
Two-Year
2 campuses, 53,267 students
Four-Year
University of Arizona (51,814)
Rank: 8

Vero Beach, FL
Airline Service
Melbourne International (MLB)
General Hospitals: 3 (676 beds)
2 accredited, 68 services
Office-Based Physicians
B   Family Medicine: 28
AA Medical Specialists: 114
AA Surgeons: 83
Public Libraries
Indian River County Library
Rank: 103

Victorville–Apple Valley, CA
Airline Service
Southern California Logistics (VCV)
General Hospitals: 17 (3,514 beds)
17 accredited, 4 teaching,
426 services
Office-Based Physicians
C   Family Medicine: 307
A   Medical Specialists: 721
A   Surgeons: 504
Public Libraries
7 independent libraries
Continuing Education
Two-Year
6 campuses, 71,545 students

★ = *one of the top 30 places for services*

Four-Year
California State University San Bernardino (20,192)
Loma Linda University (4,249)
University of Redlands (5,652)
Rank: 66

Waynesville, NC
Airline Service
Asheville Regional (AVL)
General Hospitals: 1 (113 beds)
1 accredited
Office-Based Physicians
AA Family Medicine: 25
C   Medical Specialists: 23
C   Surgeons: 21
Public Libraries
Haywood County Public Library
Continuing Education
Two-Year
1 campus, 2,680 students
Rank: 111

Wenatchee, WA
Airline Service
Pangborn Memorial (EAT)
General Hospitals: 3 (193 beds)
1 accredited, 82 services
Office-Based Physicians
AA Family Medicine: 37
B   Medical Specialists: 55
B   Surgeons: 47
Public Libraries
North Central Library
Continuing Education
Two-Year
1 campus, 5,077 students
Rank: 56

Western St. Tammany Parish, LA
Airline Service
Louis Armstrong New Orleans International (MSY)
General Hospitals: 4 (696 beds)
4 accredited, 156 services
Office-Based Physicians
C   Family Medicine: 33
AA Medical Specialists: 197
AA Surgeons: 143
Public Libraries
St. Tammany Parish Library
Continuing Education
Two-Year
1 campus, 505 students
Rank: 117

Whidbey Island, WA
Airline Service
Seattle-Tacoma International (SEA)
General Hospitals: 1 (80 beds)
1 accredited, 29 services

Office-Based Physicians
A   Family Medicine: 26
C   Medical Specialists: 21
C   Surgeons: 20
Public Libraries
Sno-Isle Library System
Rank: 133

★ Wickenburg, AZ
Airline Service
Phoenix Sky Harbor International (PHX)
General Hospitals: 28 (6,577 beds)
25 accredited, 7 teaching, 1,160 services
Office-Based Physicians
C   Family Medicine: 636
AA Medical Specialists: 1,989
AA Surgeons: 1,353
Public Libraries
Wickenburg Public Library
Continuing Education
Two-Year
10 campuses, 219,268 students
Four-Year
Arizona State University (74,452)
Midwestern University (1,288)
Ottawa University (3,776)
Thunderbird School of Management (1,852)
Rank: 24

★ Williamsburg, VA
Airline Service
Newport News/Williamsburg International (PHF)
General Hospitals: 1 (110 beds)
1 accredited, 57 services
Office-Based Physicians
AA Family Medicine: 27
B   Medical Specialists: 55
A   Surgeons: 47
Public Libraries
Williamsburg Regional Library
Continuing Education
Four-Year
College of William and Mary (8,967)
Rank: 19

Wimberley, TX
Airline Service
Austin-Bergstrom International (AUS)
General Hospitals: 1 (110 beds)
1 accredited, 40 services
Office-Based Physicians
C   Family Medicine: 22
B   Medical Specialists: 34
B   Surgeons: 26
Public Libraries
5 independent libraries

Continuing Education
Four-Year
Texas State University (30,705)
Rank: 84

Woodstock, VT

Airline Service
Lebanon Municipal (LEB)
General Hospitals: 2 (220 beds)
2 accredited, 1 teaching, 159 services
Office-Based Physicians
A   Family Medicine: 17
AA Medical Specialists: 53
B   Surgeons: 25
Public Libraries
23 independent libraries
Continuing Education
Four-Year
Vermont Law School (632)
Rank: 99

York Beaches, ME
Airline Service
Portland International Jetport (PWM)
General Hospitals: 3 (365 beds)
2 accredited, 139 services
Office-Based Physicians
B   Family Medicine: 43
B   Medical Specialists: 70
B   Surgeons: 55
Public Libraries
33 independent libraries
Continuing Education
Two-Year
1 campus, 1,371 students
Four-Year
University of New England (5,955)
Rank: 114

Yuma, AZ
Airline Service
Yuma International (YUM)
General Hospitals: 1 (277 beds)
1 accredited, 55 services
Office-Based Physicians
C   Family Medicine: 15
AA Medical Specialists: 74
AA Surgeons: 42
Public Libraries
Yuma County Library District
Continuing Education
Two-Year
1 campus, 11,857 students
Rank: 118

Services

★ = *one of the top 30 places for services*

FINDING THE RIGHT DOCTOR

Chances are good you'll have to choose a new physician at some point; even if you don't move after retirement, your doctor might. Finding a replacement for the person in whom you've put so much trust isn't always easy.

Think about the kind of doctor with whom you're most comfortable. Do you want to place complete faith in your physician? Do you have questions about your treatment? Do you like a cooperative arrangement in which you and your doctor work as a team? It's very important to most people that they have a doctor who'll listen to their complaints, worries, and concerns, rather than one who may make patients feel they're questioning the doctor's authority.

If you're planning to move, you might ask your present doctor if he or she knows anything about the doctors in the area where you're going. Or you can get names from the nearest hospital at the new location, from friends you make, from medical societies, and from new neighbors.

Warning! Doctor Shortages Ahead

It's ironic that physician shortages loom a generation after experts predicted an oversupply of doctors. Newly certified M.D.s are less likely than ever to set themselves up in solo practice, instead joining large specialty groups or going to work for hospital systems. And older physicians are retiring from their profession in large numbers.

Nationally, about 1 in 15 Medicare patients experiences trouble finding a doctor, according to a federal report. Depending on where you move and how you're paying for treatment, you may find a competent physician immediately, or you may have to wait months for your first appointment, or you may not find treatment at all. One of the important keys is how well Medicare is reimbursing the doctor.

Location Makes a Difference

Three-fourths of all doctors, according to a recent survey, have no problem accepting new Medicare patients. The other 25 percent don't care for bureaucratic paperwork or they practice specialties that may be underreimbursed by Medicare. Or they work in attractive retirement spots that have seen older adults arrive in enormous numbers from other parts of the country, driving up living costs at a time when Medicare payments stay relatively low.

You should know that the amount Medicare pays a physician for a medical procedure varies by location. Medicare pays a San Francisco internist a flat $65 and a Fargo, North Dakota, internist a flat $46 for a "moderate complexity" office visit. The disparity is due to different practice costs and liability insurance premiums. If both shoot upward, some physicians stop accepting Medicare patients until procedure payments are raised too.

But Let's Say You're Lucky

When you've decided whom you want to contact, call that doctor's office, say you're a prospective patient, and ask to speak to the doctor briefly. You may have to agree to call back, but making a connection with a professional voice is an important step. If you can't arrange this, say, if the doctor is too busy, you probably ought to be forgiving and persist. You'll need a physician who's ultimately reachable.

When you do make contact, tell the doctor enough about yourself that he or she has a good idea of who you are and what your problems may be. If the doctor sounds right to you, you could ask about fees, house calls (yes, they're again being made when necessary), and emergencies. Or you may wish to save some of these questions for a personal visit. It's important to establish through the initial phone call or visit that you and the doctor will be at ease with each other.

Evaluate the doctor's attitude. If he or she doesn't want to bother with you now, you'll probably get that don't-bother-me treatment sooner or later when dealing with specific problems. Make sure:

- You can openly discuss your feelings and personal concerns about sexual and emotional problems.

- The doctor isn't vague, impatient, or unwilling to answer all your questions about the causes and treatment of your physical problems.

- The doctor takes a thorough history on you and asks about past physical and emotional problems, family medical history, medication you're taking, and other matters affecting your health.

- The doctor doesn't always attribute your problems to getting older and he or she doesn't automatically prescribe drugs rather than deal with real causes of your medical problems.

- The doctor has an associate to whom you can turn should your doctor retire or die.

Talk with the doctor about the transfer of your medical records. Some doctors like to have them, especially if there's any specific medical problem or chronic condition. Other doctors prefer not to see them and to develop new records.

Even if you feel fine, arrange to have a physical or at least a quick checkup. This is more for the doctor's benefit than for yours, but it will help you too. Should an emergency occur, the doctor will have basic information about you and some knowledge of your needs, and you'll avoid the stress of trying to work with a doctor who has to learn about you in an emergency.

FINDING THE RIGHT LAWYER

When you move from one state to another, you enter a new legal environment. Even if your will is legal in your new state (and it may not be), it may not do the best possible job. When you resettle, see a lawyer in your new area to make certain your will is one your state will recognize. Some states, for example, require that the executor of a will be a resident of the state where the deceased lived. For a legal checkup, you may have to contact a family lawyer.

Lawyering is a competitive field. In the past, lawyers and clients usually found each other in the Rotary Club, at a church supper, or on the golf course. Since 1977, when the Supreme Court struck down laws barring the legal profession from advertising, many lawyers have gotten quite adept at promoting themselves.

Look up "Lawyers" in the Yellow Pages and you'll be surprised by the techniques many firms borrow from consumer goods advertising. Specialists for 24-hour divorces, personal bankruptcy, workers' compensation, and personal injury claims abound. Somewhere hidden among the listings is a professional who can advise you. How do you find him or her?

- **Satisfied clients:** If a friend or neighbor has used a lawyer's services, ask what sort of matter the lawyer handled. Some lawyers, especially in large

cities, specialize in a certain branch of law and aren't interested in taking on cases outside their specialty.

- **Lawyer referral service:** Most state bar associations have a referral service with a toll-free phone number. Typically, the name you're given is an attorney who practices where you live, specializes in your legal problem, and is next up in the association's database to be referred. You can have a first interview with him or her for a stated—and very modest—fee. In that interview, you can find out whether you'll need further legal services, and, if so, you can decide whether you want to continue with the lawyer to whom you were referred.

- **Local bar association:** If the state bar association referral service lists no lawyer in your area, try the local bar association. If you don't find it in the telephone book, inquire for the president's name at the county courthouse. You can then ask him or her for the name of a good lawyer. Be sure to make it clear you're asking them, in their capacity as president of the local association, for the name of a reliable attorney who can perform the kind of service you're seeking.

Don't Put Off Your Will

It's human nature to avoid thinking about the need for a will. Seven out of every 10 people die without one, and 8 of 10 who do have a will fail to keep it up-to-date. If you don't have a will when you die, the state where you live in your retirement years will write one for you according to its own statutes, and the assets you may have worked hard to accumulate will be distributed according to its laws.

Don't put off making a will because of imagined costs. A lawyer can tell you the basic fee in advance; it's usually $500 to $1,000 for a simple document. And it may save your heirs thousands. Once you have a will, make a note to yourself in your calendar to review it every year. Births, marriages, deaths, hard feelings, the patching up of hard feelings, plus changes in your finances, your health, or federal or state laws—any of these may affect your will. Periodic review helps ensure you won't forget to make needed adjustments.

If death and taxes are inevitable—as the old saying goes—so are taxes after death. But it isn't all bad. For 2007 and 2008, estates smaller than $2 million are *not* subject to federal tax; and the exemption increases to $3.5 million in 2009. State tax exemptions vary greatly and often change, another reason for keeping the document up-to-date.

Where should you keep your will? Put it in a safe place, but don't hide it behind a painting or under a rug. If you conceal it too well, a court may rule you don't have one. Your lawyer should have a signed copy, and the original should be in a logical place, such as a safe-deposit box or your desk. Be sure your spouse, a close relative, or a friend knows where both the copies and the original are.

DRIVER LICENSING

When you settle in a new state, you have to surrender your out-of-state driver's license and get a new one. The time to get this done ranges from immediately in nine states to up to 6 months in Vermont. Hawaii lets you keep your existing license until it expires.

Required Tests

For a new resident with a valid driver's license from a former state, the requirements for getting a license from the new state vary. All states now require vision testing. In Connecticut and New Hampshire, all other tests aside from vision may be waived. Washington requires you to get behind the wheel with a license examiner for a road test; in 29 other states, a road test may be waived or required at the discretion of the examiner.

Problem Drivers

Forty-six states belong to the National Driver License (NDL) Compact, an agreement among states to share information on drivers who accumulate tickets in one jurisdiction and try to escape control in another. If your license has been revoked, you won't get a new one simply by moving to another state. Every license application is checked with the National Driver Register, a federal data file of persons whose license to drive has been revoked.

Driving Danger Signals

Researching the records of insurance companies and state police agencies, Dr. Leon Pastalan of the University of Michigan found that older drivers receive a high number of tickets for the following five traffic violations:

- Rear-end collisions
- Dangerously slow driving
- Failure to yield the right-of-way
- Driving the wrong way on one-way streets
- Illegal turns

Even though people age at different rates, normal changes that affect eyesight, muscle reflexes, and hearing are the reasons older adults are ticketed for these moving violations more often than the rest of the population. Simply recognizing your limitations will help you become a better driver.

Eyesight. Ninety percent of all sensory input needed to drive a car comes through the eyes. As vision loses its sharpness, the typical rectangular black-and-white road signs become hard to read. Night driving is especially risky, because the older we get, the more illumination we need to see. For example, an 80-year-old needs three times the light that a 20-year-old needs to read. Other problems include loss of depth perception (a major cause of rear-end collisions) and limited peripheral vision (dangerous when making turns at intersections).

You can adjust to these dangers by not driving at night, having regular eye checkups, wearing gray- or green-tinted sunglasses on days with high sun glare, and replacing your car's standard rearview mirror with a wide-angle one to aid peripheral vision.

Muscle Reflexes. Many people slow down as they get older. Strength may dwindle, neck and shoulder joints may stiffen, and you may tire sooner. Most important to driving, your reflex reactions may slow. All these symptoms can affect how safely you enter a busy freeway, how cautiously you change lanes to pass a plodding 18-wheel truck, or how you avoid a rear-end fender bender.

Ask your physician if any of the medications you're taking might decrease your alertness and ability to drive defensively. On long road trips, take along a companion to share the driving, and break the day's distance into short stretches to reduce fatigue. Don't get caught on freeways and major arterial streets during morning and evening rush hours.

Hearing. One in every five persons over age 55 and one of every three persons over age 65 has impaired hearing. It's a gradual condition and can go unnoticed for a long time. When you can't hear an ambulance siren, a ticket for failing to yield the right-of-way to an emergency vehicle is the likely consequence.

You can compensate for hearing loss by having periodic checkups. When you drive, open a window,

turn off the radio, keep the air-conditioner fan on low speed, and cut unnecessary conversation.

DRIVER LICENSING & CAR REGISTRATION AFTER MOVING

A Guide for Persons with Current Paperwork from a Former Jurisdiction

STATE	DRIVER LICENSING TIME LIMIT	WRITTEN TEST	VISION TEST	ROAD TEST	VEHICLE REGISTRATION NDL COMPACT	TIME LIMIT	INSPECTION REQUIRED
Alabama	30 days	●	Yes		Yes	30 days	
Alaska	90 days	●	Yes		Yes	10 days	
Arizona	immediately	○	Yes	○	Yes	immediately	
Arkansas	30 days		Yes		Yes	10 days	s
California	10 days	●	Yes	○	Yes	20 days	e
Colorado	30 days	●	Yes	○	Yes	immediately	e
Connecticut	30 days	○	Yes	○	Yes	60 days	e
Delaware	60 days	●	Yes	○	Yes	60 days	s/e
District of Columbia	30 days	●	Yes	○	Yes	*	s/e
Florida	30 days	○	Yes	○	Yes	10 days	e
Georgia	30 days	●	Yes		No	30 days	e
Hawaii	*	●	Yes	○	Yes	10 days	s
Idaho	90 days	●	Yes		Yes	90 days	
Illinois	90 days	●	Yes		Yes	30 days	e
Indiana	60 days	●	Yes		Yes	60 days	e
Iowa	immediately	●	Yes		Yes	90 days	
Kansas	90 days	●	Yes		Yes	*	
Kentucky	immediately	●	Yes		No	15 days	
Louisiana	90 days		Yes		Yes	immediately	s/e
Maine	30 days	●	Yes	○	Yes	30 days	s
Maryland	30 days	○	Yes	○	Yes	30 days	e
Massachusetts	immediately		Yes		No	immediately	s/e
Michigan	immediately	●	Yes		No	immediately	e
Minnesota	60 days	●	Yes	○	Yes	60 days	
Mississippi	60 days	●	Yes	○	Yes	30 days	s
Missouri	immediately	●	Yes	○	Yes	30 days	s/e
Montana	90 days	○	Yes	○	Yes	immediately	
Nebraska	30 days	●	Yes	○	Yes	*	
Nevada	30 days	○	Yes	○	Yes	45 days	e
New Hampshire	60 days	○	Yes	○	Yes	60 days	s
New Jersey	60 days	●	Yes	○	Yes	60 days	s/e
New Mexico	30 days	●	Yes		Yes	30 days	
New York	30 days	●	Yes		Yes	30 days	s/e
North Carolina	30 days	●	Yes	○	Yes	immediately	s/e
North Dakota	60 days	●	Yes	○	Yes	immediately	
Ohio	30 days	●	Yes	○	Yes	immediately	e
Oklahoma	immediately	●	Yes	○	Yes	60 days	s/e
Oregon	immediately	●	Yes	○	Yes	immediately	e
Pennsylvania	60 days	●	Yes	○	Yes	60 days	s/e
Rhode Island	30 days	●	Yes		Yes	30 days	s/e
South Carolina	90 days		Yes	○	Yes	45 days	s
South Dakota	90 days	○	Yes	○	Yes	90 days	
Tennessee	30 days	○	Yes	○	Yes	immediately	
Texas	30 days	○	Yes	○	Yes	30 days	s/e
Utah	60 days	●	Yes		Yes	60 days	s/e
Vermont	6 months	○	Yes	○	Yes	6 months	s
Virginia	30 days	○	Yes		Yes	30 days	s
Washington	30 days	●	Yes	○	Yes	30 days	
West Virginia	30 days	●	Yes		Yes	30 days	s/e
Wisconsin	immediately	●	Yes	○	No	immediately	e
Wyoming	120 days		Yes	○	Yes	immediately	

● = Required; ○ = May be waived; * = Existing license or registration valid until expiration; s = Safety inspection; e = Emissions test; s/e = Both safety inspection and emissions test

Source: American Automobile Association, Digest of Motor Laws, 2006; Places Rated survey.

DRIVER AGE DISCRIMINATION?

Once you start feeling your age, will insurance companies and state highway safety committees consider you dangerous when you get behind the wheel of your automobile?

On the face of it, older drivers have a better accident record than younger drivers. People over 60 represent 1 in 8 persons in America, yet are involved in only 1 in 15 of the automobile accidents. Still, the National Safety Council notes that people over 60 drive much less than younger people and actually have a poorer accident record when comparing the number of miles driven.

The American Medical Association and the American Association of Motor Vehicle Administrators have both recommended that states reexamine older drivers more frequently than younger drivers.

Twenty-six states and Washington, D.C., now require special examinations or accelerated license renewal based solely on age. Typical restrictions prohibit nighttime driving, require the vehicle to have supplemental mirrors, or restrict driving to specified places or a limited radius from the driver's home. In addition, California, Delaware, Georgia, Nevada, New Jersey, Oregon, and Pennsylvania require doctors to report conditions that impair driving ability. Tennessee takes the opposing view: licenses issued to drivers over 65 "do not expire."

Alaska	No mail-in renewals after age 69. Vision test required at age 69.	**Louisiana**	Renew license every 4 years; mail renewal not available to people 70 and older or if prior renewal was by mail.
Arizona	License renewal every 5 years after age 65. No mail-in renewals after age 70.	**Maine**	Vision reexamination at ages 40, 52, and 62 and each subsequent year. License renewal every 4 years for drivers over age 65.
California	No mail-in renewals after age 70. Reexamination waived for "clean record" drivers under age 70. Vision and rules-of-the-road written test required at age 70.		
		Maryland	Renew license every 5 years. Vision test required for renewal at 40 and older.
Colorado	License renewal every 5 years after age 61. Mail or electronic renewal not available after age 61 or if previous renewal was not in person.	**Missouri**	License renewal every 3 years after age 70.
		Montana	License renewal every 8 years for drivers over age 68 and every 4 years for drivers over age 75. Only two successive renewals may be made by mail, regardless of age.
Connecticut	License renewal every 2 years after age 65. Showing hardship, renewals may be by mail for those 65 and older.		
Florida	Vision test required after age 80. Only two successive renewals may be made by mail, regardless of age.	**New Hampshire**	For drivers over age 75, a road test must be taken.
		New Mexico	License renewal every 4 years for drivers over age 75.
Georgia	Renewals every 5 years after age 60. Vision test required for 64 and older.	**North Carolina**	Renew license every 5 years from age 54.
Hawaii	License renewal every 2 years for drivers over age 72.	**Oregon**	Vision reexamination at 50 and over on 8-year renewal.
Idaho	Drivers over 63 must renew every 4 years. No mail-in renewals after age 69.	**Rhode Island**	License renewal every 2 years for drivers over age 70.
Illinois	Complete reexamination every 4 years for drivers age 75 to 80, every 2 years for drivers age 81 to 86; for age 87 and older there is an annual renewal. Renewal applicants over 75 must take a road test.	**South Carolina**	License renewal with vision test every 5 years for drivers over 65.
		Utah	Vision examination required at age 65 and older.
		Washington, D.C.	Vision and reaction examination for drivers over age 70; complete reexamination at age 75 and over.
Indiana	Renewal every 3 years for drivers over age 75.		
Iowa	License renewal every 2 years for drivers over age 70.	**Wisconsin**	No mail-in renewals after age 70.
Kansas	License renewal every 4 years for drivers over age 65.		

Source: Insurance Institute for Highway Safety.

COLLEGE TUITION BREAKS

Every state allows for tuition and fee waivers at public colleges and universities. The most common beneficiaries are the dependents of police or firefighters killed in the line of duty, or dependents of state higher education teachers and administrators.

Forty-two states waive or reduce tuition in their public colleges for persons who've reached a specific age. For attendance at both 2- and 4-year institutions, it's the law in 15 states; in another 7, it's a formal policy adopted by the state's Board of Regents or Board of Higher Education. California, Florida, and New York statutes cover tuition waivers only at 4-year institutions. It's common practice for individual colleges and universities in all 50 states to establish their own tuition reduction policies.

The limitations on this benefit vary. States that permit tuition waivers grant it on a space-available basis, which simply means older students who want to take advantage of the tuition break are admitted to courses only after tuition-paying students have enrolled. Eight states grant the benefit only for auditing courses (enrolling for no credit). Four states—Illinois, Indiana, Maryland, and Virginia—look at the student's income to determine eligibility.

ESTABLISHING RESIDENCY FOR TUITION BENEFITS

Legal residency not only is important for tax purposes but also is a necessary step to qualify for in-state tuition fees or tuition waivers at local public colleges.

Of the states that offer some form of tuition reduction or waiver, most require proof of at least 1 year of residency. Here are several steps to take to satisfy that requirement:

- Ask the local county clerk for a certificate of domicile.
- Get a driver's license and register your car in the new state.
- If you don't drive, ask the driver's license authority for a nondriver ID card. All states now issue them; some are similar to the driver's license format. Delaware, Illinois, and Minnesota will issue an ID card to all persons, not just nondrivers.
- File your final state income tax in your former state; file state and federal income taxes in the new state.
- At your first opportunity, register and vote in an election in your new state.

College Tuition Waivers for Older Adults

STATE	MINIMUM AGE	2-YEAR COLLEGES	4-YEAR COLLEGES
Alabama	60	○	
Alaska	60	●	●
Arkansas	60	■	■
California	60		■
Colorado	65	○	○
Connecticut	62	■	■
Delaware	60	■	○
Florida	60	○	■
Georgia	62	●	●
Hawaii	60		■
Idaho	60	○	●
Illinois	65	■	■
Indiana	60	○	○
Kansas	60	○	●
Kentucky	65	■	■
Louisiana	60	■	■
Maine	65		●
Maryland	60	■	■
Massachusetts	60	●	●
Michigan	60	●	●
Minnesota	62	○	○
Missouri	65	○	○
Montana	62	●	●
Nebraska	65	○	○
Nevada	62	●	●
New Jersey	65	■	■
New Mexico	65	■	■
New York	60		■
North Carolina	65	■	■
Ohio	60	■	■
Oklahoma	65	●	●
Oregon	65		●
Rhode Island	60	■	■
South Carolina	60	■	■
South Dakota	65		●
Tennessee	65	■	■
Texas	65	○	○
Utah	62	○	○
Vermont	62	○	○
Virginia	60	■	■
Washington	60	■	■
Wyoming	62	○	○

■ = *state statute*, ● = *formal policy*, ○ = *discretion of each institution*

Source: State Higher Education Executive Officers, State Tuition, Fees, and Financial Assistance Policies for Public Colleges and Universities, 2006; Places Rated Partners survey.

Alabama

There's no legislation or state policy to waive or reduce tuition for older adults in state-funded colleges and universities. Tuition and general student fees are waived for courses in all state-funded 2-year colleges.

Alaska

State policy waives tuition for residents 60 years or older at state-funded institutions on a space-available basis.

Arizona

There's no legislation or state policy within the university or community college system to waive or reduce tuition for older adults.

Arkansas

Tuition and general student fees are waived for credit courses on a space-available basis for older adults at any state institutions of higher learning.

California

Tuition and general student fees may be waived only at participating campuses of the California State University system for credit courses on a space-available basis.

Colorado

State higher education policy permits each state-funded institution, at its discretion, to waive or reduce tuition for older adults.

Connecticut

State law waives tuition at all state-funded 2-year colleges; unless students are admitted to degree-granting programs at state universities, tuition is waived only on a space-available basis.

Delaware

State law waives application, course, registration, and other fees for credit courses on a space-available basis. Students must be formal degree candidates.

District of Columbia

Tuition is waived in courses taken for credit or audited at all University of the District of Columbia campuses.

Florida

Tuition fees are waived for courses taken by residents over 60 who attend classes at state universities on a space-available basis. No academic credit is given under the waiver.

Georgia

State higher education policy allows tuition fees to be waived only for credit courses on a space-available basis. Dental, medical, veterinary, and law school courses are excluded.

Hawaii

Tuition and general student fees are waived at the University of Hawaii campuses for regularly scheduled credit courses on a space-available basis.

Idaho

State policy reduces the registration fee to $20, plus a $5 fee per credit hour is charged for courses on a space-available basis.

Illinois

Older persons who have been accepted in regularly scheduled credit courses, and whose income is less than $14,000, are eligible for tuition waivers on a space-available basis.

Indiana

With certain limitations, 50 percent of the tuition fee is waived for older adults who aren't working full-time and have a high-school degree.

Iowa

There's no legislation or state policy within the university or community college system to waive or reduce tuition for older adults.

Kansas

Tuition and general student fees at state-funded universities are waived only for auditing courses on a space-available basis.

Kentucky

Tuition and general student fees are waived at any state-funded institution of higher learning, for residents only, for regularly scheduled credit courses on a space-available basis.

Louisiana

Tuition and other registration fees are waived for courses on a space-available basis, provided sufficient funds are appropriated by the legislature to reimburse colleges and universities affected.

Maine

Tuition and fees are waived for undergraduate courses on a space-available basis at state-supported colleges and universities.

Maryland

Tuition fees are waived for 2-year college courses on a space-available basis, and up to three university or 4-year college courses per term on a space-available basis for students whose income is derived from retirement benefits and who aren't employed full-time.

Massachusetts

Tuition fees are waived for courses if the college or university isn't overenrolled.

Michigan

Community colleges and state colleges and universities may waive tuition for older students meeting admission requirements.

Minnesota

Except for an administration fee of $6 per credit hour, collected only when a course is taken for credit, tuition and activity fees are waived to attend courses for credit, to audit any course offered for credit, or to enroll in any noncredit adult vocational education courses on a space-available basis.

Mississippi

There's no legislation or state policy within the university or community college system to waive or reduce tuition for older adults.

Missouri

State higher education policy permits each state-funded institution, at its discretion, to waive or reduce tuition for older adults.

Montana

State higher education policy permits tuition to be waived at the discretion of the regents of the Montana university system.

Nebraska

State higher education policy permits each state-funded institution, at its discretion, to waive or reduce tuition for older adults.

Nevada

Registration fees are waived only for regularly scheduled courses that may be audited or taken for credit. Consent of the instructor may be required.

New Hampshire

There's no state legislation or policy waiving tuition fees for older adults.

New Jersey

Tuition fees may be waived for courses on a space-available basis at each public institution of higher education.

New Mexico

Tuition may be reduced to $5 per credit hour up to a maximum of six credit hours per semester for older residents on a space-available basis.

New York

Tuition fees may be waived only for auditing courses on a space-available basis at institutions of the state university system.

North Carolina

Tuition fees are waived for auditing courses or for taking courses for credit on a space-available basis.

North Dakota

There's no state legislation or policy waiving tuition fees for older adults.

Ohio

Tuition and matriculation fees are waived only for auditing courses on a space-available basis.

Oklahoma

State higher education policy allows tuition fees to be waived only for auditing courses on a space-available basis.

Oregon

Tuition fees are waived for auditing courses on a space-available basis.

Pennsylvania

There's no legislation or state policy within the university or community college system to waive or reduce tuition for older adults.

Rhode Island

Tuition and general student fees are waived for credit courses on a space-available basis at the discretion of the institution.

South Carolina

Tuition fees are waived for courses, for credit or audit, at any state-supported institution on a space-available basis.

South Dakota

Tuition fees are reduced to 50 percent of resident tuition at state universities.

Tennessee

Tuition and registration fees are waived for auditing or taking for credit courses on a space-available basis. The board of regents may charge a service fee not to exceed $50 per quarter or $75 per semester. The waiver doesn't apply at medical, dental, or pharmacy schools.

Texas

The governing board of any state-supported institution may allow tuition fees to be waived, on a space-available basis, for auditing courses or for enrolling for credit in courses up to 6 hours per term.

Utah

Tuition fees (but not quarterly registration fees) may be waived for courses on a space-available basis at each state-funded college and university.

Vermont

Tuition fees may be waived for courses on a space-available basis at each state-funded college and university.

Virginia

Tuition and registration fees are waived on a space-available basis, if the student has a federal taxable income not exceeding $10,000. Registration is limited to no more than three courses in any one term, quarter, or semester if the person isn't enrolled for academic credit.

Washington

Depending on the institution and for no more than two courses per term, tuition and general student fees may be waived for courses taken for credit and waived entirely for courses taken for audit. There may be a nominal fee of $5 charged per term for auditing.

West Virginia

There's no legislation or state policy within the university or community college system to waive or reduce tuition for older adults.

Wisconsin

There's no legislation or state policy within the university or community college system to waive or reduce tuition for older adults.

Wyoming

The university or community college system may waive or reduce tuition for older adults at each institution's discretion.

Ambience

The hardest-to-define quality of a place is its ambience. The word comes from a Latin verb meaning to turn or revolve. Centuries later, like so many things cultural, ambience now means something different: the special qualities of place—the air, the feel, the place's *genius loci,* even the way it makes you behave.

Retirement Places Rated will not claim here that it knows better than you which places have more of that subtle quality than others. But this book does attempt to measure attributes that many of us think contribute to a place's ambience: dining out, good bookstores, a visible history, the performing arts, the great outdoors, and people. For many older adults, the best places to retire boast an interesting mix of all these elements.

Like a mild and dry climate, ambience isn't distributed fairly. Chapel Hill–Carrboro, North Carolina, for example, has indoor blessings in good restaurants, bookstores, and a fine performing arts calendar, but few amenities outdoors in scenic or protected recreation land. Over in Rabun County, Georgia, hundreds of miles to the west, the situation is reversed: neither bookstores nor the lively arts, but riches in lakes and extensive natural areas. In still other places such as Middle Cape Cod, Massachusetts, or Santa Barbara, California, free-time attractions are plentiful indoors and out. For many older adults, an ideal haven balances fun and games with culture and the arts, culture and the arts with the great outdoors, and all of it in an interesting setting.

BRICKS & MORTAR

On a map of America, where do bookstores cluster? Is there any geographic pattern to good full-service restaurants? Are historic neighborhoods common? Answers: Everywhere people have some money and a taste for reading; No, nothing apparent; and No.

Good Bookstores

Any bookstore is a good bookstore because it is what sociologists call a good "third place"—a spot separate from home and work where you can spend time. Churches and bars are third places, too. But bookselling is a competitive retail business and stores strive to offer more than just books. Now in superstores you can sit at a Starbucks cafe, scan a *For Dummies* book, sample a CD, and connect wirelessly to the Internet to read your e-mail.

Almost all superstores are operated by three chains—Barnes & Noble, Borders Group, and Books-A-Million. Two chains also manage smaller stores in shopping malls—B. Daltons (Barnes & Noble) and Waldenbooks (Borders Group). At $9 billion in annual sales from some 2,200 outlets, the chains account for 70 percent of all general bookstore sales. You'll find a superstore in half of the retirement places in this book, but you'll find an independent bookseller in more.

Of course, independent stores still operate. To survive, many specialize in religious, scientific and engineering, business, or children's books. In some locations, college bookstores—for example, Penn State Bookstore in State College, Pennsylvania; University of Florida Bookstore in Gainesville, Florida; and University Bookstore in Madison, Wisconsin—operate stores as big as the chains.

Good Restaurants

The most common service establishment in this country is the one where you walk in, sit down, and order something to eat. If you enjoy an occasional dinner splurge, you may as well go to a worthwhile eatery instead of a diner or a portion-controlled *Casa de la Maison House* where distantly prepared frozen packs of beef Wellington and veal cordon bleu are microwaved, dished out, and plated at 10 times what the chef paid for them.

To learn which places have restaurants more than just a cut above average, *Retirement Places Rated* consulted the *American Automobile Association (AAA) TourBooks*. In these volumes, one out of nine of America's full-service restaurants are rated from one to five diamonds.

One AAA diamond indicates a simple meal in clean and informal surroundings. The menu is limited to specialties: fried chicken, pizza, tacos, or hamburgers. **Contrary Mary's** just west of downtown Branson, Missouri, fits this description.

Las Cruces' **La Hacienda** restaurant, serving New Mexico specialties, is a two-diamond establishment. Eateries at this level focus on presentation, that is, "common garnishes" and "styled dishware." They offer a more extensive menu. Service is attentive but informal and the decor is trendy and upbeat.

DINING OUT

Like Michelin with its three-star ratings, the *AAA TourBooks* are stingy with their five diamonds. For 2007, just 8 eateries from among the 3,155 AAA-rated full-service restaurants in places profiled in *Retirement Places Rated* earned that designation.

AAA FIVE-DIAMOND RESTAURANTS

Erna's Elderberry House—Oakhurst, California

The Dining Room in the Ritz Carlton—Naples, Florida

The Dining Room at Woodlands—Summerville, SC

Marquesa—Scottsdale, Arizona

Mary Elaine's—Scottsdale, Arizona

The Ventana Room—Tucson, Arizona

Wheatleigh's Dining Room—Lenox (Southern Berkshire County), Massachusetts

The White Barn Inn—Kennebunk (York Beaches), Maine

Three-diamond restaurants begin the upscale adult or special family dining segment. A wine and specialty-beer list, food creatively cooked to order with quality ingredients, a skilled waitstaff, and a trendy or formal ambience—these are the features that AAA's anonymous diners look for. Scottsdale, Arizona's **Windows on the Green,** specializing in American Southwest cuisine, is in this category.

Asheville, North Carolina, has 2 four-diamond establishments: **Gabrielle's** in the Richmond Hill Inn and **Horizon's** in the Grove Park Inn. Charleston, South Carolina, has 11 four-diamond eateries. The five-diamond designation represents the ultimate and most memorable adult dining experiences, with "flawless" being a key word—in food preparation and presentation, in service, and in atmosphere.

Historic Neighborhoods

In demolishing an early-19th-century orphanage in Charleston, South Carolina, in 1953, workmen lashed a heavy chain around a large marble angel atop the pediment and pulled it crashing down with a tow truck. That incident so outraged some citizens, that their campaign to save Charleston's historic buildings marked the start of civic historic preservation in the United States.

If you walk along the cobblestone streets of historic downtown Charleston, you may feel as if you've journeyed back in time to before the outbreak of the Civil War. Step into the central plaza of Santa Fe and you can imagine the days when the city was an outpost of Spain. Travel a bit outside of the New Mexico capital city and you encounter the pueblos of Native Americans as they existed before the Europeans had any idea that there was a "New World."

Charleston is quite different from Santa Fe. But one of the reasons both cities are among the top-rated retirement places is the contribution that history makes to their ambience. Santa Fe mandates the Spanish-Pueblo adobe and wood construction that recalls the city's 18th- and 19th-century past, for instance, and Charleston's zoning code protects even the most dilapidated antebellum "shotgun" shack from demolition. Their histories are different, but both places have preserved a palpable sense of their pasts, and thus have created an enticing present.

TWENTY VISIBLE HISTORIES

Just one in three retirement places with big collections of historic buildings are in the Sun Belt. But the locations that count—Savannah, Tucson, Key West, and Charleston—are among the best-known places in the country for historic preservation. Here are 20 retirement places with the most contributing buildings in historic neighborhoods.

PLACE	CONTRIBUTING BUILDINGS
Savannah, GA	5,909
Tucson, AZ	5,469
Middle Cape Cod, MA	4,202
Madison, WI	3,205
East End Long Island, NY	3,104
Litchfield Hills, CT	2,828
Lakeland–Winter Haven, FL	2,698
Key West, FL	2,690
State College, PA	2,690
Northampton–Amherst, MA	2,261
Charleston, SC	1,983
Rehoboth Bay–Indian River Bay, DE	1,884
Southern Berkshire County, MA	1,736
Burlington, VT	1,484
Woodstock, VT	1,466
Easton–St. Michaels, MD	1,464
Asheville, NC	1,356
Athens, GA	1,298
Annapolis, MD	1,240
Loudoun County, VA	1,204

Source: Derived from the National Park Service, National Register of Historic Places.

Visible history is an important component of all places' ambience. As Richard Moe, president of the National Trust for Historic Preservation, puts it, historical places are important, "not just as isolated bits of architecture and landscape, not just as lifeless monuments, but as environments where we can connect with the lives of the generations that came before us, places where we can build and maintain safe, rich, meaningful lives for ourselves and the generations that will come after us."

You don't have to live in an exceptional place like Charleston or Santa Fe to enjoy a sense of the past. Communities preserve their visible history by saving a school, a house, a hotel, or a department store that provides a link to the years gone by. And the preserved buildings don't have to be frozen as museum pieces, either. The school can become a restaurant, the house a bed-and-breakfast, the department store an apartment house, the hotel . . . well, it can still be a hotel.

Retirement Places Rated measures a community's visible history by counting the number of "contributing" residential buildings in historic districts listed on the National Register of Historic Places. The Register was established by the National Historic Preservation Act of 1966. It calls attention to districts, sites, buildings, structures, and objects that are significant in American history and culture. Contributing buildings are "unaltered, authentic historic structures" that are eligible for preservation tax credits.

SAMPLING THE LIVELY ARTS CALENDAR

How do you measure the cultural goings-on in another place? If you loved your hometown's symphony, will you, after surfacing somewhere else, have to settle for shaded seats at the annual outdoor Country Harmonica Blowoff?

Put it another way: If you exchange a big place for a smaller one, dirty air for clean, cold seasons for warm sun, and the costly for the economical, do you also risk trading the lively arts for a cultural desert?

Certainly a catalog of culture can include, among many things, art and history museums, comedy clubs, live theatre, bookstore readings, National Public Radio stations, street festivals, and charity auctions. *Retirement Places Rated* doesn't attempt such comprehensiveness. Instead, it focuses on crowd pleasers that take place in the local campus or civic auditoriums.

Touring Artists Bookings

Long before hit musicals like *Rent* and *Hairspray,* or a touring pianist, a European boys choir, or a visiting New York contemporary dance troupe comes to town for a date at the local performing arts center, the guest performer is booked by a nonprofit college or community concert association.

Does this mean you'll find the performing arts only in a big city blessed with an expensive concert hall and a nonprofit community concert association

---

ENVIABLE TOURING ARTISTS DATES

What does $40 get you in Iowa City? Two tickets to *La Bohème* at the University of Iowa's Hancher Auditorium in Orchestra I, the best seats in the house—with parking. Here are selected events from the Hancher's 2006–07 season to rebut any notion that lively arts aren't cultivated out on the prairie.

Los Hombres Calientes—Sept 29

Martha Graham Dance Company—Oct 3

Marvin Hamlisch—Oct 6

Epigraph for a Condemned Book—Oct 11

Bayanihan Philippine National Dance Company—Oct 12

Batsheva Dance Company—Oct 19

Rent—Oct 21–22

Musicians from Marlboro—Nov 1

Miami City Ballet, *Don Quixote*—Nov 10

FamilyMusik©, *Peter and the Wolf*—Nov 12

Classical Savion—Nov 15

The Western Wind, *The Chanukah Story*—Dec 3

Dianne Reeves, *Christmas Time Is Here*—Dec 8

Hamburg Symphony—Jan 21

Time for Three—Jan 24

Cashore Marionettes, *Simple Gifts*—Jan 27

The Producers—Feb 6–8

Aquila Theatre Company, *Romeo and Juliet*—Feb 13–14

Guarneri Quartet—Feb 15

Salute to Benny Goodman—Feb 24

Momix, *Lunar Sea*—Feb 27

Art Garfunkel—Mar 3

The David Sanborn Group—Mar 7

Stuttgart Chamber Orchestra—Mar 23

Hairspray—Apr 17–22

David Gonzalez, *The Frog Bride*—May 6

The Bobs—June 1

Source: www.hancher.uiowa.edu

---

bankrolled by philanthropists, managed by paid professionals, and attended by season member-subscribers? No.

The attendance growth at fine arts concerts is due not to turning up the volume and variety of performances in big cities but to popular interest in smaller cities and towns. And a good part of the interest comes from older fans. Among the 200 places in this guide, 159 benefit from 247 college and community arts series that regularly book touring artists.

Resident Ensembles

Besides taking in the touring attractions, people in some places have the additional option of attending performances of resident ensembles.

Opera. The image of horned helmets, silvery shields, and unintelligible singing is a low-brow cliché. Fans boast that operatic stagecraft is the most demanding of the performing arts because of the unique commingling of instruments and voice with theater and dance; if you're introduced to a good production, they say, you'll be hooked for life. Among the 29 places in this book with live opera, Brevard, North Carolina; Madison, Wisconsin; and Santa Fe, New Mexico, may have little else in common but they all belong to this group.

Symphony Orchestras. Orchestras are more common than opera companies; in fact, 72 places in this book have at least one. Their music is heard in woodsy state parks, high-school auditoriums, philharmonic halls, impressive new civic arts centers, and small-town bandboxes and pavilions.

OUTDOOR RECREATION ASSETS

For many, the great outdoors is one of the most important factors behind a move in retirement. It takes in a wide range of possibilities. It might mean lying on a Gulf Coast beach, tramping the Appalachian Trail, fly-casting for Rocky Mountain rainbow trout, day-sailing on Chesapeake Bay, or just getting away from it all to a cabin on the edge of a Pacific Northwest wilderness area.

Well before the time comes for shedding job obligations, many people have already identified from past family vacations the places where, when they retire, their own ideal of the great outdoors will be right outside their door.

Yes, a location's costs of living increase with its ambience. But here are 15 places in Retirement Places Rated's *top 60 percent in ambience and in low living costs.*

The Water Draw

Maryland watermen tell mainland tourists, many of whom come to Chesapeake Bay fishing villages for the oysters and soft-shell crabs, that the true length of estuarine shore reached by the Bay's tide would total more than 8,000 miles if all the kinks and bends were flattened out.

They say in Michigan's Roscommon County that the locals tend to live away from Houghton Lake, the state's biggest inland body of water, while the transplanted retired folks who've migrated up from Detroit or Cleveland or Chicago unerringly light on the shore like loons there for the duration.

And Oklahomans vaunt the state's collection of Corps of Engineer lakes. If you could tip the state a bit to the south, they say, the water would flow out and flood Texas for a good while.

There's not much connection between the migration of retired people on the one hand and the sight of water on the other, however. Water didn't play nearly

as great a part in attracting older adults during the 1980s as did a mild climate and resort development. In fact, certain Arizona, Nevada, and New Mexico counties that are desert-dry attracted retired people at a faster rate than wet counties in other parts of the country.

For all that, you'll spot lakes, ponds, and marine bays in 9 out of 10 of the 200 *Retirement Places Rated* locations. Aside from being a basic necessity for supporting life, water is regarded by most people as a scenic amenity; many regard it as a recreational amenity—as long as there is enough of it to fish in, boat on, or swim in without enduring snowmelt-cold temperatures. What's Petoskey, Michigan, without the Straits of Mackinac?

Or Cape Cod minus the Atlantic Ocean? Four out of five Americans today live within 100 miles of a coastline; in another 10 years, the Department of the Interior predicts three out of four will live within 50 miles. Not surprisingly, *65 Retirement Places Rated* havens have an ocean or Great Lakes coastline.

Counting Acres: The Public Lands

Of all the outdoor activities that older adults take to most frequently, the leading ones—pleasure driving, walking, picnicking, sightseeing, bird-watching, nature walking, and fishing—might arguably be more fun in the country's splendid system of federal- and state-run public recreation areas.

National Forests.   "Clear-Cutting Turns Off Tourists," said the bumper stickers around Ozark National Forest in northwest Arkansas a few years ago. Well, so do rumbling, crawling 18-wheel logger's trucks along U.S. 71. Although various parts of the national forests are classified as "wilderness," "primitive," "scenic," "historic," or "recreation" areas, the main purpose of the system is silviculture: growing wood, harvesting it carefully, and preserving naturally beautiful areas from the depredations of amateur chain saws, burger palaces, miniature golf, and timeshare condos.

In rainy Deschutes National Forest near Bend, Oregon, the harvest is Douglas fir. Among the widespread components of Mark Twain National Forest in the southern Missouri Ozarks, the crop is local hardwood of blackjack oak and hickory. Within Pisgah National Forest in western North Carolina near Asheville, the trees are virgin oak, beech, and black walnut.

But also within the forest system are more than a quarter of a million miles of paved roads, built not just for logging crews but for everyone. They lead to a wide variety of recreation developments: some 400 privately operated resorts, marinas, and ski lodges, plus fishing lakes and streams, campgrounds, and hiking trails. In 102 places profiled in the following pages, millions of acres are national forest lands.

National Parks.   Where multiple use is the philosophy behind national forests, the National Park Service preserves irreplaceable geographic and historic treasures for public recreation. This has been its mission ever since Congress created Yellowstone National Park back in 1872, in adjacent western corners of the old Montana and Wyoming territories, "as a public park or pleasuring ground for the benefit and enjoyment of the people."

"America's best idea," as the world knows it, is a collection of national parks, preserves, monuments, memorials, battlefields, seashores, riverways, and trails that make up the oldest and largest national park system in the world. Twelve-and-a-half million of the National Park Service's 84 million acres are found in *Retirement Places Rated* areas.

RETIREMENT PLACES OR GOLF RESORTS?

Playing a round of golf at a public course means paying your greens fees to a course open to everyone, whether its a publicly run "municipal" course or a privately run "daily fee" course. These 15 spots have fewer than 300 year-round residents per hole of public golf. When vacationers and owners of second homes return for the season, however, the population can quintuple and courses once again become crowded.

PLACE	PUBLIC GOLF HOLES
Beaufort, SC	567
Door Peninsula, WI	144
Eagle River–Woodruff, WI	72
Hilton Head Island, SC	567
Lake of the Ozarks, MO	207
Lake Placid, NY	153
Leelanau Peninsula, MI	72
McCall, ID	72
Myrtle Beach, SC	1,215
Northern Neck, VA	81
Ocean City, MD	279
Petoskey–Harbor Springs, MI	243
Silverthorne–Breckenridge, CO	99
Southern Pines–Pinehurst, NC	558
Southport–Brunswick Islands, NC	603

Source: Derived from National Golf Foundation data and Woods & Poole Economics population forecasts.

And, if you're 62 or older, for a one-time processing fee of $10, you'll have lifetime entrance to all properties administered by the National Park Service—national parks, monuments, historic sites, recreation areas, and national wildlife refuges—and a 50 percent discount on some federal-use fees charged for such facilities as camping, swimming, parking, boat launching, and tours.

National Wildlife Refuges.   Wildlife refuges protect native flora and fauna from people. This purpose hasn't changed since 1903, when Theodore Roosevelt created the first refuge, Pelican Island near Vero Beach, Florida, to save the mangrove-nesting egrets from poachers scrounging for plumage to adorn women's hats.

Most of the country's 545 refuges are open for wildlife activities, particularly photography and nature observation. In certain of the refuges and at irregular times, fishing and hunting are permitted, depending on the size of the refuge's wild populations. But you don't have to move to the sticks to be close to nature: One-third of the land area of Clark County, Nevada (where Las Vegas is the seat of government), is dedicated to wildlife refuges. Fort Myers–Cape Coral, Florida, has four refuges on 5,648 acres—Caloosahatchee, J.N. "Ding" Darling, Matlacha Pass, and Pine Island.

State Recreation Areas. The 10 million acres of state-run recreation areas are often equal in quality to the federal public lands, and in most states, older visitors get a break on entrance fees. They range from small day-use parks in wooded areas or on beaches, offering little more than picnic tables and restrooms; to large rugged parks and forests with developed hiking trails and campsites; to big-time destination resorts complete with golf courses, swimming pools, tennis courts, and full-time recreation staffs.

JUDGING: AMBIENCE

Even if we could all agree on the measurable things that contribute to a place's ambience, ranking places, let's admit, can't be done fairly. There are simply too many likes and dislikes. A Florida bass fisherman, hauling out his smoky outboard motor for a tuneup, may care less about the announced dates of a local civic concert series. A Cape Cod couple lolling on the beach may never know the joys of rehabbing a Queen Anne house in Port Townsend, Washington, nor would they ever regret the loss.

There are too many differences in taste for a rating system to suit everyone. Yet it's still possible to measure the supply of specific amenities. Chamber of Commerce brochures and state tourism promotion kits do it all the time. Travelers make their own comparisons. Hearsay may hold that winter living in the northern Michigan flatwoods is as dull and lonesome today as it was for the natives who quit the area for the city generations ago, or that there's little historical feel to sun-baked Henderson, Nevada.

Retirement Places Rated tries a more objective approach. It neither judges the quality of music by local symphonies and opera companies nor pushes the scenic benefits of the desert over seashore or forest environs. It simply indicates the presence of things that most persons agree enhance retirement living.

Each place starts with a base score of zero, to which scores are added according to the following criteria.

Good Bookstores

Stores that are part of Barnes & Noble's 806-store chain, The Borders Group's 1,147-store chain, and Books-A-Million's 179-store chain are counted, as well as those among the American Booksellers Association's 1,210 independent members. Of the retirement places covered in this book, 41 do not have a bookstore.

Good Restaurants

The number of quality diamonds is added for restaurants rated by AAA in each place. The result is then scaled against a standard where the highest figure gets 100, the average figure produces 50, and none yields 0. Charleston, South Carolina (with as many four-diamond eateries as Los Angeles), gets 100. Boone–Blowing Rock, North Carolina, and Connecticut's Litchfield Hills are tied at 50. Eight places with no restaurants rated by AAA earn 0.

Visible History

Within each place, the number of residential buildings defined by the National Register of Historic Places as "contributing" to the authentic appearance of historic districts is totaled. The result is then scaled against a standard where the greatest number of contributing homes gets 100, the average number produces 50, and none yields 0. Savannah, Georgia, with its renowned collection of historic districts and homes—some surviving from the 18th century—gets 100. Sonora–Twain Harte, in California's historic gold country, earns 50. Twenty-five other places with no historic buildings get 0.

The Lively Arts Calendar

In the calendar year, the number of dates booked for touring fine arts groups to perform at campus and civic auditoriums is added to the number of performance dates for local opera and ballet companies and symphony orchestras. The result is then scaled against a standard where the greatest number of dates gets 100, the average number produces 50, and no dates yields 0. Sarasota, Florida; Brevard, North Carolina; and 69 locations from Amador County in the California Sierras to the York Beaches on Maine's

Atlantic Coast are respectively, the best, average, and worst in the lively arts calendar.

Outdoor Recreation Assets

In the United States, a total of 18.63 percent of the land area is classified as inland or coastal water, federal protected land, or state recreation area.

Each place's own area percentage for each of these four kinds of outdoor recreation assets is totaled. The result is then scaled against a standard where the highest figure gets 100, the average figure produces 50, and none yields 0. Among the retirement places, McCall, Idaho; Bar Harbor, Maine; and Athens, Georgia, are respectively the best, average, and worst for outdoor assets.

RANKINGS: AMBIENCE

Ten factors are used to rate a place's ambience assets: (1) good bookstores; (2) good restaurants; (3) "contributing" buildings in the National Register of Historic Places; (4) campus and civic auditorium touring artist dates; (5) resident opera and symphony orchestra dates; (6) area golf courses; (7) ocean and Great Lakes coastal water areas; (8) inland water areas; (9) protected federal land; and (10) state recreation areas. Locations that are tied get the same rank and are listed alphabetically.

Retirement Places from First to Last

RANK	PLACE	SCORE
1.	Middle Cape Cod, MA	100.0
2.	Charleston, SC	99.4
3.	East End Long Island, NY	98.9
4.	Kalispell–Flathead Valley, MT	98.4
5.	Brunswick, ME	97.9
6.	Savannah, GA	97.4
7.	Sarasota, FL	96.9
8.	Tucson, AZ	96.4
9.	Laguna Beach–Dana Point, CA	95.9
10.	Henderson, NV	95.4
11.	Lower Cape May, NJ	94.9
12.	Hanover, NH	94.4
13.	Hilton Head Island, SC	93.9
14.	Scottsdale, AZ	93.4
15.	Silverthorne–Breckenridge, CO	92.9
16.	Cottonwood–Verde Valley, AZ	92.4
17.	Prescott–Prescott Valley, AZ	91.9
18.	Maui, HI	91.4
19.	Largo, FL	90.9
20.	Eugene, OR	90.4
21.	Fort Myers–Cape Coral, FL	89.9
22.	Flagstaff, AZ	88.9
22.	Sedona, AZ	88.9
24.	Bay St. Louis–Pass Christian, MS	87.9
24.	Leelanau Peninsula, MI	87.9
26.	Fort Collins–Loveland, CO	87.4
27.	Bar Harbor, ME	86.9
28.	Key West, FL	86.4
29.	Melbourne–Palm Bay, FL	85.9
30.	Madison, WI	85.4
31.	Bozeman, MT	84.9
32.	Burlington, VT	84.4
33.	Beaufort, SC	83.9
34.	Williamsburg, VA	83.4
35.	Southern Berkshire County, MA	82.9
36.	Asheville, NC	82.4
37.	Woodstock, VT	81.9

RANK	PLACE	SCORE
38.	Traverse City, MI	81.4
39.	Palm Springs–Coachella Valley, CA	80.9
40.	Naples, FL	80.4
41.	Myrtle Beach, SC	79.8
42.	Martha's Vineyard, MA	79.3
43.	Bellingham, WA	78.8
44.	Victorville–Apple Valley, CA	78.3
45.	Ocala, FL	77.8
46.	Toms River–Barnegat Bay, NJ	77.3
47.	Medford–Ashland, OR	76.8
48.	Charlottesville, VA	76.3
49.	Lakeland–Winter Haven, FL	75.8
50.	Annapolis, MD	75.3
51.	Santa Barbara, CA	74.8
52.	St. Augustine, FL	74.3
53.	Carson City–Carson Valley, NV	73.8
54.	Fairhope–Gulf Shores, AL	73.3
55.	Lake Placid, NY	72.8
56.	Petoskey–Harbor Springs, MI	72.3
57.	Rockport–Aransas Pass, TX	71.8
58.	Park City, UT	71.3
59.	Jackson Hole, WY	70.8
60.	Pensacola, FL	70.3
61.	Litchfield Hills, CT	69.8
62.	Morro Bay–Cambria, CA	69.3
63.	Santa Fe, NM	68.8
64.	Wickenburg, AZ	68.3
65.	Gainesville, FL	67.8
66.	Door Peninsula, WI	67.3
67.	Easton–St. Michaels, MD	66.8
68.	The Big Island, HI	66.3
69.	Camden, ME	65.8
70.	Wenatchee, WA	65.3
71.	Bend, OR	64.8
72.	Northampton–Amherst, MA	64.3
73.	Placer County, CA	63.8
74.	Ocean City, MD	63.3

RANK	PLACE	SCORE
75.	Ketchum–Sun Valley, ID	62.8
76.	Hot Springs, AR	62.3
77.	Bisbee, AZ	61.8
78.	St. George–Zion, UT	61.3
79.	Chapel Hill–Carrboro, NC	60.8
80.	Southern Pines–Pinehurst, NC	60.3
81.	Taos, NM	59.7
82.	Bradenton, FL	59.2
83.	Lake Conroe, TX	58.7
84.	Chestertown, MD	58.2
85.	Coeur d'Alene, ID	57.7
86.	Georgetown, TX	57.2
87.	St. Simons–Jekyll Islands, GA	56.7
88.	Carmel–Pebble Beach, CA	56.2
89.	Dare Outer Banks, NC	55.7
90.	Grand Junction, CO	55.2
91.	York Beaches, ME	54.7
92.	Iowa City, IA	54.2
93.	Port Townsend, WA	53.7
94.	Loudoun County, VA	53.2
95.	Paradise–Magalia, CA	52.7
96.	Hattiesburg, MS	52.2
97.	East Stroudsburg, PA	51.7
98.	Port Charlotte, FL	51.2
99.	Mariposa, CA	50.2
99.	Monadnock Region, NH	50.2
101.	Northern Neck, VA	49.7
102.	Rehoboth Bay–Indian River Bay, DE	49.2
103.	San Juan Islands, WA	48.7
104.	Hendersonville–East Flat Rock, NC	48.2
105.	Rio Rancho, NM	47.7
106.	Sandpoint–Lake Pend Oreille, ID	47.2
107.	Las Cruces, NM	46.7
108.	Leesburg–Mount Dora, FL	46.2
109.	Ruidoso, NM	45.7
110.	Wimberley, TX	45.2
111.	Newport–Lincoln City, OR	44.7
112.	Beaufort–Atlantic Beach, NC	44.2
113.	Sonora–Twain Harte, CA	43.7
114.	New Bern, NC	43.2
115.	Madison, MS	42.7
116.	Sullivan County, NY	42.2
117.	Fayetteville, AR	41.7
118.	Durango, CO	41.2
119.	McCall, ID	40.7
120.	Columbia, MO	40.2
121.	Charles Town–Shepherdstown, WV	39.6
122.	Anacortes, WA	39.1
123.	Athens, GA	38.6
124.	Western St. Tammany Parish, LA	38.1
125.	Boone–Blowing Rock, NC	37.6
126.	Yuma, AZ	37.1
127.	Fredericksburg, TX	36.6
128.	Fredericksburg–Spotsylvania, VA	36.1
129.	New Braunfels, TX	35.6
130.	Waynesville, NC	35.1
131.	Alpine–Big Bend, TX	34.6
132.	Port Angeles–Sequim, WA	34.1
133.	Brevard, NC	33.6
134.	Vero Beach, FL	33.1
135.	Grass Valley–Nevada City, CA	32.6
136.	Eagle River–Woodruff, WI	32.1
137.	Hamilton–Bitterroot Valley, MT	31.6

RANK	PLACE	SCORE
138.	Fairplay, CO	31.1
139.	Kingman, AZ	30.1
139.	Lake Havasu City, AZ	30.1
141.	Pagosa Springs, CO	29.6
142.	Natchitoches, LA	29.1
143.	Lake of the Ozarks, MO	28.6
144.	Kissimmee–St. Cloud, FL	28.1
145.	Mendocino–Fort Bragg, CA	27.6
146.	State College, PA	27.1
147.	Grants Pass, OR	26.6
148.	Smith Mountain Lake, VA	26.1
149.	Montrose, CO	25.6
150.	Southport–Brunswick Islands, NC	25.1
151.	Apalachicola, FL	24.6
152.	Branson, MO	24.1
153.	Payson, AZ	23.6
154.	Panama City, FL	23.1
155.	Las Vegas, NM	22.1
155.	Rabun County, GA	22.1
157.	Pike County, PA	21.6
158.	Long Beach Peninsula, WA	21.1
159.	Whidbey Island, WA	20.6
160.	Cortez, CO	20.1
161.	St. Marys, GA	19.5
162.	Crossville, TN	19.0
163.	Silver City, NM	18.5
164.	St. Jay–Northeast Kingdom, VT	18.0
165.	Summerville, SC	17.5
166.	Sebring–Avon Park, FL	17.0
167.	Brownsville, TX	16.5
168.	Maryville, TN	16.0
169.	Palmer–Wasilla, AK	15.5
170.	Pahrump Valley, NV	15.0
171.	Edenton, NC	14.5
172.	Nelson County, VA	14.0
173.	Delta County, CO	13.5
174.	Thomasville, GA	13.0
175.	Front Royal, VA	12.5
176.	Dahlonega, GA	12.0
177.	Cedar City, UT	11.5
178.	Pendleton District, SC	11.0
179.	Port St. Lucie, FL	10.5
180.	Driggs, ID	10.0
181.	Oakhurst–Coarsegold, CA	9.5
182.	McAllen–Alamo, TX	9.0
183.	Alamogordo, NM	8.5
184.	Boerne, TX	8.0
185.	Chewelah, WA	7.5
186.	Roswell, NM	7.0
187.	Eureka Springs, AR	6.5
188.	Hampshire County, WV	6.0
189.	Tryon, NC	5.5
190.	Brown County, IN	5.0
191.	Murray–Kentucky Lake, KY	4.5
192.	Amador County, CA	4.0
193.	Norfork Lake, AR	3.5
194.	Oxford, MS	3.0
195.	Marble Falls–Lake LBJ, TX	2.5
196.	Berkeley Springs, WV	2.0
197.	Conway, AR	1.5
198.	Kerrville, TX	1.0
199.	Lake of the Cherokees, OK	0.5
200.	Cedar Creek Lake, TX	0.0

Ambience

PLACE PROFILES: AMBIENCE

The following capsule profiles are selective features that contribute interest, ambience, and difference to the retirement places featured in *Retirement Places Rated*.

The profiles begin with the local number of **Good Bookstores** and **Good Restaurants.** The next entry, **Visible History,** counts registered neighborhoods (historic districts) and their "contributing buildings" as detailed in the National Register of Historic Places database. Listed underneath are selected Historic Districts that are residential—as opposed to commercial—neighborhoods, if any.

The next category, **Lively Arts Performance Dates,** counts the annual number of dates booked for touring arts groups as reported by *Musical America's* most recent survey. The number of dates for resident opera and symphony performances is also counted. If a place has no entry, then it has no established performing arts series or resident musical ensemble tracked by *Musical America.*

The next category, **Outdoor Recreation Assets,** counts (1) regulation golf holes for daily fee, municipal, or private golf courses; (2) square miles of inland water; (3) square miles of ocean or Great Lakes coastal water; (4) acres of federal protected areas; and (5) acres of state protected areas within each retirement place.

The figures for inland water include ponds and lakes if their surface areas are 40 acres or more. Streams, canals, and rivers are also counted if their width is ⅛ mile or more. The water area along irregular Great Lakes and ocean coastlines is counted, too, if the bays, inlets, and estuaries are between 1 and 10 miles in width.

A list of federal protected lands—units of the National Park Service, National Forests, and National Wildlife Refuges—is included. In this section, the following abbreviations are used:

NF: National Forest
NHP: National Historic Park

NM: National Monument
NMP: National Military Park
NP: National Park
NRA: National Recreation Area
NS: National Seashore
NST: National Scenic Trail
NWR: National Wildlife Refuge

A place's final score equally weights the **Visible History, Lively Arts Performance Dates, Outdoor Recreation Assets, Good Restaurants,** and **Good Bookstores** scores and scales the result against a standard where 100 is best, 50 average, and 0 worst. A star (★) preceding a place's name highlights it as one of the top 30 places for ambience.

Information comes from these sources: ABC Leisure Magazines, *Musical America: 2006 International Directory of the Performing Arts; American Automobile Association TourBooks* (23 volumes) 2006; American Bookseller Association, member directory (www.bookweb.org/bookstores); American Symphony Orchestra League, *Symphony Magazine,* January–February, 2006; Barnes & Noble, "Store Locator" (http://storelocator.barnesandnoble.com); Books-a-Million, "Store Finder" (www.booksamillion.com); Borders, "Store Locator" (www.bordersstores.com); National Golf Foundation (unpublished golf course data), 2006; Places Rated Partners survey of state parks and recreation departments, 2003; U.S. Department of Agriculture, *Land Areas of the National Forest System,* 2006; U.S. Department of Commerce, Bureau of the Census, unpublished land and water area measurements, 2000, and National Oceanic and Atmospheric Administration, *The Coastline of the United States,* 1975; U.S. Department of the Interior, Fish and Wildlife Service, *Annual Report,* 2006, and unpublished master deed listing, 2006, and National Park Service, *Index to the National Park System and Related Areas,* 2006; unpublished master deed listing, 2006; and unpublished National Register of Historic Places database (www.cr.nps.gov/nr), 2006.

Retirement Places Rated

Alamogordo, NM
Good Restaurants: 2
Visible History
Registered neighborhoods: 2
Contributing buildings: 209
    La Luz District
    Tularosa Original Townsite
Outdoor Recreation Assets
Golf course holes
    Daily fee: 45; Municipal: 18; Private: 9
Inland water area: 1 sq. miles
Federal protected areas: 563,752 acres
    Lincoln NF
    White Sands NM
State recreation areas: 200 acres
Rank: 183

Alpine–Big Bend, TX
Good Bookstores
Independent & College: 2
Good Restaurants: 5
Visible History
Registered neighborhoods: 2
Contributing buildings: 107
    Castolon District
    Terlingua District
Outdoor Recreation Assets
Golf course holes
    Daily fee: 27
Federal protected areas: 775,279 acres
    Big Bend NP
    Rio Grande Wild Scenic River
State recreation areas: 18,000 acres
Rank: 131

Amador County, CA
Good Restaurants: 2
Visible History
Registered neighborhoods: 1
Contributing buildings: 11
    Chichizola Family Store Complex
Outdoor Recreation Assets
Golf course holes
    Daily fee: 36
Inland water area: 12 sq. miles
Federal protected areas: 78,116 acres
    Eldorado NF
State recreation areas: 136 acres
Rank: 192

Anacortes, WA
Good Bookstores
Mall & Superstores: 1
Independent & College: 2
Good Restaurants: 19
Outdoor Recreation Assets
Golf course holes
    Daily fee: 72; Private: 18
Inland water area: 40 sq. miles
Puget Sound coastal water: 145 sq. miles
Federal protected areas: 541,740 acres
    Mt. Baker NF
    North Cascades NP

    Ross Lake NRA
    San Juan Islands NWR
State recreation areas: 3,391 acres
Rank: 122

Annapolis, MD
Good Bookstores
Mall & Superstores: 6
Independent & College: 1
Good Restaurants: 16
Visible History
Registered neighborhoods: 4
Contributing buildings: 1,240
    Colonial Annapolis District
    Davidsonville District
    Owensville District
    Woodwardville District
Lively Arts Performance Dates
Touring artists: 3
Resident ensembles: 29
Outdoor Recreation Assets
Golf course holes
    Daily fee: 117; Private: 144
Inland water area: 38 sq. miles
Chesapeake coastal water: 134 sq. miles
Federal protected areas: 432 acres
    National Capital Parks
State recreation areas: 1,772 acres
Rank: 50

Apalachicola, FL
Visible History
Registered neighborhoods: 1
Contributing buildings: 652
    Apalachicola District
Outdoor Recreation Assets
Golf course holes
    Daily fee: 18
Inland water area: 32 sq. miles
Gulf coastal water: 199 sq. miles
Federal protected areas: 35,237 acres
    Apalachicola NF
    St. Vincent NWR
State recreation areas: 1,964 acres
Rank: 151

Asheville, NC
Good Bookstores
Mall & Superstores: 5
Good Restaurants: 63
Visible History
Registered neighborhoods: 11
Contributing buildings: 1,331
    Chestnut Hill District
    Clingman Avenue District
    Grove Park District
    Montford Area District
    West End District
Lively Arts Performance Dates
Touring artists: 123
Resident ensembles: 37

continued

★ = *in the top 30 places for ambience*

Ambience

Outdoor Recreation Assets
Golf course holes
  Daily fee: 81; Municipal: 36; Private: 54
Inland water area: 4 sq. miles
Federal protected areas: 37,137 acres
  Blue Ridge Parkway
  Pisgah NF
Rank: 36

Athens, GA

Good Bookstores
Mall & Superstores: 2
Independent & College: 1
Good Restaurants: 3
Visible History
Registered neighborhoods: 12
Contributing buildings: 1,281
  Bloomfield Street District
  Boulevard District
  Buena Vista Heights District
  Cobbham District
  Dearing Street District
  Reese Street District
  West Hancock Avenue District
Lively Arts Performance Dates
Touring artists: 25
Outdoor Recreation Assets
Golf course holes
  Daily fee: 36; Private: 27
Rank: 123

★ Bar Harbor, ME

Good Bookstores
Independent & College: 5
Good Restaurants: 45
Visible History
Registered neighborhoods: 5
Contributing buildings: 381
  Blue Hill District
  Castine District
  Off-the-Neck District
  Somesville District
  West Street District
Lively Arts Performance Dates
Touring artists: 12
Outdoor Recreation Assets
Golf course holes
  Daily fee: 108
Inland water area: 299 sq. miles
Atlantic coastal water: 166 sq. miles
Federal protected areas: 41,394 acres
  Acadia NP
State recreation areas: 39,500 acres
Rank: 27

★ Bay St. Louis–Pass Christian, MS

Good Bookstores
Mall & Superstores: 6
Independent & College: 1
Good Restaurants: 24
Visible History
Registered neighborhoods: 6

Contributing buildings: 612
  Beach Boulevard District
  Scenic Drive District
  Sycamore Street District
  West Beach District
  West Central District
Lively Arts Performance Dates
Resident ensembles: 11
Outdoor Recreation Assets
Golf course holes
  Daily fee: 180; Private: 36
Inland water area: 23 sq. miles
Federal protected areas: 82,570 acres
  De Soto NF
  Gulf Islands NS
State recreation areas: 398 acres
Rank: 24

Beaufort, SC

Good Bookstores
Mall & Superstores: 2
Independent & College: 1
Good Restaurants: 40
Visible History
Registered neighborhoods: 4
Contributing buildings: 582
  Beaufort District
  Bluffton District
  Daufuskie Island District
Lively Arts Performance Dates
Touring artists: 9
Outdoor Recreation Assets
Golf course holes
  Daily fee: 567; Private: 531
Inland water area: 110 sq. miles
Atlantic coastal water: 56 sq. miles
Federal protected areas: 1,421 acres
  Ace Basin NWR
  Pinckney Island NWR
State recreation areas: 5,000 acres
Rank: 33

Beaufort–Atlantic Beach, NC

Good Bookstores
Independent & College: 2
Good Restaurants: 14
Visible History
Registered neighborhoods: 4
Contributing buildings: 204
  Beaufort District
  Cape Lookout Village District
  Morehead City District
  Portsmouth Village
Outdoor Recreation Assets
Golf course holes
  Daily fee: 36; Private: 18
Inland water area: 532 sq. miles
Atlantic coastal water: 29 sq. miles
Federal protected areas: 25,174 acres
  Cape Lookout NS
  Cedar Island NWR
  Croatan NF
State recreation areas: 654 acres
Rank: 112

★ = in the top 30 places for ambience

Bellingham, WA

Good Bookstores
Mall & Superstores: 2
Independent & College: 1
Good Restaurants: 12
Visible History
Registered neighborhoods: 3
Contributing buildings: 857
  Eldridge Avenue District
  Sehome Hill District
Lively Arts Performance Dates
Touring artists: 30
Outdoor Recreation Assets
Golf course holes
  Daily fee: 180; Municipal: 18; Private: 36
Inland water area: 55 sq. miles
Puget Sound coastal water: 328 sq. miles
Federal protected areas: 847,050 acres
  Mt. Baker NF
  North Cascades NP
  Ross Lake NRA
  San Juan Islands NWR
State recreation areas: 2,602 acres
Rank: 43

Bend, OR

Good Bookstores
Mall & Superstores: 1
Independent & College: 3
Good Restaurants: 17
Visible History
Registered neighborhoods: 2
Contributing buildings: 299
  Drake Park District
  Old Town District
Outdoor Recreation Assets
Golf course holes
  Daily fee: 207; Private: 90
Inland water area: 37 sq. miles
Federal protected areas: 984,057 acres
  Deschutes NF
State recreation areas: 4,097 acres
Rank: 71

Berkeley Springs, WV

Good Restaurants: 1
Outdoor Recreation Assets
Golf course holes
  Municipal: 18
Inland water area: 1 sq. miles
Federal protected areas: 124 acres
  Chesapeake and Ohio Canal NHP
State recreation areas: 6,119 acres
Rank: 196

The Big Island, HI

Good Bookstores
Mall & Superstores: 2
Independent & College: 1
Good Restaurants: 14
Visible History
Registered neighborhoods: 1
Contributing buildings: 30
  Bond District

Lively Arts Performance Dates
Touring artists: 6
Outdoor Recreation Assets
Golf course holes
  Daily fee: 288; Municipal: 18; Private: 90
Inland water area: 4 sq. miles
Pacific coastal water: 1,093 sq. miles
Federal protected areas: 240,646 acres
  Hakalau Forest NWR
  Hawaii Volcanoes NP
  Kaloko-Honokahau NHP
  Pu'uhonua o Honaunau NHP
State recreation areas: 1,131 acres
Rank: 68

Bisbee, AZ

Good Bookstores
Mall & Superstores: 1
Independent & College: 2
Good Restaurants: 15
Visible History
Registered neighborhoods: 7
Contributing buildings: 503
  Bisbee District
  Douglas District
  Douglas Residential District
  Douglas Sonoran District
Lively Arts Performance Dates
Touring artists: 13
Outdoor Recreation Assets
Golf course holes
  Daily fee: 90; Municipal: 27
Inland water area: 49 sq. miles
Federal protected areas: 509,733 acres
  Chiracahua NM
  Coronado NF
  Coronado NM
  Leslie Canyon NWR
  San Bernardino NWR
State recreation areas: 56 acres
Rank: 77

Boerne, TX

Good Bookstores
Independent & College: 1
Good Restaurants: 1
Visible History
Registered neighborhoods: 2
Contributing buildings: 92
  Comfort District
  Sisterdale Valley District
Outdoor Recreation Assets
Golf course holes
  Daily fee: 45; Private: 36
Inland water area: 1 sq. miles
State recreation areas: 938 acres
Rank: 184

Boone–Blowing Rock, NC

Good Bookstores
Mall & Superstores: 1
Independent & College: 2
Good Restaurants: 13

continued

Visible History
Registered neighborhoods: 2
Contributing buildings: 96
Green Park District
Valle Crucis District
Lively Arts Performance Dates
Touring artists: 15
Outdoor Recreation Assets
Golf course holes
Daily fee: 18; Private: 36
Federal protected areas: 10,470 acres
Blue Ridge Parkway
Pisgah NF
Rank: 125

Bozeman, MT
Good Bookstores
Mall & Superstores: 2
Independent & College: 1
Good Restaurants: 36
Visible History
Registered neighborhoods: 7
Contributing buildings: 678
Bon Ton District
Cooper Park District
Lindley Place District
North Tracy Avenue District
South Tracy District
South Willson District
Lively Arts Performance Dates
Touring artists: 6
Resident ensembles: 12
Outdoor Recreation Assets
Golf course holes
Daily fee: 63; Private: 54
Inland water area: 26 sq. miles
Federal protected areas: 691,320 acres
Beaverhead NF
Gallatin NF
Yellowstone NP
Rank: 31

Bradenton, FL
Good Bookstores
Mall & Superstores: 2
Good Restaurants: 29
Visible History
Registered neighborhoods: 2
Contributing buildings: 402
Braden Castle Park District
Palmetto District
Outdoor Recreation Assets
Golf course holes
Daily fee: 207; Municipal: 54; Private: 225
Inland water area: 55 sq. miles
Gulf coastal water: 47 sq. miles
Federal protected areas: 25 acres
De Soto NM
Passage Key NWR
State recreation areas: 10,733 acres
Rank: 82

Branson, MO
Good Restaurants: 41
Lively Arts Performance Dates
Outdoor Recreation Assets
Golf course holes
Daily fee: 81
Inland water area: 19 sq. miles
Federal protected areas: 65,989 acres
Mark Twain NF
State recreation areas: 294 acres
Rank: 152

Brevard, NC
Good Restaurants: 2
Lively Arts Performance Dates
Resident ensembles: 10
Outdoor Recreation Assets
Golf course holes
Daily fee: 54; Private: 45
Inland water area: 2 sq. miles
Federal protected areas: 87,718 acres
Blue Ridge Parkway
Nantahala NF
Pisgah NF
Rank: 133

Brown County, IN
Good Restaurants: 2
Outdoor Recreation Assets
Golf course holes
Daily fee: 18
Inland water area: 4 sq. miles
Federal protected areas: 18,451 acres
Hoosier NF
State recreation areas: 15,692 acres
Rank: 190

Brownsville, TX
Good Bookstores
Mall & Superstores: 2
Good Restaurants: 5
Lively Arts Performance Dates
Touring artists: 2
Outdoor Recreation Assets
Golf course holes
Daily fee: 72; Municipal: 63; Private: 54
Inland water area: 263 sq. miles
Federal protected areas: 60,386 acres
Lower Rio Grande Valley NWR
Laguna Atascosa NWR
State recreation areas: 1 acre
Rank: 167

★ **Brunswick, ME**
Good Bookstores
Mall & Superstores: 3
Independent & College: 2
Good Restaurants: 62
Visible History
Registered neighborhoods: 16
Contributing buildings: 951
Federal Street District
Lincoln Street District
Pennellville District

★ = in the top 30 places for ambience

Lively Arts Performance Dates
  Touring artists: 4
  Resident ensembles: 116
Outdoor Recreation Assets
  Golf course holes
    Daily fee: 243; Municipal: 54; Private: 99
  Inland water area: 192 sq. miles
  Atlantic coastal water: 114 sq. miles
Rank: 5

Burlington, VT
  Good Bookstores
    Mall & Superstores: 3
    Independent & College: 2
  Good Restaurants: 17
  Visible History
    Registered neighborhoods: 17
    Contributing buildings: 1,422
      Battery Street District
      Buell Street-Bradley Street District
      Main Street-College Street District
      North Street District
      Pearl Street District
      South Union Street District
      South Willard Street District
  Lively Arts Performance Dates
    Touring artists: 29
  Outdoor Recreation Assets
    Golf course holes
      Daily fee: 126; Private: 36
    Inland water area: 81 sq. miles
  Rank: 32

Camden, ME
  Good Bookstores
    Independent & College: 1
  Good Restaurants: 26
  Visible History
    Registered neighborhoods: 6
    Contributing buildings: 437
      Chestnut Street District
      High Street District
      Main Street District
      Rockland Residential District
      Rockport District
      Thomaston District
  Lively Arts Performance Dates
    Touring artists: 20
  Outdoor Recreation Assets
    Golf course holes
      Daily fee: 45; Private: 9
    Inland water area: 75 sq. miles
    Atlantic coastal water: 159 sq. miles
    Federal protected areas: 4,212 acres
      Acadia NP
    State recreation areas: 8,800 acres
  Rank: 69

Carmel–Pebble Beach, CA
  Good Bookstores
    Mall & Superstores: 4
    Independent & College: 1
  Good Restaurants: 50

Visible History
  Registered neighborhoods: 1
  Contributing buildings: 17
    Monterey Old Town District
Lively Arts Performance Dates
  Touring artists: 15
Outdoor Recreation Assets
  Golf course holes
    Daily fee: 180; Municipal: 81; Private: 162
  Inland water area: 13 sq. miles
  Pacific coastal water: 132 sq. miles
  Federal protected areas: 312,040 acres
    Los Padres NF
    Pinnacles NM
    Salinas River NWR
  State recreation areas: 14,304 acres
Rank: 88

Carson City–Carson Valley, NV
  Good Bookstores
    Mall & Superstores: 2
  Good Restaurants: 12
  Visible History
    Registered neighborhoods: 1
    Contributing buildings: 29
      Genoa District
  Lively Arts Performance Dates
    Touring artists: 22
  Outdoor Recreation Assets
    Golf course holes
      Daily fee: 135; Municipal: 36; Private: 18
    Inland water area: 40 sq. miles
    Federal protected areas: 72,192 acres
      Eldorado NF
      Toiyabe NF & Special Area
    State recreation areas: 3,692 acres
  Rank: 53

Cedar City, UT
  Good Bookstores
    Independent & College: 1
  Good Restaurants: 7
  Visible History
    Registered neighborhoods: 1
    Contributing buildings: 104
      Cedar City District
  Outdoor Recreation Assets
    Golf course holes
      Municipal: 18
    Inland water area: 4 sq. miles
    Federal protected areas: 252,453 acres
      Cedar Breaks NM
      Dixie NF
      Fishlake NF
      Zion NP
    State recreation areas: 11 acres
  Rank: 177

Cedar Creek Lake, TX
  Outdoor Recreation Assets
    Golf course holes
      Daily fee: 36; Private: 18
    Inland water area: 75 sq. miles
    State recreation areas: 566 acres
  Rank: 200

★ = in the top 30 places for ambience

Ambience

continued

153

Chapel Hill–Carrboro, NC
Good Bookstores
Mall & Superstores: 2
Good Restaurants: 33
Visible History
Registered neighborhoods: 7
Contributing buildings: 484
Cedar Grove Rural Crossroads District
Chapel Hill District
Gimghoul Neighborhood District
Hillsborough District
West Chapel Hill District
Lively Arts Performance Dates
Touring artists: 27
Outdoor Recreation Assets
Golf course holes
Daily fee: 81; Private: 45
Inland water area: 1 sq. miles
Rank: 79

★ **Charleston, SC**
Good Bookstores
Mall & Superstores: 6
Independent & College: 2
Good Restaurants: 112
Visible History
Registered neighborhoods: 8
Contributing buildings: 1,935
Old Charleston District
Hampton Park Terrace District
McClellanville District
Rockville District
William Enston Home
Lively Arts Performance Dates
Touring artists: 18
Outdoor Recreation Assets
Golf course holes
Daily fee: 234; Municipal: 18; Private: 180
Inland water area: 119 sq. miles
Atlantic coastal water: 321 sq. miles
Federal protected areas: 105,635 acres
Ace Basin NWR
Cape Romain NWR
Fort Sumter NM
Francis Marion NF
State recreation areas: 1,551 acres
Rank: 2

Charles Town–Shepherdstown, WV
Good Bookstores
Independent & College: 1
Good Restaurants: 5
Visible History
Registered neighborhoods: 9
Contributing buildings: 1,060
Old Charles Town District
Downtown Charles Town District
Harpers Ferry District
Middleway District
Shepherdstown District
Lively Arts Performance Dates
Touring artists: 14

Outdoor Recreation Assets
Golf course holes
Daily fee: 36; Private: 18
Inland water area: 2 sq. miles
Federal protected areas: 3,253 acres
Appalachian NST
Harpers Ferry NHP
Rank: 121

Charlottesville, VA
Good Bookstores
Mall & Superstores: 4
Good Restaurants: 23
Visible History
Registered neighborhoods: 6
Contributing buildings: 1,161
Advance Mills
Batesville District
Covesville District
Proffit District
Scottsville District
Southwest Mountains Rural District
Lively Arts Performance Dates
Touring artists: 56
Outdoor Recreation Assets
Golf course holes
Daily fee: 36; Municipal: 18; Private: 63
Inland water area: 3 sq. miles
Federal protected areas: 15,441 acres
Appalachian NST
Blue Ridge Parkway
Shenandoah NP
Rank: 48

Chestertown, MD
Good Bookstores
Independent & College: 1
Good Restaurants: 1
Visible History
Registered neighborhoods: 2
Contributing buildings: 641
Betterton District
Chestertown District
Lively Arts Performance Dates
Touring artists: 5
Outdoor Recreation Assets
Golf course holes
Private: 18
Inland water area: 23 sq. miles
Chesapeake coastal water: 111 sq. miles
Federal protected areas: 2,286 acres
Eastern Neck NWR
Rank: 84

Chewelah, WA
Good Restaurants: 1
Outdoor Recreation Assets
Golf course holes
Daily fee: 45
Inland water area: 62 sq. miles
Federal protected areas: 296,233 acres
Colville NF
Coulee Dam NRA
Kaniksu NF

★ = *in the top 30 places for ambience*

Little Pend Oreille NWR
Northeast Washington LUP
State recreation areas: 156 acres
Rank: 185

Coeur d'Alene, ID
Good Bookstores
Mall & Superstores: 1
Good Restaurants: 10
Visible History
Registered neighborhoods: 1
Contributing buildings: 54
Sherman Park Addition
Lively Arts Performance Dates
Touring artists: 28
Outdoor Recreation Assets
Golf course holes
Daily fee: 144; Private: 36
Inland water area: 71 sq. miles
Federal protected areas: 244,862 acres
Coeur d'Alene NF
Kaniksu NF
State recreation areas: 9,523 acres
Rank: 85

Columbia, MO
Good Bookstores
Mall & Superstores: 1
Good Restaurants: 18
Visible History
Registered neighborhoods: 2
Contributing buildings: 350
East Campus District
Rocheport
Lively Arts Performance Dates
Touring artists: 20
Outdoor Recreation Assets
Golf course holes
Daily fee: 36; Municipal: 36; Private: 45
Inland water area: 6 sq. miles
Federal protected areas: 4,142 acres
Mark Twain NF
State recreation areas: 3,371 acres
Rank: 120

Conway, AR
Good Bookstores
Independent & College: 2
Good Restaurants: 4
Lively Arts Performance Dates
Touring artists: 5
Outdoor Recreation Assets
Golf course holes
Daily fee: 9; Private: 36
Inland water area: 17 sq. miles
State recreation areas: 182 acres
Rank: 197

Cortez, CO
Good Restaurants: 4
Visible History
Registered neighborhoods: 2
Contributing buildings: 929

Outdoor Recreation Assets
Golf course holes
Municipal: 18
Inland water area: 3 sq. miles
Federal protected areas: 309,290 acres
Hovenweep NM
Mesa Verde NP
San Juan NF
Yucca House NM
Rank: 160

★ Cottonwood–Verde Valley, AZ
Good Bookstores
Mall & Superstores: 1
Independent & College: 1
Good Restaurants: 2
Visible History
Registered neighborhoods: 2
Contributing buildings: 395
Clarkdale District
Cottonwood Commercial District
Lively Arts Performance Dates
Touring artists: 6
Outdoor Recreation Assets
Golf course holes
Daily fee: 135; Municipal: 36; Private: 72
Inland water area: 5 sq. miles
Federal protected areas: 1,965,386 acres
Coconino NF
Kaibab NF
Montezuma Castle NM
Prescott NF
Tonto NF
Tuzigoot NM
State recreation areas: 1,025 acres
Rank: 16

Crossville, TN
Visible History
Registered neighborhoods: 1
Contributing buildings: 405
Cumberland Homesteads District
Lively Arts Performance Dates
Touring artists: 5
Outdoor Recreation Assets
Golf course holes
Daily fee: 108; Private: 54
Inland water area: 3 sq. miles
Federal protected areas: 50 acres
Obed Wild Scenic River
State recreation areas: 1,562 acres
Rank: 162

Dahlonega, GA
Good Restaurants: 1
Visible History
Registered neighborhoods: 1
Contributing buildings: 23
Hawkins Street District
Lively Arts Performance Dates
Touring artists: 3
Outdoor Recreation Assets
Golf course holes
Daily fee: 18

continued

Ambience

Federal protected areas: 57,233 acres
>Chattahoochee NF
State recreation areas: 1 acre
Rank: 176

Dare Outer Banks, NC

Good Bookstores
Independent & College: 1
Good Restaurants: 39
Visible History
Registered neighborhoods: 1
Contributing buildings: 41
>Nags Head Beach Cottages District
Outdoor Recreation Assets
Golf course holes
>Daily fee: 54
Inland water area: 868 sq. miles
Atlantic coastal water: 312 sq. miles
Federal protected areas: 166,472 acres
>Alligator River NWR
>Cape Hatteras NS
>Pea Island NWR
>Wright Brothers NM
State recreation areas: 385 acres
Rank: 89

Delta County, CO

Outdoor Recreation Assets
Golf course holes
>Municipal: 36
Inland water area: 6 sq. miles
Federal protected areas: 191,673 acres
>Grand Mesa NF
>Gunnison NF
>Uncompahgre NF
State recreation areas: 410 acres
Rank: 173

Door Peninsula, WI

Good Bookstores
Independent & College: 2
Good Restaurants: 15
Visible History
Registered neighborhoods: 5
Contributing buildings: 273
>Louisiana Street/Seventh Avenue District
>Namur Belgian-American District
>Third Avenue District
>Thordarson Estate District
>Welcker's Resort District
Outdoor Recreation Assets
Golf course holes
>Daily fee: 126; Municipal: 18; Private: 18
Inland water area: 25 sq. miles
Lake Michigan coastal water: 1,862 sq. miles
Federal protected areas: 29 acres
>Gravel Island NWR
>Green Bay NWR
State recreation areas: 9,303 acres
Rank: 66

Driggs, ID

Outdoor Recreation Assets
Golf course holes
>Daily fee: 18; Private: 18
Federal protected areas: 88,293 acres
>Targhee NF
Rank: 180

Durango, CO

Good Bookstores
Mall & Superstores: 1
Good Restaurants: 15
Visible History
Registered neighborhoods: 2
Contributing buildings: 184
>East 3rd Avenue District
>Main Avenue District
Lively Arts Performance Dates
Touring artists: 10
Outdoor Recreation Assets
Golf course holes
>Daily fee: 18; Private: 45
Inland water area: 8 sq. miles
Federal protected areas: 403,864 acres
>San Juan NF
State recreation areas: 334 acres
Rank: 118

Eagle River–Woodruff, WI

Good Restaurants: 7
Lively Arts Performance Dates
Touring artists: 5
Outdoor Recreation Assets
Golf course holes
>Daily fee: 36; Municipal: 36; Private: 18
Inland water area: 145 sq. miles
Federal protected areas: 54,536 acres
>Chequamegon NF
>Nicolet NF
Rank: 136

★ East End Long Island, NY

Good Bookstores
Mall & Superstores: 5
Independent & College: 8
Good Restaurants: 44
Visible History
Registered neighborhoods: 29
Contributing buildings: 2,988
>East Hampton Village District
>Pantigo Road District
>Sag Harbor Village District
>Sagaponack District
>Shelter Island Heights District
>Shore Road District
>Southampton Village District
>Southold District
Lively Arts Performance Dates
Touring artists: 17
Outdoor Recreation Assets
Golf course holes
>Daily fee: 333; Municipal: 234; Private: 558
Inland water area: 248 sq. miles

★ = *in the top 30 places for ambience*

Atlantic coastal water: 838 sq. miles
Federal protected areas: 9,230 acres
  Amagansett NWR
  Conscience Point NWR
  Elizabeth A. Morton NWR
  Fire Island NS
  Seatuck NWR
  Target Rock NWR
  Wertheim NWR
State recreation areas: 24,766 acres
Rank: 3

Easton–St. Michaels, MD
Good Bookstores
Independent & College: 1
Good Restaurants: 11
Visible History
Registered neighborhoods: 3
Contributing buildings: 1,464
  Easton District
  Oxford District
  St. Michaels District
Lively Arts Performance Dates
Touring artists: 7
Outdoor Recreation Assets
Golf course holes
  Daily fee: 18; Municipal: 18; Private: 36
Inland water area: 57 sq. miles
Chesapeake coastal water: 150 sq. miles
State recreation areas: 29 acres
Rank: 67

East Stroudsburg, PA
Good Bookstores
Mall & Superstores: 1
Independent & College: 2
Good Restaurants: 22
Visible History
Registered neighborhoods: 2
Contributing buildings: 255
  Academy Hill District
  Pocono Manor District
Outdoor Recreation Assets
Golf course holes
  Daily fee: 297; Private: 63
Inland water area: 9 sq. miles
Federal protected areas: 8,618 acres
  Appalachian NST
  Delaware Water Gap NRA
State recreation areas: 8,984 acres
Rank: 97

Edenton, NC
Good Restaurants: 2
Visible History
Registered neighborhoods: 2
Contributing buildings: 93
  Edenton Cotton Mill District
  Edenton District
Outdoor Recreation Assets
Golf course holes
  Daily fee: 18
Inland water area: 61 sq. miles
Rank: 171

★ Eugene, OR
Good Bookstores
Mall & Superstores: 4
Good Restaurants: 20
Visible History
Registered neighborhoods: 7
Contributing buildings: 871
  Amazon Family Housing Complex
  Coburg District
  East Skinner Butte District
  Eugene Blair Boulevard Historic Area
  South University District
  Washburne District
Lively Arts Performance Dates
Touring artists: 96
Outdoor Recreation Assets
Golf course holes
  Daily fee: 117; Municipal: 9; Private: 54
Inland water area: 64 sq. miles
Federal protected areas: 1,424,083 acres
  Oregon Islands NWR
  Siuslaw NF
  Umpqua NF
  Willamette NF
State recreation areas: 10,450 acres
Rank: 20

Eureka Springs, AR
Good Restaurants: 12
Visible History
Registered neighborhoods: 1
Contributing buildings: 474
  Eureka Springs District
Outdoor Recreation Assets
Golf course holes
  Daily fee: 9; Private: 18
Inland water area: 9 sq. miles
State recreation areas: 622 acres
Rank: 187

Fairhope–Gulf Shores, AL
Good Bookstores
Mall & Superstores: 2
Independent & College: 2
Good Restaurants: 17
Visible History
Registered neighborhoods: 6
Contributing buildings: 330
  Battles Wharf District
  Fairhope Bayfront District
  Fairhope Downtown District
  Foley Downtown District
  Montrose District
  Point Clear District
Lively Arts Performance Dates
Touring artists: 24
Outdoor Recreation Assets
Golf course holes
  Daily fee: 207; Municipal: 36; Private: 54
Inland water area: 98 sq. miles
Gulf coastal water: 235 sq. miles

continued

Ambience

Federal protected areas: 5,042 acres
   Bon Secour NWR
State recreation areas: 6,150 acres
Rank: 54

Fairplay, CO
Visible History
Registered neighborhoods: 4
Contributing buildings: 48
   Estabrook District
Outdoor Recreation Assets
Golf course holes
   Daily fee: 27
Inland water area: 10 sq. miles
Federal protected areas: 650,381 acres
   Arapaho NF
   Pike NF
   San Isabel NF
State recreation areas: 7,475 acres
Rank: 138

Fayetteville, AR
Good Bookstores
Mall & Superstores: 2
Independent & College: 1
Good Restaurants: 9
Visible History
Registered neighborhoods: 3
Contributing buildings: 168
   Washington-Willow District
   Wilson Park District
Lively Arts Performance Dates
Touring artists: 44
Outdoor Recreation Assets
Golf course holes
   Daily fee: 63; Private: 72
Inland water area: 6 sq. miles
Federal protected areas: 21,971 acres
   Ozark NF
State recreation areas: 1,351 acres
Rank: 117

★ Flagstaff, AZ
Good Bookstores
Mall & Superstores: 2
Good Restaurants: 75
Visible History
Registered neighborhoods: 10
Contributing buildings: 820
   Flagstaff Townsite Historic Residential District
   North End Historic Residential District
   Railroad Addition District
   Walnut Canyon National Monument
   Williams Historic Business District
   Williams Residential District
Lively Arts Performance Dates
Touring artists: 21
Outdoor Recreation Assets
Golf course holes
   Daily fee: 18; Municipal: 45; Private: 108
Inland water area: 43 sq. miles
Federal protected areas: 4,103,928 acres
   Coconino NF
   Glen Canyon NRA

   Grand Canyon NP
   Kaibab NF
   Lake Mead NRA
   Navajo NM
   Prescott NF
   Sitgreaves NF
   Sunset Crater NM
   Walnut Canyon NM
   Wupatki NM
State recreation areas: 48 acres
Rank: 22

★ Fort Collins–Loveland, CO
Good Bookstores
Mall & Superstores: 4
Independent & College: 1
Good Restaurants: 34
Visible History
Registered neighborhoods: 9
Contributing buildings: 708
   Laurel School District
Lively Arts Performance Dates
Touring artists: 8
Resident ensembles: 54
Outdoor Recreation Assets
Golf course holes
   Daily fee: 9; Municipal: 99; Private: 54
Inland water area: 33 sq. miles
Federal protected areas: 791,499 acres
   Rocky Mountain NP
   Roosevelt NF
State recreation areas: 2,689 acres
Rank: 26

★ Fort Myers–Cape Coral, FL
Good Bookstores
Mall & Superstores: 5
Independent & College: 2
Good Restaurants: 65
Visible History
Registered neighborhoods: 2
Contributing buildings: 83
Lively Arts Performance Dates
Touring artists: 13
Outdoor Recreation Assets
Golf course holes
   Daily fee: 423; Municipal: 54; Private: 738
Inland water area: 236 sq. miles
Gulf coastal water: 6 sq. miles
Federal protected areas: 6,274 acres
   Caloosahatchee NWR
   J. N. Ding Darling NWR
   Matlacha Pass NWR
   Pine Island NWR
State recreation areas: 2,975 acres
Rank: 21

Fredericksburg, TX
Good Bookstores
Independent & College: 1
Good Restaurants: 7
Visible History
Registered neighborhoods: 2

Contributing buildings: 421
Fredericksburg District
Lively Arts Performance Dates
Touring artists: 9
Outdoor Recreation Assets
Golf course holes
Daily fee: 18; Municipal: 18
Federal protected areas: 591 acres
Lyndon B. Johnson NHP
State recreation areas: 2,162 acres
Rank: 127

Fredericksburg–Spotsylvania, VA
Good Bookstores
Mall & Superstores: 4
Good Restaurants: 22
Visible History
Registered neighborhoods: 4
Contributing buildings: 370
Fredericksburg District
Spotsylvania Court House District
Washington Avenue District
Woodstock District
Outdoor Recreation Assets
Golf course holes
Daily fee: 18; Private: 36
Inland water area: 11 sq. miles
Federal protected areas: 214 acres
Fredericksburg and Spotsylvania NMP
State recreation areas: 2,000 acres
Rank: 128

Front Royal, VA
Good Restaurants: 3
Visible History
Registered neighborhoods: 1
Contributing buildings: 66
Riverton District
Outdoor Recreation Assets
Golf course holes
Daily fee: 72
Inland water area: 3 sq. miles
Federal protected areas: 21,122 acres
Appalachian NST
George Washington NF
Shenandoah NP
Rank: 175

Gainesville, FL
Good Bookstores
Mall & Superstores: 4
Independent & College: 1
Good Restaurants: 30
Visible History
Registered neighborhoods: 9
Contributing buildings: 1,110
High Springs District
Melrose District
Northeast Gainesville Residential District
Pleasant Street District
Southeast Gainesville Residential District
Waldo District
Lively Arts Performance Dates
Touring artists: 32

Outdoor Recreation Assets
Golf course holes
Daily fee: 36; Municipal: 18; Private: 54
Inland water area: 95 sq. miles
State recreation areas: 29,662 acres
Rank: 65

Georgetown, TX
Good Bookstores
Mall & Superstores: 3
Good Restaurants: 69
Visible History
Registered neighborhoods: 1
Contributing buildings: 70
Belford District
Lively Arts Performance Dates
Touring artists: 4
Resident ensembles: 32
Outdoor Recreation Assets
Golf course holes
Daily fee: 117; Municipal: 18; Private: 72
Inland water area: 12 sq. miles
Federal protected areas: 903 acres
Balcones Canyonlands NWR
Rank: 86

Grand Junction, CO
Good Bookstores
Mall & Superstores: 2
Independent & College: 1
Good Restaurants: 7
Visible History
Registered neighborhoods: 1
Contributing buildings: 27
North Seventh Street Historic Residential District
Lively Arts Performance Dates
Touring artists: 5
Outdoor Recreation Assets
Golf course holes
Daily fee: 45; Municipal: 27; Private: 18
Inland water area: 13 sq. miles
Federal protected areas: 568,371 acres
Colorado NM
Grand Mesa NF
Manti-La Sal NF
Uncompahgre NF
White River NF
State recreation areas: 1,608 acres
Rank: 90

Grants Pass, OR
Good Restaurants: 9
Lively Arts Performance Dates
Touring artists: 6
Outdoor Recreation Assets
Golf course holes
Daily fee: 54
Inland water area: 2 sq. miles
Federal protected areas: 401,568 acres
Oregon Caves NM
Rogue River NF
Siskiyou NF
State recreation areas: 1,135 acres
Rank: 147

continued

★ = in the top 30 places for ambience

Ambience

Retirement Places Rated

Grass Valley–Nevada City, CA

Good Bookstores
Independent & College: 3
Good Restaurants: 3
Visible History
Registered neighborhoods: 2
Contributing buildings: 30
Outdoor Recreation Assets
Golf course holes
Daily fee: 108; Private: 36
Inland water area: 17 sq. miles
Federal protected areas: 174,769 acres
Tahoe NF
Toiyabe NF
State recreation areas: 4,142 acres
Rank: 135

Hamilton–Bitterroot Valley, MT

Good Bookstores
Independent & College: 2
Good Restaurants: 2
Visible History
Registered neighborhoods: 2
Contributing buildings: 156
Hamilton Southside Residential District
Outdoor Recreation Assets
Golf course holes
Daily fee: 27; Private: 18
Inland water area: 6 sq. miles
Federal protected areas: 1,120,165 acres
Bitterroot NF
Lee Metcalf NWR
Lolo NF
State recreation areas: 294 acres
Rank: 137

Hampshire County, WV

Good Restaurants: 1
Visible History
Registered neighborhoods: 1
Contributing buildings: 15
Capon Springs
Outdoor Recreation Assets
Golf course holes
Private: 9
Inland water area: 3 sq. miles
Federal protected areas: 3,518 acres
George Washington NF
Rank: 188

★ Hanover, NH

Good Bookstores
Mall & Superstores: 1
Independent & College: 4
Good Restaurants: 37
Visible History
Registered neighborhoods: 8
Contributing buildings: 309
Canaan Street District
Central Square District
Enfield Shaker District
Haverhill Corner District
Hebron Village District
Lyme Common District
Orford Street District
Lively Arts Performance Dates
Touring artists: 33
Outdoor Recreation Assets
Golf course holes
Daily fee: 126; Municipal: 18; Private: 27
Inland water area: 37 sq. miles
Federal protected areas: 355,686 acres
Appalachian NST
White Mountain NF
State recreation areas: 83 acres
Rank: 12

Hattiesburg, MS

Good Bookstores
Mall & Superstores: 1
Independent & College: 1
Good Restaurants: 4
Visible History
Registered neighborhoods: 4
Contributing buildings: 775
Hattiesburg Historic Neighborhood District
North Main Street District
Oaks District
Parkhaven District
Lively Arts Performance Dates
Touring artists: 20
Outdoor Recreation Assets
Golf course holes
Daily fee: 54; Private: 36
Inland water area: 3 sq. miles
Federal protected areas: 50,644 acres
De Soto NF
State recreation areas: 744 acres
Rank: 96

★ Henderson, NV

Good Bookstores
Mall & Superstores: 13
Independent & College: 1
Good Restaurants: 7
Lively Arts Performance Dates
Touring artists: 78
Resident ensembles: 60
Outdoor Recreation Assets
Golf course holes
Daily fee: 711; Municipal: 135; Private: 243
Inland water area: 180 sq. miles
Federal protected areas: 1,720,863 acres
Desert NWR
Lake Mead NRA
Moapa Valley NWR
Toiyabe NF
Toiyabe Special Area
State recreation areas: 54,532 acres
Rank: 10

Hendersonville–East Flat Rock, NC

Good Bookstores
Mall & Superstores: 1
Good Restaurants: 15
Visible History
Registered neighborhoods: 9

★ = *in the top 30 places for ambience*

Contributing buildings: 651
  Druid Hills District
  Flat Rock District
  Hyman Heights-Mount Royal District
  Lenox Park District
  Seventh Avenue Depot District
  West Side District
Outdoor Recreation Assets
Golf course holes
  Daily fee: 90; Private: 54
Inland water area: 1 sq. miles
Federal protected areas: 17,817 acres
  Blue Ridge Parkway
  Pisgah NF
Rank: 104

★ **Hilton Head Island, SC**
Good Bookstores
Mall & Superstores: 2
Independent & College: 1
Good Restaurants: 40
Visible History
Registered neighborhoods: 2
Contributing buildings: 82
  Bluffton District
  Daufuskie Island District
Lively Arts Performance Dates
Touring artists: 9
Outdoor Recreation Assets
Golf course holes
  Daily fee: 567; Private: 531
Inland water area: 110 sq. miles
Atlantic coastal water: 56 sq. miles
Federal protected areas: 2,746 acres
  Ace Basin NWR
  Pinckney Island NWR
State recreation areas: 5,000 acres
Rank: 13

Hot Springs, AR
Good Bookstores
Mall & Superstores: 2
Good Restaurants: 12
Visible History
Registered neighborhoods: 5
Contributing buildings: 269
  Hot Springs Central Avenue District
  Pleasant Street District
  Quapaw-Prospect District
Lively Arts Performance Dates
Touring artists: 20
Outdoor Recreation Assets
Golf course holes
  Daily fee: 90; Private: 144
Inland water area: 57 sq. miles
Federal protected areas: 124,592 acres
  Hot Springs NP
  Ouachita NF
State recreation areas: 391 acres
Rank: 76

Iowa City, IA
Good Bookstores
Mall & Superstores: 2

Good Restaurants: 7
Visible History
Registered neighborhoods: 10
Contributing buildings: 771
  Brown Street District
  College Green District
  East College Street District
  Gilbert-Linn Street District
  Longfellow District
  Melrose District
Lively Arts Performance Dates
Touring artists: 35
Outdoor Recreation Assets
Golf course holes
  Daily fee: 99; Municipal: 18; Private: 9
Inland water area: 9 sq. miles
State recreation areas: 2,180 acres
Rank: 92

Jackson Hole, WY
Good Bookstores
Independent & College: 1
Good Restaurants: 23
Visible History
Registered neighborhoods: 12
Contributing buildings: 661
Outdoor Recreation Assets
Golf course holes
  Daily fee: 45; Private: 18
Inland water area: 214 sq. miles
Federal protected areas: 2,654,035 acres
  Bridger NF
  Grand Teton NP
  John D. Rockefeller Memorial Parkway
  National Elk Refuge
  Shoshone NF
  Targhee NF
  Teton NF
  Yellowstone NP
Rank: 59

★ **Kalispell–Flathead Valley, MT**
Good Bookstores
Mall & Superstores: 2
Independent & College: 2
Good Restaurants: 31
Visible History
Registered neighborhoods: 7
Contributing buildings: 1,016
  East Side District
  Main Street Commercial District
  West Side District
Outdoor Recreation Assets
Golf course holes
  Daily fee: 135; Municipal: 27; Private: 18
Inland water area: 158 sq. miles
Federal protected areas: 2,423,962 acres
  Flathead NF
  Glacier NP
  Kootenai NF
  Lolo NF
State recreation areas: 263 acres
Rank: 4

Ambience

continued

★ = *in the top 30 places for ambience*

161

Kerrville, TX
Good Restaurants: 2
Lively Arts Performance Dates
Touring artists: 6
Outdoor Recreation Assets
Golf course holes
Municipal: 18; Private: 36
Inland water area: 1 sq. miles
State recreation areas: 517 acres
Rank: 198

Ketchum–Sun Valley, ID
Good Bookstores
Independent & College: 3
Good Restaurants: 7
Visible History
Registered neighborhoods: 1
Contributing buildings: 23
Bellevue District
Lively Arts Performance Dates
Touring artists: 18
Outdoor Recreation Assets
Golf course holes
Daily fee: 36; Private: 36
Inland water area: 16 sq. miles
Federal protected areas: 506,948 acres
Challis NF
Craters of the Moon NM
Minidoka NWR
Sawtooth NF
Rank: 75

★ Key West, FL
Good Bookstores
Mall & Superstores: 1
Independent & College: 2
Good Restaurants: 76
Visible History
Registered neighborhoods: 2
Contributing buildings: 2,683
Key West District 2
Pigeon Key District
Lively Arts Performance Dates
Touring artists: 15
Outdoor Recreation Assets
Golf course holes
Daily fee: 18; Private: 72
Inland water area: 407 sq. miles
Atlantic coastal water: 541 sq. miles
Federal protected areas: 1,154,410 acres
Big Cypress N Preserve
Crocodile Lake NWR
Dry Tortugas NP
Everglades Expansion
Everglades NP
Great White Heron NWR
Key West NWR
National Key Deer NWR
State recreation areas: 5,894 acres
Rank: 28

Kingman, AZ
Good Restaurants: 18
Lively Arts Performance Dates
Touring artists: 27
Outdoor Recreation Assets
Golf course holes
Daily fee: 153; Municipal: 18
Inland water area: 158 sq. miles
Federal protected areas: 1,329,144 acres
Grand Canyon NP
Havasu NWR
Kaibab NF
Lake Mead NRA
Pipe Spring NM
State recreation areas: 11,339 acres
Rank: 139

Kissimmee–St. Cloud, FL
Good Bookstores
Mall & Superstores: 1
Good Restaurants: 14
Visible History
Registered neighborhoods: 1
Contributing buildings: 189
Kissimmee District
Outdoor Recreation Assets
Golf course holes
Daily fee: 297; Private: 36
Inland water area: 184 sq. miles
Rank: 144

★ Laguna Beach–Dana Point, CA
Good Bookstores
Mall & Superstores: 2
Independent & College: 2
Good Restaurants: 65
Visible History
Registered neighborhoods: 1
Contributing buildings: 46
Crystal Cove District
Lively Arts Performance Dates
Touring artists: 4
Outdoor Recreation Assets
Golf course holes
Daily fee: 288; Municipal: 198; Private: 369
Inland water area: 10 sq. miles
Pacific coastal water: 148 sq. miles
Federal protected areas: 59,215 acres
Cleveland NF
State recreation areas: 5,859 acres
Rank: 9

Lake Conroe, TX
Good Bookstores
Mall & Superstores: 2
Independent & College: 1
Good Restaurants: 13
Lively Arts Performance Dates
Touring artists: 6
Outdoor Recreation Assets
Golf course holes
Daily fee: 216; Municipal: 27; Private: 234
Inland water area: 33 sq. miles

★ = *in the top 30 places for ambience*

Federal protected areas: 47,800 acres
    Sam Houston NF
State recreation areas: 1,912 acres
Rank: 83

Lake Havasu City, AZ

Good Restaurants: 18

Lively Arts Performance Dates

Touring artists: 27

Outdoor Recreation Assets

Golf course holes
    Daily fee: 153; Municipal: 18
Inland water area: 158 sq. miles
Federal protected areas: 1,329,144 acres
    Grand Canyon NP
    Havasu NWR
    Kaibab NF
    Lake Mead NRA
    Pipe Spring NM
State recreation areas: 11,339 acres
Rank: 139

Lakeland–Winter Haven, FL

Good Bookstores

Mall & Superstores: 4

Good Restaurants: 8

Visible History

Registered neighborhoods: 17
Contributing buildings: 2,698
    Biltmore-Cumberland District
    Dixieland District
    East Lake Morton Residential District
    Fort Meade District
    Lake Hunter Terrace District
    Lake Wales Historic Residential District
    South Bartow Residential District
    South Lake Morton District
    Winter Haven Heights Historic Residential District

Lively Arts Performance Dates

Touring artists: 6

Outdoor Recreation Assets

Golf course holes
    Daily fee: 504; Municipal: 63; Private: 108
Inland water area: 135 sq. miles
Federal protected areas: 154 acres
    Lake Wales Ridge NWR
State recreation areas: 7,843 acres
Rank: 49

Lake of the Cherokees, OK

Outdoor Recreation Assets

Golf course holes
    Daily fee: 27
Inland water area: 52 sq. miles
State recreation areas: 228 acres
Rank: 199

Lake of the Ozarks, MO

Good Bookstores

Mall & Superstores: 1

Good Restaurants: 12

Visible History

Registered neighborhoods: 1

Contributing buildings: 42
    Camp Pin Oak District
Outdoor Recreation Assets
Golf course holes
    Daily fee: 207; Private: 18
Inland water area: 54 sq. miles
State recreation areas: 12,206 acres
Rank: 143

Lake Placid, NY

Good Bookstores

Independent & College: 2

Good Restaurants: 18

Visible History

Registered neighborhoods: 7
Contributing buildings: 500
    Amherst Avenue District
    Camp Dudley Road District
    Essex Village District
    Highland Park District
    Keeseville District

Lively Arts Performance Dates

Touring artists: 6

Outdoor Recreation Assets

Golf course holes
    Daily fee: 108; Municipal: 45; Private: 9
Inland water area: 120 sq. miles
State recreation areas: 1,724 acres
Rank: 55

★ Largo, FL

Good Bookstores

Mall & Superstores: 5
Independent & College: 2

Good Restaurants: 162

Outdoor Recreation Assets

Golf course holes
    Daily fee: 144; Municipal: 90; Private: 351
Inland water area: 65 sq. miles
Gulf coastal water: 95 sq. miles
Federal protected areas: 17 acres
    Pinellas NWR
State recreation areas: 3,114 acres
Rank: 19

Las Cruces, NM

Good Bookstores

Mall & Superstores: 1
Independent & College: 2

Good Restaurants: 16

Visible History

Registered neighborhoods: 4
Contributing buildings: 483
    Alameda-Depot District
    Dona Ana Village District
    La Mesilla District
    Mesquite Street Original Townsite District

Lively Arts Performance Dates

Touring artists: 12

Outdoor Recreation Assets

Golf course holes
    Daily fee: 63; Private: 81
Inland water area: 7 sq. miles

continued

Ambience

Federal protected areas: 52,780 acres
   San Andres NWR
   White Sands NM
State recreation areas: 140 acres
Rank: 107

Las Vegas, NM
Good Bookstores
Independent & College: 2
Good Restaurants: 4
Visible History
Registered neighborhoods: 7
Contributing buildings: 710
   Distrito de las Escuelas
   Lincoln Park District
   North New Town District
   Old Town Residential District
Outdoor Recreation Assets
Golf course holes
   Daily fee: 18
Inland water area: 19 sq. miles
Federal protected areas: 355,096 acres
   Las Vegas NWR
   Pecos NM
   Santa Fe NF
State recreation areas: 12,705 acres
Rank: 155

★ Leelanau Peninsula, MI
Good Bookstores
Independent & College: 2
Good Restaurants: 17
Visible History
Registered neighborhoods: 5
Contributing buildings: 188
   Fountain Point
   Glen Haven Village District
   Leland District
   Port Oneida Rural District
Lively Arts Performance Dates
Touring artists: 60
Outdoor Recreation Assets
Golf course holes
   Daily fee: 72; Private: 27
Inland water area: 31 sq. miles
Lake Michigan coastal water: 2,153 sq. miles
Federal protected areas: 45,835 acres
   Sleeping Bear Dunes N Lakeshore
State recreation areas: 1,300 acres
Rank: 24

Leesburg–Mount Dora, FL
Good Bookstores
Mall & Superstores: 1
Good Restaurants: 15
Lively Arts Performance Dates
Touring artists: 5
Outdoor Recreation Assets
Golf course holes
   Daily fee: 513; Private: 45
Inland water area: 203 sq. miles

Federal protected areas: 84,652 acres
   Lake Woodruff NWR
   Ocala NF
State recreation areas: 17,472 acres
Rank: 108

Litchfield Hills, CT
Good Bookstores
Independent & College: 4
Good Restaurants: 13
Visible History
Registered neighborhoods: 35
Contributing buildings: 2,800
   Canaan Village District
   Hotchkissville District
   Litchfield District
   New Milford Center District
   Pine Meadow District
   Plymouth Center District
   Sharon District
   Watertown Center District
Lively Arts Performance Dates
Touring artists: 4
Outdoor Recreation Assets
Golf course holes
   Daily fee: 90; Municipal: 18; Private: 108
Inland water area: 25 sq. miles
Federal protected areas: 5,885 acres
   Appalachian NST
State recreation areas: 373 acres
Rank: 61

Long Beach Peninsula, WA
Good Bookstores
Independent & College: 1
Good Restaurants: 11
Visible History
Registered neighborhoods: 1
Contributing buildings: 23
   Oysterville District
Outdoor Recreation Assets
Golf course holes
   Daily fee: 27
Inland water area: 16 sq. miles
Pacific coastal water: 102 sq. miles
Federal protected areas: 11,271 acres
   Willapa NWR
State recreation areas: 5,853 acres
Rank: 158

Loudoun County, VA
Good Bookstores
Mall & Superstores: 5
Independent & College: 1
Good Restaurants: 2
Visible History
Registered neighborhoods: 9
Contributing buildings: 1,201
   Bluemont District
   Catoctin Rural District
   Goose Creek District
   Hillsboro District
   Leesburg District

★ = in the top 30 places for ambience

Middleburg District
Taylorstown District
Unison District
Lively Arts Performance Dates
Touring artists: 50
Outdoor Recreation Assets
Golf course holes
Daily fee: 72; Municipal: 36; Private: 144
Inland water area: 1 sq. miles
Federal protected areas: 1,585 acres
Appalachian NST
Harpers Ferry NHP
Rank: 94

★ **Lower Cape May, NJ**
Good Bookstores
Independent & College: 2
Good Restaurants: 37
Visible History
Registered neighborhoods: 5
Contributing buildings: 878
Cape May District
Dennisville District
Marshallville District
Ocean City Residential District
South Tuckahoe District
Lively Arts Performance Dates
Touring artists: 20
Outdoor Recreation Assets
Golf course holes
Daily fee: 108; Private: 36
Inland water area: 30 sq. miles
Atlantic coastal water: 172 sq. miles
Federal protected areas: 8,099 acres
Cape May NWR
State recreation areas: 4,558 acres
Rank: 11

Madison, MS
Good Bookstores
Independent & College: 2
Good Restaurants: 23
Visible History
Registered neighborhoods: 1
Contributing buildings: 150
East Canton District
Lively Arts Performance Dates
Touring artists: 1
Resident ensembles: 116
Outdoor Recreation Assets
Golf course holes
Daily fee: 27; Private: 72
Inland water area: 23 sq. miles
Federal protected areas: 4,703 acres
Natchez Trace NST
Natchez Trace Parkway
Rank: 115

★ **Madison, WI**
Good Bookstores
Mall & Superstores: 5
Independent & College: 2
Good Restaurants: 37

Visible History
Registered neighborhoods: 20
Contributing buildings: 3,183
College Hills District
Fourth Lake Ridge District
Jenifer-Spaight District
Langdon Street District
Mansion Hill District
Nakoma District
Northwest Side District
Orton Park District
Sherman Avenue District
Shorewood District
Southwest Side District
University Heights District
West Lawn Heights District
Wingra Park District
Lively Arts Performance Dates
Touring artists: 97
Resident ensembles: 126
Outdoor Recreation Assets
Golf course holes
Daily fee: 216; Municipal: 90; Private: 126
Inland water area: 36 sq. miles
State recreation areas: 1,083 acres
Rank: 30

Marble Falls–Lake LBJ, TX
Good Restaurants: 6
Outdoor Recreation Assets
Golf course holes
Daily fee: 18; Municipal: 18
Inland water area: 25 sq. miles
Federal protected areas: 2,868 acres
Balcones Canyonlands NWR
State recreation areas: 1,841 acres
Rank: 195

Mariposa, CA
Good Bookstores
Independent & College: 3
Good Restaurants: 9
Visible History
Registered neighborhoods: 4
Contributing buildings: 624
Camp Curry District
Coulterville Main Street District
Mariposa Town District
Yosemite Village District
Outdoor Recreation Assets
Golf course holes
Daily fee: 9
Inland water area: 12 sq. miles
Federal protected areas: 440,343 acres
Sierra NF
Stanislaus NF
Yosemite NP
Rank: 99

Martha's Vineyard, MA
Good Bookstores
Independent & College: 2
Good Restaurants: 12

continued

★ = *in the top 30 places for ambience*

Visible History
Registered neighborhoods: 4
Contributing buildings: 808
Edgartown Village District
Gay Head-Aquinnah Town Center District
William Street District
Lively Arts Performance Dates
Touring artists: 12
Outdoor Recreation Assets
Golf course holes
Daily fee: 27; Private: 27
Inland water area: 18 sq. miles
Atlantic coastal water: 37 sq. miles
Rank: 42

Maryville, TN
Good Restaurants: 4
Visible History
Registered neighborhoods: 3
Contributing buildings: 158
Cades Cove District
Indiana Avenue District
Louisville District
Outdoor Recreation Assets
Golf course holes
Daily fee: 117; Private: 18
Inland water area: 8 sq. miles
Federal protected areas: 98,248 acres
Appalachian NST
Great Smoky Mountains NP
Rank: 168

★ Maui, HI
Good Bookstores
Mall & Superstores: 5
Independent & College: 1
Good Restaurants: 65
Lively Arts Performance Dates
Touring artists: 3
Outdoor Recreation Assets
Golf course holes
Daily fee: 324; Municipal: 18; Private: 9
Inland water area: 4 sq. miles
Pacific coastal water: 124 sq. miles
Federal protected areas: 27,233 acres
Haleakala NP
Kakahaia NWR
Kalaupapa NHP
State recreation areas: 561 acres
Rank: 18

McAllen–Alamo, TX
Good Bookstores
Mall & Superstores: 1
Good Restaurants: 2
Visible History
Registered neighborhoods: 1
Contributing buildings: 217
Oblate Park District
Lively Arts Performance Dates
Touring artists: 4
Outdoor Recreation Assets
Golf course holes
Daily fee: 135; Municipal: 72; Private: 45

Inland water area: 14 sq. miles
Federal protected areas: 24,267 acres
Lower Rio Grande Valley NWR
Santa Ana NWR
State recreation areas: 588 acres
Rank: 182

McCall, ID
Good Bookstores
Independent & College: 1
Good Restaurants: 2
Outdoor Recreation Assets
Golf course holes
Daily fee: 45; Municipal: 27
Inland water area: 56 sq. miles
Federal protected areas: 2,031,004 acres
Boise NF
Payette NF
Salmon NF
Rank: 119

Medford–Ashland, OR
Good Bookstores
Mall & Superstores: 2
Good Restaurants: 19
Visible History
Registered neighborhoods: 9
Contributing buildings: 1,175
Ashland Railroad Addition District
Jacksonville District
Medford Downtown District
Siskiyou-Hargandine District
Skidmore Academy District
South Oakdale District
Union Creek District
Lively Arts Performance Dates
Resident ensembles: 44
Outdoor Recreation Assets
Golf course holes
Daily fee: 72; Municipal: 9; Private: 27
Inland water area: 17 sq. miles
Federal protected areas: 452,211 acres
Crater Lake NP
Klamath NF
Rogue River NF
Umpqua NF
State recreation areas: 1,401 acres
Rank: 47

★ Melbourne–Palm Bay, FL
Good Bookstores
Mall & Superstores: 6
Independent & College: 1
Good Restaurants: 35
Visible History
Registered neighborhoods: 3
Contributing buildings: 195
Barton Avenue Residential District
Rockledge Drive Residential District
Valencia Subdivision Residential District
Lively Arts Performance Dates
Touring artists: 15

★ = in the top 30 places for ambience

Outdoor Recreation Assets
Golf course holes
Daily fee: 180; Municipal: 135; Private: 108
Inland water area: 276 sq. miles
Federal protected areas: 35,759 acres
Archie Carr NWR
Canaveral NS
St. Johns NWR
State recreation areas: 168 acres
Rank: 29

Mendocino–Fort Bragg, CA
Good Bookstores
Independent & College: 5
Good Restaurants: 16
Outdoor Recreation Assets
Golf course holes
Daily fee: 9; Municipal: 18
Inland water area: 7 sq. miles
Federal protected areas: 179,075 acres
Mendocino NF
State recreation areas: 19,448 acres
Rank: 145

★ **Middle Cape Cod, MA**
Good Bookstores
Mall & Superstores: 2
Independent & College: 6
Good Restaurants: 83
Visible History
Registered neighborhoods: 29
Contributing buildings: 4,169
Brewster Old King's Highway District 237
Cotuit District 105
Falmouth Village Green District 79
Hyannis Port District 127
Old King's Highway District 797
Old Village District 205
Wellfleet Center District 173
West Falmouth Village District 135
Lively Arts Performance Dates
Resident ensembles: 74
Outdoor Recreation Assets
Golf course holes
Daily fee: 180; Municipal: 216; Private: 198
Inland water area: 60 sq. miles
Atlantic coastal water: 466 sq. miles
Federal protected areas: 27,460 acres
Cape Cod NS
State recreation areas: 218 acres
Rank: 1

Monadnock Region, NH
Good Bookstores
Mall & Superstores: 1
Independent & College: 1
Good Restaurants: 6
Visible History
Registered neighborhoods: 11
Contributing buildings: 703
Chesham Village District 13
Dublin Lake District 64
Dublin Village District 55
Fitzwilliam Common District 19

Harrisville District 135
Jaffrey Center District 34
Silver Lake District 76
Troy Village District 225
Lively Arts Performance Dates
Touring artists: 8
Outdoor Recreation Assets
Golf course holes
Daily fee: 72; Private: 27
Inland water area: 22 sq. miles
State recreation areas: 942 acres
Rank: 99

Montrose, CO
Good Bookstores
Independent & College: 1
Good Restaurants: 6
Outdoor Recreation Assets
Golf course holes
Daily fee: 54
Inland water area: 2 sq. miles
Federal protected areas: 368,753 acres
Black Canyon of the Gunnison NM
Curecanti NRA
Gunnison NF
Manti-La Sal NF
Uncompahgre NF
State recreation areas: 9 acres
Rank: 149

Morro Bay–Cambria, CA
Good Bookstores
Mall & Superstores: 2
Independent & College: 3
Good Restaurants: 62
Lively Arts Performance Dates
Touring artists: 105
Resident ensembles: 15
Outdoor Recreation Assets
Golf course holes
Daily fee: 144; Municipal: 54; Private: 18
Inland water area: 19 sq. miles
Federal protected areas: 190,402 acres
Los Padres NF
State recreation areas: 15,616 acres
Rank: 62

Murray–Kentucky Lake, KY
Good Bookstores
Independent & College: 1
Good Restaurants: 1
Visible History
Registered neighborhoods: 1
Contributing buildings: 62
Murray Commercial District
Lively Arts Performance Dates
Touring artists: 4
Outdoor Recreation Assets
Golf course holes
Daily fee: 18; Private: 36
Inland water area: 25 sq. miles
State recreation areas: 3,146 acres
Rank: 191

continued

Ambience

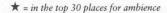
★ = *in the top 30 places for ambience*

Myrtle Beach, SC
Good Bookstores
Mall & Superstores: 5
Good Restaurants: 94
Visible History
Registered neighborhoods: 2
Contributing buildings: 117
Myrtle Heights-Oak Park District
Lively Arts Performance Dates
Touring artists: 5
Outdoor Recreation Assets
Golf course holes
Daily fee: 1,197; Municipal: 18; Private: 72
Inland water area: 12 sq. miles
Atlantic coastal water: 11 sq. miles
State recreation areas: 312 acres
Rank: 41

Naples, FL
Good Bookstores
Mall & Superstores: 3
Independent & College: 1
Good Restaurants: 51
Visible History
Registered neighborhoods: 1
Contributing buildings: 66
Naples District
Lively Arts Performance Dates
Touring artists: 100
Outdoor Recreation Assets
Golf course holes
Daily fee: 216; Private: 1,098
Inland water area: 91 sq. miles
Gulf coastal water: 18 sq. miles
Federal protected areas: 561,225 acres
Big Cypress National Preserve
Everglades NP
Florida Panther NWR
State recreation areas: 72,945 acres
Rank: 40

Natchitoches, LA
Good Bookstores
Independent & College: 1
Good Restaurants: 5
Visible History
Registered neighborhoods: 1
Contributing buildings: 390
Natchitoches District
Lively Arts Performance Dates
Touring artists: 4
Outdoor Recreation Assets
Golf course holes
Daily fee: 9; Municipal: 18
Inland water area: 43 sq. miles
Federal protected areas: 130,474 acres
Cane River Creole NHP
Kisatchie NF
State recreation areas: 67 acres
Rank: 142

Nelson County, VA
Visible History
Registered neighborhoods: 1
Contributing buildings: 130
Lovingston District
Outdoor Recreation Assets
Golf course holes
Daily fee: 63
Inland water area: 2 sq. miles
Federal protected areas: 30,007 acres
Appalachian NST
Blue Ridge Parkway
George Washington NF
Rank: 172

New Bern, NC
Good Bookstores
Mall & Superstores: 2
Good Restaurants: 7
Visible History
Registered neighborhoods: 3
Contributing buildings: 643
Ghent District
New Bern District
Riverside District
Outdoor Recreation Assets
Golf course holes
Daily fee: 108; Private: 54
Inland water area: 66 sq. miles
Atlantic coastal water: 26 sq. miles
Federal protected areas: 63,068 acres
Croatan NF
Rank: 114

New Braunfels, TX
Good Bookstores
Independent & College: 1
Good Restaurants: 18
Visible History
Registered neighborhoods: 1
Contributing buildings: 23
Gruene District
Lively Arts Performance Dates
Touring artists: 52
Outdoor Recreation Assets
Golf course holes
Daily fee: 54; Municipal: 18; Private: 18
Inland water area: 13 sq. miles
State recreation areas: 1,000 acres
Rank: 129

Newport–Lincoln City, OR
Good Bookstores
Independent & College: 2
Good Restaurants: 21
Outdoor Recreation Assets
Golf course holes
Daily fee: 63
Inland water area: 13 sq. miles
Federal protected areas: 174,603 acres
Oregon Islands NWR
Siletz Bay NWR
Siuslaw NF
State recreation areas: 3,120 acres
Rank: 111

★ = in the top 30 places for ambience

Norfork Lake, AR

Good Restaurants: 1

Outdoor Recreation Assets

Golf course holes

Daily fee: 36

Inland water area: 32 sq. miles

Federal protected areas: 64,200 acres

Buffalo NR

Ozark NF

State recreation areas: 663 acres

Rank: 193

Northampton–Amherst, MA

Good Bookstores

Mall & Superstores: 1

Independent & College: 1

Good Restaurants: 9

Visible History

Registered neighborhoods: 32

Contributing buildings: 2,242

Elm Street District

Hadley Center District

Hatfield Center District

Huntington Village District

Mill-Prospect Street District

Upper Main Street District

Lively Arts Performance Dates

Resident ensembles: 22

Outdoor Recreation Assets

Golf course holes

Daily fee: 90; Municipal: 45; Private: 36

Inland water area: 16 sq. miles

State recreation areas: 8,548 acres

Rank: 72

Northern Neck, VA

Good Bookstores

Independent & College: 1

Good Restaurants: 4

Visible History

Registered neighborhoods: 4

Contributing buildings: 315

Heathsville District

Irvington

Lancaster Court House District

Reedville District

Outdoor Recreation Assets

Golf course holes

Daily fee: 81; Private: 18

Inland water area: 41 sq. miles

Atlantic coastal water: 150 sq. miles

Rank: 101

Oakhurst–Coarsegold, CA

Good Bookstores

Independent & College: 1

Good Restaurants: 4

Outdoor Recreation Assets

Golf course holes

Daily fee: 54; Municipal: 18; Private: 18

Inland water area: 15 sq. miles

Federal protected areas: 481,974 acres

Devils Postpile NM

Inyo NF

San Joaquin River NWR

Sierra NF

Yosemite NP

State recreation areas: 3,323 acres

Rank: 181

Ocala, FL

Good Bookstores

Mall & Superstores: 2

Independent & College: 2

Good Restaurants: 19

Visible History

Registered neighborhoods: 7

Contributing buildings: 567

Dunnellon Boomtown District

Lake Lillian Neighborhood District

McIntosh District

Ocala District

Tuscawilla Park District

West Ocala District

Outdoor Recreation Assets

Golf course holes

Daily fee: 297; Municipal: 45; Private: 72

Inland water area: 84 sq. miles

Federal protected areas: 275,590 acres

Ocala NF

State recreation areas: 5,834 acres

Rank: 45

Ocean City, MD

Good Bookstores

Independent & College: 1

Good Restaurants: 30

Visible History

Registered neighborhoods: 1

Contributing buildings: 622

Pocomoke City District

Outdoor Recreation Assets

Golf course holes

Daily fee: 252; Municipal: 27

Inland water area: 111 sq. miles

Atlantic coastal water: 11 sq. miles

Federal protected areas: 7,803 acres

Assateague Island NS

Chincoteague NWR

State recreation areas: 1,670 acres

Rank: 74

Oxford, MS

Good Bookstores

Independent & College: 2

Good Restaurants: 5

Lively Arts Performance Dates

Touring artists: 23

Outdoor Recreation Assets

Golf course holes

Municipal: 18

Inland water area: 48 sq. miles

Federal protected areas: 40,041 acres

Holly Springs NF

Rank: 194

continued

★ = *in the top 30 places for ambience*

Pagosa Springs, CO

Good Bookstores
Independent & College: 1
Good Restaurants: 3
Outdoor Recreation Assets
Golf course holes
Daily fee: 27
Inland water area: 5 sq. miles
Federal protected areas: 429,853 acres
Rio Grande NF
San Juan NF
State recreation areas: 2,672 acres
Rank: 141

Pahrump Valley, NV

Good Restaurants: 8
Outdoor Recreation Assets
Golf course holes
Daily fee: 45
Inland water area: 12 sq. miles
Federal protected areas: 1,867,675 acres
Ashe Meadows NWR
Death Valley NM
Humboldt NF
Toiyabe NF
State recreation areas: 1,134 acres
Rank: 170

Palmer–Wasilla, AK

Good Bookstores
Mall & Superstores: 1
Independent & College: 1
Good Restaurants: 2
Visible History
Registered neighborhoods: 2
Contributing buildings: 27
Lively Arts Performance Dates
Touring artists: 6
Outdoor Recreation Assets
Golf course holes
Daily fee: 18; Municipal: 18
Inland water area: 261 sq. miles
Federal protected areas: 1,733,618 acres
Chugach NF
Denali National Preserve
Denali NP
Lake Clark NP
Rank: 169

Palm Springs–Coachella Valley, CA

Good Bookstores
Mall & Superstores: 10
Independent & College: 1
Good Restaurants: 63
Visible History
Registered neighborhoods: 1
Lively Arts Performance Dates
Touring artists: 7
Resident ensembles: 176
Outdoor Recreation Assets
Golf course holes
Daily fee: 1,224; Municipal: 162; Private: 1,017
Inland water area: 96 sq. miles

Federal protected areas: 447,347 acres
Cleveland NF
Coachella Valley NWR
Joshua Tree NM
San Bernardino NF
State recreation areas: 70,571 acres
Rank: 39

Panama City, FL

Good Bookstores
Mall & Superstores: 2
Good Restaurants: 1
Lively Arts Performance Dates
Touring artists: 10
Outdoor Recreation Assets
Golf course holes
Daily fee: 144; Private: 54
Inland water area: 119 sq. miles
Gulf coastal water: 15 sq. miles
State recreation areas: 1,268 acres
Rank: 154

Paradise–Magalia, CA

Good Bookstores
Mall & Superstores: 1
Independent & College: 1
Good Restaurants: 14
Visible History
Registered neighborhoods: 1
Contributing buildings: 114
South of Campus Neighborhood
Lively Arts Performance Dates
Touring artists: 18
Outdoor Recreation Assets
Golf course holes
Daily fee: 54; Municipal: 18; Private: 36
Inland water area: 38 sq. miles
Federal protected areas: 136,034 acres
Lassen NF
North Central Valley NWR
Plumas NF
Sacramento River NWR
State recreation areas: 32,000 acres
Rank: 95

Park City, UT

Good Bookstores
Mall & Superstores: 2
Good Restaurants: 32
Visible History
Registered neighborhoods: 1
Contributing buildings: 47
Park City Main Street District
Outdoor Recreation Assets
Golf course holes
Daily fee: 18; Municipal: 90; Private: 90
Inland water area: 39 sq. miles
Federal protected areas: 945,362 acres
Ashley NF
Uinta NF
Wasatch NF
State recreation areas: 25,851 acres
Rank: 58

★ = in the top 30 places for ambience

Payson, AZ
Good Restaurants: 5
Visible History
Registered neighborhoods: 2
Contributing buildings: 70
    Globe Downtown District
    Pine District
Outdoor Recreation Assets
Golf course holes
    Daily fee: 45; Municipal: 9; Private: 36
Inland water area: 28 sq. miles
Federal protected areas: 1,703,136 acres
    Coconino NF
    Tonto NF
    Tonto NM
State recreation areas: 160 acres
Rank: 153

Pendleton District, SC
Good Bookstores
Independent & College: 1
Good Restaurants: 1
Visible History
Registered neighborhoods: 3
Contributing buildings: 181
    Newry District
    Pendleton District
    Seneca District
Outdoor Recreation Assets
Golf course holes
    Daily fee: 63; Private: 36
Inland water area: 49 sq. miles
Federal protected areas: 84,574 acres
    Sumter NF
State recreation areas: 2,679 acres
Rank: 178

Pensacola, FL
Good Bookstores
Mall & Superstores: 3
Independent & College: 1
Good Restaurants: 12
Visible History
Registered neighborhoods: 3
Contributing buildings: 490
    Sullivan Lumber Company Residential District
    North Hill Preservation District
    Pensacola District
Lively Arts Performance Dates
Touring artists: 153
Resident ensembles: 26
Outdoor Recreation Assets
Golf course holes
    Daily fee: 99; Municipal: 18; Private: 45
Inland water area: 88 sq. miles
Gulf coastal water: 14 sq. miles
Federal protected areas: 23,212 acres
    Gulf Islands NS
State recreation areas: 983 acres
Rank: 60

Petoskey–Harbor Springs, MI
Good Bookstores
Independent & College: 2

Good Restaurants: 18
Visible History
Registered neighborhoods: 3
Contributing buildings: 761
    Bay View
    East Mitchell Street District
    Four Mile Clearing Rural District
Outdoor Recreation Assets
Golf course holes
    Daily fee: 243; Private: 99
Inland water area: 16 sq. miles
Lake Michigan coastal water: 398 sq. miles
State recreation areas: 8,591 acres
Rank: 56

Pike County, PA
Good Bookstores
Independent & College: 1
Good Restaurants: 6
Visible History
Registered neighborhoods: 1
Contributing buildings: 397
    Milford District
Outdoor Recreation Assets
Golf course holes
    Daily fee: 63; Private: 63
Inland water area: 20 sq. miles
Federal protected areas: 17,589 acres
    Delaware Water Gap NRA
    Upper Delaware National Scenic River
State recreation areas: 5,700 acres
Rank: 157

Placer County, CA
Good Bookstores
Mall & Superstores: 3
Independent & College: 3
Good Restaurants: 10
Visible History
Registered neighborhoods: 1
Contributing buildings: 45
    Dutch Flat District
Lively Arts Performance Dates
Touring artists: 9
Outdoor Recreation Assets
Golf course holes
    Daily fee: 180; Municipal: 36; Private: 144
Inland water area: 96 sq. miles
Federal protected areas: 352,944 acres
    Eldorado NF
    Tahoe NF
State recreation areas: 37,796 acres
Rank: 73

Port Angeles–Sequim, WA
Good Bookstores
Independent & College: 1
Good Restaurants: 23
Outdoor Recreation Assets
Golf course holes
    Daily fee: 27; Private: 36
Inland water area: 35 sq. miles
Pacific coastal water: 702 sq. miles

continued

★ = *in the top 30 places for ambience*

Federal protected areas: 528,532 acres
  Dungeness NWR
  Flattery Rocks NWR
  Olympic NF
  Olympic NP
  Protection Island NWR
  Quillayute Needles NWR
  State recreation areas: 3,075 acres
Rank: 132

Port Charlotte, FL
Good Bookstores
  Mall & Superstores: 2
Good Restaurants: 10
Visible History
  Registered neighborhoods: 1
  Contributing buildings: 126
    Punta Gorda Residential District
Lively Arts Performance Dates
  Touring artists: 7
Outdoor Recreation Assets
  Golf course holes
    Daily fee: 135; Private: 72
  Inland water area: 122 sq. miles
  Gulf coastal water: 4 sq. miles
  Federal protected areas: 20 acres
    Island Bay NWR
  State recreation areas: 346 acres
Rank: 98

Port St. Lucie, FL
Good Restaurants: 4
Visible History
  Registered neighborhoods: 1
  Contributing buildings: 34
    St. Lucie Village District
Outdoor Recreation Assets
  Golf course holes
    Daily fee: 126; Municipal: 54; Private: 90
  Inland water area: 43 sq. miles
  Atlantic coastal water: 73 sq. miles
  State recreation areas: 1,543 acres
Rank: 179

Port Townsend, WA
Good Bookstores
  Independent & College: 1
Good Restaurants: 7
Visible History
  Registered neighborhoods: 1
  Contributing buildings: 760
    Port Townsend District
Outdoor Recreation Assets
  Golf course holes
    Daily fee: 45; Private: 9
  Inland water area: 63 sq. miles
  Pacific coastal water: 169 sq. miles
  Federal protected areas: 708,777 acres
    Olympic NF & NP
    Protection Island NWR
    Quillayute Needles NWR
  State recreation areas: 2,685 acres
Rank: 93

★ Prescott–Prescott Valley, AZ
Good Bookstores
  Mall & Superstores: 1
  Independent & College: 1
Good Restaurants: 59
Visible History
  Registered neighborhoods: 14
  Contributing buildings: 1,074
    East Prescott District
    Fleury's Addition District
    Joslin and Whipple District
    Pine Crest District
    South Prescott Townsite
    West Prescott District
    Whipple Heights District
Lively Arts Performance Dates
  Touring artists: 6
Outdoor Recreation Assets
  Golf course holes
    Daily fee: 135; Municipal: 36; Private: 72
  Inland water area: 5 sq. miles
  Federal protected areas: 1,965,387 acres
    Coconino NF
    Kaibab NF
    Montezuma Castle NM
    Prescott NF
    Tonto NF
    Tuzigoot NM
  State recreation areas: 1,025 acres
Rank: 17

Rabun County, GA
Good Restaurants: 3
Visible History
  Registered neighborhoods: 1
  Contributing buildings: 14
    Hambidge Center District
Outdoor Recreation Assets
  Golf course holes
    Daily fee: 36; Municipal: 9; Private: 18
  Inland water area: 6 sq. miles
  Federal protected areas: 149,048 acres
    Chattahoochee NF
  State recreation areas: 4,534 acres
Rank: 155

Rehoboth Bay–Indian River Bay, DE
Good Bookstores
  Independent & College: 1
Good Restaurants: 33
Visible History
  Registered neighborhoods: 8
  Contributing buildings: 1,884
    Bridgeville District
    Fort Miles District
    Laurel District
    Lewes District
    Milton District
    South Milford District
Outdoor Recreation Assets
  Golf course holes
    Daily fee: 108; Private: 108
  Inland water area: 41 sq. miles

★ = *in the top 30 places for ambience*

Atlantic coastal water: 123 sq. miles
Federal protected areas: 8,818 acres
  Prime Hook NWR
State recreation areas: 8,278 acres
Rank: 102

Rio Rancho, NM

Good Bookstores
Independent & College: 1
Good Restaurants: 9
Outdoor Recreation Assets
Golf course holes
  Daily fee: 63; Private: 27
Inland water area: 5 sq. miles
Federal protected areas: 409,748 acres
  Bandelier NM
  Cibola NF
  Santa Fe NF
  Valles Caldera NP
State recreation areas: 945 acres
Rank: 105

Rockport–Aransas Pass, TX

Good Bookstores
Independent & College: 1
Good Restaurants: 25
Lively Arts Performance Dates
Touring artists: 24
Outdoor Recreation Assets
Golf course holes
  Daily Private: 18
Inland water area: 207 sq. miles
Gulf coastal water: 7 sq. miles
Federal protected areas: 53,195 acres
  Aransas NWR
State recreation areas: 322 acres
Rank: 57

Roswell, NM

Good Restaurants: 4
Visible History
Registered neighborhoods: 1
Contributing buildings: 12
  The Caverns District
Lively Arts Performance Dates
Touring artists: 5
Outdoor Recreation Assets
Golf course holes
  Daily fee: 18; Municipal: 18; Private: 18
Inland water area: 16 sq. miles
Federal protected areas: 181,440 acres
  Carlsbad Caverns NP
  Lincoln NF
State recreation areas: 6,900 acres
Rank: 186

Ruidoso, NM

Good Restaurants: 10
Visible History
Registered neighborhoods: 1
Contributing buildings: 28
  Lincoln District
Lively Arts Performance Dates
Touring artists: 30

Outdoor Recreation Assets
Golf course holes
  Daily fee: 36; Municipal: 9; Private: 36
Federal protected areas: 398,908 acres
  Cibola NF
  Lincoln NF
State recreation areas: 3 acres
Rank: 109

St. Augustine, FL

Good Bookstores
Mall & Superstores: 1
Good Restaurants: 50
Visible History
Registered neighborhoods: 4
Contributing buildings: 1,130
  Abbott Tract District
  Lincolnville District
  Model Land Company District
  St. Augustine Town Plan District
Outdoor Recreation Assets
Golf course holes
  Daily fee: 198; Municipal: 27; Private: 135
Inland water area: 64 sq. miles
Atlantic coastal water: 15 sq. miles
Federal protected areas: 248 acres
  Castillo de San Marcos NM
  Fort Matanzas NM
State recreation areas: 5,140 acres
Rank: 52

St. George–Zion, UT

Good Bookstores
Mall & Superstores: 1
Independent & College: 1
Good Restaurants: 11
Visible History
Registered neighborhoods: 4
Contributing buildings: 173
  Grafton District
  Hurricane District
  Oak Creek District
  Zion Lodge District
Lively Arts Performance Dates
Touring artists: 10
Outdoor Recreation Assets
Golf course holes
  Daily fee: 54; Municipal: 108; Private: 18
Inland water area: 3 sq. miles
Federal protected areas: 525,395 acres
  Dixie NF
  Zion NP
State recreation areas: 9,965 acres
Rank: 78

St. Jay–Northeast Kingdom, VT

Good Bookstores
Independent & College: 3
Good Restaurants: 6
Visible History
Registered neighborhoods: 7
Contributing buildings: 346
  Downtown Hardwick Village District
  Maple Street-Clarks Avenue District

continued

Ambience

★ = in the top 30 places for ambience

Retirement Places Rated

Peacham Corner District
St. Johnsbury District
Summer Street District
Outdoor Recreation Assets
Golf course holes
Daily fee: 18
Inland water area: 7 sq. miles
Rank: 164

St. Marys, GA
Good Restaurants: 6
Visible History
Registered neighborhoods: 4
Contributing buildings: 134
Dungeness District
High Point-Half Moon Bluff District
St. Marys District
Woodbine District
Outdoor Recreation Assets
Golf course holes
Daily fee: 72
Inland water area: 56 sq. miles
Atlantic coastal water: 11 sq. miles
Federal protected areas: 18,849 acres
Cumberland Island NS
State recreation areas: 500 acres
Rank: 161

St. Simons–Jekyll Islands, GA
Good Bookstores
Mall & Superstores: 1
Independent & College: 2
Good Restaurants: 15
Visible History
Registered neighborhoods: 3
Contributing buildings: 370
Brunswick Old Town District
Outdoor Recreation Assets
Golf course holes
Daily fee: 180; Private: 72
Inland water area: 61 sq. miles
Atlantic coastal water: 6 sq. miles
Federal protected areas: 239 acres
Fort Frederica NM
State recreation areas: 1,268 acres
Rank: 87

Sandpoint–Lake Pend Oreille, ID
Good Bookstores
Independent & College: 1
Good Restaurants: 5
Lively Arts Performance Dates
Touring artists: 9
Outdoor Recreation Assets
Golf course holes
Daily fee: 63
Inland water area: 182 sq. miles
Federal protected areas: 472,655 acres
Coeur d'Alene NF
Kaniksu NF
Kootenai NF
State recreation areas: 1,612 acres
Rank: 106

San Juan Islands, WA
Good Bookstores
Independent & College: 2
Good Restaurants: 9
Visible History
Registered neighborhoods: 2
Contributing buildings: 29
Camp Nor'Wester
Roche Harbor
Outdoor Recreation Assets
Golf course holes
Daily fee: 27
Inland water area: 81 sq. miles
Puget Sound coastal water: 362 sq. miles
Federal protected areas: 379 acres
San Juan Islands NWR
State recreation areas: 6,699 acres
Rank: 103

Santa Barbara, CA
Good Bookstores
Mall & Superstores: 5
Independent & College: 3
Good Restaurants: 54
Lively Arts Performance Dates
Touring artists: 3
Resident ensembles: 192
Outdoor Recreation Assets
Golf course holes
Daily fee: 117; Municipal: 36; Private: 126
Inland water area: 13 sq. miles
Federal protected areas: 699,100 acres
Channel Islands NP
Los Padres NF
State recreation areas: 4,222 acres
Rank: 51

Santa Fe, NM
Good Bookstores
Mall & Superstores: 2
Good Restaurants: 64
Visible History
Registered neighborhoods: 7
Contributing buildings: 579
Camino del Monte Sol District
Don Gaspar District
Madrid District
Plaza del Cerro
Santa Fe District
Lively Arts Performance Dates
Touring artists: 22
Resident ensembles: 59
Outdoor Recreation Assets
Golf course holes
Daily fee: 45; Municipal: 18; Private: 45
Inland water area: 2 sq. miles
Federal protected areas: 247,690 acres
Bandelier NM
Pecos NHP
Santa Fe NF
State recreation areas: 355 acres
Rank: 63

174   ★ = *in the top 30 places for ambience*

★ **Sarasota, FL**
Good Bookstores
Mall & Superstores: 6
Good Restaurants: 69
Visible History
Registered neighborhoods: 8
Contributing buildings: 459
Burns Court District
Central-Cocoanut District
Eagle Point District
Edgewood District
Overtown District
Venezia Park District
Lively Arts Performance Dates
Touring artists: 3
Resident ensembles: 1,521
Outdoor Recreation Assets
Golf course holes
Daily fee: 387; Municipal: 36; Private: 342
Inland water area: 34 sq. miles
Gulf coastal water: 12 sq. miles
State recreation areas: 20,102 acres
Rank: 7

★ **Savannah, GA**
Good Bookstores
Mall & Superstores: 3
Independent & College: 1
Good Restaurants: 84
Visible History
Registered neighborhoods: 12
Contributing buildings: 5,907
Ardsley Park-Chatham Crescent District
Cuyler-Brownville District
Daffin Park-Parkside Place District
Eastside District
Gordonston District
Savannah District
Savannah Victorian District
Thomas Square Streetcar District
Lively Arts Performance Dates
Touring artists: 16
Outdoor Recreation Assets
Golf course holes
Daily fee: 99; Municipal: 45; Private: 135
Inland water area: 56 sq. miles
Atlantic coastal water: 19 sq. miles
Federal protected areas: 20,942 acres
Fort Pulaski NM
Savannah Coastal NWR
Wassaw NWR
State recreation areas: 8,755 acres
Rank: 6

★ **Scottsdale, AZ**
Good Bookstores
Mall & Superstores: 2
Independent & College: 2
Good Restaurants: 76
Lively Arts Performance Dates
Touring artists: 10
Resident ensembles: 42

Outdoor Recreation Assets
Golf course holes
Daily fee: 360; Private: 531
Inland water area: 21 sq. miles
Federal protected areas: 657,695 acres
Tonto NF
Rank: 14

Sebring–Avon Park, FL
Visible History
Registered neighborhoods: 1
Contributing buildings: 13
Avon Park District
Lively Arts Performance Dates
Touring artists: 18
Outdoor Recreation Assets
Golf course holes
Daily fee: 243; Municipal: 18
Inland water area: 78 sq. miles
Federal protected areas: 504 acres
Lake Wales Ridge NWR
State recreation areas: 370 acres
Rank: 166

★ **Sedona, AZ**
Good Bookstores
Mall & Superstores: 2
Good Restaurants: 75
Lively Arts Performance Dates
Touring artists: 51
Outdoor Recreation Assets
Golf course holes
Daily fee: 18; Municipal: 45; Private: 108
Inland water area: 43 sq. miles
Federal protected areas: 4,103,928 acres
Coconino NF
Glen Canyon NRA
Grand Canyon NP
Kaibab NF
Lake Mead NRA
Navajo NM
Prescott NF
Sitgreaves NF
Sunset Crater NM
Walnut Canyon NM
Wupatki NM
State recreation areas: 48 acres
Rank: 22

Silver City, NM
Good Bookstores
Independent & College: 1
Good Restaurants: 4
Visible History
Registered neighborhoods: 5
Contributing buildings: 227
Chihuahua Hill District
Pinos Altos District
San Lorenzo District
Silver City District
Outdoor Recreation Assets
Golf course holes
Municipal: 18

continued

Ambience

★ = *in the top 30 places for ambience*

Inland water area: 2 sq. miles
Federal protected areas: 883,507 acres
Gila NF
Rank: 163

★ Silverthorne–Breckenridge, CO
Good Bookstores
Mall & Superstores: 1
Independent & College: 1
Good Restaurants: 33
Visible History
Registered neighborhoods: 1
Contributing buildings: 225
Breckenridge District
Outdoor Recreation Assets
Golf course holes
Daily fee: 72; Municipal: 27
Inland water area: 11 sq. miles
Federal protected areas: 309,728 acres
San Isabel NF
White River NF
Rank: 15

Smith Mountain Lake, VA
Good Restaurants: 6
Visible History
Registered neighborhoods: 5
Contributing buildings: 693
Bedford District
Cahas Mountain Rural District
Cifax Rural District
Franklin District
Rocky Mount District
Outdoor Recreation Assets
Golf course holes
Daily fee: 117; Private: 54
Inland water area: 34 sq. miles
Federal protected areas: 28,534 acres
Appalachian NST
Blue Ridge Parkway
Booker T. Washington NM
Jefferson NF
State recreation areas: 21,506 acres
Rank: 148

Sonora–Twain Harte, CA
Good Bookstores
Independent & College: 2
Good Restaurants: 6
Visible History
Registered neighborhoods: 3
Contributing buildings: 352
Columbia District
Yosemite Valley
Outdoor Recreation Assets
Golf course holes
Daily fee: 45
Inland water area: 39 sq. miles
Federal protected areas: 1,041,093 acres
Stanislaus NF
Yosemite NP
State recreation areas: 796 acres
Rank: 113

Southern Berkshire County, MA
Good Bookstores
Mall & Superstores: 3
Independent & College: 3
Good Restaurants: 16
Visible History
Registered neighborhoods: 28
Contributing buildings: 1,691
Elm-Maple-South Streets District
Main Street District
North Egremont District
Sheffield Center District
Sheffield Plain District
South Egremont Village District
South Lee District
Taconic and West Avenues District
Lively Arts Performance Dates
Touring artists: 5
Outdoor Recreation Assets
Golf course holes
Daily fee: 180; Private: 72
Inland water area: 15 sq. miles
Federal protected areas: 5,110 acres
Appalachian NST
State recreation areas: 90,397 acres
Rank: 35

Southern Pines–Pinehurst, NC
Good Bookstores
Mall & Superstores: 1
Independent & College: 1
Good Restaurants: 7
Visible History
Registered neighborhoods: 7
Contributing buildings: 816
Aberdeen District
Cameron District
Carthage District
Lakeview District
Pinehurst District
Southern Pines District
Lively Arts Performance Dates
Touring artists: 12
Outdoor Recreation Assets
Golf course holes
Daily fee: 558; Private: 135
Inland water area: 8 sq. miles
State recreation areas: 628 acres
Rank: 80

Southport–Brunswick Islands, NC
Good Restaurants: 8
Visible History
Registered neighborhoods: 1
Contributing buildings: 161
Southport District
Outdoor Recreation Assets
Golf course holes
Daily fee: 603; Private: 18
Inland water area: 40 sq. miles
Atlantic coastal water: 16 sq. miles
Rank: 150

★ = in the top 30 places for ambience

State College, PA

Good Bookstores

Mall & Superstores: 2

Good Restaurants: 11

Visible History

Registered neighborhoods: 14

Contributing buildings: 2,677

  Aaronsburg District
  Bellefonte District
  Boalsburg District
  College Heights District
  Holmes-Foster-Highlands District
  Lemont District
  Linden Hall District
  Millheim District
  Oak Hall District
  Philipsburg District
  Rebersburg District
  Unionville District

Lively Arts Performance Dates

Touring artists: 21

Resident ensembles: 11

Outdoor Recreation Assets

Golf course holes

  Daily fee: 63; Private: 54

Inland water area: 4 sq. miles

State recreation areas: 9,986 acres

Rank: 146

Sullivan County, NY

Good Bookstores

Independent & College: 1

Good Restaurants: 7

Visible History

Registered neighborhoods: 3

Contributing buildings: 169

  Liberty Downtown District
  Liberty Village District
  Mamakating Park District

Outdoor Recreation Assets

Golf course holes

  Daily fee: 153; Municipal: 36

Inland water area: 27 sq. miles

Federal protected areas: 7 acres

  Upper Delaware Scenic River

State recreation areas: 2,076 acres

Rank: 116

Summerville, SC

Good Restaurants: 10

Visible History

Registered neighborhoods: 4

Contributing buildings: 856

  Ashley River District
  Summerville District

Outdoor Recreation Assets

Golf course holes

  Daily fee: 81; Municipal: 27

Inland water area: 2 sq. miles

State recreation areas: 1,213 acres

Rank: 165

Taos, NM

Good Bookstores

Independent & College: 1

Good Restaurants: 27

Visible History

Registered neighborhoods: 5

Contributing buildings: 173

  La Loma Plaza District
  Las Trampas District
  Ranchos de Taos Plaza
  Taos Downtown District

Lively Arts Performance Dates

Touring artists: 41

Outdoor Recreation Assets

Golf course holes

  Daily fee: 18

Inland water area: 1 sq. miles

Federal protected areas: 482,251 acres

  Carson NF

Rank: 81

Thomasville, GA

Good Bookstores

Independent & College: 2

Good Restaurants: 1

Visible History

Registered neighborhoods: 10

Contributing buildings: 1,121

  Dawson Street Residential District
  East End District
  Metcalfe District
  Paradise Park District
  Stevens Street District
  Thomasville District
  Tockwotton-Love Place District

Lively Arts Performance Dates

Touring artists: 6

Outdoor Recreation Assets

Golf course holes

  Municipal: 18; Private: 18

Inland water area: 4 sq. miles

State recreation areas: 1 acre

Rank: 174

Toms River–Barnegat Bay, NJ

Good Bookstores

Mall & Superstores: 3

Independent & College: 1

Good Restaurants: 18

Visible History

Registered neighborhoods: 5

Contributing buildings: 908

  Bay Head District
  Beach Haven District
  Double Trouble District
  Island Heights District
  Whitesbog District

Lively Arts Performance Dates

Touring artists: 20

Outdoor Recreation Assets

Golf course holes

  Daily fee: 90; Municipal: 54; Private: 99

continued

★ = *in the top 30 places for ambience*

Ambience

Inland water area: 121 sq. miles
Atlantic coastal water: 16 sq. miles
Federal protected areas: 17,452 acres
    Edwin B. Forsythe NWR
State recreation areas: 9,825 acres
Rank: 46

Traverse City, MI
Good Bookstores
Mall & Superstores: 2
Independent & College: 1
Good Restaurants: 19
Visible History
Registered neighborhoods: 2
Contributing buildings: 633
    Boardman Neighborhood District
    Central Neighborhood District
Lively Arts Performance Dates
Touring artists: 60
Outdoor Recreation Assets
Golf course holes
    Daily fee: 144; Private: 36
Inland water area: 26 sq. miles
Lake Michigan coastal water: 110 sq. miles
Federal protected areas: 2 acres
    Manistee NF
State recreation areas: 745 acres
Rank: 38

Tryon, NC
Good Bookstores
Independent & College: 1
Good Restaurants: 1
Lively Arts Performance Dates
Touring artists: 4
Outdoor Recreation Assets
Golf course holes
    Daily fee: 18; Private: 9
Inland water area: 1 sq. miles
Rank: 189

★ Tucson, AZ
Good Bookstores
Mall & Superstores: 5
Independent & College: 1
Good Restaurants: 106
Visible History
Registered neighborhoods: 19
Contributing buildings: 5,443
    Armory Park Historic Residential District
    Blenman-Elm District
    Catalina Vista District
    El Encanto Estates Residential District
    El Montevideo District
    El Presidio District
    Iron Horse Expansion District
    Pie Allen District
    Sam Hughes Neighborhood District
    San Clemente District
    Speedway-Drachman District
    West University District
    Winterhaven District

Lively Arts Performance Dates
Touring artists: 111
Resident ensembles: 206
Outdoor Recreation Assets
Golf course holes
    Daily fee: 405; Municipal: 108; Private: 234
Inland water area: 2 sq. miles
Federal protected areas: 1,336,181 acres
    Buenos Aires NWR
    Cabeza Prieta NWR
    Coronado NF
    Grand Canyon NP
    Organ Pipe Cactus NM
    Saguaro NM
State recreation areas: 5,511 acres
Rank: 8

Vero Beach, FL
Good Bookstores
Mall & Superstores: 3
Independent & College: 1
Good Restaurants: 6
Visible History
Registered neighborhoods: 1
Contributing buildings: 28
    Old Town Sebastian District 28
Lively Arts Performance Dates
Touring artists: 4
Outdoor Recreation Assets
Golf course holes
    Daily fee: 45; Municipal: 54; Private: 261
Inland water area: 37 sq. miles
Atlantic coastal water: 7 sq. miles
Federal protected areas: 127 acres
    Archie Carr NWR
    Pelican Island NWR
State recreation areas: 557 acres
Rank: 134

Victorville–Apple Valley, CA
Good Bookstores
Mall & Superstores: 9
Independent & College: 1
Good Restaurants: 44
Lively Arts Performance Dates
Touring artists: 7
Outdoor Recreation Assets
Golf course holes
    Daily fee: 252; Municipal: 81; Private: 171
Inland water area: 45 sq. miles
Federal protected areas: 2,447,835 acres
    Angeles NF
    Death Valley NP
    Joshua Tree NP
    Mojave Desert National Preserve
    San Bernardino NF
State recreation areas: 14,475 acres
Rank: 44

Waynesville, NC
Good Bookstores
Independent & College: 1
Good Restaurants: 11

★ = in the top 30 places for ambience

Visible History
Registered neighborhoods: 1
Contributing buildings: 34
    Canton Main Street District
Outdoor Recreation Assets
Golf course holes
    Daily fee: 99; Private: 18
Inland water area: 1 sq. mile
Federal protected areas: 132,194 acres
    Appalachian NST
    Blue Ridge Parkway
    Great Smoky Mountains NP
    Pisgah NF
Rank: 130

Wenatchee, WA
Good Bookstores
Independent & College: 2
Good Restaurants: 18
Visible History
Registered neighborhoods: 2
Contributing buildings: 62
    Buckner Homestead District
    Cottage Avenue District
Outdoor Recreation Assets
Golf course holes
    Daily fee: 63; Municipal: 36
Inland water area: 72 sq. miles
Federal protected areas: 1,454,265 acres
    Lake Chelan NRA
    North Cascades NP
    Wenatchee NF
State recreation areas: 1,428 acres
Rank: 70

Western St. Tammany Parish, LA
Good Bookstores
Mall & Superstores: 3
Independent & College: 2
Good Restaurants: 11
Visible History
Registered neighborhoods: 2
Contributing buildings: 350
    Abita Springs District
    Division of St. John District
Outdoor Recreation Assets
Golf course holes
    Daily fee: 72; Private: 90
Inland water area: 260 sq. miles
Gulf coastal water: 10 sq. miles
Federal protected areas: 36,846 acres
    Big Branch Marsh NWR
    Bogue Chitto NWR
State recreation areas: 2,979 acres
Rank: 124

Whidbey Island, WA
Good Bookstores
Independent & College: 1
Good Restaurants: 9
Visible History
Registered neighborhoods: 1
Contributing buildings: 103
    Central Whidbey Island District

Outdoor Recreation Assets
Golf course holes
    Daily fee: 36; Private: 36
Inland water area: 13 sq. miles
Puget Sound coastal water: 295 sq. miles
Federal protected areas: 1,711 acres
    Ebey's Landing NHR
    San Juan Islands NWR
State recreation areas: 4,446 acres
Rank: 159

Wickenburg, AZ
Good Restaurants: 2
Outdoor Recreation Assets
Golf course holes
    Daily fee: 27
Inland water area: 21 sq. miles
Federal protected areas: 657,695 acres
    Tonto NF
Rank: 64

Williamsburg, VA
Good Bookstores
Mall & Superstores: 4
Independent & College: 1
Good Restaurants: 43
Visible History
Registered neighborhoods: 2
Contributing buildings: 41
    Norge District
Lively Arts Performance Dates
Touring artists: 8
Outdoor Recreation Assets
Golf course holes
    Daily fee: 144; Private: 90
Inland water area: 22 sq. miles
Gulf coastal water: 15 sq. miles
Federal protected areas: 2,892 acres
    Colonial NHP
State recreation areas: 2,505 acres
Rank: 34

Wimberley, TX
Good Bookstores
Mall & Superstores: 1
Good Restaurants: 68
Visible History
Registered neighborhoods: 3
Contributing buildings: 60
    Belvin Street District
    Downtown Buda District
Lively Arts Performance Dates
Touring artists: 5
Resident ensembles: 332
Outdoor Recreation Assets
Golf course holes
    Daily fee: 63
Inland water area: 2 sq. miles
Rank: 110

Woodstock, VT
Good Bookstores
Independent & College: 3
Good Restaurants: 40

continued

Ambience

Visible History
Registered neighborhoods: 23
Contributing buildings: 1,431
  Bethel Village District
  Chester Village District
  Hartford Village District
  Jericho Rural District
  Norwich Village District
  Parker Hill Rural District
  Quechee Historic Mill District
  South Royalton District
  South Woodstock Village District
  Weston Village District
  White River Junction District
  Wilder Village District
  Woodstock Village District
Lively Arts Performance Dates
Touring artists: 6
Outdoor Recreation Assets
Golf course holes
  Daily fee: 90; Private: 36
Inland water area: 5 sq. miles
Federal protected areas: 26,548 acres
  Appalachian NST
  Green Mountain NF
  Marsh-Billings NHP
State recreation areas: 984 acres
Rank: 37

York Beaches, ME
Good Bookstores
Independent & College: 1
Good Restaurants: 52
Visible History
Registered neighborhoods: 13

Contributing buildings: 808
  Cape Arundel Summer Colony District
  Isles of Shoals
  Kennebunk District
  Kennebunkport District
  Limerick Upper Village District
  Limington District
  Saco District
  York District
Outdoor Recreation Assets
Golf course holes
  Daily fee: 198; Private: 27
Inland water area: 32 sq. miles
Atlantic coastal water: 20 sq. miles
State recreation areas: 396 acres
Rank: 91

Yuma, AZ
Good Bookstores
Mall & Superstores: 1
Good Restaurants: 11
Visible History
Registered neighborhoods: 2
Contributing buildings: 117
  Brinley Avenue District
  Century Heights District
Lively Arts Performance Dates
Touring artists: 20
Outdoor Recreation Assets
Golf course holes
  Daily fee: 81; Municipal: 18; Private: 18
Inland water area: 5 sq. miles
Federal protected areas: 972,281 acres
  Cabeza Prieta NWR
  Kofa NWR
State recreation areas: 9 acres
Rank: 126

ET CETERA: AMBIENCE

RETIREMENT PLACES WITH THE BEST BASS FISHING

All varieties of black bass, the premier game fish in North America, are found in lakes and rivers in every state but Alaska. They aren't abundant in all areas, however, and some regions do not have the large bass-holding waters that can withstand extensive public attention. One or more of *Field & Stream*'s 50 best fishing spots in the United States and Canada are within the following retirement places.

Burlington, Vermont

With the Green Mountains on the east and the Adirondack Mountains on the west, 120-mile-long Lake Champlain, a natural lake on the Vermont–New York border, is nestled in the midst of some outstanding country. The principal game fish is smallmouth bass, especially in the northern sector. Largemouth bass are abundant, too, particularly in weedy bays. In addition, walleye, trout, salmon, and perch fishing is excellent.

Henderson, Nevada

Near this suburban Las Vegas community and backed by the Hoover Dam, Lake Mead has lots of good bass cover, resulting in an abundance of 1- to 3-pound largemouth bass. Stripers, too, benefit from the expanded forage base and are popular on this lake, with small fish up to 10 pounds being plentiful.

INLAND WATER

Aside from ocean or Great Lakes coastal bays and river estuaries, big lakes in the interior are a recreation draw for miles around. More than 5 percent of the surface area is big-lake water in the 15 locations below.

PLACE	BIG-LAKE WATER AREA
Eagle River–Woodruff, WI	14.2%
Burlington, VT	13.0%
Sandpoint–Lake Pend Oreille, ID	9.5%
Cedar Creek Lake, TX	7.9%
Hot Springs, AR	7.8%
Lake of the Ozarks, MO	7.6%
Pendleton District, SC	7.3%
Oxford, MS	7.1%
Sebring–Avon Park, FL	7.1%
Lakeland–Winter Haven, FL	6.7%
Lake of the Cherokees, OK	6.6%
Murray–Kentucky Lake, KY	6.1%
Norfork Lake, AR	5.5%
Coeur d'Alene, ID	5.4%
Jackson Hole, WY	5.1%

Source: Bureau of the Census, unpublished area measurements.

Hot Springs, Arkansas

Lake Ouachita, a Corps of Engineers lake about 35 miles from Hot Springs, is part of the Ouachita National Forest and is known for a variety of good fishing. Largemouth and spotted (locally called "Kentucky") bass are plentiful here. Stripers, too, are abundant among the rotting timber left standing in this lake when it was flooded.

Kissimmee–St. Cloud, Florida

There are numbers of shallow, grassy lakes in Florida's Kissimmee River chain. Lake Kissimmee (the largest) and East and West Tohopekaliga are among the most prominent. West Tohopekaliga is rated one of the best places for trophy bass, which is high praise in a state that has many trophy largemouth waters.

Lake Havasu City, Arizona

Lake Mohave, an impoundment on the Colorado River downstream from Lake Mead (see Henderson, Nevada, above), is an excellent largemouth bass lake, providing good fishing on points, cliffs, brush, and other habitats that are typical of these weedless desert lakes. Cold water issuing from Hoover Dam makes the upper 15 miles more suitable for trout, but the rest of the 67-mile-long lake offers plenty of bass fishing opportunities.

Lakeland–Winter Haven, Florida

The Florida Phosphate Pits, which are flooded, reclaimed phosphate-mining areas of varying size, possess an abundance of chunky largemouth bass, including plenty of trophy-size fish. There are lots of pits in the south-central mining country, and the newest publicly accessible ones are in the Tenoroc State Reserve outside of Lakeland.

Murray, Kentucky

Kentucky Lake and Barkley Lake, immediately east of this small college town, are magnets for warm water anglers throughout the Midwest. Combined, they are the second-largest man-made water system in America, and their 3,500 miles of shoreline provide countless coves, bays, finders, and hideaways for bass. Largemouth and spotted (Kentucky) bass are plentiful, and smallmouth bass have become especially prominent in recent years.

Norfork Lake, Arkansas

Norfork Lake and nearby Bull Shoals are among the best largemouth bass waters in the Ozarks, have excellent spring and fall fishing, and provide good angling throughout the year for a variety of species, including white bass and crappies. Trout and smallmouth bass are also present.

Northampton–Amherst, Massachusetts

Located in a wilderness setting just east of Amherst, the 25,000-acre Quabbin Reservoir is the largest body of water in Massachusetts and a principal source of Boston's water supply. In addition to trout and salmon, it sports a good fishery for bass, particularly smallmouth, and is tightly managed for fishing and boating.

Ambience

Ocala, Florida

Good largemouth fishing can be had in many areas of Florida's lengthy and renowned St. Johns River, particularly Rodman Reservoir at the northern edge of the Ocala National Forest and Lake George, upriver yet south of Rodman Reservoir.

Table Rock Lake, Missouri

Table Rock Lake, an impoundment of the White River in southeastern Missouri, is surrounded by the Mark Twain National Forest. Its 43,100 acres are spread out in a meandering, mazelike configuration of coves and creeks that hide many bass.

Costs of Living

You get what you pay for, some economists say. High living costs are a sign of high quality of life. Expensive places, like a new BMW or Lexus automobile, are more desirable. Cheaper places are less so.

Tell that to the thousands of older Californians who've fled to low-cost Nevada next door, or to New Yorkers who hit I-95 south for a reasonably priced Florida retirement.

Because of windowed envelopes—interest, dividends, annuities, pensions, and Social Security checks—that can be sent to any forwarding address, you needn't remain stuck in a place you can't afford. The best economic reason you'll need for leaving home is the potential savings you'll find living somewhere else.

RETIREMENT INCOME: GETTING IT

"Money's no problem," a witty accountant will tell you. "Lack of money . . . now *that's* a problem." Lack of enough money causes many people to cling to unsatisfying jobs. For those who do retire, the lack of money crimps plans for travel or for life in a sunny, clean-air place where the bass fishing is good. It indefinitely defers the dream of a small part-time business, the book you've been meaning to write, or the boat you want to build.

Can you afford to stop working? More to the point, can you swing retirement where you're living now, or maybe there is somewhere else where you can do it more easily?

The Checks Are in the Mail

In retirement, you'll likely have not one source of income, but many. Apart from Social Security, there are annuities, Individual Retirement Accounts (IRAs) and Keogh Plans, thousands of government-employee plans (federal civil service, military, state, and municipal), and nearly a million private pension plans, each of which has different rules for age of eligibility, years of service required, payouts, and how spouses are covered.

For most of us, the main income sources—in descending dollar amounts—are Social Security benefits, income from an employer's defined-benefit plan or 401k plan, and asset income. More and more persons also will count on earnings from a job or self-employment.

Social Security Benefits. Benefits are paid out by the federal government at the end of each month to persons who paid into the system during at least 10 years of working.

Annual earnings up to the year you become eligible for Social Security are averaged and adjusted for inflation to derive an Average Index of Monthly Earnings (AIME). A benefit formula is then applied to the AIME to determine your Primary Insurance Amount (PIA). How much of the PIA you actually get depends on when you retire.

In the past, you were eligible for 100 percent of your PIA when you turned 65, the full retirement age defined by the Social Security program back in 1935. Because we're all living longer, this full retirement age is gradually rising to 67 over the next several decades.

You can collect 75 percent of your PIA at age 62. If you put off claiming your benefits for each of the first 36 months afterward, the early retirement penalty is cut by 0.555 percent, or 6.67 percent a year. Your full PIA is earned at age 66. If you stay on the job after that, you receive a delayed retirement credit of 8 percent a year. If you work and put off claiming Social Security benefits until you're 70, for instance, you would receive benefits equal to 132 percent of your PIA.

In 2007, the maximum monthly Social Security check is $2,116 for a single worker, $3,174 for a couple with one dependent spouse, and $4,232 for a couple when both spouses are eligible. These amounts assume the worker made maximum contributions and retires at full retirement age. The average amount mailed out each month to a couple is much less—$1,713, or $20,556 a year.

Pensions. Pensions are contributed to by everyone working in government, but just half of all workers in the private sector are covered by an employer pension plan. And only half of these will ever see the money because of vesting requirements. Not for nothing are persons who are getting benefits from their former employer called "the pension elite."

Unlike the Social Security system to which workers contribute no matter how many different jobs they hold, private pensions are the equivalent of a corporate loyalty test—at least for the standard 8 or 10 years of service required before an employee is vested and shares in a pension fund.

Unlike Social Security, too, most employer pension plans don't have a cost-of-living escalator clause. The typical amount from a private pension is $13,950

REPLACING INCOME: PART ONE

A rule of thumb in retirement planning states: "If your retirement income is 70 to 75 percent of what it was in the last year of work, you'll hardly notice a change in your standard of living." The rule applies mainly to job incomes of between $45,000 and $70,000.

To keep up your standard of living after you retire, you'll need:

A MINIMUM OF . . .	OR . . .	OF YOUR JOB INCOME OF . . .
$13,400	90%	$15,000
$17,000	85%	$20,000
$20,400	82%	$25,000
$23,700	79%	$30,000
$30,700	77%	$40,000
$36,600	73%	$50,000
$42,800	71%	$60,000
$48,800	70%	$70,000
$54,400	68%	$80,000
$59,000	66%	$90,000

Income figures are pretax amounts. The percent "replacement rates" do not reflect the impact of future inflation, longevity, and healthcare costs, and assume that the household doesn't relocate after retirement to a low-cost area.

for a married couple age 62 to 65 that is eligible for payments. While the amount isn't paltry, it isn't lavish, either. According to a recent study from the Social Security Administration, just 7 out of 100 couples with pensions can rely on them for at least half their income.

Assets. Assets include income from dividends from stock investments you've made over the years; rents from real estate you own; royalties from your invention, song, computer software, book, or oil well; and interest from IRAs, Keogh Plans, CDs, passbook savings accounts, and loans.

Like private pensions and earnings from a job, income from assets supplements Social Security for a more comfortable later life. Six out of every 10 households over 65 count on money from these sources.

Earnings. Earnings from a job or self-employment are the only sure way of boosting your income after you retire. Once you start collecting Social Security and pension checks, there's almost nothing you can do on your own to increase their amounts (Social Security provides an annual cost of living increase based on the Consumer Price Index; for 2007, it's 3.3 percent).

A job, from part-time or seasonal work all the way to a 50-week-a-year new career, can make the difference between living in your daughter's basement and living comfortably on your own.

Scraping By on $73,500 a Year

One simple way to judge whether you can stop work and take your money and run to another part of the country is to compare your income with incomes in other places.

In 2007, the estimated income for a two-person household in the United States is $73,500. Among the locations profiled in *Retirement Places Rated,* the average is $65,000. The highest is $168,100 in Jackson Hole, Wyoming, and the lowest is $35,300 in McAllen–Alamo, Texas.

Households can be a husband and wife, a single parent and child, or two unrelated people. Average amounts tend to be high because most households aren't retired and count on earnings and interest and dividends from more than one member. Still, the figures are useful for making comparisons.

"Replacement Rates"

How much your Social Security benefits, pension, and asset income will replace your preretirement income is one variety of replacement rate. Another is the rate at which your postretirement income replaces different household incomes around the country.

Just as you want your income after retirement to come close to your earnings at work, you may want to relocate to where your retirement income comes close to local income. This is likelier in parts of the mountain West and interior Texas than it is in wealthy beach communities and ski resorts. The two tables below show places rated in this book with the lowest and highest income.

Lowest Income

PLACE	INCOME
McAllen–Alamo, TX	$35,300
Brownsville, TX	$38,100
Cedar City, UT	$43,100
Driggs, ID	$43,800
Yuma, AZ	$43,900

Highest Income

PLACE	INCOME
Jackson Hole, WY	$168,100
Park City, UT	$109,200
Ketchum–Sun Valley, ID	$100,300
Easton–St. Michaels, MD	$100,300
Naples, FL	$98,600

Source: Woods & Poole Economics, Inc., household income forecasts. Figures are two-person household incomes.

WHERE THE MONEY COMES FROM

The following table indicates the primary sources of retirement income and the percentage of newly retired couples in the United States who depend on each source:

INCOME SOURCE	PERCENT OF NEWLY RETIRED COUPLES IN U.S.
Social Security	93%
Assets	63%
Private pensions	43%
Earnings	21%
Government pensions	20%

Source: Derived from Social Security Administration, Income of the Population 55 and Over.

In locations in Rio Grande Country, the Ozarks and Ouachitas, the Rocky Mountains, and the Southern Highlands, for example, your income may go a lot further in replacing local household incomes than it would back home in, say, New York, Denver, or Altoona.

Retired persons who move tend to quit richer areas with high costs for places with more modest average incomes. They are in search of spots where their own money can be stretched—in short, where costs are lower.

RETIREMENT INCOME: SPENDING IT

Do household incomes reflect local prices? For the most part, they do indeed. A Bureau of Labor Statistics study showed that two-thirds of the difference in incomes between, say, Traverse City, Michigan, and Tucson, Arizona, indicates their different costs of living. The rest is due to different employers, worker skills, and prevailing wages.

"Elite" homes cost more than three-quarters of all homes in an area. Among Retirement Places Rated's *200 locations, elite home prices average $416,000. In these 15, they top $750,000.*

Local Costs of Living

If you're thinking of moving, consider how far your income would stretch elsewhere. Household incomes in different places provide the first clue. Comparing actual costs completes the picture.

It's a "black hole," the *Wall Street Journal* noted on just what everyone means by cost of living. How much will $50,000 get you in Asheville, North Carolina, versus Annapolis, Maryland? The figures you get from online cost-of-living calculators are all over the map, one might say.

The government's monthly Consumer Price Index (CPI) offers no help. It reports price inflation, but quotes no prices. While the CPI has gone up 14-fold since the start of World War II, it offers no insights on the money you'd need to get by in southern California versus a small town in the Ozarks.

A few years ago, a group of experts appointed by the Department of Labor to look into better ways to measure cost differences between places threw in the towel. Given the infinite range of consumer tastes and household tactics for saving a dollar, they noted, the few ways to pin down why life in one place is more expensive than in another come down to the following: focus on the weather's effect on clothing costs and household utility bills, and then look at taxes.

Taxes certainly do make a difference. But clothing and home energy bills? Not that much. According to one retailer, the price difference between cotton and synthetic wardrobes in the Sun Belt and woolen and down-filled Frost Belt clothing amounts to less than 1 percent of a household's annual budget. As for the comparative costs of keeping warm in the North Woods winter and staying cool in the Florida Interior, often the only difference is the season during which local residents pay most of their bill.

One firm that counsels transferred employees uses an 80/20 rule. In its experience, 80 percent of the difference in living costs between where you've come from and where you're going comes down to two items: housing and taxes. The other 20 percent comes from hundreds of things such as spin-balancing the wheels on your car; a six-pack of beer; soap flakes; greens fees for a weekend round of golf; and a shampoo, trim, and blow-dry at a salon.

To measure what it costs to live in each place, *Retirement Places Rated* prices major expenses that a $60,000-a-year retired couple may experience in different places around the country. In some locations, that couple's income wouldn't be enough to bid on a lower-priced house. In other spots, the income is more than enough to live comfortably.

Housing: The Difference That Makes a Difference

"You can't get too much housing," real estate salespeople say with one hand on the steering wheel and the other on their listings as they drive prospective buyers about for a windshield tour of neighborhoods.

True enough, you never need the space until you don't have it, and there are still tax and investment advantages to owning a home on your own piece of ground. Older adults are no different from everyone else in the kind of roof they prefer overhead: townhouse, apartment, mobile home, or the common detached house. The latter is the overwhelming favorite.

Having said all that, between a mortgage, property taxes, and utilities, owning a home takes up the lion's share of that $60,000-a-year retired couple's budget. The following outlines these and other expected costs.

Home Mortgage.   Claiming an average 24.3 percent of income (or $14,568) among the retirement places profiled here, the mortgage is certainly the most expensive item on the older household's budget. When the real estate broker touts location, location, location, you may answer rent, rent, rent. While it adds nothing to your net worth, renting permits you to avoid most of the cost differences among places and gives you flexibility. Good rental markets include large college towns and large, seasonal resorts.

Property Taxes.   Nevertheless, if you're like most older newcomers, you'll eventually end up owning. Typical property taxes among our 200 retirement places amount to $1,146 on a median-priced home and will account for 1.9 percent of your household budget for as long as you own, unless you settle in a state with (1) low effective tax rates, or (2) generous homestead exemptions for older people with no income tests, or (3) both. Bear in mind, too, that taxes tend to be much lower when the property lies beyond the corporate limits of cities and towns.

Transportation.   At 14.84 percent, the cost of getting from one place to another, $8,908, is the second-highest category here. Ask yourself whether you really need more

than one car, as a good part of the size of this budget item reflects financing two late-model cars. Get rid of one vehicle and you'll save about 30 percent. Make do with one vehicle that's paid for, and you save about 50 percent.

Since there is a national market for cars, meaning you can buy one anywhere for a similar price, the cost of purchasing one doesn't vary much by location. What do vary are taxes, insurance, title and registration fees, and gasoline excise taxes.

Food.   This category, which includes groceries *and* dining out, claims another 10.33 percent, or $6,202. While prices for packaged prepared foods generally don't vary enough to hit household budgets around the country with dramatic effect, prices for fresh fruits, vegetables, and dairy products do. In places with an agricultural hinterland, you'll save if you spend money at farmers' markets and roadside produce stands on the back of pickup trucks.

Healthcare.   Medical expenses with Medicare coverage in the year immediately after retiring will still take 6.98 percent, or $4,193, and will require more and more of your income each year as you get older. True, basic Medicare covers hospital bills after you turn 65, but it won't cover things such as an outpatient diagnostic visit, a prescription painkiller, or a splint for a broken thumb. Most importantly, Medicare doesn't cover physician fees.

To measure costs in each place, *Retirement Places Rated* looks at the amounts that Medicare permits five doctors to charge their older patients for specific services. Charges for a semiprivate room in the area's largest acute-care hospital are also part of this factor.

Utilities.   These costs claim 5.72 percent, or $3,427 of the household's expenses, and cover everything from water and telephone to electricity, piped-in natural gas, and heating oil. Unlike consumer packaged goods, monthly electric bills vary widely around the country. Climate determines how much money will be needed to keep interiors comfortable. Customer density, distance from oil and coal fuel sources, age of the power plant, and the type and size of equipment used in generating electricity also play a part in the charges to consumers.

Recreation.   This catchall covers everything from a health club membership, weekday play at an 18-hole public or semiprivate golf course, overnight camping at a state park, and movie tickets. It claims 4.04 percent, or $2,429. Like the dining-out part of the food budget, enjoying yourself can be a controllable expense. Costs at large resort areas are highest.

State Income Taxes. Though you've chucked the tie and briefcase and bid goodbye to the commuting hassles that go with working full-time, you won't be completely immune from paying taxes, in spite of the many tax breaks coming along when you turn 65. Yes, your tax bracket will be lower after you leave work, but *federal income taxes* may still hit you with the same impact whether you surface in Bellingham, Washington; Ocala, Florida; or Brownsville, Texas. But *state income taxes* vary tremendously. Among the 151 retirement places within states that tax income, they amount to 2.58 percent of the household budget, or $1,545.

Should you move only to one of the handful of no-income-tax states and ignore the alternatives? That may be a mistake. It's better to broaden your search to include other states with two characteristics: (1) a favorable tax treatment of retirement income (see the table "State Tax Exclusion of Pension Income," later in this chapter) and (2) lower costs of living that offset the state's income tax.

Sales Taxes. Finally, for all the annoyance that sales taxes cause, they exact less than 1.2 percent, or under $700, of our retired couple's expenses on average in the states that levy the tax. In the age of Internet mail-order and cross-border shopping, this tax is increasingly seen as easily avoidable.

You'll notice that the major items above add up to 72 percent of the retired household budget. Where does the other 28 percent go? Savings, investments, gifts to your grandchildren, tuition for a course at a community college, federal income taxes, a *Wall Street Journal* subscription, a new windbreaker, a bottle of Merlot. Aside from federal income taxes, these are discretionary expenses and their amounts aren't greatly influenced by geography.

A Caution

Let's admit here that pricing the costs of living for all people for all the time is impossible. The number of unique items that fill a shopping cart trundled by a household over a year's time comes close to a thousand.

Some of us trade at Wal-Mart and others at convenience stores, some at eBay and other Internet retailers, and still others at Costco, Price Club, BJ's Wholesale, and Burlington Coat Factory. Having said that, *Retirement Places Rated* nevertheless makes a reasonable attempt at coming up with average household expenses for each of the 200 retirement places.

JUDGING: COSTS OF LIVING

Will your income stretch farther in the Rio Grande Country than in the Desert Southwest? Do prices really vary tremendously among different places, or can sharp-pencil budgeting and bargain-price shopping keep your head above water in Maui or Laguna Beach or anywhere else you choose to live?

To help you compare each place's differences, for each location, *Retirement Places Rated* measures nine expenses on the budget for a hypothetical retired couple with $60,000 income: (1) **home mortgage,** (2) **transportation,** (3) **food,** (4) **utilities,** (5) **healthcare,** (6) **recreation,** (7) **property taxes,** (8) **state income taxes,** and (9) **state and local sales taxes.**

The expenses are totaled and the result is then compared with all 200 places to get a percent score. The higher the score, the less expensive the retirement place. Carmel–Pebble Beach, California, gets a score of 0, thanks to whopping homeowner costs. Camden, Maine, comes closest to the average score of 50. A location on the lower Rio Grande in southernmost Texas—McAllen–Alamo—gets 100, the best for costs of living.

RANKINGS: COSTS OF LIVING

Nine items on a typical retired household's budget are used to rank retirement places for costs of living: (1) **mortgage payments** on a median-priced home; (2) that home's **property taxes;** (3) **utilities,** including water, telephone, electricity, and home heating; (4) **food;** (5) **healthcare;** (6) **recreation;** (7) **transportation;** (8) **state income taxes;** and (9) **state and local sales taxes.** A place's score is its percent on a scale of 0 to 100 corresponding to its rank. Lower scores mean more expensive places, and higher scores mean less expensive places. Places that are tied get the same rank and are listed alphabetically.

Retirement Places from Least to Most Expensive

RANK	PLACE	SCORE		RANK	PLACE	SCORE
1.	McAllen–Alamo, TX	100.0		68.	Kingman, AZ	66.4
2.	Brownsville, TX	99.5		69.	Hendersonville–East Flat Rock, NC	65.9
3.	Natchitoches, LA	99.0		70.	Beaufort–Atlantic Beach, NC	65.4
4.	Alpine–Big Bend, TX	98.5		71.	Boerne, TX	64.9
5.	Thomasville, GA	98.0		72.	Western St. Tammany Parish, LA	64.4
6.	Roswell, NM	97.5		73.	Leelanau Peninsula, MI	63.9
7.	Lake of the Cherokees, OK	97.0		74.	Ocala, FL	63.4
8.	Alamogordo, NM	96.5		75.	Yuma, AZ	62.9
9.	Cedar Creek Lake, TX	96.0		76.	Iowa City, IA	62.4
10.	Silver City, NM	95.5		77.	Bisbee, AZ	61.9
11.	Murray–Kentucky Lake, KY	95.0		78.	Lakeland–Winter Haven, FL	61.4
12.	Hattiesburg, MS	94.5		79.	Hamilton–Bitterroot Valley, MT	60.9
13.	Eureka Springs, AR	94.0		80.	Eagle River–Woodruff, WI	60.4
14.	Crossville, TN	93.5		81.	Door Peninsula, WI	59.8
15.	Hampshire County, WV	93.0		82.	Kalispell–Flathead Valley, MT	59.3
16.	Norfork Lake, AR	92.5		83.	Monadnock Region, NH	58.8
17.	Kerrville, TX	92.0		84.	Lake Placid, NY	58.3
18.	Rockport–Aransas Pass, TX	91.5		85.	Southport–Brunswick Islands, NC	57.8
19.	Fayetteville, AR	91.0		86.	Sandpoint–Lake Pend Oreille, ID	57.3
20.	Maryville, TN	90.5		87.	Pagosa Springs, CO	56.8
21.	Conway, AR	90.0		88.	Southern Pines–Pinehurst, NC	56.3
22.	Pendleton District, SC	89.5		89.	Nelson County, VA	55.8
23.	Fredericksburg, TX	89.0		90.	Pensacola, FL	55.3
24.	Las Cruces, NM	88.5		91.	Hanover, NH	54.8
25.	Waynesville, NC	88.0		92.	Boone–Blowing Rock, NC	54.3
26.	Marble Falls–Lake LBJ, TX	87.5		93.	Coeur d'Alene, ID	53.8
27.	Oxford, MS	87.0		94.	Chewelah, WA	53.3
28.	Edenton, NC	86.5		95.	Dare Outer Banks, NC	52.8
29.	Berkeley Springs, WV	86.0		96.	Lake Conroe, TX	52.3
30.	Las Vegas, NM	85.5		97.	Lake Havasu City, AZ	51.8
31.	Delta County, CO	85.0		98.	Rehoboth Bay–Indian River Bay, DE	51.3
32.	Branson, MO	84.5		99.	Taos, NM	50.8
33.	Summerville, SC	84.0		100.	State College, PA	50.3
34.	New Braunfels, TX	83.5		101.	Camden, ME	49.8
35.	Cortez, CO	83.0		102.	St. George–Zion, UT	49.3
36.	Brown County, IN	82.5		103.	Grants Pass, OR	48.8
37.	Montrose, CO	82.0		104.	Palmer–Wasilla, AK	48.3
38.	Hot Springs, AR	81.5		105.	Panama City, FL	47.8
39.	St. Marys, GA	81.0		106.	Payson, AZ	47.3
40.	Grand Junction, CO	80.5		107.	Bozeman, MT	46.8
41.	Rabun County, GA	79.9		108.	Fairplay, CO	46.3
42.	Petoskey–Harbor Springs, MI	79.4		109.	Bar Harbor, ME	45.8
43.	Madison, MS	78.9		110.	Port St. Lucie, FL	45.3
44.	New Bern, NC	78.4		111.	Front Royal, VA	44.8
45.	Dahlonega, GA	77.9		112.	McCall, ID	44.3
46.	Brevard, NC	77.4		113.	Southern Berkshire County, MA	43.8
47.	Traverse City, MI	76.9		114.	Durango, CO	43.3
48.	Fairhope–Gulf Shores, AL	76.4		115.	Apalachicola, FL	42.8
49.	Ruidoso, NM	75.9		116.	Port Angeles–Sequim, WA	42.3
50.	Charles Town–Shepherdstown, WV	75.4		117.	Pike County, PA	41.8
51.	Bay St. Louis–Pass Christian, MS	74.9		118.	Fort Collins–Loveland, CO	41.3
52.	Athens, GA	74.4		119.	Melbourne–Palm Bay, FL	40.8
53.	Asheville, NC	73.9		120.	Medford–Ashland, OR	40.3
54.	Savannah, GA	73.4		121.	Driggs, ID	39.7
55.	Columbia, MO	72.9		122.	York Beaches, ME	39.2
56.	Rio Rancho, NM	72.4		123.	Eugene, OR	38.7
57.	Sebring–Avon Park, FL	71.9		124.	Bellingham, WA	38.2
58.	St. Jay–Northeast Kingdom, VT	71.4		125.	Leesburg–Mount Dora, FL	37.7
59.	Tryon, NC	70.9		126.	Smith Mountain Lake, VA	37.2
60.	Wimberley, TX	70.4		127.	Largo, FL	36.7
61.	Georgetown, TX	69.9		128.	Gainesville, FL	36.2
62.	Cedar City, UT	69.4		129.	Sullivan County, NY	35.7
63.	Lake of the Ozarks, MO	68.9		130.	East Stroudsburg, PA	35.2
64.	Charleston, SC	68.4		131.	Wenatchee, WA	34.7
65.	Myrtle Beach, SC	67.9		132.	Woodstock, VT	34.2
66.	St. Simons–Jekyll Islands, GA	67.4		133.	Port Charlotte, FL	33.7
67.	Long Beach Peninsula, WA	66.9				*continued*

Costs of Living

189

Retirement Places from Least to Most Expensive (cont.)

RANK	PLACE	SCORE		RANK	PLACE	SCORE
134.	Brunswick, ME	33.2		168.	Middle Cape Cod, MA	16.1
135.	Tucson, AZ	32.7		169.	Henderson, NV	15.6
136.	Charlottesville, VA	32.2		170.	Victorville–Apple Valley, CA	15.1
137.	Vero Beach, FL	31.7		171.	Mariposa, CA	14.6
138.	Newport–Lincoln City, OR	31.2		172.	Sonora–Twain Harte, CA	14.1
139.	Kissimmee–St. Cloud, FL	30.7		173.	Carson City–Carson Valley, NV	13.6
140.	Bradenton, FL	30.2		174.	Lower Cape May, NJ	13.1
141.	Pahrump Valley, NV	29.7		175.	St. Augustine, FL	12.6
142.	Ocean City, MD	29.2		176.	Amador County, CA	12.1
143.	Madison, WI	28.7		177.	Annapolis, MD	11.6
144.	Northern Neck, VA	28.2		178.	Silverthorne–Breckenridge, CO	11.1
145.	Cottonwood–Verde Valley, AZ	27.7		179.	Naples, FL	10.6
146.	Northampton–Amherst, MA	27.2		180.	Palm Springs–Coachella Valley, CA	10.1
147.	Flagstaff, AZ	26.7		181.	Park City, UT	9.6
148.	Santa Fe, NM	26.2		182.	Williamsburg, VA	9.1
149.	Chapel Hill–Carrboro, NC	25.7		183.	Loudoun County, VA	8.6
150.	Chestertown, MD	25.2		184.	Mendocino–Fort Bragg, CA	8.1
151.	Fort Myers–Cape Coral, FL	24.7		185.	Hilton Head Island, SC	7.6
152.	Bend, OR	24.2		186.	Scottsdale, AZ	7.1
153.	Sarasota, FL	23.7		187.	Ketchum–Sun Valley, ID	6.6
154.	Anacortes, WA	23.2		188.	San Juan Islands, WA	6.1
155.	Port Townsend, WA	22.7		189.	Sedona, AZ	5.6
156.	Whidbey Island, WA	22.2		190.	Grass Valley–Nevada City, CA	5.1
157.	Burlington, VT	21.7		191.	Maui, HI	4.6
158.	Fredericksburg–Spotsylvania, VA	21.2		192.	Martha's Vineyard, MA	4.1
159.	Oakhurst–Coarsegold, CA	20.7		193.	Placer County, CA	3.6
160.	Beaufort, SC	20.2		194.	Morro Bay–Cambria, CA	3.1
161.	Wickenburg, AZ	19.6		195.	Key West, FL	2.6
162.	Easton–St. Michaels, MD	19.1		196.	Jackson Hole, WY	2.1
163.	Prescott–Prescott Valley, AZ	18.6		197.	Santa Barbara, CA	1.6
164.	The Big Island, HI	18.1		198.	East End Long Island, NY	1.1
165.	Paradise–Magalia, CA	17.6		199.	Laguna Beach–Dana Point, CA	0.6
166.	Toms River–Barnegat Bay, NJ	17.1		200.	Carmel–Pebble Beach, CA	0.0
167.	Litchfield Hills, CT	16.6				

PLACE PROFILES: COSTS OF LIVING

The pages that follow detail costs-of-living factors used to rate each place—three costs of homeownership and six other living costs—for a hypothetical couple, age 65, with a gross income of $60,000. The entry at the right, **Expenses per Month,** is one-twelfth the sum of annual expenses listed. Expenses listed are estimated at 72 percent of a retired couple's total expenses. Single retired persons' Expenses per Month aren't one-half of a couple's, but more likely 66 to 75 percent.

The data mainly come from Places Rated Partners tax and consumer price surveys in early 2007. In addition, a number of sources were used. These include American Automobile Association, *Digest of Motor Laws* (state motor vehicle license, registration fees, and gasoline excise taxes), 2006; American Gas Association, *Gas Facts* (residential gas bills), 2006; Commerce Clearing House, *State Tax Guide* (state income and sales tax rates), 2007; Fodor's Travel

Publications, *Mobil Travel Guide* (state park fees, dining-out costs), 2006; National Golf Foundation (public golf course fees), 2006; U.S. Department of Health and Human Services, Health Care Financing Administration, unpublished medical procedures costs, geographic adjustment factors, and county managed-care capitation rates, 2006; U.S. Department of Labor, Bureau of Labor Statistics, unpublished data, *Consumer Expenditure Survey* (budget expense weights), 2005, and *Consumer Price Index*, final quarter 2006; U.S. General Services Administration, *Federal Travel Directory* (local per diems for food away from home), monthly, 2006; U.S. Department of the Treasury, Internal Revenue Service, *Publication 600* (state sales tax expenses by income level); and Woods & Poole Economics, Inc., unpublished household income figures, 2007.

A star (★) preceding a place's name indicates it is one of the top 30 places for low costs of living.

	Taxes, $60K Household		Annual Housing Costs			Other Annual Expenses					
PLACE	LOCAL INCOME	INCOME	SALES	MORTGAGE	UTILITIES	TAXES	FOOD	HEALTH-CARE	TRANS-PORTATION	RECREATION	EXPENSES PER MONTH	RANK
★Alamogordo, NM	$44,000	$1,255	$710	$7,392	$2,401	$766	$5,901	$3,630	$7,697	$1,336	$2,407	8
★Alpine–Big Bend, TX	$57,000	$0	$830	$5,163	$2,520	$1,009	$5,901	$3,630	$9,141	$1,724	$2,301	4
Amador County, CA	$60,700	$1,973	$856	$21,297	$3,118	$2,727	$5,901	$4,629	$9,621	$1,606	$4,073	176
Anacortes, WA	$69,300	$0	$863	$17,484	$2,894	$3,259	$6,202	$4,032	$8,690	$2,087	$3,572	154
Annapolis, MD	$95,000	$1,494	$606	$20,476	$3,074	$3,735	$6,563	$5,594	$8,978	$1,477	$4,098	177
Apalachicola, FL	$52,800	$0	$746	$14,315	$3,064	$1,550	$6,262	$4,382	$9,256	$1,570	$3,195	115
Asheville, NC	$64,300	$1,927	$572	$9,563	$2,761	$1,242	$6,202	$3,733	$8,534	$1,469	$2,789	53
Athens, GA	$54,200	$1,571	$463	$8,977	$3,030	$1,270	$6,082	$4,286	$9,041	$1,434	$2,781	52
Bar Harbor, ME	$70,700	$1,866	$506	$11,147	$2,919	$1,961	$6,563	$3,630	$8,991	$2,566	$3,123	109
Bay St. Louis–Pass Christian, MS	$63,500	$947	$1,150	$7,392	$3,240	$801	$6,202	$5,743	$8,520	$2,100	$2,760	51
Beaufort, SC	$81,900	$1,346	$770	$17,601	$4,516	$1,530	$6,202	$3,991	$9,434	$2,170	$3,618	160
Beaufort–Atlantic Beach, NC	$65,100	$1,927	$572	$9,915	$3,205	$955	$6,021	$3,804	$9,565	$1,998	$2,919	70
Bellingham, WA	$61,900	$0	$863	$15,900	$2,855	$2,854	$6,202	$3,630	$7,199	$1,998	$3,240	124
Bend, OR	$63,300	$2,499	$0	$15,489	$2,600	$2,867	$6,202	$3,630	$9,627	$2,292	$3,569	152
★Berkeley Springs, WV	$58,900	$1,452	$1,000	$7,568	$2,403	$709	$6,082	$4,089	$8,722	$1,338	$2,597	29
The Big Island, HI	$52,700	$1,984	$706	$20,711	$2,700	$882	$6,443	$3,821	$8,233	$1,751	$3,730	164
Bisbee, AZ	$53,000	$980	$710	$10,854	$2,519	$1,563	$6,082	$4,507	$8,900	$1,570	$2,948	77
Boerne, TX	$62,600	$0	$830	$10,795	$2,558	$2,375	$6,202	$3,630	$9,587	$1,465	$2,925	71
Boone–Blowing Rock, NC	$57,700	$1,927	$572	$11,089	$2,633	$757	$5,901	$3,630	$9,627	$2,562	$3,024	92
Bozeman, MT	$62,300	$1,652	$0	$14,139	$2,578	$2,471	$5,901	$3,630	$7,682	$1,638	$3,111	107
Bradenton, FL	$76,500	$0	$746	$16,252	$3,434	$2,925	$6,082	$4,246	$8,221	$1,880	$3,387	140
Branson, MO	$55,400	$1,305	$528	$7,744	$2,506	$761	$6,202	$4,153	$9,587	$1,414	$2,659	32
Brevard, NC	$60,200	$1,927	$572	$9,739	$2,816	$916	$5,841	$3,630	$7,199	$2,680	$2,728	46
Brown County, IN	$71,700	$1,297	$703	$8,272	$2,940	$916	$6,202	$3,630	$9,167	$1,784	$2,685	36
★Brownsville, TX	$38,100	$0	$830	$4,107	$2,618	$1,117	$5,841	$3,865	$9,141	$1,136	$2,188	2
Brunswick, ME	$85,200	$1,866	$506	$13,494	$2,991	$3,504	$6,202	$3,630	$9,041	$1,391	$3,324	134
Burlington, VT	$85,000	$1,452	$496	$14,550	$3,064	$4,748	$6,623	$4,382	$8,900	$1,588	$3,583	157
Camden, ME	$70,100	$1,866	$506	$11,558	$3,125	$2,521	$6,202	$3,630	$9,041	$1,391	$3,081	101
Carmel–Pebble Beach, CA	$75,200	$1,973	$856	$93,579	$2,616	$9,619	$6,623	$4,717	$9,621	$4,298	$10,959	200
Carson City–Carson Valley, NV	$91,400	$0	$792	$23,175	$3,216	$2,753	$6,925	$3,684	$9,127	$1,612	$4,028	173
Cedar City, UT	$43,100	$1,724	$775	$9,622	$2,540	$1,013	$6,202	$3,630	$9,247	$2,072	$2,875	62
★Cedar Creek Lake, TX	$54,200	$0	$830	$5,808	$3,245	$1,052	$5,841	$4,679	$9,141	$1,430	$2,421	9
Chapel Hill–Carrboro, NC	$79,500	$1,927	$572	$14,257	$3,018	$2,620	$6,563	$4,503	$9,587	$1,551	$3,486	149
Charleston, SC	$72,200	$1,346	$770	$10,737	$3,589	$1,008	$6,202	$4,436	$8,520	$1,324	$2,887	64
Charles Town–Shepherdstown, WV	$60,300	$1,452	$1,000	$9,857	$2,764	$1,015	$5,901	$3,668	$8,609	$1,273	$2,750	50
Charlottesville, VA	$79,600	$1,827	$616	$13,787	$2,933	$2,382	$6,563	$3,952	$9,032	$1,728	$3,344	136
Chestertown, MD	$77,900	$1,494	$606	$14,844	$3,276	$2,197	$6,563	$5,594	$8,978	$1,477	$3,502	150
Chewelah, WA	$47,300	$0	$863	$11,441	$2,300	$1,915	$6,322	$4,298	$9,434	$1,945	$3,034	94
Coeur d'Alene, ID	$56,500	$1,569	$790	$11,910	$2,299	$2,023	$6,082	$3,630	$8,631	$1,500	$3,027	93
Columbia, MO	$65,700	$1,305	$528	$8,859	$2,829	$1,475	$6,262	$4,323	$9,078	$1,704	$2,814	55
★Conway, AR	$57,500	$1,544	$911	$7,568	$2,958	$864	$6,021	$3,630	$8,650	$1,042	$2,540	21
Cortez, CO	$56,100	$1,300	$319	$8,566	$2,471	$855	$6,623	$4,046	$8,814	$1,461	$2,683	35
Cottonwood–Verde Valley, AZ	$50,600	$980	$710	$17,014	$2,579	$1,944	$5,841	$3,630	$8,978	$1,524	$3,403	145
★Crossville, TN	$54,000	$165	$1,115	$7,275	$2,601	$449	$5,841	$4,178	$8,592	$1,986	$2,485	14
Dahlonega, GA	$51,200	$1,571	$463	$8,977	$2,660	$1,062	$5,841	$4,729	$8,064	$1,739	$2,722	45
Dare Outer Banks, NC	$67,000	$1,927	$572	$10,971	$3,505	$1,248	$6,202	$4,064	$9,587	$1,622	$3,041	95
Delta County, CO	$50,700	$1,300	$319	$9,094	$2,578	$776	$5,841	$3,788	$8,814	$1,379	$2,627	31
Door Peninsula, WI	$72,200	$1,784	$670	$10,150	$2,471	$2,256	$6,082	$3,630	$9,250	$1,614	$2,970	81
Driggs, ID	$43,800	$1,569	$790	$13,201	$2,889	$1,389	$6,925	$4,080	$8,631	$1,888	$3,226	121
Durango, CO	$71,000	$1,300	$319	$14,491	$2,568	$980	$6,623	$4,046	$8,814	$1,461	$3,187	114
Eagle River–Woodruff, WI	$56,600	$1,784	$670	$10,091	$2,376	$2,053	$6,082	$3,630	$9,250	$1,837	$2,966	80
East End Long Island, NY	$88,700	$2,232	$472	$66,004	$3,820	$29,546	$6,864	$5,436	$10,358	$2,860	$10,341	198
Easton–St. Michaels, MD	$100,300	$1,494	$606	$19,185	$3,374	$2,027	$6,202	$3,893	$8,690	$2,041	$3,702	162
East Stroudsburg, PA	$57,200	$1,152	$711	$12,203	$2,784	$3,597	$6,202	$4,535	$9,100	$1,816	$3,296	130
★Edenton, NC	$57,600	$1,927	$572	$6,806	$3,364	$813	$5,901	$3,630	$9,587	$1,622	$2,595	28
Eugene, OR	$61,200	$2,499	$0	$14,668	$2,311	$2,679	$6,202	$3,630	$7,199	$1,704	$3,231	123
★Eureka Springs, AR	$44,900	$1,544	$911	$6,864	$2,604	$894	$6,021	$3,630	$8,633	$1,053	$2,481	13
Fairhope–Gulf Shores, AL	$63,800	$1,170	$590	$9,974	$3,196	$498	$6,021	$4,466	$8,281	$1,685	$2,746	48
Fairplay, CO	$69,500	$1,300	$319	$13,553	$2,274	$1,311	$5,279	$4,731	$8,025	$2,728	$3,120	108
★Fayetteville, AR	$56,400	$1,544	$911	$7,334	$2,746	$998	$6,021	$3,630	$8,650	$1,042	$2,530	19
Flagstaff, AZ	$59,100	$980	$710	$17,542	$2,330	$1,754	$5,841	$3,630	$8,978	$1,524	$3,429	147
Fort Collins–Loveland, CO	$75,000	$1,300	$329	$13,656	$2,784	$1,765	$6,423	$3,843	$8,814	$2,084	$3,204	118
Fort Myers–Cape Coral, FL	$73,800	$0	$746	$15,372	$3,430	$3,156	$6,563	$4,742	$9,627	$2,198	$3,557	151

continued

Costs of Living

PLACE	LOCAL INCOME	Taxes, $60K Household INCOME	Taxes, $60K Household SALES	Annual Housing Costs MORTGAGE	Annual Housing Costs UTILITIES	Annual Housing Costs TAXES	Other Annual Expenses FOOD	Other Annual Expenses HEALTH-CARE	Other Annual Expenses TRANS-PORTATION	Other Annual Expenses RECREATION	EXPENSES PER MONTH	RANK
★ Fredericksburg, TX	$62,300	$0	$830	$8,214	$2,576	$1,646	$6,021	$3,630	$9,141	$1,019	$2,560	23
Fredericksburg-Spotsylvania, VA	$66,000	$1,827	$616	$15,724	$3,194	$2,820	$6,383	$4,339	$9,032	$2,174	$3,598	158
Front Royal, VA	$58,900	$1,827	$616	$12,614	$2,683	$1,522	$6,262	$4,173	$9,078	$1,784	$3,175	111
Gainesville, FL	$60,900	$0	$746	$13,259	$2,951	$2,934	$6,202	$4,463	$9,627	$1,663	$3,262	128
Georgetown, TX	$66,600	$0	$830	$9,636	$2,620	$3,251	$6,443	$3,630	$8,977	$1,477	$2,872	61
Grand Junction, CO	$61,100	$1,300	$319	$9,387	$2,440	$1,152	$6,202	$3,630	$8,814	$1,379	$2,699	40
Grants Pass, OR	$51,800	$2,499	$0	$13,377	$2,338	$1,640	$6,082	$3,630	$7,199	$2,468	$3,091	103
Grass Valley-Nevada City, CA	$75,000	$1,973	$856	$28,514	$3,276	$3,816	$6,082	$4,249	$9,621	$2,241	$4,802	190
Hamilton-Bitterroot Valley, MT	$51,300	$1,652	$0	$13,201	$2,390	$1,693	$5,901	$3,630	$7,682	$1,638	$2,966	79
★ Hampshire County, WV	$46,700	$1,452	$1,000	$6,630	$2,328	$499	$6,082	$4,089	$8,722	$1,338	$2,501	15
Hanover, NH	$82,300	$237	$0	$11,265	$3,003	$4,310	$6,563	$3,689	$7,073	$2,854	$3,020	91
★ Hattiesburg, MS	$57,400	$947	$1,150	$5,515	$2,894	$752	$5,841	$4,543	$9,067	$1,695	$2,479	12
Henderson, NV	$71,900	$0	$792	$19,889	$2,878	$2,863	$6,623	$5,066	$9,127	$1,753	$3,863	169
Hendersonville-East Flat Rock, NC	$64,600	$1,927	$572	$10,385	$2,578	$1,015	$6,202	$3,630	$9,587	$1,446	$2,915	69
Hilton Head Island, SC	$81,900	$1,346	$770	$26,343	$4,516	$2,290	$6,563	$3,991	$8,520	$3,933	$4,511	185
Hot Springs, AR	$59,400	$1,544	$911	$6,982	$3,018	$729	$6,202	$4,385	$8,650	$2,605	$2,688	38
Iowa City, IA	$72,600	$1,522	$675	$10,033	$3,018	$2,198	$6,082	$3,630	$9,167	$1,802	$2,947	76
Jackson Hole, WY	$168,100	$0	$586	$36,669	$4,750	$2,757	$6,925	$4,340	$8,722	$2,319	$5,226	196
Kalispell-Flathead Valley, MT	$61,100	$1,652	$0	$12,438	$2,281	$2,328	$6,082	$3,630	$7,682	$1,661	$2,972	82
★ Kerrville, TX	$66,400	$0	$830	$7,451	$2,884	$1,621	$6,202	$3,630	$9,141	$1,042	$2,513	17
Ketchum-Sun Valley, ID	$100,300	$1,569	$790	$28,631	$3,503	$2,342	$6,925	$4,080	$8,631	$1,888	$4,596	187
Key West, FL	$91,900	$0	$746	$32,855	$4,824	$4,692	$6,383	$4,674	$9,612	$1,731	$5,091	195
Kingman, AZ	$47,100	$980	$710	$10,795	$2,526	$1,473	$5,841	$4,718	$8,978	$1,230	$2,911	68
Kissimmee-St. Cloud, FL	$45,900	$0	$746	$13,494	$2,759	$2,587	$6,202	$5,584	$9,627	$2,104	$3,381	139
Laguna Beach-Dana Point, CA	$92,800	$1,973	$856	$90,645	$2,226	$11,370	$6,925	$5,695	$9,621	$2,535	$10,817	199
Lake Conroe, TX	$71,100	$0	$830	$8,859	$2,693	$2,644	$6,202	$6,616	$9,141	$2,006	$3,044	96
Lake Havasu City, AZ	$47,100	$980	$710	$12,145	$2,526	$1,657	$6,021	$4,718	$8,978	$1,230	$3,054	97
Lakeland-Winter Haven, FL	$59,500	$0	$746	$11,323	$2,946	$1,879	$6,082	$3,804	$9,627	$1,763	$2,956	78
★ Lake of the Cherokees, OK	$51,200	$1,459	$704	$6,336	$2,646	$611	$5,901	$3,980	$7,772	$1,491	$2,373	7
Lake of the Ozarks, MO	$63,000	$1,305	$528	$10,267	$2,564	$863	$6,563	$4,497	$8,224	$2,096	$2,880	63
Lake Placid, NY	$54,700	$2,232	$472	$8,331	$2,940	$2,387	$6,142	$4,340	$9,790	$1,748	$2,974	84
Largo, FL	$78,800	$0	$746	$13,142	$3,245	$2,526	$6,082	$4,973	$9,627	$1,763	$3,261	127
★ Las Cruces, NM	$47,400	$1,255	$710	$8,507	$2,601	$1,102	$6,202	$3,686	$7,697	$1,477	$2,571	24
★ Las Vegas, NM	$48,000	$1,255	$710	$8,448	$2,950	$869	$6,383	$3,672	$7,832	$1,927	$2,612	30
Leelanau Peninsula, MI	$71,700	$1,075	$736	$11,969	$2,819	$1,540	$6,202	$3,857	$8,277	$1,337	$2,936	73
Leesburg-Mount Dora, FL	$59,100	$0	$746	$13,670	$2,763	$2,302	$5,841	$4,423	$9,627	$2,104	$3,245	125
Litchfield Hills, CT	$86,900	$1,855	$621	$16,017	$3,321	$4,740	$6,925	$4,528	$9,222	$1,837	$3,835	167
Long Beach Peninsula, WA	$53,800	$0	$863	$10,502	$2,696	$1,825	$6,202	$3,703	$9,565	$1,845	$2,894	67
Loudoun County, VA	$82,800	$1,827	$616	$23,233	$2,978	$3,804	$6,044	$5,146	$9,352	$2,728	$4,417	183
Lower Cape May, NJ	$81,000	$1,317	$738	$16,134	$3,479	$4,870	$6,563	$5,388	$9,554	$3,592	$4,037	174
Madison, MS	$81,700	$947	$1,150	$9,387	$2,948	$911	$5,841	$3,630	$8,991	$1,536	$2,720	43
Madison, WI	$85,500	$1,784	$670	$12,321	$2,370	$4,494	$6,322	$3,690	$9,345	$1,855	$3,390	143
★ Marble Falls-Lake LBJ, TX	$57,100	$0	$830	$7,216	$3,135	$1,577	$6,202	$3,959	$9,141	$1,747	$2,578	26
Mariposa, CA	$54,400	$1,973	$856	$19,654	$2,686	$2,519	$6,443	$4,380	$9,627	$1,641	$3,943	171
Martha's Vineyard, MA	$94,900	$2,112	$526	$30,215	$3,366	$2,919	$6,322	$4,841	$9,167	$2,426	$4,901	192
★ Maryville, TN	$60,000	$165	$1,115	$8,272	$2,746	$813	$5,841	$3,987	$8,592	$1,422	$2,536	20
Maui, HI	$63,900	$1,984	$706	$33,677	$3,073	$1,521	$6,443	$3,821	$8,233	$1,751	$4,866	191
★ McAllen-Alamo, TX	$35,300	$0	$830	$4,048	$2,326	$1,168	$5,841	$3,865	$9,141	$1,136	$2,185	1
McCall, ID	$66,600	$1,569	$790	$13,963	$2,645	$1,551	$6,262	$3,630	$8,631	$1,536	$3,179	112
Medford-Ashland, OR	$62,300	$2,499	$0	$14,550	$2,438	$2,519	$6,202	$3,630	$7,199	$1,704	$3,209	120
Melbourne-Palm Bay, FL	$66,800	$0	$746	$12,849	$2,973	$2,417	$6,082	$4,888	$9,627	$1,645	$3,208	119
Mendocino-Fort Bragg, CA	$60,500	$1,973	$856	$23,585	$2,916	$2,879	$6,925	$4,674	$9,612	$2,319	$4,422	184
Middle Cape Cod, MA	$89,300	$2,112	$526	$17,777	$3,214	$3,005	$6,262	$4,814	$8,989	$2,415	$3,847	168
Monadnock Region, NH	$69,700	$237	$0	$10,854	$3,079	$4,823	$6,443	$3,630	$7,565	$1,855	$2,972	83
Montrose, CO	$54,800	$1,300	$319	$9,563	$2,594	$954	$5,841	$3,630	$8,814	$1,614	$2,688	37
Morro Bay-Cambria, CA	$70,600	$1,973	$856	$31,858	$2,458	$4,141	$6,925	$3,845	$9,621	$1,653	$5,090	194
★ Murray-Kentucky Lake, KY	$56,300	$1,513	$684	$6,395	$2,614	$752	$5,901	$3,918	$8,679	$1,434	$2,458	11
Myrtle Beach, SC	$58,200	$1,346	$770	$9,857	$2,800	$696	$6,202	$4,031	$8,520	$2,993	$2,887	65
Naples, FL	$98,600	$0	$746	$22,881	$4,398	$3,310	$6,623	$4,522	$9,627	$1,786	$4,155	179
★ Natchitoches, LA	$48,900	$1,113	$531	$6,102	$3,111	$294	$6,021	$4,089	$7,565	$1,588	$2,297	3
Nelson County, VA	$57,200	$1,827	$616	$11,030	$2,239	$1,228	$6,563	$3,952	$9,032	$1,728	$3,014	89
New Bern, NC	$66,900	$1,927	$572	$7,686	$3,336	$905	$6,021	$3,664	$9,587	$1,998	$2,720	44
New Braunfels, TX	$63,900	$0	$830	$9,035	$2,548	$1,961	$6,202	$3,630	$9,141	$1,101	$2,676	34

★ = in the top 30 places for low costs of living

PLACE	LOCAL INCOME	Taxes, $60K Household		Annual Housing Costs			Other Annual Expenses				EXPENSES PER MONTH	RANK
		INCOME	SALES	MORTGAGE	UTILITIES	TAXES	FOOD	HEALTH-CARE	TRANS-PORTATION	RECREATION		
Newport-Lincoln City, OR	$60,400	$2,499	$0	$15,489	$2,310	$2,853	$6,202	$3,630	$7,199	$2,186	$3,354	138
★ Norfork Lake, AR	$56,600	$1,544	$911	$6,864	$2,593	$701	$5,841	$3,681	$8,650	$1,724	$2,511	16
Northampton-Amherst, MA	$67,300	$2,112	$526	$14,139	$2,859	$3,563	$6,082	$4,016	$8,679	$1,710	$3,422	146
Northern Neck, VA	$78,300	$1,827	$616	$15,254	$3,118	$1,189	$6,021	$4,211	$9,032	$2,409	$3,402	144
Oakhurst-Coarsegold, CA	$46,000	$1,973	$856	$16,486	$2,835	$2,214	$6,082	$4,125	$9,621	$1,606	$3,600	159
Ocala, FL	$54,900	$0	$746	$11,089	$2,506	$1,895	$6,082	$4,073	$9,627	$1,587	$2,942	74
Ocean City, MD	$72,600	$1,494	$606	$15,606	$3,340	$2,005	$6,563	$3,673	$8,690	$1,747	$3,389	142
★ Oxford, MS	$56,300	$947	$1,150	$8,096	$3,098	$680	$5,841	$3,630	$8,991	$1,536	$2,594	27
Pagosa Springs, CO	$47,300	$1,300	$319	$13,201	$2,410	$1,296	$5,901	$3,630	$8,814	$1,461	$3,010	87
Pahrump Valley, NV	$58,700	$0	$792	$15,548	$2,139	$1,886	$6,202	$4,577	$9,127	$2,341	$3,388	141
Palmer-Wasilla, AK	$63,600	$0	$0	$11,969	$3,085	$2,497	$6,623	$4,949	$8,900	$1,962	$3,097	104
Palm Springs-Coachella Valley, CA	$56,900	$1,973	$856	$20,300	$2,936	$3,181	$6,864	$5,133	$9,621	$2,828	$4,250	180
Panama City, FL	$60,700	$0	$746	$12,731	$2,831	$1,567	$6,202	$4,620	$9,627	$1,499	$3,102	105
Paradise-Magalia, CA	$56,000	$1,973	$856	$18,012	$2,884	$2,434	$6,563	$4,402	$9,621	$1,312	$3,784	165
Park City, UT	$109,200	$1,724	$775	$25,463	$2,606	$2,380	$6,563	$3,630	$9,256	$1,998	$4,334	181
Payson, AZ	$53,900	$980	$710	$12,321	$2,678	$1,573	$5,841	$4,638	$8,978	$2,053	$3,110	106
★ Pendleton District, SC	$60,400	$1,346	$770	$8,038	$2,845	$545	$5,901	$3,630	$8,520	$1,536	$2,544	22
Pensacola, FL	$58,600	$0	$746	$11,675	$2,856	$1,493	$6,262	$4,619	$9,621	$1,552	$3,017	90
Petoskey-Harbor Springs, MI	$68,100	$1,075	$736	$9,505	$2,781	$1,620	$6,202	$3,630	$8,094	$1,420	$2,709	42
Pike County, PA	$55,900	$1,152	$711	$11,499	$2,586	$3,173	$6,202	$4,535	$9,100	$1,816	$3,200	117
Placer County, CA	$82,500	$1,973	$856	$29,628	$2,851	$4,332	$6,082	$4,249	$9,621	$2,241	$4,935	193
Port Angeles-Sequim, WA	$63,600	$0	$863	$13,611	$2,666	$2,343	$6,202	$3,703	$9,565	$1,845	$3,196	116
Port Charlotte, FL	$62,200	$0	$746	$13,201	$2,996	$2,735	$6,202	$5,210	$9,627	$1,822	$3,316	133
Port St. Lucie, FL	$51,400	$0	$746	$11,734	$3,035	$2,722	$6,082	$4,649	$9,627	$1,810	$3,135	110
Port Townsend, WA	$70,900	$0	$863	$17,542	$3,151	$2,962	$6,082	$3,867	$9,565	$1,833	$3,581	155
Prescott-Prescott Valley, AZ	$50,600	$980	$710	$20,065	$2,579	$2,292	$6,202	$3,630	$8,978	$1,536	$3,717	163
Rabun County, GA	$53,700	$1,571	$463	$9,035	$2,863	$726	$5,841	$4,729	$8,064	$1,739	$2,701	41
Rehoboth Bay-Indian River Bay, DE	$61,000	$1,714	$0	$13,259	$2,908	$1,001	$6,082	$4,433	$8,125	$1,798	$3,055	98
Rio Rancho, NM	$59,300	$1,255	$710	$10,854	$2,559	$1,201	$6,563	$3,630	$7,697	$1,771	$2,825	56
★ Rockport-Aransas Pass, TX	$58,200	$0	$830	$6,102	$3,173	$1,366	$6,202	$4,665	$9,141	$1,724	$2,525	18
★ Roswell, NM	$56,500	$1,255	$710	$6,043	$2,593	$465	$6,202	$3,630	$8,010	$1,820	$2,363	6
Ruidoso, NM	$48,600	$1,255	$710	$10,150	$2,944	$972	$6,383	$3,630	$7,697	$1,924	$2,747	49
St. Augustine, FL	$79,300	$0	$746	$21,591	$2,816	$3,659	$6,202	$4,634	$9,627	$1,822	$4,043	175
St. George-Zion, UT	$46,100	$1,724	$775	$12,027	$2,739	$1,134	$6,202	$3,630	$9,247	$2,072	$3,087	102
St. Jay-Northeast Kingdom, VT	$60,400	$1,452	$496	$8,683	$2,799	$2,980	$6,082	$3,630	$8,571	$1,853	$2,832	58
St. Marys, GA	$52,600	$1,571	$463	$6,864	$2,515	$1,223	$6,082	$4,988	$8,534	$2,327	$2,688	39
St. Simons-Jekyll Islands, GA	$68,000	$1,571	$463	$9,211	$3,126	$1,277	$6,082	$4,988	$8,534	$2,327	$2,893	66
Sandpoint-Lake Pend Oreille, ID	$50,000	$1,569	$790	$12,321	$2,473	$1,461	$5,901	$3,630	$8,631	$1,536	$3,004	86
San Juan Islands, WA	$92,000	$0	$863	$29,804	$3,324	$3,184	$5,901	$3,630	$9,565	$1,951	$4,598	188
Santa Barbara, CA	$79,500	$1,973	$856	$40,600	$2,605	$3,892	$6,623	$3,882	$9,621	$1,830	$5,791	197
Santa Fe, NM	$73,300	$1,255	$710	$17,777	$3,009	$1,256	$6,563	$3,630	$7,697	$2,382	$3,460	148
Sarasota, FL	$98,500	$0	$746	$16,604	$3,435	$3,201	$6,202	$4,536	$9,627	$1,645	$3,571	153
Savannah, GA	$70,000	$1,571	$463	$7,627	$3,276	$1,619	$6,202	$4,997	$8,534	$2,292	$2,798	54
Scottsdale, AZ	$70,200	$980	$710	$27,223	$3,083	$3,512	$6,563	$4,869	$8,978	$1,747	$4,570	186
Sebring-Avon Park, FL	$52,000	$0	$746	$9,915	$2,566	$1,697	$5,841	$4,397	$9,627	$1,528	$2,830	57
Sedona, AZ	$59,100	$980	$710	$31,271	$2,330	$3,127	$6,202	$3,656	$8,978	$1,230	$4,696	189
★ Silver City, NM	$49,700	$1,255	$710	$8,272	$2,443	$504	$5,841	$3,630	$7,697	$1,359	$2,456	10
Silverthorne-Breckenridge, CO	$77,900	$1,300	$319	$24,993	$3,893	$1,634	$5,279	$4,731	$8,025	$2,728	$4,111	178
Smith Mountain Lake, VA	$57,500	$1,827	$616	$14,726	$2,293	$1,380	$5,841	$3,630	$9,032	$1,798	$3,253	126
Sonora-Twain Harte, CA	$57,100	$1,973	$856	$20,769	$3,234	$2,706	$5,901	$3,996	$9,621	$1,606	$3,975	172
Southern Berkshire County, MA	$75,800	$2,112	$526	$11,617	$3,116	$2,670	$6,082	$4,701	$8,679	$1,534	$3,182	113
Southern Pines-Pinehurst, NC	$74,100	$1,927	$572	$10,443	$3,028	$1,094	$6,563	$3,630	$9,587	$2,057	$3,011	88
Southport-Brunswick Islands, NC	$55,100	$1,927	$572	$10,150	$3,336	$1,036	$6,202	$4,178	$9,587	$1,974	$2,992	85
State College, PA	$61,200	$1,152	$711	$11,206	$2,758	$2,417	$6,202	$4,034	$9,100	$1,839	$3,074	100
Sullivan County, NY	$63,000	$2,232	$472	$10,033	$3,335	$4,259	$6,142	$4,340	$9,790	$1,748	$3,275	129
Summerville, SC	$56,100	$1,346	$770	$8,624	$3,179	$1,013	$6,202	$3,758	$8,633	$1,409	$2,668	33
Taos, NM	$49,400	$1,255	$710	$14,139	$2,819	$636	$6,202	$3,630	$7,697	$2,358	$3,072	99
★ Thomasville, GA	$59,200	$1,571	$463	$6,160	$2,929	$782	$5,841	$3,718	$8,064	$1,034	$2,323	5
Toms River-Barnegat Bay, NJ	$72,500	$1,317	$738	$15,372	$3,150	$5,555	$6,202	$4,829	$9,554	$1,947	$3,815	166
Traverse City, MI	$68,700	$1,075	$736	$9,446	$2,483	$1,711	$6,202	$3,977	$8,094	$1,361	$2,734	47
Tryon, NC	$72,100	$1,927	$572	$8,918	$2,710	$836	$5,841	$3,630	$9,587	$2,445	$2,832	59
Tucson, AZ	$60,200	$980	$710	$14,139	$2,655	$2,498	$6,202	$4,616	$8,978	$1,747	$3,341	135
Vero Beach, FL	$92,600	$0	$746	$14,139	$3,385	$2,846	$6,082	$4,649	$9,627	$1,810	$3,348	137

continued

★ = *in the top 30 places for low costs of living*

PLACE	LOCAL INCOME	Taxes, $60K Household		Annual Housing Costs			Other Annual Expenses				EXPENSES	
		INCOME	SALES	MORTGAGE	UTILITIES	TAXES	FOOD	HEALTH-CARE	TRANS-PORTATION	RECREATION	PER MONTH	RANK
Victorville–Apple Valley, CA	$55,300	$1,973	$856	$18,246	$2,589	$2,850	$6,563	$5,299	$9,621	$1,653	$3,940	170
★Waynesville, NC	$56,400	$1,927	$572	$7,920	$2,574	$873	$5,841	$3,630	$7,199	$2,680	$2,571	25
Wenatchee, WA	$64,500	$0	$863	$15,137	$2,489	$2,610	$5,901	$3,630	$9,565	$1,739	$3,304	131
Western St. Tammany Parish, LA	$73,800	$1,113	$531	$10,737	$3,435	$549	$6,202	$6,277	$8,125	$1,326	$2,929	72
Whidbey Island, WA	$65,100	$0	$863	$17,836	$3,030	$2,692	$6,262	$3,630	$9,565	$1,880	$3,582	156
Wickenburg, AZ	$70,200	$980	$710	$18,481	$3,083	$2,384	$5,841	$4,869	$8,978	$1,818	$3,693	161
Williamsburg, VA	$85,500	$1,827	$616	$24,524	$3,328	$1,920	$6,563	$4,406	$9,032	$3,292	$4,372	182
Wimberley, TX	$52,700	$0	$830	$9,974	$2,588	$2,893	$5,841	$3,777	$9,141	$1,747	$2,868	60
Woodstock, VT	$73,400	$1,452	$496	$11,382	$2,909	$4,078	$6,383	$3,630	$8,571	$3,463	$3,308	132
York Beaches, ME	$68,000	$1,866	$506	$12,614	$2,898	$2,837	$6,202	$3,640	$9,041	$1,767	$3,226	122
Yuma, AZ	$43,900	$980	$710	$10,502	$2,959	$1,735	$6,021	$4,568	$8,978	$1,583	$2,944	75

ET CETERA: COSTS OF LIVING

PROPERTY TAXES

If the size of your home's property tax bill inched upward with each reassessment since 2000, there is one big reason for it: The house is worth a lot more money. But take some comfort in knowing that the long-term *rate* at which homes are being taxed is actually going down.

Over the years, while the prices of existing homes were rising, the average effective property tax rate (the tax bill expressed as a percentage of a home's fair market value) dropped from 2 percent to about 1 percent nationwide. Experts expect the downward trend to continue.

Nowhere in the United States can you own a home and escape property taxes without specific income and age qualifications. But homeowners in certain states, such as Louisiana, where the statewide average property tax rate is 0.25 percent, shoulder less of a burden than do homeowners in other states such as New Jersey, which has an average effective tax rate of 2.4 percent, or almost 10 times that of Louisiana.

Homestead Exemptions

When you shop for favorable property taxes around the country, be a little circumspect when you hear of states that give retired people additional property tax relief. Are any of these perks, by themselves, worth the move? Read on.

Homestead exemptions are specific dollar amounts deducted from a home's assessed value. The assessed value minus the exemption equals the amount of taxable

value for computing property tax. Homeowners in Florida get a $25,000 exemption, for example, while Hawaiians get a $40,000 exemption if their home is their principal residence. A related break is the *homestead credit,* an amount subtracted from the property tax rather than from the assessed value. Ten states also allow additional exemptions or credits to older homeowners without income qualifications.

Do exemptions translate into much hard cash? Except in Alaska—where you can virtually forget property taxes once you turn 65—not really. Based on statewide average property tax rates, you'll save $204 in Hawaii ($255 if you're over 70), $54 in Illinois, $160 in Kentucky, $144 in South Carolina, and $138 in West Virginia.

Property tax exemptions can be an extra benefit in retirement, but if you're planning a move, you'd do well to put other considerations first, such as energy costs and house prices.

STATE/LOCAL SALES TAXES

Sometimes called retail taxes or consumption taxes, sales taxes are levied by some 11,000 jurisdictions and are collected on the purchase of goods at the store level. After income taxes, sales taxes account for the largest source of revenue for states and governments. Unlike property taxes, however, they were not deductible from your federal tax return. This changed in tax year 2006, when the IRS allowed taxpayers to deduct either the dollars paid in state income taxes or the dollars paid in state sales taxes (but not both).

STATE & LOCAL SALES TAX RATES

STATE	FOOD TAXED	STATE	LOCAL MAXIMUM	STATE/LOCAL MAXIMUM
Alabama	●	4.00%	7.00%	11.00%
Arizona		5.60%	4.50%	10.10%
Arkansas	●	6.00%	5.50%	11.50%
California		6.25%	2.65%	8.90%
Colorado		2.90%	7.00%	9.90%
Connecticut *		6.00%		6.00%
District of Columbia		5.75%		5.75%
Florida		6.00%	1.50%	7.50%
Georgia		4.00%	3.00%	7.00%
Hawaii *	●	4.00%		4.00%
Idaho	●	6.00%	3.00%	9.00%
Illinois	●	6.25%	3.00%	9.25%
Indiana *		6.00%		6.00%
Iowa		5.00%	2.00%	7.00%
Kansas	●	5.30%	3.00%	8.30%
Kentucky *		6.00%		6.00%
Louisiana *		4.00%	6.25%	10.25%
Maine *		5.00%		5.00%
Maryland *		5.00%		5.00%
Massachusetts *		5.00%		5.00%
Michigan *		6.00%		6.00%
Minnesota		6.50%	1.00%	7.50%
Mississippi	●	7.00%	0.25%	7.25%
Missouri	●	4.225%	4.50%	8.725%
Nebraska		5.50%	1.50%	7.00%
Nevada		6.50%	1.00%	7.50%
New Jersey *		6.00%		6.00%
New Mexico		5.00%	2.25%	7.25%
New York		4.00%	4.50%	8.75%
North Carolina		4.50%	3.00%	7.50%
North Dakota		5.00%	2.50%	7.50%
Ohio		6.00%	2.00%	8.00%
Oklahoma		4.50%	6.00%	10.50%
Pennsylvania		6.00%	1.00%	7.00%
Rhode Island *		7.00%		7.00%
South Carolina	●	5.00%	2.00%	7.00%
South Dakota	●	4.00%	2.00%	6.00%
Tennessee	●	7.00%	2.75%	9.75%
Texas		6.25%	2.00%	8.25%
Utah	●	4.75%	2.25%	7.00%
Vermont		6.00%	1.00%	7.00%
Virginia	●	4.00%	1.00%	5.00%
Washington *		6.50%	2.40%	8.90%
West Virginia *	●	6.00%		6.00%
Wisconsin		5.00%	0.60%	5.60%
Wyoming	●	4.00%	2.00%	6.00%

Source: Federation of Tax Administrators

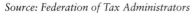 indicates groceries are taxable. Prescription drugs are tax-exempt everywhere but Illinois and New Mexico.

* indicates a flat state sales tax rate. All other states have local additions to their base tax rate.

Nationally, the median sales tax rate is 5.6 percent. If you're living in Mississippi, Rhode Island, or Tennessee, you're paying the nation's highest state rate at 7 percent. But combined state and local sales taxes, in the 34 states that allow it, can top 10 percent.

Alaska, Delaware, Montana, New Hampshire, and Oregon collect no sales taxes at all. To a retired couple, this could mean saving $500 to $900 a year. But you can avoid much of that cost in states where medicine, clothing, and especially groceries are exempt.

STATE RETIREMENT INCOME TAXES

Question: Where in America can you find rock-bottom property taxes; no personal income tax on any of your retirement income; no sales tax on the basics you'll need, such as food and medicine; no inheritance taxes for your heirs to pay; and a minimum of nickel-and-dime fees for licensing a car or for taking out a fishing license?

Answer: Dream on. The ideal tax haven would have to have the low property taxes of Louisiana,

Alaska's forgiveness of taxes on personal income, and the absence of sales taxes as in Montana. Unfortunately, you just can't find all these tax breaks together in any one state.

The ways states raise revenue differ dramatically. Sales taxes, excise taxes, license taxes, income taxes, intangibles taxes, property taxes, estate taxes, and inheritance taxes are just some of the forms their levies take. Depending on where you live, you may encounter all or only a few.

When federal income taxes were enacted in 1914, two states—Mississippi and Wisconsin—were already collecting income taxes on their own. It was only during the 1920s and 1930s that the majority of states began to raise cash by tapping personal incomes. Today, 41 states impose the tax. Two—New Hampshire and Tennessee—apply it only to income from interest and dividends. Seven—Alaska, Florida, Nevada, South Dakota, Texas, Washington, and Wyoming—don't tax income at all.

Of the 41 states with a broad-based income tax, 35 base the taxes on federal returns, typically taking a portion of what you pay the IRS or using your federal adjusted gross income or taxable income as the starting point for their own computation. Just four states—Hawaii, Illinois, Mississippi, and Pennsylvania—fully exempt Social Security and any pensions from taxation. The remaining states take differing views on taxing Social Security, government pensions, and private employer pensions.

The following descriptions of how states tax income include specific features regarding their treatment of retirement income. The best way to learn what your income taxes will be in a new state is to visit the state's Department of Revenue website for a *resident* (not nonresident) income tax form and instructions, fill it out, and compare the bottom line with that of your current state. See the "Relocation Resources" section in the Appendix for Internet addresses. Of course, you should always consult a tax advisor for help with complex tax issues.

Personal Exemptions and Standard Deductions. Most states specify amounts for taxpayers and each of their dependents that can be used as an offset in determining taxable income. And most of these also specify additional exemptions or deductions for persons over 65.

Social Security Exemption. Of the 41 states with a broad-based income tax, 26 fully exempt Social Security. The others tax benefits if they are subject to the federal income tax. They are Colorado, Connecticut, Iowa, Kansas, Minnesota, Missouri, Montana, Nebraska, New Mexico, North Dakota, Rhode Island, Utah, Vermont, West Virginia, and Wisconsin.

Public Pension Exemption. Because of legal challenges in the late 1980s and early 1990s, pensions paid by federal, state, and local governments are now treated identically in most states. For example, a state-government pension cannot be taxed more favorably than a federal-government pension. Eleven states now fully exempt public pensions.

Private Pension Exemption. States typically exempt only defined-benefit (qualified) plans, that is, pensions that provide a specific amount to a retired employee based on years of employment and compensation received. Aside from full exemptions in Mississippi, New Hampshire, Pennsylvania, and Tennessee, states tend to treat private employer pensions less favorably than public pensions.

As indicated in the following table, "State Tax Exclusion of Pension Income," some states have two exemption levels, which are based on factors such as age or disability.

State Tax Exclusion of Pension Income

STATE*	PRIVATE	STATE/LOCAL	FEDERAL/CIVILIAN	MILITARY
Alabama	State Calculation	Most exempt	Exempt	Exempt
Arizona	None	$2,500	$2,500	$2,500
Arkansas	$6,000	$6,000	$6,000	$6,000
California	None	None	None	None
Colorado	$20,000/$24,000	$20,000/$24,000	$20,000/$24,000	$20,000/$24,000
Connecticut	None	None	None	None
Delaware	$2,000/$12,500	$2,000/$12,500	$2,000/$12,500	$2,000/$12,500
District of Columbia	None	$3,000	$3,000	$3,000
Georgia	$15,000	$15,000	$15,000	$15,000
Hawaii	State Calculation	Exempt	Exempt	Exempt
Idaho	None	$23,268/$34,902	$23,268/$34,902	$23,268/$34,902
Illinois	State Calculation	Exempt	Exempt	Exempt

State Tax Exclusion of Pension Income

STATE*	PRIVATE	STATE/LOCAL	FEDERAL/CIVILIAN	MILITARY
Indiana	None/$5,250	None/$5,250	$2,000/$7,250	$2,000/$5,250
Iowa	$6,000	$6,000	$6,000	$6,000
Kansas	None	Some exempt	Exempt	Exempt
Kentucky	$41,110	State Calculation	State Calculation	State Calculation
Louisiana	$6,000	$6,000/Exempt	Exempt	Exempt
Maine	$6,000	$6,000	$6,000	$6,000
Maryland	$21,500	$21,500	$21,500	$21,500
Massachusetts	None	Exempt	Exempt	Exempt
Michigan	$39,570	Exempt	Exempt	Exempt
Minnesota	None	None	None	None
Mississippi	Exempt	Exempt	Exempt	Exempt
Missouri	$6,000	$6,000	$6,000	$6,000
Montana	$3,600	$3,600	$3,600	$3,600
Nebraska	None	None	None	None
New Hampshire	Exempt	Exempt	Exempt	Exempt
New Jersey	$15,000	$15,000	$15,000	Exempt
New Mexico	None	None	None	None
New York	$20,000	Exempt	Exempt	Exempt
North Carolina	$2,000	$4,000/Exempt	$4,000	$4,000
North Dakota	None	None/$5,000	$200 credit	$200 credit
Ohio	$200 credit	$200 credit	$200 credit	$200 credit
Oklahoma	$7,500	$7,500	$7,500	$7,500
Oregon	9% credit	9% credit	9% credit/pre-1991 exempt	9% credit
Pennsylvania	Exempt	Exempt	Exempt	Exempt
Rhode Island	None	None	None	None
South Carolina	$3,000/$10,000	$3,000/$10,000	$3,000/$10,000	$3,000/$10,000
Tennessee	Exempt	Exempt	Exempt	Exempt
Utah	$4,800/$7,500	$4,800/$7,500	$4,800/$7,500	$4,800/$7,500
Vermont	None	None	None	None
Virginia	None	None	None	Most taxable
West Virginia	None	$2,000	$2,000	$22,000
Wisconsin	None	Pre-1964 Exempt	Pre-1964 Exempt	Exempt

* Alaska, Florida, Nevada, South Dakota, Texas, Washington, and Wyoming have no income tax.

Source: Wisconsin Legislative Fiscal Bureau

Housing

Consider this: In retirement, your shelter choices are greater than those of any other age group. Your job, dependent children, commute, and career no longer determine how and where you'll live.

When the children up and leave, your household shrinks and you needn't stay on in the ark of a family home. To simplify life, you can sell the house and lease a small apartment nearby; it's surprising how many older adults go this route. Because school quality is no longer an issue, you can buy into a trendy condo development created out of old warehouses in a downtown district. You can even hit the road full-time in a motor home and stay in touch by e-mail.

DISTANT SHELTER CHOICES

If you're thinking of moving to a place hundreds of miles distant, it helps to know what kinds of common shelter choices are available. Because most of us eventually end up buying a single-family home, your first issue to consider is what the average homeowner costs are that you'll encounter there.

Single Houses

If you walk through the front door of the typical American home, you'll find yourself in a structure that was built in 1979 and has a single-level, 1,950-square-foot floor plan enclosing three bedrooms, two full baths, living room, dining room, and a complete kitchen; no basement; and an insulated attic and storm windows to conserve the heat from its gas-fired, warm-air furnace. This house is kept cool during hot spells by a central air-conditioning unit. It is also connected to city water and sewerage lines.

So much for national composites. Among the 70 million single houses in the United States (and particularly among the newer suburban homes), a buyer can choose from many building styles—Cape Cods and Queen Annes; mountain A-frames; cabins of peeled pine log; desert adobes; Greek revivals; American and Dutch colonials; Puget Sounds; catslides; exotic glass solaria; futuristic earth berms; Victorian revivals; plantation cottages; and the ever-present split-levels, ranch ramblers, and California bungalows.

In retirement places, the proportion of single homes you'll actually find among all the other options—apartments, condominiums, and mobile homes—varies considerably. So expensive is raw land in the Hamptons at the eastern end of Long Island, New York, and on Martha's Vineyard offshore of Cape Cod, Massachusetts, that single houses crowd out mobile homes and apartments. But elsewhere—southern college towns, for instance, or low-cost spots in the desert southwest—life in apartments and in mobile home parks is much more common.

Condominiums

"Condominium" was nothing more than an obscure Latin word before a new legal concept for owning real estate was imported from Puerto Rico to the U.S. mainland in 1960. Under the arrangement, you could own outright an apartment, townhouse, or single house in a multiple-unit development. You could also sell, lease, bequeath, and furnish that legally described cube of air space independent of other unit owners.

Moreover, you owned the elevators, heating plant, streets, parking spaces, garden landscaping, tennis courts, swimming pool, lights, and walkways in common with the rest of the development's residents.

Throughout the years, condominiums were heavily promoted to either "newlywed or nearly dead" buyers, as some brokers called them. Indeed, young couples and singles making their way out of the rental market and retired couples who wanted to unload a large house for a smaller one were major reasons for the number of condominium units growing from zero in 1960 to more than 4 million today.

If you've been reluctantly tearing rental payments from your checkbook and are weighing the purchase of a home for the first time, you might consider a condominium as a compromise between apartment living and the tax advantages of owning a single-family home. With a condominium, you have freedom from house and yard maintenance, a ready-made social life, and common recreation facilities. You also receive the tax advantages of ownership, often at a lower cost than buying a house would entail.

On the minus side, condo owners complain of ticky-tacky construction, parking problems, thin party walls, and living cheek by jowl with renters or other unfamiliar neighbors.

Condos can be high-rise (vertical) or low-rise (horizontal), depending on local zoning laws and available land. You'll find residential condominiums in places where land is scarce and where the prices of single detached homes are out of reach for people looking to buy a first home. This form of real estate covers the slopes around Silverthorne–Breckenridge, a ski area in the Colorado Rockies. In several of Florida's resort-and-vacation areas, there is an oversupply of investor-owned condominiums that can be rented at reasonable rates.

Mobile Homes

The major advantage of a mobile home is price. It takes a typical contractor's crew several months to build a typical three-bedroom house, whereas a mobile home takes not much more than 100 hours. In 2007, when the average cost of building a conventional home was $95 per square foot, exclusive of land, the cost of manufacturing a mobile home was $36 per square foot.

This doesn't mean that mobile homes lack quality. Since World War II, when many defense workers were housed in 300-square-foot sheet-metal boxes with ersatz cooking facilities and no plumbing, mobile homes have gradually shaken their reputation for tackiness. Mobile homes now are at least 14 feet wide. Seventy-foot-long double-wides can enclose three bedrooms, two baths, a living room, dining room, kitchen, and closets. New mobile homes are usually sold complete; appliances, furniture, draperies, lamps, and carpeting are all included in the price, as are built-in plumbing, heating, air-conditioning, and electrical systems.

The value of a mobile home, however, may depreciate in many areas where conventional homes increase in value. Arbitrary evictions from mobile home parks are not uncommon in many states, nor are restrictive zoning laws that confine this kind of housing to the urban/rural fringe.

The only time the mobile home is actually mobile is when it leaves the factory and is towed by a truck in one or more sections to a concrete foundation, whether on the owner's land or at one of 24,000 trailer parks in the country. When it arrives, the wheels, axle, and towing tongue are removed, and all that still resembles a trailer is the I-beamed chassis, which quickly becomes hidden structural reinforcement once the unit is winched onto the foundation and plumbed. After that, the mobile home becomes more or less permanent; no more than 3 percent of them are ever moved again.

Half of all new mobile homes are sold in just eight states: California, Florida, Georgia, Louisiana, North Carolina, Oklahoma, South Carolina, and Texas. You're more likely to find permissive zoning regulations and a wider choice of mobile home parks in smaller metro areas of the Sun Belt. You're less likely to find them in large metro areas where the high cost of residential land offsets any economic benefits of owning a mobile home.

Apartments

Looking for digs close to downtown, with reasonable rent, tenants similar to yourself, a pleasant landlord, off-street parking, ambience, and all the other items on your checklist, might turn out to be a quest that stops when the lease is signed but starts up again on the lease's anniversary. Still, for younger newcomers, renting is the main style of housing tenure. And for older newcomers with invested equity from their former home, renting is recommended until they become familiar with the local real estate market.

As a renter you remain flexible, since you need not stay in an apartment beyond the term of the lease

should your income slump or your inclinations take you to another part of the country. You don't need to come up with a down payment; taxes, insurance, repairs, and sometimes utilities are the landlord's headaches.

But you also miss out on such ownership benefits as growing equity, property appreciation, and tax deductions for mortgage interest, while being subject to condo conversion or arbitrary rent hikes in times of low vacancy rates.

Many of us tend to think that apartments are available only in blocks of large, high-rise tower complexes near a large metro area's central business district. In fact, only 1 out of 50 apartments is in a building of 13 stories or more, and only 1 out of 10 is in a building higher than 3 stories. Moreover, apartments make up as large a part of occupied housing in smaller areas dominated by state universities as they do in locations that are much larger in population.

BUYING THAT SINGLE-FAMILY HOME

Despite the growing number of options in housing, the single-family home is still the most common (81 percent of owner-occupied housing units are single-family homes) and the most popular (in a recent poll, 81 percent of current owners and 70 percent of renters expecting to move within 5 years said they planned to buy a detached home). In fact, two-thirds of us eventually *do* buy a single-family home.

Where are the least expensive markets for prospective buyers? You might guess that a consequence of the country's west-by-south population shift would be dramatically inflated home prices in the same direction. But some of the highest prices estimated for 2007 are found in places where homes have always been expensive: Middle Cape Cod, Massachusetts; Maui, Hawaii; Connecticut's Litchfield Hills or the eastern edge of Long Island, both areas convenient to New York City; and, since 1975, most of California.

Will we never again see the 55 percent home price rises seen in this country over the past 5 years? Never say never. During one decade, the 1970s, prices went up 178 percent. At the start of 2007, according to the National Association of Realtors, an existing single house had a median price of $220,000. This does not mean that a house can't be found for half that much. It can, in areas of Alabama, Indiana, Missouri, and Texas.

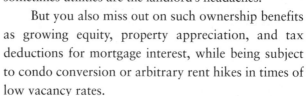

HOUSING IN BRIEF

Statistics show that many lifelong renters, if they move to a new destination after they retire, eventually buy the first house they've ever owned. Statistics also show that many lifelong owners rent in the new hometown for as long as it takes to become the equal of local sellers in their knowledge and power over the real estate market.

Most of us eventually buy a home. An appreciating investment, acquired with leveraged financing, offering tax advantages, and serving as a roof over one's head, is hard to beat. But in lawyer-speak, you'll want to come out whole.

Don't focus entirely on prices. Consider other things. Will the home appreciate? The best indicator of that is the quality of construction and long-term outlook for employment.

Next, make sure the home is not just affordable to you, but also affordable to local residents so that you needn't depend on a newcomer to buy your house.

Look for locations with a variety of owner- and renter-occupied housing styles. Housing variety implies turnover. At this point in your life, a condominium may be a great timesaver. You may want to rent for a while to rehearse your role in the new location. A local household may outgrow a rented apartment and buy your house—all of which is to the good.

EXPENSIVE NEIGHBORHOODS

Median home prices mark a point where half the homes are more expensive and half are less. Among places in *Retirement Places Rated,* the figure is $177,000. Here are locations where half the homes cost more than $400,000. In fact, the top quarter of homes in six of them top $1 million.

PLACE	MEDIAN PRICE
Carmel–Pebble Beach, CA	$1,595,000
Laguna Beach–Dana Point, CA	$1,545,000
East End Long Island, NY	$1,125,000
Santa Barbara, CA	$692,000
Jackson Hole, WY	$625,000
Maui, HI	$574,000
Key West, FL	$560,000
Morro Bay–Cambria, CA	$543,000
Sedona, AZ	$533,000
Martha's Vineyard, MA	$515,000
San Juan Islands, WA	$508,000
Placer County, CA	$505,000
Ketchum–Sun Valley, ID	$488,000
Grass Valley–Nevada City, CA	$486,000
Scottsdale, AZ	$464,000
Hilton Head Island, SC	$449,000
Park City, UT	$434,000
Silverthorne–Breckenridge, CO	$426,000
Williamsburg, VA	$418,000
Mendocino–Fort Bragg, CA	$402,000

Source: Places Rated Partners survey.

WHAT A DIFFERENCE AGE MAKES

Anyone watching the speed at which houses can be put up on pricey lots in suburbia or in cheap-jack developments near the industrial fringe might well agree with old-timers who have seen large, balloon-framed homes built with a good deal of craftsmanship. "They don't build them the way they used to," some of them might mutter.

No, they don't. Except for Victorian Revival houses, wraparound porches are rarely found. A porch is now merely a recessed space at the entrance of a house. The 10-foot interior ceilings common before World War II have been replaced with an 8-foot standard. The kind of formal stairway with well-turned balusters and waxed rails that Andy Hardy (played by Mickey Rooney in a series of 16 family movies in the late 1930s and early 1940s) used to slide down are no longer necessary—most new homes are built on a single level. Milled red oak fascias and moldings have become too expensive for common use; walls are envelopes of ⅜-inch gypsum board nailed to studs rather than the old "mud jobs" of plaster on lath; and solid six-panel doors have lost out to hollow-core flush doors of hemlock veneer.

On the other hand, copper and polyvinyl chloride water pipes have replaced galvanized iron plumbing; knob-and-tube wiring has surrendered to safer electrical circuitry; cast-iron radiators no longer interfere with furniture arrangement; pressure-treated wood has eliminated termite and dry-rot risks; and the seasonal problem of cellar flooding arises less often because there aren't many cellars being excavated. Indeed, as much as 20 percent of a new home's breathtaking price tag is due to vastly superior building materials, according to a Prudential Insurance Company study.

One useful indication of the quality of an area's housing stock is the median age of houses. Although an older house isn't necessarily on the verge of tumbling down, age can signal functional obsolescence and looming maintenance headaches. Clapboards do need scraping and repainting every 3 years, clogged sewer drains must be snaked, furnaces do wear out, and storm windows must be retrofitted.

JUDGING: HOUSING

Rating retirement places by prices, the lower the better, doesn't tell the entire housing story. Instead, *Retirement Places Rated* considers four factors and weights them the same.

Affordability. This factor captures how many times local personal income must be multiplied to meet local median house prices. The national median home price is $220,000, or almost six times the national per capita income of $36,300. In some retirement places it's a lot more, meaning that the market depends on affluent newcomers to keep prices high.

These places are ranked among the top 35 percent in Retirement Places Rated's *chapter on the economy and among the top 35 percent in housing affordability. In other words, they show promising signs of price appreciation.*

Appreciation Potential. This key factor is based on the 10-year forecast for job growth (see the earlier chapter on "The Economy"). Places that see healthy home price appreciation have expanding economies; it's as simple as that.

Quality. This factor is broadly determined by U.S. Census Bureau data on a typical home's age, number of bedrooms, total number of rooms, and price.

Variety. This important factor considers how closely the retirement place matches the nation in choices for apartment renting or for living in a home, condominium, or mobile home. Some retirement places are dominated by mobile home parks. Others have an oversupply of condominiums. Still others offer little choice to the newcomer but buying a home.

RANKINGS: HOUSING

Retirement Places Rated uses four equally weighted criteria to rank places for housing: (1) **affordability,** (2) **appreciation potential,** (3) **quality,** and (4) **variety.**

Places with tie scores get the same rank and are listed alphabetically.

Retirement Places from First to Last

RANK	PLACE	SCORE
1.	Madison, MS	100.0
2.	Conway, AR	99.4
3.	Georgetown, TX	98.9
4.	McAllen–Alamo, TX	98.4
5.	Fayetteville, AR	97.9

RANK	PLACE	SCORE
6.	St. Marys, GA	97.4
7.	Jackson Hole, WY	96.9
8.	Columbia, MO	96.4
9.	Brownsville, TX	95.9
	continued	

Retirement Places from First to Last (cont.)

Retirement Places Rated

RANK	PLACE	SCORE	RANK	PLACE	SCORE
10.	Wimberley, TX	95.4	77.	Marble Falls–Lake LBJ, TX	61.8
11.	Bay St. Louis–Pass Christian, MS	94.9	78.	Melbourne–Palm Bay, FL	61.3
12.	Lake Conroe, TX	94.4	79.	Eureka Springs, AR	60.8
13.	Myrtle Beach, SC	93.9	80.	Southern Berkshire County, MA	60.3
14.	Oxford, MS	93.4	81.	Palm Springs–Coachella Valley, CA	59.7
15.	Charleston, SC	92.9	82.	Wickenburg, AZ	59.2
16.	Madison, WI	92.4	83.	York Beaches, ME	58.7
17.	Fort Myers–Cape Coral, FL	91.9	84.	Lake Havasu City, AZ	58.2
18.	Palmer–Wasilla, AK	91.4	85.	Placer County, CA	57.7
19.	Iowa City, IA	90.9	86.	Petoskey–Harbor Springs, MI	57.2
20.	St. George–Zion, UT	90.4	87.	Rockport–Aransas Pass, TX	56.7
21.	Naples, FL	89.9	88.	Lake of the Ozarks, MO	56.2
22.	Fort Collins–Loveland, CO	89.4	89.	Tucson, AZ	55.7
23.	Chapel Hill–Carrboro, NC	88.9	90.	Cedar Creek Lake, TX	55.2
24.	New Bern, NC	88.4	91.	San Juan Islands, WA	54.7
25.	Panama City, FL	87.9	92.	Pendleton District, SC	54.2
26.	Crossville, TN	87.4	93.	Fredericksburg–Spotsylvania, VA	53.7
27.	Branson, MO	86.9	94.	Asheville, NC	52.7
28.	Savannah, GA	86.4	94.	Port St. Lucie, FL	52.7
29.	Kissimmee–St. Cloud, FL	85.9	96.	Port Charlotte, FL	52.2
30.	Bradenton, FL	85.4	97.	East Stroudsburg, PA	51.2
31.	Flagstaff, AZ	84.9	97.	Monadnock Region, NH	51.2
32.	Fairhope–Gulf Shores, AL	84.4	99.	St. Augustine, FL	50.7
33.	Charlottesville, VA	83.9	100.	Morro Bay–Cambria, CA	50.2
34.	Rio Rancho, NM	83.4	101.	Boerne, TX	49.7
35.	Pahrump Valley, NV	82.9	102.	Scottsdale, AZ	49.2
36.	Dare Outer Banks, NC	82.4	103.	Litchfield Hills, CT	48.7
37.	Cedar City, UT	81.9	104.	Edenton, NC	48.2
38.	Athens, GA	81.4	105.	Victorville–Apple Valley, CA	47.7
39.	Traverse City, MI	80.9	106.	Boone–Blowing Rock, NC	47.2
40.	Park City, UT	80.4	107.	State College, PA	46.7
41.	Summerville, SC	79.8	108.	Camden, ME	46.2
42.	Bozeman, MT	79.3	109.	Leesburg–Mount Dora, FL	45.7
43.	Hanover, NH	78.8	110.	Alpine–Big Bend, TX	45.2
44.	New Braunfels, TX	78.3	111.	St. Jay–Northeast Kingdom, VT	44.7
45.	Coeur d'Alene, ID	77.8	112.	Silverthorne–Breckenridge, CO	44.2
46.	Burlington, VT	76.8	113.	Brevard, NC	43.7
46.	Las Cruces, NM	76.8	114.	Oakhurst–Coarsegold, CA	43.2
48.	Lakeland–Winter Haven, FL	76.3	115.	Williamsburg, VA	42.2
49.	Carson City–Carson Valley, NV	75.8	115.	Woodstock, VT	42.2
50.	Bend, OR	75.3	117.	Northampton–Amherst, MA	41.7
51.	Gainesville, FL	74.8	118.	Pagosa Springs, CO	41.2
52.	Vero Beach, FL	74.3	119.	Key West, FL	40.7
53.	Pensacola, FL	73.8	120.	Hendersonville–East Flat Rock, NC	39.6
54.	Murray–Kentucky Lake, KY	72.8	120.	Sebring–Avon Park, FL	39.6
54.	Yuma, AZ	72.8	122.	Bellingham, WA	39.1
56.	Hattiesburg, MS	72.3	123.	Anacortes, WA	38.6
57.	Grand Junction, CO	71.8	124.	Hot Springs, AR	38.1
58.	Beaufort–Atlantic Beach, NC	71.3	125.	McCall, ID	37.6
59.	Maryville, TN	70.8	126.	Bisbee, AZ	37.1
60.	Thomasville, GA	70.3	127.	Sullivan County, NY	36.6
61.	Western St. Tammany Parish, LA	69.8	128.	Lake Placid, NY	36.1
62.	Dahlonega, GA	69.3	129.	Cottonwood–Verde Valley, AZ	35.6
63.	Henderson, NV	68.8	130.	Port Townsend, WA	35.1
64.	Loudoun County, VA	68.3	131.	Norfork Lake, AR	34.6
65.	Durango, CO	67.3	132.	Berkeley Springs, WV	34.1
65.	Southport–Brunswick Islands, NC	67.3	133.	Natchitoches, LA	33.6
67.	Ketchum–Sun Valley, ID	66.8	134.	Prescott–Prescott Valley, AZ	33.1
68.	Medford–Ashland, OR	66.3	135.	Hilton Head Island, SC	32.6
69.	Kingman, AZ	65.8	136.	Wenatchee, WA	32.1
70.	St. Simons–Jekyll Islands, GA	65.3	137.	Lake of the Cherokees, OK	31.6
71.	Kalispell–Flathead Valley, MT	64.8	138.	Roswell, NM	31.1
72.	Sarasota, FL	64.3	139.	Fairplay, CO	30.1
73.	Southern Pines–Pinehurst, NC	63.8	139.	Easton–St. Michaels, MD	30.1
74.	Kerrville, TX	63.3	141.	Eugene, OR	29.6
75.	Santa Fe, NM	62.8	142.	Door Peninsula, WI	29.1
76.	Ocala, FL	62.3	143.	Carmel–Pebble Beach, CA	28.6

Retirement Places from First to Last

RANK	PLACE	SCORE
144.	Cortez, CO	28.1
145.	Maui, HI	27.6
146.	Sedona, AZ	27.1
147.	Lower Cape May, NJ	26.6
148.	Ruidoso, NM	26.1
149.	Santa Barbara, CA	25.6
150.	Whidbey Island, WA	25.1
151.	Middle Cape Cod, MA	24.6
152.	Annapolis, MD	24.1
153.	Bar Harbor, ME	23.6
154.	Rabun County, GA	23.1
155.	Largo, FL	22.6
156.	Paradise–Magalia, CA	22.1
157.	Payson, AZ	21.6
158.	Silver City, NM	21.1
159.	Rehoboth Bay–Indian River Bay, DE	20.6
160.	Tryon, NC	20.1
161.	Montrose, CO	19.5
162.	Alamogordo, NM	19.0
163.	Apalachicola, FL	18.5
164.	Grass Valley–Nevada City, CA	18.0
165.	Waynesville, NC	17.5
166.	Brunswick, ME	17.0
167.	Martha's Vineyard, MA	16.5
168.	Brown County, IN	16.0
169.	Fredericksburg, TX	15.5
170.	Pike County, PA	15.0
171.	Driggs, ID	14.5
172.	Las Vegas, NM	14.0

RANK	PLACE	SCORE
173.	Ocean City, MD	13.5
174.	Grants Pass, OR	12.5
174.	Sandpoint–Lake Pend Oreille, ID	12.5
176.	Hamilton–Bitterroot Valley, MT	11.5
176.	Toms River–Barnegat Bay, NJ	11.5
178.	Beaufort, SC	11.0
179.	Newport–Lincoln City, OR	10.5
180.	Delta County, CO	10.0
181.	Hampshire County, WV	9.5
182.	Eagle River–Woodruff, WI	9.0
183.	Taos, NM	8.5
184.	Smith Mountain Lake, VA	8.0
185.	Leelanau Peninsula, MI	7.5
186.	Charles Town–Shepherdstown, WV	6.5
186.	Port Angeles–Sequim, WA	6.5
188.	The Big Island, HI	6.0
189.	Chestertown, MD	5.5
190.	Front Royal, VA	5.0
191.	Amador County, CA	4.5
192.	Nelson County, VA	4.0
193.	Sonora–Twain Harte, CA	3.5
194.	Laguna Beach–Dana Point, CA	3.0
195.	Mendocino–Fort Bragg, CA	2.5
196.	Long Beach Peninsula, WA	2.0
197.	Chewelah, WA	1.5
198.	East End Long Island, NY	1.0
199.	Northern Neck, VA	0.5
200.	Mariposa, CA	0.0

PLACE PROFILES: HOUSING

The following snapshots of 200 housing markets begin with **Shelter Choices**—the local mix of houses, condominiums, apartments, and mobile homes—expressed as percents of all occupied housing. Houses are detached, single structures. Condominiums are owner-occupied housing in multiunit structures. Apartments are renter-occupied housing in structures of five units or more. Mobile homes are factory-manufactured dwelling units transported to a site and semipermanently attached. Percentages don't add up to 100 because occupied duplexes, triplexes, fourplexes, boats, and RVs are excluded. Figures for condominiums and apartments may be slightly understated.

The next heading, **House Prices,** shows estimated prices for smaller and older *Starter Homes,* which are in the bottom quarter of local home prices, and larger and newer *Elite Homes,* which are in the upper quarter.

The next heading, **Move-Up Home for Sale,** considers selected features in an invented real estate ad for a local median-priced three-bedroom, two-bath home.

Age is the area's median age subtracted from 2007; **Main Utility** refers to primary heating source common in the area; a large majority of homes feature a **Garage;** and **Price** is the local median price (that is, half the homes are more expensive and half are less expensive).

Figures are derived from the National Association of Realtors, fourth-quarter 2006 house prices report (national median price); Places Rated Partners survey, winter 2007; U.S. Department of Commerce, U.S. Census Bureau, 2000 Census and 2005 American Community Survey (home prices and median features) and Residential Construction Branch, *Characteristics of New Housing;* U.S. Department of Housing and Urban Development, Office of Federal Housing Enterprise Oversight, fourth-quarter 2006 Home Price Index (price inflation).

A star (★) preceding a place's name indicates it is one of the top 30 places for housing.

Housing

205

| PLACE | Shelter Choices | | | | House Prices | | Move-Up Home for Sale | | | | |
	HOUSES	CONDOS	APARTMENTS	MOBILE HOMES	STARTERS	ELITE	AGE	MAIN UTILITY	GARAGE	PRICE	RANK
Alamogordo, NM	64%	0%	4%	27%	$92,000	$201,000	26	gas	■	$151,200	162
Alpine–Big Bend, TX	62%	0%	7%	24%	$56,000	$152,000	31	gas	■	$105,600	110
Amador County, CA	84%	0%	4%	9%	$291,000	$567,000	26	gas	■	$435,600	191
Anacortes, WA	72%	0%	9%	12%	$237,000	$475,000	28	gas	■	$357,600	123
Annapolis, MD	82%	3%	11%	2%	$275,000	$578,000	28	electric	■	$418,800	152
Apalachicola, FL	63%	0%	0%	28%	$144,000	$498,000	24	electric		$292,800	163
Asheville, NC	66%	2%	9%	19%	$114,000	$267,000	29	electric	■	$195,600	94
Athens, GA	50%	1%	26%	6%	$113,000	$248,000	27	electric	■	$183,600	38
Bar Harbor, ME	76%	0%	5%	12%	$140,000	$334,000	33	oil heat	■	$228,000	153
★Bay St. Louis–Pass Christian, MS	68%	1%	11%	14%	$88,000	$212,000	24	electric	■	$151,200	11
Beaufort, SC	83%	4%	9%	4%	$178,000	$583,000	39	electric		$360,000	178
Beaufort–Atlantic Beach, NC	68%	2%	3%	22%	$118,000	$297,000	20	electric	■	$202,800	58
Bellingham, WA	66%	3%	15%	10%	$216,000	$423,000	26	gas	■	$325,200	122
Bend, OR	72%	0%	7%	15%	$201,000	$445,000	20	electric	■	$316,800	50
Berkeley Springs, WV	77%	0%	0%	18%	$96,000	$199,000	25	electric	■	$154,800	132
The Big Island, HI	84%	2%	9%	0%	$234,000	$588,000	23	gas	■	$423,600	188
Bisbee, AZ	64%	0%	8%	22%	$136,000	$299,000	26	gas	■	$222,000	126
Boerne, TX	79%	0%	3%	14%	$126,000	$311,000	18	electric	■	$220,800	101
Boone–Blowing Rock, NC	65%	2%	15%	12%	$128,000	$309,000	24	oil heat	■	$226,800	106
Bozeman, MT	63%	3%	9%	13%	$189,000	$377,000	24	gas	■	$289,200	42
★Bradenton, FL	59%	8%	10%	16%	$197,000	$460,000	24	electric	■	$332,400	30
★Branson, MO	57%	3%	10%	24%	$99,000	$228,000	20	electric	■	$158,400	27
Brevard, NC	75%	0%	0%	18%	$115,000	$271,000	25	electric	■	$199,200	113
Brown County, IN	86%	0%	0%	11%	$112,000	$224,000	28	LP gas	■	$169,200	168
★Brownsville, TX	71%	2%	9%	11%	$45,000	$125,000	22	electric	■	$84,000	9
Brunswick, ME	67%	5%	14%	14%	$178,000	$366,000	39	oil heat	■	$276,000	166
Burlington, VT	62%	6%	13%	5%	$199,000	$369,000	31	oil heat	■	$297,600	46
Camden, ME	75%	0%	6%	9%	$145,000	$339,000	43	oil heat	■	$236,400	108
Carmel–Pebble Beach, CA	69%	2%	17%	4%	$1,152,000	$2,517,000	55	gas	■	$1,914,000	143
Carson City–Carson Valley, NV	70%	0%	11%	12%	$305,000	$656,000	20	gas	■	$474,000	49
Cedar City, UT	71%	0%	11%	9%	$131,000	$251,000	20	gas	■	$196,800	37
Cedar Creek Lake, TX	62%	0%	3%	32%	$63,000	$178,000	23	electric	■	$118,800	90
★Chapel Hill–Carrboro, NC	59%	2%	22%	10%	$162,000	$423,000	24	electric	■	$291,600	23
★Charleston, SC	64%	2%	15%	9%	$115,000	$339,000	28	electric	■	$219,600	15
Charles Town–Shepherdstown, WV	78%	0%	8%	11%	$125,000	$275,000	26	electric	■	$201,600	186
Charlottesville, VA	55%	3%	25%	1%	$170,000	$390,000	42	gas	■	$282,000	33
Chestertown, MD	81%	0%	9%	4%	$186,000	$430,000	36	oil heat	■	$303,600	189
Chewelah, WA	70%	0%	4%	23%	$144,000	$300,000	27	gas	■	$234,000	197
Coeur d'Alene, ID	73%	1%	7%	13%	$162,000	$323,000	22	gas	■	$243,600	45
★Columbia, MO	60%	2%	15%	8%	$114,000	$247,000	25	gas	■	$181,200	8
★Conway, AR	66%	0%	8%	18%	$99,000	$206,000	18	electric	■	$154,800	2
Cortez, CO	65%	0%	3%	28%	$107,000	$238,000	26	gas	■	$175,200	144
Cottonwood–Verde Valley, AZ	75%	0%	1%	24%	$204,000	$475,000	15	gas	■	$348,000	129
★Crossville, TN	73%	0%	2%	19%	$87,000	$217,000	19	gas	■	$148,800	26
Dahlonega, GA	69%	0%	2%	24%	$116,000	$248,000	16	LP gas	■	$183,600	62
Dare Outer Banks, NC	81%	0%	2%	11%	$135,000	$308,000	17	electric	■	$224,400	36
Delta County, CO	75%	0%	0%	19%	$120,000	$243,000	30	gas	■	$186,000	180
Door Peninsula, WI	81%	0%	5%	8%	$119,000	$316,000	32	gas	■	$207,600	142
Driggs, ID	81%	0%	0%	14%	$170,000	$342,000	16	gas	■	$270,000	171
Durango, CO	68%	1%	7%	18%	$188,000	$398,000	23	gas	■	$296,400	65
Eagle River–Woodruff, WI	88%	0%	3%	5%	$120,000	$306,000	29	gas	■	$206,400	182
East End Long Island, NY	97%	0%	2%	0%	$639,000	$2,113,000	57	oil heat	■	$1,350,000	198
Easton–St. Michaels, MD	82%	0%	6%	3%	$224,000	$664,000	30	electric	■	$392,400	139
East Stroudsburg, PA	86%	1%	3%	5%	$158,000	$308,000	22	oil heat	■	$249,600	97
Edenton, NC	69%	0%	3%	20%	$83,000	$212,000	29	LP gas	■	$139,200	104
Eugene, OR	67%	1%	14%	11%	$197,000	$380,000	31	electric	■	$300,000	141
Eureka Springs, AR	73%	0%	0%	17%	$82,000	$200,000	24	gas	■	$140,400	79
Fairhope–Gulf Shores, AL	71%	2%	4%	19%	$120,000	$290,000	17	electric	■	$204,000	32
Fairplay, CO	93%	0%	0%	4%	$179,000	$348,000	18	LP gas	■	$277,200	139
★Fayetteville, AR	67%	1%	15%	8%	$98,000	$209,000	23	gas	■	$150,000	5
Flagstaff, AZ	61%	0%	14%	17%	$207,000	$478,000	17	gas	■	$358,800	31
★Fort Collins–Loveland, CO	72%	3%	12%	6%	$186,000	$361,000	24	gas	■	$277,200	22
★Fort Myers–Cape Coral, FL	62%	10%	9%	13%	$187,000	$447,000	20	electric	■	$314,400	17
Fredericksburg, TX	78%	0%	4%	15%	$100,000	$244,000	27	gas	■	$168,000	169
Fredericksburg–Spotsylvania, VA	50%	0%	40%	1%	$184,000	$439,000	35	electric	■	$321,600	93
Front Royal, VA	86%	0%	5%	4%	$170,000	$320,000	29	electric	■	$258,000	190

★ = in top 30 places for housing

	Shelter Choices				House Prices		Move-Up Home for Sale				
PLACE	HOUSES	CONDOS	APARTMENTS	MOBILE HOMES	STARTERS	ELITE	AGE	MAIN UTILITY	GARAGE	PRICE	RANK
Gainesville, FL	53%	2%	24%	11%	$158,000	$383,000	23	electric	■	$271,200	51
★ Georgetown, TX	79%	0%	11%	5%	$127,000	$251,000	15	gas	■	$199,200	3
Grand Junction, CO	72%	2%	8%	12%	$122,000	$251,000	26	gas	■	$192,000	57
Grants Pass, OR	69%	0%	4%	20%	$172,000	$352,000	27	electric	■	$273,600	174
Grass Valley-Nevada City, CA	83%	0%	5%	8%	$370,000	$767,000	23	LP gas	■	$583,200	164
Hamilton-Bitterroot Valley, MT	75%	0%	3%	16%	$167,000	$342,000	24	gas	■	$270,000	176
Hampshire County, WV	72%	0%	3%	23%	$82,000	$168,000	24	electric	■	$135,600	181
Hanover, NH	67%	4%	11%	9%	$143,000	$315,000	32	oil heat	■	$230,400	43
Hattiesburg, MS	64%	0%	16%	10%	$61,000	$155,000	30	electric	■	$112,800	56
Henderson, NV	78%	2%	16%	3%	$277,000	$497,000	13	gas	■	$406,800	63
Hendersonville-East Flat Rock, NC	72%	2%	2%	19%	$126,000	$275,000	23	electric	■	$212,400	120
Hilton Head Island, SC	74%	12%	9%	5%	$322,000	$768,000	22	electric	■	$538,800	135
Hot Springs, AR	70%	2%	7%	16%	$79,000	$222,000	27	gas	■	$142,800	124
★ Iowa City, IA	56%	3%	26%	7%	$130,000	$270,000	28	gas	■	$205,200	19
★ Jackson Hole, WY	66%	0%	12%	6%	$410,000	$1,357,000	20	electric	■	$750,000	7
Kalispell-Flathead Valley, MT	71%	0%	5%	17%	$157,000	$336,000	26	gas	■	$254,400	71
Kerrville, TX	68%	0%	7%	20%	$87,000	$217,000	24	electric	■	$152,400	74
Ketchum-Sun Valley, ID	74%	5%	6%	7%	$289,000	$1,015,000	23	gas	■	$585,600	67
Key West, FL	57%	6%	8%	18%	$383,000	$959,000	26	electric	■	$672,000	119
Kingman, AZ	83%	0%	9%	7%	$148,000	$299,000	13	electric	■	$220,800	69
★ Kissimmee-St. Cloud, FL	65%	1%	13%	14%	$188,000	$355,000	16	electric	■	$276,000	29
Laguna Beach-Dana Point, CA	81%	5%	13%	2%	$1,084,000	$2,505,000	46	gas	■	$1,854,000	194
★ Lake Conroe, TX	69%	0%	8%	20%	$101,000	$266,000	17	electric	■	$181,200	12
Lake Havasu City, AZ	90%	3%	5%	3%	$168,000	$340,000	13	electric	■	$248,400	84
Lakeland-Winter Haven, FL	61%	2%	7%	24%	$138,000	$315,000	23	electric	■	$231,600	48
Lake of the Cherokees, OK	64%	0%	1%	31%	$71,000	$206,000	24	LP gas	■	$129,600	137
Lake of the Ozarks, MO	76%	4%	2%	14%	$116,000	$290,000	20	electric	■	$210,000	88
Lake Placid, NY	74%	0%	5%	10%	$107,000	$223,000	48	oil heat	■	$170,400	128
Largo, FL	46%	9%	19%	26%	$165,000	$392,000	30	electric	■	$268,800	155
Las Cruces, NM	57%	1%	8%	27%	$105,000	$248,000	22	gas	■	$174,000	46
Las Vegas, NM	59%	0%	3%	32%	$107,000	$239,000	28	LP gas	■	$172,800	172
Leelanau Peninsula, MI	89%	0%	1%	6%	$138,000	$392,000	27	gas	■	$244,800	185
Leesburg-Mount Dora, FL	63%	1%	5%	27%	$172,000	$386,000	19	electric	■	$279,600	109
Litchfield Hills, CT	76%	6%	7%	1%	$207,000	$442,000	42	oil heat	■	$327,600	103
Long Beach Peninsula, WA	68%	1%	5%	23%	$129,000	$302,000	31	electric	■	$214,800	196
Loudoun County, VA	85%	4%	10%	0%	$307,000	$643,000	13	gas	■	$475,200	64
Lower Cape May, NJ	73%	8%	6%	3%	$188,000	$461,000	33	gas	■	$330,000	147
★ Madison, MS	72%	0%	13%	7%	$106,000	$289,000	17	gas	■	$192,000	1
★ Madison, WI	60%	3%	26%	1%	$171,000	$312,000	31	gas	■	$252,000	16
Marble Falls-Lake LBJ, TX	71%	0%	2%	21%	$81,000	$229,000	24	electric	■	$147,600	77
Mariposa, CA	69%	0%	4%	24%	$265,000	$484,000	25	LP gas	■	$402,000	200
Martha's Vineyard, MA	91%	0%	0%	0%	$367,000	$877,000	26	oil heat	■	$618,000	167
Maryville, TN	75%	1%	7%	14%	$105,000	$225,000	25	electric	■	$169,200	59
Maui, HI	75%	8%	13%	0%	$426,000	$919,000	23	electric	■	$688,800	145
★ McAllen-Alamo, TX	71%	1%	7%	16%	$43,000	$121,000	18	electric	■	$82,800	4
McCall, ID	78%	0%	0%	15%	$170,000	$376,000	23	gas	■	$285,600	125
Medford-Ashland, OR	67%	1%	9%	15%	$190,000	$390,000	28	electric	■	$297,600	68
Melbourne-Palm Bay, FL	70%	6%	11%	9%	$165,000	$375,000	22	electric	■	$262,800	78
Mendocino-Fort Bragg, CA	72%	0%	8%	13%	$305,000	$661,000	31	gas	■	$482,400	195
Middle Cape Cod, MA	86%	4%	5%	0%	$235,000	$513,000	29	oil heat	■	$363,600	151
Monadnock Region, NH	69%	0%	11%	8%	$148,000	$278,000	41	oil heat	■	$222,000	97
Montrose, CO	66%	0%	5%	24%	$126,000	$240,000	26	gas	■	$195,600	161
Morro Bay-Cambria, CA	71%	1%	10%	10%	$401,000	$872,000	26	gas	■	$651,600	100
Murray-Kentucky Lake, KY	67%	0%	6%	15%	$79,000	$176,000	30	electric	■	$130,800	54
★ Myrtle Beach, SC	57%	6%	8%	23%	$122,000	$271,000	17	electric	■	$201,600	13
★ Naples, FL	54%	22%	11%	7%	$268,000	$765,000	16	electric	■	$468,000	21
Natchitoches, LA	67%	0%	7%	20%	$65,000	$178,000	29	gas	■	$124,800	133
Nelson County, VA	83%	0%	0%	14%	$126,000	$336,000	24	electric	■	$225,600	192
★ New Bern, NC	70%	0%	6%	17%	$96,000	$228,000	24	electric	■	$157,200	24
New Braunfels, TX	74%	0%	7%	16%	$106,000	$260,000	20	electric	■	$184,800	44
Newport-Lincoln City, OR	64%	1%	9%	18%	$190,000	$427,000	28	electric	■	$316,800	179
Norfork Lake, AR	75%	1%	3%	16%	$87,000	$189,000	25	electric	■	$140,400	131
Northampton-Amherst, MA	64%	6%	15%	1%	$192,000	$355,000	41	oil heat	■	$289,200	117
Northern Neck, VA	87%	0%	1%	10%	$150,000	$565,000	30	electric	■	$312,000	199
Oakhurst-Coarsegold, CA	80%	0%	7%	7%	$206,000	$427,000	23	gas	■	$337,200	114
Ocala, FL	64%	1%	4%	26%	$140,000	$305,000	19	electric	■	$226,800	76

continued

★ = in top 30 places for housing

PLACE	Shelter Choices				House Prices		Move-Up Home for Sale				
	HOUSES	CONDOS	APARTMENTS	MOBILE HOMES	STARTERS	ELITE	AGE	MAIN UTILITY	GARAGE	PRICE	RANK
Ocean City, MD	75%	6%	7%	7%	$191,000	$440,000	22	electric	■	$319,200	173
★ Oxford, MS	62%	1%	11%	17%	$85,000	$244,000	21	electric	■	$165,600	14
Pagosa Springs, CO	71%	0%	6%	19%	$165,000	$370,000	15	LP gas	■	$270,000	118
Pahrump Valley, NV	41%	0%	2%	51%	$198,000	$388,000	14	electric	■	$318,000	35
★ Palmer-Wasilla, AK	80%	0%	0%	7%	$152,000	$296,000	18	gas	■	$244,800	18
Palm Springs-Coachella Valley, CA	70%	1%	12%	12%	$246,000	$544,000	21	gas	■	$415,200	81
★ Panama City, FL	65%	2%	8%	17%	$159,000	$376,000	22	electric	■	$260,400	25
Paradise-Magalia, CA	63%	1%	11%	16%	$223,000	$462,000	29	gas	■	$368,400	156
Park City, UT	82%	3%	6%	4%	$302,000	$756,000	14	gas	■	$520,800	40
Payson, AZ	67%	1%	2%	26%	$133,000	$373,000	25	gas	■	$252,000	157
Pendleton District, SC	65%	0%	3%	27%	$95,000	$255,000	23	electric	■	$164,400	92
Pensacola, FL	73%	2%	9%	9%	$139,000	$329,000	27	electric	■	$238,800	53
Petoskey-Harbor Springs, MI	76%	0%	8%	10%	$112,000	$282,000	28	gas	■	$194,400	86
Pike County, PA	91%	0%	1%	5%	$148,000	$298,000	22	electric	■	$235,200	170
Placer County, CA	81%	1%	9%	5%	$383,000	$794,000	21	gas	■	$606,000	85
Port Angeles-Sequim, WA	72%	0%	7%	17%	$168,000	$366,000	27	electric	■	$278,400	186
Port Charlotte, FL	76%	6%	4%	12%	$165,000	$385,000	20	electric	■	$270,000	96
Port St. Lucie, FL	72%	7%	4%	11%	$156,000	$314,000	19	electric	■	$240,000	94
Port Townsend, WA	75%	0%	4%	15%	$215,000	$527,000	23	electric	■	$358,800	130
Prescott-Prescott Valley, AZ	75%	2%	12%	11%	$250,000	$550,000	15	gas	■	$410,400	134
Rabun County, GA	72%	0%	3%	22%	$105,000	$282,000	21	LP gas	■	$184,800	154
Rehoboth Bay-Indian River Bay, DE	69%	1%	4%	24%	$161,000	$371,000	22	electric	■	$271,200	159
Rio Rancho, NM	84%	0%	4%	10%	$144,000	$288,000	16	gas	■	$222,000	34
Rockport-Aransas Pass, TX	64%	2%	5%	24%	$67,000	$198,000	24	electric	■	$124,800	87
Roswell, NM	74%	0%	5%	17%	$71,000	$171,000	37	gas	■	$123,600	138
Ruidoso, NM	65%	0%	2%	27%	$120,000	$314,000	22	gas	■	$207,600	148
St. Augustine, FL	70%	4%	7%	14%	$245,000	$673,000	18	electric	■	$441,600	99
★ St. George-Zion, UT	77%	0%	7%	10%	$156,000	$314,000	13	gas	■	$246,000	20
St. Jay-Northeast Kingdom, VT	68%	0%	7%	11%	$118,000	$215,000	40	oil heat	■	$177,600	111
★ St. Marys, GA	65%	0%	8%	17%	$91,000	$190,000	15	electric	■	$140,400	6
St. Simons-Jekyll Islands, GA	69%	2%	10%	14%	$96,000	$315,000	27	electric	■	$188,400	70
Sandpoint-Lake Pend Oreille, ID	72%	0%	3%	20%	$148,000	$337,000	25	gas	■	$252,000	174
San Juan Islands, WA	80%	0%	0%	10%	$315,000	$951,000	20	electric	■	$609,600	91
Santa Barbara, CA	65%	3%	18%	6%	$372,000	$1,306,000	34	gas	■	$830,400	149
Santa Fe, NM	69%	1%	10%	16%	$223,000	$536,000	22	gas	■	$363,600	75
Sarasota, FL	70%	9%	8%	9%	$201,000	$505,000	24	electric	■	$339,600	72
★ Savannah, GA	69%	1%	13%	6%	$95,000	$236,000	32	gas	■	$156,000	28
Scottsdale, AZ	74%	5%	20%	1%	$305,000	$864,000	17	electric	■	$556,800	102
Sebring-Avon Park, FL	67%	2%	4%	22%	$125,000	$266,000	21	electric	■	$202,800	120
Sedona, AZ	77%	1%	5%	16%	$380,000	$989,000	17	gas	■	$639,600	146
Silver City, NM	64%	0%	2%	28%	$103,000	$236,000	29	gas	■	$169,200	158
Silverthorne-Breckenridge, CO	55%	14%	22%	4%	$316,000	$716,000	20	gas	■	$511,200	112
Smith Mountain Lake, VA	76%	0%	1%	19%	$179,000	$401,000	21	electric	■	$301,200	184
Sonora-Twain Harte, CA	75%	0%	5%	15%	$279,000	$546,000	26	LP gas	■	$424,800	193
Southern Berkshire County, MA	64%	7%	10%	3%	$149,000	$319,000	53	oil heat	■	$237,600	80
Southern Pines-Pinehurst, NC	73%	1%	3%	19%	$116,000	$307,000	22	electric	■	$213,600	73
Southport-Brunswick Islands, NC	63%	1%	1%	34%	$119,000	$292,000	17	electric	■	$207,600	65
State College, PA	62%	1%	23%	7%	$142,000	$305,000	32	electric	■	$229,200	107
Sullivan County, NY	69%	2%	8%	12%	$134,000	$274,000	39	oil heat	■	$205,200	127
Summerville, SC	68%	0%	8%	18%	$107,000	$242,000	21	electric	■	$176,400	41
Taos, NM	69%	0%	1%	25%	$142,000	$428,000	24	gas	■	$289,200	183
Thomasville, GA	67%	0%	5%	22%	$66,000	$189,000	28	electric	■	$126,000	60
Toms River-Barnegat Bay, NJ	86%	4%	6%	2%	$192,000	$398,000	28	gas	■	$314,400	176
Traverse City, MI	75%	0%	8%	11%	$122,000	$262,000	26	gas	■	$193,200	39
Tryon, NC	71%	2%	4%	20%	$102,000	$258,000	26	electric	■	$182,400	160
Tucson, AZ	63%	1%	18%	12%	$179,000	$405,000	25	gas	■	$289,200	89
Vero Beach, FL	68%	11%	8%	10%	$171,000	$457,000	20	electric	■	$289,200	52
Victorville-Apple Valley, CA	74%	1%	13%	6%	$224,000	$482,000	26	gas	■	$373,200	105
Waynesville, NC	74%	0%	2%	20%	$99,000	$233,000	30	oil heat	■	$162,000	165
Wenatchee, WA	69%	0%	8%	12%	$194,000	$400,000	31	electric	■	$309,600	136
Western St. Tammany Parish, LA	80%	1%	5%	11%	$128,000	$297,000	20	electric	■	$219,600	61
Whidbey Island, WA	76%	0%	7%	11%	$244,000	$497,000	24	electric	■	$364,800	150
Wickenburg, AZ	70%	2%	10%	18%	$211,000	$486,000	17	electric	■	$378,000	82

★ = in top 30 places for housing

	Shelter Choices				House Prices		Move-Up Home for Sale				
PLACE	HOUSES	CONDOS	APARTMENTS	MOBILE HOMES	STARTERS	ELITE	AGE	MAIN UTILITY	GARAGE	PRICE	RANK
Williamsburg, VA	57%	0%	27%	1%	$211,000	$762,000	32	gas	■	$501,600	115
★ Wimberley, TX	61%	0%	15%	15%	$119,000	$270,000	18	electric	■	$204,000	10
Woodstock, VT	70%	3%	7%	9%	$147,000	$307,000	37	oil heat	■	$232,800	115
York Beaches, ME	70%	4%	7%	8%	$165,000	$337,000	31	oil heat	■	$258,000	83
Yuma, AZ	53%	1%	9%	30%	$140,000	$286,000	20	electric	■	$214,800	54

ET CETERA: HOUSING

RESALE HOUSES & NEW HOUSES

If a single, detached home is your preferred form of housing, consider the pluses and minuses of resale houses versus new houses.

In most markets, resale homes are less expensive than equivalent new homes and are available in broader price ranges, with more architectural styles and locations in town. Resale homes usually have had minor defects, often unforeseen when the home was new, corrected by the seller.

But the age of the structure may signal problems. Repairs to the roof, floor coverings, appliances, and mechanical systems, which have depreciated over the years, may be necessary during the first 2 years you own the house. More important, as a neighborhood matures, some homes are maintained better than others and price disparities develop, which can affect your own home's value.

New houses in new, homogeneous neighborhoods portend more rapid appreciation in value over equivalent resale houses. You can have a new house covered by an extended homeowner warranty to protect you from major structural defects. If timing permits, you also can customize the house with options and extras and have the opportunity to select colors, appliance brands, and technological features such as heating and air-conditioning systems.

But the drawback to new homes in many communities is their 10 to 20 percent price premium over equivalent resale homes. Buying a new home is more complicated, too, since many more decisions have to be made about finish details and landscaping, all of which may mean frequent site visits to confer with the builder.

A GEOGRAPHY OF NEW HOME FEATURES

For decades, housing experts at the U.S. Census Bureau have followed regional trends in new single-family home construction. Here's a look at regional differences in certain home features.

Stories. The use of the word "story" to refer to flights of buildings may have originated with tiers of stained-glass or painted windows that described a special event. The common definition today is the space between the floor and the ceiling, roof, or the floor above, in the case of a multistory home. It has nothing to do with the height of a house; a house that appears from the outside to be two stories may actually be a single-story with a cathedral ceiling.

A generation ago, more than 75 percent of new houses were either one story or split level, that is, having floors on more than one level when the difference in floor levels was less than one story. Today, new split-level homes have disappeared from the American

THE DUAL NATURE OF DUPLEXES

If you're a first-time investor considering a home for rental income, a duplex (a house divided into apartments for two households) often is a better buy than a single house because of a better relation between price and income. A duplex may be bought for 8 to 10 times its annual rental income, whereas a single house may cost 13 to 15 times what it could bring in rent.

You may want to consider buying a duplex, renting one of the apartments, and occupying the other yourself. This is particularly attractive in college towns. From Charlottesville, Virginia, to Athens, Georgia, to Madison, Wisconsin, college towns have more rental properties and renters than other places. Aside from the income and depreciation you would have from the rental unit, if you live alone, congenial tenants—perhaps a graduate student and family—can watch the house should you want to do some traveling. You can also trade lower rent for maintenance help.

Housing

scene. Countrywide, 4 out of 10 new homes are built on a single level; the rest are two or more stories.

Construction and Exterior. In frame construction, the wood frame supports the floors and roof; in masonry construction, the exterior masonry wall serves as the support. Masonry construction using local stone has virtually disappeared in new houses. Concrete block construction, however, is a common technique in Arizona (40 percent of new homes have it) and Florida (85 percent), where the exterior is either spray-painted or stuccoed. Everywhere else, the majority of new houses are of frame construction.

Aluminum siding has disappeared thanks to tougher and more easily maintained vinyl siding. The exterior's biggest market is in the Midwest, where two-thirds of new homes have it, and in the Northeast, where 90 percent of new homes have it. The majority (86 percent) of all homes being built with brick exteriors in the United States are in the South. Stucco over cinder block is the predominant choice in the West, especially in California and Nevada.

Basements. The basement is an area of full-story height below the first floor that is not meant for year-round living. Only a third of new houses have basements because they are expensive to excavate. In six states, however, two out of three new houses come with some kind of basement, reflecting a pattern of locating the furnace below grade and a preference for extra living space. These states are Illinois, Iowa, Michigan, Minnesota, New York, and Pennsylvania.

Most new houses without basements either have a crawl space (an unfinished, accessible space below the first floor that is usually less than full-story height) or are simply resting on a concrete slab poured on the ground. In the United States, crawl spaces are preferred only in the Pacific Northwest and the Carolinas. Concrete slab footings support almost all new houses in the Sun Belt states of Arizona, Arkansas, Georgia, Louisiana, Mississippi, Oklahoma, and Texas.

Floor Area. New homes have gotten much larger over the past 25 years—from 1,660 square feet to 2,434 square feet on average, or enough difference to equal the size of a small condo. Interestingly, during that time, the floor area of new homes in the Northeast went from smallest to largest in the country. Why the expansion there and in other regions? More bedrooms, plus a bathroom for every bedroom.

Bedrooms. A bedroom is a finished room with closet specifically designed for sleeping. A den, a space in the attic, or a convertible basement aren't counted as bedrooms. A one-room house is considered to have one bedroom. The proportion of new homes with two bedrooms or less hasn't changed in decades, but the proportion of new homes with four bedrooms or more has almost doubled.

Bathrooms. Bathrooms are either full (a tub or shower stall, a sink, and a toilet) or half (just a sink and a toilet). A generation ago, one-quarter of new houses had one and a half baths or less. Today, one-quarter of new homes have three baths or more. In the West, the figure approaches one-third.

Fireplaces. Like dinettes and rumpus rooms, flueless imitation fireplaces are memories of the 1950s. Twenty-five years ago, most new homes had no working fireplace. Today, half of all new American homes have working fireplaces and chimneys. Unfortunately, many fireplaces in these new homes aren't used because of smoke problems caused by short chimneys. For a good fireplace draft, the chimney cap should be at least 20 feet above the hearth.

Homes with two fireplaces can be found more frequently in the northern timber states of Idaho, Minnesota, Montana, Oregon, and Washington, and also in North Carolina and Pennsylvania.

THE OTHER SIDE OF AMBIENCE

Most of us live in homes built years ago that were bought, lived in, and sold by a succession of owners. We all confirm the "filtering theory" of housing, which states that houses filter down from high-income first owners to middle-income buyers to lower-income owners. To put it another way, many high-income families live in newer homes, and most lower-income households occupy older homes. So what else is new?

However, when the real estate section of *Preservation* magazine and the weekend editions of large daily newspapers around the country advertise old homes on the market for $1 million or more, you're looking at big exceptions to this theory. Nowhere is this more apparent than in several places that rate high in *Retirement Places Rated*'s "Ambience" chapter: Charleston, South Carolina; Savannah, Georgia; Key West, Florida; and Annapolis, Maryland. Homes in historic neighborhoods there have some of the biggest prices in the country. Still, the filtering theory holds true for most of America's retirement places: The older the housing, the lower the price.

Porches, Patios, and Decks. A porch is a covered addition or recessed space elevated above the ground at the home's entrance. These Main Street lookouts almost disappeared after World War II, but are fast returning in new home markets. You'll find an enclosed porch attached to half of new homes in this country, and more than that in the South and West.

A patio is a floored area with or without a roof that sits directly on the ground. They predominate in the South and West, where the climate allows longer use. Decks, on the other hand, are roofless floored areas not sitting directly on the ground and are more preferred in the Northeast than any other region.

Garages and Carports. Garages, as everyone knows, are completely enclosed shelters for automobiles; carports are roofed shelters that aren't completely enclosed. Detached garages are a feature of older homes and were typically built behind the home, invisible from the street. Attached two-car garages, which became a popular feature on new homes during the 1950s, now are a standard feature on two-thirds of all newly built homes. And the carport? Except on older homes in the South and West, it has disappeared along with the once-popular split-level design.

Swimming Pools. You won't find new tract houses anywhere with in-ground swimming pools. Builders have learned that few buyers shop for shelter and a swimming pool at the same time. Moreover, local ordinances can require expensive liability insurance and a 4-foot-high fence around the pool's perimeter to prevent accidents.

A RENTER'S MISCELLANY

The kind of apartment building you choose to live in definitely makes a difference in your monthly costs, according to the latest Institute of Real Estate Management survey. Rents for a typical four-room, 850-square-foot unit are much higher in high-rise elevator buildings (U.S. median rent $950) than in garden apartments (U.S. median rent $715), defined by the institute as a group of low-rise apartment buildings on a large landscaped lot under one manager. The least expensive kind of building is the low-rise or walk-up building with fewer than 24 units (U.S. median rent $675).

You'll find that the annual turnover rate, defined as newly occupied apartments as a percent of all the apartments in the building in a year's time, also varies by the kind of building. Around the country, high-rise elevator buildings have the lowest turnover rate (U.S. median 22 percent), whereas the turnover rate in walk-ups and elevator buildings of three or fewer stories is more than twice this (U.S. median 49 percent). The kind of apartment building with the most transient population is the garden apartment, in which 62 percent of tenants moved in within the previous 12 months.

The Rule of 156

One useful way of determining the rent for a house is to divide its market value by 156. This *rule of 156* was developed by the city of San Francisco as a way of specifying the fair value of an apartment being converted into a condo for a tenant who had been renting it. As the landlord might put it, the price equals 156 times your monthly rent, take it or leave it.

What the rule implies in reverse is that landlords can expect a 156-month (or 13-year) payback on houses they rent. Using this rule plus the prices of *move-up* houses given in the Place Profiles, it isn't difficult to figure roughly what it would cost you to rent a house in a given metro area, assuming that the landlord has realistic expectations for the rate of return on property.

In Alamogordo, New Mexico, the rent would be $800; in Gainesville, Florida, $1,450; in Santa Barbara, California, $4,430. The rule of 156 may seem unfair to landlords, since there is only an 8 percent return, from which maintenance and taxes must be paid. Bear in mind, however, that those landlords rarely buy houses for the rental income they may bring; rather, they buy them for their ultimate market appreciation and rent them during the interim to cover expenses and generate a modest cash flow.

Renters' Rights

In some states with large renter populations, laws concerning relations between landlords and tenants give rights to the landlord while imposing obligations on the tenant.

Fifteen states, however, have passed landlord-tenant laws based on the Uniform Residential Landlord and Tenant Act (1972), a model law drawn up by the National Conference of Commissioners on Uniform State Laws. The act removes the landlord and tenant relationship from property law and establishes it on the basis of contract law with all the rights and remedies. These states are Alaska, Arizona, Florida, Hawaii, Iowa, Kansas, Kentucky, Montana, Nebraska, New Mexico, Oregon, Rhode Island, South Carolina, Tennessee, and Virginia.

This law defines rights and obligations of both parties to a lease on an apartment or a house, and it also specifies the way disputes can be resolved. Among its provisions are the following:

- The landlord cannot demand a security deposit greater than the amount of one month's rent.

- The landlord may enter the dwelling unit without consent of the tenant in case of emergency. In all other cases, the tenant may not unreasonably withhold consent to enter the dwelling unit for purposes of inspection, repair, and improvement.

- If your dispute with a landlord leads you to complain to the local housing board, to join a tenants' group, or to sue your landlord, the landlord cannot retaliate by cutting services, raising your rent, or evicting you.

- If the landlord doesn't make needed repairs, and the cost of the repairs is no more than $100 or half the rent (whichever is greater), you may make the repairs and deduct the expense from your monthly rent.

- After you vacate the apartment or house, any money you've deposited as security must be returned. If there are any deductions from the deposit for damages or other reasons, these deductions must be itemized.

- If your landlord doesn't live up to the lease's terms, you can recover damages in small claims court.

Personal Safety

Some time ago in Chapel Hill, North Carolina, the cops were worried about gun thefts in town and in nearby Carrboro. Several sporting-goods shops had been hit, and in many home burglaries the take included a rifle or handgun. Everyone noted the irony: Houses are broken into for the guns that homeowners bought to protect themselves from a rash of break-ins. The rising spiral meant more guns on the street.

In Barnstable District Court on Cape Cod one spring day, two dozen persons were arraigned for offenses that wouldn't open the eyes of a reporter on the *Las Vegas Sun* police beat: possession of marijuana and conspiracy to violate controlled substance laws, operating under the influence and speeding, breaking and entering with intent to commit a felony, giving a false name to a police officer, and assault and battery.

In a coffee shop up in Wisconsin's Door County peninsula, the talk one winter morning concerned a condo break-in. Missing were a shopping bag of Pampers and a baby's crib. Left behind were a state-of-the-art stereo system, Waterford crystal, the silver, and a closet full of high-fashion ski wear. Maybe we should all start locking our doors, the locals in the coffee shop agreed.

Chapel Hill does have a modest crime problem, Door County has none, and Cape Cod hasn't much of one until the summer tourists come. Indeed, the odds of your being a crime victim in 3 out of 4 of the 200 places profiled in *Retirement Places Rated* are below the national average.

Check the police log printed in the newspapers of some places or the website of the local police department (see the sidebar "E-Blotters," below) and you'll wonder whether anything interesting goes on there at all. A drunk-and-disorderly, a car break-in, a bar fight that spills out into the parking lot, a graffiti artist loose downtown, a husband-wife donnybrook—all are just occasional items hidden among the traffic accidents, animal complaints, and fishing violations.

Some places seem so safe you couldn't pay someone to punch you. Others, by comparison, are just plain dangerous. If you decide on settling in rural Brown County, Indiana, the rough odds of your being involved in a violent crime are 1 in 3,861. Should you settle in Myrtle Beach, the chances rise to 1 in 113, or slightly worse than being injured in your own home. One could say that life along South Carolina's Grand Strand is more than 34 times more dangerous than it is in the rolling limestone belt in south-central Indiana.

EVERYONE'S A VICTIM

But quoting raw odds distorts the crime picture. In spite of the popular idea that older persons are the preferred targets of crooks, you are more likely to have your pocket picked or your purse snatched than you are of being victimized by all other crimes. So why the need for a chapter on personal safety if your retirement years are statistically safer than all the years preceding?

The simple answer is that you are a different kind of crime victim whenever you have to trim back shrubbery along your home's foundation to limit a thief's potential hiding places, or have to get rid of the mailbox and install a mail slot in your front door, or have to check your car's door locks when driving down a darkened avenue, or have to keep feeling for your wallet at street festivals, or have to use only empty elevators, or have to stay indoors evenings more than you really care to. In some places such tactics are advised, in others they are merely prudent, and in still others they may not be necessary at all.

CRIME RISK: SEVERAL CONNECTIONS

Why some places are safer than others is a subject certain to get politicians, police, and citizens into arguments. For all the debate, experts recognize several factors.

Climate Has a Striking Effect

Police respond to more disturbance calls on the day after summer temperatures are highest than on any other days of the year. The numbers of burglaries, vandalisms, and rapes increase with ambient temperatures up to 85°F. Southern locations with longer, hotter summer seasons see more criminal activity than Northern locations.

But whether in the Sun Belt or in the Frost Belt, cops and criminals are busiest throughout July and August, when all crimes except robbery are the likeliest to happen. Since people spend more time outdoors during these months, they are more exposed. Homes, too, are more unprotected during this time of year because they are left with open windows and unlocked doors. Robbery is the cold-weather exception. It is highest in December, when shoppers and retail stores doing brisk holiday business make tempting targets.

Consider crime rates carefully. If they are quoted in promotion brochures or on websites, it is usually the FBI's single number (the "Crime Index") and then only if it is under the national average. But most offenses are either against property or against people. The latter, designated *violent crime,* is more serious.

After years of trending downward, violent crime suddenly increased 4 percent in 2006. Proceed with caution. There are many defensive tactics you can use to avoid being a crime victim in a new location, the best of which are detailed in the "Et Cetera" section of this chapter. Ultimately, a prudent selection of neighborhoods makes all the difference. The local police department's community relations officer can help by identifying dangerous areas for you. He or she can also do a quick security check of your new home.

Consider geographic connections that experts have noted. Sun Belt resorts such as Palm Springs, California, and Myrtle Beach, South Carolina, and even Branson in the Missouri Ozarks, see tens of thousands of visitors year-round and have serious *property crime* problems. Peaceful places along the notorious "drug highways" of I-5, I-10, I-75, and I-95 are sometimes caught up in drug trafficking and occasional gunplay. Places with large military bases see a much higher rate of aggravated assaults.

The Time & Length of the Day Counts

After sundown is the time most cars are stolen, most persons and businesses are robbed, most persons are assaulted, and most thefts are committed. Burglaries, purse snatchings and pocket pickings, on the other hand, happen more often during daylight hours. Some police dispatchers contend that the number of daylight minutes is a predictor of the kind of 911 calls they will handle.

Size Matters

Population size and density is closely tied to crime rates. Safer places—Fredericksburg in the Texas Hill Country and the Leelanau Peninsula in northern Michigan, for instance—are rural. More dangerous places are urban. There are exceptions, certainly. Ocean City, Maryland, and Natchitoches, Louisiana, have crime rates resembling those of Tucson, Arizona.

Even Traffic Plays a Role

The ease with which a criminal can drive off down the street, escape onto an arterial road, and disappear among commuters on the interstate is an encouragement. One reason retirement places on islands and peninsulas have lower crime rates is that few crooks are dumb enough to commit robberies if their only escape is over a long bridge or causeway.

Age & Sex Figure

Some 4 million persons in this country have arrest records for misdeeds other than traffic violations. The proportion of suspects who are male is much higher than their proportion in the general population. Half the persons picked up by police for violent and property crimes are under 20 years of age and four-fifths are male. None of this should be taken to mean that persons hold up convenience stores, boost Chevrolet Camaros, or duke it out in disco parking lots because they are young and male, but these characteristics are associated with other factors in crime.

The Economy Plays a Role

In most places, each time the unemployment rate goes up, the police make more arrests. But joblessness and loss of income won't automatically make a place unsafe. Many of the safer places in this book are poorer than average and suffer job losses during business slumps. More affluent areas, given similar sets of circumstances, aren't nearly as safe as they seem: Rich offenders are arrested less often than poor ones, especially on suspicion. Once arrested, they are convicted with less frequency. This is especially true in juvenile cases involving thefts and break-ins.

Transience Lifts Crime

A warning sign for crooks is a stable neighborhood where people know one another and look out for one another's safety and property no matter how many police cruise the area. High neighborhood turnover leading to more strangers living next to each other leads to higher crime rates. Resort areas that draw transients—Branson, Missouri; Myrtle Beach, South Carolina; or Pensacola, Florida, for instance—have serious crime problems. When visitors are added to the year-round residents, the higher population betters the odds that victim and crook will meet.

Police Strength

In Manhattan, there are 1,300 police officers per square mile; in most rural counties there are between 1 and 3 sworn uniformed officers for every 1,000 residents. In parts of the sparsely settled Rocky Mountains and in parts of the California Desert well east of Los Angeles, however, state police need an average 30 minutes or more to respond to calls.

It's natural to think personal safety in a place rises or falls with the size of the local police force, but it just isn't so. Police enforce traffic codes, investigate accidents, find lost children, and calm down fighting spouses. They battle crime too, but most of what they do is after the fact. They respond to complaints; they interview victims and fill out reports, they follow up

E-BLOTTERS

The local newspaper isn't the only source of information on criminal activity, nor even the best. The facts now come directly from 24-hour crime reports on the police department's website. Consider three sample items in the investigating officer's own words:

- **Shoplifting in Myrtle Beach, South Carolina:** "A 48-year-old woman was arrested after she put a pair of Tommy Hilfiger overalls under her dress at Belk at Myrtle Square Mall. As she ran out of the store, the overalls fell onto the floor. Police arrested her."
- **Burglary in Santa Fe, New Mexico:** "Someone broke into a gray 1989 Saab between 3 p.m. Monday and midnight Tuesday on the 2600 block of Cerrillos Road. A Social Security card and a Kenwood stereo were reported stolen."
- **Assault in Annapolis, Maryland:** "Officers responded to an assault report at a restaurant and found an adult male victim suffering from a cut on his left ear. The victim told the officers that his companion threw a baked potato that struck a nearby adult male, staining his shirt. They got into a physical fight with blows being exchanged."

To find these and similar accounts, simply do an Internet search for the term "police department" before or after your city's name. Electronic crime blotters are the most popular part of the police department's website. Some departments even e-mail the 24-hour reports free of charge to subscribers throughout the world.

on tips, and they collar suspects and bring them to book. A large number of police per capita, however, is usually an indication of a high-crime area rather than an area where crime is being foiled.

CRIME VS. OTHER EVENTS IN LIFE

The rates for some crimes are higher than those of other harmful events. For instance, over your life the risk of losing something to a thief is higher than that of needing medical attention for an injury. The risk of having your car stolen is higher than that of dying from stroke, diabetes, Alzheimer's disease, and Parkinson's disease combined.

Everyone runs a greater risk of being a violent crime victim, with or without injury, than being hurt in a traffic accident. In the following table, crimes are in bold.

EVENT RATE PER 100,000 PEOPLE

Personal Theft	**2,286**
Medically attended injury, all causes	1,150
Death, all causes	801
Burglary	**726**
Auto Theft	**416**
Divorce	360
Aggravated Assault	**291**
Death from heart disease	222
Death from cancer	189
Robbery	**141**
Death from stroke	51
Death from chronic lower respiratory disease	42
Accidental death, all circumstances	38
Death from diabetes mellitus	26
Death from Alzheimer's disease	23
Death from influenza and pneumonia	22
Accidental death in an automobile	16
Death from kidney disease	15
Death from septicemia (blood disease)	11
Suicide	11
Death from hypertension	8
Accidental poisoning death	7
Death from Parkinson's disease	6
Accidental death by falling	6
Murder	**6**
Accidental death from drowning	2
Accidental death from fire	1
Accidental death from aircraft crash	.2
Death from hot weather	.002
Death from lightning	.001

Source: Centers for Disease Control; FBI; National Safety Council. All figures are rounded.

Other factors related to criminal activity include the practices of local prosecutors, judges, juries, and parole boards; the attitudes of the community toward crime; and the willingness of ordinary citizens to report crime.

CRIME INDEXES

Every year some 17,000 police departments send figures on the number of crimes reported in their cities and towns to the FBI in Washington. Because of their seriousness, frequency, and probability of being reported, eight crimes make up the FBI's Crime Index. Four are classified as "violent" crimes; the other four are "property" crimes.

Violent Crime

It seemed too good to be true: Throughout the 1990s, violent crime rates dropped to their lowest level in a generation. Police chiefs and mayors celebrated in front of television cameras and declared that strategies like community policing, zero tolerance, reclaiming public spaces, rapid deployment, accurate intelligence, and relentless follow-up were working. In most regions of the country, for the rest of the decade and into the new millennium, each year was safer than the one before.

But 2001 ended the optimism. That year, the rates for major crimes shot up. Some criminologists predicted that parolees returning to the streets from their convictions during the crack-cocaine epidemic, plus surging numbers of teenagers (historically the age group likeliest to commit crime) and joblessness would mark the end of good news for some time to come.

Of all criminal offenses, *murder* is the likeliest to be reported and has the highest rate of charges being brought. Half of all murdered persons knew their killers, perhaps even sat across from them at the breakfast table the morning of the crime or loaned them money the week before. Among the retirement places profiled in this book, Savannah, Georgia, has the highest murder rate. Typical of southern cities, killings here are often the result of soured drug deals or new slights and old scores settled with a gun or knife.

Victims and killers around the country are becoming less connected, however. One murder in 8 involves a victim and a stranger, 1 in 20 a juvenile gang killing. Based on the number of unsolved killings each year and an increase in slayings involving strangers, the FBI estimates at least 25 serial killers are on the loose.

Rape, too, frequently involves acquainted victims and aggressors. It is the most underreported of crimes and also has the highest proportion of "unfounded" complaints. Rape victims are always female by current crime reporting standards.

Thanks to branch bank and convenience store holdups, as well as attempted stickups in nightclub parking lots, the *robbery* rate in Annapolis, Maryland, is three times that of the typical retirement place profiled in *Retirement Places Rated.* It is the one violent crime that most often involves more than one criminal, and the one committed less out of impulsive anger than as a way of making a living. It differs from common theft because it involves force or threat, thereby placing the victim in fear.

Assault is simply an attempt, successful or not, to injure another person. Its rate is highest in August and lowest in February, higher in the West than in other parts of the country, and higher in areas with resort or military economies. A high rate of assault, like that in Palmer–Wasilla, AK, more often indicates strictly enforced domestic-abuse laws than it does bar fights.

Property Crime

Santa Fe, New Mexico, isn't just America's oldest capital city. "The City Different" (a trademarked name) has one of the highest burglary rates among the 200 retirement places profiled here.

Burglary can be forcible entry, unlawful entry in which no force is used, or attempted forcible entry—all to commit a felony or theft. Most burglaries, say professional crooks in prison, are planned for hours and pulled off in minutes. The typical target is the home or apartment. In resorts like Branson, Missouri, or Myrtle Beach, South Carolina, it's the parked car. Nearly half of the incidents involve simply walking in rather than breaking in. The typical time is between 9 and 11 a.m. or between 1 and 3 p.m., when you're least likely to be inside.

Larceny-theft, after drunk driving and drug offenses, is the most common crime in North America. Skipping out of a self-serve gas station is one example. Shoplifting a Russian sable coat is another. Except for snatched purses and picked pockets, in almost all of the larceny-theft cases the victim never sees the offender.

Auto theft, it's been said, is a victimless crime because you get over your loss with a check from the insurance company. The typical incident, peaking in the summer during school recess, involves an unlocked car in a parking lot at a shopping mall, hospital, discount store, or movie theater. In the Phoenix suburbs and in larger cities along Interstate 10 in the California desert, stealing cars is an underground art. Along the Rio Grande in southernmost Texas, 8 of 10 cars stolen in the McAllen–Alamo area are driven over international bridges to Mexico, often before the victims realize their cars are gone.

Arson was added to the Crime Index in 1979 following a congressional mandate. It includes any willful or malicious burning or attempt to burn, with or without the intent to defraud, a building or a vehicle or personal property of someone else. It doesn't include fires of suspicious or unknown origin.

Caveats

Crime rates are derived from the number of offenses actually reported to local police. But more than 60 percent of all crime goes *unreported,* according to victim surveys, and that percentage varies from one place to another.

DEFENDING FLORIDA

Before the FBI began collecting national crime data in 1930, the best source of figures on causes of death was the life insurance industry. When it came to murder, Florida had the highest rate.

Seventy-five years later, a lot has changed. Several of Florida's large cities rank near the bottom in personal safety, but 16 states now have higher murder rates than the Sunshine State. Moreover, Florida has given up its decades-long record for having the highest rates of violent crime *and* property crime.

But the lawless image sticks, thanks to Miami. The state continues as the tropical backdrop for *Miami Herald* columnists Edna Buchanan's and Carl Hiaasen's best-selling crime fiction. A movie remake of *Miami Vice,* a bloody television series in the 1980s in which hip undercover narcs and drug lords brandished locally made TEC-9 machine pistols at each other, came out in 2006. Sightseeing buses still trundle by the sites of Gianni Versace's murder, the FDR assassination attempt, the Candy Mossler murder case, and the Barbara Mackle kidnapping.

Florida draws millions of visitors who stay for a good part of the year. A fairer way to measure its crime, notes Florida's Department of Law Enforcement, would be to add the average daily number of tourists to its number of year-round residents, and *then* determine the per capita rate. The results would make Florida look like Iowa and improve its national image.

FIFTEEN PEACEABLE PLACES

These smaller places, mainly outside the Sun Belt, have the lowest combination of property and violent crime among all 200 locations profiled in Retirement Places Rated.

Because victims often believe it futile to file complaints, many crimes never become known. This affects the accuracy of the Crime Index. Even if a complaint is filed, the investigating officer's definition of the crime may affect the numbers. A snatched purse, for instance, is either a robbery or a larceny depending on the jurisdiction. Likewise, a slap in the face is either an aggravated assault or a simple assault depending on motive.

Moreover, some police departments have padded the figures to oust a judge considered soft on crime or to persuade the city council to increase the department's budget, or they've fudged the number of crimes to create an image of effective law enforcement.

In some rural areas, too, car thefts and parking-lot fights growing out of teenage high jinks aren't added to the statistics. Wise sheriffs punish the offenders informally with a night in jail, restitution, and some community service.

It's important to distinguish between the *incidence* of crime and the crime *rate*. Incidence is simply how many crimes are reported in a given place. The more people living in a place, the greater the crime incidence.

Police in greater Tucson log 5,700 violent crimes a year. Far to the east, their counterparts in Gainesville investigate 1,800. Is Tucson more dangerous than Gainesville? Hardly. Tucson's violent crime rate per 100,000 residents is 685; Gainesville's is 961. Although Tucson is safer than Gainesville, neither one has a violent crime rate below the national average—343.

JUDGING: PERSONAL SAFETY

The one crime that cops file the most reports on is theft: a stolen bike, a necklace missing from a jewelry retailer's display case, hubcaps disappearing from a used-car lot, a customer skipping out of a fast food restaurant. Yet these heists are counted as heavily as homicides to determine crime rates. When it comes to comparing places, this method doesn't show relative danger.

A more realistic way to grade for personal safety is simple: For each place, *Retirement Places Rated* averages the rates for violent and property crimes for the latest 5-year period, but since property crimes are much less serious than crimes against people, they get one-tenth the weight of violent crimes. *Note:* Although arson is a property crime, arson figures aren't included in the scoring because they aren't available for many retirement places. Each place's score begins with the addition of two factors:

1. **Violent crime rate:** The rates for murder, robbery, and aggravated assault are added together.

2. **Property crime rate:** The rates for burglary, theft, and auto theft are totaled, and the result is divided by 10.

This sum is then scaled against a standard in which the average for all 200 places is set at 50. Iowa City, a college town on the prairie in eastern Iowa with a score of 50.3, is the typical retirement place for relative freedom from crime.

Places with *lower* crime rates than the average earn scores *greater* than 50. Brown County, a quiet spot just outside the Big Ten college town of Bloomington, Indiana, gets a perfect 100 score.

Places with *higher* crime rates than average get scores *lower* than 50. Though not as crime-ridden as other locations in the United States, Myrtle Beach, South Carolina, does have a high assault rate and a shockingly high property crime rate—the main reason this golf resort midway between New York and Miami earns the worst score, 0.0.

JUDGING EXAMPLES

A New England college town, a Texas college town, and a spa in the Arkansas Ouachitas demonstrate the scoring method for crime.

Northampton–Amherst, Massachusetts

If higher crime rates go with younger populations, Northampton–Amherst is certainly an exception to that rule. One of every four people here is a student at the Five Colleges—Amherst, Hampshire, Mount Holyoke, Smith, and the University of Massachusetts. Yet the area sees crime rates far below the national average. Moreover, crime rates that fell throughout the

1990s continued to fall throughout the early years of the 21st century.

Among the 3,300 crimes reported to the police in a typical year, over one-half involve theft. Comparing Northampton–Amherst's violent crime rate (264) and one-tenth its property crime rate (184) against the average for all retirement places produces a score of 66.4, or 68th among all 200 retirement places in personal safety.

Alpine–Big Bend, Texas

This small place in low, dry, green mountains 3 hours southeast of El Paso has, in Sul Ross State University, a higher portion of college students in its population than Northampton–Amherst. The area experiences few stickups and break-ins. Escape only leads out into empty Chihuahua Desert ranching country, where you may outrun a Ford Crown Victoria police cruiser but you won't outrun Motorola or a Texas Department of Public Safety helicopter.

Alpine has had several sensational murders, but none in the past 5 years. In spite of the town's location near the Rio Grande River and Mexico, auto theft is negligible. Recently, prisoners in the county lockup were moved to more secure facilities in a neighboring county seat to cut down on drug smuggling. The area's violent crime rate (234) and one-tenth the property crime rate (185) give the area a better-than-average score of 70.9, or 59th among all 200 places in personal safety.

Hot Springs, Arkansas

Sun Belt resorts are saddled with high property crime rates, and this one is no exception. Adding Hot Springs's modest rate for violent crime (551) to one-tenth its rising property crime rate (689) results in a total of 1,240, an unflattering record good for a score of 4.6, or 191st in personal safety among 200 places profiled here.

Up until 1967, when Governor Winthrop Rockefeller ordered state troopers to break up the craps tables, bulldoze the slot machines into a gravel pit, and close down the brothels, Hot Springs had a 100-year, wide-open tradition for lawlessness. Can the spot be returning to the norm?

Hardly, the locals will tell you: One-third of all the annual crime occurs during the thoroughbred racing season at Oaklawn Park every spring. They also claim that the only other thing that distinguishes this retirement place in the eyes of the law is the phenomenal

number of speeding tickets handed out on I-30 and on U.S. 270 by the Arkansas Highway Patrol's Troop K.

RANKINGS: PERSONAL SAFETY

To rank each place for freedom from crime, *Retirement Places Rated* adds two numbers: (1) the **Violent Crime Rate** and (2) the **Property Crime Rate** divided by 10. The lower this total figure, the better. A place's score is

its percentile on a scale of 0 to 100 corresponding to its rank. Places with tie scores get the same rank and are listed in alphabetical order.

Retirement Places from First to Last

RANK	PLACE	SCORE
1.	Brown County, IN	100.0
2.	Whidbey Island, WA	99.5
3.	Fairplay, CO	99.0
4.	Charles Town–Shepherdstown, WV	98.5
5.	Oxford, MS	98.0
6.	Leelanau Peninsula, MI	97.5
7.	Northern Neck, VA	97.0
8.	Berkeley Springs, WV	96.5
9.	San Juan Islands, WA	96.0
10.	Monadnock Region, NH	95.5
11.	Door Peninsula, WI	95.0
12.	Fredericksburg, TX	94.5
13.	Pike County, PA	94.0
14.	Smith Mountain Lake, VA	93.5
15.	Woodstock, VT	93.0
16.	Nelson County, VA	92.5
17.	Eureka Springs, AR	92.0
18.	St. Jay–Northeast Kingdom, VT	91.5
19.	Kalispell–Flathead Valley, MT	91.0
20.	Laguna Beach–Dana Point, CA	90.5
21.	Boerne, TX	90.0
22.	Hanover, NH	89.5
23.	Lake Placid, NY	89.0
24.	Bar Harbor, ME	88.5
25.	York Beaches, ME	88.0
26.	Ketchum–Sun Valley, ID	87.5
27.	State College, PA	87.0
28.	Litchfield Hills, CT	86.5
29.	Hamilton–Bitterroot Valley, MT	86.0
30.	Camden, ME	85.5
31.	Park City, UT	85.0
32.	Martha's Vineyard, MA	84.5
33.	Dahlonega, GA	84.0
34.	St. George–Zion, UT	83.5
35.	Toms River–Barnegat Bay, NJ	83.0
36.	Montrose, CO	82.5
37.	Delta County, CO	82.0
38.	Loudoun County, VA	81.5
39.	Morro Bay–Cambria, CA	81.0
40.	Fairhope–Gulf Shores, AL	80.5
41.	Front Royal, VA	79.9
42.	Petoskey–Harbor Springs, MI	79.4
43.	Rabun County, GA	78.9
44.	Sandpoint–Lake Pend Oreille, ID	78.4
45.	Chewelah, WA	77.9
46.	Norfork Lake, AR	77.4
47.	Williamsburg, VA	76.9
48.	East End Long Island, NY	76.4

RANK	PLACE	SCORE
49.	Georgetown, TX	75.9
50.	Hampshire County, WV	75.4
51.	Tryon, NC	74.9
52.	Cedar City, UT	74.4
53.	Boone–Blowing Rock, NC	73.9
54.	Marble Falls–Lake LBJ, TX	73.4
55.	Fredericksburg–Spotsylvania, VA	72.9
56.	East Stroudsburg, PA	72.4
57.	Driggs, ID	71.9
58.	Taos, NM	71.4
59.	Alpine–Big Bend, TX	70.9
60.	Silver City, NM	70.4
61.	Brunswick, ME	69.9
62.	Wimberley, TX	69.4
63.	Durango, CO	68.9
64.	Grass Valley–Nevada City, CA	68.4
65.	Traverse City, MI	67.9
66.	Eagle River–Woodruff, WI	67.4
67.	Pagosa Springs, CO	66.9
68.	Northampton–Amherst, MA	66.4
69.	Brevard, NC	65.9
70.	Southern Berkshire County, MA	65.4
71.	Alamogordo, NM	64.9
72.	Kerrville, TX	64.4
73.	Lake of the Ozarks, MO	63.9
74.	Southern Pines–Pinehurst, NC	63.4
75.	Chestertown, MD	62.9
76.	Las Cruces, NM	62.4
77.	Hendersonville–East Flat Rock, NC	61.9
78.	Murray–Kentucky Lake, KY	61.4
79.	Waynesville, NC	60.9
80.	Silverthorne–Breckenridge, CO	60.4
81.	Placer County, CA	59.8
82.	Henderson, NV	59.3
83.	Burlington, VT	58.8
84.	Port Townsend, WA	58.3
85.	Madison, MS	57.8
86.	Madison, WI	57.3
87.	Rio Rancho, NM	56.8
88.	Port Angeles–Sequim, WA	56.3
89.	Grants Pass, OR	55.8
90.	Edenton, NC	55.3
91.	Fort Collins–Loveland, CO	54.8
92.	The Big Island, HI	54.3
93.	Jackson Hole, WY	53.8
94.	Lake of the Cherokees, OK	53.3
95.	Beaufort–Atlantic Beach, NC	52.8
96.	Hattiesburg, MS	52.3

RANK	PLACE	SCORE
97.	Lake Havasu City, AZ	51.8
98.	Sullivan County, NY	51.3
99.	McCall, ID	50.8
100.	Iowa City, IA	50.3
101.	Conway, AR	49.8
102.	Bozeman, MT	49.3
103.	Pahrump Valley, NV	48.8
104.	Southport–Brunswick Islands, NC	48.3
105.	Scottsdale, AZ	47.8
106.	Bend, OR	47.3
107.	Amador County, CA	46.8
108.	Carson City–Carson Valley, NV	46.3
109.	Coeur d'Alene, ID	45.8
110.	New Braunfels, TX	45.3
111.	Long Beach Peninsula, WA	44.8
112.	Wickenburg, AZ	44.3
113.	Charlottesville, VA	43.8
114.	Easton–St. Michaels, MD	43.3
115.	Crossville, TN	42.8
116.	Western St. Tammany Parish, LA	42.3
117.	Fayetteville, AR	41.8
118.	Cortez, CO	41.3
119.	Thomasville, GA	40.8
120.	Grand Junction, CO	40.3
121.	Lake Conroe, TX	39.7
122.	Maryville, TN	39.2
123.	Columbia, MO	38.7
124.	Middle Cape Cod, MA	38.2
125.	Mariposa, CA	37.7
126.	Naples, FL	37.2
127.	Asheville, NC	36.7
128.	Apalachicola, FL	36.2
129.	Santa Barbara, CA	35.7
130.	Paradise–Magalia, CA	35.2
131.	Port Charlotte, FL	34.7
132.	Sonora–Twain Harte, CA	34.2
133.	St. Augustine, FL	33.7
134.	New Bern, NC	33.2
135.	St. Marys, GA	32.7
136.	Wenatchee, WA	32.2
137.	Vero Beach, FL	31.7
138.	Dare Outer Banks, NC	31.2
139.	Medford–Ashland, OR	30.7
140.	Mendocino–Fort Bragg, CA	30.2
141.	Chapel Hill–Carrboro, NC	29.7
142.	Las Vegas, NM	29.2
143.	Prescott–Prescott Valley, AZ	28.7
144.	Payson, AZ	28.2
145.	Bellingham, WA	27.7
146.	Maui, HI	27.2
147.	Eugene, OR	26.7
148.	Sarasota, FL	26.2

RANK	PLACE	SCORE
149.	Sebring–Avon Park, FL	25.7
150.	Bay St. Louis–Pass Christian, MS	25.2
151.	Cedar Creek Lake, TX	24.7
152.	Lower Cape May, NJ	24.2
153.	Rehoboth Bay–Indian River Bay, DE	23.7
154.	Roswell, NM	23.2
155.	Oakhurst–Coarsegold, CA	22.7
156.	Carmel–Pebble Beach, CA	22.2
157.	Pendleton District, SC	21.7
158.	Yuma, AZ	21.2
159.	Summerville, SC	20.7
160.	Kingman, AZ	20.2
161.	Lakeland–Winter Haven, FL	19.6
162.	Victorville–Apple Valley, CA	19.1
163.	Leesburg–Mount Dora, FL	18.6
164.	Anacortes, WA	18.1
165.	Fort Myers–Cape Coral, FL	17.6
166.	Port St. Lucie, FL	17.1
167.	Ruidoso, NM	16.6
168.	Largo, FL	16.1
169.	Kissimmee–St. Cloud, FL	15.6
170.	Branson, MO	15.1
171.	Flagstaff, AZ	14.6
171.	Sedona, AZ	14.6
173.	Newport–Lincoln City, OR	13.6
174.	Ocala, FL	13.1
175.	Santa Fe, NM	12.6
176.	Brownsville, TX	12.1
177.	Pensacola, FL	11.6
178.	McAllen–Alamo, TX	11.1
179.	Athens, GA	10.6
180.	Key West, FL	10.1
181.	Bisbee, AZ	9.6
182.	Melbourne–Palm Bay, FL	9.1
183.	Cottonwood–Verde Valley, AZ	8.6
184.	St. Simons–Jekyll Islands, GA	8.1
185.	Panama City, FL	7.6
186.	Palm Springs–Coachella Valley, CA	7.1
187.	Beaufort, SC	6.6
187.	Hilton Head Island, SC	6.6
189.	Ocean City, MD	5.6
190.	Gainesville, FL	5.1
191.	Hot Springs, AR	4.6
192.	Natchitoches, LA	4.1
193.	Rockport–Aransas Pass, TX	3.6
194.	Savannah, GA	3.1
195.	Tucson, AZ	2.6
196.	Bradenton, FL	2.1
197.	Charleston, SC	1.6
198.	Palmer–Wasilla, AK	1.1
199.	Annapolis, MD	0.6
200.	Myrtle Beach, SC	0.0

PLACE PROFILES: PERSONAL SAFETY

The following Place Profiles show each retirement place's average annual rates for seven crimes: murder, rape, robbery, aggravated assault, burglary, theft, and motor-vehicle theft for the latest 5 years for which data are available. The rates for these crimes are grouped into **Violent** and **Property** categories.

The next-to-last column indicates the crime trend over 5 years: 15 places have arrows pointing up (↑), meaning their *Retirement Places Rated* crime rates rose more than 15 percent; 128 places have an arrow pointing down (↓), meaning their crime rates have dropped more than 15 percent. A dash for the remaining 54 places means their crime rates have neither risen nor fallen more than 15 percent.

The rightmost column shows each retirement place's rank from 1 (safest, least crime) to 200 (more dangerous, more crime).

All figures are derived from the FBI's unpublished "Crime by County" annual reports for the latest 5 years for which data is available. A star (★) preceding a place's name highlights it as one of the top 30 places for personal safety.

| PLACE | Violent Crime Rates | | | | Property Crime Rates | | | | |
	MURDER	RAPE	ROBBERY	ASSAULT	BURGLARY	THEFT	AUTO THEFT	TREND	RANK
200 Retirement Places	3.5	31.7	72.6	276.4	774	2,551	287		
Alamogordo, NM	6.3	15.8	17.4	213.2	404	1,570	84	↓	71
Alpine–Big Bend, TX	0.0	21.3	10.6	202.1	532	1,287	32	–	59
Amador County, CA	5.3	50.4	18.6	246.7	960	1,743	342	↑	107
Anacortes, WA	1.8	60.6	56.1	135.7	1,165	5,179	421	↑	164
Annapolis, MD	8.2	35.6	457.5	695.9	866	3,534	690	↑	199
Apalachicola, FL	9.8	68.5	68.5	224.9	528	2,416	176	↓	128
Asheville, NC	3.7	22.2	131.9	149.5	1,010	2,338	410	↓	127
Athens, GA	4.7	47.4	158.4	238.1	1,159	4,750	350	↓	179
★ Bar Harbor, ME	1.9	0.0	7.5	62.0	447	1,643	103	↓	24
Bay St. Louis–Pass Christian, MS	4.7	44.0	137.0	101.9	1,280	3,513	282	↓	150
Beaufort, SC	3.0	35.0	113.9	605.7	1,185	2,784	304	↓	187
Beaufort–Atlantic Beach, NC	4.9	37.2	38.8	179.5	836	2,109	136	–	95
Bellingham, WA	2.2	50.4	53.7	138.3	1,000	3,914	359	–	145
Bend, OR	1.5	39.0	32.9	98.7	904	3,219	312	↓	106
★ Berkeley Springs, WV	0.0	0.0	12.9	77.1	366	649	103	↓	8
The Big Island, HI	1.9	54.1	33.3	93.0	730	2,725	272	↓	92
Bisbee, AZ	5.6	36.6	39.8	657.0	675	2,440	374	↑	181
★ Boerne, TX	3.9	19.4	7.8	104.7	295	1,144	70	–	21
Boone–Blowing Rock, NC	2.3	16.1	13.8	94.1	753	1,923	135	↓	53
Bozeman, MT	5.4	46.0	14.9	209.5	430	2,552	232	–	102
Bradenton, FL	4.5	33.7	175.9	643.2	1,212	3,410	389	–	196
Branson, MO	7.2	35.9	23.9	543.5	591	3,136	194	↓	170
Brevard, NC	0.0	23.4	13.4	207.5	686	1,249	107	↓	69
★ Brown County, IN	6.5	0.0	6.5	13.0	182	246	13	–	1
Brownsville, TX	3.5	29.7	80.0	341.4	976	4,553	253	–	176
Brunswick, ME	1.0	33.8	39.5	68.5	535	2,198	121	↓	61
Burlington, VT	4.7	32.1	27.4	106.3	649	2,495	96	↓	83
★ Camden, ME	0.0	19.6	2.5	61.3	314	1,955	69	–	30
Carmel–Pebble Beach, CA	7.9	30.8	172.0	289.6	625	2,259	489	↓	156
Carson City–Carson Valley, NV	1.0	0.0	34.8	315.7	591	1,887	304	–	108
Cedar City, UT	1.8	14.7	14.1	93.6	480	2,190	139	↓	52
Cedar Creek Lake, TX	6.4	16.5	29.3	448.0	955	1,789	302	↑	151
Chapel Hill–Carrboro, NC	3.3	18.1	116.3	193.8	1,072	2,952	172	↓	141
Charleston, SC	5.7	48.9	221.7	750.3	933	3,574	524	↓	197
★ Charles Town–Shepherdstown, WV	2.2	6.5	12.9	51.7	246	716	86	↓	4
Charlottesville, VA	3.9	50.0	68.7	234.2	345	2,347	183	↓	113
Chestertown, MD	0.0	15.1	40.3	236.7	705	1,068	146	–	75
Chewelah, WA	2.4	58.2	7.3	29.1	768	1,862	187	↓	45
Coeur d'Alene, ID	1.7	42.6	15.0	222.0	822	2,451	221	↓	109
Columbia, MO	0.7	18.3	84.3	265.5	466	2,468	143	↓	123
Conway, AR	3.6	37.9	26.3	171.1	559	2,791	178	↓	101
Cortez, CO	12.2	4.1	12.2	345.4	569	2,146	171	↑	118
Cottonwood–Verde Valley, AZ	4.8	48.2	48.2	463.2	1,042	3,850	415	↑	183
Crossville, TN	0.0	20.0	12.0	244.5	1,004	2,409	331	–	115
Dahlonega, GA	6.3	16.2	8.1	84.6	612	1,623	128	–	33
Dare Outer Banks, NC	3.0	50.5	20.8	187.3	1,391	3,118	169	↓	138
Delta County, CO	0.8	33.2	10.6	141.2	355	1,241	105	–	37
★ Door Peninsula, WI	0.0	35.0	3.5	31.5	234	1,238	45	–	11
Driggs, ID	0.0	69.5	13.9	166.7	375	1,209	69	↑	57
Durango, CO	2.1	25.7	12.8	111.2	488	2,122	167	↓	63
Eagle River–Woodruff, WI	9.0	9.0	13.5	117.2	590	2,028	234	–	66
East End Long Island, NY	1.9	8.9	65.1	117.8	294	1,504	188	–	48
Easton–St. Michaels, MD	2.9	25.7	85.8	283.0	495	1,915	103	↓	114
East Stroudsburg, PA	3.2	26.9	37.7	119.6	523	1,587	169	↓	56
Edenton, NC	13.6	20.5	81.8	156.9	1,118	1,507	68	↓	90
Eugene, OR	1.6	33.4	78.0	163.7	903	3,589	502	↓	147
★ Eureka Springs, AR	3.8	15.0	7.5	82.6	421	1,135	143	↓	17

★ = in top 30 places for personal safety

PLACE	MURDER	RAPE	ROBBERY	ASSAULT	BURGLARY	THEFT	AUTO THEFT	TREND	RANK
200 Retirement Places	3.5	31.7	72.6	276.4	774	2,551	287		
Fairhope-Gulf Shores, AL	0.7	28.1	25.5	112.5	478	1,404	86	↓	40
★ Fairplay, CO	8.0	8.0	0.0	73.3	303	456	72	↓	3
Fayetteville, AR	5.2	64.4	26.4	233.9	533	2,564	182	−	117
Flagstaff, AZ*	5.8	53.5	57.6	401.3	725	3,873	268	−	171
Fort Collins-Loveland, CO	0.7	65.8	16.4	132.4	494	2,582	193	↓	91
Fort Myers-Cape Coral, FL	6.2	34.8	150.5	386.6	918	2,272	439	↓	165
★ Fredericksburg, TX	0.0	8.8	0.0	57.5	265	1,336	40	↓	12
Fredericksburg-Spotsylvania, VA	5.4	17.8	34.0	152.4	138	1,776	127	↓	55
Front Royal, VA	0.0	35.1	29.2	73.1	225	1,918	175	−	41
Gainesville, FL	3.5	68.7	135.6	621.8	1,108	2,653	326	↓	190
Georgetown, TX	1.3	31.1	27.8	130.3	387	1,541	105	−	49
Grand Junction, CO	2.4	39.7	22.2	211.0	762	2,872	276	−	120
Grants Pass, OR	7.5	25.1	52.6	76.4	702	2,710	362	↓	89
Grass Valley-Nevada City, CA	1.0	23.7	19.5	198.5	523	1,174	196	↓	64
★ Hamilton-Bitterroot Valley, MT	2.6	20.5	2.6	184.4	123	883	26	↓	29
Hampshire County, WV	9.4	23.5	0.0	258.1	385	620	99	↑	50
★ Hanover, NH	0.0	33.0	11.8	61.3	340	1,423	61	↓	22
Hattiesburg, MS	3.9	19.4	87.8	76.1	933	2,761	186	↓	96
Henderson, NV*	3.1	26.4	57.2	116.6	749	1,529	615	↓	82
Hendersonville-East Flat Rock, NC	2.1	44.1	51.4	99.7	742	1,942	207	−	77
Hilton Head Island, SC	3.0	35.0	113.9	605.7	1,185	2,784	304	↓	187
Hot Springs, AR	8.7	27.1	104.2	411.6	2,049	4,393	451	↑	191
Iowa City, IA	1.7	40.5	51.7	219.9	545	2,123	97	↓	100
Jackson Hole, WY	0.0	79.7	15.9	164.7	547	2,370	133	−	93
★ Kalispell-Flathead Valley, MT	0.0	3.7	8.7	100.9	127	1,500	80	↓	19
Kerrville, TX	0.0	21.7	28.2	154.1	536	2,014	93	−	72
★ Ketchum-Sun Valley, ID	0.0	9.4	0.0	113.2	514	1,198	90	−	26
Key West, FL	1.2	54.5	112.8	401.5	980	3,698	455	↓	180
Kingman, AZ	5.7	14.7	36.9	290.9	1,211	3,514	523	−	160
Kissimmee-St. Cloud, FL	2.4	48.5	105.0	409.6	1,407	2,529	301	↓	169
★ Laguna Beach-Dana Point, CA	1.7	8.5	25.5	91.3	306	1,150	133	↓	20
Lake Conroe, TX	2.9	25.7	62.6	284.1	682	2,024	214	↓	121
Lake Havasu City, AZ	4.0	15.8	19.8	158.2	647	2,828	346	↓	97
Lakeland-Winter Haven, FL	2.9	26.3	97.9	348.6	1,043	2,667	328	↓	161
Lake of the Cherokees, OK	5.1	33.5	2.6	337.3	584	1,104	183	↑	94
Lake of the Ozarks, MO	10.3	10.3	20.7	111.1	703	2,382	129	↓	73
★ Lake Placid, NY	0.0	18.5	2.6	153.5	439	686	29	↓	23
Largo, FL*	2.7	41.2	105.8	453.6	832	2,483	351	↓	168
Las Cruces, NM	2.7	48.7	62.2	108.1	463	2,041	134	↓	76
Las Vegas, NM	3.3	46.5	56.4	424.9	564	1,517	183	↓	142
★ Leelanau Peninsula, MI	13.8	23.0	4.6	45.9	257	758	51	↓	6
Leesburg-Mount Dora, FL	3.6	32.6	53.7	552.6	849	1,576	221	↓	163
★ Litchfield Hills, CT	3.4	8.5	18.7	95.3	334	1,351	125	↓	28
Long Beach Peninsula, WA	0.0	18.7	18.7	173.3	1,709	2,403	206	−	111
Loudoun County, VA	1.1	20.0	27.1	113.4	184	1,656	122	↓	38
Lower Cape May, NJ	2.9	26.3	77.0	258.4	951	3,333	151	↓	152
Madison, MS	9.1	27.5	65.5	134.1	501	1,987	218	−	85
Madison, WI	0.7	29.2	77.4	137.7	439	2,053	166	↓	86
Marble Falls-Lake LBJ, TX	0.0	15.5	10.3	162.7	579	1,457	152	↓	54
Mariposa, CA	5.6	38.9	0.0	410.9	655	1,488	122	↓	125
Martha's Vineyard, MA	0.0	12.9	6.4	179.9	186	1,253	58	↓	32
Maryville, TN	4.4	52.4	25.7	314.3	710	1,808	238	−	122
Maui, HI	1.5	11.8	51.4	132.9	1,315	3,916	532	−	146
McAllen-Alamo, TX	6.2	25.2	93.4	375.0	1,167	3,942	390	−	178
McCall, ID	0.0	50.7	0.0	202.6	861	2,090	342	−	99
Medford-Ashland, OR	2.6	32.8	34.4	249.0	686	3,154	274	−	139
Melbourne-Palm Bay, FL	3.3	45.9	112.2	566.1	888	2,488	252	−	182
Mendocino-Fort Bragg, CA	6.7	31.3	35.8	454.3	770	1,221	162	↓	140
Middle Cape Cod, MA	3.1	25.3	35.8	380.0	751	1,470	130	↓	124
★ Monadnock Region, NH	0.0	33.9	13.0	60.0	248	704	76	↓	10
Montrose, CO	0.0	38.5	8.2	104.4	311	1,605	124	↓	36
Morro Bay-Cambria, CA	0.0	19.1	19.1	143.0	372	1,325	86	↓	39
Murray-Kentucky Lake, KY	5.7	40.1	28.6	100.3	888	2,051	186		78
Myrtle Beach, SC	6.1	67.5	196.4	703.1	1,406	5,390	694	↓	200
Naples, FL	4.8	32.1	74.4	338.2	529	1,661	142	↓	126
Natchitoches, LA	5.1	20.4	79.1	648.4	1,864	2,977	186	−	192

continued

★ = in top 30 places for personal safety

PLACE	Violent Crime Rates				Property Crime Rates			TREND	RANK
	MURDER	RAPE	ROBBERY	ASSAULT	BURGLARY	THEFT	AUTO THEFT		
200 Retirement Places	3.5	31.7	72.6	276.4	774	2,551	287		
★ Nelson County, VA	6.6	6.6	13.3	66.3	345	1,073	133	↓	16
New Bern, NC	6.4	22.5	63.3	231.7	1,059	2,672	158	↓	134
New Braunfels, TX	1.1	46.3	19.9	217.3	725	2,653	126	↓	110
Newport-Lincoln City, OR	2.2	46.6	39.9	412.4	1,111	3,576	361	↑	173
Norfork Lake, AR	0.0	32.9	2.5	103.8	319	2,051	109	↑	46
Northampton-Amherst, MA	1.3	31.0	27.2	204.9	546	1,154	141	–	68
★ Northern Neck, VA	4.0	4.0	8.0	47.9	331	906	64	↓	7
Oakhurst-Coarsegold, CA	5.2	25.9	117.0	387.4	844	1,504	575	↓	155
Ocala, FL	5.9	58.3	72.6	567.5	839	2,000	230	↓	174
Ocean City, MD	0.0	42.0	83.9	675.4	641	3,451	184	–	189
★ Oxford, MS	0.0	9.9	9.9	46.9	165	990	59	↓	5
Pagosa Springs, CO	0.0	78.7	8.7	96.2	857	1,644	122	↑	67
Pahrump Valley, NV	0.0	5.4	10.8	258.0	1,250	1,739	290	–	103
Palmer-Wasilla, AK	0.0	15.4	54.0	972.4	556	5,503	494	↓	198
Palm Springs-Coachella Valley, CA	5.4	30.5	161.0	403.7	1,864	3,112	804	–	186
Panama City, FL	6.9	61.1	102.7	519.4	1,029	3,463	326	–	185
Paradise-Magalia, CA	3.7	40.9	64.7	225.0	1,014	2,013	568	–	130
Park City, UT	0.0	25.3	13.6	35.1	493	2,076	134	↓	31
Payson, AZ	0.0	30.2	18.9	407.9	957	1,875	204	–	144
Pendleton District, SC	5.8	47.6	41.8	429.6	884	2,101	203	↑	157
Pensacola, FL	6.3	44.3	122.3	507.2	943	2,484	259	↓	177
Petoskey-Harbor Springs, MI	0.0	63.3	24.1	84.4	443	1,514	57	↓	42
★ Pike County, PA	5.7	26.8	19.1	42.0	610	673	96	↓	13
Placer County, CA	1.6	18.3	35.2	147.4	625	1,925	347	↓	81
Port Angeles-Sequim, WA	4.4	69.4	23.6	152.2	588	1,905	188	–	88
Port Charlotte, FL	3.2	26.1	52.3	321.4	808	1,989	173	↑	131
Port St. Lucie, FL	3.7	43.1	111.8	450.5	1,065	2,237	273	↓	166
Port Townsend, WA	0.0	46.4	7.1	107.0	963	2,339	146	↓	84
Prescott-Prescott Valley, AZ	1.5	31.0	39.9	291.0	682	3,024	257	↓	143
Rabun County, GA	0.0	0.0	6.3	138.2	515	1,564	239	↓	43
Rehoboth Bay-Indian River Bay, DE	0.6	45.5	80.0	406.9	825	1,934	128	↓	153
Rio Rancho, NM	4.0	26.7	22.8	257.5	602	1,212	191	↓	87
Rockport-Aransas Pass, TX	13.1	21.8	61.0	461.8	1,851	4,944	227	↑	193
Roswell, NM	7.7	61.2	45.9	258.3	1,475	2,828	216	↓	154
Ruidoso, NM	9.7	29.1	33.9	596.1	1,057	1,711	228	↓	167
St. Augustine, FL	1.4	7.5	46.6	377.3	684	1,904	177	↓	133
St. George-Zion, UT	0.0	22.7	1.9	137.1	407	1,323	181	↓	34
★ St. Jay-Northeast Kingdom, VT	0.0	23.3	13.3	63.2	509	1,211	113	↓	18
St. Marys, GA	4.9	24.1	56.6	313.7	693	2,325	158	–	135
St. Simons-Jekyll Islands, GA	5.6	36.5	197.8	157.1	1,321	5,393	332	↓	184
Sandpoint-Lake Pend Oreille, ID	2.5	20.0	2.5	120.2	463	1,698	163	↓	44
★ San Juan Islands, WA	0.0	6.7	6.7	33.5	362	1,098	107	↓	9
Santa Barbara, CA	1.7	31.4	78.7	330.6	576	1,607	264	–	129
Santa Fe, NM	7.4	57.5	59.7	487.8	1,804	1,897	341	↓	175
Sarasota, FL	1.4	24.4	71.1	308.3	861	2,667	226	↓	148
Savannah, GA	11.7	35.1	316.1	331.1	1,212	3,914	682	–	194
Scottsdale, AZ	1.8	28.1	58.8	119.9	930	2,493	587	↓	105
Sebring-Avon Park, FL	4.6	26.7	104.0	322.9	1,120	2,015	223	↓	149
Sedona, AZ	5.8	53.5	57.6	401.3	725	3,873	268	–	171
Silver City, NM	3.3	23.1	19.8	102.4	958	1,708	106	↓	60
Silverthorne-Breckenridge, CO	0.0	7.9	7.9	66.9	311	3,701	79	↓	80
★ Smith Mountain Lake, VA	1.8	23.0	4.4	76.2	223	983	100	–	14
Sonora-Twain Harte, CA	3.5	12.2	22.6	285.7	1,322	2,088	406	↓	132
Southern Berkshire County, MA	0.0	42.1	18.1	242.9	451	924	129	↓	70
Southern Pines-Pinehurst, NC	6.2	9.9	42.2	175.1	847	1,440	149	↓	74
Southport-Brunswick Islands, NC	3.6	35.0	38.6	132.7	1,567	2,099	296	–	104
★ State College, PA	2.1	23.2	19.0	66.9	258	1,624	50	↓	27
Sullivan County, NY	3.5	30.9	45.9	281.8	656	1,460	79	↓	98
Summerville, SC	3.9	41.8	100.1	385.7	698	2,326	262		159
Taos, NM	3.1	15.7	37.8	179.5	627	1,153	31	↓	58
Thomasville, GA	0.0	17.8	55.8	214.1	872	2,674	216	↓	119
Toms River-Barnegat Bay, NJ	2.0	9.3	35.1	117.3	381	1,421	95	↓	35
Traverse City, MI	0.0	80.1	10.9	139.5	369	1,574	82	–	65
Tryon, NC	5.2	20.9	41.8	146.4	716	972	183	–	51
Tucson, AZ	8.8	52.3	194.1	385.0	991	5,063	881	–	195
Vero Beach, FL	0.8	45.5	52.8	303.7	706	2,360	179	↓	137

★ = in top 30 places for personal safety

| | Violent Crime Rates | | | | Property Crime Rates | | | | |
PLACE	MURDER	RAPE	ROBBERY	ASSAULT	BURGLARY	THEFT	AUTO THEFT	TREND	RANK
200 Retirement Places	3.5	31.7	72.6	276.4	774	2,551	287		
Victorville–Apple Valley, CA	5.1	26.4	177.1	243.0	966	2,727	773	↓	162
Waynesville, NC	1.4	24.2	24.2	191.6	800	1,503	155	−	79
Wenatchee, WA	2.9	66.9	37.8	129.4	829	3,725	252	↓	136
Western St. Tammany Parish, LA	2.4	25.9	48.9	279.9	533	2,208	211	↓	116
★ Whidbey Island, WA	1.3	16.8	5.2	37.5	199	665	35	↓	2
Wickenburg, AZ	0.0	18.2	18.2	181.8	945	2,763	545	↓	112
Williamsburg, VA	1.5	39.6	24.3	91.3	236	1,999	113	↓	47
Wimberley, TX	0.9	24.9	34.3	132.2	438	1,757	170	↓	62
★ Woodstock, VT	8.6	13.8	5.2	46.5	499	1,146	74	↓	15
★ York Beaches, ME	0.5	29.5	21.5	55.6	343	1,434	83	↓	25
Yuma, AZ	1.7	23.3	38.0	479.2	741	1,912	447	−	158

ET CETERA: PERSONAL SAFETY

ARE NEWCOMERS MORE VULNERABLE THAN LOCALS?

As we age, our dread of crime can grow out of proportion to the odds of actually ending up a victim. But the outcomes of a burglary, robbery, or fraud are certainly deeper and longer lasting for older adults than they are for younger persons.

Aside from staying away from unfamiliar dark streets, locking your doors and windows, not talking to strangers, and being alert, aware, and accompanied when going out, here are other common-sense tactics for avoiding crime that are drawn from police departments in several retirement places. The time for unlocking your doors or leaving the keys in your car in a new destination comes—if ever—only after you've become the equal of the natives in your knowledge of what's safe and what isn't.

Burglary Defenses

For most homes, minimum security—defined by police as foiling entry into a home through any door or window except by destructive force—is enough to stop all but the dumbest or most dogged burglars. It's usually *after* they've been burglarized, experts note, that people learn additional ways to make their homes secure.

If your home is going to be hit, the chances are greater that it will happen during the day while you are out—even if you're gardening in the backyard—than at night when you're asleep. The probability is high, too, that the burglar will be an unemployed young person who knows the neighborhood, and that the job will be done on the spur of the moment because the home looks empty and easy to enter.

From the viewpoint of the crook, the job's quick rewards also entail the risk of doing time in jail. He may turn back at any of three points:

Casing the House. If doors and windows are in plain sight and the sounds are unmistakable that someone is inside, most intruders will turn down the risk and search for an easier target. Here are some defensive tactics:

- If you leave the house during the day, walk out to the sidewalk and turn and wave at the front door whether or not the house is occupied.

- Close the garage door if you are away—an empty garage is a sign of absent people. If you'll be away for more than a day or two, unplug the garage door opener, lock the garage door, and leave the house through the front door. Using high-tech apparatus, expert crooks can crack electronic codes for garage door openers.

- Turn down the ringer on the telephone—an unanswered telephone is a giveaway. And don't announce your absence on your telephone answering-machine or voice-mail greeting.

- Plant thorny bushes under windows and near doors or trim back existing shrubbery to limit an intruder's potential hiding places.

- Leave your air-conditioner's fan on when you are out. Most burglaries occur in August and a silent air-conditioner is the crook's tip to an empty house.

- Tune in a radio or a television to a talk program, and turn on a porch light and yard light and one or two interior lights—the bathroom is one of the best rooms in which to leave a light on—if you are going out for the evening.

Entering the House. Even if the front door is unlocked, an intruder commits a crime once he is inside the house—whether or not anything is stolen. If doors and windows are locked and it looks as if it will take time and energy to break in, he will often go elsewhere.

Prowling the House. A burglar inside a target house is a very dangerous person to confront. He may be discouraged if he cannot quickly find loot or if he thinks the police are on their way. Here are several defensive tactics:

- Maintain a secure closet (not a safe) with an outward-opening door for storing furs, cameras, guns, silverware, and jewelry; on the door, install a 1-inch deadbolt lock. Place an annunciator alarm on the inside. If the door is paneled or of hollow-core construction, strengthen it with ¾-inch plywood or galvanized sheet steel backing.

- Install a telephone extension in your bedroom and add a rim lock with a 1-inch deadbolt to the interior side of the bedroom door (ideally, a "thumb turn" with no exterior key); then if you hear an intruder, you can retreat to the bedroom, lock the door, and call the police.

  In addition, avoid:

- Displaying guns on interior walls that can be seen from the street. Guns are big drawing cards for burglars.

- Hiding door keys in the mailbox, under the door-mat, atop the door casing, in a flowerpot, or any secret place seasoned burglars search first.

- Keeping a safe in your house. If an intruder finds a safe, he will assume you have something of great value and may come back later and force you to open it.

- Leaving window fans and air-conditioners in unlocked windows when you are away from home.

- Entering your home or calling out if you find a window or door forced when you return home.

Go to a neighbor and call the police. Wait there until the police come.

- Attaching tags on your key ring that identify you, your car, or your address.

Personal Larceny Defenses

Personal larceny with contact, a police blotter term for purse snatching and pocket picking, is the only crime that strikes older adults more frequently than the rest of the population. It is a common way a street crook gets cash in a hurry. The target is the person who looks the easiest to attack, has the most money or valuables to lose, and appears the least likely to give chase.

- **Purses:** If you can do without a purse, do without it. Instead, tuck money and credit cards in an inside pocket. If you must carry a purse, carry it under your arm with its opening facing down; if you're attacked, let the purse's contents fall to the ground, then sit down on the sidewalk before you are knocked down.

- **Wallets:** Never carry a wallet in your back pocket; even an amateur can lift it and escape before you realize what's happening. Carry it in the front pocket of your trousers. Wrap a large rubber band around the wallet so that it can't be withdrawn smoothly and can't fall through if your pocket is cut by a razor blade.

  In addition, you should avoid:

- Walking without energy, purpose, or assurance. Predators sense vulnerability if you lack confidence.

- Letting strangers stop you for conversation.

- Approaching cars parked on the street with motors running.

- Flashing your jewelry or cash. This is a signal to street thugs, especially if you seem neither strong nor quick. They may follow you to a more convenient spot for a holdup.

- Walking close to building entrances or shrubbery.

- Getting separated from your purse or wallet in a crowded restroom or other public place, or leaving your purse or wallet unattended in a shopping cart, or on a counter.

- Mingling with adolescents leaving school or groups of adolescents anywhere.

- Using shortcuts, alleys, or dark ways, and walking through sparsely traveled areas or near thick trees and shrubs.

SECURE HOUSING DEVELOPMENTS

If you are considering life in a development—whether a high-rise apartment or condominium, mobile home park, townhouse complex, housing tract, or enclosed dwelling with adjoining courtyards and interior patios—check for these basic security factors.

Opportunity for Surveillance

The ease with which residents and police patrols can watch what is going on is determined by the design of the building complex. The ability to see and question strangers depends on how each residence is designed and its relationship to neighboring dwellings. The nearness of elevator doors to apartment entrances, the number of apartments opening onto each landing, the location and nearness of parking lots and open spaces, the layout of streets and walkways, the evenness and intensity of exterior and interior lighting—all of these factors affect ease of surveillance.

All entryways and walkways should be clearly visible to residents and police at any time of day or night. This means the landscaping surrounding them should be low and free from obstacles and heavy foliage. Walkways should be evenly illuminated at night with lamps that are not so bright as to cause light "tunnels."

Clustered housing units where residents know their neighbors encourages watchfulness. In large buildings, if only a few apartments open onto a common landing or hallway, the same sort of neighborly concern is promoted.

Differentiation of Space & Territory

The most dangerous places within large buildings are interior public areas with no definite territorial boundaries. Areas seemingly belonging to no one are, in effect, open to everyone. When places are definitely marked off, an intruder will be more obvious, and

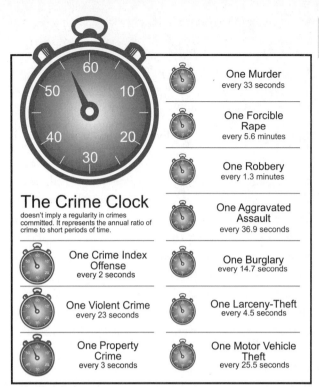

The Crime Clock doesn't imply a regularity in crimes committed. It represents the annual ratio of crime to short periods of time.

One Murder every 33 seconds

One Forcible Rape every 5.6 minutes

One Robbery every 1.3 minutes

One Aggravated Assault every 36.9 seconds

One Crime Index Offense every 2 seconds

One Burglary every 14.7 seconds

One Violent Crime every 23 seconds

One Larceny-Theft every 4.5 seconds

One Property Crime every 3 seconds

One Motor Vehicle Theft every 25.5 seconds

owners and neighbors will be alerted to potential danger more quickly.

Access Control

Obviously, the quality of locks, doors, door frames, and windows affects the ease with which your residence can be entered. Yet many builders give little attention to these details. Still less attention may be given to entrances, a surprising fact when you consider that the design and layout of entrances are crucial elements in security, since they define territory and boundaries to residents, visitors, and intruders.

Entrances and exits to a complex should be limited in number, and entrance routes should pass near activity areas so that many people can observe those who come and go. An increasingly popular type of retirement community designed for metropolitan areas high in crime—like many found in Florida or Texas—consists of an enclosed complex of either condominium townhouses or cluster homes surrounded by a wall or secure fence and connected by courtyards and terraces. Entrance in these developments is usually through a single gate guarded by a watchman who has closed-circuit television and an elaborate communications system.

Personal Safety

Siting & Clustering

The placement of buildings on the grounds and their relationship to one another affect the ease of access. The opportunity for crime increases in complexes where the design allows anyone to wander at will between dwellings or through courtyards. When residences are clustered so that entrances face each other and access is limited, strangers are less likely to wander through and are more apt to be questioned if they do. The practice of clustering units together, then, limits access naturally and unobtrusively, while at the same time providing a setting for the casual social contacts between neighbors that ensures security.

Despite the feeling of safety that walls, fences, guard posts, and television scanners provide for persons in a community setting, too heavy a concentration of these may be a warning flag. Security measures piled on top of one another, such as excessive numbers of police with attack dogs, indicate high crime in the area. If you sense an excessive preoccupation with security, it's wise to ask about crime or simply eliminate the community from your list altogether.

TYPICAL FRAUDS

P.T. Barnum is credited with the wise but cynical comment that there is "a sucker born every minute and two [con men] to take advantage of him." He spoke from bitter experience; twice in his lifetime he was the victim of swindlers.

Why do older adults fall for con games? The answer is that the proposals sound too good to pass up and are presented with urgency by persons who appear to be honest and sincere. The favorite targets of these crooks are older adults who are likely to have liquid assets in their savings accounts.

It's hard to believe that people can still be taken in by the "pigeon drop," a scam thousands of years old in which the "mark" is expected to ante up some of his or her own money in order to be cut in on an imaginary find of a small fortune. A similar game involves persuading a victim to help bank examiners and the FBI catch an embezzler by withdrawing some of his or her funds and turning them over to the supposed law enforcement officer.

Both of these scams have been exposed time after time, yet victims continue to be bilked out of millions of dollars every year. Consumer and business frauds, too, net billions for their perpetrators. Here are some common examples.

Building Inspector & Contractor Scams

Crooks working in tandem pull off code violation frauds with newcomers as their frequent victims. One poses as a building inspector who "discovers" serious violations and the need for immediate repairs to a homeowner's furnace. Shortly afterward the accomplice arrives, pretending to be a repairman who can perform the needed work at low cost. Typically, little or nothing is done to the furnace, but the victim gets a bill for several hundred dollars.

Home improvement swindles are played by con men who usually show up late in the day offering to perform some service such as installing insulation at half-price. They claim they have just finished a job in the neighborhood and have material left over, which accounts for the good deal they can pass on to you. You have to make up your mind on the spot and pay immediately. The job probably never gets finished, and the materials used are worth even less than the bargain price you paid.

Work-at-Home Scams

Older adults who respond to print advertisements such as the following actual examples noted in a recent U.S. House of Representatives mail-fraud hearing are prime targets for work-at-home scams:

IDEAS, INVENTIONS, new products needed by innovative manufacturers. Marketing assistance available to individuals, tinkerers, universities, companies. Call free: 1-800-528-6050. Arizona residents: 1-800-352-0458, extension 831.

EARN $200 weekly, part-time taking short phone messages at home. Call 1-615-779-3235 extension 267.

Assemble electronic devices in your home during spare time. $300.00 to $600.00/week possible. Experience, knowledge, not necessary. No investment. Write for free information. Electronic Development Lab, Drawer 1560-L, Pinellas Park, FL 33565.

The ads promise extra income each month, all yours for addressing envelopes, making wreaths or plaques in your living room, knitting baby booties, assembling fishing tackle in your basement, growing earthworms, watching television, or raising houseplants at home. U.S. Postal Service investigators, who

It is possible to see a crime in progress without recognizing it as such. Here are some situations that might be observed in any neighborhood. These are situations a trained police officer would investigate if he or she were making the observation.

Situations Involving Vehicles

SITUATION	POSSIBLE SIGNIFICANCE
Moving vehicles, especially if moving slowly without lights, following an aimless or repetitive course.	Casing for a place to rob or burglarize; drug pusher, sex offender, or vandal.
Parked, occupied vehicle, especially at an unusual hour.	Lookout for burglary in progress (sometimes two people masquerading as lovers).
Vehicle parked in neighbor's drive being loaded with valuables, even if the vehicle looks legitimate, i.e., moving van or commercial van.	Burglary or larceny in progress.
Abandoned vehicle with or without license plate.	Stolen or abandoned after being used in a crime.
Persons loitering around parked cars.	Burglary of vehicle contents, theft of accessories, vandalism.
Persons detaching accessories and mechanical parts.	Theft or vandalism.
Apparent business transactions from a vehicle near school, park, or quiet residential neighborhood.	Drug sales.
Persons being forced into a vehicle.	Kidnapping, rape, robbery.
Objects thrown from a moving vehicle.	Disposal of contraband.

Situations Involving Property

SITUATION	POSSIBLE SIGNIFICANCE
Property in homes, garages, or storage areas, especially if several items of the same kind such as TVs and bicycles.	Storage of stolen property.
Property in vehicles, especially meaningful at night or if property is household goods, appliances, unmounted tape decks, stereo equipment.	Stolen property, burglary in progress.
Property being removed from a house or building; meaningful if residents are at work, are on vacation, or are known to be absent.	Burglary or larceny in progress.
Open doors, broken doors or windows, or other signs of a forced entry.	Burglary in progress or the scene of a recent burglary.

Situations Involving Persons

SITUATION	POSSIBLE SIGNIFICANCE
Door-to-door solicitors—especially significant if one goes to the back of the house and one stays in front. Can be men or women, clean-cut and well dressed.	Casing for burglary, burglary in progress, soliciting violation.
Waiting in front of a house.	Lookout for burglary in progress.
Forced entry or entry through window.	Burglary, vandalism, theft.
Persons shortcutting through yards.	Fleeing the scene of a crime.
Persons running, especially if carrying items of value.	Fleeing the scene of a crime.
Person carrying property, especially if property isn't boxed or wrapped.	Offender leaving the scene of a burglary, robbery, or larceny.
High volume of human traffic in and out of residence.	Drug sales, vice activities, "fence" operation.

Personal Safety

have been looking into these scams for years, say that they haven't encountered one legitimate work-at-home offer that requires payment from the person who responds to the ad.

That's the key to work-at-home scams: A fee is required in order for the person to get in on the opportunity. The promoter claims that the money is for a start-up kit or for other expenses. The promise is that the promoter will buy back the finished product or that he will arrange for it to be purchased by others in the marketplace. Unfortunately, the promoter seldom if ever buys back the products, and the consumer is not only robbed of his or her initial cash outlay but also stuck with a large quantity of products for which there is no market.

Commodities Sales

Commodities swindles have become one of the biggest consumer frauds in years. Government investigators estimate these schemes are defrauding the public of as much as $1 billion a year.

The term *commodities* refers to a wide range of investments, from metals and gems to wholesale food products and foreign currencies. Although most investment firms are reputable, there are a growing number of firms that illegally sell or exchange investments to the unwary. Because commodity issues are complex, even highly educated persons are taken in. Indeed, convicted swindlers have testified in recent congressional hearings that the preferred customer is a retired physician, engineer, college professor, or military officer. Moreover, according to these crooks, the best telephone area codes in the country to call are in the Midwest and West because, they allege, people there are less cynical.

Commodity investments are perfect vehicles for swindlers, since the payment of profits to investors can often be deferred for 6 months to a year, leaving plenty of time for the operators to skip town before the investors suspect a scam. Moreover, since commodities are by nature very complicated and risky investments, many investors are never sure whether they've been had.

There are two basic ways to invest in commodities. The first is to pay the full price and take immediate possession of the items. The second is to buy on margin, which involves putting up a percentage of the total purchase price with the balance being due on a future date.

A commodities scheme typically involves a boiler room full of telephones in which 10 to 100 salespeople make calls to persons who responded to newspaper advertising. The salespeople work on commission and high-pressure pitches are the name of the game. In many cases, a sale is consummated on the telephone. If the person called doesn't agree to purchase anything in the initial call, he or she will be inundated with literature and harassed until a sale is made. The salesperson usually requires the deposit to be wired from the investor's bank, leaving no time for second thoughts.

Putting It All Together

Is there really an ideal place for retirement in America? Various chambers of commerce, real estate promoters, and state tourism and economic development agencies may claim the title for their own backyards. After all, with more than 30 million persons between 50 and 60 years of age giving thought to where they'll live after they retire, attracting the footloose among them to the Leisure Villages, Palm Shores, and Mountain Homes of this country is a highly promising growth industry.

By *Retirement Places Rated*'s criteria, however, the ideal place would have the climate of Maui, Hawaii, where a southerly latitude and the Pacific Ocean keeps the air temperature from ever dropping below 65°F or from topping 90°F much of the time.

It would have to be a rural place if it were to match the low crime rate of Rabun County in the northeast Georgia mountains, or the inexpensive housing around Roswell in southeastern New Mexico cattle country.

Yet the ideal spot would also have to be a large college town to match the full range of healthcare facilities and continuing education opportunities available in Gainesville, Florida, or Chapel Hill, North Carolina.

For ambience, you may choose a place like Middle Cape Cod, Massachusetts, which has not only good restaurants and a calendar of symphony orchestra performances and guest artist dates, but opportunities for outdoor activities as well—all in a setting filled with reminders of a historic past.

For finding part-time work, the place should have the prospects of Henderson, Nevada, and Loudoun County, Virginia, for job growth in the retail trade; services; and finance, insurance, and real estate (FIRE) industries.

Finally, the ideal place should offer retired persons the low living costs of McAllen–Alamo on the north bank of the Rio Grande in southernmost Texas.

A HOLY GRAIL?

Obviously, this ideal haven is a fiction. You can explore the geography at length and with care, but you will never find the single place that combines all the firsts according to this book's criteria. Moreover, because one person's haven can often

IF YOU READ THIS CHAPTER FIRST

Readers who've skipped ahead to see how it all comes out may be surprised by many of the results shown in the chart on the upcoming pages. If you're curious about how a place is rated in a particular category, see the explanation of the scoring system in the appropriate chapter. Bear in mind that:

- The chapters on Economy, Services, and Ambience favor larger places. Climate is neutral. Smaller places have the edge in Costs of Living and Personal Safety. Housing's *variety* and *quality* components help big places but the chapter's *affordability* part favors smaller ones.

- Scores are expressed in percentages in which 50 is average, 100 best, and 0 worst.

- When you review the rankings in each of the chapters, be sure to note the close groupings of scores. With such close results, ranking places from 1 to 200 may give the impression of greater differences among them than actually exist.

- Throughout this guide, the places compared aren't towns or cities. Almost all of them are counties where older newcomers settle in town, suburb, and rural hinterland.

- Though this guide does not profile every desirable retirement destination in America, each of the 200 places it does include are among the country's best.

AMERICA'S TOP 30 RETIREMENT PLACES

RANK	RETIREMENT PLACE	MEAN SCORE
1.	Georgetown, TX	72.9
2.	St. George–Zion, UT	72.1
3.	Fort Collins–Loveland, CO	71.9
4.	Charleston, SC	71.9
4.	Henderson, NV	71.9
6.	Kalispell–Flathead Valley, MT	70.3
7.	Fairhope–Gulf Shores, AL	68.8
8.	Scottsdale, AZ	68.7
9.	Laguna Beach–Dana Point, CA	67.9
10.	Sarasota, FL	67.7
11.	Wickenburg, AZ	67.4
12.	Traverse City, MI	67.3
13.	Fayetteville, AR	67.2
14.	Fort Myers–Cape Coral, FL	67.2
15.	Morro Bay–Cambria, CA	66.3
16.	Hanover, NH	66.2
17.	Savannah, GA	66.2
18.	Las Cruces, NM	66.1
19.	Charlottesville, VA	65.4
20.	Naples, FL	65.3
20.	Tucson, AZ	65.3
22.	Wimberley, TX	65.2
23.	Madison, WI	65.1
24.	Bay St. Louis–Pass Christian, MS	64.4
25.	Myrtle Beach, SC	64.1
26.	Placer County, CA	63.8
27.	Medford–Ashland, OR	63.7
28.	Asheville, NC	63.5
29.	Bend, OR	63.5
30.	Iowa City, IA	63.4

Because of rounding, the list above appears to indicate several ties, but there are actually only two ties.

be another's purgatory and your rural retreat someone else's boondocks, one can argue that there really is no such thing as the ideal place.

Your retirement years will amount to one-quarter of your life. Choosing where to spend these years isn't easy. The first tactic is to focus on *your own* preferences and needs. The chapter "Making *Retirement Places Rated* Work for You," at the front of the book, can help you identify what these preferences and needs might be. Having said all this, one can still try to discover which of the 200 places come close to the ideal.

FINDING THE BEST ALL-AROUND PLACES

The method for determining the best all-around retirement places in the United States is simple: The scores of each place for all seven factors—Climate, the Economy, Services, Ambience, Costs of Living, Housing, and Personal Safety—are averaged for a final score. Georgetown, Texas, for instance, has a score of 63.3 in Climate, 99.4 in The Economy, 45.7 in Services, 57.2 in

Ambience, 69.9 in Costs of Living, 98.9 in Housing, and 75.9 in Personal Safety. The average of all these scores is 72.9.

Because the system is based on scores, the higher the mean score, the better the place is judged to be all-around—Georgetown places first overall. The list in the sidebar above, "America's Top 30 Retirement Places," highlights the places that rise to the top as the better spots for retirement in America.

In some respects, the top 30 list in this edition of *Retirement Places Rated* resembles that of the previous edition, published in 2004. Although their rankings have changed, 13 of the places in this edition's top 30 were in the previous edition's top 30.

By no means are the top 30 perfect. Seventeen rank in the bottom 20 percent in one or more of the seven categories. Myrtle Beach, South Carolina, for example, is last in Personal Safety, and Carmel–Pebble Beach, California, is one place from last in Costs of Living. Just one of the top 30—St. George–Zion, Utah—ranks in the upper half in all categories. Hanover, New Hampshire; Iowa City, Iowa; and Traverse City, Michigan, rank in the upper half in all the categories except Climate.

Back to the main point: There isn't an ideal retirement haven in America. Aside from a fault or two, many come close through a combination of strengths. Whether their strengths are vital or unimportant, or whether their faults are knockout factors or trivial considerations, is for you to decide.

RANKINGS: PUTTING IT ALL TOGETHER

The following chart gives each place's score in each of *Retirement Places Rated*'s seven chapters. On the right side, the average of the seven scores is shown, as is the place's overall rank—the higher the average, the higher the rank. For example, Asheville's average score of 63.5 places it 28th overall among 200 locations. The best possible average score is 100.0, meaning perfection in all seven categories. Scores that are truly tied get the same rank. Because of rounding, there are fewer ties than indicated. A star (★) in front of a place's name identifies it as one of the overall top 30.

Within each column, the entries in orange represent the top 30 places within that particular category. For example, Alpine–Big Bend, Texas; The Big Island, Hawaii; Bisbee, Arizona; Bradenton, Florida; and Carmel–Pebble Beach, California, all rank among the top 30 for Climate.

RETIREMENT PLACE	CLIMATE	THE ECONOMY	SERVICES	AMBIENCE	COSTS OF LIVING	HOUSING	PERSONAL SAFETY	MEAN SCORE	RANK
Alamogordo, NM	74.3	22.6	31.1	8.5	96.5	19.0	64.9	45.3	131
Alpine–Big Bend, TX	89.9	6.0	30.1	34.6	98.5	45.2	70.9	53.6	81
Amador County, CA	83.9	50.7	6.0	4.0	12.1	4.5	46.8	29.7	189
Anacortes, WA	64.3	68.3	52.7	39.1	23.2	38.6	18.1	43.5	142
Annapolis, MD	32.1	93.9	78.8	75.3	11.6	24.1	0.6	45.2	132
Apalachicola, FL	72.3	4.0	3.0	24.6	42.8	18.5	36.2	28.8	192
★ Asheville, NC	40.2	67.3	91.4	82.4	73.9	52.7	36.7	63.5	28
Athens, GA	60.8	47.2	87.4	38.6	74.4	81.4	10.6	57.2	64
Bar Harbor, ME	8.5	16.5	32.6	86.9	45.8	23.6	88.5	43.2	143
★ Bay St. Louis–Pass Christian, MS	48.2	87.9	32.1	87.9	74.9	94.9	25.2	64.4	24
Beaufort, SC	56.7	94.9	62.8	83.9	20.2	11.0	6.6	48.0	114
Beaufort–Atlantic Beach, NC	44.7	32.1	23.6	44.2	65.4	71.3	52.8	47.7	115
Bellingham, WA	63.8	66.3	94.4	78.8	38.2	39.1	27.7	58.3	58
★ Bend, OR	62.8	84.4	85.4	64.8	24.2	75.3	47.3	63.5	29
Berkeley Springs, WV	5.5	2.0	1.0	2.0	86.0	34.1	96.5	32.4	183
The Big Island, HI	94.4	36.1	52.7	66.3	18.1	6.0	54.3	46.8	124
Bisbee, AZ	88.9	53.2	29.1	61.8	61.9	37.1	9.6	48.8	105
Boerne, TX	68.3	25.1	30.6	8.0	64.9	49.7	90.0	48.1	113
Boone–Blowing Rock, NC	23.6	33.6	86.9	37.6	54.3	47.2	73.9	51.0	95
Bozeman, MT	23.1	63.3	77.3	84.9	46.8	79.3	49.3	60.6	43
Bradenton, FL	88.4	96.4	59.2	59.2	30.2	85.4	2.1	60.1	46
Branson, MO	20.1	58.7	62.3	24.1	84.5	86.9	15.1	50.2	99
Brevard, NC	38.1	14.0	49.2	33.6	77.4	43.7	65.9	46.0	128
Brown County, IN	1.5	15.0	4.0	5.0	82.5	16.0	100.0	32.0	184
Brownsville, TX	72.8	52.7	43.7	16.5	99.5	95.9	12.1	56.2	66
Brunswick, ME	3.5	73.3	83.4	97.9	33.2	17.0	69.9	54.0	77
Burlington, VT	3.0	64.8	92.9	84.4	21.7	76.8	58.8	57.5	62
Camden, ME	12.5	30.1	33.1	65.8	49.8	46.2	85.5	46.1	127
Carmel–Pebble Beach, CA	99.4	89.4	76.3	56.2	0.0	28.6	22.2	53.2	84
Carson City–Carson Valley, NV	89.4	60.3	66.8	73.8	13.6	75.8	46.3	60.9	40
Cedar City, UT	19.0	47.7	50.2	11.5	69.4	81.9	74.4	50.6	98
Cedar Creek Lake, TX	50.2	35.6	23.1	0.0	96.0	55.2	24.7	40.7	154
Chapel Hill–Carrboro, NC	49.2	86.9	100.0	60.8	25.7	88.9	29.7	63.0	32

continued

★ = in the overall top 30 places to retire; **orange text** = in the top 30 places in that category

RETIREMENT PLACE	CLIMATE	THE ECONOMY	SERV-ICES	AMBI-ENCE	COSTS OF LIVING	HOUSING	PERSONAL SAFETY	MEAN SCORE	RANK
★ Charleston, SC	59.7	**88.9**	**92.4**	**99.4**	68.4	**92.9**	1.6	**71.9**	4
Charles Town–Shepherdstown, WV	30.1	6.5	26.6	39.6	75.4	6.5	**98.5**	40.5	156
★ Charlottesville, VA	37.6	**86.4**	**97.4**	76.3	32.2	83.9	43.8	**65.4**	19
Chestertown, MD	11.0	4.5	61.3	58.2	25.2	5.5	62.9	32.7	181
Chewelah, WA	13.5	8.5	21.6	7.5	53.3	1.5	77.9	26.3	198
Coeur d'Alene, ID	22.6	78.8	71.8	57.7	53.8	77.8	45.8	58.3	58
Columbia, MO	2.0	62.3	**98.9**	40.2	72.9	**96.4**	38.7	58.8	53
Conway, AR	32.6	80.4	65.3	1.5	**90.0**	**99.4**	49.8	59.9	47
Cortez, CO	43.7	16.0	12.5	20.1	83.0	28.1	41.3	35.0	177
Cottonwood–Verde Valley, AZ	**87.4**	71.3	83.9	**92.4**	27.7	35.6	8.6	58.1	60
Crossville, TN	28.1	39.1	54.7	19.0	**93.5**	**87.4**	42.8	52.1	90
Dahlonega, GA	45.7	35.1	55.2	12.0	77.9	69.3	84.0	54.2	76
Dare Outer Banks, NC	22.1	43.2	9.5	55.7	52.8	82.4	31.2	42.4	145
Delta County, CO	59.2	10.0	14.0	13.5	85.0	10.0	82.0	39.1	162
Door Peninsula, WI	19.0	15.5	24.1	67.3	59.8	29.1	**95.0**	44.3	137
Driggs, ID	17.0	8.0	10.0	10.0	39.7	14.5	71.9	24.4	200
Durango, CO	52.2	65.8	84.9	41.2	43.3	67.3	68.9	60.5	44
Eagle River–Woodruff, WI	16.0	27.1	2.0	32.1	60.4	9.0	67.4	30.6	187
East End Long Island, NY	25.1	73.3	61.8	**98.9**	1.1	1.0	76.4	48.2	112
Easton–St. Michaels, MD	36.6	23.6	40.7	66.8	19.1	30.1	43.3	37.2	168
East Stroudsburg, PA	9.5	60.8	52.7	51.7	35.2	51.2	72.4	47.6	116
Edenton, NC	37.1	3.0	18.0	14.5	**86.5**	48.2	55.3	37.5	167
Eugene, OR	50.2	59.2	**89.4**	90.4	38.7	29.6	26.7	54.9	72
Eureka Springs, AR	27.6	5.5	9.0	6.5	**94.0**	60.8	**92.0**	42.2	147
★ Fairhope–Gulf Shores, AL	45.2	69.8	51.7	73.3	76.4	84.4	80.5	**68.8**	7
Fairplay, CO	18.5	30.6	0.0	31.1	46.3	30.1	**99.0**	36.5	172
★ Fayetteville, AR	24.1	79.8	**94.4**	41.7	**91.0**	**97.9**	41.8	**67.2**	13
Flagstaff, AZ	59.7	74.3	**89.9**	88.9	26.7	84.9	14.6	62.7	35
★ Fort Collins–Loveland, CO	42.7	**91.9**	**95.9**	87.4	41.3	**89.4**	54.8	**71.9**	3
★ Fort Myers–Cape Coral, FL	90.4	**95.9**	59.7	89.9	24.7	**91.9**	17.6	**67.2**	14
Fredericksburg, TX	67.3	12.5	25.1	36.6	**89.0**	15.5	**94.5**	48.6	108
Fredericksburg–Spotsylvania, VA	31.1	78.3	76.3	36.1	21.2	53.7	72.9	52.8	87
Front Royal, VA	10.5	13.0	20.6	12.5	44.8	5.0	79.9	26.6	197
Gainesville, FL	76.3	55.7	**97.9**	67.8	36.2	74.8	5.1	59.1	52
★ Georgetown, TX	63.3	**99.4**	45.7	57.2	69.9	**98.9**	75.9	**72.9**	1
Grand Junction, CO	53.2	50.2	74.8	55.2	80.5	71.8	40.3	60.9	41
Grants Pass, OR	82.9	26.6	67.8	26.6	48.8	12.5	55.8	45.9	129
Grass Valley–Nevada City, CA	74.8	69.3	48.2	32.6	5.1	18.0	68.4	45.2	133
Hamilton–Bitterroot Valley, MT	51.2	31.1	16.0	31.6	60.9	11.5	**86.0**	41.2	150
Hampshire County, WV	12.0	0.5	3.5	6.0	**93.0**	9.5	75.4	28.6	193
★ Hanover, NH	10.0	54.2	81.9	**94.4**	54.8	78.8	**89.5**	**66.2**	16
Hattiesburg, MS	39.1	25.6	**86.4**	52.2	**94.5**	72.3	52.3	60.3	45
★ Henderson, NV	**91.4**	**100.0**	77.8	90.4	15.6	68.8	59.3	**71.9**	4
Hendersonville–East Flat Rock, NC	36.1	41.2	82.9	48.2	65.9	39.6	61.9	53.7	80
Hilton Head Island, SC	58.2	**94.9**	62.8	**93.9**	7.6	32.6	6.6	50.9	96
Hot Springs, AR	54.7	29.1	**88.9**	62.3	81.5	38.1	4.6	51.3	93
★ Iowa City, IA	2.5	83.9	**99.4**	54.2	62.4	**90.9**	50.3	**63.4**	30
Jackson Hole, WY	17.0	81.9	63.8	70.8	2.1	**96.9**	53.8	55.2	71
★ Kalispell–Flathead Valley, MT	44.2	68.3	65.8	**98.4**	59.3	64.8	**91.0**	**70.3**	6
Kerrville, TX	70.3	17.0	42.2	1.0	**92.0**	63.3	64.4	50.0	101
Ketchum–Sun Valley, ID	33.1	72.8	15.0	62.8	6.6	66.8	**87.5**	49.2	103
Key West, FL	58.7	48.7	46.7	**86.4**	2.6	40.7	10.1	42.0	148
Kingman, AZ	**92.9**	82.4	38.6	30.1	66.4	65.8	20.2	56.6	65
Kissimmee–St. Cloud, FL	77.8	**87.4**	19.0	28.1	30.7	**85.9**	15.6	49.2	104
★ Laguna Beach–Dana Point, CA	**98.9**	92.9	**93.4**	95.9	0.6	3.0	**90.5**	67.9	9
Lake Conroe, TX	61.8	93.9	37.1	58.7	52.3	**94.4**	39.7	62.6	36
Lake Havasu City, AZ	**96.4**	82.4	38.6	30.1	51.8	58.2	51.8	58.5	55
Lakeland–Winter Haven, FL	77.3	61.3	46.2	75.8	61.4	76.3	19.6	59.7	48
Lake of the Cherokees, OK	31.6	17.5	13.0	0.5	**97.0**	31.6	53.3	34.9	178
Lake of the Ozarks, MO	11.0	42.7	24.6	28.6	68.9	56.2	63.9	42.3	146
Lake Placid, NY	0.5	10.5	10.5	72.8	58.3	36.1	**89.0**	39.7	160
Largo, FL	84.4	75.8	81.9	90.9	36.7	22.6	16.1	58.3	57
★ Las Cruces, NM	71.3	48.2	68.8	46.7	**88.5**	76.8	62.4	**66.1**	18
Las Vegas, NM	55.7	11.5	28.1	22.1	**85.5**	14.0	29.2	35.2	176
Leelanau Peninsula, MI	1.0	12.0	11.5	**87.9**	63.9	7.5	**97.5**	40.2	158
Leesburg–Mount Dora, FL	79.8	46.2	54.2	46.2	37.7	45.7	18.6	46.9	122

★ = *in the overall top 30 places to retire*; **orange text** = *in the top 30 places in that category*

RETIREMENT PLACE	CLIMATE	THE ECONOMY	SERV-ICES	AMBI-ENCE	COSTS OF LIVING	HOUSING	PERSONAL SAFETY	MEAN SCORE	RANK
Litchfield Hills, CT	15.5	45.7	29.6	69.8	16.6	48.7	**86.5**	44.6	135
Long Beach Peninsula, WA	34.6	1.5	18.5	21.1	66.9	2.0	44.8	27.1	196
Loudoun County, VA	5.0	**98.9**	25.6	53.2	8.6	68.3	81.5	48.7	106
Lower Cape May, NJ	38.6	23.6	11.0	**94.9**	13.1	26.6	24.2	33.1	180
Madison, MS	41.7	77.8	28.1	42.7	78.9	**100.0**	57.8	61.0	38
★ Madison, WI	3.5	**89.9**	**98.4**	**85.4**	28.7	**92.4**	57.3	**65.1**	23
Marble Falls–Lake LBJ, TX	61.3	39.6	14.5	2.5	**87.5**	61.8	73.4	48.7	107
Mariposa, CA	81.4	7.5	1.5	50.2	14.6	0.0	37.7	27.6	195
Martha's Vineyard, MA	14.0	20.1	31.6	79.3	4.1	16.5	84.5	35.7	174
Maryville, TN	25.1	77.3	70.3	16.0	**90.5**	70.8	39.2	55.6	70
Maui, HI	**93.9**	84.9	35.6	**91.4**	4.6	27.6	27.2	52.2	88
McAllen–Alamo, TX	76.8	81.4	49.7	9.0	**100.0**	**98.4**	11.1	60.9	39
McCall, ID	21.1	11.0	0.5	40.7	44.3	37.6	50.8	29.4	190
★ Medford–Ashland, OR	79.3	83.4	69.3	76.8	40.3	66.3	30.7	**63.7**	27
Melbourne–Palm Bay, FL	**86.9**	67.8	75.8	**85.9**	40.8	61.3	9.1	61.1	37
Mendocino–Fort Bragg, CA	**95.4**	9.5	60.3	27.6	8.1	2.5	30.2	33.4	179
Middle Cape Cod, MA	16.5	55.2	57.7	**100.0**	16.1	24.6	38.2	44.0	138
Monadnock Region, NH	0.0	27.6	47.7	50.2	58.8	51.2	**95.5**	47.3	119
Montrose, CO	57.7	28.1	34.1	25.6	82.0	19.5	82.5	47.1	121
★ Morro Bay–Cambria, CA	**98.4**	80.9	80.9	69.3	3.1	50.2	81.0	**66.3**	15
★ Murray–Kentucky Lake, KY	33.6	22.1	**91.9**	4.5	**95.0**	72.8	61.4	54.5	74
★ Myrtle Beach, SC	53.7	**88.4**	64.8	79.8	67.9	**93.9**	0.0	**64.1**	25
★ Naples, FL	**85.4**	**97.4**	56.2	80.4	10.6	**89.9**	37.2	**65.3**	20
Natchitoches, LA	40.7	4.5	44.2	29.1	**99.0**	33.6	4.1	36.5	173
Nelson County, VA	18.0	0.0	12.0	14.0	55.8	4.0	**92.5**	28.0	194
New Bern, NC	26.6	54.7	47.2	43.2	78.4	**88.4**	33.2	53.1	85
New Braunfels, TX	66.3	57.7	73.8	35.6	83.5	78.3	45.3	62.9	33
Newport–Lincoln City, OR	65.3	13.5	27.1	44.7	31.2	10.5	13.6	29.4	191
Norfork Lake, AR	28.6	20.6	70.8	3.5	92.5	34.6	77.4	46.9	123
Northampton–Amherst, MA	15.0	44.2	79.8	64.3	27.2	41.7	66.4	48.4	111
Northern Neck, VA	24.1	2.5	26.1	49.7	28.2	0.5	**97.0**	32.6	182
Oakhurst–Coarsegold, CA	80.9	66.8	5.5	9.5	20.7	43.2	22.7	35.6	175
Ocala, FL	73.8	57.2	42.7	77.8	63.4	62.3	13.1	55.8	69
Ocean City, MD	33.6	19.5	7.0	63.3	29.2	13.5	5.6	24.5	199
Oxford, MS	42.2	41.2	74.3	3.0	**87.0**	**93.4**	**98.0**	62.7	34
Pagosa Springs, CO	46.7	33.1	6.5	29.6	56.8	41.2	66.9	40.1	159
Pahrump Valley, NV	84.4	65.3	4.5	15.0	29.7	82.9	48.8	47.2	120
Palmer–Wasilla, AK	13.0	38.1	8.0	15.5	48.3	**91.4**	1.1	30.8	186
Palm Springs–Coachella Valley, CA	**97.4**	**93.4**	60.8	80.9	10.1	59.7	7.1	58.5	54
Panama City, FL	66.8	76.8	64.3	23.1	47.8	**87.9**	7.6	53.5	83
Paradise–Magalia, CA	**93.4**	42.2	81.4	52.7	17.6	22.1	35.2	49.2	102
Park City, UT	29.6	76.3	22.6	71.3	9.6	80.4	85.0	53.5	82
Payson, AZ	80.4	53.7	13.5	23.6	47.3	21.6	28.2	38.3	165
Pendleton District, SC	56.2	32.6	21.1	11.0	**89.5**	54.2	21.7	40.9	152
Pensacola, FL	41.2	**85.9**	**85.9**	70.3	55.3	73.8	11.6	60.6	42
Petoskey–Harbor Springs, MI	4.5	36.6	75.3	72.3	79.4	57.2	79.4	57.8	61
Pike County, PA	20.6	24.6	5.0	21.6	41.8	15.0	**94.0**	31.8	185
★ Placer County, CA	**91.9**	**96.9**	72.8	63.8	3.6	57.7	59.8	**63.8**	26
Port Angeles–Sequim, WA	**86.4**	28.6	71.3	34.1	42.3	6.5	56.3	46.5	126
Port Charlotte, FL	78.8	72.3	37.6	51.2	33.7	52.2	34.7	51.5	91
Port St. Lucie, FL	69.3	37.1	45.2	10.5	45.3	52.7	17.1	39.6	161
Port Townsend, WA	**85.9**	37.6	40.2	53.7	22.7	35.1	58.3	47.6	116
Prescott–Prescott Valley, AZ	**87.9**	71.3	83.9	**91.9**	18.6	33.1	28.7	59.3	49
Rabun County, GA	43.2	1.0	17.5	22.1	79.9	23.1	78.9	38.0	166
Rehoboth Bay–Indian River Bay, DE	30.6	45.2	66.3	49.2	51.3	20.6	23.7	41.0	151
Rio Rancho, NM	55.2	**89.9**	8.5	47.7	72.4	83.4	56.8	59.1	51
Rockport–Aransas Pass, TX	62.3	3.5	2.5	71.8	**91.5**	56.7	3.6	41.7	149
Roswell, NM	49.7	31.6	20.1	7.0	**97.5**	31.1	23.2	37.2	168
Ruidoso, NM	78.3	7.0	36.1	45.7	75.9	26.1	16.6	40.8	153
St. Augustine, FL	82.4	59.7	57.2	74.3	12.6	50.7	33.7	52.9	86
★ St. George–Zion, UT	67.8	79.3	73.3	61.3	49.3	**90.4**	83.5	**72.1**	2
St. Jay–Northeast Kingdom, VT	8.5	9.0	39.6	18.0	71.4	44.7	**91.5**	40.4	157
St. Marys, GA	71.8	40.2	22.1	19.5	81.0	**97.4**	32.7	52.1	89
St. Simons–Jekyll Islands, GA	83.4	51.2	69.8	56.7	67.4	65.3	8.1	57.4	63
Sandpoint–Lake Pend Oreille, ID	7.5	34.6	35.1	47.2	57.3	12.5	78.4	38.9	163
San Juan Islands, WA	69.8	29.6	15.0	48.7	6.1	54.7	**96.0**	45.7	130

continued

★ = *in the overall top 30 places to retire;* **orange text** = *in the top 30 places in that category*

RETIREMENT PLACE	CLIMATE	THE ECONOMY	SERV-ICES	AMBI-ENCE	COSTS OF LIVING	HOUSING	PERSONAL SAFETY	MEAN SCORE	RANK
Santa Barbara, CA	100.0	75.3	95.4	74.8	1.6	25.6	35.7	58.3	56
Santa Fe, NM	56.7	85.4	68.3	68.8	26.2	62.8	12.6	54.4	75
★ Sarasota, FL	90.9	92.4	79.3	96.9	23.7	64.3	26.2	67.7	10
★ Savannah, GA	65.8	56.7	80.4	97.4	73.4	86.4	3.1	66.2	17
★ Scottsdale, AZ	97.9	97.9	87.9	93.4	7.1	49.2	47.8	68.7	8
Sebring–Avon Park, FL	73.3	19.0	38.1	17.0	71.9	39.6	25.7	40.7	155
Sedona, AZ	75.8	74.3	89.9	88.9	5.6	27.1	14.6	53.7	79
Silver City, NM	68.8	14.5	51.2	18.5	95.5	21.1	70.4	48.6	109
Silverthorne–Breckenridge, CO	27.1	56.2	7.5	92.9	11.1	44.2	60.4	42.8	144
Smith Mountain Lake, VA	46.2	21.1	27.6	26.1	37.2	8.0	93.5	37.1	170
Sonora–Twain Harte, CA	92.4	26.1	55.7	43.7	14.1	3.5	34.2	38.5	164
Southern Berkshire County, MA	14.5	38.6	52.2	82.9	43.8	60.3	65.4	51.1	94
Southern Pines–Pinehurst, NC	46.7	44.7	56.7	60.3	56.3	63.8	63.4	56.0	67
Southport–Brunswick Islands, NC	54.2	70.8	36.6	25.1	57.8	67.3	48.3	51.4	92
State College, PA	29.1	58.2	78.3	27.1	50.3	46.7	87.0	53.8	78
Sullivan County, NY	7.0	23.1	16.5	42.2	35.7	36.6	51.3	30.3	188
Summerville, SC	35.1	49.2	19.5	17.5	84.0	79.8	20.7	43.7	141
Taos, NM	51.2	34.1	34.6	59.7	50.8	8.5	71.4	44.3	136
Thomasville, GA	70.3	52.2	96.9	13.0	98.0	70.3	40.8	63.1	31
Toms River–Barnegat Bay, NJ	21.6	62.8	58.7	77.3	17.1	11.5	83.0	47.4	118
★ Traverse City, MI	6.0	64.3	93.9	81.4	76.9	80.9	67.9	67.3	12
Tryon, NC	52.7	18.5	17.0	5.5	70.9	20.1	74.9	37.1	171
★ Tucson, AZ	81.9	91.4	96.4	96.4	32.7	55.7	2.6	65.3	20
Vero Beach, FL	75.3	61.8	48.7	33.1	31.7	74.3	31.7	50.9	97
Victorville–Apple Valley, CA	95.9	90.9	67.3	78.3	15.1	47.7	19.1	59.2	50
Waynesville, NC	39.6	21.1	44.7	35.1	88.0	17.5	60.9	43.8	139
Wenatchee, WA	35.1	43.7	71.8	65.3	34.7	32.1	32.2	45.0	134
Western St. Tammany Parish, LA	48.7	46.7	41.7	38.1	64.4	69.8	42.3	50.2	99
Whidbey Island, WA	64.8	40.7	33.6	20.6	22.2	25.1	99.5	43.8	140
★ Wickenburg, AZ	94.9	97.9	87.9	68.3	19.6	59.2	44.3	67.4	11
Williamsburg, VA	25.1	63.3	90.9	83.4	9.1	42.2	76.9	55.8	68
★ Wimberley, TX	47.7	70.3	57.7	45.2	70.4	95.4	69.4	65.2	22
Woodstock, VT	7.5	18.0	50.7	81.9	34.2	42.2	93.0	46.8	125
York Beaches, ME	6.5	49.2	43.2	54.7	39.2	58.7	88.0	48.5	110
Yuma, AZ	96.9	51.7	40.7	37.1	62.9	72.8	21.2	54.8	73

RETIREMENT REGIONS

If your sights are set on southwestern desert retirement, parts of five states will qualify. If you're tending toward mountain living, even more states fill the bill. Considering retirement somewhere near a blue-water ocean coastline? Join the three out of five Americans in 26 states who are already there. Rather than focusing on states, why not think of regions?

Here are 18 regions that look, feel, talk, and act differently from one another, yet the places within them share a number of characteristics. Few of their boundaries match the political borders you'll find in your road atlas. Most of them embrace parts of more than one state. Some states are apportioned among more than one region.

On the following pages, *Retirement Places Rated* describes these regions into which the 200 places geographically and culturally seem to fall. Some regions are known as resort country and have been such for well

over a century. Some have unsophisticated, small-town manners. Others are relatively new and heavily promoted. One—the Florida Interior—is nationally synonymous with retirement.

Still others aren't associated with retirement by anyone but savvy residents of nearby metropolitan areas. The North Woods country of Michigan and Wisconsin is such a place for Chicagoans, Milwaukeeans, and Detroiters. So are some of the New England locations of coastal Maine and rural New Hampshire and Vermont to Bostonians and New Yorkers.

Each region's heading is accompanied by a thumbnail map showing its general location, plus the places within the region listed by their overall rank. The 30 best all-around retirement places are all over the map. The Desert Southwest and Gulf Coast regions each have five; the rest are spread in ones, twos, and threes among 13 other regions.

★ = in the overall top 30 places to retire; **orange text** = in the top 30 places in that category

Please remember that the number of older adults voting with their feet means that the 200 places profiled throughout this book are each in their own way preferred destinations. Whether you decide to move to any of them, or to one not profiled, or end up staying right where you are, *Retirement Places Rated* hopes that your later years will rank among your best.

California Coast

Laguna Beach–Dana Point, CA (9)
Morro Bay–Cambria, CA (15)
Santa Barbara, CA (56)
Carmel–Pebble Beach, CA (84)
Mendocino–Fort Bragg, CA (179)

For all its troubles—earthquakes; fires; flooding; budget deficits; flush times, followed by slumps, followed by flush times; and political turmoil—California still has long-term strengths. For some, it is also a fine state for retirement; just ask the many native older adults who've returned after a disappointing period in Las Vegas or Phoenix.

California's settled coast certainly isn't a homogeneous area, stretching as it does from the Border Beach on the Mexican boundary all the way up to the wine country north of San Francisco and beyond. About the only natural features these five California Coast places have in common are a Pacific shoreline and a mild climate that moves from Mediterranean to marine as you head north.

All five places in this region rank highest in their mild climates but also for their available services and long-term prospects for job growth. The locations get middling marks for crime and for ambience. After price declines through the early 1990s, the region once again saw rapid home price appreciation in the new century. Expensive real estate sets this region apart from all the others. Consequently, all five California Coast retirement places cluster near the bottom in costs of living and how far typical retirement incomes will stretch.

For all that, the California Coast has been popular for retirement since the end of World War II. One in 7 retired Navy officers lives somewhere within San Diego County, as does 1 in 50 retired physicians. For decades, San Luis Obispo County was one of the most populous areas in the country without a large central city. Much of its current growth comes from attracting older persons.

Nonetheless, because of the high cost of living, a limited supply of water, and restrictions on development, population growth along the California Coast has slowed. Indeed, some experts predict the area will continue to lose more retired persons than it will attract. The living may be easy, but it is not cheap.

The essential take: This region is the best of all the retirement areas profiled in *Retirement Places Rated* in average scores across six of the seven categories. The seventh? Costs of Living.

Desert Southwest

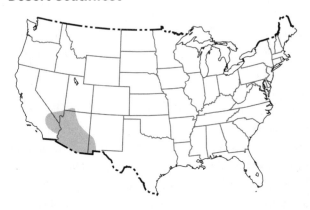

St. George–Zion, UT (2)
Henderson, NV (4)
Scottsdale, AZ (8)
Wickenburg, AZ (11)
Tucson, AZ (20)
Prescott–Prescott Valley, AZ (49)
Victorville–Apple Valley, CA (50)
Palm Springs–Coachella Valley, CA (54)
Lake Havasu City, AZ (55)
Cottonwood–Verde Valley, AZ (60)
Kingman, AZ (65)
Yuma, AZ (73)
Sedona, AZ (79)

Bisbee, AZ (105)
Silver City, NM (109)
Pahrump Valley, NV (120)
Payson, AZ (165)

This region generally sits in the southern end of the Great Basin between the country's two highest mountain ranges, the Rockies to the east and the Sierra Nevadas to the west. The two mountain ranges not only add beauty, grandeur, and ruggedness to the region but also block moist air coming from either the Pacific Ocean or the Gulf of Mexico. The entire region is high, mountainous, and dry. The valleys are dusty, with scant vegetation. The mountains and cliffsides, eroded by wind and sand, are jagged, angular, and knife-sharp.

If it's sun you're after, this is the place. One location, Yuma, is officially designated America's sunniest by federal climate record keepers. Hot, bright, cloudless days followed by cool, even chilly, nights are the rule here. This means you can enjoy outdoor activities in the daytime and still get a good night's rest under a blanket or two.

Rapidly growing Arizona is the typical Sun Belt state. To the alarm of many, suburban Tucson and suburban Phoenix will meet somewhere along I-10 in the next decade. Tucson has a high degree of ambience by *Retirement Places Rated*'s standards. The "Valley of the Sun" takes in Scottsdale, a highly ranked suburban city.

Many parts of the Desert Southwest suffer from high crime rates. Large areas such as Tucson, Palm Springs, and even smaller areas such as Kingman all rank near the bottom in that category. The supply of healthcare facilities varies greatly from location to location. Indeed, newcomers to Prescott–Prescott Valley and Cottonwood–Verde Valley report difficulties finding a physician, and residents of the Pahrump Valley in Nevada must drive 50 miles to Las Vegas for specialized care.

Despite its rapid population growth (the counties surrounding the 17 places profiled above together have gained nearly 4.5 million persons in the past 10 years, for example), this is thinly settled land. There is so much space here, with such great distances even between small towns, that people who have lived in thickly populated regions such as the Great Lakes or the Northeast may find it difficult to adjust to the feeling of isolation.

Florida Interior

Lakeland–Winter Haven, FL (48)
Gainesville, FL (52)
Ocala, FL (69)
Kissimmee–St. Cloud, FL (104)
Leesburg–Mount Dora, FL (122)
Sebring–Avon Park, FL (155)

Perhaps because they so recently hailed from other places, few of Florida's residents are aware of the state's long and engaging history. The land was first claimed by Spain in the 16th century, wrested away by the British, taken back by Spain, declared an independent republic by a group of ragtag Americans, and finally turned over by Spain to the United States in 1819.

Very little happened in this remote, mosquito-infested outpost until the real estate boom of the 1920s. Then, dream cities sprouted up everywhere as the pitch of the real estate promoter was heard in the land. Property values increased from hour to hour, and thousands of persons bought unseen acres, many under saltwater. It took three disasters—the hurricanes of 1926 and 1928 and the crash of 1929—to burst the bubble. But by then, the lure of Florida had been implanted in the American soul.

Florida has been elevated to its so-called "megastate" niche by a migration unique in American history. In 1950, the state had 2 million people. When the year 2010 figures are tallied, the number is forecast to top 20 million, surpassing New York as the third-largest state behind California and Texas. Nearly all of the increase is coming from people moving in from other states.

If you're determined to find whatever it is you're searching for in retirement, you'll find it somewhere in Florida. Florida is the number one tourist destination in the world. It has nine distinct media markets, two coasts, snow, perpetual sunshine, swamps, islands, new no-down-payment homes for $65,000, and houses you can't afford if you have to ask the price. If there are three factors that account for the numbers of highly rated places here, they are low living costs, climate, and the near-term outlook for employment. Two factors that mar their ratings unquestionably, however, are crime and a slight lack of ambience—qualities that *Retirement Places Rated* admits are difficult to define.

Gulf Coast

Fairhope–Gulf Shores, AL (7)

Sarasota, FL (10)

Fort Myers–Cape Coral, FL (14)

Naples, FL (20)

Bay St. Louis–Pass Christian, MS (24)

Pensacola, FL (42)

Bradenton, FL (46)

Largo, FL (57)

Panama City, FL (83)

Port Charlotte, FL (91)

Western St. Tammany Parish, LA (99)

Rockport–Aransas Pass, TX (149)

Apalachicola, FL (192)

The Gulf Coast, along with the Desert Southwest, has 5 of the top 30 retirement places. Extending along a 1,700-mile arc from Naples, Florida, westward to Brownsville, Texas, opposite Mexico on the Rio Grande, this region is the longest reach of American coast within a single climate zone. View it on a clear night from space shuttle height and you'd see most of the illumination coming from a stretch of Florida coast below Tampa Bay, another stretch from Panama City to New Orleans, and the enormous Houston galaxy.

Here is where tropical storms and hurricanes historically batter Texas, Louisiana, Mississippi, and Alabama, but spare a good stretch of Florida. After 2 years, Hurricane Katrina's devastation is still evident

between New Orleans and Mobile. In spite of the threat, this region is the fastest-growing part of each of the states that front the Gulf.

Except for lower scores for Rockport–Aransas Pass on an empty stretch above Corpus Christi, and for Apalachicola, in the isolated center of Florida's panhandle, each Gulf Coast retirement place ranks among the best in employment growth. Aside from several Florida locations—Fort Myers, Naples, Sarasota—each ranks among the top half in living costs. Many newcomers find summer weather wearyingly hot and regularly stormy, which accounts for the region's modest scores for Climate.

Hawaii

Maui, HI (88)

The Big Island, HI (124)

The last state to join the Union (1959), Hawaii is also the southernmost state. Just below 22 degrees of latitude, Honolulu, the capital, is as far south as middle Mexico. The state of 120 islands is 2,400 airline miles from mainland United States. Let's use the word *paradise* only once to note where it sits in the American mind. The word aptly fits. Then again, it doesn't.

This is the only state in the tropical climate zone, officially defined as anywhere temperatures never fall below 64°F. Orchids grow wild here, the sun shines most of the time, the Pacific trade winds keep the islands temperate, the beaches are superb, and the water is deep and blue.

Hawaii is one of just four states to exclude public and private pensions from its income tax. The cost of living, however, is so high that this is the only state to discourage mainland persons from moving in for retirement. From the Commission on Aging on down to pitchmen on the street selling condominiums to visitors, you're going to hear the discouraging word. Though the islands are relatively inexpensive to visit, they are unaffordable for year-round living for most retired persons. Here, Housing and Urban Development, the federal agency subsidizing housing costs, reports the country's highest fair-market rent.

Still, they come. Honolulu, like San Diego and San Antonio, is extremely popular with ex-military. Maui and the Big Island of Hawaii are now drawing older newcomers at a faster rate than Honolulu. Apropos of their size, the neighboring islands have middling ranks in services and prospects for employment growth. They also experience a surprisingly high level of ambience.

Heartland

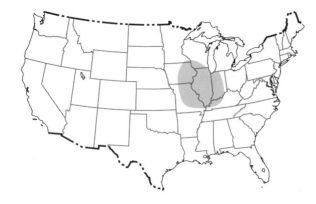

Madison, WI (23)
Iowa City, IA (30)
Columbia, MO (53)
Murray–Kentucky Lake, KY (74)
Brown County, IN (184)

Heartland, Middle Earth, Breadbasket—the names sometimes given to the central states evoke the change of seasons on featureless farmland or an area mostly flown over by persons bound for either coast.

Though farming is important here, industry is more so in certain parts. The land seems plain from the air, but it is far from being homogeneous. One way to find choice retirement spots is to home in on large universities, such as those of the Big Ten. Four cities—Columbus, Ohio; Lansing–East Lansing, Michigan; Madison, Wisconsin; and Minneapolis–St. Paul, Minnesota—are also homes of state government. Two—Ann Arbor, Michigan, and Evanston, Illinois—are suburbs of major metropolitan areas. Another four—Champaign, Illinois; Columbia, Missouri (home of the Big 12's University of Missouri); Iowa City, Iowa; and West Lafayette, Indiana—are towns where the academic calendar dominates community life. While Brown County in south-central Indiana isn't a college town, it is next door and minutes away from one of the country's best: Bloomington, home of Indiana University.

It isn't conjecture that Heartland college towns make up a distinct retirement region of their own. The proportion of persons 65 and over tends to be greater here than it is in the nation as a whole. Large land-grant universities in the Heartland have huge alumni organi-

zations, and many of these alums from the 1950s and 1960s are returning for the benefits of the college town they knew years ago: past friendships, the cultural and recreational amenities, the youthful population, and the human services usually found only in larger cities.

If hot summers and cold, snowy winters weren't factors, Columbia, Missouri; Iowa City, Iowa; and Madison, Wisconsin, would likely rank among the top 10 retirement places in this edition of *Retirement Places Rated*.

Inner South

Thomasville, GA (31)
Chapel Hill–Carrboro, NC (32)
Oxford, MS (34)
Madison, MS (38)
Hattiesburg, MS (45)
Athens, GA (64)
Southern Pines–Pinehurst, NC (67)
Natchitoches, LA (173)

This region is neither north nor, with the exception of Thomasville, so far south to be thoroughly Dixie. It's mainly in the center of the country's eastern half and includes North Carolina's and Georgia's Piedmont (but not their mountains—they are part of *Retirement Places Rated*'s Southern Highlands region) and most of Kentucky, Mississippi, and Tennessee.

Middle Tennessee, hemmed in by the looping Tennessee River, is gently rolling bluegrass country: fertile, well-watered, and famous for its fine livestock. The heart of the state, it is rich in tradition and history and its rural people keep up southern folkways.

Kentucky encompasses mountains in its sandstone area, deep gorges and caves in its limestone region, and swampy flats and oxbow lagoons in the far western part of the state. This end of Kentucky is called the Purchase, after the Jackson Purchase, which bought 8,500 square miles in Kentucky and Tennessee from the Chickasaw Tribe. Although Kentucky always had plenty of navigable rivers, it wasn't until the Tennessee Valley Authority (TVA) projects of the 1930s and 1940s that it had a large number of lakes. These impoundments, created by dams on the Tennessee River and its tributaries, have transformed both Kentucky and Tennessee into front-runners for fishing and water recreation.

Two of Mississippi's three locations in this region—Hattiesburg and Oxford—are prominent college towns. The third, Madison, is a suburb of the state capital at Jackson. Each attracts older adults from throughout the country thanks to "Mississippi Hometown Retirement," a marketing program to bring northerners into the state for retirement.

Why is the Inner South such an attractive retirement region? For one thing, the region lies north of more established retirement areas of the Sun Belt. Although the Sun Belt still remains a big drawing card for older adults, the "Retirement Belt" seems to be widening north. People are discovering the benefits of being closer to their former homes in the Midwest or Northeast; the desirability of mild, four-season climates as opposed to the monotony of the semitropical varieties; and the great advantages of low costs and low crime rates compared with many retirement areas farther south.

Furthermore, the gently rolling terrain with its pleasant scenery, the unhurried pace of life that is far less manic than in many parts of Florida, and the outdoor recreational options and the weather to enjoy them make the Inner South a winner.

Mid-Atlantic Metro Belt

Charlottesville, VA (19)
Williamsburg, VA (68)
State College, PA (78)

Fredericksburg–Spotsylvania, VA (87)
Loudoun County, VA (106)
East End Long Island, NY (112)
East Stroudsburg, PA (116)
Toms River–Barnegat Bay, NJ (118)
Annapolis, MD (132)
Rehoboth Bay–Indian River Bay, DE (151)
Charles Town–Shepherdstown, WV (156)
Lake Placid, NY (160)
Easton–St. Michaels, MD (168)
Lower Cape May, NJ (180)
Chestertown, MD (181)
Northern Neck, VA (182)
Berkeley Springs, WV (183)
Pike County, PA (185)
Sullivan County, NY (188)
Hampshire County, WV (193)
Nelson County, VA (194)
Front Royal, VA (197)
Ocean City, MD (199)

The area south from New York City to Washington and through the northern Virginia suburbs to Richmond is the most densely settled in America. Many cities here—notably Newark, Trenton, Philadelphia, Wilmington, Baltimore, and Washington—have been losing population for years.

In the midst of urban stagnation, however, one can easily overlook the pockets of suburban and rural retirement growth not visible from the Amtrak rails or I-95: the Atlantic beach counties, Chesapeake Bay, the Catskills, and small-scale metro areas such as State College, Pennsylvania, and Charlottesville, Virginia, home of major state universities.

The 127 miles of New Jersey's sandy Atlantic coastline, particularly from the tip of Cape May north to Toms River, has rebounded after years of decline. One in five residents of Ocean County is over age 65, compared with the U.S. average of one in nine.

The retired newcomers among them didn't have to come far; they are often New Yorkers and Philadelphians, some returning after a disappointing stint in Florida. Many planned retirement communities have been built or are being developed here, though people who want less structure can find many small seaside towns, particularly south of Atlantic City and west of the Garden State Parkway.

Farther south, you'll find retirement destinations within hailing distance of Washington and Baltimore on the Delmarva Peninsula and the shores of Chesapeake

Bay. Many of the bigger summer resorts resemble Miami Beach rather than the charming, small seaside communities they once were before the opening of the Chesapeake Bay Bridge in 1952. Delaware's Rehoboth Beach, which has a winter population of 2,040 and a summer population of 50,000, calls itself the nation's summer capital because so many federal workers crowd its beaches. Ocean City, just over the border in Maryland, is also a popular resort among Washington and Baltimore residents.

With 23 locations, the Mid-Atlantic Metro Belt embraces the most retirement places in this book. These locations are a kind of compromise between aging in places in greater New York, Philadelphia, Baltimore, or Washington and moving a long distance to Florida. Places in this region score above average in Personal Safety, Services, and the visible history and lively arts factors of the Ambience category. Its faults, for many, are winter weather and high living costs.

New England

Hanover, NH (16)
Burlington, VT (62)
Brunswick, ME (77)
Southern Berkshire County, MA (94)
York Beaches, ME (110)
Northampton–Amherst, MA (111)
Monadnock Region, NH (119)
Woodstock, VT (125)
Camden, ME (127)
Litchfield Hills, CT (135)
Middle Cape Cod, MA (138)
Bar Harbor, ME (143)
St. Jay–Northeast Kingdom, VT (157)
Martha's Vineyard, MA (174)

In New England, the preferred retirement destinations aren't in heavily urbanized Connecticut, Massachusetts,

or Rhode Island. To find the most popular retirement places, look in the rural pockets of the north, in Maine, New Hampshire, and Vermont. One big exception is Massachusetts' Barnstable County (Cape Cod), where one in three residents over the past 20 years has been a newcomer and where one in five is now over age 65. Two future exceptions may be in Hampshire County (Northampton–Amherst) in western Massachusetts and Litchfield County in northwest Connecticut.

In the decades since 1960, Maine's population has jumped 40 percent. By Sun Belt standards, that kind of growth seems paltry. For the Pine Tree State, though, it's been the fastest gain since the mid–19th century.

Most retired newcomers choose the rocky Atlantic coast over the hard-going farm areas and rough-cut paper- and lumber-mill towns in Maine's interior. Within the seascape counties—Hancock, Knox, Lincoln, and York—the places that draw retired people are the small lobster ports and summer resort towns off old U.S. 1, places with names like Camden, Bar Harbor, Ellsworth, Wiscasset, and Rockland.

New Hampshire is growing, too. Indeed, it is growing the most quickly of all the northeastern states—mainly at the expense of Massachusetts, its heavily taxed neighbor. You'll pay neither income nor sales taxes here. The only other state where this is still possible is Alaska. But you will pay handsomely for real estate around Hanover, home of Dartmouth College, and in the Monadnock Region in the southeastern part of the state.

For all its attraction for disaffected New Yorkers and Pennsylvanians who come to live year-round, Vermont remains the most rural state in America according to the U.S. Census Bureau. Two of every three residents here live beyond the built-up limits of cities. Much of the state unmistakably remains a 19th-century Currier & Ives landscape of sugar maples, dairy farms, and steepled white Congregational churches that dominate every green town common. In early October, the brilliant fall foliage draws busloads of weekenders from Boston and New York.

Of all 18 retirement regions, New England received the highest average ratings for Ambience, for Services such as medical care and continuing education, and also for its relative freedom from crime. The region's harsh winter climate and relatively high living costs, however, are reasons behind the slow growth in its retirement places.

North Woods

Traverse City, MI (12)
Petoskey–Harbor Springs, MI (61)
Door Peninsula, WI (137)
Leelanau Peninsula, MI (158)
Eagle River–Woodruff, WI (187)

One region violating the "Law of Thermodemographics" (warm bodies eventually head south to the Sun Belt and stay) has got to be the land that includes the northern counties of Michigan's Lower Peninsula and the Wisconsin counties in Packer country near Green Bay. Spring, summer, and fall here are lovely seasons but all too short. Winters are long and cold and are the main reason behind the low marks in Climate for the above five places.

During the 1970s, this area saw a population increase unequaled since waves of Finns, Germans, Czechs, and Poles arrived 120 years previously. Growth continues, but at a slower pace. On any summer weekend, campers, RVs, and boat-trailing cars crowd the northbound lanes of I-75 out of Detroit, I-94 out of Chicago, and I-43 out of Milwaukee. The traffic offers a clue to why the formerly depressed North Woods, forested with hemlock and Norway pine, have come back.

The area's pull is strong for many vacationers from the big industrial cities of the Great Lakes. Many later winterize their rural lakefront or flatwoods second home and retire year-round. It's said in Traverse City, Michigan, that if you want to know why it costs Ford and GM so much to make cars, the answer is the costly pension and healthcare benefits that retired autoworkers living up here are getting.

This is recreation land with a rugged, Paul Bunyan flavor, not only in the summer months, when the population doubles, but also during the fall deer-hunting and winter skiing seasons. Most of Michigan's 11,000 and Wisconsin's 15,000 lakes are up here. "In some lakes," the *New York Times* reported in a profile of Eagle River and its environs, "the fishermen can see 30 feet down in waters forest green, or black, or blue, depending on the time of day or the perspective, and can retrieve dropped eyeglasses or snagged fishing lures."

In spite of high personal income and property taxes in these two North Woods states, the cost of living is still lower than in most other retirement regions. The crime rate is low, too. Except for small cities such as Sturgeon Bay in Wisconsin and Traverse City and Petoskey in Michigan, though, you won't find much in the way of structured retirement activities or a full range of healthcare facilities. Nor will you find expanding job prospects. Do expect to drive a good distance for retail shopping; this is rough, beautiful, but sparsely settled country.

Ozarks & Ouachitas

Fayetteville, AR (13)
Conway, AR (47)
Hot Springs, AR (93)
Branson, MO (99)
Norfork Lake, AR (123)
Lake of the Ozarks, MO (146)
Eureka Springs, AR (147)
Lake of the Cherokees, OK (178)

After the Texas Interior, the Ozarks and Ouachitas region has the lowest average rating for Ambience and for Services, but the highest for low living costs. Its record for freedom from crime runs from middling to good.

Like the Southern Highlands region, the Ozarks and Ouachitas of southern Missouri, northern and western Arkansas, and eastern Oklahoma are a highland area with distinct folkways and geology that are undergoing rapid changes. In both areas, country craft galleries and bluegrass music festivals abound, and the mountain roads that wind through small towns also wind through some of the nation's prettiest countryside.

Here, an automobile is a virtual necessity. Many Ozark and Ouachita natives can trace their family names all the way back to Carolina and Virginia mountain roots.

Three million people live in these hilly Ozark plateaus and ridge-and-valley Ouachita Mountains. Wal-Mart (the corporate headquarters, not the many superstores) is the major employer here. Mention this region and you evoke an image of small-scale subsistence farming, chickens roosting in the hickory tree out back, shoeless springs and summers, moonshining, poverty, and isolation. Applied to the rural counties, the image was accurate until the 1960s and still is in some isolated pockets.

When the public utilities built hydroelectric dams, they produced a series of large impounded lakes in hardwood forests, which in turn produced resorts and a steady migration of retired people from Des Moines, Omaha, Tulsa, Oklahoma City, Memphis, Kansas City, St. Louis, and especially Chicago.

Some of the newcomers are what some call the new gentry—professional people with good incomes who see themselves doing a bit of farming on a small section of land. Others are the new peasantry, back-to-the-land types interested in raising their own food, promoting conservation, maintaining rural values, and using alternative fuel sources.

Lately, this region has been waking up to the problems that come with growth. Concerns about the loss of a special way of life are increasingly voiced; some locals say it may have already passed from the scene, never to be revived, despite local folk culture institutes and craft schools. The areas outside the biggest cities—Fayetteville and Fort Smith, Arkansas, and Springfield and Joplin, Missouri—aren't densely populated, yet some of the lakes are having pollution problems, and some of the better-known resorts are acquiring a tacky patina of liquor stores, fast-food outlets, tourist attractions, and New Age crystal shops.

Pacific Northwest

Medford–Ashland, OR (27)
Bend, OR (29)
Bellingham, WA (58)
Eugene, OR (72)
Port Townsend, WA (116)
Port Angeles–Seqium, WA (126)
Grants Pass, OR (129)
San Juan Islands, WA (130)
Wenatchee, WA (134)
Whidbey Island, WA (140)
Anacortes, WA (142)
Palmer–Wasilla, AK (186)
Newport–Lincoln City, OR (191)
Long Beach Peninsula, WA (196)
Chewelah, WA (198)

In the 1970s, no other state made so clear its desire to discourage immigration as did Oregon when its popular governor, Tom McCall, urged tourists to give the state a try. "But for heaven's sake," he quickly added, "don't come to live here." This awareness of the harm that rapid population growth can bring to beautiful, pristine land is commonly felt elsewhere in the Pacific Northwest.

Nevertheless, the near collapse of the lumber industry in Oregon and Washington in the early 1980s caused local planners to behave like their counterparts in other states and compete for industrial development and population growth.

Certain rural areas are being pitched as retirement havens—ironic, because older adults from the Great Lakes, the distant Northeast, and even sun-baked Southern California have been coming to this area for years to enjoy the clear air, quiet, and uncrowded space.

In Washington, retirement destinations are most often the islands reached by bridge or ferry from downtown Seattle, and places such as Port Angeles, Port Townsend, Sequim, and Bellingham with salt-water frontages. The area, with the tall Cascades and Olympic mountains in view, has a somewhat wet marine climate, low crime rates, and outstanding outdoor recreation endowments.

In Oregon, retired persons settle along the spectacular but damp Pacific Coast and in the forested cities and towns along I-5 between Portland and the California border.

A well-known demographer once observed that the popularity of the Pacific Northwest Cloud Belt just goes to show that "'Sun Belt' is a very imperfect synonym for population growth." Since the 1970s, for example, Bend and the surrounding forested environs in Deschutes County, Oregon, has been one of the fastest-growing places outside of Florida. Of more than 3,100 counties in the United States, the ones along Puget Sound in Washington ranked among the top in rate of growth over the same period.

Rio Grande Country

Las Cruces, NM (18)
McAllen–Alamo, TX (39)
Rio Rancho, NM (51)
Brownsville, TX (66)
Santa Fe, NM (75)
Alpine–Big Bend, TX (81)
Alamogordo, NM (131)
Taos, NM (136)
Ruidoso, NM (153)
Roswell, NM (168)
Las Vegas, NM (176)

The Rio Grande River rises in the Rocky Mountains in southwestern Colorado, flows south through the center of New Mexico west of Santa Fe, continues through Albuquerque and Las Cruces, and serves as a 1,240-mile boundary between Texas and Mexico before emptying into the Gulf of Mexico some 60 miles downriver from Brownsville.

This area has a large ethnic population. Two of every 5 persons are Mexican-American, and 1 in 10 is Native American. Like the Delta South, too, Rio Grande Country is distinguished by low incomes, large families, poor housing, joblessness, low levels of education, and other social problems.

Along the river's southward progress are a few pockets of phenomenal retirement growth. Not only Albuquerque and suburban Rio Rancho but also Las Cruces and the settled areas around them have all seen their number of residents over age 65 jump at three or more times the average national rate. Even with the well-publicized growth that most of semiarid New

Mexico has experienced, there are still fewer than eight persons per square mile. The desert-mesa vastness is imposing, the distances between towns great, and the loneliness outside city limits a little scary to retired persons hailing from large cities.

The lower valley in southernmost Texas isn't lonely at all. This is the number one winter tourist destination in all of Texas. Since 1990, Cameron County (Brownsville) and Hidalgo County (McAllen–Alamo) have together seen their population grow 34 percent. Many of the new residents are retired Midwesterners who found a climate as mild as Florida's and living costs nearly as low as Mexico's.

Rocky Mountain

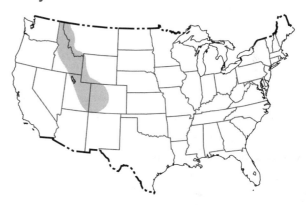

Fort Collins–Loveland, CO (3)
Kalispell–Flathead Valley, MT (6)
Flagstaff, AZ (35)
Grand Junction, CO (41)
Bozeman, MT (43)
Durango, CO (44)
Coeur d'Alene, ID (58)
Jackson Hole, WY (71)
Park City, UT (82)
Cedar City, UT (98)
Ketchum–Sun Valley, ID (103)
Montrose, CO (121)
Silverthorne–Breckenridge, CO (144)
Hamilton–Bitterroot Valley, MT (150)
Pagosa Springs, CO (159)
Delta County, CO (162)
Sandpoint–Lake Pend Oreille, ID (163)
Fairplay, CO (172)
Cortez, CO (177)
McCall, ID (190)
Driggs, ID (200)

What does green and rugged Coeur d'Alene in Idaho's panhandle have in common with sun-baked Silver City in southwestern New Mexico? Very little. Yet the Census Bureau lumps them together in a region it labels Mountain. By better reasoning, Silver City with its desert flavor more properly belongs in the Desert Southwest. When it comes to certain foothill-and-mountain counties in Arizona, Colorado, Idaho, and Montana, however, the feel is definitely high-country, definitely Rocky Mountains.

In spite of the reservations many older adults have about high altitudes and cold winters, the Rockies are emerging from their vacation-only status, becoming an area where older adults are moving for year-round living. After the Desert Southwest region, this high, rugged, and beautiful region has the greatest number of places profiled in *Retirement Places Rated*. Alas, just two places here are among the Top 30.

The area is distinguished by middling marks in Services, the Economy, and Costs of Living, and a poor one for winter climate. It is above average only in Ambience and Personal Safety.

In Colorado, one can easily distinguish between the Eastern Slope and Western Slope areas. Large cities such as Colorado Springs (in a setting that reminds many of Asheville in the North Carolina mountains) and Fort Collins are Eastern Slope. Grand Junction, near the Utah border, is the population center of the Western Slope. The two slopes have different political orientations (conservative Western Slope versus urban Denver–Boulder liberalism) and different growth rates.

In Idaho, where the population has risen by more than one-quarter since 1990, retired newcomers head for the city of Coeur d'Alene, within commuting distance of Spokane, Washington, or they settle near ski country—Driggs, Ketchum–Sun Valley, or McCall. In Montana, the spectacular but sparsely settled western counties—particularly Flathead, Lake, Missoula, and Ravalli—are the ones drawing older newcomers.

South Atlantic

Charleston, SC (4)
Savannah, GA (17)
Myrtle Beach, SC (25)
Melbourne–Palm Bay, FL (37)
St. Simons–Jekyll Islands, GA (63)
New Bern, NC (85)
St. Augustine, FL (86)
St. Marys, GA (89)
Southport–Brunswick Islands, NC (92)
Hilton Head Island, SC (96)
Vero Beach, FL (97)
Beaufort, SC (114)
Beaufort–Atlantic Beach, NC (115)
Summerville, SC (141)
Dare Outer Banks, NC (145)
Key West, FL (148)
Port St. Lucie, FL (161)
Edenton, NC (167)

The retirement places along the South Atlantic coast have a special appeal and flavor. Although the coastline is dotted with cities such as Charleston and Savannah, whose history began centuries ago, it first experienced rapid growth during the 1970s. In the intervening years, in spite of cyclical downturns, the growth has not stopped.

Most of these resort-retirement areas lie in low, marshy land either on the mainland itself or on nearby barrier islands. Palmetto palms, scrub oak, dune grass, and Spanish moss swaying in the sea breezes impart a languid, relaxed mood. Fishing shanties lie scattered near the piers where shrimpers, crabbers, and trawlers moor. Stately planter-style cottages set back from the narrow street are almost hidden behind tall hedges and are surrounded by massive live oaks. Streets paved with old oyster and clam shells; small gift shops, boutiques, and shops offering seafood, gumbo, and chicory coffee; taverns and inns of all ages and sizes—these are what you'll find in every metro area, town, and village of the coastal islands.

The South Atlantic resorts are less crowded and have lower living costs than most comparable places on the Florida peninsula. Furthermore, their summer months, while sometimes uncomfortable, are less rugged than those farther south. You are likely to find newer buildings and younger people here than in some older retirement havens.

On the minus side, crime rates are high. Of the 18 retirement places in this region, only 2 in North

Carolina—Edenton and Beaufort–Atlantic Beach—have above-average ratings for Personal Safety. Healthcare facilities can be inadequate, and while housing costs are generally low for the region, places such as the Dare Outer Banks are joining Hilton Head and Beaufort as expensive havens. Finally, these low-lying oceanside locations are subject to damage from severe tropical storms.

Southern Highlands

Asheville, NC (28)
Maryville, TN (70)
Dahlonega, GA (76)
Hendersonville–East Flat Rock, NC (80)
Crossville, TN (90)
Boone–Blowing Rock, NC (95)
Brevard, NC (128)
Waynesville, NC (139)
Pendleton District, SC (152)
Rabun County, GA (166)
Smith Mountain Lake, VA (170)
Tryon, NC (171)

There is a 600-mile stretch of Appalachian Mountains from Frederick County in Virginia to Hall County in Georgia that absorbed a good deal of antipoverty money during the 1960s and 1970s. Much of the area is still poor. Much of it, too, is as scenic as any place in the nation.

This is a land of peaks and ridges, rushing streams, and thundering waterfalls. In the earliest spring days, the hillsides burst with flowering trees and shrubs: rhododendron, azalea, dogwood, and magnolia. The George Washington, Pisgah, and Chattahoochee national forests stand tall with black walnut, pine, beech, poplar, birch, and oak. The mountain vistas, especially along the Blue Ridge Parkway, show row after spectacular row of parallel mountain ridges.

Distant parts of what you see from the road are so inaccessible that it is unlikely humans have regularly hiked more than 10 percent of the topography.

Because the area is bookended by Atlanta in the south and Washington in the north, it isn't at all unusual to encounter former urbanites from these major cities among the retired persons in places such as Rabun County in north Georgia, Asheville and Hendersonville in western North Carolina, and Smith Mountain Lake in Virginia. What is interesting is the number of retired northerners who settle here after a disappointing stint in Florida.

The Southern Highlands are a major destination for retired persons. Many of the region's communities are ideal for retirement living, offering a wide range of special services for older residents. The Appalachian counties generally combine low costs of living and housing, low crime rates, adequate healthcare facilities in most places, and some of the country's mildest four-season climates.

You're going to need a car to get around comfortably in much of this region, though. It is a rough wilderness area abundant in natural beauty, yet it is located within reach of major eastern population centers, which eliminates the feeling of isolation so often associated with wilderness areas.

Tahoe Basin & Sierras

Placer County, CA (26)
Carson City–Carson Valley, NV (40)
Paradise–Magalia, CA (102)
Grass Valley–Nevada City, CA (133)
Sonora–Twain Harte, CA (164)
Oakhurst–Coarsegold, CA (175)
Amador County, CA (189)
Mariposa, CA (195)

More than 24 million Californians live either in the hugely populated Southland (greater Los Angeles; Orange, Riverside, and San Bernardino counties; and greater San Diego) or in the hugely populated Bay Area (greater San Francisco, Oakland, and San Jose). Everyone else lives in a part of the state the Beach Boys seem never to have sung about.

You might call it the Other California. Parts of it—the Mother Lode Country and the area surrounding Lake Tahoe in both California and Nevada—are seeing a growing number of retired newcomers, most of whom are Californians. Sacramento, California, and Reno, Nevada, 110 miles apart, are the major cities.

Mother Lode Country, the interior marked by the Sierra Mountains, with alpine meadows, blizzard-filled passes, clear lakes, trout streams, and magnificent scenery, was once a hard-worked mining area. Now it is a tourist haven. Donner Lake, a popular summer beach resort, also doubles as a winter ski area. Even in midsummer, this high mountain lake tends to be on the chilly side. Tuolumne County, roughly 100 miles to the south, contains spectacular Yosemite National Park, with all of the opportunities for outstanding outdoor recreation.

Although the gold rush is long over, the scenery, mountain climate, and open spaces attract people for year-round life in their former vacation cabins. Places such as Grass Valley, Nevada City, Mariposa, and Twain Harte are seeing higher living costs, especially those associated with owning a home.

The essential take: mild, four-season Climate; expanding Economy; high Costs of Living; and middling scores in the Services, Ambience, and Personal Safety categories.

Texas Interior

Georgetown, TX (1)
Wimberley, TX (22)
New Braunfels, TX (33)
Lake Conroe, TX (36)
Kerrville, TX (101)
Marble Falls–Lake LBJ, TX (107)
Fredericksburg, TX (108)
Boerne, TX (113)
Cedar Creek Lake, TX (154)

Of all the states, Texas occupies the most unique place in the American mind. To paraphrase a bragging guidebook published by the state during the depression, Texas is so large that if it could be folded up and over, using its northernmost boundary as a hinge, McAllen would be plunked down in the middle of North Dakota. If it were folded eastward, El Paso would lie just off the coast of Florida.

Admission to statehood over a century and a half ago carried with it federal assurance that it could subdivide into five separate states should circumstances require. Out in the country, there are indeed more internally sharp contrasts here than in any other state. Northeast Texas looks like Arkansas. East Texas is deeply southern with small farms bringing in sugar cane, cotton, and rice. Southwest Texas is mainly lonely open-range cattle country at the top of a desert that begins in Mexico. Northwest Texas is high, dry, and broken, with occasional winter blizzards, looking like parts of New Mexico.

You'll find contrasting retirement regions too. The lower Rio Grande Valley is distinctly Hispanic and has winters as mild as Florida's. So do the Gulf Coast beaches, from South Padre Island up to just above Corpus Christi. Then there's an area in the middle of the state encompassing the lovely cedar-scented Hill Country along with greater Austin and greater San Antonio.

Austin, state capital and home of the University of Texas, seems to have the same terrain and natural vegetation as New England for many visitors. Metropolitan Austin has expanded so quickly that its population is triple what it was 30 years previously. The negative housing-price appreciation due to the slumping Texas economy is long over. Housing costs here are affordable by national standards but rising. Austin is a books and bureaucrats city, drawing a good many retired University of Texas alumni from all over the nation along with Texas government employees.

Wimberley, Georgetown, and Marble Falls are each close by.

San Antonio's appeal as a retirement destination, on the other hand, has five causes: Brooks, Kelly, Lackland, and Randolph Air Force bases, and Fort Sam Houston. Many veterans who were posted to them during the 1950s and 1960s have returned for the mild San Antonio winters, low living costs, and pleasant Hispanic atmosphere. Nearby are New Braunfels and Boerne, two suburban retirement destinations.

West of Austin and northwest of San Antonio, the Hill Country towns of Fredericksburg and Kerrville have spic-and-span layouts in their old sections. These are towns settled by Germans who fled their homeland in the mid–19th century. So attractive is this area that much of it is experiencing second-home development by prosperous Texans and Californians.

Appendix

RELOCATION RESOURCES

We hope that *Retirement Places Rated* has helped you figure out where you wish to spend your retirement years. However, you may find you still need more information about a place or you may want to do your own research. In this appendix you'll find some resources—print and electronic—that will help.

HOW PLACES PRESENT THEMSELVES

Local chamber of commerce organizations promote the benefits of living and doing business within the 200 places profiled in this book (see the section titled "Retirement Contacts & Place Finder," later in this appendix, for names and Web addresses or other contact information of the major chambers). Contacting chambers of commerce for their "newcomer's pack" produces a collection of promotional brochures, maps, business statistics, cost-of-living data, and events calendars, and may also trigger mail and telephone calls from real estate brokers. The annual *World Chamber of Commerce Directory* lists the chamber name, address, and telephone number, as well as the name of the chamber's contact person, for over 4,000 locations in the United States. It is available in larger libraries. By far, the most authoritative, clutter-free, noncommercial Internet gateway is www.uschamber.com, the website of the U.S. Chamber of Commerce.

Be aware that some chambers promptly respond to your inquiry with useful materials while others do not respond at all. Frequently, you'll receive more material if you identify yourself as a prospective new resident than you will if you say you're retired.

WHAT REALLY GOES ON IN OTHER PLACES

If you've identified a few likely locations, a short-term subscription to their local newspapers is invaluable (see "Retirement Contacts & Place Finder" later in this appendix for names and Web addresses or other contact information for each place's primary newspapers). After reading a month's worth, you'll have an excellent idea of consumer prices, political issues, and other matters on the mind of residents.

For the name, address, telephone number, monthly subscription cost, special features, and politics (typically independent) of each of the country's 1,635 daily newspapers, the best source is *Editor & Publisher's International Yearbook*. Good Internet gateways to online newspapers include The Internet Public Library (www.ipl.org) and NewsVoyager (www. newspaperlinks.com).

Note: You'll learn that one or two newspapers arriving in the mail every day quickly becomes overwhelming. A weekend edition is adequate for keeping up with local happenings. Most dailies publish Sunday editions and will fill "Sunday Only" subscriptions. Whether you want a daily or just a Sunday subscription, be sure to tell the circulation department that you want to receive the classified sections and shopping inserts. To save postage, newspapers omit these sections in mail subscriptions.

For similar information on the 6,890 semiweekly and weekly newspapers (often the only publications covering rural areas), *Gale's Directory of Publications* is an alternative source.

CHECKING IN WITH THE STATES

A variety of state agencies can be valuable resources for further research about the places described in this book. Whether your interest is planning a fact-finding vacation to a place or reviewing which states offer the best public services for the over-55 set, getting in touch with state agencies can help solidify your retirement place decision. The upcoming table, "State Agency Contact Information," lists phone numbers and Web addresses (where applicable) for the following state agency resources:

Aging & Retirement Agencies. Don't be put off by the bureaucratic titles. State aging offices are gold mines of information on government services, job openings, self-employment opportunities, volunteer activities and programs, and taxes. They also put you in touch with other local public and private organizations for retired persons.

Climate Centers. Here you can find state climatologists, who are persons appointed by the state government and who are also recognized by the director of the National Climatic Data Center of the National Oceanic and Atmospheric Administration as the chief climatologist of a particular state. The Internet gateway is www.stateclimate.org.

Tax & Revenue Divisions. After housing prices, the biggest cost difference between places in differing states is taxes. The best way to learn what your income tax will be in a new state is to write for its *resident* (not its *out-of-state*) income tax form and instructions, fill it out, and compare the bottom line with that of your current state income tax return. Even better, download the state's tax form from the Internet and e-mail the director of revenue if you have questions. The best Internet gateway is maintained by the Federation of Tax Administrators, a professional association of revenue department officials from each of the states: www.taxadmin.org/fta/link.

Travel & Recreation Offices. Free, quality travel guides abound. Attracting tourists is a competitive aspect of state government, and more than a few realize that capturing new residents is a happy consequence of strong travel promotion. You'll find that many of the contacts listed below can send you information on local retirement, in addition to a state travel guide, events calendar, and official road map.

State Agency Contact Information

STATE	AGENCY	PHONE NUMBER	WEB ADDRESS
Alabama	Aging & Retirement	334/242-5743	www.adss.state.al.us
	Climate Center	256/961-7752	www.atmos.uah.edu/aosc
	Taxes & Revenue	334/242-2677	www.ador.state.al.us
	Travel & Recreation	800/252-2262	www.touralabama.org
Alaska	Aging & Retirement	907/465-4879	www.alaskaaging.org
	Climate Center	907/264-7471	http://climate.uaa.alaska.edu
	Taxes & Revenue	907/269-6620	www.tax.state.ak.us
	Travel & Recreation	907/929-2200	www.travelalaska.com

STATE	AGENCY	PHONE NUMBER	WEB ADDRESS
Arizona	Aging & Retirement	602/542-4446	www.de.state.az.us/aaa
	Climate Center	480/965-6165	www.public.asu.edu/~aunjs/index.html
	Taxes & Revenue	520/628-6442	www.azdor.gov
	Travel & Recreation	800/842-8257	www.arizonaguide.com
Arkansas	Aging & Retirement	501/682-2441	www.arkansas.gov/dhhs/aging
	Climate Center		www.srcc.lsu.edu
	Taxes & Revenue	501/682-1100	www.arkansas.gov/dfa
	Travel & Recreation	800/628-8725	www.arkansas.com
California	Aging & Retirement	916/419-7500	www.aging.ca.gov
	Climate Center	916/574-2830	www.climate.water.ca.gov
	Taxes & Revenue	800/852-5711	www.ftb.ca.gov/
	Travel & Recreation	800/862-2543	www.gocalif.ca.gov
Colorado	Aging & Retirement	303/866-2800	www.cdhs.state.co.us/aas
	Climate Center	970/491-8545	http://ccc.atmos.colostate.edu
	Taxes & Revenue	303/238-7378	www.revenue.state.co.us
	Travel & Recreation	800/265-6723	www.colorado.com
Connecticut	Aging & Retirement	860/424-5274	www.ct.gov/agingservices
	Climate Center	860/486-0135	www.cag.uconn.edu/nrme/cscc
	Taxes & Revenue	860/297-5962	www.ct.gov/drs
	Travel & Recreation	800/282-6863	www.ctbound.org
Delaware	Aging & Retirement	302/255-9390	www.dhss.delaware.gov/dhss
	Climate Center	302/381-2294	www.udel.edu/leathers/stclim.html
	Taxes & Revenue	302/577-8200	www.state.de.us
	Travel & Recreation	800/441-8846	www.visitdelaware.net
District of Columbia	Aging & Retirement	202/724-5622	www.dcoa.dc.gov/dcoa
	Climate Center	None	
	Taxes & Revenue	202/727-1000	www.otr.cfo.dc.gov
	Travel & Recreation	202/789-7000	www.washington.org
Florida	Aging & Retirement	850/414-2000	http://elderaffairs.state.fl.us
	Climate Center	850/644-3417	www.coaps.fsu.edu/climate_center
	Taxes & Revenue	800/352-3671	http://dor.myflorida.com/dor
	Travel & Recreation	888/735-2872	www.flausa.com
Georgia	Aging & Retirement	404/657-5258	www.aging.dhr.georgia.gov
	Climate Center	706/542-6067	http://climate.engr.uga.edu
	Taxes & Revenue	706/542-6058	www.etax.dor.ga.gov
	Travel & Recreation	800/847-4842	www.georgia.org
Hawaii	Aging & Retirement	808/586-0100	www4.hawaii.gov/eoa
	Climate Center	808/956-2324	http://lumahai.soest.hawaii.edu/Hsco
	Taxes & Revenue	808/587-4242	www.state.hi.us
	Travel & Recreation	800/464-2924	www.gohawaii.com
Idaho	Aging & Retirement	208/334-3833	www.idahoaging.com
	Climate Center	208/885-6184	http://snow.ag.uidaho.edu/index.html
	Taxes & Revenue	800/972-7660	www.tax.idaho.gov
	Travel & Recreation	800/635-7820	www.visitid.org
Illinois	Aging & Retirement	217/785-2870	www.state.il.us/aging
	Climate Center	217/333-0729	www.sws.uiuc.edu/atmos/statecli
	Taxes & Revenue	800/732-8866	www.revenue.state.il.us
	Travel & Recreation	800/226-6632	www.enjoyillinois.com
Indiana	Aging & Retirement	317/232-7123	www.in.gov/fssa/elderly
	Climate Center	765/494-6574	www.agry.purdue.edu/climate
	Taxes & Revenue	317/233-4018	www.in.gov/dor
	Travel & Recreation	888/365-6946	www.enjoyindiana.com
Iowa	Aging & Retirement	515/725-3301	www.state.ia.us/elderaffairs
	Climate Center	515/281-8981	www.agriculture.state.ia.us/climatology.htm
	Taxes & Revenue	515/281-3114	www.iowa.gov
	Travel & Recreation	800/345-4692	www.traveliowa.com
Kansas	Aging & Retirement	785/296-5222	www.k4s.org/kdoa
	Climate Center	785/532-7019	www.oznet.ksu.edu/wdl
	Taxes & Revenue	785/296-8458	www.ksrevenue.org
	Travel & Recreation	800/252-6727	www.travelks.com
Kentucky	Aging & Retirement	502/564-6930	www.chfs.ky.gov
	Climate Center	270/745-5983	http://kyclim.wku.edu
	Taxes & Revenue	502/564-4581	www.revenue.ky.gov/forms
	Travel & Recreation	800/225-8747	www.kentuckytourism.com
Louisiana	Aging & Retirement	225/342-7100	www.portal.louisiana.gov/elderlyaffairs
	Climate Center	225/578-6870	www.losc.lsu.edu
	Taxes & Revenue	225/219-0102	www.rev.state.la.us
	Travel & Recreation	800/677-4082	www.louisianatravel.com

continued

STATE	AGENCY	PHONE NUMBER	WEB ADDRESS
Maine	Aging & Retirement	207/287-9200	www.state.me.us/dhs/beas
	Climate Center	207/581-3441	www.umaine.edu/maineclimate
	Taxes & Revenue	207/287-2076	www.maine.gov/revenue
	Travel & Recreation	888/624-6345	www.visitmaine.com
Maryland	Aging & Retirement	410/767-1100	www.mdoa.state.md.us
	Climate Center	301/405-7223	www.atmos.umd.edu/~climate
	Taxes & Revenue	410/260-7980	http://individuals.marylandtaxes.com
	Travel & Recreation	800/634-7386	www.mdisfun.org
Massachusetts	Aging & Retirement	617/222-7451	www.state.ma.us/elder
	Climate Center	978/664-5372	
	Taxes & Revenue	617/887-6367	www.mass.gov
	Travel & Recreation	800/447-6277	www.mass-vacation.com
Michigan	Aging & Retirement	517/373-8230	www.mdch.state.mi.us/mass/masshome.html
	Climate Center	517/355-0231	http://climate.geo.msu.edu
	Taxes & Revenue	517/373-3200	www.michigan.gov/taxes
	Travel & Recreation	888/784-7328	www.michigan.org
Minnesota	Aging & Retirement	651/431-2500	www.mnaging.org
	Climate Center	651/296-4214	www.climate.umn.edu
	Taxes & Revenue	651/296-3781	www.taxes.state.mn.us
	Travel & Recreation	800/657-3700	www.exploreminnesota.com
Mississippi	Aging & Retirement	601/359-4925	www.mdhs.state.ms.us/aas.html
	Climate Center	662/325-3915	www.msstate.edu/dept/GeoSciences/climate
	Taxes & Revenue	601/923-7000	www.mstc.state.ms.us
	Travel & Recreation	800/927-6378	www.visitmississippi.org
Missouri	Aging & Retirement	573/751-6400	www.dhss.mo.gov
	Climate Center	573/882-5908	www.mcc.missouri.edu
	Taxes & Revenue	573/751-4450	www.dor.mo.gov/tax
	Travel & Recreation	800/877-1234	www.missouritourism.org
Montana	Aging & Retirement	406/444-7788	www.dphhs.state.mt.us/sltc
	Climate Center	406/243-6622	http://climate.ntsg.umt.edu
	Taxes & Revenue	406/444-6900	www.mt.gov/revenue
	Travel & Recreation	800/847-4868	www.visitmt.com
Nebraska	Aging & Retirement	402/471-2307	www.hhs.state.ne.us/ags/agsindex.htm
	Climate Center	402/472-5206	www.nebraskaclimateoffice.unl.edu
	Taxes & Revenue	800/742-7474	www.revenue.state.ne.us
	Travel & Recreation	800/228-4307	www.visitnebraska.org
Nevada	Aging & Retirement	775/687-4210	www.aging.state.nv.us
	Climate Center	775/784-1723	www.climate.unr.edu
	Taxes & Revenue	775/684-2000	www.tax.state.nv.us
	Travel & Recreation	800/638-2328	www.travelnevada.com
New Hampshire	Aging & Retirement	603/271-4394	www.dhhs.state.nh.us
	Climate Center	603/862-7052	www.unh.edu/stateclimatologist
	Taxes & Revenue	603/271-2191	www.nh.gov/revenue
	Travel & Recreation	800/386-4664	www.visitnh.gov
New Jersey	Aging & Retirement	609/292-4027	www.state.nj.us./health
	Climate Center	732/445-4741	http://climate.rutgers.edu/stateclim
	Taxes & Revenue	609/292-6400	www.state.nj.us/treasury
	Travel & Recreation	800/847-4865	www.visitnj.org
New Mexico	Aging & Retirement	505/476-4799	www.nmaging.state.nm.us
	Climate Center	505/646-2104	http://weather.nmsu.edu
	Taxes & Revenue	505/827-0700	www.tax.state.nm.us
	Travel & Recreation	800/545-2040	www.newmexico.org
New York	Aging & Retirement	518/474-7012	www.aging.state.ny.us/nysofa
	Climate Center	607/255-3034	http://nysc.eas.cornell.edu
	Taxes & Revenue	800/225-5829	www.tax.state.ny.us
	Travel & Recreation	800/225-5697	http://iloveny.state.ny.us
North Carolina	Aging & Retirement	919/733-3983	www.dhhs.state.nc.us
	Climate Center	919/515-3056	www.nc-climate.ncsu.edu
	Taxes & Revenue	877/252-4052	www.dor.state.nc.us
	Travel & Recreation	800/847-4862	www.visitnc.com
North Dakota	Aging & Retirement	701/328-4601	www.nd.gov/humanservices
	Climate Center	701/231-6577	www.soilsci.ndsu.nodak.edu/ndawn
	Taxes & Revenue	701/328-2770	www.nd.gov/tax
	Travel & Recreation	800/435-5663	www.ndtourism.com

STATE	AGENCY	PHONE NUMBER	WEB ADDRESS
Ohio	Aging & Retirement	614/466-7246	www.state.oh.us/age
	Climate Center	614/292-0148	www.geography.ohio-state.edu/faculty/ rogers/statclim.html
	Taxes & Revenue	800/282-1780	www.tax.ohio.gov
	Travel & Recreation	800/282-5393	http://consumer.discoverohio.com
Oklahoma	Aging & Retirement	405/521-2281	www.okdhs.org
	Climate Center	405/325-2541	www.ocs.ou.edu
	Taxes & Revenue	405/521-3160	www.tax.ok.gov
	Travel & Recreation	800/652-6552	www.travelok.com
Oregon	Aging & Retirement	503/945-5811	www.oregon.gov/DHS
	Climate Center	541/737-5705	www.ocs.oregonstate.edu/index.html
	Taxes & Revenue	503/378-4988	www.oregon.gov/DOR
	Travel & Recreation	800/547-7842	www.traveloregon.com
Pennsylvania	Aging & Retirement	717/783-1550	www.aging.state.pa.us
	Climate Center	814/865-8732	www.climate.psu.edu
	Taxes & Revenue	717/787-8201	www.revenue.state.pa.us
	Travel & Recreation	800/847-4872	www.experiencepa.com
Rhode Island	Aging & Retirement	401/462-0500	www.dea.ri.gov
	Climate Center	None	
	Taxes & Revenue	401/222-1040	www.tax.state.ri.us
	Travel & Recreation	800/556-2484	www.visitrhodeisland.com
South Carolina	Aging & Retirement	803/734-9900	www.aging.sc.gov
	Climate Center	803/734-9568	www.dnr.sc.gov/climate/sco
	Taxes & Revenue	843/556-1780	www.sctax.org
	Travel & Recreation	800/346-3634	www.travelsc.com
South Dakota	Aging & Retirement	605/773-3656	www.state.sd.us
	Climate Center	605/688-5678	www.climate.sdstate.edu
	Taxes & Revenue	605/773-3311	www.state.sd.us
	Travel & Recreation	800/732-5682	www.travelsd.com
Tennessee	Aging & Retirement	615/741-2056	www.state.tn.us/comaging
	Climate Center	865/632-4222	www.srcc.lsu.edu
	Taxes & Revenue	615/253-0600	www.tennessee.gov/revenue
	Travel & Recreation	800/462-8366	http://state.tn.us/tourdev
Texas	Aging & Retirement	512/438-3030	www.texas.gov
	Climate Center	979/845-5044	www.met.tamu.edu/met/osc/osc.html
	Taxes & Revenue	512/463-4865	www.window.state.tx.us
	Travel & Recreation	800/888-8839	www.traveltex.com
Utah	Aging & Retirement	801/538-3910	www.hsdaas.utah.gov
	Climate Center	435/797-2664	http://climate.usurf.usu.edu
	Taxes & Revenue	801/297-2200	www.tax.utah.gov/forms
	Travel & Recreation	800/200-1160	www.utah.com
Vermont	Aging & Retirement	802/241-2400	www.dad.state.vt.us
	Climate Center	802/656-3060	www.uvm.edu/~ldupigny/sc/index.html
	Taxes & Revenue	866/828-2865	www.state.vt.us/tax
	Travel & Recreation	800/837-6668	www.vermontvacation.com
Virginia	Aging & Retirement	804/662-9333	http://vda.virginia.gov
	Climate Center	434/924-0548	www.climate.virginia.edu
	Taxes & Revenue	804/367-8031	www.tax.virginia.gov
	Travel & Recreation	800/934-9184	www.virginia.org
Washington	Aging & Retirement	360/902-7797	www.aasa.dshs.wa.gov
	Climate Center	206/543-3145	www.climate.washington.edu
	Taxes & Revenue	800/647-7706	www.dor.wa.gov
	Travel & Recreation	800/544-1800	www.tourism.wa.gov
West Virginia	Aging & Retirement	304/558-3317	www.state.wv.us
	Climate Center	304/766-3257	www.wvclimate.org
	Taxes & Revenue	304/558-3333	www.state.wv.us/taxrev
	Travel & Recreation	800/225-5982	www.state.wv.us/tourism
Wisconsin	Aging & Retirement	608/266-2536	www.dhfs.state.wi.us
	Climate Center	608/263-2374	www.aos.wisc.edu/~sco
	Taxes & Revenue	608/266-2772	www.revenue.wi.gov
	Travel & Recreation	800/432-8747	www.travelwisconsin.com
Wyoming	Aging & Retirement	307/777-7986	http://wdh.state.wy.us
	Climate Center	307/766-6659	www.wrds.uwyo.edu/wrds/wsc/wsc.html
	Taxes & Revenue	307/777-7961	http://revenue.state.wy.us
	Travel & Recreation	800/225-5996	www.wyomingtourism.org

Appendix

Immediately under each retirement place's heading is the name of one of America's 210 Designated Market Areas (DMAs) to which it belongs according to Nielsen Media Research, the firm that produces television audience ratings. A DMA, or media market, is simply an area where people get the same TV and radio station offerings and other kinds of media including newspapers and Internet content.

Next are entries that show the Internet address of the largest local newspaper, the official website of the principal city, and the website of the principal city's chamber of commerce.

Listed next are cities, towns, villages, and unincorporated places with more than 1,000 people within each retirement place's boundaries. Population figures are in parentheses to the right of each name. In instances where an area has just one place over 1,000 persons, the largest places are listed.

Incorporated areas are in plain text. They have official boundaries and have met legal requirements for incorporation as municipalities. Unincorporated areas are shown in *italics*. These entries are populated places identified as having local recognition but no legal boundaries.

ALAMOGORDO, NM (OTERO COUNTY)

DMA: Albuquerque–Santa Fe

Alamogordo C/C
www.alamogordo.com
City of Alamogordo
www.ci.alamogordo.nm.us
Alamogordo Daily News
www.alamogordonews.com

Populated Places
Alamogordo (36,245)
Boles Acres (1,172)
La Luz (1,615)
Mescalero (1,233)
Tularosa (2,858)

ALPINE–BIG BEND, TX (BREWSTER COUNTY)

DMA: Odessa–Midland

Alpine C/C
www.alpinetexas.com
City of Alpine
www.ci.alpine.tx.us
Alpine Avalanche
www.alpineavalanche.com

Populated Places
Alpine (6,065)

AMADOR COUNTY, CA (AMADOR COUNTY)

DMA: Sacramento–Stockton–Modesto

Amador County C/C
www.amadorcountychamber.com

City of Amador
www.amador-city.com
City of Jackson
www.ci.jackson.ca.us
Amador Ledger Dispatch
www.ledger-dispatch.com

Populated Places
Ione (7,607)
Jackson (4,303)
Plymouth (1,072)
Sutter Creek (2,748)

ANACORTES, WA (SKAGIT COUNTY)

DMA: Seattle–Tacoma

Anacortes C/C
www.anacortes.org
Anacortes American
www.goanacortes.com

Populated Places
Anacortes (16,083)
Big Lake (1,153)
Burlington (8,247)
Mount Vernon (29,271)
Sedro-Woolley (10,045)

ANNAPOLIS, MD (ANNE ARUNDEL COUNTY)

DMA: Baltimore

Annapolis & Anne Arundel County
www.annapolischamber.com
City of Annapolis
www.ci.annapolis.md.us
The Capital
www.capitalonline.com

Populated Places
- Annapolis (36,300)
- *Arden-on-the-Severn* (1,971)
- *Arnold* (23,422)
- *Brooklyn Park* (10,938)
- *Cape St. Claire* (8,022)
- *Crofton* (20,091)
- *Crownsville* (1,670)
- *Deale* (4,796)
- *Ferndale* (16,056)
- *Green Haven* (17,415)
- *Herald Harbor* (2,313)
- *Hillsmere Shores* (2,977)
- *Jessup* (7,865)
- *Lake Shore* (13,065)
- *Linthicum* (7,539)
- *Londontowne* (7,595)
- *Maryland City* (6,814)
- *Mayo* (3,153)
- *Odenton* (20,534)
- *Parole* (14,031)
- *Pasadena* (12,093)
- *Pumphrey* (5,317)
- *Riva* (3,966)
- *Riviera Beach* (12,695)
- *Selby-on-the-Bay* (3,674)
- *Severn* (35,076)
- *Severna Park* (28,507)
- *Shady Side* (5,559)
- *South Gate* (28,672)

APALACHICOLA, FL (FRANKLIN COUNTY)

DMA: Panama City

Apalachicola C/C
www.apalachicolabay.org
Apalachicola Times
http://comm.emeraldcoast.com/times

Populated Places
- Apalachicola (2,340)
- Carrabelle (1,290)
- *Eastpoint* (2,158)

ASHEVILLE, NC (BUNCOMBE COUNTY)

DMA: Greenville–Spartanburg–Asheville

Asheville Area C/C
www.ashevillechamber.org
City of Asheville
www.asheville.nc.us
Asheville Citizen-Times
www.citizen-times.com

Populated Places
- Asheville (72,231)
- *Avery Creek* (1,405)
- *Bent Creek* (1,389)
- Biltmore Forest (1,497)
- Black Mountain (7,650)
- *Fairview* (2,495)
- *Royal Pines* (5,334)
- *Swannanoa* (4,132)
- Weaverville (2,508)
- Woodfin (3,277)

ATHENS, GA (CLARKE COUNTY)

DMA: Atlanta

Athens Area C/C
www.athenschamber.net
City & County Unified
www.athensclarkecounty.com
Athens Banner Herald/Daily News
www.onlineathens.com

Populated Places
- Athens (103,238)
- Winterville (1,059)

BAR HARBOR, ME (HANCOCK COUNTY)

DMA: Bangor

Bar Harbor C/C
www.barharbormaine.gov
City of Bar Harbor
www.ci.bar-harbor.me.us
Bar Harbor Times
www.mainecoastnow.com

Populated Places
- Bar Harbor (5,118)
- Blue Hill (2,314)
- Bucksport (4,961)
- Castine (1,392)
- Dedham (1,490)
- Deer Isle (1,903)
- Ellsworth (7,021)
- Franklin (1,446)
- Gouldsboro (2,017)
- Hancock (2,270)
- Lamoine (1,662)
- Mount Desert (2,197)
- Orland (2,078)
- Penobscot (1,405)
- Sedgwick (1,067)
- Southwest Harbor (1,983)
- Stonington (1,164)
- Sullivan (1,249)
- Surry (1,453)
- Tremont (1,643)
- Trenton (1,466)

BAY ST. LOUIS–PASS CHRISTIAN, MS (HANCOCK & HARRISON COUNTIES)

DMA: New Orleans

City of Bay Saint Louis
www.ci.bay-st-louis.ms.us
City of Pass Christian
www.ci.pass-christian.ms.us
Mississippi Gulf Coast C/C
www.mscoastchamber.com
The Sea Coast Echo
www.seacoastecho.com

Populated Places
   Bay St. Louis (8,317)
   Diamondhead (5,912)
   Long Beach (17,283)
   Pass Christian (6,851)
   Waveland (7,227)

BEAUFORT, SC (BEAUFORT COUNTY)

DMA: Savannah

Beaufort Regional C/C
www.beaufortsc.org
City of Beaufort
www.cityofbeaufort.org
Beaufort Gazette
www.beaufortgazette.com

Populated Places
   Beaufort (12,058)
   Bluffton (2,341)
   Burton (7,180)
   Laurel Bay (6,625)
   Port Royal (9,347)
   Shell Point (2,856)

BEAUFORT–ATLANTIC BEACH, NC (CARTERET COUNTY)

DMA: Greenville–New Bern–Washington

Carteret County C/C
www.nccoastchamber.com
City of Atlantic Beach
www.atlanticbeach-nc.com
City of Beaufort
www.beaufortnc.org
The Beaufort Gazette
www.beaufortgazette.com

Populated Places
   Atlantic Beach (1,803)
   Beaufort (4,119)
   Cape Carteret (1,400)
   Emerald Isle (3,686)
   Harkers Island (1,525)
   Morehead City (8,847)
   Newport (3,840)
   Pine Knoll Shores (1,570)

BELLINGHAM, WA (WHATCOM COUNTY)

DMA: Seattle–Tacoma

Bellingham-Whatcom C/C & Ind.
www.bellingham.com
Bellingham Herald
www.bellinghamherald.com

Populated Places
   Bellingham (74,547)
   Birch Bay (4,961)
   Blaine (4,330)
   Everson (2,067)
   Ferndale (9,977)
   Geneva (2,257)
   Lynden (10,697)
   Sudden Valley (4,165)
   Sumas (1,069)

BEND, OR (DESCHUTES COUNTY)

DMA: Bend

Bend C/C
www.bendchamber.org
City of Bend
www.bend.or.us
The Bulletin
www.bendbulletin.com

Populated Places
   Bend (67,152)
   Deschutes River Woods (4,631)
   La Pine (5,799)
   Redmond (19,771)
   Sisters (1,212)
   Terrebonne (1,469)
   Three Rivers (2,445)

BERKELEY SPRINGS, WV (MORGAN COUNTY)

DMA: Washington, D.C.

C/C of Martinsburg & Berkeley
www.berkeleycounty.org
City of Berkeley Springs
www.berkeleysprings.com
The Morgan Messenger
www.morganmessenger.com

Populated Places
Berkeley Springs (703)
Paw Paw (507)

THE BIG ISLAND, HI (HAWAII COUNTY)

DMA: Honolulu

Downtown Hilo
www.downtownhilo.com
Hawaii Island C/C
www.gohilo.com
Hawaii Tribune-Herald
www.hawaiitribune-herald.com

Populated Places
Ainaloa (1,910)
Captain Cook (3,206)
Hawaiian Acres (1,776)
Hawaiian Beaches (3,709)
Hawaiian Ocean View (2,178)
Hawaiian Paradise Park (7,051)
Hilo (40,759)
Holualoa (6,107)
Honalo (1,987)
Honokaa (2,233)
Kailua (9,870)
Kalaoa (6,794)
Kapaau (1,159)
Keaau (2,010)
Kealakekua (1,645)
Kurtistown (1,157)
Leilani Estates (1,046)
Mountain View (2,799)
Nanawale Estates (1,073)
Orchidlands Estates (1,731)
Pahala (1,378)
Papaikou (1,414)
Pepeekeo (1,697)
Volcano (2,231)
Waikoloa Village (4,806)
Waimea (7,028)
Wainaku (1,227)

BISBEE, AZ (COCHISE COUNTY)

DMA: Tucson

Bisbee C/C
www.bisbeearizona.com
City of Bisbee
www.cityofbisbee.com
The Bisbee Observer
www.thebisbeeobserver.com

Populated Places
Benson (4,934)
Bisbee (6,177)
Douglas (16,791)

Huachuca City (1,890)
Pirtleville (1,550)
Sierra Vista (41,908)
St. David (1,744)
Tombstone (1,569)
Whetstone (2,354)
Willcox (3,769)

BOERNE, TX (KENDALL COUNTY)

DMA: San Antonio

City of Boerne
www.ci.boerne.tx.us
Greater Boerne Area C/C
www.boerne.org
The Boerne Star
www.boernestar.com

Populated Places
Boerne (8,054)
Comfort (2,358)

BOONE–BLOWING ROCK, NC (WATAUGA COUNTY)

DMA: Charlotte

Blowing Rock C/C
www.blowingrock.com/chamber.php
Boone Area C/C
www.boonechamber.com
City of Blowing Rock
www.townofblowingrock.com
City of Boone
www.townofboone.net
The Mountain Times
www.mountaintimes.com
The Watauga Democrat
www.wataugademocrat.com

Populated Places
Blowing Rock (1,463)
Boone (13,192)

BOZEMAN, MT (GALLATIN COUNTY)

DMA: Butte–Bozeman

Bozeman Area C/C
www.bozemanchamber.com
City of Bozeman
www.bozeman.net
Bozeman Daily Chronicle
www.bozemandailychronicle.com

Populated Places
Belgrade (7,033)
Big Sky (1,221)
Bozeman (33,535)
Four Corners (1,828)
Manhattan (1,465)
Three Forks (1,845)
West Yellowstone (1,223)

BRADENTON, FL (MANATEE COUNTY)

DMA: Tampa–St. Petersburg

City of Bradenton
www.cityofbradenton.com
Manatee C/C
www.manateechamber.com
Bradenton Herald
www.bradenton.com

Populated Places
Anna Maria (1,867)
Bayshore Gardens (17,350)
Bradenton (53,917)
Bradenton Beach (1,561)
Cortez (4,491)
Ellenton (3,142)
Holmes Beach (5,100)
Memphis (7,264)
Palmetto (13,510)
Samoset (3,440)
South Bradenton (21,587)
West Bradenton (4,444)
West Samoset (5,507)
Whitfield (2,984)

BRANSON, MO (TANEY COUNTY)

DMA: Springfield

Branson/Lakes Area C/C
www.explorebranson.com
City of Branson
www.branson.com
Branson Daily News
www.bransondailynews.com

Populated Places
Branson (7,008)
Forsyth (1,706)
Hollister (3,835)
Merriam Woods (1,133)

BREVARD, NC (TRANSYLVANIA COUNTY)

DMA: Greenville–Spartanburg–Asheville

City of Brevard
www.cityofbrevard.com
Transylvania Brevard C/C
www.brevardncchamber.org
Hendersonville Times-News
www.hendersonvillenews.com

Populated Places
Brevard (6,643)

BROWN COUNTY, IN (BROWN COUNTY)

DMA: Indianapolis

Brown County C/C
www.browncounty.org
Brown County Democrat
www.browncountyindiana.com

Populated Places
Nashville (804)

BROWNSVILLE, TX (CAMERON COUNTY)

DMA: Harlingen–Weslaco–Brownsville

Brownsville C/C
www.brownsvillechamber.com
City of Brownsville
www.brownsville.org
Brownsville Herald
www.brownsvilleherald.com

Populated Places
Brownsville (167,493)
Cameron Park (5,961)
Combes (2,840)
Harlingen (62,318)
La Feria (6,815)
Laguna Heights (1,990)
Laguna Vista (2,600)
Laureles (3,285)
Los Fresnos (5,192)
Los Indios (1,194)
Olmito (1,198)
Palm Valley (1,282)
Port Isabel (5,373)
Primera (3,200)
Rancho Viejo (1,799)
Rio Hondo (2,082)
San Benito (24,699)
Santa Rosa (2,946)
South Padre Island (2,588)
South Point (1,118)

BRUNSWICK, ME (CUMBERLAND COUNTY)

DMA: Portland–Auburn

City of Brunswick
www.brunswickme.org
Southern Midcoast Maine C/C
www.midcoastmaine.com
The Times Record
www.timesrecord.com

Populated Places
Baldwin (1,373)
Bridgton (5,216)
Brunswick (21,820)
Cape Elizabeth (8,922)
Casco (3,649)
Cumberland (7,656)
Falmouth (10,601)
Freeport (8,066)
Gorham (15,300)
Gray (7,376)
Harpswell (5,242)
Harrison (2,355)
Naples (3,561)
New Gloucester (5,291)
North Windham (4,568)
North Yarmouth (3,485)
Portland (63,889)
Pownal (1,586)
Raymond (4,578)
Scarborough (18,897)
Sebago (1,495)
South Portland (23,742)
Standish (9,915)
Westbrook (16,108)
Windham (16,371)
Yarmouth (8,257)
Yarmouth (3,560)

BURLINGTON, VT (CHITTENDEN COUNTY)

DMA: Burlington–Plattsburgh

City of Burlington
www.ci.burlington.vt.us
Lake Champlain Regional C/C
www.vermont.org
Burlington Free Press
www.burlingtonfreepress.com

Populated Places
Burlington (38,531)
Charlotte (3,651)
Colchester (17,165)
Essex (19,146)
Essex Junction (8,841)
Hinesburg (4,425)
Huntington (1,939)
Jericho (5,068)

Milton (10,169)
Richmond (4,110)
Shelburne (6,995)
South Burlington (16,993)
Underhill (3,020)
Westford (2,129)
Williston (8,243)
Winooski (6,353)

CAMDEN, ME (KNOX COUNTY)

DMA: Portland–Auburn

Camden-Rockport-Lincolnville C/C
www.camdenme.org
City of Camden
www.town.camden.me.us
Camden Herald
www.camdenherald.com

Populated Places
Appleton (1,334)
Camden (5,341)
Cushing (1,289)
Friendship (1,206)
Hope (1,447)
Owls Head (1,644)
Rockland (7,658)
Rockport (3,504)
South Thomaston (1,503)
St. George (2,706)
Thomaston (4,169)
Union (2,350)
Vinalhaven (1,322)
Warren (3,804)
Washington (1,425)

CARMEL–PEBBLE BEACH, CA (MONTEREY COUNTY)

DMA: Monterey–Salinas

Carmel Valley C/C
www.carmelcalifornia.org
City of Carmel by the Sea
www.ci.carmel.ca.us
Carmel Pine Cone
www.carmelpinecone.com

Populated Places
Carmel Valley Village (4,700)
Carmel-by-the-Sea (3,994)
Del Monte Forest (4,531)
Del Rey Oaks (1,584)
Las Lomas (3,078)
Marina (19,006)

CARSON CITY–CARSON VALLEY, NV (CARSON CITY & DOUGLAS COUNTY)

DMA: Reno

Carson City Area C/C
www.carsoncitychamber.com
City of Carson City
www.carson-city.nv.us
Nevada Appeal
www.nevadaappeal.com

Populated Places
Carson City (56,062)
Gardnerville Ranchos (11,054)
Indian Hills (4,407)
Johnson Lane (4,837)
Kingsbury (2,624)
Minden (2,836)
Stateline (1,215)

CEDAR CITY, UT (IRON COUNTY)

DMA: Salt Lake City

Cedar City Area C/C
www.chambercedarcity.org
City of Cedar City
www.cedarcity.org
Cedar City Review
www.cedarcityreview.com

Populated Places
Cedar City (23,983)
Enoch (4,167)
Parowan (2,532)

CEDAR CREEK LAKE, TX (HENDERSON COUNTY)

DMA: Dallas–Ft. Worth

Greater Cedar Creek Lake C/C
www.cclake.net
Cedar Creek Pilot
www.cedarcreekpilot.com

Populated Places
Athens (12,559)
Chandler (2,470)
Gun Barrel City (5,962)
Malakoff (2,370)
Seven Points (1,251)
Tool (2,452)
Trinidad (1,147)

CHAPEL HILL–CARRBORO, NC (ORANGE COUNTY)

DMA: Raleigh–Durham

City of Chapel Hill
www.ci.chapel-hill.nc.us
Hillsborough/Orange County C/C
www.hillsboroughchamber.com
Chapel Hill News
www.chapelhillnews.com

Populated Places
Carrboro (16,425)
Chapel Hill (49,439)
Hillsborough (5,382)

CHARLESTON, SC (CHARLESTON COUNTY)

DMA: Charleston

Charleston CVB
www.charlestoncvb.com
City of Charleston
www.ci.charleston.sc.us
Charleston City Paper
www.charlestoncitypaper.com

Populated Places
Awendaw (1,187)
Charleston (107,505)
Folly Beach (2,263)
Hollywood (4,307)
Isle of Palms (4,579)
Kiawah Island (1,128)
Ladson (13,264)
Meggett (1,344)
Mount Pleasant (57,932)
North Charleston (85,430)
Ravenel (2,306)
Seabrook Island (1,213)
Sullivan's Island (1,897)

CHARLES TOWN–SHEPHERDSTOWN, WV (JEFFERSON COUNTY)

DMA: Washington, D.C.

City of Charles Town
www.charlestownwv.us
Jefferson County C/C
www.jeffersoncounty.com
Shepherdstown Chronicle
www.shepherdstownchronicle.com

Populated Places
Bolivar (1,080)
Charles Town (3,704)
Corporation of Ranson (3,793)
Shepherdstown (1,158)

CHARLOTTESVILLE, VA (CHARLOTTESVILLE CITY & ALBEMARLE COUNTY)

DMA: Charlottesville

Charlottesville Regional C/C
www.cvillechamber.org
City of Charlottesville
www.charlottesville.org
Daily Progress
www.dailyprogress.com

Populated Places
Charlottesville (40,437)

CHESTERTOWN, MD (KENT COUNTY)

DMA: Baltimore

Kent County C/C
www.kentchamber.org
The Star Democrat
www.stardem.com

Populated Places
Chestertown (4,673)
Rock Hall (2,566)

CHEWELAH, WA (STEVENS COUNTY)

DMA: Spokane

Chewelah C/C
www.chewelah.org
City of Chewelah
www.cityofchewelah.com
The Independent
www.chewelah.org/indep

Populated Places
Chewelah (2,285)
Colville (5,029)
Kettle Falls (1,588)

COEUR D'ALENE, ID (KOOTENAI COUNTY)

DMA: Spokane

City of Coeur d'Alene
www.coeurdaleneidaho.org
Coeur d'Alene Area C/C
www.cdachamber.com
Coeur d'Alene Press
www.cdapress.com

Populated Places
Coeur d'Alene (40,059)
Dalton Gardens (2,400)
Hayden (11,906)
Post Falls (23,162)
Rathdrum (5,740)
Spirit Lake (1,500)

COLUMBIA, MO (BOONE COUNTY)

DMA: Columbia–Jefferson City

City of Columbia
www.gocolumbiamo.com
Columbia C/C
www.columbiamochamber.com
Columbia Daily Tribune
www.showmenews.com

Populated Places
Ashland (2,175)
Centralia (3,657)
Columbia (91,814)

CONWAY, AR (FAULKNER COUNTY)

DMA: Little Rock–Pine Bluff

City of Conway
www.cityofconway.org
Conway C/C
www.conwayarkcc.org
Log Cabin Democrat
www.thecabin.net

Populated Places
Conway (51,999)
Greenbrier (3,615)
Mayflower (1,900)
Vilonia (2,719)

CORTEZ, CO (MONTEZUMA COUNTY)

DMA: Albuquerque–Santa Fe

Cortez C/C
www.cortezchamber.org
City of Cortez
www.cityofcortez.com
Cortez Journal
www.cortezjournal.com

Populated Places
Cortez (8,244)
Mancos (1,183)
Towaoc (1,097)

COTTONWOOD–VERDE VALLEY, AZ (YAVAPAI COUNTY)

DMA: Phoenix

City of Cottonwood
www.ci.cottonwood.az.us
Cottonwood/Verde Valley C/C
www.cottonwood.verdevalley.com
The Verde Independent
http://verdenews.com

Populated Places
Camp Verde (10,155)
Clarkdale (3,753)
Cottonwood (10,894)

CROSSVILLE, TN (CUMBERLAND COUNTY)

DMA: Knoxville

City of Crossville
www.crossvilletn.gov
Crossville-Cumberland County C/C
www.crossvilleedb.com
Crossville Chronicle
www.crossville-chronicle.com

Populated Places
Crossville (10,424)
Fairfield Glade (4,885)
Lake Tansi (2,621)

DAHLONEGA, GA (LUMPKIN COUNTY)

DMA: Atlanta

City of Dahlonega
www.cityofdahlonega.com

Dahlonega-Lumpkin County CVB
800.231.5543
The Dahlonega Nugget
www.thedahloneganugget.com

Populated Places
Dahlonega (4,519)

DARE OUTER BANKS, NC (DARE COUNTY)

DMA: Norfolk–Portsmouth–Newport News

Outer Banks C/C
www.outerbankschamber.com
Outer Banks Sentinel
www.obsentinel.womacknewspapers.com

Populated Places
Kill Devil Hills (6,550)
Kitty Hawk (3,358)
Manteo (1,301)
Nags Head (3,076)
Southern Shores (2,642)
Wanchese (1,527)

DELTA COUNTY, CO (DELTA COUNTY)

DMA: Grand Junction–Montrose

City of Delta
www.delta-co.gov
Delta Area C/C
www.deltami.org
Delta County Independent
www.deltacountyindependent.com

Populated Places
Cedaredge (2,148)
Delta (8,135)
Hotchkiss (1,043)
Orchard City (3,053)
Paonia (1,584)

DOOR PENINSULA, WI (DOOR COUNTY)

DMA: Green Bay–Appleton

Door County C/C
www.doorcounty.com
Door County Advocate
www.doorcountydailynews.com
Door County Magazine
www.doorcountymagazine.com

Populated Places
Brussels (1,271)
Egg Harbor (1,457)
Forestville (1,219)
Gardner (1,265)
Gibraltar (1,044)
Liberty Grove (1,820)
Nasewaupee (1,970)
Sevastopol (2,631)
Sturgeon Bay (9,180)

DRIGGS, ID (TETON COUNTY)

DMA: Idaho Falls–Pocatello

City of Driggs
www.driggs.govoffice.com
Teton Valley C/C
www.tetonvalleychamber.com
Jackson Hole News & Guide
www.jacksonholenet.com

Populated Places
Driggs (1,197)
Victor (1,365)

DURANGO, CO (LA PLATA COUNTY)

DMA: Albuquerque–Santa Fe

City of Durango
www.durangogov.org
Durango Area Chamber
www.durango.org
The Herald
www.durangoherald.com

Populated Places
Bayfield (1,639)
Durango (15,501)

EAGLE RIVER–WOODRUFF, WI (VILAS COUNTY)

DMA: Wausau–Rhinelander

City of Eagle River
www.eagleriver.govoffice2.com
Eagle River C/C
www.eagleriver.org
Vilas County News-Review
www.vilascountynewsreview.com

Populated Places
Arbor Vitae (3,320)
Boulder Junction (1,028)

Conover (1,221)
Eagle River (1,608)
Lac du Flambeau (3,158)
Lac du Flambeau (1,646)
Lincoln (2,686)
Phelps (1,460)
St. Germain (2,011)
Washington (1,648)

EAST END LONG ISLAND, NY (SUFFOLK COUNTY)

DMA: New York

Sag Harbor C/C
www.sagharborchamber.com
Long Island Press
www.longislandpress.com

Populated Places
East Hampton (21,267)
Riverhead (34,240)
Sag Harbor (2,368)
Shelter Island (2,443)
Southampton (58,756)
Southold (21,781)
Westhampton Beach (1,957)
Westhampton (2,869)

EASTON–ST. MICHAELS, MD (TALBOT COUNTY)

DMA: Baltimore

Talbot County C/C
www.talbotchamber.org
The Star Democrat
www.stardem.com

Populated Places
Easton (13,447)
St. Michaels (1,121)
Trappe (1,137)

EAST STROUDSBURG, PA (MONROE COUNTY)

DMA: Wilkes Barre–Scranton

C/C Pocono Mountains
www.poconochamber.net
Pocono Record
www.poconorecord.com

Populated Places
Arlington Heights (5,132)
Brodheadsville (1,637)
East Stroudsburg (10,621)
Mount Pocono (2,997)
Mountainhome (1,169)
Pocono Pines (1,013)
Stroudsburg borough (6,264)

EDENTON, NC (CHOWAN COUNTY)

DMA: Norfolk–Portsmouth–Newport News

Edenton-Chowan C/C
www.edenton.com/chamber
The Chowan Herald
252/482-4418

Populated Places
Edenton (5,001)

EUGENE, OR (LANE COUNTY)

DMA: Eugene

City of Eugene
www.eugene-or.gov
Eugene Area C/C
www.eugenechamber.com
The Register-Guard
www.registerguard.com

Populated Places
Cottage Grove (8,724)
Creswell (4,632)
Dunes City (1,257)
Eugene (144,515)
Florence (7,841)
Junction City (5,369)
Oakridge (3,147)
Springfield (55,641)
Veneta (3,477)

EUREKA SPRINGS, AR (CARROLL COUNTY)

DMA: Springfield, MO

City of Eureka Springs
www.eurekasprings.com
Eureka Springs C/C
www.eurekaspringschamber.com
Times-Echo (Carroll County News)
www.eurekaspringstimesecho.com

Populated Places
Berryville (4,935)
Eureka Springs (2,350)
Green Forest (2,859)

FAIRHOPE–GULF SHORES, AL (BALDWIN COUNTY)

DMA: Mobile–Pensacola

Alabama Gulf Coast Area C/C
www.alagulfcoastchamber.com
City of Fairhope
www.cofairhope.com
Fairhope Courier
www.topix.net/city/fairhope-al

Populated Places
Bay Minette (7,808)
Daphne (18,581)
Fairhope (15,391)
Foley (11,419)
Gulf Shores (7,263)
Loxley (1,435)
Orange Beach (5,055)
Point Clear (1,876)
Robertsdale (4,681)
Spanish Fort (5,642)

FAIRPLAY, CO (PARK COUNTY)

DMA: Denver

South Park C/C
www.parkchamberofcommerce.org
The Flume
www.theflume.com

Populated Places
Alma (183)
Fairplay (661)

FAYETTEVILLE, AR (WASHINGTON COUNTY)

DMA: Ft. Smith–Fayetteville–Springdale–Rogers

City of Fayetteville
www.accessfayetteville.org
Fayetteville C/C
www.fayettevillear.com
Northwest Arkansas Times
www.nwanews.com

Populated Places
Elkins (1,890)
Elm Springs (1,162)
Farmington (4,376)
Fayetteville (66,655)
Greenland (1,061)
Johnson (2,746)
Lincoln (1,904)
Prairie Grove (2,996)
Springdale (55,791)
Tontitown (1,621)
West Fork (2,195)

FLAGSTAFF, AZ (COCONINO COUNTY)

DMA: Phoenix

City of Flagstaff
www.flagstaff.az.gov
Flagstaff C/C
www.flagstaffchamber.com
Arizona Daily Sun
www.azdailysun.com

Populated Places
Flagstaff (57,391)
Fredonia (1,051)
Grand Canyon Village (1,460)
Kachina Village (2,664)
Kaibito (1,607)
Lechee (1,606)
Mountainaire (1,014)
Munds Park (1,250)
Page (6,794)
Parks (1,137)
Williams (3,094)

FORT COLLINS-LOVELAND, CO (LARIMER COUNTY)

DMA: Denver

City of Fort Collins
www.ci.fort-collins.co.us
City of Loveland
www.ci.loveland.co.us
Fort Collins Area C/C
www.fortcollinschamber.com
Loveland C/C
www.loveland.org
Coloradoan
www.coloradoan.com

Populated Places
Berthoud (4,887)
Campion (1,832)
Estes Park (5,812)
Fort Collins (128,026)
Laporte (2,691)
Loveland (59,563)
Wellington (3,469)
Windsor (1,035)

FORT MYERS–CAPE CORAL, FL (LEE COUNTY)

DMA: Fort Myers–Naples

Cape Coral C/C
www.capecoralchamber.com
City of Cape Coral
www.capecoral.net
City of Fort Myers
www.cityftmyers.com
Greater Fort Myers C/C
www.fortmyers.org
News-Press
www.news-press.com

Populated Places
Alva (2,182)
Bokeelia (1,997)
Bonita Springs (37,992)
Buckingham (3,742)
Burnt Store Marina (1,271)
Cape Coral (140,010)
Cypress Lake (12,072)
Estero (9,503)
Fort Myers (58,428)
Fort Myers Beach (6,834)
Fort Myers Shores (5,793)
Gateway (2,943)
Harlem Heights (1,065)
Iona (11,756)
Lehigh Acres (33,430)
Lochmoor Waterway Estates (3,858)
McGregor (7,136)
North Fort Myers (40,214)
Olga (1,398)
Palmona Park (1,353)
Pine Island Center (1,721)
Pine Manor (3,785)
Punta Rassa (1,731)
San Carlos Park (16,317)
Sanibel (6,072)
St. James City (4,105)
Suncoast Estates (4,867)
Three Oaks (2,255)
Tice (4,538)
Villas (11,346)
Whiskey Creek (4,806)

FREDERICKSBURG, TX (GILLESPIE COUNTY)

DMA: Austin

City of Fredericksburg
www.fbgtx.org
Fredericksburg C/C
www.fredericksburg-texas.com
Fredericksburg Standard-Radio Post
www.fredericksburgstandard.com

Populated Places
Fredericksburg (10,432)
Harper (1,006)

FREDERICKSBURG–SPOTSYLVANIA, VA (SPOTSYLVANIA COUNTY)

DMA: Washington, D.C.

City of Fredericksburg
www.fredericksburgva.gov
Fredericksburg Regional C/C
www.fredericksburgchamber.org
Free Lance-Star
www.fredericksburg.com

Populated Places
Fredericksburg (20,732)

FRONT ROYAL, VA (WARREN COUNTY)

DMA: Washington, D.C.

City of Front Royal
www.ci.front-royal.va.us
Front Royal Warren County C/C
www.frontroyalchamber.com
Warren Sentinel
540/635-4174

Populated Places
Front Royal (14,499)

GAINESVILLE, FL (ALACHUA COUNTY)

DMA: Gainesville

City of Gainesville
www.cityofgainesville.org
Gainesville Area C/C
www.gainesvillechamber.com
Gainesville Sun/Eclipse
www.gainesville.com

Populated Places
Alachua (7,557)
Archer (1,288)
Gainesville (108,184)
Hawthorne (1,443)
High Springs (4,157)
Newberry (3,804)

GEORGETOWN, TX (WILLIAMSON COUNTY)

DMA: Austin

City of Georgetown
www.georgetown.org
Georgetown C/C
www.georgetownchamber.org
Austin American-Statesman
www.statesman.com
The Austin Chronicle
www.austinchronicle.com

Populated Places
Anderson Mill (8,953)
Brushy Creek (15,371)
Florence (1,109)
Georgetown (39,015)
Granger (1,331)
Hutto (7,401)
Jarrell (1,406)
Jollyville (15,813)
Liberty Hill (1,491)
Serenada (1,847)
Taylor (15,014)

GRAND JUNCTION, CO (MESA COUNTY)

DMA: Grand Junction–Montrose

City of Grand Junction
www.gjcity.org
Grand Junction Area C/C
www.gjchamber.org
Daily Sentinel
www.gjsentinel.com

Populated Places
Clifton (17,345)
Fruita (6,878)
Fruitvale (6,936)
Grand Junction (45,299)
Orchard Mesa (6,456)
Palisade (2,683)
Redlands (8,043)

GRANTS PASS, OR (JOSEPHINE COUNTY)

DMA: Medford–Klamath Falls

City of Grants Pass
www.ci.grants-pass.or.us
Grants Pass/Josephine County C/C
www.grantspasschamber.org
Grants Pass Daily Courier
www.thedailycourier.com

Populated Places
Cave Junction (1,380)
Grants Pass (28,882)
Redwood (5,844)

GRASS VALLEY–NEVADA CITY, CA (NEVADA COUNTY)

DMA: Sacramento–Stockton–Modesto

City of Grass Valley
www.cityofgrassvalley.com
Grass Valley C/C
www.grassvalleychamber.com
Nevada City C/C
www.nevadacitychamber.com
The Union
www.theunion.com

Populated Places
Alta Sierra (6,522)
Grass Valley (12,449)
Lake of the Pines (3,956)
Lake Wildwood (4,868)
Nevada City (3,032)
Penn Valley (1,387)
Truckee (15,737)

HAMILTON–BITTERROOT VALLEY, MT (RAVALLI COUNTY)

DMA: Missoula

Bitterroot Valley C/C
www.bitterrootvalleychamber.com
City of Hamilton
www.cityofhamilton.net
Ravalli Republic
www.ravallirepublic.com

Populated Places
Hamilton (4,443)
Stevensville (1,855)

HAMPSHIRE COUNTY, WV (HAMPSHIRE COUNTY)

DMA: Washington, D.C.

Hampshire County C/C
www.hampshirecountychamber.com
Hampshire Review
www.hampshirereview.com

Populated Places
Romney (1,975)

HANOVER, NH (GRAFTON COUNTY)

DMA: Burlington–Plattsburgh

City of Hanover
www.hanovernh.org
Hanover Area C/C
www.hanoverchamber.org
Valley News
www.vnews.com

Populated Places
Ashland (2,004)
Bethlehem (2,381)
Bristol (3,118)
Campton (2,947)
Canaan (3,452)
Enfield (4,830)
Hanover (11,156)
Haverhill (4,553)
Holderness (2,065)
Lebanon (12,606)
Littleton (6,139)
Lyme (1,704)
Orford (1,071)
Plymouth (6,204)
Thornton (2,021)
Woodstock (1,171)

HATTIESBURG, MS (FORREST COUNTY)

DMA: Hattiesburg–Laurel

City of Hattiesburg
www.hattiesburgms.com
Mississippi Economic Development
www.medc.ms
Hattiesburg American
www.hattiesburgamerican.com

Populated Places
Hattiesburg (47,463)
Petal (10,088)

HENDERSON, NV (CLARK COUNTY)

DMA: Las Vegas

City of Henderson
www.cityofhenderson.com
Henderson C/C
www.hendersonchamber.com
Las Vegas Sun
www.lasvegassun.com

Populated Places
  Henderson (232,146)

HENDERSONVILLE–EAST FLAT ROCK, NC (HENDERSON COUNTY)

DMA: Greenville–Spartanburg–Asheville

City of Hendersonville
www.cityofhendersonville.org
Henderson County C/C
www.hendersonvillechamber.org
Times-News
www.hendersonvillenews.com

Populated Places
  Balfour (1,200)
  Barker Heights (1,237)
  East Flat Rock (4,151)
  Etowah (2,766)
  Flat Rock (2,750)
  Fletcher (4,522)
  Hendersonville (11,396)
  Laurel Park (2,083)
  Mills River (5,979)
  Mountain Home (2,169)
  Valley Hill (2,137)

HILTON HEAD ISLAND, SC (BEAUFORT COUNTY)

DMA: Savannah

Hilton Head Island-Bluffton C/C
www.hiltonheadisland.org
Hilton Head Island Packet
www.islandpacket.com

Populated Places
  Bluffton (2,341)
  Burton (7,180)
  Hilton Head Island (34,497)
  Laurel Bay (6,625)
  Port Royal (9,347)
  Shell Point (2,856)

HOT SPRINGS, AR (GARLAND COUNTY)

DMA: Little Rock–Pine Bluff

City of Hot Springs
www.ci.hot-springs.ar.us
Greater Hot Springs C/C
www.hotspringschamber.com
The Sentinel-Record
www.hotsr.com

Populated Places
  Hot Springs (37,847)
  Hot Springs Village (8,397)
  Lake Hamilton (1,609)
  Piney (3,988)
  Rockwell (3,024)

IOWA CITY, IA (JOHNSON COUNTY)

DMA: Cedar Rapids–Waterloo–Iowa City–Dubuque

City of Iowa City
www.icgov.org
Iowa City Area C/C
www.iowacityarea.com
The Press-Citizen
www.press-citizen.com

Populated Places
  Coralville (17,811)
  Iowa City (62,887)
  Lone Tree (1,081)
  North Liberty (8,808)
  Solon (1,352)
  Tiffin (1,473)

JACKSON HOLE, WY (TETON COUNTY)

DMA: Idaho Falls–Pocatello

City of Jackson
www.ci.jackson.wy.us
Jackson Hole C/C
www.jacksonholechamber.com
Jackson Hole News & Guide
www.jacksonholenews.com

Populated Places
  Hoback (1,453)
  Jackson (9,038)
  Moose Wilson Road (1,439)
  Rafter J Ranch (1,138)
  Wilson (1,294)

KALISPELL–FLATHEAD VALLEY, MT (FLATHEAD COUNTY)

DMA: Missoula

City of Kalispell
www.kalispell.com
Kalispell Area C/C
www.kalispellchamber.com
Daily Inter Lake
www.dailyinterlake.com

Populated Places
Bigfork (1,421)
Columbia Falls (4,440)
Evergreen (6,215)
Kalispell (18,480)
Lakeside (1,679)
Whitefish (7,067)

KERRVILLE, TX (KERR COUNTY)

DMA: San Antonio

City of Kerrville
www.kerrville.org
Kerrville Area C/C
www.kerrvilletx.com
Kerrville Daily Times
www.dailytimes.com

Populated Places
Ingram (1,838)
Kerrville (22,010)

KETCHUM–SUN VALLEY, ID (BLAINE COUNTY)

DMA: Twin Falls

City of Ketchum
www.ci.ketchum.id.us
Sun Valley-Ketchum CVB
www.visitsunvalley.com
Idaho Mountain Express
www.sunvalleycentral.com/index.php

Populated Places
Bellevue (2,203)
Hailey (7,583)
Ketchum (3,145)
Sun Valley (1,444)

KEY WEST, FL (MONROE COUNTY)

DMA: Miami–Ft. Lauderdale

City of Key West
www.keywestcity.com
Key West C/C
www.keywestchamber.org
The Citizen
www.keysnews.com

Populated Places
Big Coppitt Key (2,595)
Big Pine Key (5,032)
Cudjoe Key (1,695)
Key Largo (11,886)
Key West (23,935)
Marathon (9,822)
North Key Largo (1,049)
Stock Island (4,410)
Tavernier (2,173)

KINGMAN, AZ (MOHAVE COUNTY)

DMA: Phoenix

City of Kingman
www.ci.kingman.az.us
Kingman Area C/C
www.kingmanchamber.org
Kingman Daily Miner
www.kingmandailyminer.com

Populated Places
Golden Valley (4,515)
Kingman (25,547)

KISSIMMEE–ST. CLOUD, FL (OSCEOLA COUNTY)

DMA: Orlando–Daytona Beach–Melbourne

City of St. Cloud
www.stcloud.org
Kissimmee/Osceola County C/C
www.kissimmeechamber.com
Osceola News-Gazette
www.aroundosceola.com

Populated Places
Campbell (2,677)
Celebration (2,736)
Kissimmee (59,364)
St. Cloud (22,508)
Yeehaw Junction (21,778)

LAGUNA BEACH–DANA POINT, CA (ORANGE COUNTY)

DMA: Los Angeles

Dana Point C/C
www.danapoint-chamber.com
City of Dana Point
www.danapoint.org
City of Laguna Beach
www.lagunabeachcity.net
Laguna Beach C/C
www.lagunabeachchamber.org
Coastline Pilot
www.coastlinepilot.com

Populated Places
    Dana Point (35,867)
    Laguna Beach (24,127)
    Laguna Hills (32,198)
    Laguna Niguel (64,664)
    Laguna Woods (18,293)
    Mission Viejo (94,982)

LAKE CONROE, TX (MONTGOMERY COUNTY)

DMA: Houston

City of Conroe
www.cityofconroe.org
Greater Conroe/Lake Conroe Area
www.conroe.org
Conroe Courier
www.thecourier-online.com

Populated Places
    Conroe (47,042)
    Cut and Shoot (1,244)
    Magnolia (1,187)
    Oak Ridge North (3,306)
    Panorama Village (2,341)
    Patton Village (1,505)
    Pinehurst (4,266)
    Porter Heights (1,490)
    Roman Forest (2,950)
    Shenandoah (1,715)
    Splendora (1,394)
    The Woodlands (55,649)
    Willis (4,172)
    Woodbranch (1,377)

LAKE HAVASU CITY, AZ (MOHAVE COUNTY)

DMA: Phoenix

City of Lake Havasu City
www.lhcaz.gov

Lake Havasu City C/C
www.havasuchamber.com
Havasu Sun News
www.havasunews.com

Populated Places
    Bullhead City (39,101)
    Colorado City (4,371)
    Desert Hills (2,183)
    Dolan Springs (1,867)
    Golden Valley (4,515)
    Lake Havasu City (55,338)
    Mohave Valley (13,694)

LAKELAND–WINTER HAVEN, FL (POLK COUNTY)

DMA: Tampa–St. Petersburg

City of Lakeland
www.lakelandgov.net
City of Winter Haven
www.mywinterhaven.com
Lakeland Area C/C
www.lakelandchamber.com
Winter Haven Area C/C
www.winterhavenfl.com
The Ledger
www.theledger.com

Populated Places
    Auburndale (12,381)
    Babson Park (1,182)
    Bartow (16,278)
    Combee Settlement (5,436)
    Crooked Lake Park (1,682)
    Crystal Lake (5,341)
    Cypress Gardens (8,844)
    Davenport (2,017)
    Dundee (3,064)
    Eagle Lake (2,489)
    Fort Meade (5,742)
    Frostproof (2,950)
    Fussels Corner (5,313)
    Gibsonia (4,507)
    Haines City (16,371)
    Highland City (2,051)
    Inwood (6,925)
    Jan Phyl Village (5,633)
    Kathleen (3,280)
    Lake Alfred (3,930)
    Lake Hamilton (1,414)
    Lake Wales (12,964)
    Lakeland (88,713)
    Lakeland Highlands (12,557)
    Loughman (1,385)
    Medulla (6,637)
    Mulberry (3,233)
    Polk City (1,522)
    Wahneta (4,731)

Waverly (1,927)
Willow Oak (4,917)
Winston (9,024)
Winter Haven (29,501)

LAKE OF THE CHEROKEES, OK (DELAWARE COUNTY)

DMA: Tulsa

Grand Lake Area C/C
www.grandlakechamber.org
The Grove Sun Daily
www.grovesun.com

Populated Places
Cleora (1,113)
Copeland (1,448)
Grove (5,752)
Jay (2,840)

LAKE OF THE OZARKS, MO (CAMDEN COUNTY)

DMA: Springfield

Lake of the Ozarks C/C
www.odd.net/ozarks
Lake Sun Leader
www.lakesunleader.com

Populated Places
Camdenton (3,061)
Osage Beach (3,921)
Village of Four Seasons (1,579)

LAKE PLACID, NY (ESSEX COUNTY)

DMA: Burlington–Plattsburgh

Lake Placid/Essex County CVB
www.lakeplacid.com
The Press Republican
www.pressrepublican.com

Populated Places
Chesterfield (2,355)
Crown Point (2,013)
Elizabethtown (1,286)
Jay (2,303)
Keene (1,052)
Lake Placid (2,757)
Lewis (1,170)
Moriah (4,708)
North Elba (9,029)

Port Henry (1,089)
Saranac Lake (2,162)
Schroon (1,772)
St. Armand (1,307)
Ticonderoga (5,091)
Westport (1,316)
Willsboro (1,880)
Wilmington (1,150)

LARGO, FL (PINELLAS COUNTY)

DMA: Tampa–St. Petersburg

City of Largo
www.largo.com
Largo Mid-Pinellas C/C
www.largochamber.com
Largo Leader
www.tbnweekly.com/pubs/largo_leader

Populated Places
Largo (74,473)

LAS CRUCES, NM (DONA ANA COUNTY)

DMA: El Paso

City of Las Cruces
www.las-cruces.org
Greater Las Cruces C/C
www.lascruces.org
Sun-News
www.lcsun-news.com

Populated Places
Anthony (7,904)
Chaparral (6,117)
Dona Ana (1,379)
Hatch (1,654)
Las Cruces (82,671)
Mesilla (2,205)
Radium Springs (1,518)
Santa Teresa (2,607)
Sunland Park (14,089)
University Park (2,732)
Vado (3,003)

LAS VEGAS, NM (SAN MIGUEL COUNTY)

DMA: Albuquerque–Santa Fe

Las Vegas/San Miguel C/C
www.lasvegasnm.org
Review-Journal
www.reviewjournal.com

Populated Places
Las Vegas (14,020)
Pecos (1,407)

Tavares (11,621)
Umatilla (2,647)
Yalaha (1,175)

LEELANAU PENINSULA, MI (LEELANAU COUNTY)

DMA: Traverse City–Cadillac

Leelanau Peninsula C/C
www.leelanau.com/chamber
Leelanau Enterprise
www.leelanaunews.com

Populated Places
Binghamship (2,520)
Centervilleship (1,181)
Clevelandship (1,119)
Elmwood chartership (4,358)
Empireship (1,156)
Greilickville (1,415)
Kassonship (1,739)
Leelanauship (2,240)
Lelandship (2,136)
Solonship (1,652)
Suttons Bayship (3,094)

LEESBURG–MOUNT DORA, FL (LAKE COUNTY)

DMA: Orlando–Daytona Beach–Melbourne

City of Leesburg
www.leesburgflorida.gov
City of Mount Dora
www.ci.mount-dora.fl.us
Leesburg Area C/C
www.leesburgchamber.com
Mount Dora C/C
www.mountdora.com
Daily Commercial
www.dailycommercial.com

Populated Places
Astatula (1,629)
Astor (1,487)
Clermont (11,617)
Eustis (17,683)
Fruitland Park (3,578)
Groveland (5,205)
Howey-in-the-Hills (1,194)
Lady Lake (13,244)
Leesburg (19,086)
Mascotte (4,647)
Minneola (8,665)
Mount Dora (11,474)
Mount Plymouth (2,814)
Silver Lake (1,882)

LITCHFIELD HILLS, CT (LITCHFIELD COUNTY)

DMA: Hartford–New Haven

City of Litchfield
www.litchfieldct.com
Northwest Connecticut C/C
www.litchfieldhills.com
Litchfield County Times
www.countytimes.com

Populated Places
Barkhamsted (3,711)
Bethlehem (3,596)
Bridgewater (1,898)
Canaan (1,101)
Colebrook (1,540)
Cornwall (1,489)
Goshen (3,092)
Harwinton (5,571)
Kent (2,962)
Litchfield (8,684)
Morris (2,393)
New Hartford (6,746)
New Milford (28,667)
Norfolk (1,676)
North Canaan (3,392)
Plymouth (12,183)
Roxbury (2,327)
Salisbury (4,083)
Sharon (3,052)
Thomaston (7,938)
Warren (1,361)
Washington (3,693)
Watertown (22,330)
Winchester (10,857)
Woodbury (9,734)

LONG BEACH PENINSULA, WA (PACIFIC COUNTY)

DMA: Seattle–Tacoma

City of Long Beach
www.longbeachwa.gov
Washington Coast C/C
www.washingtoncoastchamber.org
Chinook Observer
www.chinookobserver.com

Populated Places
Long Beach (1,386)
Ocean Park (1,459)
Raymond (2,995)
South Bend (1,831)

LOUDOUN COUNTY, VA (LOUDOUN COUNTY)

DMA: Washington, D.C.

City of Leesburg
www.leesburgva.org
Loudoun County C/C
www.loudounchamber.org
Leesburg Today/Journal of Loudoun
www.leesburg2day.com

Populated Places
Leesburg (36,269)
Lovettsville (1,160)
Purcellville (4,680)

LOWER CAPE MAY, NJ (CAPE MAY COUNTY)

DMA: Philadelphia

C/C of Greater Cape May
www.capemaychamber.com
Cape May Star & Wave
www.starandwave.com

Populated Places
Avalon borough (2,133)
Cape May (3,760)
Cape May Court House (4,704)
Erma (2,088)
North Cape May (3,618)
North Wildwood (4,778)
Ocean City (15,330)
Rio Grande (2,444)
Sea Isle City (2,968)
Stone Harbor borough (1,062)
Villas (9,064)
West Cape May borough (1,038)
Wildwood (5,291)
Wildwood Crest borough (3,872)
Woodbine borough (2,569)

MADISON, MS (MADISON COUNTY)

DMA: Jackson

City of Madison
www.madisonthecity.com
Madison County C/C
www.madisoncountychamber.com
Madison County Herald
www.mcherald.com

Populated Places
Canton (12,507)
Flora (1,478)
Madison (16,737)
Ridgeland (21,236)

MADISON, WI (DANE COUNTY)

DMA: Madison

City of Madison
www.ci.madison.wi.us
Greater Madison C/C
www.greatermadisonchamber.com
Capital Times
www.madison.com

Populated Places
Albion (1,895)
Belleville (1,982)
Berry (1,190)
Black Earth (1,283)
Blooming Grove (1,755)
Bristol (2,745)
Burke (3,001)
Cambridge (1,108)
Christiana (1,419)
Cottage Grove (5,271)
Cross Plains (3,418)
Dane (1,085)
Deerfield (2,202)
DeForest (8,438)
Dunkirk (2,042)
Dunn (5,320)
Fitchburg (22,040)
Madison (221,551)
Maple Bluff (1,297)
Marshall (3,561)
Mazomanie (1,528)
McFarland (7,383)
Medina (1,340)
Middleton (15,816)
Monona (7,716)
Montrose (1,237)
Mount Horeb (6,188)
Oregon (8,493)
Pleasant Springs (3,127)
Roxbury (1,803)
Rutland (1,991)
Shorewood Hills (1,671)
Springdale (1,634)
Springfield (2,880)
Stoughton (12,646)
Sun Prairie (25,392)
Verona (10,166)
Vienna (1,408)
Waunakee (10,360)
Westport (3,616)
Windsor (5,322)

MARBLE FALLS–LAKE LBJ, TX (BURNET COUNTY)

DMA: Austin

City of Marble Falls
www.ci.marble-falls.tx.us
Marble Falls–Lake LBJ C/C
www.marblefalls.org
Burnet Bulletin
www.burnetbulletin.com

Populated Places
   Bertram (1,304)
   Burnet (5,562)
   Cottonwood Shores (1,090)
   Granite Shoals (2,336)
   Horseshoe Bay (3,337)
   Marble Falls (6,745)
   Meadowlakes (1,714)

MARIPOSA, CA (MARIPOSA COUNTY)

DMA: Fresno–Visalia

Mariposa County C/C
www.mariposachamber.org
Mariposa Gazette
www.mariposagazette.com

Populated Places
   Bootjack (1,588)
   Mariposa (1,373)

MARTHA'S VINEYARD, MA (DUKES COUNTY)

DMA: Boston

Martha's Vineyard C/C
www.mvy.com
Vineyard Gazette
www.mvgazette.com

Populated Places
   Edgartown (3,935)
   Oak Bluffs (3,787)
   Tisbury (3,812)
   Vineyard Haven (2,048)
   West Tisbury (2,671)

MARYVILLE, TN (BLOUNT COUNTY)

DMA: Knoxville

Blount County C/C
www.blountchamber.com
City of Maryville
www.maryvillegov.com
Daily Times
www.thedailytimes.com

Populated Places
   Alcoa (8,388)
   Eagleton Village (4,883)
   Louisville (2,157)
   Maryville (25,851)
   Seymour (8,850)

MAUI, HI (MAUI COUNTY)

DMA: Honolulu

Maui C/C
www.mauichamber.com
The Maui News
www.mauinews.com

Populated Places
   Kaanapali (1,375)
   Kahului (20,146)
   Kaunakakai (2,726)
   Kihei (16,749)
   Kualapuu (1,936)
   Lahaina (9,118)
   Lanai City (3,164)
   Makawao (6,327)
   Paia (2,499)
   Pukalani (7,380)
   Waikapu (1,115)
   Wailuku (12,296)

MCALLEN–ALAMO, TX (HIDALGO COUNTY)

DMA: Harlingen–Weslaco–Brownsville

City of McAllen
www.mcallen.net
McAllen C/C
mcallenchamber.com
The Monitor
www.themonitor.com

Populated Places
   Alamo (15,976)
   Alton (7,057)
   Cesar Chavez (1,469)
   Doffing (4,256)
   Donna (15,846)

Doolittle (2,358)
Edcouch (4,426)
Edinburg (62,735)
Elsa (6,458)
Heidelberg (1,586)
Hidalgo (10,889)
Indian Hills (2,036)
La Blanca (2,351)
La Homa (10,433)
La Joya (4,486)
La Villa (1,455)
Llano Grande (3,333)
Lopezville (4,476)
McAllen (123,622)
Mercedes (14,185)
Mila Doce (4,907)
Mission (60,146)
Monte Alto (1,611)
Muniz (1,106)
North Alamo (2,061)
Nurillo (5,056)
Olivarez (2,445)
Palmhurst (4,991)
Palmview (4,421)
Penitas (1,182)
Pharr (58,986)
Progreso (5,082)
San Carlos (2,650)
San Juan (30,773)
Scissors (2,805)
South Alamo (3,101)
Sullivan City (4,346)
Weslaco (31,442)
West Sharyland (2,947)

MCCALL, ID (VALLEY COUNTY)

DMA: Boise

City of McCall
www.mccall.id.us
McCall C/C
www.mccallchamber.org
The Star-News
www.webdms.com/~starnews

Populated Places
Cascade (1,005)
McCall (2,415)

MEDFORD–ASHLAND, OR (JACKSON COUNTY)

DMA: Medford–Klamath Falls

Ashland C/C
www.ashlandchamber.com
Chamber of Medford/Jackson County
www.medfordchamber.com

City of Ashland
www.ashland.or.us
City of Medford
www.ci.medford.or.us
Medford Mail Tribune
www.mailtribune.com
Ashland Daily Tidings
www.dailytidings.com

Populated Places
Ashland (20,829)
Central Point (15,672)
Eagle Point (7,496)
Gold Hill (1,062)
Jacksonville (2,230)
Medford (70,147)
Phoenix (4,375)
Rogue River (1,941)
Shady Cove (2,301)
Talent (6,018)
White City (5,466)

MELBOURNE–PALM BAY, FL (BREVARD COUNTY)

DMA: Orlando–Daytona Beach–Melbourne

C/C Melbourne Palm Bay Area
www.melpb-chamber.org
City of Melbourne
www.melbourneflorida.org
City of Palm Bay
www.palmbayflorida.org
Florida Today
www.flatoday.com

Populated Places
Cape Canaveral (10,523)
Cocoa (16,898)
Cocoa Beach (12,435)
Indialantic (3,076)
Indian Harbour Beach (8,441)
June Park (4,367)
Malabar (2,772)
Melbourne (76,646)
Melbourne Beach (3,314)
Merritt Island (36,090)
Micco (9,498)
Mims (9,147)
Palm Bay (92,833)
Port St. John (12,112)
Rockledge (24,245)
Satellite Beach (9,811)
Sharpes (3,415)
South Patrick Shores (8,913)
Titusville (43,767)
West Melbourne (15,054)

MENDOCINO–FORT BRAGG, CA (MENDOCINO COUNTY)

DMA: San Francisco–Oakland–San Jose

City of Fort Bragg
http://ci.fort-bragg.ca.us
Mendocino Coast C/C
www.mendocinocoast.com
Mendocino Beacon
www.mendocinobeacon.com

Populated Places
Covelo (1,175)
Fort Bragg (6,814)
Laytonville (1,301)
Talmage (1,141)
Ukiah (15,463)
Willits (5,066)

MIDDLE CAPE COD, MA (BARNSTABLE COUNTY)

DMA: Boston

Cape Cod C/C
www.ecapechamber.com
Cape Cod Chronicle
www.capecodchronicle.com

Populated Places
Barnstable Town (47,826)
Bourne (19,356)
Bourne (1,443)
Brewster (10,242)
Buzzards Bay (3,549)
Chatham (6,832)
Dennis (15,891)
Eastham (5,551)
Falmouth (33,644)
Forestdale (3,992)
Harwich (12,675)
Mashpee (14,280)
Orleans (6,458)
Sandwich (20,726)
Teaticket (1,907)
Truro (2,164)
Wellfleet (2,822)
Yarmouth (24,621)

MONADNOCK REGION, NH (CHESHIRE COUNTY)

DMA: Boston

City of Jaffrey
www.town.jaffrey.nh.us

City of Keene
www.ci.keene.nh.us
Greater Keene C/C
www.keenechamber.com
Jaffrey C/C
www.jaffreychamber.com
Ledger-Transcript
www.ledgertranscript.com

Populated Places
Alstead (2,026)
Chesterfield (3,866)
Dublin (1,556)
Fitzwilliam (2,297)
Harrisville (1,113)
Hinsdale (4,207)
Jaffrey (5,711)
Keene (22,778)
Marlborough (2,094)
Marlborough (1,089)
Richmond (1,165)
Rindge (6,302)
Swanzey (7,313)
Troy (2,061)
Walpole (3,703)
West Swanzey (1,118)
Westmoreland (1,894)
Winchester (4,281)

MONTROSE, CO (MONTROSE COUNTY)

DMA: Grand Junction–Montrose

City of Montrose
www.cityofmontrose.org
Montrose C/C
www.montrosechamber.com
Montrose Daily Press
www.montrosepress.com

Populated Places
Montrose (15,479)
Olathe (1,679)

MORRO BAY–CAMBRIA, CA (SAN LUIS OBISPO COUNTY)

DMA: Santa Barbara–San Marcos–San Luis Obispo

Cambria C/C
www.cambriachamber.org
City of Morro Bay
www.morro-bay.ca.us
Morro Bay C/C
www.morrobay.org
San Luis Obispo County Tribune
www.sanluisobispo.com

Populated Places
Arroyo Grande (16,315)
Atascadero (27,130)
Cambria (6,232)
Cayucos (2,943)
El Paso de Robles (Paso Robles)
Grover Beach (12,887)
Lake Nacimiento (2,176)
Morro Bay (10,208)
Nipomo (12,626)
Oceano (7,260)
Pismo Beach (8,419)
San Luis Obispo (43,509)
San Miguel (1,427)
Templeton (4,687)

MURRAY–KENTUCKY LAKE, KY (CALLOWAY COUNTY)

DMA: Paducah–Cape Girardeau

City of Murray
www.murrayky.gov
Murray-Calloway County C/C
www.murraylink.com/chamber
Murray Ledger & Times
www.murrayledger.com

Populated Places
Murray (15,538)

MYRTLE BEACH, SC (HORRY COUNTY)

DMA: Florence–Myrtle Beach

City of Myrtle Beach
www.cityofmyrtlebeach.com
Myrtle Beach Area CVB
www.mbchamber.com
Sun News
www.myrtlebeachonline.com

Populated Places
Bucksport (1,117)
Conway (13,442)
Forestbrook (3,391)
Garden City (9,357)
Little River (7,027)
Loris (2,305)
Myrtle Beach (26,593)
North Myrtle Beach (14,096)
Red Hill (10,509)
Socastee (14,295)
Surfside Beach (4,772)

NAPLES, FL (COLLIER COUNTY)

DMA: Fort Myers–Naples

City of Naples
www.naplesgov.com
Greater Naples C/C
www.napleschamber.org
Naples Daily News
www.naplesnews.com

Populated Places
Golden Gate (20,951)
Immokalee (19,763)
Lely (3,857)
Lely Resort (1,426)
Marco Island (16,109)
Naples (21,709)
Naples Manor (5,186)
Naples Park (6,741)
Pelican Bay (5,686)
Pine Ridge (1,965)
Vineyards (2,232)

NATCHITOCHES, LA (NATCHITOCHES PARISH)

DMA: Shreveport

City of Natchitoches
www.ci.natchitoches.la.us
Natchitoches Area C/C
www.natchitocheschamber.com
Natchitoches Times
318/s352-3618

Populated Places
Campti (1,054)
Natchitoches (17,701)

NELSON COUNTY, VA (NELSON COUNTY)

DMA: Roanoke–Lynchburg

Nelson County CVB
www.nelsoncounty.com
Nelson County Times
www.nelsoncountytimes.com

Populated Places
Livingston district (4,928)
Massies Mill district (2,377)
Rockfish (4,525)
Schuyler (2,615)

NEW BERN, NC (CRAVEN COUNTY)

DMA: Greenville–New Bern–Washington

City of New Bern
www.ci.new-bern.nc.us
New Bern Area C/C
www.newbernchamber.com
Sun-Journal
www.newbernsj.com

Populated Places
  Brices Creek (2,060)
  Fairfield Harbour (1,983)
  Havelock (21,827)
  James City (5,420)
  Neuse Forest (1,426)
  New Bern (24,106)
  River Bend (2,755)
  Trent Woods (3,961)

NEW BRAUNFELS, TX (COMAL COUNTY)

DMA: San Antonio

City of New Braunfels
830.608.2100
New Braunfels C/C
www.nbcham.org
New Braunfels Herald & Zeitung
www.herald-zeitung.com

Populated Places
  Bulverde (4,446)
  Canyon Lake (16,870)
  Garden Ridge (2,538)
  New Braunfels (48,979)

NEWPORT–LINCOLN CITY, OR (LINCOLN COUNTY)

DMA: Portland

City of Lincoln City
www.lincolncity.org
City of Newport
www.thecityofnewport.net
Greater Newport C/C
www.newportchamber.org
Lincoln City C/C
www.lcchamber.com
Lincoln City News Guard
www.thenewsguard.com
Newport News-Times
www.newportnewstimes.com

Populated Places
  Depoe Bay (1,363)
  Lincoln Beach (2,078)
  Lincoln City (7,849)
  Newport (9,833)
  Rose Lodge (1,708)
  Siletz (1,132)
  Toledo (3,434)
  Waldport (2,094)

NORFORK LAKE, AR (BAXTER COUNTY)

DMA: Springfield, MO

City of Norfork
www.norfork.net/city.htm
Mountain Home Area C/C
www.mtnhomechamber.com
The Baxter Bulletin
www.baxterbulletin.com

Populated Places
  Cotter (1,032)
  Gassville (1,931)
  Mountain Home (11,896)

NORTHAMPTON–AMHERST, MA (HAMPSHIRE COUNTY)

DMA: Springfield–Holyoke

Amherst Area C/C
www.amherstarea.com
City of Northampton
www.city.northampton.ma.us
Northampton C/C
www.explorenorthampton.com
Daily Hampshire Gazette
www.gazettenet.com

Populated Places
  Amherst (34,047)
  Belchertown (13,958)
  Chesterfield (1,272)
  Easthampton (16,004)
  Granby (6,344)
  Hadley (4,822)
  Hatfield (3,282)
  Huntington (2,182)
  Northampton (28,715)
  Pelham (1,416)
  South Hadley (17,063)
  Southampton (5,841)
  Ware (10,005)
  Westhampton (1,568)
  Williamsburg (2,434)
  Worthington (1,292)

NORTHERN NECK, VA (LANCASTER & NORTHUMBERLAND COUNTIES)

DMA: Richmond–Petersburg

Lancaster County C/C
www.lancasterva.com
Northern Neck Tourism Council
www.northernneck.org
The Daily News Record
www.dnronline.com

Populated Places
    Kilmarnock (1,168)

OAKHURST-COARSEGOLD, CA (MADERA COUNTY)

DMA: Fresno–Visalia

Oakhurst Area C/C
www.oakhurstchamber.com
Sierra Star
www.sierrastar.com

Populated Places
    Chowchilla (16,525)
    Madera (52,147)
    Madera Acres (7,741)
    Oakhurst (2,868)
    Parksdale (2,688)
    Parkwood (2,119)
    Yosemite Lakes (4,160)

OCALA, FL (MARION COUNTY)

DMA: Orlando–Daytona Beach–Melbourne

City of Ocala
www.ocalafl.org
Ocala-Marion County C/C
www.ocalacc.com
Ocala Star Banner
www.ocala.com

Populated Places
    Belleview (3,856)
    Dunnellon (1,971)
    Ocala (49,745)
    Silver Springs Shores (6,690)

OCEAN CITY, MD (WORCESTER COUNTY)

DMA: Salisbury

City of Ocean City
www.town.ocean-city.md.us
Ocean City C/C
www.oceancity.org
The Daily Times
www.delmarvanow.com

Populated Places
    Berlin (3,711)
    Ocean City (7,049)
    Ocean Pines (10,496)
    Pocomoke City (3,909)
    Snow Hill (2,323)
    West Ocean City (3,311)

OXFORD, MS (LAFAYETTE COUNTY)

DMA: Memphis

City of Oxford
www.oxfordms.net
Oxford C/C
www.oxfordms.com
Oxford Eagle
www.oxfordeagle.com

Populated Places
    Oxford (13,618)

PAGOSA SPRINGS, CO (ARCHULETA COUNTY)

DMA: Denver

City of Pagosa Springs
www.townofpagosasprings.com
Pagosa Springs Area C/C
www.pagosaspringschamber.com
Pagosa Springs Sun
www.pagosasun.com

Populated Places
    Pagosa Springs (1,628)

PAHRUMP VALLEY, NV (NYE COUNTY)

DMA: Las Vegas

Pahrump Valley C/C
www.pahrumpchamber.com
Valley Times
www.pahrumpvalleytimes.com

Populated Places
Beatty (1,154)
Pahrump (24,631)
Tonopah (2,627)

PALMER–WASILLA, AK (MATANUSKA–SUSITNA COUNTY)

DMA: Anchorage

City of Palmer
www.cityofpalmer.org
City of Wasilla
www.cityofwasilla.com
Greater Palmer C/C
www.palmerchamber.org
Mat-Su CVB
www.alaskavisit.com
Mat-Su Valley Frontiersman
www.frontiersman.com

Populated Places
Big Lake (2,635)
Butte (2,561)
Gateway (2,952)
Houston (1,614)
Lazy Mountain (1,158)
Meadow Lakes (4,819)
Palmer (6,920)
Tanaina (4,993)
Wasilla (8,471)
Willow (1,658)

PALM SPRINGS–COACHELLA VALLEY, CA (RIVERSIDE COUNTY)

DMA: Los Angeles

City of Palm Springs
www.ci.palm-springs.ca.us
Palm Springs C/C
www.pschamber.org
Desert Sun
www.desert-sun.com

Populated Places
Cathedral City (51,713)
Coachella (32,432)
Desert Hot Springs (20,492)
Indian Wells (4,933)
Indio (70,542)
La Quinta (38,232)
Murrieta Hot Springs (2,948)
Palm Desert (47,058)
Palm Springs (47,082)
Rancho Mirage (16,514)
Thousand Palms (5,120)

PANAMA CITY, FL (BAY COUNTY)

DMA: Panama City

Bay County C/C
www.panamacity.org
City of Panama City
www.panamacity-fl.gov
News Herald
www.newsherald.com

Populated Places
Callaway (14,437)
Cedar Grove (5,226)
Laguna Beach (2,909)
Lower Grand Lagoon (4,082)
Lynn Haven (15,677)
Mexico Beach (1,192)
Panama City (37,188)
Panama City Beach (11,477)
Parker (4,672)
Pretty Bayou (3,519)
Springfield (9,043)
Upper Grand Lagoon (10,889)

PARADISE–MAGALIA, CA (BUTTE COUNTY)

DMA: Chico–Redding

City of Paradise
www.townofparadise.com
Paradise C/C
www.paradisechamber.com
Chico Enterprise-Record
www.chicoer.com

Populated Places
Biggs (1,803)
Chico (71,427)
Concow (1,095)
Durham (5,220)
Gridley (5,588)
Magalia (10,569)
Oroville (13,468)
Palermo (5,720)
Paradise (26,517)
South Oroville (7,695)
Thermalito (6,045)

PARK CITY, UT (SUMMIT & WASATCH COUNTIES)

DMA: Salt Lake City

City of Park City
www.parkcity.org
Park City C/C
www.parkcityinfo.com

The Park Record
www.parkrecord.com

Populated Places
Coalville (1,451)
Heber (9,147)
Kamas (1,502)
Midway (2,737)
Oakley (1,228)
Park City (8,065)
Summit Park (6,597)

PAYSON, AZ (GILA COUNTY)

DMA: Phoenix

Rim Country Regional C/C
www.rimcountrychamber.com
Town of Payson
www.ci.payson.az.us
Payson Patriot
www.paysonpatriot.com

Populated Places
Canyon Day (1,092)
Claypool (1,794)
Globe (7,187)
Miami (1,841)
Payson (14,729)
Peridot (1,266)
Pine (1,931)
San Carlos (3,716)
Strawberry (1,028)
Sun Valley (1,536)

PENDLETON DISTRICT, SC (OCONEE COUNTY)

DMA: Greenville–Spartanburg–Asheville

Greater Seneca C/C
www.senecachamber.com
Daily Journal
www.dailyjm.com

Populated Places
Seneca (7,962)
Utica (1,322)
Walhalla (3,727)
Westminster (2,669)

PENSACOLA, FL (ESCAMBIA COUNTY)

DMA: Mobile–Pensacola

City of Pensacola
www.ci.pensacola.fl.us
Pensacola Bay Area C/C
www.pensacolachamber.com
News Journal
www.pensacolanewsjournal.com

Populated Places
Bellview (21,201)
Brent (22,257)
Century (1,799)
Ensley (18,752)
Ferry Pass (27,176)
Gonzalez (11,365)
Goulding (4,484)
Molino (1,312)
Myrtle Grove (17,211)
Pensacola (54,055)
Warrington (15,207)
West Pensacola (21,939)

PETOSKEY–HARBOR SPRINGS, MI (EMMET COUNTY)

DMA: Traverse City–Cadillac

City of Harbor Springs
www.cityofharborsprings.com
City of Petoskey
www.ci.petoskey.mi.us
Harbor Springs C/C
www.harborspringschamber.com
Petoskey Regional C/C
www.petoskey.com
Petoskey News-Review
www.petoskeynews.com

Populated Places
Harbor Springs (1,594)
Petoskey (6,198)

PIKE COUNTY, PA (PIKE COUNTY)

DMA: New York

Pike County C/C
www.pikechamber.com
TriState Observer
www.tristateobserver.com

Populated Places
Matamoras borough (2,591)
Milford borough (1,214)

PLACER COUNTY, CA (PLACER COUNTY)

DMA: Sacramento–Stockton–Modesto

City of Roseville
www.roseville.ca.us
Government
www.placer.ca.gov
Auburn Journal
www.auburnjournal.com

Populated Places
Auburn (12,912)
Colfax (1,720)
Dollar Point (1,539)
Foresthill (1,791)
Granite Bay (19,388)
Kings Beach (4,037)
Lincoln (32,804)
Loomis (6,577)
Meadow Vista (3,096)
North Auburn (11,847)
Rocklin (49,626)
Roseville (105,940)
Tahoe Vista (1,668)

PORT ANGELES–SEQUIM, WA (CLALLAM COUNTY)

DMA: Seattle–Tacoma

City of Port Angeles
www.cityofpa.us
Port Angeles C/C
www.portangeles.org
Sequim-Dungeness C/C
www.cityofsequim.com
Peninsula Daily News
www.peninsuladailynews.com

Populated Places
Forks (3,192)
Port Angeles (18,927)
Sequim (5,162)

PORT CHARLOTTE, FL (CHARLOTTE COUNTY)

DMA: Fort Myers–Naples

Charlotte County C/C
www.charlottecountychamber.org
Charlotte Sun Herald
www.sun-herald.com

Populated Places
Charlotte Harbor (3,647)
Charlotte Park (2,182)
Cleveland (3,268)
Englewood (16,196)
Grove City (2,092)
Harbour Heights (2,873)
Manasota Key (1,345)
Port Charlotte (46,451)
Punta Gorda (17,111)
Rotonda (6,574)
Solana (1,011)

PORT ST. LUCIE, FL (ST. LUCIE COUNTY)

DMA: West Palm Beach–Ft. Pierce

City of Port St. Lucie
www.cityofpsl.com
Port St. Lucie C/C
www.stluciechamber.org
TC Palm/Port St. Lucie News
www.tcpalm.com

Populated Places
Fort Pierce (38,552)
Indian River Estates (5,793)
Lakewood Park (10,458)
Port St. Lucie (131,692)
White City (4,221)

PORT TOWNSEND, WA (JEFFERSON COUNTY)

DMA: Seattle–Tacoma

Port Townsend C/C
www.ptchamber.org
Port Townsend & Jefferson County Leader
www.ptleader.com

Populated Places
Port Ludlow (1,968)
Port Townsend (9,001)

PRESCOTT–PRESCOTT VALLEY, AZ (YAVAPAI COUNTY)

DMA: Phoenix

City of Prescott
www.cityofprescott.net
Prescott C/C
www.prescott.org
Prescott Valley C/C
www.pvchamber.org
Prescott Daily Courier/Valley Tribune
www.prescottaz.com

Populated Places
Prescott (40,360)
Prescott Valley (33,068)

RABUN COUNTY, GA (RABUN COUNTY)

DMA: Atlanta

Rabun County C/C
www.gamountains.com
The Clayton Tribune
www.theclaytontribune.com

Populated Places
Clayton (2,100)

REHOBOTH BAY–INDIAN RIVER BAY, DE (SUSSEX COUNTY)

DMA: Salisbury

Lewes C/C
www.leweschamber.com
Sussex County C/C
www.sussexcountychamber.org
Cape Gazette
www.capegazette.com
Delaware Coast Press
www.delmarvanow.com

Populated Places
Bridgeville (1,578)
Delmar (1,483)
Georgetown (4,911)
Laurel (3,822)
Lewes (3,116)
Long Neck (1,629)
Milford (4,103)
Millsboro (2,505)
Milton (1,791)
Ocean View (1,094)
Rehoboth Beach (1,556)
Seaford (6,997)
Selbyville (1,742)

RIO RANCHO, NM (SANDOVAL COUNTY)

DMA: Albuquerque–Santa Fe

City of Rio Rancho
www.ci.rio-rancho.nm.us
Rio Rancho CVB
www.rioranchonm.org
The Observer
www.observer-online.com

Populated Places
Bernalillo (6,938)
Corrales (7,638)
Jemez Pueblo (1,953)
Placitas (3,452)
Rio Rancho (66,594)
San Felipe Pueblo (2,080)
Santo Domingo Pueblo (2,550)

ROCKPORT–ARANSAS PASS, TX (ARANSAS COUNTY)

DMA: Corpus Christi

City of Rockport
www.cityofrockport.com
Rockport-Fulton Area C/C
www.rockport-fulton.org
The Rockport Pilot
www.rockportpilot.com

Populated Places
Aransas Pass (8,065)
Fulton (1,663)
Rockport (9,041)

ROSWELL, NM (EDDY COUNTY)

DMA: Albuquerque–Santa Fe

Roswell C/C
www.roswellnm.org
Roswell Daily Record
www.roswell-record.com

Populated Places
Artesia (10,481)
Carlsbad (25,300)
Loving (1,313)

RUIDOSO, NM (LINCOLN COUNTY)

DMA: Albuquerque–Santa Fe

City of Ruidoso
www.voruidoso.com
Ruidoso Valley C/C
www.ruidosonow.com
Ruidoso News
www.ruidosonews.com

Populated Places
Capitan (1,500)
Carrizozo (1,063)
Ruidoso (8,812)
Ruidoso Downs (1,972)

ST. AUGUSTINE, FL (ST. JOHNS COUNTY)

DMA: Jacksonville

City of Saint Augustine
www.ci.st-augustine.fl.us
St. Augustine/St. Johns County C/C
www.staugustinechamber.com
St. Augustine Record
www.staugustine.com

Populated Places
Butler Beach (4,436)
Fruit Cove (16,077)
Palm Valley (19,860)
Sawgrass (4,942)
St. Augustine (12,263)
St. Augustine Beach (5,753)
St. Augustine Shores (4,922)
Villano Beach (2,533)

ST. GEORGE–ZION, UT (WASHINGTON COUNTY)

DMA: Salt Lake City

City of Saint George
www.sgcity.org
St. George Area C/C
www.stgeorgechamber.com
The Spectrum
www.thespectrum.com

Populated Places
Enterprise (1,419)
Hildale (1,973)
Hurricane (10,989)
Ivins (6,738)
La Verkin (4,105)
Santa Clara (5,864)
St. George (64,201)
Toquerville (1,118)
Washington (13,669)

ST. JAY–NORTHEAST KINGDOM, VT (CALEDONIA COUNTY)

DMA: Burlington–Plattsburgh

City of Saint Johnsbury
www.town.st-johnsbury.vt.us
Northeast Kingdom C/C
www.nekchamber.com
Caledonian-Record
www.caledonianrecord.com

Populated Places
Barnet (1,768)
Burke (1,676)
Danville (2,287)
Hardwick (3,230)
Lyndon (5,602)
Lyndonville (1,222)
Ryegate (1,194)
St. Johnsbury (7,495)
Sutton (1,056)
Waterford (1,216)

ST. MARYS, GA (CAMDEN COUNTY)

DMA: Jacksonville

City of St. Marys
www.ci.st-marys.ga.us
Tribune & Georgian
www.tribune-georgian.com

Populated Places
Kingsland (12,063)
St. Marys (16,404)
Woodbine (1,353)

ST. SIMONS–JEKYLL ISLANDS, GA (GLYNN COUNTY)

DMA: Jacksonville

Brunswick-Golden Isles C/C
www.brunswick-georgia.com
Glynn County News and Media
www.glynncounty.com/News_and_Medi

Populated Places
Country Club Estates (7,594)
Dock Junction (6,951)
St. Simons (13,381)

SANDPOINT–LAKE PEND OREILLE, ID (BONNER COUNTY)

DMA: Spokane

City of Sandpoint
www.cityofsandpoint.com
Greater Sandpoint C/C
www.sandpointchamber.org
Bonner County Daily Bee
www.bonnercountydailybee.com

Populated Places
Priest River (1,909)
Sandpoint (8,105)

SAN JUAN ISLANDS, WA (SAN JUAN COUNTY)

DMA: Seattle–Tacoma

City of Friday Harbor
www.fridayharbor.org
San Juan Island C/C
www.sanjuanisland.org
San Juan Journal
www.sanjuanjournal.com

Populated Places
Friday Harbor (2,096)

SANTA BARBARA, CA (SANTA BARBARA COUNTY)

DMA: Santa Barbara–San Marcos–San Luis Obispo

City of Santa Barbara
www.santabarbaraca.gov
Santa Barbara Region C/C
www.sbchamber.org
Santa Barbara News Press
www.sbcoast.com

Populated Places
Buellton (4,293)
Carpinteria (13,549)
Goleta (29,367)
Guadalupe (6,346)
Isla Vista (18,344)
Lompoc (39,985)
Los Alamos (1,372)
Mission Canyon (2,610)
Mission Hills (3,142)
Montecito (10,000)
Orcutt (28,830)
Santa Barbara (85,899)
Santa Maria (84,346)
Santa Ynez (4,584)
Solvang (5,141)
Summerland (1,545)
Toro Canyon (1,697)
Vandenberg Village (5,802)

SANTA FE, NM (SANTA FE COUNTY)

DMA: Albuquerque–Santa Fe

City of Santa Fe
www.santafenm.gov
Santa Fe County C/C
www.santafechamber.com
Santa Fe New Mexican
www.freenewmexican.com

Populated Places
Agua Fria (2,051)
Chimayo (2,924)
Edgewood (1,791)
El Valle de Arroyo Seco (1,149)
Eldorado at Santa Fe (5,799)
Espanola (2,754)
La Cienega (3,007)
La Puebla (1,296)
Pojoaque (1,261)
Santa Fe (70,631)

SARASOTA, FL (SARASOTA COUNTY)

DMA: Tampa–St. Petersburg

City of Sarasota
www.sarasotagov.com
Greater Sarasota C/C
www.sarasotachamber.com
Sarasota Herald Tribune
www.heraldtribune.com

Populated Places
Bee Ridge (8,744)
Desoto Lakes (3,198)
Englewood (16,196)
Fruitville (12,741)
Gulf Gate Estates (11,647)
Kensington Park (3,720)
Lake Sarasota (4,458)
Laurel (8,393)
Longboat Key (7,583)
Nokomis (3,334)
North Port (42,253)
North Sarasota (6,738)
Osprey (4,143)
Plantation (4,168)
Ridge Wood Heights (5,028)
Sarasota (53,711)
Sarasota Springs (15,875)
Siesta Key (7,150)
South Gate Ridge (5,655)
South Sarasota (5,314)
South Venice (13,539)
Southgate (7,455)
The Meadows (4,423)
Vamo (5,285)
Venice (20,974)
Venice Gardens (7,466)
Warm Mineral Springs (4,811)

SAVANNAH, GA (CHATHAM COUNTY)

DMA: Savannah

City of Savannah
www.ci.savannah.ga.us
Savannah Area C/C
www.savannahchamber.com

Savannah Morning News/ Evening Press
www.savannahnow.com

Populated Places
    Bloomingdale (2,677)
    Garden City (9,550)
    Georgetown (10,599)
    Isle of Hope (2,605)
    Montgomery (4,134)
    Pooler (10,019)
    Port Wentworth (3,238)
    Savannah (128,453)
    Skidaway Island (6,914)
    Thunderbolt (2,467)
    Tybee Island (3,614)
    Whitemarsh Island (5,824)
    Wilmington Island (14,213)

SCOTTSDALE, AZ (MARICOPA COUNTY)

DMA: Phoenix

City of Scottsdale
www.scottsdaleaz.gov
Scottsdale Area C/C
www.scottsdalechamber.com
Scottsdale Tribune
www.scottsdaletribune.com

Populated Places
    Scottsdale (226,013)

SEBRING–AVON PARK, FL (HIGHLANDS COUNTY)

DMA: Tampa–St. Petersburg

Avon Park C/C
www.apfla.com
City of Avon Park
www.avonpark.cc
Greater Sebring C/C
www.sebringflchamber.com
News Sun
www.newssun.com

Populated Places
    Avon Park (8,872)
    Lake Placid (1,784)
    Placid Lakes (3,054)
    Sebring (10,431)

SEDONA, AZ (COCONINO COUNTY)

DMA: Phoenix

City of Sedona
www.sedonaaz.gov
Sedona C/C
www.visitsedona.com
Red Rock News
www.redrocknews.com

Populated Places
    Sedona (10,220)

SILVER CITY, NM (GRANT COUNTY)

DMA: Albuquerque–Santa Fe

City of Silver City
www.townofsilvercity.org
Silver City-Grant County C/C
www.silvercity.org
Silver City Sun-News
www.scsun-news.com

Populated Places
    Bayard (2,397)
    Hurley (1,378)
    Santa Clara (1,842)
    Silver City (9,999)

SILVERTHORNE–BRECKENRIDGE, CO (SUMMIT COUNTY)

DMA: Denver

City of Breckenridge
www.townofbreckenridge.com
The Summit Chamber
www.summitchamber.org
Summit Daily News
www.summitdaily.com

Populated Places
    Breckenridge (2,680)
    Frisco (2,418)
    Silverthorne (3,610)

SMITH MOUNTAIN LAKE, VA (BEDFORD & FRANKLIN COUNTIES)

DMA: Roanoke–Lynchburg

Bedford County C/C
www.bedfordareachamber.com

Franklin County C/C
www.franklincountyva.org
The Lake
www.roanoke.com/smithmountainlake

Populated Places
Ferrum (1,313)
Forest (8,006)
North Shore (2,112)
Rocky Mount (4,568)

SONORA–TWAIN HARTE, CA (TUOLUMNE COUNTY)

DMA: Sacramento–Stockton–Modesto

Sonora C/C
www.sonorachamber.com
Tuolumne County C/C
www.tcchamber.com
Twain Harte C/C
www.twainhartecc.com
Union Democrat
www.uniondemocrat.com

Populated Places
Columbia (2,405)
East Sonora (2,078)
Jamestown (3,017)
Mi-Wuk Village (1,485)
Mono Vista (3,072)
Sonora (4,668)
Soulsbyville (1,729)
Tuolumne City (1,865)
Twain Harte (2,586)

SOUTHERN BERKSHIRE COUNTY, MA (BERKSHIRE COUNTY)

DMA: Albany–Schenectady–Troy

C/C Southern Berkshire
www.greatbarrington.org
Berkshire Eagle
www.berkshireeagle.com

Populated Places
Becket (1,786)
Egremont (1,356)
Great Barrington (7,441)
Lanesborough (2,953)
Lee (5,885)
Lenox (5,156)
Sheffield (3,366)

SOUTHERN PINES–PINEHURST, NC (MOORE COUNTY)

DMA: Raleigh–Durham

City of Pinehurst
www.villageofpinehurst.org
City of Southern Pines
www.southernpines.net
Moore County C/C
www.moorecountychamber.com
Southern Pines Pilot
www.thepilot.com

Populated Places
Aberdeen (4,794)
Carthage (1,935)
Pinebluff (1,220)
Pinehurst (11,437)
Robbins (1,217)
Seven Lakes (3,214)
Southern Pines (11,881)
Whispering Pines (2,137)

SOUTHPORT–BRUNSWICK ISLANDS, NC (BRUNSWICK COUNTY)

DMA: Wilmington

Southport-Oak Island Area C/C
www.southport-oakisland.com
The Brunswick Beacon
www.brunswickbeacon.com

Populated Places
Boiling Spring Lakes (4,107)
Carolina Shores (1,621)
Leland (4,440)
Navassa (1,594)
Oak Island (7,679)
Shallotte (1,588)
Southport (2,725)
Sunset Beach (2,176)

STATE COLLEGE, PA (CENTRE COUNTY)

DMA: Johnstown–Altoona

Chamber of Business & Industry of Centre
www.cbicc.org
City of State College
www.statecollege.com
Centre Daily Times
www.centredaily.com

Populated Places
Bellefonte borough (6,161)
Boalsburg (3,578)
Centre Hall borough (1,080)
Houserville (1,809)
Lemont (2,116)
Milesburg borough (1,149)
Park Forest Village (8,830)
Philipsburg borough (2,942)
Pine Grove Mills (1,141)
Pleasant Gap (1,611)
Ramblewood (1,054)
State College borough (38,720)
Stormstown (1,602)
Zion (2,054)

SULLIVAN COUNTY, NY (SULLIVAN COUNTY)

DMA: New York

Sullivan County C/C
www.catskills.com
Sullivan County Democrat
www.sc-democrat.com

Populated Places
Bethel (4,522)
Callicoon (3,146)
Cochecton (1,381)
Delaware (2,857)
Fallsburg (12,788)
Fremont (1,401)
Highland (2,520)
Liberty (9,589)
Livingston Manor (1,355)
Lumberland (2,064)
Mamakating (11,497)
Monticello (6,649)
Neversink (3,643)
Rockland (3,989)
South Fallsburg (2,061)
Thompson (14,786)
Tusten (1,491)
Woodridge (1,047)
Wurtsboro (1,263)

SUMMERVILLE, SC (DORCHESTER COUNTY)

DMA: Charleston

City of Summerville
www.summerville.sc.us
Greater Summerville-Dorchester County C/C
www.gsdcchamber.org
Summerville Journal Scene
www.summervillejournalscene.com

Populated Places
Ridgeville (1,960)
St. George (2,119)
Summerville (35,676)

TAOS, NM (TAOS COUNTY)

DMA: Albuquerque–Santa Fe

City of Taos
www.taosgov.com
Taos C/C
www.taoschamber.com
Taos News
www.taosnews.com

Populated Places
Questa (1,913)
Ranchos de Taos (2,390)
Taos (5,126)
Taos Pueblo (1,264)

THOMASVILLE, GA (THOMAS COUNTY)

DMA: Tallahassee–Thomasville

Thomasville/Thomas County C/C
www.thomasvillechamber.com
Thomasville Times-Enterprise
www.timesenterprise.com

Populated Places
Boston (1,449)
Meigs (1,077)
Thomasville (18,725)

TOMS RIVER–BARNEGAT BAY, NJ (OCEAN COUNTY)

DMA: New York

City of Brick
www.twp.brick.nj.us
Toms River-Ocean County C/C
www.oc-chamber.com
Ocean County's Observer
www.ocobserver.com

Populated Places
Barnegat (1,690)
Bay Head borough (1,259)
Beach Haven borough (1,352)
Beach Haven West (4,444)
Beachwood borough (10,738)
Cedar Glen Lakes (1,617)
Cedar Glen West (1,376)

Crestwood Village (8,392)
Forked River (4,914)
Holiday Heights (2,389)
Island Heights borough (1,861)
Lakehurst borough (2,683)
Lakewood (36,065)
Lavallette borough (2,747)
Leisure Knoll (2,467)
Leisure Village (4,443)
Little Egg Harbor (19,834)
Long Beach (3,461)
Manahawkin (2,004)
Manchester (41,902)
Mystic Island (8,694)
New Egypt (2,519)
North Beach Haven (2,427)
Ocean Acres (13,155)
Ocean Gate borough (2,109)
Ocean (7,820)
Pine Beach borough (2,025)
Pine Ridge at Crestwood (2,025)
Plumsted (8,047)
Point Pleasant Beach borough (5,397)
Point Pleasant borough (19,861)
Seaside Heights borough (3,220)
Seaside Park borough (2,301)
Ship Bottom borough (1,418)
Silver Ridge (1,211)
South Toms River borough (3,698)
Stafford (25,522)
Surf City borough (1,527)
Toms River (86,327)
Tuckerton borough (3,780)
Waretown (1,582)

TRAVERSE CITY, MI (GRAND TRAVERSE COUNTY)

DMA: Traverse City–Cadillac

City of Traverse City
www.ci.traverse-city.mi.us
Traverse City Area C/C
www.tcchamber.org
Traverse City Record-Eagle
www.record-eagle.com

Populated Places
East Bay (10,241)
Fife Lake (2,558)
Garfield (15,801)
Grant (1,191)
Green Lake (5,332)
Kingsley (1,524)
Long Lake (7,912)
Mayfield (1,595)
Paradise (4,730)
Peninsula (5,450)
Traverse City (14,365)
Whitewater (2,799)

TRYON, NC (POLK COUNTY)

DMA: Greenville–Spartanburg–Asheville

City of Tryon
www.tryon-nc.com
Polk County C/C
www.polkchamber.org
Tryon Daily Bulletin
www.tryondailybulletin.com

Populated Places
Tryon (1,752)

TUCSON, AZ (PIMA COUNTY)

DMA: Tucson

City of Tucson
www.tucsonaz.gov
Tucson Metropolitan C/C
www.tucsonchamber.org
Tucson Citizen
www.tucsoncitizen.com/daily/front

Populated Places
Ajo (3,705)
Avra Valley (5,038)
Casas Adobes (54,011)
Catalina (7,025)
Catalina Foothills (53,794)
Drexel Heights (23,849)
East Sahuarita (1,419)
Flowing Wells (15,050)
Green Valley (17,283)
Littletown (1,010)
Marana (26,098)
Oro Valley (38,438)
Picture Rocks (8,139)
Sahuarita (9,007)
Sells (2,799)
South Tucson (5,562)
Summit (3,702)
Tanque Verde (16,195)
Three Points (5,273)
Tortolita (3,740)
Tucson (515,526)
Tucson Estates (9,755)
Vail (2,484)

VERO BEACH, FL (INDIAN RIVER COUNTY)

DMA: West Palm Beach–Ft. Pierce

City of Vero Beach
www.covb.org
Indian River County C/C
www.indianriverchamber.com

Press-Journal
www.tcpalm.com

Populated Places
Fellsmere (4,800)
Florida Ridge (15,217)
Gifford (7,599)
Indian River Shores (3,550)
Roseland (1,775)
Sebastian (19,643)
South Beach (3,457)
Vero Beach (17,078)
Wabasso Beach (1,075)

VICTORVILLE–APPLE VALLEY, CA (SAN BERNARDINO COUNTY)

DMA: Los Angeles

Apple Valley C/C
www.avchamber.org
City of Apple Valley
www.applevalley.org
City of Victorville
www.ci.victorville.ca.us
Victorville C/C
www.vvchamber.com
Daily Press
www.vvdailypress.com

Populated Places
Adelanto (24,360)
Apple Valley (65,156)
Barstow (23,737)
Big Bear City (5,779)
Big Bear Lake (6,158)
Big River (1,266)
Bloomington (19,318)
Chino (77,578)
Chino Hills (75,722)
Colton (51,350)
Crestline (10,218)
Fontana (163,860)
Grand Terrace (12,342)
Hesperia (77,984)
Highland (50,892)
Joshua Tree (4,207)
Lake Arrowhead (8,934)
Lenwood (3,222)
Loma Linda (20,901)
Mentone (7,803)
Montclair (35,474)
Morongo Valley (1,929)
Mountain View Acres (2,521)
Muscoy (8,919)
Needles (5,348)
Ontario (172,679)
Rancho Cucamonga (169,353)
Redlands (69,995)
Rialto (99,513)

Running Springs (5,125)
San Antonio Heights (3,122)
San Bernardino (198,550)
Searles Valley (1,885)
Twentynine Palms (28,409)
Upland (73,589)
Victorville (91,264)
Wrightwood (3,837)
Yucaipa (49,100)
Yucca Valley (19,696)

WAYNESVILLE, NC (HAYWOOD COUNTY)

DMA: Greenville–Spartanburg–Asheville

City of Waynesville
www.townofwaynesville.org
Haywood County C/C
www.haywood-nc.com
Smoky Mountain News
www.smokymountainnews.com

Populated Places
Canton (4,002)
Clyde (1,357)
Lake Junaluska (2,675)
Waynesville (9,386)
West Canton (1,156)

WENATCHEE, WA (CHELAN COUNTY)

DMA: Seattle–Tacoma

City of Wenatchee
www.cityofwenatchee.com
Wenatchee Valley C/C
www.wenatchee.org
Wenatchee World
www.wenworld.com

Populated Places
Cashmere (2,985)
Chelan (3,684)
Leavenworth (2,206)
Sunnyslope (2,521)
Wenatchee (29,374)
West Wenatchee (1,681)

WESTERN ST. TAMMANY PARISH, LA (ST. TAMMANY PARISH)

DMA: New Orleans

Mandeville C/C
504/624-8388
St. Tammany West C/C
www.sttammanychamber.org

St. Tammany News Banner
www.thesttammanynews.com

Populated Places
Abita Springs (2,211)
Covington (9,347)
Eden Isle (6,261)
Lacombe (7,518)

WHIDBEY ISLAND, WA (ISLAND COUNTY)

DMA: Seattle–Tacoma

Central Whidbey C/C
www.centralwhidbeychamber.com
Oak Harbor C/C
www.oakharborchamber.org
News-Times
www.whidbeynewstimes.com

Populated Places
Camano (13,347)
Coupeville (1,813)
Freeland (1,313)
Langley (1,018)
Oak Harbor (22,327)

WICKENBURG, AZ (MARICOPA COUNTY)

DMA: Phoenix

City of Wickenburg
www.ci.wickenburg.az.us
Wickenburg C/C
www.wickenburgchamber.com
Wickenburg Sun
www.wickenburgsun.com

Populated Places
Wickenburg (6,224)

WILLIAMSBURG, VA (WILLIAMSBURG CITY & JAMES CITY COUNTY)

DMA: Norfolk–Portsmouth–Newport News

City of Williamsburg
www.ci.williamsburg.va.us
Greater Williamsburg C/C
www.williamsburgcc.com
Virginia Gazette
www.vagazette.com

Populated Places
Williamsburg (11,751)

WIMBERLEY, TX (HAYS COUNTY)

DMA: Austin

Wimberley C/C
www.wimberley.org
City of Wimberley
www.vil.wimberley.tx.us
Wimberley Valley News & Views
www.wimberleyhometownnews.com

Populated Places
Buda (3,948)
Dripping Springs (1,666)
Kyle (17,770)
San Marcos (45,523)
Wimberley (2,712)
Woodcreek (1,460)

WOODSTOCK, VT (WINDSOR COUNTY)

DMA: Burlington–Plattsburgh

Woodstock Area C/C
www.woodstockvt.com
Vermont Standard
802/457-1313

Populated Places
Bethel (1,980)
Cavendish (1,435)
Chester (3,112)
Hartford (10,822)
Hartland (3,155)
Ludlow (1,037)
Norwich (3,567)
Rochester (1,170)
Royalton (2,542)
Sharon (1,384)
Springfield (8,891)
Weathersfield (2,853)
West Windsor (1,116)
White River Junction (2,569)
Windsor (3,735)
Woodstock (3,224)

YORK BEACHES, ME (YORK COUNTY)

DMA: Portland–Auburn

Yorks C/C
www.gatewaytomaine.org
York Weekly
www.yorkweekly.com

Populated Places

Acton (2,273)
Alfred (2,818)
Arundel (4,031)
Berwick (7,348)
Biddeford (22,072)
Buxton (8,163)
Cape Neddick (2,997)
Cornish (1,392)
Dayton (2,016)
Eliot (6,413)
Hollis (4,556)
Kennebunk (11,510)
Kennebunkport (4,033)
Kittery (10,453)
Lebanon (5,561)
Limerick (2,544)
Limington (3,678)
Lyman (4,173)
Newfield (1,504)
North Berwick (4,802)
Ogunquit (1,295)
Old Orchard Beach (9,350)
Parsonsfield (1,742)
Saco (18,230)
Sanford (21,734)
Shapleigh (2,509)

South Berwick (7,304)
Waterboro (7,233)
Wells (10,088)
York (13,490)
York Harbor (3,321)

YUMA, AZ (YUMA COUNTY)

DMA: Yuma

City of Yuma
www.ci.yuma.az.us
Yuma County C/C
www.chambercommerce.com
Yuma Sun
www.yumasun.com

Populated Places

Fortuna Foothills (20,478)
San Luis (21,646)
Somerton (10,071)
Wellton (1,862)
Yuma (84,688)

Retirement Places Rated

INDEX

Index

Index